pulled

DATE DUE

billing

CIVIL WAR MEDICINE

Care & Comfort of the Wounded

ROBERT E. DENNEY

STERLING PUBLISHING CO., INC.
NEW YORK

ACKNOWLEDGMENTS

First, I'd like to express my thanks to that grand old man Eldon (Josh) Billings for lending me so many of his books, which I used to develop this one.

Next, I express my gratitude and appreciation to the many employees of the Library of Congress, the National Archives, and the National Library of Medicine, who assisted me in my research at their wonderful facilities.

Special thanks, again, go to my friend and magician at the Library of Congress, Gayle Harris, and her daughter, Elinda, for their assistance and encouragement.

Last, but certainly not least, my gratitude to my editor, Keith L. Schiffman, for his patience, guidance, and wonderful sense of humor.

Library of Congress Cataloging-in Publication Data
Denney, Robert E.
Civil War medicine : care & comfort of the wounded / by Robert E. Denney.
    p.   cm.
Includes bibliographical references and index.
ISBN 0-8069-0879-3
1. United States—History—Civil War, 1861-1865—Medical care.
2. Medicine, Military—United States—History—19th century. I. Title.
E621.D44   1994   94-16737
973.7'75—dc20 CIP

10 9 8 7 6 5 4 3 2 1

Published by Sterling Publishing Company, Inc.
387 Park Avenue South, New York, N.Y. 10016
©1994 by Robert E. Denney
Distributed in Canada by Sterling Publishing
c/o Canadian Manda Group, One Atlantic Avenue, Suite 105
Toronto, Ontario, Canada M6K 3E7
Distributed in Great Britain and Europe by Cassell PLC
Villiers House, 41/47 Strand, London WC2N 5JE, England
Distributed in Australia by Capricorn Link (Australia) Pty Ltd.
P.O. Box 6651, Baulkham Hills, Business Centre, NSW 2153, Australia
Manufactured in the United States of America

Sterling ISBN 0-8069-0879-3

This book is dedicated to the many medical
personnel of the United States Armed Forces, who, in battle,
have given their devotion, and often their lives, to provide
CARE & COMFORT
to the wounded and helpless.
I have, on two occasions, been the recipient of such
ministrations, for which I'll be eternally grateful.

CONTENTS

"Still the battle continues … the grape and canister fill the air as they go screaming on their fearful errand; the sight of that field is perfectly appalling; men tossing their arms wildly calling for help; there they lie bleeding , torn and mangled; legs, arms and bodies are crushed and broken as if smitten by thunderbolts; the ground is crimson with blood; it is terrible to witnes.…"
—Emma Edmonds, Union field nurse, Battle of First Manassas, Va., July 21, 1861

"The theater of the bloody drama was almost a wilderness.… At no time … were the conveniences for the establishment of large general hospitals to be found; in fact, the drugs, medicines and hospital stores absolutely essential for the field were with difficulty obtained.…"
—Surg. John Brinton, Med. Dir., Army of the Tennessee, at Ft. Henry, Tenn., Feb. 15, 1862

"… Washington looked like a mammoth masquerade. Spanish hats, scarlet-lined riding cloaks, swords and sashes, high boots and bright spurs.… The men rode as if the safety of the nation depended on their speed alone."
—Louisa May Alcott, Nurse at the Union Hospital in Georgetown, Washington, D.C., Jan. 18, 1863

"The stench from the hospitals … is almost insupportable.… The board of health believe[s that] the great number of cases of fever now in Danville proceeds from the cause above.…"
—Petition of the citizens of Danville, Va., to the Confederate Secy. of War, to remove the prison hospital from that city, Feb. 1, 1864

1865

"In two or three open sheds and in one railroad building were six hundred men without even straw for bedding, and no blankets to protect them from the rain which soaked through these long wards of misery.... There were moanings and cries for help, to all of which it was impossible to respond...."
—Wm. H. Reed, Union Nurse, at Burke's Station, Va., following Gen. Lee's surrender to Grant, April 10, 1865

PROLOGUE

THE STATE OF MEDICINE IN 1861

Medicine was far different in 1861 from what it is today. The existence of microbes and germs hadn't yet been accepted; surgery was in the same state that it had been in for the 50 years before; operating methods were primitive and wholly unsanitary in most cases; most sickness was treated at home, hospitals being but rarely used; local medicines were preferred to unknown (and untested) pharmaceuticals; and the training of doctors was only very basic. It was, indeed, an inauspicious time for someone to be wounded in war.

The state of public health had made some headway, primarily in cities such as New York, Philadelphia, and Chicago. In rural communities, public health remained the way it had been for over 100 years; the survivors of childhood diseases lived to an average age of 55. Little was known about the causes of disease. Galen's ancient theory of "humors" and the later theory of miasma odors emanating from the earth were the most popular ideas accepted to describe the origins of disease. Many diseases were common, including typhoid, typhus, measles, mumps, smallpox, malaria, yellow fever, and dengue ("breakbone") fever. One of the worst, and the most dreaded, was smallpox.

Ancient records show that smallpox existed before the Roman Empire, in China and the Middle East. Armies had been decimated by the pox many times in history, and little was done about it until vaccination was discovered in (as some believe) China. Over the centuries, vaccination was used effectively, and in 1798 the use of cowpox vaccination proved to be a more stable and better vaccination method than using a serum derived from human smallpox victims. This vaccine became widely used, and did much to eradicate the disease. In 1776, Gen. George Washington ordered that all his troops be vaccinated against smallpox. Napoléon had his entire army vaccinated in 1805, thereby gaining an advantage that he later lost to typhus and typhoid.

Among the European armies of the early 19th century, the use of discipline was the greatest deterrent to the spread of such diseases as typhus, typhoid, and smallpox. Bathing and delousing played a major role in the improvement of those armies' health. The armies that fought the American Civil War lost more men to disease than to combat.

ON THE EVE OF BATTLE—1861

For the first time in its history, the United States would assemble very large armies; the staff system for the armies' medical departments hadn't yet been tested. When the war first started, only one assistant surgeon was assigned to a regiment of twelve hundred men, and so little was thought of the qualifications necessary that almost anyone could get the job—even some quacks who sold "snake oil" were appointed. The mobilization of the Union Army in 1861 led to many immediate problems, not the least of which was the availability of doctors for the combat units. The impression among the general populace that was any good civilian physician was capable of performing as a military medical surgeon. It was quickly found that this wasn't true. The Regular Army Medical Service used its normal procedure of inducting medical doctors who'd recently completed medical schools. The newly inducted surgeons didn't have the background for handling military matters, and the most serious problems were getting these new medical officers, North and South, used to the idea of regimentation and adherence to the chain of command to accomplish their mission.

The states, responsible for the mobilization of the regiments, appointed their own doctors to them. In many cases, the doctor, like the colonel commanding the regiment, was appointed based on political favoritism and not necessarily on qualifications. Some of the governors of the states required examinations, some didn't. Among the troops from the western states (Indiana, Ohio, Iowa, Wisconsin, Minnesota, Kansas, etc.) the doctors from Ohio were among the best. In New England, those from Vermont and Massachusetts were better screened than were those from the other states.

THE HEALTH OF THE UNION ARMY

One of the major duties of the regimental doctors was the examination of their state's enlistees before these men were mustered into service. Of the first-call volunteers in April 1861, about 20 percent were discharged for disabilities suffered prior to entering the Army. These disabled men included syphilitics, men older than 60, those with hernias, those with no teeth, some with missing fingers. One case was reported where a doctor "examined" over 90 recruits in one hour. In one Chicago regiment the doctor had the men parade past him, and he passed the entire group *en masse.* Most often these unfit personnel clogged the hospitals and took needed facilities from the troops who were sick or injured after coming into the service. One state, New York, conducted a reexamina-

tion of the troops furnished to the Federal service. Of the 47,417 men initially accepted for service, a special board of doctors weeded out 5554. It was unfortunate that more states didn't emulate New York's example.

Dr. Charles S. Tripler, the first surgeon appointed to the Army of the Potomac, found that "for the most part, physicians taken suddenly from civil life, with little knowledge of their duties ... had to be taught them from the very alphabet. The line officers were equally ignorant with themselves in this respect, and hence confusion, conflict of authority and discontent, very seriously impaired efficiency in the medical department. The general idea seemed to be that it was the duty of the doctor to physic every man who chose to report sick, and to sign such papers as the colonel directed him to sign. To superintend the sanitary condition of the regiment, to call upon the commanding officers to abate nuisances, to take measures for the prevention of disease, was, in many instances, considered impertinent and obtrusive, and the suggestions of the medical officer to these ends were too frequently disregarded and ignored."

By May 1861, about 30 percent of all the troops mustered had been on the sick list at least once, most complaining of "acute diarrhea." The health of the troops from the eastern states was better than that of those from the western states, especially concerning communicable diseases, such as measles, chicken pox, mumps, and smallpox. In the rural western states, cities were small, towns and villages even smaller, and most of the population lived on farms in isolated or semi-isolated areas. These people came into contact with few others, and rarely with strangers. The eastern states, such as New York, Massachusetts, Pennsylvania, etc., with their large cities provided a more fertile ground for those "childhood" diseases that self-immunized the citizenry. Many soldiers, east and west, were very sick, and often mortally so, with viral-type diseases that the doctors knew little about.

A major problem in the initial stages of the war, for both North and South, was the training of the troops in field sanitation. Because most of the troops from the western states, and those from the South as well, were from farms, their idea of personal hygiene and their use of toilet facilities was somewhat lacking.

This problem was less important in those units officered by current or former Regular Army officers. Sherman, upon taking command of a regiment early in the war, immediately indoctrinated his junior officers in the use of field latrines, and he demanded enforcement of good sanitation measures. He personally inspected his troops' living and mess areas. Consequently, the sick rate in his units was low.

The Sanitary Commission prepared pamphlets for issue to the troops on the preparation and use of latrines, as well as on personal hygiene—bathing, etc. Field sanitation was to be the responsibility of the line officer—from the colonel down through the lieutenant.

Surg. Tripler, early in 1861, stated, "It is a singular fact, but one as to which I believe all military surgeons of experience will agree with me, that the sick report of a regiment, under ordinary circumstances, is a constant quantity; that after a regiment has been in the field a month, that quantity will be ascertained; and, that if the regimental hospital is evacuated, in a short time it will be found to contain again its habitual number of inmates, so that we may have as many successive crops of sick as we choose, by repeating the process of evacuating the regimental upon the general hospitals."

Intestinal infections increased dramatically over the course of the war. In 1861, typhoid fever, caused by polluted water (polluted usually by human feces) caused 17 percent of all military deaths. By 1865, the mortality rate of typhoid had reached 56 percent of all those who'd contracted it. Diarrhea and dysentery caused a high sick rate of 64 percent of all the troops in the first year of the war, and this increased to 99.5 percent in 1862. Better field-sanitation conditions brought this rate down dramatically.

FOOD AND CLOTHING FOR THE TROOPS

A major cause of poor health was the clothing and food issued to the troops. Initially, the states were responsible for the "outfitting" of the regiments—i.e., providing them with proper uniforms (including undergarments), blankets, eating utensils, and weapons, and when the states' regiments were mustered into Federal service, the states presented the bill to the Federal government for such costs. Governments being what they are, this worked well in some cases, not so well in others. Some troops were provided shoddy uniforms, and state "contractors" were paid the full sum for the equipment.

Once the troops went into camp, food became a major problem. Rather than use a common kitchen for an entire company of 100 men, the men formed into informal "messes," where resources were pooled, and the individual who knew how to boil water was appointed cook. If no one knew how to boil water, the men drew straws. The results of this arrangement can be imagined. The food, in most cases, was almost inedible after being cooked. The food was usually a hard-baked (water, salt, and flour) cracker, salt pork in various stages of preservation, beans, and coffee. The hardtack crackers had to be soaked in water, coffee, or some other liquid to make them even chewable. Sometimes they were ground using stones (or by using one-half of an old mess kit with nail holes in it to make a grater) and added to other items, or combined with water, formed into cakes, and fried in bacon fat. The troops fried rice and beans, they fried beef, they fried everything they could get into their skillets. These skillets generally made up one-half of their mess kit. The doctors often referred to their ailments as "death from the frying pan."

Seldom were fresh vegetables issued. If they were available locally, the price was usually much higher than normal—due to price gouging by the local farmers. The Federals tried a new dried mixture called "desiccated vegetables"—also referred to by the troops as "decimated vegetables." It was described variously as "not fit for the hogs," or "tasteless to the extreme." It wasn't too popular with the troops. It did have one advantage: It stored well, and thousands of tons of it were issued for the Union troops from Virginia to Georgia. The results of the troops' diet could have been easily predicted—stomach ailments, scurvy in some cases, and general ill health.

Another major food problem, North and South, was that the rations were issued for several days at a time, and a soldier would eat his three days of food in one day. He then went hungry for the following two days. There were numerous instances where soldiers in formation would faint from weakness because they hadn't eaten for two or three days.

TRANSPORTATION OF
THE SICK AND WOUNDED

Transportation of the sick and wounded was another problem facing the medical departments, and one that had been truly neglected before the war and that would remain so even into the early stages of the fight.

Prior to the Civil War, the U.S. Army had never provided vehicles expressly designed for the transportation of the sick and wounded. In 1859, a Board assembled by the Secretary of War adopted, as an experiment, a four-wheel carriage and two models of two-wheel carriage. The four-wheel carriage had been tested upon the plains, in an expedition to New Mexico, and had been favorably reported upon by the medical officer in charge. A few of the two-wheeled units had been built, but never used. Some doubts were voiced about the suitability of the two-wheel vehicles, but these carriages were adopted and recommended as the best transport for badly wounded men, although such vehicles were largely untested. Experience, however, showed that the two-wheelers were utterly unfit for any such purpose. When the war came, the quartermaster's department ordered carriages to be built as fast as possible, in quantities designated by the Surgeon General, and in a ratio of five two-wheel units to one four-wheel. The two-wheel units were to be the backbone of the fleet of ambulances available; this was most unfortunate for the patients who were to ride in them.

Initial distribution of the two-wheel carriages in the Washington area was made, and very soon they were being used as pleasure-carts for the officers and to carry people into, and around, the city. The vehicles rapidly broke down. The Surgeon of the Army of the Potomac, Dr. Charles S. Tripler, stopped such use of the carriages before even more of them broke down. In the western theatre of operations, the four-wheel carriage was more readily available, and more widely used.

Another experiment, copied from the French army, was tried for ambulances. This experimental vehicle was called a *cacolet*. It carried two men, one on each side of a horse. This rig weighed about 140 pounds and was very bulky. The main advantage of this device was that patients could be carried anywhere a horse or mule could travel. The

great disadvantage was that the patients had to ride sitting up, because the motion of the animal created dizziness when the patient was lying down. In addition, the *cacolet* provided no protection from inclement weather. Not many of these conveyances were ever used.

CONFEDERATE MEDICAL SERVICE

The Confederate government had entirely different problems, and it came up with short-sighted solutions. In 1861, there were no established offices or channels for the Southern military medical profession. An organization had to be created using what personnel had formerly served in the U.S. Army, and using the volunteers available. To compound this problem, the Confederate Congress appropriated only $50,000 for the establishment and operation of military hospitals.

While rapid progress was made in most areas of organization and administration, the greatest advance was in the creation of the hospital system throughout the South. By the end of 1863, approximately 18 months after the First Battle of Bull Run (Manassas), the medical service had organized principal hospitals in many locations. Among these were Virginia (39), North Carolina (21), South Carolina (12), Georgia (50), Alabama (23), Mississippi (3), Florida (4) and Tennessee (2).

The number of personnel flowing in and out of the Confederate hospitals equalled the number in the North, and surpassed it in many ways. The South's largest hospital, the Chimborazo in Richmond, had a very impressive record regarding treatment and humanity. Always working with limited resources, during the two-year period Nov. 1, 1861-1863 that hospital admitted 47,176 patients, of whom 17,384 were transferred, 17,845 returned to duty, 4378 furloughed, 635 discharged, 846 deserted, and 3031 died. This was a very low mortality rate (a little over 6%), considering the conditions. The number of desertions was surprisingly low. The number returned to duty during this two-year period represents two Confederate Corps or more.

Within the Dept. of Virginia, during the period Sept. 1862-Dec. 1863 the 39 hospitals in service processed 293,165 patients, a number equal to all of Lee's army being admitted to the hospital three times. Of this number, 95,875 were returned to duty, 2807 discharged as unfit for duty, 4446 deserted, and 19,248 died. The toll in human suffering was vast and far-reaching.

The South had a real problem with obtaining medicine after the U.S. naval blockade began to tighten in early 1862, and the Confederacy had to resort to some unusual methods of treatment. The *Confederate States Medical and Surgical Journal* of July 1864 listed a *Standard Supply Table of Indigenous Remedies for Field Service and Sick in General Hospital* which contained lists of herbs and plants that could be used medicinally when manufactured medicines weren't available. Many stimulants, listed for diverse purposes, were derivatives of the calamus, Virginia snakeroot, partridgeberry, sassafras, lavender, tulip tree, or Seneca snakeroot plants. Astringents were made variously from the bearberry, marsh rosemary, sumac, and white-oak leaves and bark. Tonics came from such things as dogwood (astringent), persimmon, American colombo, American gentian, hop, Georgia bark, wild cherry, white oak, blackberry or dewberry, American centaury, white willow, and sage. No restraint was cautioned when applying native medicines to the sick and wounded. Considering what was available, it's amazing that the Southern doctors did so well.

CIVILIAN EFFORTS, NORTH AND SOUTH

The origin and growth during the early part of the war of the Sanitary Commission in the North, and the various Relief Societies in the South, present a study in organizational capabilities. Originally, there were several organizations (and these grew rapidly in number) that provided much-needed succor to the troops. In the South, no major agency was formed to coordinate all activities, whereas in the North the United States Sanitary Commission and the Northwest Sanitary Commission rapidly became the controlling forces needed to coordinate relief efforts.

The original agencies were formed by women, usually mothers, sisters, or wives of soldiers, who felt that they should do "their part" in the war. The initial efforts in the North were to manufacture and organize the supply of hospital necessities, such as bandages and lint. This spread further to the making of shirts, drawers, hospital gowns, bedding kits,

etc., as well as to the collection of money to furnish such items as sewing kits, writing paper, and stamped envelopes.

In the North, at the beginning, there was much duplication of effort, resulting in a glut of some items and extreme shortages of others. Too, the packing of the items was somewhat less than efficient, and many items were spoiled when food (packed along with clothing) turned rancid or rotted. The Commissions in the North eventually organized depots where local relief organizations sent their contributions. At these places *all* packages were opened, examined, and repackaged. Like items were packed together—shirts with shirts, drawers with drawers, etc.—and all items clearly stamped with indelible ink stating that they were from the Commission. Packages were clearly labelled with their contents and with Commission markings. This identification prevented the looting of the supplies by transportation handlers, etc., who sold the items to the soldiers for a profit. The South never consolidated its relief efforts as well as had been done in the North.

The object of the U.S. Sanitary Commission was to cut through government red tape and provide the necessary support in a flexible and efficient manner, something no government had ever yet achieved. The Commission began with Dr. Bellows, who visited Washington in 1861, and then went back to New York with a plan of organization and the blessings of the President and the Secretary of War. The highest officials of the government felt that the Commission could do no harm.

All its major "officials" were medical professionals, who devoted much time and money to the Commission's efforts. Its doctors were sent to inspect the camps and the mess facilities to garner information on which to base recommendations. Their primary concern was the health of the troops. Early in the war the Commission published some 18 pamphlets dealing with field sanitation in the camps, handling of the sick and wounded, the use and storage of medicines, etc. The knowledge imparted by these pamphlets proved invaluable to the government in the control of disease and the alleviation of suffering.

Several innovations were instituted by the U.S. Sanitary Commission. Among these were the development and use of wheeled kettles in which soup was prepared in the rear areas of the battlefield. The soup could be served to the wounded or injured even while the battle was raging.

The organizations, North and South, also established a series of "Soldier's Homes" or "Soldier's Rests" along the routes to and from the battle areas. A forerunner of the USO as we know it, these "rest stops" furnished dormitory sleeping, good food, libraries, bathing and laundry facilities, etc., to all who needed these services. In the North during the war, over 800,000 soldiers availed themselves of the services, eating over 4,500,000 meals and staying over for 1,000,000 nights' lodgings. All of this hospitality was furnished to the troops free of charge; the cost was paid for by the communities, and from donations of food and services.

There were no Federal allotments of money to the families of the troops during the war. Some states did provide a small allowance, but this practice was uncommon. The Sanitary Commission established a "Claim Agency" to help soldiers obtain their bounty money when such payments were in arrears. A "Pension Agency" was also established to aid the soldier who was discharged for disability (often because of an amputation) in order to get his pension straightened out with a laggard government agency. It also had a "Back Pay Agency" which helped the soldier whose paybook was lost (or otherwise unusable) to gain his money. These were very useful services in an army where many were illiterate.

A locator service called the "Hospital Directory" was established in the North, and something similar in the South, where information could be found about patients and invalids in the 233 general hospitals. These directory services were established in Washington, Philadelphia, New York, and Louisville, where the names of more than 600,000 men were registered.

During a battle or engagement the Commission was usually on the battlefield to care for the wounded and, as much as possible, to relieve the suffering.

THE OVERALL EFFECT

The Civil War caused untold misery for many thousands of military and civilian personnel from battle casualties, sickness, displacement, and poor living conditions. Many thousands died needlessly because of inattention, lack of medicine, lack of facilities and, in some cases, cruelty.

In this volume, the chronicle unfolds.

1861

In Washington, the New Year's spirit was somewhat subdued. With the election of Abraham Lincoln as President, South Carolina had seceded from the Union and declared her sovereignty. The country was in political turmoil and war clouds gathered on the horizon.

In the North, the United States Army and Navy were wholly unprepared for war. Years of neglect and ingrained bureaucracy, combined with budget cuts and miserly appropriations from Congress, had left the War and Navy Depts. ineffectual.

The United States Navy had few ships, and many of them were in foreign ports, supporting American diplomatic missions.

Medical services within the two departments, Army and Navy, were almost nonexistent. The Chief Medical Officer of the Army, Col. Thomas Lawson, also a veteran of the War of 1812, was a martinet; he was extremely harsh on his own staff and on the doctors serving in the far-flung posts throughout the country. He didn't believe in extravagances, such as medical textbooks, and he was enraged when it was reported that one military post actually had *two* sets of surgical instruments.

The overall medical staff at the beginning of the war consisted of the Surgeon General, 30 surgeons, and 83 assistant surgeons. Of these, 3 surgeons and 21 assistant surgeons resigned to go with the Confederacy, and 3 assistant surgeons were dismissed for disloyalty to the Union. This was somewhat balanced by the fact that 5 Southern surgeons and 8 Southern assistant surgeons chose to remain in the Union Army. The war began with a total of 98 medical personnel to support 16,000 Regular Army troops.

During the early period of 1861, little was done to augment the medical services in the North, because no one believed that the war, if it would actually come, would last long. In the South, the Confederate government moved to organize a medical service within the army using as a cadre those officers who'd "gone South," and newly recruited doctors. For some period, resources on both sides were limited.

Overall, things remained somewhat quiet, until Lincoln's call in April for troops, after Ft. Sumter was fired upon.

April 1 (Monday)

Tension was extremely high at this time. The Confederacy, having organized its own government based in Montgomery, Ala., was threatening war over the status of Ft. Sumter in Charleston Harbor, S.C. The South had taken most of the Federal forts located in their respective states, with the exception of Forts Sumter and Pickens. Southern hotheads were calling for firing on Ft. Sumter; cooler heads, preaching patience, seemed to be outnumbered.

April 9 (Tuesday)

Mary A. Livermore, a Boston native, was destined to play a major role in the work of the Sanitary Commission in the (then) western part of the United States. Livermore, a very intelligent woman, had moved to Chicago with her husband, who was a Universalist clergyman. In Chicago, Dr. Livermore founded a successful weekly newspaper, called the *New Covenant*, which was distributed throughout the (then) Northwest. Mrs. Livermore's prominent position in the society of the time would be an invaluable asset in her work with the Commission.

An intellectual snob, Mary had a strong sense of superiority to those with less education than she had. She was usually very condescending to all she met—not traits that would make her popular! However, she worked in an earnest, forthright manner and she was very good at seeing things accomplished, bringing order and efficiency to where none had existed. Well travelled, she was at home, east or west, and could command the attention of society in either place. An ideal choice for member of the Western Sanitary Commission, she was destined to meet someone of similar capabilities, albeit from a more common environment, in the very near future: Mary Ann Bickerdyke of Galesburg, Ill.

Far from Boston, in Knoxville, Tenn., Henry Melvil Doak enlisted in the "Knoxville Guards," which became part of the Confederates' 19th Tennessee Regiment. Doak was to have a very different career, destined to serve in both the Army and Navy of the Confederacy. A well-educated young man of 20 years, he had, before the war, studied law, taught school, and farmed. Assigned as Adjutant, he was with the regiment at Cumberland Gap, Fishing Creek, Ky., Lebanon, Ky., Murfreesboro, Tenn., and finally Decatur, Ala., where he became ill. He rejoined his regiment at Corinth, Miss., the day before the Battle of Shiloh, on April 5, 1862.

April 12 (Friday)

Shortly past midnight of this day, four men were sent out in a boat flying a white flag to Ft. Sumter to again confer with Union Maj. Robert Anderson about the surrender of the fort. Anderson replied that he'd evacuate the fort on the 15th, unless he received additional instructions or supplies, not realizing that a relief fleet was lying just outside the harbor awaiting daylight to enter. To his visitors, anything less than immediate surrender was unacceptable. They then informed Anderson that firing would commence within one hour if he didn't capitulate. Realizing what was coming, Anderson shook their hands and told them, "If we do not meet again in this world, I hope we may meet in the better one." The boat left, returning for Cummings Point about 3:20 A.M., arriving there at 4 A.M.

At Cummings Point, Roger Pryor, a Virginian, was offered the honor of firing the first shot, but he declined. Another Virginian, a 67-year-old fire-eater and avid secessionist named Edmund Ruffin, gladly accepted the honor, and at 4:30 A.M. pulled the lanyard on the gun. Sumter was fired upon. The war had begun.

April 13 (Saturday)

The firing on Sumter continued into this day, until at last, honor satisfied, Anderson capitulated to Confederate Gen. P. G. T. Beauregard, his former artillery student, and agreed to the surrender terms offered on Thursday, the 11th. The Confederate Roger Pryor returned to Sumter to participate in the ceremonies, which took place in the fort hospital. No casualties had occurred on either side, despite the weight of all the iron thrown about. The surrender was signed, and Anderson was permitted to fire a fifty-gun salute to his flag, during which a burning ember fell in some powder. The resulting explosion killed Pvt. Daniel Hough and wounded five other Federal soldiers, the first real casualties of the war. The flag was lowered and given to Anderson, who packed it with his personal effects. Sumter was lost to the Union.

Livermore, Mary, Boston, Mass.:

The opening of the War of the Rebellion found me in Boston, my native city. My own home had been in Chicago for years, but my aged father was thought to be dying, and the stern speech of the telegram had summoned me to his bedside.... The daily papers teemed with the dreary records of secession. The Southern press blazed with hatred of the North, and with fierce contempt for her patience and her avowed desire for peace. Northern men and women were driven from Southern homes, leaving behind all their possessions, and thankful to escape with life....

The day after arrival, came the news that Ft.

Sumter was attacked, which increased the feverish anxiety ... therefore, the telegraph, which had registered for the astounded nation the hourly progress of the bombardment, announced the lowering of the stars and stripes, and the surrender of the beleaguered garrison, the news fell on the land like a thunderbolt....

Also in Boston on this day was Amy Morris Bradley, who'd been in Charleston, S.C., and had seen Ft. Sumter. Bradley wrote in her diary of the people weeping in Boston's streets when it was announced that Sumter had been fired upon.

Amy Morris Bradley was born of Quaker ancestry on September 12, 1823, in East Vassalboro, Me. Her mother having died when she was seven years old, Amy learned quickly the art of housekeeping. Amy has been described as short, thin, and delicate-looking. Grey eyes looked out from a serious face marked by a high, broad forehead, sharp nose, and prominent mouth. She had light, sandy hair and a tendency to freckle. Amy referred to her looks as "plain, but lovable."

At an early age, Amy began teaching school in the local neighborhood, developing a real knack for controlling unruly boys. She'd held various teaching jobs and positions in the Massachusetts area, until 1853, when she took a teaching position in Costa Rica. Her experience there and her visits to the antebellum South during this period would hold her in good stead during the Civil War. She left Costa Rica in 1857, after a sojourn of more than three years. Amy, back in Boston in 1859, used the language skills she'd acquired in Costa Rica to obtain a well-paying position. She took courses in bookkeeping, and taught Spanish on the side.

Amy served during the war as a nurse and a hospital matron. Following the war, she went to Wilmington, N.C., and become principal of a school. Amy died on January 15, 1904, at her cottage on the Tileston School grounds in Wilmington. One of her students, Henry Bacon, was the architect of the Lincoln Memorial, in Washington, D.C.

April 14 (Sunday)

Livermore, Mary, Boston, Mass.:

The pulpits thundered with denunciations of the rebellion. Congregations applauded sermons such as were never before heard in Boston, not even from radical preachers.... There was an end of patience,

and in its stead was aroused a determination to avenge the insult offered the nation. Conservative and peaceful counsel shrivelled in the blaze of belligerent excitement.

April 15 (Monday)

In Washington, Lincoln issued a call for 75,000 volunteers to serve for three months, and he called for a special session of Congress for July 4th.

In Bridgeport, Conn., the women of the town organized the first of many "societies" to be formed with the idea of affording relief and comfort to the Union volunteers. This group was followed on the same day by a group at Charlestown, Mass., and by another at Lowell, Mass., a few days later. The stated purposes of these societies was to "... provide clothing, provisions, and matters of comfort not supplied by Government regulations, to send books and newspapers to the camps, to preserve a record of the services of each soldier, and to hold constant communication with the officers of the regiments, in order that they might be kept informed of the condition of their friends."

Livermore, Mary, Boston, Mass.:

April 15. Who that saw that day will ever forget it! For now, drowning the exaltations of the triumphant South, louder than their boom of cannon, heard above their clang of bells and blare of trumpets, there rang out the voice of Abraham Lincoln calling for seventy-five thousand volunteers for three months.... This proclamation was like the first peal of a surcharged thunder-cloud, clearing the murky air. The South received it as a declaration of war; the North as a confession that civil war had begun; and the whole North arose as one man....

During this momentous month, William G. Ewin of Nashville, Tenn., enlisted in the "Hickory Guards," which later became Co. A, 20th Tennessee Infantry Regiment. Ewin would serve with the regiment in its travels through eastern Tennessee, southern Kentucky, and northern Alabama to its meeting with Union forces at Shiloh, on April 6, 1862.

April 16 (Tuesday)

Throughout the North, the states began recruitment drives, bringing in volunteer companies and holding them in camps until a regiment could be formed and outfitted for transfer to Federal service. The quality of medical care in these camps varied with the location. Some states provided immediate medical service with doctors present and with some hospital facilities, while other states didn't perform so well. One of the major problems in all locations was the almost total lack of sanitary control within the camps. The officers of the companies weren't trained military men and they had no real experience in the administration and discipline necessary to prevent disease and sickness. The simplest problems, such as the use of latrine pits, and the burial of garbage and offal from the animals slaughtered for rations, were neglected. It was a popular belief that *volunteer* troops wouldn't accept the rigid discipline then enforced on the Regular Army without rebelling against authority. Further, it was thought that the innate traits that made the American volunteer so patriotic would protect him from the evils of the undisciplined camp, notwithstanding the lessons of the recent war in the Crimea, where tens of thousands had died of disease, until Florence Nightingale convinced the English Parliament that action was necessary from the central government. The absolute powers granted the British Sanitary Commission over the hospitals and sanitary control of the camps saved thousands of soldiers from death in 1855. The United States Army Medical Service hadn't learned the lesson of the Crimea.

Livermore, Mary, Boston, Mass.:

To my father this uprising of the country was the very elixir of life. The blood came again to his cheek, and vigor to his system. And when, on the morning of Tuesday, volunteers began to arrive in Boston, and Faneuil Hall, the old "Cradle of Liberty," was opened for their accommodation, he insisted on being lifted into a carriage, and on going to witness their arrival and reception. As they marched from the railroad stations, they were escorted by crowds cheering vociferously. Merchants and clerks rushed out from stores, bareheaded, saluting them as they passed. Windows were flung up; and women leaned out into the rain, waving flags and handkerchiefs....

As the men filed into Faneuil Hall, in solid columns, the enthusiasm knew no bounds. Men, women, and children seethed in a fervid excite-

ment.... I saw the dear banner of my country, rising higher and higher to the top of the flagstaff, fling out fold after fold to the damp air, and float proudly over the hallowed edifice. Oh, the roar that rang out from ten thousand throats! Old men, with white hair and tearful faces, lifted their hats to the national ensign, and reverently saluted it. Young men greeted it with fierce and wild hurrahs....

I had never seen anything like this before.... I was weak with the new tides of feeling coursing through my being.

That day cartridges were made for the regiments by the hundred thousand. Army rifles were ordered from the Springfield Armory. Fifteen hundred workmen were engaged for the Charlestown Navy Yard. Enlistments of hardy-looking men went on vigorously, and hundreds of wealthy citizens pledged pecuniary aid to the families of the soldiers....

April 17 (Wednesday)

Late this day the 6th Mass. Volunteer Infantry departed Boston for Washington. Mary Livermore witnessed the departure.

On the afternoon of the next day, the 6th Massachusetts, a full regiment one thousand strong, started from Boston by rail, leaving the Fourth Massachusetts to follow.

An immense concourse of people gathered in the neighborhood of the Boston and Albany railroad station to witness their departure. The great crowd was evidently under the influence of deep feeling, but it was repressed, and the demonstrations were not noisy.... Tears ran down not only the cheeks of women, but those of men; but there was no faltering....

"Fall into line!" was the unfamiliar order that rang out clear and distinct, with a tone of authority. The blue-coated soldiers released themselves tenderly from the clinging arms of affection, kissed again, and again, and again, the faces upturned to theirs, white with the agony of parting, formed in long lines, company by company, and were marched into the cars.... Ah, how little they, or we, foresaw the reception awaiting them in the streets of Baltimore!

April 18 (Thursday)

In Washington, five companies of troops arrived from Pennsylvania for the defense of the capital.

Coming through Baltimore, they met cold stares and ugly looks, but they passed through unharmed. They arrived unarmed, untrained, and wholly unprepared.

At Charles Town, western Virginia, E. A. Craighill, a new medical doctor, enlisted as a private in the Botts Grays for the duration of the war. The Grays were later to become Company G, 2nd Virginia Infantry, a part of the famed Stonewall Brigade. This company, with 104 young men, contained most of the local professionals and young gentlemen. These men were among the richest and best educated in the area, and over the next four years many of them would transfer to other organizations to become outstanding commanders and officers. Some would be killed in the fight for the Confederacy; most would survive.

April 19 (Friday)

The 6th Massachusetts Vol. Infantry Regiment arrived in Baltimore and was marching from one station to another, en route to Washington, when a large crowd of Southern sympathizers began to throw rocks and bricks, and fired into the ranks of the troops. These troops, unlike those of the day before, were armed, and returned the fire, killing twelve civilians and wounding several more. The troops picked up their four dead, packed them in ice, sent them home, and then went on to the capital with their 17 wounded.

In Cleveland, Ohio, the ladies of the city organized a group whose object was the care of the families of the volunteers.

April 20 (Saturday)

Mary Livermore left Boston for Chicago, and was greeted in Albany by newspapers telling the story of the adventures of the 6th Massachusetts in Baltimore. Shocked by the news, Livermore notes that one person was reported to have said, "Waal, now, them Southern fire-eaters *have* gone and done it—that's a fact!"…

The United States Army, prior to the war, was stationed throughout the west, often in small groups of a company, manning lonely outposts on the routes to California and Oregon. Such a post was Camp Davis, Tex., which was on the southern overland mail route, about 450 miles northwest of San Antonio, Tex.

A part of the garrison of Camp Davis was a medical detachment headed by Asst. Surg. D. C. Peters, USA, who'd been at Davis for many months prior to the secession of Texas from the Union in February of this year. In April, Peters was directed to join the command of Brevet Lt. Col. I. V. D. Reeve, USA, as it moved with companies of the 8th U.S. Infantry from New Mexico and Arizona through Texas to join the Union. Peter's account sheds light on one little-known action.

Peters, D. C., Asst. Surg., USA, en route through Texas:

In the month of April 1861, Col. Reeve's forces, numbering over three hundred men arrived, and I immediately reported to that officer. We proceeded on our route, and were not molested until we reached Ft. Clark, Texas, where we found the road barricaded, and the fort in readiness to resist our approach. Two of our officers had been dispatched ahead, to obtain supplies of which we stood in need, and which we were to receive at the different military stations on the route; but they were here detained as prisoners until our command came up.

A conference was held between our commanding officer and the person in charge of the fort. The latter informed us that war had been declared, and had already commenced, between the Northern and Southern states; that Ft. Sumter had been captured, and other feats had been performed by the Rebels. He, however, released our officers, furnished us provisions, and gave as an excuse for hostile conduct, that they had heard we were advancing with our troops and several thousand Indian allies, to recapture Ft. Clark.

April 21 (Sunday)

Livermore, Mary, Chicago, Ill.:

On Sunday night, eight days after the fall of Sumter, troops were despatched from Chicago to Cairo, the southern terminus of the state, and a point of great strategic importance. At that time a muddy little town, it is situated at the confluence of the Ohio and Mississippi rivers, and is the key to the navigation of both.… Southern leaders were well aware of its value as a railway and river centre, and were hurrying preparations to take possession of it.

They were forestalled in their action by Chicago. In less than forty-eight hours a force of infantry and a company of artillery were ready to march from that city. It was a citizen-corps, made up mainly of young men, most of them belonging to the best families of the state.... They left in haste, little time being accorded them to leave-taking.... The long train of twenty-six cars stood waiting them at the station, with two powerful engines attached.... As the precious train moved slowly out along the pier, the tens of thousands who lined the lake-shore bade them farewell with deafening cheers.... They were none too soon in their occupation of Cairo....

April 22 (Monday)

On this date, Illinois troops arrived at Cairo, Ill., and occupied the point at the confluence of the Ohio and Mississippi rivers. Many of these troops were from the Galesburg, Ill., area.

April 25 (Thursday)

S. Emma E. Edmonds, a native of New Brunswick, Canada, had been travelling in the American west prior to the Civil War. She was in Chicago when the news broke of the fall of Ft. Sumter, and she immediately decided to support the Union. After watching the departure of Union troops for Washington, she left Chicago, arriving in the capital on April 27, ten days after Lincoln's call for troops. Once in Washington, she was employed as a "field nurse."

April 27 (Saturday)

Edmonds, S. Emma E., Union field nurse, Washington, D.C.:

Soon after reaching Washington, I commenced visiting the temporary hospitals which were prepared to receive the soldiers who arrived there sick. The troops came pouring in so fast, and the weather being extremely warm, all the general hospitals were soon filled.... After walking through the streets for hours on a sultry southern day in search of one of those temporary hospitals, I would find a number of men there delirious with fever—others had been sunstruck and carried there—but no physician to be found in attendance.... A certain number of surgeons were detailed every morning to visit those hospitals,... but the number of hospitals and patients were increasing so fast that it required all day to make the tour.

… another great evil was to be remedied—there were thousands of sick men to be taken care of—but for these the Government had made no provision as regards more delicate kinds of food—nothing but hard bread, coffee, and pork for sick and well alike. The Sanitary Commission had not yet come into operation and the consequence was our poor sick soldiers suffered unspeakably from want of proper nourishment....

April 28 (Sunday)

On the streets of New York, the chance meeting of the Rev. Dr. Henry Whitney Bellows, a Unitarian minister, and Dr. Elisha Harris resulted in a lengthy discussion about the problems facing the government in caring for the soldiers' comfort and the prevention of disease. In his report on the Sanitary Commission, Charles J. Stillé recorded the events which followed:

They were induced to attend a meeting, which had been called at the "Infirmary for Women," with the view of devising some means of contributing to [the war effort]. They found there a number of ladies, full of zeal and enthusiasm in the cause, most desirous of information as to the best mode of making themselves useful, but very much divided in opinion as to the best means which they should adopt, and with a very imperfect idea of organization. It was suggested, after some consultation, that an association, upon a wider basis, embracing the churches, schools, and all societies of women in the city, already engaged in any way in the work of relief to the army, should be attempted, and it was decided to call a general meeting to be held at the Cooper Institute, to perfect this plan. The invitation, or call for this meeting, which was prepared by Dr. Bellows, and which is somewhat remarkable as containing the first public announcement of principles of relief which afterwards became familiar from their practical application by the Sanitary Commission, was signed by ninety-two of the best known and most influential ladies in New York....

Events moved apace, and the meeting was held at Cooper Union, resulting in the organization of the "Women's Central Association of Relief," which became the groundwork for the establishment of the

Sanitary Commission. The stated goals were to "… collect and disseminate information upon the actual and prospective wants of the army; establish recognized relations with the Medical Staff, and act as an auxiliary to it; that they will maintain a central depot of stores, and open a bureau for the examination and registration of nurses."

May 1 (Wednesday)

Dr. Bellows, on behalf of the "Women's Central Association of Relief," made application to the headquarters of the U.S. Army's Medical Dept. in New York to obtain information on how the Association could assist the government. Surg. R. C. Saterlee, the Medical Purveyor (purchasing agent) for the area, let Dr. Bellows know that "in the opinion of the representative of the Medical Bureau, the plans proposed by the women could prove of no practical value whatever to the Army." Undaunted, Dr. Bellows prepared lists of possible needs of the troops which might be met by the work of the Association. To this suggestion, Dr. Saterlee's response was that "… the Medical Staff thought the zeal of the women and the activity of the men assisting them superfluous, obtrusive, and likely to grow troublesome, and that the sphere of the public in the work of aiding and relieving the army was predestined to be a very small one."

May 3 (Friday)

Stillé, Charles J., U.S. Sanitary Commission, Washington, D.C.:

During the months of May and June, 1861, regiment after regiment arrived at the National Capital in a most unsatisfactory condition, so far as concerned their real efficiency as soldiers. These regiments had made their journey in cattle cars, as crowded and as ill-provided as if they were carrying beasts to the shambles; while most of them were utterly unprovided with any means of relief for those of their number who had become ill or exhausted from their long exposure. On arriving, no preparations had been made for their reception. Men stood for hours in the broiling sun or drenching rain, waiting in vain for rations and shelter, while their ignorant and inexperienced Commissaries and Quartermasters were slowly and painfully learning

the duties of their positions. At last, utterly worn-out and disgusted, they reached their camps, where they received rations as unwholesome as distasteful to them, and endeavored to recruit their wasted energies while lying upon rotten straw, wrapped in a shoddy blanket. The reality of all this fearful misery in such striking contrast with the gay and cheerful scenes which they had just left, soon taught the soldier, who was in earnest, that true military discipline was not only essential to his efficiency but to his safety, and indeed to his very existence, as part of this vast human machine.…

May 5 (Sunday)

Craighill, E. A., Pvt., Co. G, 2nd Virginia, Harpers Ferry, western Virginia:

… early in May, all the Virginia soldiers were organized into regiments, and the First Brigade was formed, consisting of the 2nd, 4th, 5th and 27th and later the 33rd and the Rockbridge Battery (Pendleton's) from Lexington. This Brigade was commanded by Col. Thomas Jonathan Jackson, and not long after, was ordered from Harpers Ferry, it being such a dangerous place for the assembling of troops. After encamping and drilling for a time on Bolivar Heights, one of the Virginia hills overlooking the Ferry, this brigade was sent to different neighborhoods in Jefferson, Berkeley and Frederick counties.…

May 6 (Monday)

In New York, in addition to the "Women's Central Association of Relief," the "Physicians and Surgeons of the Hospitals of New York" and the "New York Medical Association for Furnishing Hospital Supplies" were formed and held various meetings. The latter organization opened a depot for receiving, storing, and supplying lint and bandages. The Women's Central Association of Relief and the Physicians and Surgeons groups prepared for the examination and selection of suitable nurses for the military hospitals. Extensive and elaborate arrangements were made to supply a corps of specially qualified individuals to perform nursing duties for the sick and wounded which would replace the soldiers detailed from the ranks to perform such tasks who had no prior training.

May 9 (Thursday)

Peters, D. C., Asst. Surg., USA, San Antonio, Tex.:

Acting under our instructions,... we advanced down the country, and were not again seriously molested until within ten miles of San Antonio, where we were surrounded by several thousand Texan soldiers and a demand was made for an unconditional surrender. Our commander having already suspected treachery, had selected for his position a hill on which was a stone house, and every preparation was made to give the enemy battle.

A flag of truce came in from Gen. Van Dorn, stating that the force surrounding us were Confederate soldiers, and we must yield to his superior numbers or suffer the consequences. He allowed Col. Reeve to send an experienced officer to ride through his lines and estimate his strength. On returning, this officer reported the enemy in great force and well supplied with artillery. Our own troops were but poorly furnished with ammunition, had but a scanty amount of provisions, and were without artillery. At least seventy of the men were completely broken-down by scurvy and chronic diarrhea, and all were more or less worn by continuous marches over several hundred miles of desert country. At a council of war, it was decided that it would be a useless sacrifice of life to resist.... It was reluctantly decided to yield to the demands.... After the surrender, the command was detained in San Antonio. I was allowed quarters for a hospital, and, with the means at my disposal, made the sick as comfortable as possible.

On giving up our arms, it was understood that the soldiers were to be paroled and allowed the limits of the county of Bexar, and the officers the limits of the so-called southern confederacy. These paroles were not afterward fully recognized, as the surrender took place on the 9th of May, 1861, and in the following month of June, the soldiers were marched off to a camp, where they were kept under guard and all intercourse between them and their officers was, by order of the authorities, suspended. After twenty-two months of confinement these men were exchanged. Finding myself of no further use to our men, I applied for, and obtained, permission to proceed to Richmond, Virginia, where I was in hopes of being released, on the ground, that as a surgeon, I might not be considered as an actual combatant.... My application met with approval, and I was furnished with the necessary papers, to protect me while traveling....

May 10 (Friday)

There were many problems attendant to raising a large army. Among them were the clothing for the troops, and their rations. The clothing problem for a time was met by the troops themselves. There were many strange-looking uniforms during the early stages of the war. In the east, many favored the Zouave costume, which consisted of baggy pants, tight jackets, and a fez with a tassel on the top. In the west, anything and everything was seen, sometimes in one unit. The major problem was in getting the uniforms made and to the troops. Contractors, as usual, often shipped shoddy merchandise, at elevated prices, and the clothing fell apart within a few weeks. Obtaining blankets was also a major problem, and in the west the men were asked to bring their own—some arriving carrying a multicolored quilt from their bed at home.

Food was another problem. The Regular Army had its own way of doing things and that method was carried over into the volunteer organizations. There were no "company messes" as such, nor were there any "company cooks." The rations were issued to the individual, and he was supposed to be able to fix his own in whatever manner he chose. At this time in the war, the ration consisted of:

Pork or bacon, 12 oz.; fresh or salt beef, 1 lb. 8 oz.; flour, 1 lb. 2 oz., or 12 oz. hard bread, or cornmeal, 1 lb. 4 oz. For each 100 rations there was added beans or rice, 10 lbs., or 9 lbs. 12 oz. desiccated potatoes; mixed vegetables, 6 lbs. 4 oz.; green coffee, 10 lbs.; sugar, 5 lbs.; vinegar, 1 gal.; and 1 lb. of candles.

Not all items were available every day, so the troops saw mostly bacon, hard bread, and beans. The vinegar was to combat scurvy, which disease was a real threat to the men during most seasons of the year. The desiccated vegetables, commonly referred to as "decimated vegetables," weren't a popular item, and fresh vegetables were seldom, if ever, issued. No fruit was available except what could be stolen from orchards or bought from local farmers.

Desiccated vegetables consisted of potatoes, cabbages, turnips, carrots, parsnips, beets, tomatoes, onions, peas, beans, lentils, celery, etc. These vegetables were cleaned, dried, and pressed into a compact "brick" form, sealed in tin boxes, and then packed in wooden crates. A "brick" was one foot square and two inches thick, weighed about seven pounds, and contained about 112 rations of one ounce. This mess, when reconstituted, would swell to 16 times its compressed bulk! It was to provide vegetables for 100 men for one meal.

The rice issued wasn't long-grain rice, but was either brown rice, or short- to medium-grain white rice. The salt issued was in a variety of forms, from coarse mined salt, to finely milled salt. This was usually measured by the "handful," which converted to about 1/2 cup of modern measure. Usually too much salt was used in cooking, resulting in dietary problems.

The beef or pork not issued fresh was preserved with salt, and usually packed in barrels. Much spoilage occurred, and not a little of it was from bad meat sold by dishonest contractors. Bread was issued in a 22-ounce loaf per man for the day, or the equivalent made up with 18 ounces of hardtack crackers. A "marching ration" in the Union Army consisted of 16 ounces of meat, 22 ounces of bread, and 4 ounces each of coffee and sugar. Usually some of the meat was cooked and some taken as issued—i.e., salted.

The cooking utensils issued to the soldiers were extremely basic. Usually they consisted of iron camp kettles, with a handle, and varying in size from four to seven gallons, iron mess pans, about 12 inches in diameter and sloping to the bottom. Everything else consisted of whatever could be made available.

The "volunteers" who did the cooking were mostly from homes where cooking was considered "woman's work," and no self-respecting man would be found in the kitchen, unless he were a chef. The result was poor food, made even worse by improper preparation, which led to stomach ailments such as diarrhea and dysentery.

The army didn't look at the food in the same way as the recipients did. In the booklet published by the Army of the Potomac entitled *Culinary Hints for the Soldier*, the army proclaimed that "No army in the world is so well provided for, in the shape of food, either as to quantity or quality, as the army of the United States, and very little attention on the part of the cook will enable him to lay up a liberal amount weekly.... No one man can consume his daily ration,

although many waste it; and a systematic issue will, in a great measure, prevent unnecessary extravagance."

May 12 (Sunday)

At the outset of the war, Mrs. Letitia Tyler Semple, daughter of a former President of the United States, John Tyler, was in New York with her husband, who was paymaster for the U.S. Navy there. They immediately left for Virginia, stopping in Philadelphia to visit friends en route. One of her friends remarked that more soldiers died of disease than wounds, and that hospitals should be the military's first order of business.

Upon her arrival in Richmond, she met with her father, then a member of the Confederate Congress, and they went to see the Secretary of War to obtain permission to establish a hospital. Secretary Leroy P. Walker gladly assented to the establishment of a hospital at Williamsburg, Va., and Mrs. Semple departed for that town immediately. There, she was met by enthusiastic women who helped start the hospital at the Female Seminary, which stood on the site of the old colonial capitol building.

The ladies went to work, and soon there were seventy-five cots available, the first being made up by Mrs. Semple. Drs. Tinsley and Shields were assigned as the surgeons for the newly organized institution. Shortly thereafter, Mrs. Semple left Williamsburg for Richmond to attend to family business.

May 16 (Thursday)

Believing that the real root of the problem in getting the Army to accept the services of the civilian volunteer agencies lay in Washington, a group consisting of Dr. Van Buren (Physicians and Surgeons), Dr. Jacob Harsen (Lint and Bandage Association), and Drs. Bellow and Elisha Harris (Women's Central Association) arrived in that city from New York to confront the situation. What they found was confusion. Communication between the future Sanitary Commission and the U.S. Army in New York had only just been reestablished. The masses of troops filling the city were poorly led, fed, and sheltered. Above all, the government was receiving well-meaning advice from all quarters, mostly unsolicited. The New York delegation only added to the bedlam, and with no "official" sanction, it had major problems getting to see anyone in authority.

The delegation's first stop was to see Gen. Winfield Scott, the aged commander of all Army forces. The purpose was to get Scott to agree to reexamine the volunteers to weed out the diseased, disabled, and unfit before they became a major burden. The logic of this was readily apparent, and Scott agreed immediately. Another problem then arose. So many of the men who were already in uniform were so obviously unfit that their dismissal might cause some panic in the country. A compromise, of sorts, was reached whereby some of the men were retained temporarily—this led to later problems in the early battles. Some good was realized from this effort, however, because more stringent examinations were adopted to preclude a repetition of the situation.

The next call was on Acting Surgeon General Robert C. Wood, whose reception was cordial, but noncommittal. The Surgeon General, Dr. Lawson, was ill and couldn't perform his duties. Wood's opinion was that the current crisis was only a repeat of the Seminole and Mexican wars, except on a larger scale.

May 17 (Friday)

Having been named commander of the Confederate troops at Harpers Ferry on the 15th, Gen. Joseph E. Johnston arrived to find that only 60 percent of his troops were fit for duty—the remainder being sick with measles or mumps. These diseases had arrived mainly with new troops sent as reinforcements to that strategic location. Things didn't improve much over the next few months. By July, when Johnston was ordered east to Manassas, his troop strength had been reduced by illness to less than half. One Tennessee regiment, the Third, with 1100 men, had more than 600 cases of measles over a two-month period.

May 21 (Tuesday)

The United States Sanitary Commission made a formal request to the Secretary of War, Simon Cameron, outlining the powers requested for the Commission in its efforts to aid the Medical Dept. The Commission stated:

> The Commission being organized for the purposes only of inquiry and advice, asks for no legal powers, but only the official recognition and moral countenance of the Government, which will be secured by its public appointment....

> The Commission seeks no pecuniary remuneration from the Government....

> The Commission asks leave to sit through the war, either in Washington or when and where it may find it most convenient and useful; but it will disband should experience render its operations embarrassing to the Government, or less necessary and useful than it is now supposed they will prove.

> As the Government may select its own Commissioners—the persons named in the recommendation of the Medical Bureau being wholly undesirous, however willing to serve, if other persons more deserving of the confidence of the Government and of the public can be nominated....

Plainly, the Commission wasn't a self-aggrandizing group, but one which only sought to lend its experience to the solution to a major problem—albeit one the Army Medical Dept. didn't wholly recognize. The request was taken under advisement by the Secretary of War, who recommended adoption. On June 9, 1861, the approval was obtained from both Secretary Cameron and Pres. Lincoln, although Lincoln called the establishment of the Commission "adding a fifth wheel to the coach."

May 22 (Wednesday)

Just when things seemed to be in hand with the authorization of the Sanitary Commission, the Surgeon General of the Army, Dr. Thomas Lawson, died and Dr. Clement Alexander Finley, the ranking medical officer, became the new Surgeon General. Finley, born in 1797, was a man of rigid ideas and stern discipline. He informed Secretary of War Cameron that he *didn't* concur with the agreement with the newly formed Sanitary Commission. He met his nemesis in Dr. Bellows, who could charm anyone, and Finley was finally convinced to agree with the Commission's scope of operations. However, Finley's hostility towards the Commission remained.

May 23 (Thursday)

On July 19, 1817, in Knox County, Ohio, Mary Ann Ball was born to Hiram and Annie Ball. Seventeen months later, Annie died, and Mary Ann was sent to her mother's parents in Richland County, Ohio, until her father remarried a few years later. At the age of twelve, she decided to go to live with her uncle, Henry Rodgers.

In 1833, she moved to Oberlin, Ohio, and from there moved to Hamilton County, near Cincinnati. In 1847, at age 30, and considered a spinster in that day, she married Robert Bickerdyke, a widower with small children. In 1856, the Bickerdykes moved to Galesburg, Ill., taking their two sons, James and Hiram, eight and six years old, and leaving in the Cincinnati area the three children from Robert's previous marriage. The Bickerdykes still lived in Galesburg when Robert died three years later.

During her stay in Hamilton County, and before Mary Ann married Robert Bickerdyke, it is believed that she received some training in botanic medicine and did, indeed, graduate from a local Cincinnati school which taught the subject. Shortly after Robert's death, Mary Ann put up a sign on her cottage which proclaimed to all the world that "M. A. Bickerdyke, Botanic Physician" was available for consultation. Mrs. Bickerdyke became well known in the town as a woman of courage, honesty, and kindness, although she was *quite* outspoken.

May 25 (Saturday)

In Washington, the War Dept. issued General Orders No. 25, in which the President directed that a surgeon and an assistant surgeon should be appointed, for each regiment of volunteers, by the governors of their respective states, and that these officers should be examined by boards, to be appointed by the governors, as to their qualifications, the appointments to be subject to the approval of the Secretary of War.

May 26 (Sunday)

In Galesburg, Ill., it was time for services at the Brick Congregational Church, where Dr. Edward Beecher, of *the* famous Beechers, was the current minister. Dr. Beecher began with a prayer, and then he read a letter from Dr. Benjamin Woodward, a local physician who, having had volunteered in response to Lincoln's call, was currently at Cairo, Ill., with about 500 of Galesburg's (and the county's) finest.

While the war had just begun, the troops, including those from Galesburg, were dying like flies from disease and poor treatment in the hospitals. Medical supplies were poor, or nonexistent, and Dr. Woodward despaired of any improvement. His written narrative, spoken by Dr. Beecher, touched the hearts

of all the people, especially those who had sons in Cairo. Dr. Beecher asked that the congregation do something to alleviate the suffering of the men, but what could be done? After some serious debate, it was decided that they would send a representative to Cairo, along with money and some obviously needed supplies, at the earliest possible moment. The next question was: Who to send? Dr. Beecher called for a silent prayer to ask for guidance on the matter.

At the end of the prayer, one lady arose to speak. She was the wife of one of the local college professors and the current president of the Ladies Aid Circle at the church. The name she proposed was that of Sister Mary Ann Bickerdyke, who truly possessed all of the attributes the people were looking for in their representative, and more. A tall, broad-shouldered, plain-looking woman, she'd never been known to flinch from any job, or fail to complete the job once it was undertaken. An ideal candidate. Reportedly, her response was blunt and practical. She proposed to go to Cairo and "clean things up down there," calling it the "Lord's work."

In this simple church in the small town of Galesburg, Ill., was born the mission of one of the most courageous women to serve in the Civil War. Mary Livermore, her friend and co-worker in the Sanitary Commission, described Mary Ann Bickerdyke.

Livermore, Mary, Chicago, Ill.:

She was unique in method, extraordinary in executive ability, enthusiastic in devotion, and indomitable in will…. She gave herself to the rank and file of the army—the private soldiers—for whom she had unbounded tenderness, and developed almost limitless resources of help and comfort.

To them she was strength and sweetness; and for them she exercised sound, practical sense, a ready wit, and a rare intelligence, that made her a power in the hospital or on the field. There was no peril she would not dare for a sick and wounded man, no official red tape of formality for which she cared more than for a common tow string, if it interfered with her in her work of relief. To their honor be it said, the "boys" reciprocated her affection most heartily. "That homely figure, clad in calico, wrapped in a shawl, and surmounted with a 'Shaker' bonnet, is more to this army than the Madonna to a Catholic!" said an officer, pointing to Mother Bickerdyke, as she emerged from the Sanitary Commission headquarters, in Memphis, laden with an assortment of supplies.... To the entire army of the West she was emphatically "*Mother* Bickerdyke."

May 30 (Thursday)

Among the many things the new soldier had to learn was how to prepare food. A tract published for the Army of the Potomac explained to the soldier how to cook bacon.

Bacon should be well washed and scraped and put to soak all night. In the morning, put it to boil slowly; simmering is better. After it has once boiled, throw the water off and fill up with fresh water; then let it simmer for three hours. When thoroughly done, the rind comes off easily, and the meat tastes fresh and sweet.

The above assumes that there is time for the soldier to do all the soaking and boiling; that the bacon isn't so maggot-infested as to be inedible; and that the tools to do all this will be at hand. To add to this, directions were given for frying bacon.

The great secret in frying is to have the fat as hot as the fire will make it before putting the article to be cooked into it. The object is to close up the pores of the flesh at once, and prevent the fat from penetrating it, rendering it greasy and indigestible. After the bacon is well soaked, cut it into thin slices, and fry it crisp. If it is cold bacon, slice it into a pan, cover it with bread crumbs—stale bread grated—add very little fat, and put it over a quick fire for four or five minutes; then turn it, and cook the other side.

June 5 (Wednesday)

The surgeon in charge of the Military Hospital at Richmond, Va., Dr. Gibson, sent a message to the Sisters of Charity—the "white caps," or Cornette Sisters—at Emmitsburg, Md., to come to the relief of the sick and wounded in the Confederate capital. After the bureaucracy did its turn, the Sisters were allowed to begin their work at a facility that became known as St. Anne's Military Hospital. The buildings of the hospital weren't finished, walls were unplastered, but the majority of the structure was complete enough to use.

When the Sisters arrived at the hospital, they found about 300 patients there in wards containing from 12 to 14 men. Arriving at about noon, they found that none of the patients had been fed that day. The women immediately went to the kitchen and *organized* the staff. Many of the wounded were from the western Virginia campaign.

June 7 (Friday)

The supply of "white caps" from the Sisters of Charity at Emmitsburg, Md., was further exhausted when a request reached the Mother House from Confederate authorities to send nurses to Harpers Ferry. Although it caused a severe strain on available resources, the Superiors sent three Sisters on the 9th.

June 9 (Sunday)

In one of the most far-reaching documents ever published by the War Dept., Secretary of War Simon Cameron and Pres. Abraham Lincoln authorized the creation of the U.S. Sanitary Commission, and defined its relationship to the Medical Dept. of the United States Army. The document, in part, stated:

The Secretary of War has learned, with great satisfaction, that at the instance and in pursuance of the suggestion of the Medical Bureau ... consented, in connection with such others as they may choose to associate with them, to act as "A Commission of Inquiry and Advice in respect of the Sanitary Interests of the United States Forces," and without remuneration from the Government....

The Commission, in connection with a Surgeon of the U.S.A., to be designated by the Secretary, will direct its inquiries to the principles and practices connected with the inspection of recruits and enlisted men; the sanitary condition of the volunteers; to the means of preserving and restoring the health, and of securing the general comfort and efficiency of troops; to the proper provision of cooks, nurses, and hospitals; and to other subjects of like nature....

A room with necessary conveniences will be provided in the City of Washington for the use of the Commission....

The Commission will exist until the Secretary of War shall otherwise direct, unless sooner dissolved by its own action.

With the approval of the Government, the Sanitary Commission immediately concentrated on getting its offices open. To do this they recruited one man who would have a profound effect on the Commission and its work—Frederick Law Olmsted.

Frederick Law Olmsted (F.L.O., as he was commonly referred to) was born on April 26, 1822, in Hartford, Conn. His English ancestors had come to the American colonies in September 1632. F.L.O., after visits to England and other parts of the United States, toured the South, 1852-53, visiting most of the major cities, but spending more time in the countryside, studying agricultural methods and the South's "peculiar institution"—slavery. His later visits to west Texas with his brother John left him with more impressions of the strength of the nation. He'd become an accomplished writer, and his works were published in several papers and monthlies. He also wrote a book, *The Cotton Kingdom*. In the late 1850s he entered the competition to design Central Park in New York and won—despite his inexperience in either farming or gardening. It would be this work that would bring his organizational ability to the fore and bring him to the notice of many influential people in New York and New England. Olmsted's presence would have a major impact on the operation of the United States Sanitary Commission in the near future.

Three Sisters of Charity left Emmitsburg, Md., for Harpers Ferry shortly after daylight. They were to have been furnished an orderly to serve as a guide and to get them through the Federal pickets surrounding Harpers Ferry, but the guide and the Sisters passed each other on the road without knowing it. Their journey, by stagecoach, was uncomfortable due to the heat, which was such that one of the horses gave out and had to be replaced prior to reaching Frederick City. The railroad to Harpers Ferry wasn't in operation at the time, so they continued on by coach, becoming stuck outside Maryland Heights on the outskirts of Harpers Ferry. After some delay, the coach was freed and the journey continued. At dusk, they were stopped by the first of three Confederate picket lines and finally passed on to the town over a bridge that had already been charged with powder to blow it up in the event of retreat.

On Bolivar Heights, another hill across the town from Maryland Heights, a military hospital had been established near a small Catholic church. The hospital was already filled with the sick, and hundreds more, in slightly better condition, lay in tents awaiting space in the hospital. Finding a place to eat and rest, the Sisters retired for the night.

On this date, Mary Ann Bickerdyke left the Illinois Central train at Cairo, Ill., after spending a sleepless night en route from Galesburg. She'd arrived to "clean up the mess." After supervising the unloading of her meager baggage, and the boxes and crates she'd brought with her, which were many, she waited for Dr. Woodward to come and collect her. Meanwhile, she looked around Cairo and wasn't impressed. The town, what there was of it, was surrounded by high levees on three sides to keep out the Ohio and Mississippi rivers. Drainage was poor, and the recent rains had left the streets a quagmire.

Eventually, Dr. Woodward arrived, in uniform, driving his own horse and buggy. He seemed to be the only one in uniform, since the government had yet to issue uniforms to the enlisted personnel at Cairo. After some discussion, all of the woman's baggage was loaded into the buggy and they left for Ft. Defiance—a name given the local fort.

En route, Dr. Woodward informed Bickerdyke that she had a pass to visit the fort only for that day. All civilians, especially women, had to be out by sundown. Bickerdyke only commented, "We'll see about that, I'll leave when my work is done." After passing the sentry at the gate, the doctor drove to where three tents were set apart from the others. This was the regimental hospital, such as it was. Before entering the first tent, the doctor told Bickerdyke that conditions were very bad and that she might be shocked when she saw what the tent arrangement was like.

The situation was much worse than what she'd been led to believe by Dr. Woodward's letter to the people at Galesburg. Inside the first tent were ten men, only one or two with cots, the remainder on straw pallets on the ground covered with a blanket or an overcoat. The men lay so close together that there was little room to move between them. The dirt floor of the tent, the part that wasn't covered with human bodies, was covered with human excrement, and flies swarmed over the sick men. The men lay only partly clothed, most only in shirts and underwear, which were covered with filth and vomit and smelly with stale sweat. Near the door sat a human scarecrow with a dipper and an empty pail near his feet. This was the nurse for the remainder of the patients in the tent.

Bickerdyke's inspection continued through all the tents before she asked how many of the men were dying, not soon, but today. The reply came: two men with bloody flux, and one starving to death because he couldn't keep anything in his stomach. Bickerdyke looked thoughtful.

Outside, Bickerdyke found several empty barrels. She asked the doctor to get her several healthy men to help her work. He demurred, saying that he was only a junior surgeon, and that he'd never given direction to any, other than nurses and patients. Bickerdyke, scorning Woodward's indecision, went to the nearest camp fire and bribed the men there with a future meal of chicken and bread if they'd help her. She immediately had volunteers.

First, Bickerdyke had the men saw the barrels in half and scrub them out with hot water. Next, she opened some of the boxes she'd brought with her, and out came cakes of lye soap. With hot water in the tubs, Bickerdyke then went to the first tent with the doctor and a few of her volunteers. There she chided the patients into wanting a bath and bribed them all with a promise of fried chicken if they could walk to the tubs. Those who couldn't walk were carried. Once there, the patients were turned over to Dr. Woodward, who had firm directions from Bickerdyke to scrub the men thoroughly and to cut their hair and beards down to the skin to get rid of the lice. The patients' clothing was to be burned, as was the straw they had been lying on. She'd brought new clothing for the men. The doctor objected that the baring of the skin of the patients who had temperatures might do them harm. This notion was immediately countered by Bickerdyke with the fact that it was 90° outside, and that it would do the men no harm to take off their clothes.

Organizing some of the other volunteers, Bickerdyke took a spade and began to scoop out the top layer of dirt from inside the first tent until she reached a solid, clean level. While the volunteers completed the other tents, Bickerdyke organized the spreading of clean straw on the floor of the first tent. While the other tents were being prepared, the remainder of the patients were being scrubbed and dressed in clean clothing. By late afternoon, all of the patients were back in their tents under clean sheets and feeling much better.

When all were in bed, Bickerdyke passed out the food she'd brought from Galesburg, patients first, and then the volunteers. As the sunset gun time approached, Bickerdyke took two pails to each of the tents. One pail was filled with water and the other had lime in the bottom of it to be used as a latrine. The doctor admonished Bickerdyke that she'd miss her train if they didn't hurry, to which she replied that she wasn't going back until the job was done. Meanwhile, she'd find a place to stay in town. Off she went with a pleasant "Goodnight," leaving a very befuddled Dr. Woodward.

June 10 (Monday)

At Cairo, Ill., Mary Ann Bickerdyke had found lodging by knocking on doors and asking. Finding a room, she settled in and wrote a long letter back to Galesburg, Ill., to explain the situation and to organize more funding and supplies. Several things she considered essential, such as soap, soda, underwear, and zinc chamber pots. Blankets, skillets, pots (large), pans (also large), and washboards were also essential.

When she returned to Ft. Defiance on this day, Mrs. Bickerdyke found that Dr. Woodward was also responsible for five other hospitals in the area. She immediately visited them and found them to be as bad, if not worse, than the first. Within a short period of time she had those five in much better shape, much to the amazement and pleasure of the patients, and the bewilderment of the hospital administrators, who felt as though they'd been hit by a cyclone.

One such hospital was at Bird's Point, where a civilian contract doctor was in charge of the patients. He "managed" to fit these patients into his regular schedule of civilian patients, which meant that the soldiers seldom saw him. As a result, the Bird's Point hospital was the worst of the lot, being the filthiest, most poorly run, and with the most deaths. On one of Mrs. Bickerdyke's visits, the doctor happened to be there, and she berated him on his treatment of the patients. In the middle of the hospital, in front of the patients and staff, she told him in no uncertain terms that he was incompetent, inefficient, and not fit to treat the patients in that hospital. The doctor went immediately to Brig. Gen. Benjamin M. Prentiss to complain. The civilian doctor screamed at Gen.

Prentiss that a "cyclone in calico" had come into his hospital and had created chaos.

Prentiss, an Illinois businessman, and a veteran of the Mexican War, had been asked by the governor of the state to command state troops. Prentiss was an intelligent man and was given to tackling problems head-on, and today he got his chance. First, he listened to the doctor and couldn't make sense of the complaint. Prentiss had never heard of Mrs. Bickerdyke, at least not yet. The doctor explained that Bickerdyke had been brought into camp in an unauthorized manner by Dr. Woodward. The general, knowing that women weren't allowed in the camp, told the doctor that the solution was simple, that she'd have to leave, and that *he'd* see to it. The messenger sent to get Dr. Woodward found both the doctor and Mrs. Bickerdyke outside Gen. Prentiss' tent, because they'd followed the contract doctor to headquarters. The conversation wasn't recorded, but when the doctor and Mrs. Bickerdyke left Prentiss' tent, she had a semiofficial status in the organization. In effect, she took over, and she organized a diet kitchen which served all the hospitals in the area.

The first serious battle of the war was fought today at Big Bethel, Va., between 2500 Federals from Ft. Monroe and 1200 Confederates. The Federals lost the match, losing 18 dead. The Confederates lost one man.

When the news of the battle at Big Bethel reached Richmond, Mrs. Letitia Tyler Semple immediately left for Williamsburg, and the hospital she'd helped found there last month. There had been so many refugees from Hampton and other places, and so many sick soldiers needing attention, that William and Mary College, the Court House, and several churches were taken for hospitals. Dr. Willis Westmoreland was now in charge of the overall medical operation, and he sent a message to Mrs. Semple asking her to inspect the various facilities to see what was needed. On her tour she found that many things were lacking, and she left for Richmond to get them as quickly as possible. Once in Richmond, she visited Surg. Gen. Moore, who provided all that he could at that time, and then she turned to the local populace for assistance. The people of Richmond, Petersburg, and other cities and towns gave generously, and she had all the materials sent to Williamsburg.

The first death in the hospital was that of a young man named Ball, from Fairfax County, Va. Mrs. Semple continued her good works for several months until the area was evacuated when Union troops arrived in spring 1862.

June 13 (Thursday)

Edmonds, S. Emma E., Union field nurse, Washington, D.C.:

Typhoid fever began to make its appearance in camp, as the burning sun of June came pouring down on us, and the hospitals were soon crowded with its victims.... I shall notice, briefly, the manner in which the hospitals are conducted in camp. There are large tents furnished for hospital purposes, which will accommodate from twenty to twenty-five men. These tents are usually put up in the most pleasant and shady part of the camp; the inside is nicely leveled, and board floors laid, if boards can be procured, if not, rubber blankets are laid down instead. Sometimes there are straw ticks and cot bedspreads furnished, but not in sufficient quantity to supply all the hospitals. Along each side of the tent the sick are laid, on blankets or cots, leaving room to pass between the beds.... The hospital corps consists of a surgeon, an assistant surgeon, a hospital steward, a ward master, four nurses, two cooks, and a man of all work to carry water, cut wood, and make himself generally useful....

Draining the grounds is a very important part of hospital duty, for when those terrible thunderstorms come, which are so frequent in the South, it is ... impossible to keep the tent floors from being flooded.... Great excitement prevails in camp during these tempests—the rain comes down in torrents, while the wind blows a hurricane—lifting the tents from the ground, and throwing everything into wild confusion. I have seen a dozen men stand for hours around one hospital, holding down the ropes and tent poles to prevent the sick from being exposed to the raging elements....

June 15 (Saturday)

Gen. Joseph E. Johnston, CSA, commanded the troops holding Harpers Ferry and had been worried for several days about holding that town against a Federal advance. Finally, he made up his mind and ordered the evacuation and the movement of the troops to Winchester, Va. The Sisters of Charity from Emmitsburg, Md., had been working with the sick at the town since their arrival on the 9th, and they were alerted for movement. Finally at 11 P.M. on the 14th, a wagon was sent for the Sisters and their baggage to take them to the railroad for movement south. They were placed in a small hut next to the river until 4 A.M. on this date, when they boarded the train and left for Winchester, arriving there about 10 A.M., without breakfast. These three Sisters served at Winchester for several weeks before being sent on to Richmond, where they served for the remainder of the war.

June 18 (Tuesday)

One of the major problems that the Sanitary Commission had to deal with, east and west, was the shipment of food to the soldiers in the camps. The friends and relatives of these men meant well but they sent the wrong things, which were packed the wrong way, causing unnecessary losses and creating messes. Mary Livermore tells it best:

> Women rifled their storerooms and preserve closets of canned fruit and pots of jam and marmalade, which they packed with clothing and blankets, books and stationery and photographs. Baggage cars were soon flooded with fermenting sweetmeats and broken pots of jelly. Decaying fruit and vegetables, pastry and cake, badly canned meats and soups ruined clothing and papers.

In Cairo, Ill., Mrs. Bickerdyke salvaged what she could of the mess arriving from the families, and used it in her hospitals. Never having enough delicate food for the patients, she took to browbeating the healthy soldiers out of their packages for the sick ones. One other advantage she had was that the troops moved about frequently and packages addressed to a soldier who'd left for parts unknown weren't forwarded. These she "claimed" for her sick "boys." In fact, anything that wasn't nailed down and had no obvious owner was taken by Mrs. Bickerdyke, and, in short order, she had people helping her identify what was available, knowing that it was going to a good cause.

As more experience was gained by the Sanitary Commissions, east and west, the Ladies' Aid Societies and Soldiers' Aid Societies sent the packages to the Commission warehouses for distribution. Here the packages were all opened, the contents collected by type, i.e., clothing in one place (by size and type), blankets in another, food in yet another stack, etc. All items were then marked with the Sanitary Commission's identification in indelible ink and repacked in boxes also marked with the Commission's identification. This was a much more efficient operation, and one that saved many a donation from the trash heap.

June 20 (Thursday)

Dr. Bellows of the newly founded Sanitary Commission asked F. L. Olmsted to become the Executive Secretary of the Sanitary Commission, to be based in Washington, D.C. Olmsted was almost forty, lame, and in poor health.

June 21 (Friday)

In Richmond, Brig. Gen. John H. Winder began his duties by becoming familiar with the city and its environs. His duties included the fitting out of the soldiers with uniforms and weapons before the men were sent to the field, processing discharges of those unfit for service, capturing and returning soldiers deserting their units, and the care of the wounded and sick soldiers in the area. Quite a task, considering that the population of Richmond had doubled in less than four months. The city was now full of office seekers, drunken soldiers, gamblers, prostitutes, and saloons. To do his task, Winder discovered a truth that would haunt him for the entire war—he'd never have adequate staff to accomplish his mission.

June 22 (Saturday)

Having obtained a parole, Asst. Surg. Peters now had to make his own way to Richmond, Va., where he hoped to obtain his release and return to the United States.

Peters, D. C., Asst. Surg., USA, paroled prisoner, en route to Richmond, Va.:

> I started my journey on June 22, 1861, in company with two other officers. We travelled to Galveston, Texas, and found the port blockaded.... From Galveston we travelled several hundred miles overland by a circuitous route to New Orleans, Louisiana. During this part of our journey we were subjected to innumerable hardships and privations,

and ran no small risk of losing our lives, as we found the people excited against the general government, and under very little civil restraint. On arriving in Richmond, Virginia, I reported myself, according to promise, as a prisoner of war. My effort to obtain an unconditional release was fruitless, but instead, after some delay, I was granted a very rigid parole, and was informed that my only alternative was to accept it or remain a prisoner. After duly considering the subject, I signed the paper, and was ordered to proceed north by Nashville, Tennessee....

June 26 (Wednesday)

Olmsted left for Washington, D.C., passing through a rather placid countryside. His first sight of Union soldiers was at Havre de Grace, Md., where he saw several volunteers in shirt sleeves and dirty havelocks guarding the bridge crossings of the Susquehanna, where it flows into Chesapeake Bay. The troops were poorly dressed and, obviously, poorly disciplined.

June 27 (Thursday)

About 6 P.M., Olmsted arrived in Washington. The main thoroughfare, Pennsylvania Avenue, was still unpaved. During the rainy season, the Avenue was a mud trench, and a dust bowl during the dry season. The south side of the Avenue was lined with cheap stores and boardinghouses, livery stables, shacks, and open-air markets. The north side contained a brick sidewalk, the better shops, and the better hotels. Among the latter was the Willard, which Olmsted checked into upon arrival. The red-turreted Smithsonian Institution stood on the south side of the Mall, the only respectable building there. The Washington Monument was only half-finished, and it stood like a giant truncated pole.

Olmsted was met at the Willard Hotel by George E. Waring, Jr., with whom he'd worked on the Central Park project. Waring was a sanitary engineer by profession and an excellent designer of drainage systems. In a burst of enthusiasm, Waring had enlisted in the Garibaldi Guards, which were formed in New York, and he had been sent to Washington with that regiment. The two met in the lobby of the Willard, which was crowded with lobbyists, politicians, and office-seekers. The floor of the lobby was filthy with litter and tobacco juice.

June 28 (Friday)

Waring had obtained a pass for Olmsted to move about the camps since security was (supposedly) tight. Olmsted was to inspect the camps, beginning with those of the Garibaldi Guards, which were located about two miles east of the Capitol. He found the camp to be rows of tents and brushwood tumbledowns. The troops weren't in uniform, most wearing what they pleased, or had with them. Olmsted spent the night in Waring's bed, sleeping badly. The following day he returned to the Willard for further consultations. He'd begin a round of inspections of the other camps in the area the following day. These inspections would continue for about 10 days.

July 2 (Tuesday)

In one of the less celebrated actions of the war, the first contact between the Confederate and Union forces in northern Virginia occurred on this day near Williamsport, Md., at Falling Waters, where Col. George H. Thomas, USA, and Col. Thomas J. Jackson, CSA, collided in a sharp engagement for about an hour. Jackson retreated, chased by Thomas's cavalry. There were only about 8 killed and 15 wounded on the Union side. Those wounded were initially treated locally and then sent to the hospital established at Hagerstown, Md.

July 7 (Sunday)

Having breakfast at Wormeley's, a catering shop owned by a free mulatto, Olmsted listened to Senator Henry Wilson of the Military Affairs Committee rail against the Army, the Administration, and Gen. Scott. Nothing, according to Wilson, was being done right.

Near the White House, Olmsted had passed Lincoln, who was walking with two or three men, whom Olmsted described as "other loafers." Olmsted commented:

He looked much younger than I had supposed, dressed in a cheap & nasty French black cloth suit just out of [a] tight carpet bag. Looked as if he'd be an applicant for a Broadway squad policemanship, but a little too smart and careless. Turned and laughed familiarly at a joke upon himself which he overheard from my companion en passant.

July 8 (Monday)

At the end of the inspection tour, Olmsted prepared his report to the Sanitary Commission. In general, it contained little good news. The camps were located in poor areas with no provision for drainage around the tents; latrines were usually just trenches about 30 feet long without a pole or rail, the stench almost overpowering; the men's clothing was filthy and no attempt had been made to get the men to a bathing facility; the weapons were in poor condition and should be replaced; the food was issued daily, being of good quality but poorly prepared by the troops. Olmsted predicted that, given the living conditions, outbreaks of scurvy and dysentery would break out soon. Too often the officers of the more than seventy regiments around Washington were to be found in the barroom of Willard's Hotel or the other establishments in the city. The troops were left to fend for themselves.

July 10 (Wednesday)

The Sanitary Commission, being assigned office space in the Treasury Building, held its first meeting in the Grand Room. These meetings lasted for three days, usually running for three hours in the morning and another 4 to 5 hours in the evening. They appointed inspectors for the Commission, adopted a code of sanitation for distribution to the Army, drew up recommendations on the establishment of rest facilities for incoming troops at the railhead, and made other recommendations for the general welfare and health of the troops. As a possible enforcement of their recommendations, it was suggested that the Senate Military Affairs Committee direct that all officers comply with the recommendations or forward their reasons for not doing so.

One innovation the Sanitary Commission advocated was providing a means for the soldiers to send home part of their pay—an early allotment system. The Commission also recommended that a military-police force be set up to keep the soldiers out of the bars, brothels, and gambling dens. Its most important recommendation was to establish the proper sanitary conditions among the camps.

Wright, J. J. B., Surg., USA, Battle of Rich Mountain, western Virginia:

The attack on the enemy's work at Rich Mountain was made by infantry against artillery, cavalry, and infantry. The wounds, therefore, were inflicted by round shot, grape, and minié balls, and were of every description and character. A large three story house on the battlefield was occupied temporarily as an hospital, and tents were pitched in the vicinity. Having organized this hospital,… I proceeded to join the headquarters at Beverly, distant seven miles…. A general hospital was established in several commodious houses in this town…. So soon as transportation could be furnished, the wounded from Carrick's Ford were transferred to this hospital. The enemy's wounded received the same attention as our own, though they were, for the most part kept separate.…

July 11 (Thursday)

King, W. S., Surg., USA, prior to the Battle of Bull Run, Arlington, Va.:

In preparing for the expected battle, a limited number of ambulances which had been furnished, were distributed with great care, so as to equalize the amount of transportation among the regiments. I made an estimate of twenty wagons for our medical supplies, which, although approved … did not result in their being sent.

A few days before the forward movement, directions were issued by the General commanding to have the army put in light marching order…. As the conveyances estimated had not been furnished, these arrangements made it impossible to transport any medical supplies except such as could be placed in the ambulances or forage wagons.…

July 16 (Tuesday)

Edmonds, S. Emma E., Union field nurse, Washington, D.C.:

Marching orders received today—two days more, and the Army of the Potomac will be on its way to Bull Run. I find this registered in my journal July 15th, 1861.… All the sick in camp now were sent to Washington, clothes changed, knapsacks packed, letters written home, packages sent to the express office, etc.… There was one patient, however, we did not put into an ambulance, and who was a great source of anxiety to us. He lay there upon a stretcher close by, waiting to be carried to a house not far distant. He was young, not seventeen, with clear blue eyes, curly auburn hair, and a broad, white brow; his mother's pride, and an only son. Two weeks previously he'd been attacked with typhoid fever. The surgeon said, "You may do all you can for him, but it is a hopeless case."…

The ambulances started with their freight of emaciated, suffering men. Slowly that long train wound its way toward the city looking like a great funeral procession.…

July 17 (Wednesday)

McDowell's army reached Fairfax C.H. this night, where the army found large quantities of supplies left by the retreating Rebels. Discipline on the march hadn't improved.

King, W. S., Surg., USA, en route to the Battle of Bull Run, Fairfax, Va.:

… the advance was resumed. The day was unusually hot,… The road we found impassable in many places, owing to felled trees which the Rebels had placed in our way. Arriving at length near Fairfax, we discovered that the enemy had abandoned their works, and that a small force, left evidently to watch our movements, had just gone, leaving behind, in their haste, carpet-bags, trunks, a keg of whiskey, and half eaten meals.…

Edmonds, S. Emma E., Union field nurse, en route to Manassas, Va.:

The 17th of July dawned bright and clear, and everything being in readiness, the Army of the Potomac took up its line of march for Manassas. In gay spirits the army moved forward, the air resounding with the music of the regimental bands, and patriotic songs of the soldiers.… I felt strangely out of harmony with the wild, joyous spirit which pervaded the troops.… The main column reached Fairfax toward evening and encamped for the night. Col. R.'s wife of the Second ———, Mrs. B. and myself were, I think, the only three females who reached Fairfax that night.… The troops were in high spirits, and immediately began preparing supper. Some built fires while others went in search of, and appropriated, every available article which might in any way add to the comfort of hungry and fatigued men. The whole neighborhood was ransacked for milk, butter, eggs, poultry, etc., which were found in insufficient quantity to supply the wants of such a multitude. There might have been heard some stray shots fired in the direction of a field where a drove of cattle were quietly grazing; and soon after the odor of fresh steak was issuing from every part of the camp.… Supper being over, pickets posted, and camp guards detailed, all became quiet for the night.

E. A. Craighill had served his time as an infantryman in Jackson's Brigade and found it not necessarily to his liking. After being at Harpers Ferry for some time, he was called into the company "orderly room" and told that he was detailed as a medical steward to Dr. Hunter McGuire, the Brigade Surgeon. Craighill wasn't unwilling to do this, because he doubted his overall ability as an infantryman.

Craighill went to Winchester, Va., and reported to Dr. McGuire, and was put to work using his newly acquired medical knowledge. The medical staff remained in Martinsburg, Va., during the month of June and moved back to Winchester in early July. On July 17th, they left Winchester for Manassas, arriving there on the evening of the 20th.

July 18 (Thursday)

It was noon when McDowell's army approached Centreville, 22 miles and two and one-half days after leaving his camps around Alexandria. The temperature was nearing 90°, the men were out of water and didn't have the cooked rations they were to have had before they left Alexandria. Confederate Gen. Joseph E. Johnston was hurrying from the Shenandoah Valley.

McDowell sent a brigade-size force from Brig. Gen. Daniel Tyler's division to Blackburn Ford, where Col. I. B. Richardson took the force farther than it was supposed to go, and slammed into Beauregard's troops in a bloody clash which accomplished little, but caused the Federals to retreat.

King, W. S., Surg., USA, Battle of Bull Run, Centreville, Va.:

In the afternoon, heavy firing was heard on our left, towards Blackburn's Ford.… We pursued our course on the road leading to the ford, and soon met the ambulances with the dead, wounded, and disabled men. One soldier had his face shot away completely. Some in the ambulances were not wounded, but were disabled from sunstroke or exhaustion. The ambulances were stained with blood, evincing the terrible earnestness with which the Rebels had commenced their struggle. I dispatched Assistant Surgeon Magruder to … select suitable buildings for hospital purposes.… A hotel, a church, and a large dwelling were selected … some wounded were placed in them before my arrival.… An unexpected difficulty was now encountered, in the great scarcity of water. There were few wells in Centreville, and these had been so exhausted by our thirsty men that they were nearly dry. Water, procured with great difficulty and placed in basins for the purpose of washing the wounded, was snatched up and drank by stragglers, as they passed, before they could be prevented.…

To give an idea of some of our difficulties on this night, I might mention that the hospital in the church, as soon as emptied, became filled again by men stepping out of the ranks as they passed, in search of their companions, or for something to eat or drink.… As soon as Gen. Tyler, who commanded the division … arrived, I sought him and obtained a sufficient number of men as a guard for all our hospitals, and to procure a supply of water for our wounded.…

I had directed an ambulance with two wounded soldiers to be taken to a large dwelling selected as a hospital, and to have them placed in charge of the medical officer in attendance. Passing some hours after, I found these men still in the ambulance, and, on inquiry, was informed that the surgeon had declined to receive them because they did not belong to his regiment. I requested the surgeon, who appeared at the door, to inform me why he had not taken the soldiers into the hospital.… He was proceeding, in the most serious and empathic manner, to justify his course, when I cut short his argument by promptly ordering the removal of the men from the ambulance, and I remained long enough to see that they received the necessary attention.…

Edmonds, S. Emma E., Union field nurse, en route to Manassas, Va.:

Early the next morning the reveille beat, the whole camp was soon in motion, and after a slight breakfast from our haversacks the march was resumed. The day was very hot, and we found great difficulty in obtaining water, the want of which caused the troops much suffering. Many of the men were sunstruck, and others began to drop out of the ranks from exhaustion. All such as were not able to march were put into ambulances and sent back to Washington.… Considerable excitement prevailed through-

out the day, as we were every hour in expectation of meeting the enemy. Carefully feeling its way, however, the army moved steadily on, investigating every field, building, and ravine, for miles in front and to the right and left until it reached Centreville, where we halted for the night.

Several regiments had been supplied with new shoes the day before leaving camp, and they found by sad experience, that they were not the most comfortable things to march in, as their poor blistered feet testified; in many cases their feet were literally raw, the thick woolen stockings having chafed the skin off. Mrs. B. and I, having provided ourselves before leaving camp, with a quantity of linen, bandages, lint, ointment, etc. found it very convenient now, even before a shot had been fired.…

July 19 (Friday)

At Centreville, Va., the day was spent getting McDowell's army fed and regrouped. Stragglers came in at all hours.

At nearby Manassas Junction, Gen. Thomas J. Jackson arrived with his brigade as the advance of Joe Johnston's force moving from Winchester. The battle loomed.

July 20 (Saturday)

McDowell's officers spent the day doing reconnaissance of the proposed battlefield, assigning approaches, etc. Gen. Joe Johnston arrived from the Shenandoah Valley at about noon, and the remainder of his troops arrived as fast as they could be transported by rail from camps south of Winchester.

McDowell started moving his troops after dark, and they were all in motion by about 2:30 the following morning. The tactics of both commanders called for a strike against the enemy's left flank, which would have resulted in the armies doing a wheel in a macabre dance of death.

King, W. S., Surg., USA, Battle of Bull Run, Centreville, Va.:

The 19th and 20th of July were occupied in camp, waiting for the arrival of supplies. We embraced the opportunity to repair our ambulances, and again to visit the hospitals at Centreville.… I felt it my duty to make known our needs to the Surgeon General, stating … my anxiety that nothing should be wanting on my part ... that everything should be sent without stint.... I was informed the needed supplies would be sent next day to Fairfax Station, seven miles distant.... All our wounded in the Blackburn's Ford affair that could be removed were forwarded, on July 20th, in ambulances with a proper escort, to Fairfax Station, to be sent to Alexandria....

Edmonds, S. Emma E., Union field nurse, en route to Manassas, Va.:

Our surgeons began to prepare for the coming battle, by appropriating several buildings and fitting them up for the wounded—among others the stone church at Centreville—a church which many a soldier will remember, as long as memory lasts....

July 21 (Sunday)

King, W. S., Surg., USA, Battle of Bull Run, Centreville, Va.:

On the morning of July 21st, 1861, the General commanding,... passed, at daylight through our columns already moving in the direction of Bull Run.... I perceived that our troops marched at double quick, and some at a full run, while many, overcome by the heat, threw away their blankets and haversacks. I expressed my opinion to the General, that owing to their rapid movement, the men would be exhausted before they arrived on the scene of action. In this view he acquiesced, and directed that the men were not to run; but, as the officers behind, from an idea that great haste was necessary, constantly repeated the command to close up, the troops were kept at a run a great part of the way. The weather was excessively hot, and, as one of the causes of the Bull Run failure, I desire to record my belief that the exhaustion of our forces,... contributed as much as anything else to the disasters of the day. The comparative freshness of the Rebel troops gave them great and decided advantage....

Our troops ... hurried forward, the artillery was placed in position, and the action soon became general.... I thought it would be a small task,... to make out a list of the killed and wounded, and with notebook in hand I began to count the number of each. It is a singular fact that I observed near one hundred dead before one wounded!... I directed Asst. Surg. Magruder,... to proceed to Sedley Church, which was nearby, yet out of the line of fire, and to prepare

it and if necessary, a couple of houses close to the church, for the reception of our wounded.

Twice our men drove the Rebels over the crest of the hill, and victory seemed, for a brief period, to perch upon our banners.... But this exultation was of short duration: The Rebels again appeared, and their artillery opened more fiercely than ever. Our men could not again be rallied, from sheer exhaustion mostly, I believe, and we commenced slowly, and sadly, to retire.... We arrived at Centreville, tired and disappointed, near sundown ... we left at half-past ten o'clock P.M., for Fairfax, where we intended to remain till morning.

... the dust of the turnpike, between Centreville and Fairfax, raised by our soldiers and wagons in passing, floated over the road like a thick fog, and made it impossible to see for a distance of more than ten paces. In this passage, horse, foot, and vehicles were jammed in great confusion; upturned wagons and their contents blocked the way at short intervals, making it necessary for horsemen to leave the road and return again in order to go round the obstructions.... So slow was our progress that we did not reach Fairfax, a distance of only seven miles, till two o'clock in the morning....

Gray, C. C., Asst. Surg., USA, Manassas Battlefield, Va.:

I was attached to Col. Porter's Brigade of Gen. Hunter's Division.... The cavalry not being brought into action, I left them, by permission, and gave assistance to the wounded of Col. Burnside's Brigade, immediately in advance of us and suffering severely. Few ambulances could come up, and our attentions consisted chiefly in conveying the injured men into the shade, giving them water, extracting balls, etc. About two in the afternoon, I received an order from Asst. Surg. Magruder, USA, to report immediately at Sedley Church, a small building surrounded by farmhouses, about half a mile in the rear of Bull Run. Here was the principal depot for wounded. I remained here till the retreat commenced, about five in the afternoon. At that time not more than a tenth of the wounded had received attention, and I determined to remain, if practicable....

I went out to meet the advance of the Rebels ... to ask permission to continue [treating the wounded] unmolested, for shot were beginning to fly near the hospital. The officer to whom I surrendered, a lieutenant of Virginia cavalry, was an unreasonable man, and would neither permit me to return to our wounded, nor promise any protection for our hospital. I was compelled to accompany his party to Manassas Junction, eight miles distant, which place we reached about ten at night, where I was turned over to the chief medical officer, Dr. Gaston, of South Carolina. Observing my exhausted condition, he obtained permission for me to sleep on the floor of a Confederate hospital.

Edmonds, S. Emma E., Union field nurse, Manassas Battlefield, Va.:

After ascertaining the position of the enemy, Gen. McDowell ordered forward three divisions.... Sunday morning before dawn, those three divisions moved forward, presenting a magnificent spectacle, as column after column wound its way over the green hills and through the hazy valleys, with the soft moonlight falling on the long lines of shining steel. Not a drum or bugle was heard during the march, and the deep silence was only broken by the rumbling of artillery....

Mrs. B. and myself took our position on the field, according to orders, in connection with Gen. Heintzelman's division.... I imagine now, I see Mrs. B. as she stood there, looking as brave as possible with her narrow-brimmed leghorn hat, black cloth riding habit, shortened to walking length by the use of a page, a silver-mounted seven-shooter in her belt, a canteen of water swung over one shoulder and a flask of brandy over the other, and a haversack with provision, lint, bandages, adhesive plaster, etc. hanging by her side. She was tall and slender, with dark brown hair, pale face, and blue eyes.

The first man I saw killed was a gunner belonging to Col. R.'s command. A shell had burst in the midst of the battery, killing one and wounding three men and two horses.... Now the battle began to rage with terrible fury. Nothing could be heard save the thunder of artillery, the clash of steel, and the continuous roar of musketry.... I was hurried off to Centreville, a distance of seven miles, for a fresh supply of brandy, lint, etc. When I returned, the field was literally strewn with wounded, dead and dying. Mrs. B. was nowhere to be found. Had she been killed or wounded? A few moments ... and then I saw her coming toward me, running her horse with all possible speed, with about fifty canteens hanging from the pommel of her saddle.... "Don't stay to care for the wounded now; the troops are famishing with thirst and are beginning to fall back." Mr. B. then rode up with the same order, and we three started for a spring a mile distant, having gathered up the empty canteens which lay strewn on the field.... We filled our canteens while the Minnie balls fell thick and fast around us, and returned in safety to distribute the fruits of our labor among the exhausted men. We spent three hours in this manner, while the tide of battle rolled on more fiercely than before.... Mrs. B. and I dismounted and went to work again among the wounded.

Still the battle continues without cessation; the grape and canister fill the air as they go screaming on their fearful errand; the sight of that field is perfectly appalling; men tossing their arms wildly calling for help; there they lie bleeding, torn and mangled; legs, arms and bodies are crushed and broken as if smitten by thunderbolts; the ground is crimson with blood; it is terrible to witness....

Magruder, D. S., Asst. Surg., USA, Battle of Bull Run, Centreville, Va.:

After only a short search, I found and took possession of a stone church, pleasantly situated in a grove of timber, directly on the side and to the right of the road we had passed on advancing to the attack....

Upon taking possession of the church, I set men to work at removing the seats from the body of the church, with as little injury to them as practicable; had the floor covered with what blankets could be found, buckets of water brought, instruments and dressings placed in convenient places for use, and operating table improvised, and sent off men to the fields nearby to bring hay for bedding. Very soon after the work of fitting up the building had begun, the ambulances commenced returning from the field loaded with wounded men. In about two hours, the church, both upon the main floor and in the gallery, was completely filled, and I was obliged to take possession of three other unoccupied buildings, which are situated about seventy-five paces farther down and on the opposite side of the road towards the creek. So soon as I could get them cleared out, wounded men were carried into them until they were filled also. For want of other buildings, I was obliged to order many of the wounded to be laid under the trees, in the grove immediately around the church....

Craighill, E. A., Medical Steward, Jackson's Brigade, Manassas, Va.:

From at first having nothing to do, it was not long before I had more than I could possibly do, because on the bloody field, very soon the wounded needed all my attention and until late into the night of that eventful day, my every minute was occupied with the dead and the wounded, I having escaped all injury. I was reported in the Richmond papers as "missing," having failed to answer to my name at roll call. That night we established a temporary hospital at a farmhouse about a half mile in the rear of the battlefield owned by a Mr. Pringle whose house was full of dead and wounded men, and there, day and night for weeks I worked on those, first of my company, my friends, and when I could, from the brigade, or indeed from any of the army. Many poor fellows were desperately wounded, some of my close friends died that night. Six of my company were killed outright, one of whom was a physician (Tom Briscoe) we all called him. Some that it seemed to me were fatally wounded recovered; others that seemed not so badly wounded, died within a short time.

Of course, there were surgeons in our army older than I was, who had had much more experience, but none of us up to that time had seen much of gunshot wounds, and we had to unlearn what we had been taught at college, in books, as almost worthless, and only experience was useful in treatment and forming a correct or even an approximate opinion of results from wounds particularly and sometimes from disease....

... far into the night, wet, hungry, and weary. I attended again to my wounded, making them as comfortable as I could. I had had not a mouthful since breakfast and tried to find something to eat, at which I was not successful. I next thought of getting a little rest, and sleep if possible, knowing there was a strenuous day ahead of me the next day. There was no place under shelter for a well man, and my only hope was to find the sheltering arms of a friendly tree. It was raining, but not heavily, and wandering in the dark, I was attracted by a fire under one of the trees in the Pringle yard, around which there were a number of men, with their feet to the fire.... My teeth were chattering with the cold and it would be hard to imagine a more miserable human being. Seeing the fire and the men I concluded that here was

my opportunity to get warm and ... finding a place between two sleeping soundly, I crawled in and in less time than it takes to tell it, I was sound asleep....

The next morning when I awoke the sun was high in the sky, but I noticed that neither of the men I was between had stirred, and upon examination found they were stone dead.... They did not belong to our brigade, but to some Georgia regiment, I think.

July 22 (Monday)

The Federals' speed in fleeing the Manassas Battlefield was such that they covered the same ground in less than one day that had taken them two and one-half days to cover getting there. The wounded straggled badly, with all the ambulances having returned to Washington, and it took some of the wounded three days to return on their own. Some walked the distance with half their jaws shot away, legs badly mauled, broken arms, head wounds, and many other injuries. Even when they arrived in Washington, they found that the medical service wasn't prepared to handle such a large group of wounded; chaos reigned there.

King, W. S., Surg., USA, Battle of Bull Run, Centreville, Va.:

... we lay down in a field close by till daylight. As soon as the morning dawned, we saddled our horses, and finding the whole army on the march to Washington, we followed, overtaking the General on the roadside, about seven miles from the city.... Our retreat from the ground occupied, operated like a curtain to conceal from view all knowledge of the subsequent history of our cases....

Gray, C. C., Asst. Surg., USA, prisoner, Manassas, Va.:

In the morning, [Dr. Gaston] sent me, with Dr. Lewis of the Wisconsin Volunteers, with a captured two-wheeled ambulance of the Collidge pattern, to assist in collecting and caring for our wounded on the field. It was raining, and, on reaching the battleground, we found these unfortunates suffering much from cold. We soon found ... we were obliged to select such for immediate removal as it seem possible to save by treatment and shelter. We ... bore most of the patients to a farmhouse called the Lewis House, already nearly full of Rebel wounded.... The house and outbuildings were soon packed with wounded, and still many were left on the field, and numbers doubtless died for want of timely assistance. We were unable to operate in many cases urgently requiring, as our instruments had been taken from us. We suffered much for want of food, water, and blankets. For the first, we were dependent upon the ... knapsacks of the dead; for the second, upon a small muddy spring half-mile distant, a broken pitcher being our best means of transportation. We had blankets for but five or six men. We found a large supply of linen in a chest of drawers, and turned it to account for dressings.... Our instructions were to forward the patients to Manassas, as fast as possible, for removal to Richmond; and a peculiar vehicle, known as a Virginia wagon, and eminently adapted for an instrument of torture, called daily to take such as could be moved....

Sternberg, G. M., Asst. Surg., USA, prisoner, Battle of Bull Run, Centreville, Va.:

On Monday, July 22d, a small quantity of cornmeal was obtained from a house near the church, and some gruel was made. A cup of this was given to nearly every man, and this was all the food we were able to obtain for them till Monday evening, when all the medical officers were taken from Sedley Church to Manassas. How the wounded fared after we were taken from them I do not know. At Manassas we were lodged in a barn with some thirty or forty other prisoners, officers and privates, under guard....

The 1st New York Volunteer Cavalry arrived in Washington, four days after it had been mustered in. Their ride from New York had been in boxcars fitted with plain board benches arranged to get the most men in the car, regardless of comfort. Holes had been cut into the sides and ends of the car to provide ventilation, and also provided an entry for dust, soot, and ashes from the train. No provision for water, toilet facilities, or rest stops was provided. Upon arrival, many of the men were sick from dehydration and constipation. The next few days were spent getting fitted out with mounts and equipment and setting up camp. They were sent into Virginia on August 7th, and they had their first taste of combat on August 18th, just one month after being mustered in.

F. L. Olmsted had returned to New York to handle some problems in the Central Park project. Upon learning of the disaster at Manassas, he immediately left for Washington, D.C. He found the city swarming with groups of dirty soldiers who were begging food door-to-door and camping in the streets. The officers of these men could be found in the bars and restaurants, totally ignoring the plight of their troops.

In Boston, Miss Amy Bradley had decided that she'd become a nurse with the Third Maine Volunteers, now in Washington, these volunteers having participated in the action at Manassas, Va. She had every qualification for a nurse of that day—she was a skilled sickroom attendant, and was "over thirty and very plain-looking," as was required by Dorothea Dix, who was the head of the female nursing corps for the Union. Amy, characteristically, took the most direct route and wrote the regimental commander seeking a position as nurse. In fact, she flooded the mail with her requests to Drs. George E. Brickett and Gideon S. Palmer, who were with the regiment, and who knew her well from her teaching days in Maine.

July 23 (Tuesday)

Edmonds, S. Emma E., Union field nurse, Georgetown Hospitals, Washington, D.C.:

Washington at that time presented a picture striking illustrative of military life in its most depressing form. To use the words of Capt. Noyes, "There were stragglers sneaking along through the mud inquiring for their regiments, wanderers driven in by the pickets, some with guns and some without, while everyone you met had a sleepy, downcast appearance, and looked as if he would like to hide his head from all the world." Every barroom and groggery seemed filled to overflowing with officers and men, and military discipline was nearly, or quite, forgotten for a time in the army of the Potomac....

The hospitals in Washington, Alexandria and Georgetown were crowded with wounded, sick, discouraged soldiers. That extraordinary march from Bull Run, through rain, mud, chagrin, did more toward filling the hospitals than did the battle itself.... Measles, dysentery and typhoid fever were the prevailing diseases after the retreat....

Sternberg, G. M., Asst. Surg., USA, prisoner, Battle of Bull Run, Centreville, Va.:

On Tuesday, all but three of our number took a parole not to serve again during the war. Those of us who refused to take this parole, were shortly after allowed to go out and attend our wounded upon giving a parole not to attempt to escape for five days. I found a large number of wounded lying under a shed by the railroad depot, and more were constantly brought in from the field....

July 25 (Thursday)

The Sanitary Commission acted quickly and devised a list of seventy-five questions to be asked of the unit commanders returning from Manassas. These questions dealt entirely with the "state of readiness" of the units at the time the battle began. Seven inspectors visited the thirty regiments encamped around the city to complete the survey. Even before the results could be tabulated, Olmsted fixed the blame on the lack of discipline among the volunteers.

Sternberg, G. M., Asst. Surg., USA, escaped prisoner, Battle of Bull Run, Centreville, Va.:

On July 25th, I was sent to Centreville, where I found a number of men who were wounded at the affair at Blackburn's Ford They were generally doing well.... On Sunday evening, the 28th July, my parole having expired the evening before, and a favorable opportunity offering, I made my escape from Centreville, and, after a tedious tramp, arrived in Washington on the following Tuesday, July 30th, 1861, footsore and weary.

July 28 (Sunday)

Gray, C. C., Asst. Surg., USA, prisoner, Manassas, Va.:

In a week all of our surviving patients, excepting Col. Wilcox and Capt. Ricketts, had been sent to Manassas Junction, and on Sunday, July 28th, I accompanied the last load to that depot. At Manassas, I met Surg. Thomas H. Williams, medical director of Gen. Beauregard's army, and was informed by him that I should remain at the Station and assist in placing our wounded, as they arrived, upon the cars destined to transport them to Richmond.... Our wounded arriv-

ing from the field, from which they came crowded in rough army wagons, and under a scorching sun, had to be thrust into freight cars, in which they were obliged to lie on the bare floor. Often they had been a whole day without food, and time was barely allowed us to furnish them with water. These railroad cars, having no right of track, were sometimes two days in reaching Richmond. Numbers died on the road.... I proceeded to Richmond on a train with Col. Wilcox and about sixty wounded privates. Two of the latter died, exhausted, before reaching the end of the journey, the trip taking twenty-four hours; neither food, water, nor medicine were provided. At Richmond, I was sent by Gen. Winder to assist in the treatment of our wounded at the tobacco warehouse hospital, now become historical and infamous, at which place I remained, with some eight or ten Federal surgeons, till the 10th of September, when an order having been issued to send South all field and regular officers able to travel. I was included in a party of thirty-three officers and about one hundred privates, to go to Ft. Pinckney, Charleston Harbor....

At Richmond, our wounded, except those that were crowded, were as well cared for as could have been expected. The few medicines we needed were at command. Water was abundant, a bathtub on each floor; dressings were, generally, plentiful; and food, though coarse and lacking in variety, was supplied in sufficient quantity....

July 29 (Monday)

The Sanitary Commission, having completed its tabulation of the survey, presented their findings to Maj. Gen. George B. McClellan, recently appointed commander of the Army of the Potomac. Olmsted indicated that of all the officers with whom the problems were discussed, McClellan was the only one who readily understood the gravity of the situation.

In Richmond, a diarist would record. scenes of misery and suffering throughout the war and his account would be published in 1866, shortly after his death. John B. Jones, originally from New Jersey, just across the river from Philadelphia, was a strong Southern supporter in his writings and his newspaper. Early on, he'd been severely criticized by his neighbors on his stance, and had even been threatened with bodily harm. In April 1861 he went South, and volunteered to work in the Confederate government with the purpose of writing a chronicle of events. He later published that chronicle as a book. Jones was an astute observer. Although somewhat slanted and colored, his diary provides a good insight into the war.

Jones, John B., Rebel War Clerk, Confederate War Dept., Richmond, Va.:

Today quite a number of our wounded men on crutches, and with arms in splints, made their appearance in the streets, and created a sensation. A year hence, and we shall be accustomed to such spectacle.

In Salisbury, N.C. (population about 2400 in 1860), the ladies of the town met at the Rowan County courthouse and organized the Ladies' Relief Society for the Sick and Wounded Soldiers. They elected officers and began efforts to send nurses to aid the North Carolina wounded. They published an appeal in the local newspaper, the *Carolina Watchman*, for assistance and issued a long list of needed supplies.

August 1 (Thursday)

In Richmond, Surgeon General S. P. Moore visited the buildings being occupied by the Union prisoners. His report to the Confederate Secretary of War, raised the spectre of epidemic:

I visited the buildings occupied by the prisoners yesterday afternoon. The upper building has on [its] first floor fifty-two officers, including five surgeons; the latter are assisting the medical officer in his attendance on sick prisoners. The second and third floors contain 261 men. In the lower building are 551 prisoners. The police of these building is very bad, especially the lower one. The yard of the upper building requires much policing. From the crowded state of these buildings it is feared that a pestilence may make its appearance, and if it should the city would be the sufferer. It is therefore recommended that an additional building be had so as to make a more proper distribution for these men....

August 3 (Saturday)

Edmonds, S. Emma E., Union field nurse, Georgetown Hospitals, Washington, D.C.:

Have been on duty all day. John C. is perfectly wild with delirium and keeps shouting at the top of his voice some military command, or, when vivid recol-

lections of the battlefield come to his mind, he enacts a pantomime of the terrible strife. He goes through the whole manual of arms as correctly as if he were in the ranks.... When we tell him the enemy has retreated, he persists in pursuing....

My friend, Lieut. M. is extremely weak and nervous, and the wild ravings of J. C. disturb him exceedingly. I requested Surg. P. to have him removed to a more quiet ward, and received in reply, "This is the most quiet ward in the whole building." There are five hundred patients here who require constant attention, and not half enough nurses to take care of them.... While I write there are three being carried past the window to the dead room....

August 6 (Tuesday)

Today, in Washington, an act of Congress was passed that required vacancies among the volunteer medical officers to be filled by state governors in the same manner as the original appointments were made. Some of the state authorities had appointed the qualification boards, but many others had entirely neglected it. The Secretary of War had also accepted what were termed independent regiments, the colonels of which asserted the right to appoint their own medical officers, and, notwithstanding the act of Congress, to fill the vacancies.

In some cases, the colonels of state regiments refused to accept the medical officers appointed to them in conformity with the law and the orders of the President. Some even went so far as to eject these medical personnel from the camps to which they were sent. Some state authorities, especially those of New York and Pennsylvania, which had good qualification boards, strongly objected to the ejection of the doctors and took their case to the Secretary of War, Simon Cameron, who was slow to do much. There were also cases where the regimental commanders decided to leave their surgeons at home, for almost any reason, when the regiment was mustered into federal service. The medical situation in the Union Army at this stage was somewhat chaotic.

The Sanitary Commission began a rapid expansion of its areas of responsibility throughout the army. Early on, they established a means of gathering data which could be presented in tabular form and then statistically analyzed. They managed to obtain permission to have their printing done at the Government Printing Office (GPO) at government expense.

The Sanitary Commission also published a medical library which, in turn, was printed by the GPO. Such material was to be made available to the surgeons in the field. Many monographs were published and distributed during the course of the war.

August 10 (Saturday)

Today, the first major battle in the western theatre was fought among the rolling hills and densely overgrown gullies near Wilson's Creek, about nine miles south of Springfield, Mo. From the beginning, the battle had all the makings of a Union defeat. Union forces were commanded by the headstrong, but capable, Gen. Nathaniel Lyon, who began the attack by dividing his inferior force, sending Col. Franz Sigel to make a rear attack on the Confederates. Sigel, 37, a German graduate of Karlsruhe Military Academy, wasn't familiar with American military practices, and was an unknown factor. Independent command wasn't, and never would be, one of his strong points.

Sigel's troops were routed, and he was out of the battle without having contributed much except confusion. The Confederates were driven back at first but rallied, and, with their superior numbers, eventually won the day as Lyon lay dead on the field of battle. With Lyon dead, the Federals withdrew and the Confederates failed to follow up the advantage. The Federals left 1317 of their troops along Bloody Ridge, nearly 25 percent of their original force, and withdrew all the way to Rolla, southwest of St. Louis, conceding a large part of the state to the secessionist forces. The medical aspects of the battle were recorded by one of the assistant surgeons.

Sprague, H. M., Asst. Surg., USA, Battle of Wilson's Creek, Mo. :

The limited time given to the different regiments to prepare themselves for the fight, and the small supply of the purveyor at St. Louis at the time the regiments were organized, forced each surgeon to rely on his private instruments. But if any regiments lacked medicines and medical stores, it was through the inefficiency of the medical officers. Of ambulances, there were but two in the command. These were large spring wagons drawn by six mules. It was only

at the earnest solicitation of Maj. Sturgis, that even these were allowed to move with the troops, so great was the fear of Gen. Lyon that the rumbling of teams might give notice to the enemy of our approach.... As many of the wounded as could walk came across the open field, and were cared for at a ravine back of the line of battle. Col. Sigel's wounded were left on the field, and were brought in during the night following the battle. The attention shown the wounded was good, but not specially praiseworthy. The only medical officer that I knew to be actually on the field of battle was Surg. Cornyn, 1st Missouri Volunteers. Asst. Surg. Patee and myself were at the hospital station in the ravine. The supply of water was abundant, a large stream running through the valley. There were no subsistence supplies except the cooked rations in the haversacks of the men.... Most of the wounded were removed to Springfield. About two hundred were carried along with the troops in their retreat.... Not only the slightly wounded, but those with compound fractures, wounds through the chest and testes, were conveyed on baggage wagons, caissons, and the six-mule spring wagons. Through a flag of truce, an arrangement was made to remove all of the wounded who could be moved between half-past eleven A.M. of the day of the fight, and midnight. Most of them were provided for before the truce expired.... At no time during the engagement was the situation of the ambulances considered safe.... No one acted as medical director, and there was no drilled ambulance corps, and the wounded were not systematically carried from the field. The severely wounded could only be moved on stretchers, and were not carried off until after the engagement.... The percentage of casualties was very large....

White, W. H., Surg., USV, 22d Iowa Vols., Battle of Wilson's Creek, Mo.:

As to the condition of medical supplies, ambulances, and hospital tents, the 1st Iowa Volunteers will furnish a fair specimen. Our medical supplies consisted of a few drugs, stored away in a dry-goods box. My instruments were good, as I had my own general operating and pocket cases. My transportation for the wounded consisted of a single wagon. I had no hospital tents. I partially supplied the deficiency by giving up my own wall tent. Personally, I was without assistance, my assistant surgeon being inefficient.... On the field I was on the descending ground back of the line of battle of the 1st Iowa Volunteers. The wounded were brought back to me by their comrades. I had them placed in three divisions, forming a triangle, and I passed from one to another, simply stopping to check hemorrhage, or to apply primary dressings.... I removed most of the wounded, a half an hour before the battle terminated, to a ravine.... From this place they were removed by commissary wagons to Springfield, and were placed in a large brick hotel, a church, and two private dwellings....

Davis, Philip C., Asst. Surg., USA, Battle of Wilson's Creek, Mo.:

This battle was the most severe and well contested that had occurred up to that time ... the fight raged furiously for six or seven hours.... About noon the fire of both sides slackened, the enemy fell back a mile, and our forces retreated to Springfield.... We succeeded in carrying away everything except the medicines, hospital stores, and supplies.... Our dead and wounded fell into the hands of the enemy.... I was ordered by Col. Sigel to remain to assist in taking care of the wounded. Our column having retreated towards Rolla, the enemy came in about daybreak and took possession of the village, and immediately proceeded to appropriate everything that was deemed by them necessary, either for their comfort or convenience, and we were consequently left without many articles for the benefit of the wounded under our charge. Our supplies of medicines, hospital stores, &c., were taken, and but little to work with was left us. The wounded were brought from the field in wagons, carriages, ambulances, litters, and, in fact, every kind of conveyance which could be brought into requisition. Our ambulances were few, and it occupied five or six days before they were all brought in, as, after the enemy arrived, they took all the means of transportation that could be found in the neighborhood.... The churches, hotels, court house, and nearly all of the private dwellings were filled with wounded of both sides....

Melcher, S. H., Asst. Surg., 5th Missouri Vols., Wilson's Creek, Mo.:

The Third and Fifth Missouri Volunteers, with two companies of artillery recently organized, had marched from Rolla to Carthage, by way of Neosho, in eighteen days. The distance was over two hundred

miles. On one day, not less than twenty men fell, sunstruck, on the road....

The wounded were sent to the rear in wagons as the fight progressed. The attendance they received was trifling, consisting of water dressings or adhesive plasters.... The flies were exceedingly troublesome after the battle, maggots forming in the wounds in less than an hour after dressing them, and also upon any clothing or bedding soiled by blood or pus. The wounded left on the field in the enemy's hands were swarming with maggots when brought in. After several ineffectual attempts to extirpate these pests, I succeeded perfectly by sprinkling calomel freely over the wounded surface. When the sloughs separated, clean granulating surfaces were presented, and by using balsam of [copaiba] as a dressing, smearing the bandages with this oleoresin, I could keep the wounds free from maggots....

August 11 (Sunday)

In Washington, D.C., the Sanitary Commission had expanded its scope again to include the inspection of hospitals. The Commission had already provided bedding, nightshirts, medicines, and food to the hospitals of the area. Now they focused on the building of new hospitals to supplant the hotels, schools, and private houses serving as hospitals. The Army Medical Service, so confident that it could handle the situation, was overwhelmed with the number of wounded coming back from Manassas, and it floundered.

August 12 (Monday)

Surg. Charles S. Tripler, born in 1806, was active in the Army at the start of the war. His early work was mainly in the organization (from a medical viewpoint) of the Army of the Potomac following the action at First Manassas. His was to be the burden of the Peninsular Campaign conducted by McClellan in early 1862. After the battle of Fair Oaks, he was assigned as Medical Inspector General for the Army, and he returned to Washington, turning over his duties in the Army of the Potomac to Jonathan Letterman.

Tripler, Charles S., Med. Dir., Army of the Potomac, Washington, D.C.:

I joined the Army of the Potomac August 12th, 1861, and was immediately charged with the organization of the medical department. At that time, the three-months volunteers were mustered out of service, and the new levies were rapidly assembled in Washington and its vicinity.… There were some five or six hotels, seminaries, and infirmaries in Washington and Georgetown occupied as general hospitals, and one or two in Alexandria, the fruits of the exigencies of the three months campaign. These were under capable officers, were well regulated and conducted; but with no system in reference to the admission or discharge of patients. Every regimental surgeon sent what men he pleased to the general hospitals without knowing whether there was room for them or not, and men were discharged from the hospitals with no means provided to ensure their return to their regiments. It wasn't an unusual circumstance for sick men to pass the night in ambulances, wandering the streets from hospital to hospital seeking admission. I could find no information anywhere as to what regiments were present, or whether they had medical officers or not. My first endeavor was to find out.…

August 14 (Wednesday)

The Confederate troops in western Virginia were undergoing their "baptism of sickness." Gen. W. W. Loring's inspector general noted that nearly one-third of the brigade was on the sick list, the troops being afflicted with measles and a malignant type of fever. One regiment from North Carolina could only muster 200 of its 1000 men for duty. The 16th Tennessee left a trail of sick wherever it moved, mostly suffering from malaria and typhoid fever. The 1st Tennessee filled the hotels at Warm Springs with its sick and dying. Rations were very short and the regiment was reduced to eating local cattle (with little salt) and picking local blackberries. The incessant rain didn't help matters much, reducing communication and movement of the sick to places where they could be cared for properly. By the 23rd of the month, the camp looked like "a Tennessee hog pen." Gen. Lee wrote of the conditions:

We have a great deal of sickness among the soldiers, and now those on the sick list would form an army. The measles is still among them, though I hope it is dying out. But it is a disease which though light in childhood is severe in manhood, and prepares the system for other attacks. The constant rains, with no shelter but tents, have aggravated it. All these drawbacks, with impassible roads, have paralyzed our efforts.

August 16 (Friday)

Throughout the summer, Mary Ann Bickerdyke spent her days doing the rounds of the various hospitals around Cairo, making sure the kitchens were run properly and "sorting out" those cooks who needed a little "help." One thing she did at the Cairo hospital was to dismiss the inefficient nurses (who were really convalescing soldiers) and replace them with able-bodied men who were doing time in the guardhouse for minor infractions. This was good for everyone. The troops serving time were free and occupied doing useful work, which made them feel good, and the work was being done, which made the patients feel good.

In Cairo that summer a young woman from Vermont was visiting her brother, the most important banker in town, and she became involved in working at the Cairo hospital when she could. Miss Mary Safford was a well-educated, beautiful, and romantic young woman who captured the heart of every patient, as well as the hearts of the staff, in the hospital. Lacking the homemaking and organizational skills of Bickerdyke, she spent her time consoling the patients, writing letters for them, hanging curtains in the windows, smoothing fevered brows, and being an angel. The patients loved her to distraction, and Mrs. Bickerdyke used her to the fullest in her role. In addition, Mrs. Bickerdyke taught her the less glamorous side of nursing. Safford learned to cook, wash the patient's clothing, wash and iron the sheets, and make beds. The patients and staff called Mrs. Bickerdyke "Mother," and they called Mary Safford "The Angel of Cairo," which much pleased Mother Bickerdyke.

August 18 (Sunday)

At Camp Dennison, Ohio, the 8th Ohio had gone through a real bout of measles and typhoid fever. The latter malady was referred to by the soldiers as "the disease of Camp Maggotty Hollow." By this date the regiment was in so sad a shape that another regiment had to be called in its stead for active service. McClellan's western Virginia campaign was sorely deterred by sickness. Chronic dysentery, diarrhea, malaria, typhoid fever, measles, and rheumatism took out over 20,000 men from July to October, rendering many regiments wholly unfit for duty.

August 19 (Monday)

Tripler, Charles S., Med. Dir., Army of the Potomac, Washington, D.C.:

I directed all the prisoners at the Capitol prison to be vaccinated, a bath to be fitted up for their use, and such outdoor exercise to be allowed them as was consistent with their safekeeping....

August 20 (Tuesday)

Operations in western Virginia during the summer and into the early fall were complicated by both terrain and the lack of roads. The mountainous country left few places for large bodies of troops to camp, and the rain runoff drained the camp latrines and offal dumping grounds into the nearest body of water, which water was often used by other troops downstream. Further complications came in the evacuation of the wounded and sick to hospitals. Often the roads were preempted by military traffic and ambulances were scarce. The unfortunate wounded soldiers either had to wait for assistance or attempt to make it to the hospitals on their own.

August 22 (Thursday)

Surg. Tripler, of the Army of the Potomac, in Washington, today sent one of his surgeons to the camp of the Pennsylvania Cavalry on 7th Street to direct the cleanup of the camp. The cavalry commander had allowed his area to become extremely odious.

This same day, Surg. Tripler recommended that the troops being quartered on the flats (present site of Arlington Cemetery and the Pentagon) near Arlington, Lee's old home, be moved to higher ground. Some 33 percent of the troops there were reported sick with diarrhea, typhoid, and intermittent fevers.

Tripler, Charles S., Med. Dir., Army of the Potomac, Washington, D.C.:

I represented to the Adj. General that ... I thought it practicable to remove the camps beyond the first crest, so as to afford the protection of the hills against infected currents of air. Ascertaining, by personal inquiry and inspection, that the men were turned out long before sunrise and were hours in waiting for

their breakfasts, and feeling that this had much to do with the prevalence of malarial fevers, I asked for and obtained an order, that reveille should not be beat till after sunrise, and that hot coffee should be issued to the men immediately after roll call.... In one week after the hot coffee was ordered, a regimental surgeon complained to me that green coffee was issued to his men, without the means of properly roasting it, and they could not get the extra rations ordered. Col. Clark, to whom I referred the complaint, promptly replied that green coffee was always issued, that it should be roasted in a mess pan, or Dutch oven, or other vessel, purchased with the company funds; that the quantity issued was fixed by law, and was deemed ample; and so it was, but it required the exercise of a little judgment to discover it....

At the camp of the Third Maine Regiment in Claremont, Va., Dr. George E. Brickett, acting surgeon for the regiment, wrote Miss Amy Morris Bradley, then in Boston:

Yours of the 22nd [July] is just received. In answer I would say that the chances for you to do good are good. You would be in your element here as an angel of mercy. But I am fearful that you would be deprived of many comforts and even necessities of life, which you have been accustomed to, and that you would be sorry you had left those comforts for the rough life of the Camp.

If you are willing to run your risk, we will give you employment, and enough to eat.

Dr. Gideon S. Palmer, also of the Third Maine Regiment, wrote to Amy:

I can assure you that you can do much good here and we should all be very much pleased to see you. I should for one, and what I say, you know I mean ... you shall have the rations and fare as well as we do, if you come. There are many hardships to endure in camp life of which I would have you thoroughly apprised.... Let us know by letter at what hour you will reach Washington, and we will send an ambulance—the best mode of conveyance we have—for you....

Enclosed with the letter from Dr. Palmer was Amy's official appointment, which read:

I hereby appoint Miss Amy M. Bradley of Maine, Nurse in the 3rd Regt. of Maine Vols. She will please report herself at the Hospital of said regiment as soon as possible.

August 24 (Saturday)

F. L. Olmsted joined in the inspection of the local hospitals of the Washington area, taking with him John Russell (an Englishman), who'd seen the debacle in the Crimea. Because of Russell's experience, his suggestions and recommendations were invaluable to both to Olmsted and to the Sanitary Commission.

August 26 (Monday)

Tripler, Charles S., Med. Dir., Army of the Potomac, Washington, D.C.:

First among the causes assigned for the number on the sick report ... was the recklessness with which the men had been enlisted. General Orders No. 51, War Dept., August 3d, 1861, commanded, that when volunteers were mustered in, they should be minutely examined by the surgeon and assistant surgeon of the regiment as to their physical qualifications. I question whether this most important order has ever received the adequate attention from the persons whose duty it was to execute it.... The surgeon of the 61st New York reported to me as a reason for his large sick report, that he had a large number of broken-down men; many sixty to seventy years old, many afflicted with hernia, old ulcers, epilepsy, and the like. Another acting brigade surgeon reported that there has been no medical examination of many of the regiments before they were enrolled; another, that there were eighty men with hernia and epilepsy in the 5th New York Cavalry....

August 28 (Wednesday)

In Lynchburg, Va., another revolution of sorts was taking place. Mrs. Lucy Wilhelmina Otey, the 60-year-old mother of seven Confederate soldiers, took on the Confederate military establishment on the subject of nursing the wounded and sick. She won! She took over the old Union Hotel in Lynchburg, at the corner of 6th and Main Streets, and converted it into the Ladies' Relief Hospital. She, and many of the more affluent women of the town, staffed the hospital with 500 volunteers and provided *all* the nursing staff—a major break with tradition, North or South. The hospital was to be very

successful in treating the wounded, so much so that the most serious cases were always sent there for care and treatment. Although the hospital was fitted for only 100 beds, during the next three years it often exceeded that capacity by at least 50 percent.

Mrs. Otey, in a head-to-head battle with Dr. W. O. Owen, the military head of medical services in Lynchburg, sensed that she wouldn't be able to break Dr. Owen's hidebound traditional approach of not allowing women in the hospitals. Off she went to Richmond on the canal boat to talk to Jeff Davis about this problem. Whatever was said in that meeting isn't known. The result was that Mrs. Otey returned to Lynchburg with full authority to open her hospital and run it *outside* military authority.

The ladies of the hospital took great care of their charges, providing many more of the niceties to the patients than were available in the military hospitals. They reported directly to Richmond on their statistics, bypassing the local authorities. Soldiers who died in their hospital were formally dressed for burial, and a lock of hair was sent to the mother of the deceased. Touches such as these weren't normally found in any hospital of the era.

August 29 (Thursday)

On this morning, Amy M. Bradley left East Cambridge, Mass., went to Boston, and entrained for New York. Arriving there, she stayed at the Astor House.

August 30 (Friday)

At 6:30 A.M., Amy M. Bradley, in the company of Lt. William O'Neil of the 7th Massachusetts Volunteers, travelled to Washington from New York. Arriving in the capital, she found the city alive with uniforms, tented encampments everywhere, and indescribably filthy.

August 31 (Saturday)

Today, Amy M. Bradley took a tour of the sights of Washington, a city she'd never visited. As a part of her "tour," she went to the Treasury Building, where the U.S. Sanitary Commission was then located. Here she made herself known to the Rev. Frederick N. Knapp, the head of the organization. This contact would provide Amy with much-needed support during the war.

At about 4 P.M., Amy boarded an ambulance from the Third Maine Regimental Hospital for her trip across the river to Claremont, Va. Amy recorded the experience:

Bradley, Amy M., Nurse, Third Maine Regt., Claremont, Va.:

It was a pleasant ride along the banks of the beautiful Potomac now studded with the white tents of the Federal Army protected by Fts. Runyon, Jackson, and Ellsworth, the latter being near our encampment. Twilight found me safe with the regiment. Old familiar faces welcomed me which made me feel quite at home. It was teatime; the band was playing a lively national air. I was ushered into the tent of our worthy surgeon, Dr. G. S. Palmer, and introduced to Col. [Oliver Otis] Howard, Lieut. Col. Tucker, Adjt. Hall, Mrs. Sampson, the Matron, and Miss Graves who is, like myself, a nurse in the hospital. When we were seated at the table, Col. Howard meekly bowed his head and asked our Father's blessing upon the food before us. What, thought I, is this the rough life of the Camp, which has so often [been] pictured to me. And, I said, No, this reminds me of a 'camp meeting' only more quiet.…

September 1 (Sunday)

At Claremont, Va., Amy Bradley spent her first full day of official activity as a nurse for the Third Maine Regiment.

Dr. Palmer called at my tent, a bright sunshiny Sabbath morning and asked me if I would like to accompany him through the hospital tents—my hat was quickly donned—and we started. He was intending to select some of the sickest ones … to be sent to the General Hospital in Alexandria. There were four large hospital tents filled with fever cases, resulting from the long-to-be-remembered Battle of Bull Run, July 21, 1861. They were lying on mattresses placed on the ground. How sick they looked—no comfortable bed, no soft pillows—O … it was terrible to look at! We passed through the first tent, the doctor prescribing for each as we passed along.

As we stood by the bedside of one, I spoke to him. He looked up as if he had never heard the voice before. Said I, "Would you like to have anything?"

He looked again, and as if he was thinking of some journey he was to take and said, "I would like

to see my mother and sister before I go home."

I burst into tears and said, "Please, Doctor, do not send him away, but let me take care of him for his mother and sister until he goes home!" For I knew by his looks he could not live but a few days—so it was decided that he should remain.

The doctor saying, "If that is what you came for, we will give you plenty of work! I have another boy in a similar condition in another tent—I will have him brought in here and you may take care of him for his mother," adding, "if he lives you shall have the credit of saving him. I think he was one of your scholars when you taught school in Gardiner—William Sturtevant!"

"O, yes, that is true and now I have got to fill his mother's place by his sickbed," thus I commenced my work.

In Salisbury, N.C., the Ladies' Relief Society for the Sick and Wounded Soldiers, organized in late July, issued another appeal for assistance, and again published a long list of needed articles in the *Carolina Watchman*.

September 2 (Monday)

Olmsted had completed the report on the inspection tours immediately following the Battle of Manassas, and was ready to provide a formal report to the entire Sanitary Commission board His report disclosed a major criticism of the War Dept. The findings showed that only eight regiments went into the battle in reasonably good physical condition. The others suffered from lack of food, water, and sleep. A long, hard march immediately before the battle further devastated the troops' ability and morale. The report concluded that those regiments who had good discipline in camp before going to Manassas fared very well, the others, having less responsible officers, did poorly.

The directors of the Sanitary Commission were aghast at the report, which laid the blame on the "imbecility of the government." The military members of the Commission threatened to resign if the report were made public. Olmsted relented and directed that the report be rewritten, and not distributed. The report would have wide-ranging effects on the course of the Medical Dept. of the Army, for now, embarrassed into action, it would try to correct the deficiencies.

September 3 (Tuesday)

In Claremont, Va., Amy Bradley had found her calling, working as a nurse in the hospital of the Third Maine Regiment. She was on the go from "reveille to taps" every day nursing her patients and giving them the same tender treatment their mothers would. One of her first actions was to organize a letter-writing campaign to get things from Maine to the patients. Cots for use in the tents were the first items needed.

September 5 (Thursday)

In St. Louis, the *Western* Sanitary Commission was authorized by Special Orders No. 159 to work with the Union forces. This order established the role of the Commission regarding its relationship with the various military commands, defined its authority, and limited its scope of influence. This order was at the direction of Maj. Gen. J. C. Frémont, and was later confirmed and expanded by successive commanders of the area and, indeed, by the Secretary of War. The area defined was all that west of the Appalachians, except for western Virginia. Under this mantle of authority, the Western Sanitary Commission began its operations.

September 7 (Saturday)

The problem of unqualified surgeons and assistant surgeons in the Army of the Potomac had become increasingly worse. Surg. Tripler decided to act.

Tripler, Charles S., Med. Dir., Army of the Potomac, Washington, D.C.:

To remedy the irregular and doubtful appointments made by colonels, and to give the troops confidence in their medical officers, I determined to assemble boards for the examination of the incompetent, as rapidly as their cases were brought to my notice. This I did under authority of General Order No. 35, War Dept., June 26th, 1861. On September 7th, 1861, I assembled such a board and ordered twelve medical officers before it for examination. From that time forward, whenever a medical officer was complained of for incompetency, a board was ordered. In many cases the complaints were ascertained to be well founded, and the officers were discharged....

September 10 (Tuesday)

The Medical Dept. of the U.S. Army was doing business as usual. Not being used to stockpiling medicines and medical supplies or equipment, almost immediately they fell far behind in the support of the Army of the Potomac. Although another engagement was expected at any time, the Surgeon General took no action to increase his supplies and equipment *before* the battle. When the Sanitary Commission objected to this philosophy, the Surgeon General replied that supplies could be had from New York, and that contract personnel could be hired to make the beds when needed. The Surgeon General had never coped with large numbers of casualties, or for that matter, having 150,000 men to care for medically.

Tripler, Charles S., Med. Dir., Army of the Potomac, Washington, D.C.:

Having thus established some order and system in the "personnel" of the medical department, and some method in instructing the officers in their duties, my attention was turned to the means of keeping them supplied with medicines, instruments, and stores. In this I met with many difficulties. The volunteer medical officers could not readily accommodate themselves to the rigid system of the army in regard to their supplies.... The medical purveyor was restricted by the regulations, and although my order ought to have been sufficient to relieve him from all responsibility, still, to be perfectly safe, he'd refer such requisitions to the Surgeon General; the consequence was, my orders were countermanded, and he was finally ordered by the Surgeon General not to issue anything disallowed by the supply table, without the sanction of the Surgeon General previously obtained....

Another difficulty was encountered in getting the supplies to the regiments after the stores were assembled. Ordinarily, the purveyor turns over his supplies to the quartermaster, and it is the duty of that officer to transport them to their destination. It was soon perceived that this mode would not answer in the confusion then reigning in Washington; the regular quartermasters were charged with duties considered of more importance, the volunteer quartermasters did not know how to perform what was required. We were therefore obliged to require the medical officers to call for and to transport their own supplies to their camps....

September 12 (Thursday)

Tripler, Charles S., Med. Dir., Army of the Potomac, Washington, D.C.:

Another difficulty ... was the supplying the regiments with hospital tents. I determined to issue three of these tents to a regiment; which would accommodate comfortably thirty men.... I approved of requisitions for this number, whenever they were presented, and I ordered requisitions to be made in all cases, when I discovered it had been neglected. These tents, however, were frequently taken, by arbitrary authority, for other purposes, such as stores tents, guard tents, and the like. Whenever an abuse of this sort was brought to my notice, I took every means in my power to correct it.... When the medical officers reported to me, I required them to submit to me an inventory of the supplies of all sorts they had on hand. These were carefully reviewed, and whenever they were defective, requisitions were immediately called to meet the deficiencies. Great difficulty was experienced in enforcing obedience to this simple requirement....

September 13 (Friday)

At the Third Maine Regimental Hospital in Claremont, Va., Amy Bradley had received "two or three dozen" bed cots from Maine and now went to the U.S. Sanitary Commission to get the bedding to complete the beds for her patients. She'd already tapped the resources of the Commission for hospital clothing and dietary foods for the patients. Within a short time "her hospital" was "up to snuff."

September 14 (Saturday)

Major problems in the health of the Army of the Potomac were getting worse as the summer dragged on. The heat of September in the Washington camps caused thousands of men to succumb to the various fevers rampant in that region. McClellan's Surg. Gen. Tripler made light of the reports he received to some degree, leading the commanders to believe that the problem was less severe than it actually was. Not all the commanders bought this theory, having firsthand knowledge of the readiness of their troops. Some commanders, notably Joseph Hooker, decided to build cabins for the sick rather than leave their men to suffer the elements.

Allen, J. M., Surg., 54th Pennsylvania Vols., Washington, D.C.:

This regiment is on duty in the valley of the Potomac. This region of Virginia is proverbial for almost every variety of miasmatic fever, and when the peculiar nature of the climate, hot days and cold nights, is taken into consideration in connection with frequent overflows and rank undergrowth, the cause may be easily explained. The diseases incident to the vicinity are remittent, typhoid and congestive fevers, pneumonia, diarrheal and bronchial affections.

September 15 (Sunday)

One myth about the Civil War was that Union troops used Christ Church, in Alexandria, Va., as billets, or to stable horses. The church was used for religious services, as Miss Amy M. Bradley attests.

Bradley, Amy M., Nurse, Third Maine Regt., Claremont, Va.:

The day was bright and beautiful ... so we all arrayed ourselves in our best camp suit. Dr. Palmer, Dr. Hildreth, the Chaplain, Mrs. Sampson, Miss Graves, and myself put some chairs in a four-wheeled ambulance, and started. We passed Ft. Ellsworth where we had a splendid view of Washington and Alexandria with the lovely Potomac rolling majestically. Our driver drove slowly, that we might enjoy all the beauties of the prospects before us.

We arrived at the church entrance soon after the bell began to ring. I wish I could describe my feelings as I stepped upon the threshold where Washington once stood, but my pen would fail to tell the deep emotions that filled my soul. We listened to a very good sermon well delivered by a Chaplain of one of the New York regiments. After services we passed through the church. The inside of the church including every pew but that of the Father of his Country, has been remodeled. Washington's pew is left untouched. You who have seen the square pews in Dr. Channing's Church in Boston can imagine how this looks. For a moment we are all seated there, and each wondered (childlike) if he or she was sitting where he sat. To us it was an interesting event in our life's history to sit in that pew, sacred because of its former ownership.

The church outside is literally covered with the graceful ivy so common in England. We gathered a few sprigs, with some leaves from the graveyard adjoining, and then started for Camp, where we soon arrived safely, the distance being about two miles.

September 16 (Monday)

In Chicago, after a long, hot summer of organizing the Western Sanitary Commission's offices, Mary Livermore and Mrs. Jane Hoge occupied the facilities located at McVicker's Theater on Madison Street. Mrs. Eliza Porter, the wife of another minister, took charge of the visitors coming to the facility and managed to get them to donate much more money to the Commission's efforts than they had originally intended. Here, at the theatre, all donations were received and assorted into their various categories. From here, the boxes were shipped to the various points in the west that had requested such supplies. The Western Sanitary Commission was at last in business.

September 22 (Sunday)

In Richmond, Brig. Gen. John H. Winder was trying to cope with a major problem that was increasing in scope. As a part of the duties of his office as Inspector-General for the Richmond area, he was charged with the discharge of soldiers who'd been rendered unfit for military service, for whatever reason. Following the Battle of Manassas in July, the numbers of wounded overwhelmed the Richmond hospitals. The obvious solution was to treat and discharge those who wouldn't be able to perform further service, amputees, in particular. As a first-time effort, the red tape involved in this process between the Inspector-General's Office, the Surgical Board, and the area Quartermaster's office delayed such discharge, and hence removal from Richmond, of hundreds of Confederate soldiers. The bad publicity resulting from this bungling fell primarily on Winder, causing a further rift between his office and the city.

September 30 (Monday)

Surg. William J. Sloan, USA, inspected the quarters of the prisoners from Cape Hatteras and wrote the following report to Col. G. Loomis, commanding Ft. Columbus, N.Y.:

Sir: I have the honor to report that the condition of the Ft. Hatteras prisoners in the castle at this post is such as to require the immediate attention of the Government. They are crowded into an ill-ventilated building which has always been an unhealthy one when occupied by large bodies of men. There are no conveniences for cooking except in the open air, no means of heating the lower tier of gun rooms and no privies within the area. As the winter approaches I cannot see how these 630 men can be taken care of under the above circumstances. These men are without clothing and are not disposed to use the means prescribed by me for the prevention of disease unless compelled to do so. Everything necessary in a sanitary point of view has been urged upon them but is only carried out by the persistent efforts of the officer in charge of the castle. Under all these circumstances with the effect of change of climate and the depression resulting from their situation disease must be the result.

There are now upwards of eighty cases of measles amongst them, a number of cases of typhoid fever, pneumonia, intermittent fever, &c. I have taken the worst cases into my hospital and am preparing it with beds to its full capacity for other cases. Every building upon the island being crowded with troops, with a large number of tents, I know not how the condition of these prisoners can be improved except by a change of location to some other place for all or a portion of them, the present condition of things resulting principally from deficiency of quarters and not from causes within our control.

At Claremont, Va., Amy M. Bradley had been notified that the Third Maine Regiment's brigade would be relocated. Col. Oliver Otis Howard, recently promoted to brigadier general, was also reassigned as Brigade Commander, and would be leaving the regiment. Before leaving, Gen. Howard gave Amy a lock of his thick ash-brown hair threaded with silver—not an unusual gift in that era.

Amy's concern, because of their physical condition, was for her patients' being moved. This problem was solved by setting up a temporary hospital across the road in the Powell House, combining the patients of the Maine regiment and the 40th New York (the Mozart Regiment). Iron bedframes were placed in the rooms and two sofas were found for the hall. Amy handpicked two soldiers to act as male nurses, and a cook was assigned.

October 3 (Thursday)

The varieties of fevers that plagued the troops weren't always diagnosed properly, if at all. One of the major problems was the tools available to the doctors. Thermometers were available, but not generally used for diagnosis. Few, if any, laboratories were available to assist the doctors. The fever that laid so many low in the area of the Potomac was called, naturally, the Potomac Fever. The problem in diagnosis was its identity. Was it typhus, malaria, remittent, bilious, or some other fever?

The Army of the Potomac decided to appoint a Board of Inquiry to determine the cause of the fevers and to recommend steps to prevent them. One such board studied the epidemic that was prevalent in the 10th Massachusetts (then camped on Kalorama Heights, outside of Washington). After due consideration, it was reported that the fevers were due to the climatic change, the men having come from cool western Massachusetts, and to the overwork of the men in building fortifications. No mention was made of the water supply (one of the real culprits), or of the method in which latrines and garbage pits were used (another culprit). Their only recommendation was to reduce the number of men in each of the tents from 16 to 10. This was a good idea in any event, personal hygiene being what it was at that time.

October 5 (Saturday)

Tripler, Charles S., Med. Dir., Army of the Potomac, Washington, D.C.:

When I took charge of the Army of the Potomac [medical department], I supposed that the general hospitals within the limits of that army were under my control, and that it devolved upon me … to provide accommodations for the number of sick and wounded that we should be likely to have. The buildings already provided and occupied were … totally inadequate. The entire hospital establishments in Washington, Georgetown, Alexandria, Baltimore, and Annapolis contained but two thousand seven hundred beds. A Sanitary Commission being in session at Washington about the 1st of September, an invitation was extended to me to assist, which I accepted. They were then discussing the subject of general hospitals. They seemed to be of the opinion that there should be as many as five thousand beds in

Washington. I explained to the gentlemen at some length my views upon the subject, and endeavored to show them that twenty thousand beds, at least, would be required. After several days' consideration, the commission decided to … request … frame buildings erected sufficient to accommodate fifteen thousand men.…

I was … decidedly in favor of putting up cheap frame buildings, expressly designed for hospitals, in preference to relying upon hotels, schoolhouses, and the like … I fully believed suitable buildings could be erected at a cost not exceeding $25 per bed. The Commission … agreeing to send me a much better plan.… After tedious delays, their drawings were at last sent to Washington. They were the design of an architect in New York.… The expense, as estimated by the architect, was $75 per bed. Time pressing, and it being too late to wait for other plans, I reluctantly decided to adopt it, after having made certain modifications that would … reduce the cost to about $60 per bed. To the plan proposed [20,000 beds] … on account of the expense … one-fourth of the buildings I had recommended might be put up.

When the Quartermaster General advertised for proposals to put up the new buildings, instead of $15,000 for each two hundred beds, as estimated by the architect, the bids ranged from $30,000 to $80,000. This expense couldn't be incurred, and two, only, of the buildings, sufficient for four hundred men, were attempted, and it was many months before they were completed.

When Ft. Sumter was fired upon in April 1861, Regular Army Surg. George E. Cooper was on duty at Ft. Mackinac, Mich., and remained there until the ice broke up on the lakes on April 28, 1861, when he departed for Washington, D.C. His initial assignment was with Union troops in the area of Harpers Ferry, Va., and Chambersburg, Pa. During this period, he was directed to move the hospital at Chambersburg to Hagerstown, Md., which was accomplished. He was then assigned as purveyor of medical supplies under Gen. Patterson in the lower Shenandoah Valley, and later at Baltimore, Md. On this date, Surg. Cooper was sent to Annapolis, where the Hilton Head expedition was assembling.

Cooper, George E., Surg., USA, Annapolis, Md.:

In accordance with these orders, I reported to Brig.

Gen. T. W. Sherman in Washington, and accompanied him to Annapolis, where the troops for the expedition were assembling.... These troops remained at Annapolis from ten days to two weeks, and were, a day prior to sailing, joined by the 79th New York Volunteers.... The 47th and 48th New York regiments were not composed of as good material as the other regiments. The men were weakly, and many were mere boys taken to fill the ranks; many, too, were old and decrepit, and habitual drunkards. During the sojourn of the troops at Annapolis, the men were encamped in the grounds of the Naval Academy, on the banks of the Severn, to the rear of the college grounds, and on a farm to the west of the city.... Being all, with the exception of the battery, new levies, they knew nothing of camp life, and, consequently, paid but little regard to their own comfort. The result was the advent of catarrh, fevers, and derangements of the digestive system. The men were entirely regardless of all hygienic rules, and paid no attention to the advice of their medical officers. It was a common subject of remark, that men, who but a few weeks before, occupied positions in society demanding cleanliness and a care for personal appearance, now disregarded it, and either from apathy or laziness, neither washed their persons nor the clothing they carried upon them. The fevers attacking the men were mostly of a malarious type, and particularly so among those regiments which had been encamped for a time, prior to coming to Annapolis, in the vicinity of Washington. Some of the fevers, too, were of the type denominated typhoid. Many, too, which at first were of the malarious type, in a short time presented typhoid symptoms; but, as no autopsies were made, I am not able to say whether or not they assumed the character, in the intestines, of mesenteric fever....

Some three days previous to the embarkation of the troops, variola made its appearance among the 8th Maine Volunteers. Orders were immediately issued to remove not only the sufferers, but all who had been in contact with them. In consequence of these precautions, the disease did not spread. Vaccine virus too, was procured from the Surgeon General's Office, and all the men of the regiment were vaccinated, as well as those who were encamped in the vicinity....

October 7 (Monday)

Amy M. Bradley had just put the Powell House in good working order when it was decided to move the patients to the General Hospital in Alexandria, Va. Amy was very worried about her patients, but she could do nothing about the move.

It was hard for both nurse and sick ones to be separated, but tears must be choked back and heart wishes hushed when orders come from Headquarters. We soon had them ready to be moved. Then two-by-two they were placed in an ambulance and carried from me.

October 8 (Tuesday)

The 7th Connecticut Volunteers, passing through Washington, were fed at the Soldier's Rest facility near the railroad station. The catering was done by contractors, and the troops reported flies on the food, boiled beef infested with maggots, and worms in the hardtack.

October 10 (Thursday)

With Powell House out of business, Amy M. Bradley spent part of October at Mt. Eagle, nursing a very bad cold. The house, built in the late 18th century, had many glass windows. She managed to visit "her" patients in the Alexandria General Hospitals three times during her stay at Mt. Eagle.

October 11 (Friday)

The most famous of all Confederate hospitals, the Chimborazo with a capacity of over 8000 patients, opened on this date on Chimborazo Heights overlooking the James in Richmond. The site had an excellent view, good drainage on three sides, and a readily available supply of good water. The facility was really five separate hospitals, each being divided into thirty buildings, or wards. Each building could accommodate up to 60 patients, the buildings being 100 feet long and 30 feet wide on a one-story plan. The streets were wide, and adequate space between buildings was allowed for good ventilation. The facility had five soup houses, five icehouses, bathhouses, a 10,000-loaf-a-day bakery, a 400-keg-capacity brewery, and its own cemetery. A two-hundred-acre farm next door provided pasture for about 200 cows and for about 300 to 500 goats. Chimborazo was by far the best medical facility, North or South.

October 13 (Sunday)

In Richmond, Brig. Gen. John H. Winder was the subject of an article in the Richmond *Examiner* in which charges were made that the Confederate dead weren't being given proper burial, and that Winder was personally responsible for this situation. The charges were totally false, but the newspaper didn't bother to correct the mistake. In fact, the *Examiner* was extremely hostile to both Winder and Pres. Davis's administration during the entire war.

October 15 (Tuesday)

At Cairo, Ill., Mrs. Bickerdyke had found that the supplies arriving at that station from the Sanitary Commission offices in Chicago were first-rate and packed so that the contents wouldn't be destroyed en route. As the boxes arrived, Bickerdyke took immediate charge of them for her hospitals and for the sick. No one objected to this arrangement since she had already proven to everyone's satisfaction that she was the best one to make the most of the contents.

October 17 (Thursday)

At about this time, Amy M. Bradley was asked by Dr. Brickett to take charge of the Fifth Maine Regiment hospital at Camp Franklin, Va., located south and west of Washington.

Bradley, Amy M., Nurse, Fifth Maine Regt., Camp Franklin, Va.:

I am the only lady in the Regiment who works for the sick, tho there are several of the officers who have their wives. I like Camp Life very much, just excitement enough to suit me. Let me describe a day!

At half past five in the morning we are awakened by sweet music—the reveille—when we dress and prepare for the duties of the day. My first work is to run into the Hospital to see my sick boys and wish them good morning. Then I go to the tent and assist in preparing their breakfast. Then eat my own, since I came here it has consisted of poor coffee boiled in a very black kettle—drunk without milk—potatoes and fried pork, bread and molasses. Dinner, ditto,

Supper the same with occasionally a variation of butter. I weigh 105 pounds, enjoy excellent health.

During the day, the different Regiments of our Brigade are regularly drilled in sight of my tent. Our Brigade (the 7th) consists of the 16th, 26th, 27th New York Volunteers and the 5th Maine, 4000 men all encamped a short distance from each other. O, I wish you could behold these tented fields—an intensely interesting picture to me! Camp meeting on a large scale—preaching quite different music also, still I am reminded of those Methodist encampments in Maine.

The greatest trouble I have is to keep my feet still when the bands are playing. I am not sure, but I shall take to dancing soon!

The scenery in Virginia is fine, but the houses are far inferior to our New England tenements, and the farms are almost ruined now. The roads are miserable! As our army advances, they fell the trees, making fearful havoc with the woodlands. There are now 32 forts around Washington—we are encamped near Ft. Worth, about three miles from Munson's Hill [current site of Bailey's Crossroads, Va.].

… [at night I rest my] weary limbs in our somewhat hard beds in our little tent … I sleep very soundly, seldom dreaming, therefore, when morning comes I am perfectly refreshed and ready to begin the duties of the hour.

October 18 (Friday)

Following the Battle of Manassas in July, E. A. Craighill worked in the hospitals in and around Manassas, often going into the town of Manassas on business. On one of his trips there, he met Surg. Thomas H. Williams, a former U.S. Army Surgeon, and they became acquainted. Dr. Williams had many contacts within the Confederate Army Medical Service and recommended that Craighill "stand for the examination" to become a surgeon. This Craighill readily consented to do, and so it was arranged. On this date Craighill was appointed a Captain in the Confederate Army and a Surgeon, probably the youngest surgeon in the army, being younger than 21 at the time.

Craighill, E. A., Surg., CSA, near Manassas, Va.:

When I got my orders to report to Gen. Early, who was only a few miles from Manassas, I was feeling

very badly, and prudence would have dictated waiting a few days, which I could easily have done before
reporting.... Notwithstanding I was sick, [I] reported the next day, believing and hoping my bad feeling was temporary, and that I would be all right in a
few days. In this I was mistaken ... I really suffered
terribly but kept on duty, telling no one. After a
week or so of this experience, I was compelled to
take to my cot, a very poor excuse for a bed, and
sent for our hospital Steward ... and asked him ...
to get the surgeon, Dr. Hicks, to come to my tent. I
stated my case as well as I could, and he then for the
first time examined me, and said, I was "a very sick
man," ordered the ambulance and had me sent to
Manassas. I at once looked up my friend, Dr.
Williams and related my experience, which he confirmed upon examination. He ordered me to a hospital in Richmond. I asked him if it would be all the
same to him, if I went home instead. He said, while
he could recommend a sick man a furlough, he
could not grant it, but seeing how sick I was, rather
winked at the irregularity....

    ... instead of going to the rear to a hospital where
I expect I certainly would have died, I took the train
for Strasburg, the then-terminus of the Manassas Gap
railroad ... where I had to take the stage for Winchester.... How I survived the trip I do not know, but
about daylight the stage drew up in front of the Taylor
Hotel, having taken ... about fifteen hours to make
the trip from Manassas to Winchester....

Craighill finally arrived at home with a very
advanced case of typhoid pneumonia. It would be
months before he fully recovered and returned to
his duties.

October 21 (Monday)

The action at Ball's Bluff, on the Virginia side of
the Potomac, west of Washington, was of little military value for either side. It was decidedly a disaster
for the Union and a great morale booster for the
Confederates. The action took place at the top of a
steep bluff which faced Harrison's Island, the island
being located about a mile downriver from Conrad's
Ferry. About 250 yards separated the island from the
Maryland shore, and the channel between the island
and the Virginia shore was about 75 yards wide,
with a very swift current. The Union forces crossed
to the island and then to the Virginia shore, went up

the bluff, and engaged the Confederate forces. Of
the total Union force, not all were engaged and the
Confederates defeated them piecemeal, with the
bluecoats scrambling to descend the bluff and the
Rebels firing down it into the mass of men at the
bottom trying to cross the swift channel to the
island. There were other problems in evacuating the
wounded, as reported by the Union surgeons.

Crosby, A. B., Surg., USV, Ball's Bluff, Va.:

Early in the day, anticipating an action, I ordered
forty-two fresh beds made in the brigade hospital, at
the time nearly completed, and took possession of
two large halls in town and caused them to be abundantly supplied with fresh straw. An ambulance train
was ordered to Edward's Ferry, and another to Conrad's Ferry, to await orders.... We arrived when the
retreat had fairly commenced, and each boat coming
from the island brought wounded men. A house and
barn on the island were used as a hospital, where the
severest injuries were cared for. The difficulties in the
way of getting off the wounded were very great. They
were to be transported from the Virginia shore to the
island, thence to the mainland, where they were
landed on the towpath of the canal. The towpath was
entirely filled with artillery, and unfortunately, the
regimental ambulances had been taken across the
canal on to the bank of the river by a flatboat, which
was afterwards put into the river to transport troops,
so that they were rendered useless.... A skiff being
discovered farther down the canal, I ordered the
wounded to be put across the canal as rapidly as possible.... I went through an arch under the canal, and
ordered the ambulance train there to take down the
fences and to drive to the point where the wounded
were being put across the canal. It was now quite
dark, but we were so fortunate as to find two barns
about a mile from this point. These were rapidly
cleared, and the floors covered with straw.... Directions were given that all the wounded on the island
should be removed and transported by canal boat to
Edward's Ferry during the night, and thence, by
ambulance to Poolesville.

    The whole number comprised in the list of
wounded is one hundred and sixty-nine.... Under
wounds of the chest, several wounds of the lungs are
included. None of these cases have proved fatal....
All of the wounds of the abdomen which penetrated

the cavity, some four or five, proved fatal.... The wounds of the shoulders were, generally, not severe.... Of the wounds of the knee, only two penetrated the joint; one of these I amputated above the knee, and the patient is making a most rapid recovery.... The remaining case of particular interest is one where a ball passed through the left buttock, through the scrotum, grazing the testicle, and entering the penis at its anterior third, ploughed its way out through the urethra.... The case is doing well....

Surg. Crosby reported the wounds by category, which included 93 wounds of the head and face out of a total of 169, a very large proportion. This was probably caused by the Confederate firing down the side of the bluff at the Union troops attempting to escape across the narrow passage to the island.

Lidell, John A., Surg., USV, Baker's Brigade, Ball's Bluff, Va.:

I established a hospital at a farmhouse near the Virginia shore at Harrison's Island; but such wounded as could walk I directed to cross the island to a barn near the Maryland shore and our ferry.... Fighting ceased at dark. The enemy had no artillery, and most of the wounds of our men were inflicted by round musket balls. About two hundred wounded had to be provided for. I determined to remove them that night, lest they might be captured the next morning.... Late that night, accompanied by Surg. Martin Rizer, 72d Pennsylvania Volunteers, I carefully searched the Virginia shore of the island for any wounded that might have been overlooked. The enemy's pickets did not fire on us, though we were less than one hundred yards distant, and carried lanterns. We were evidently recognized as searching for the wounded. We were much delayed in the removal of the wounded by the stragglers, who crowded our boats with their worthless carcasses.... At midnight I crossed to the Maryland shore. Most of the wounded were sent to Edward's Ferry by canal boat, and thence by the brigade ambulance train to the general hospital at Poolesville....

After long delays, the plan of Gen. Winfield Scott to blockade the South Carolina coast was under way. Since the 1st of October regiments had been arriving at camps near Annapolis and placed under the command of Brig. Gen. Thomas W. Sherman.

These were, for the most part, raw recruits, and as yet not "blooded" with the camp diseases. On this date they sailed for Ft. Monroe, Va., for further deployment south.

October 22 (Tuesday)

Tripler, Charles S., Med. Dir., Army of the Potomac, Washington, D.C.:

The prophylactic use of quinine and whiskey having been suggested as a means of preventing malarial disease, I determined to test its efficacy. There being no warrant for such an issue in the regulations of the army, I procured a small quantity from a sanitary aid society, and received favorable reports of its effects. Upon representing this to the Surgeon General, I was authorized to issue it, in reasonable quantities, to regiments whose conditions seemed most to demand it.... The surgeon of the Cameron dragoons reported that by its use he'd reduced his sick report from 126 to 74, in two weeks. The surgeon of the 62nd Pennsylvania reported as favorably, and stated that two companies of the regiment, who had used it faithfully for two weeks, presented a sick report of only four men. Much prejudice and aversion, however, had to be overcome in inducing the men to take this medicine, and I scarcely think it would have been practicable to have forced it upon the whole army. Fortunately, there was no necessity for this.

This was probably the only case in recorded history where a soldier had to be induced to drink whiskey!

October 25 (Friday)

Tripler, Charles S., Med. Dir., Army of the Potomac, Washington, D.C.:

Protection of the men against the contagion of smallpox, of course, received constant attention. While the Army of the Potomac was in process of organization, smallpox was prevailing rather extensively in several of the districts from which the troops were recruited. It was unsafe to travel, without protection, over any railway in the country. The city of Washington was infected, as I know from the number of applications made to me by the authorities for the use of our smallpox ambulances to convey city patients to the pesthouse....

Orders were issued and reiterated for the vaccination of all volunteers unprotected. I also recommended that an order should be published, requiring that all recruits ... be vaccinated before they were started from their rendezvous; and that they should be carefully inspected as to this immediately upon their arrival....

October 29 (Tuesday)

In a fleet of 77 vessels, the largest Federal fleet assembled to date, Brig. Gen. Sherman's 16,000 troops sailed from Ft. Monroe on Hampton Roads for Pt. Royal, S.C., under command of Flag Officer DuPont. The intent of this massive array of armament was to take Pt. Royal for a refuelling and servicing station for the blockading Union squadrons. The fleet consisted of an odd mixture of vessels, including steamers, sail ships, tugs, barges, and almost anything that would float. Many were loaded with live cattle to be used for rations.

Cooper, George E., Surg., USA, Ft. Monroe, Va.:

On Sunday evening, October 20th, 1861, the troops were embarked on the steam transports, and on Monday morning, they sailed for Ft. Monroe.... The troops remained at Ft. Monroe from the 22d of October until the 29th of the same month and were kept on shipboard during that time, with the exception of one brigade, which was put on shore in a drill, which was for the purpose of instructing them in disembarking in surfboats....

Supplies of medicines and hospital stores for three months had been put up at the purveyor's depot in New York, in quantities sufficient for ten regiments, but they had been stored away in the hold of one of the transports and could not be come at. Some boxes of Kidwell's disinfectant had been turned over to the quartermaster for the use of the transports, when at Annapolis, with the request that it would be divided among the ships; but instead of making this use of it, it was placed aboard the steamship *Winfield Scott*, and, in the storm of November 1, 1861, the greater part was thrown overboard...

October 31 (Thursday)

Cooper, George E., Surg., USA, at sea, en route to Pt. Royal, S.C.:

On the morning of the 31st, the signal officer on board the steamship *Vanderbilt* notified the general

commanding that a case of variola had made its appearance in the 8th Michigan regiment. Instructions were sent to isolate the patient as much as possible. This was done, and the disease did not spread during the time the men remained on board, though, some three weeks later, it broke out in the crew of the vessel, and several were attacked by variola and varioloid....

In the early stages of the war, the medical officers were learning to cope with "red tape," involved when reporting numbers of sick, etc. Surg. Tripler, the senior medical officer of the Army of the Potomac, finally received complete reports in October. Men were still being discharged for disabilities that existed prior to entry into the service, seven months after the first troops were called.

Tripler, Charles S., Med. Dir., Army of the Potomac, Washington, D.C.:

I received for October, reports from one hundred and twenty-nine regiments, seven battalions, fourteen batteries, and eight general hospitals. The aggregate strength of the force from which these reports were received was one hundred and sixteen thousand seven hundred and sixty-three. Of these, thirty-eight thousand two hundred and forty-eight were under treatment during the month in the field and general hospitals; twenty-seven thousand nine hundred and eighty-three were returned to duty; two hundred and ninety-five died, and seven thousand four hundred and forty-three remained under treatment at the end of the month; five hundred and ten were discharged on surgeon's certificates of disability. These men never should have been enlisted. They were simply impositions upon the government, and were received through the carelessness or incompetency of the recruiting or inspecting officers....

November 1 (Friday)

Flag Officer DuPont's 77-ship fleet that had sailed from Hampton Roads on October 29th was struck by a violent storm off Cape Hatteras. The ships were scattered, and one ship carrying beef cattle was sunk, as was the transport *Governor*, but Maj. John G. Reynolds and his battalion of marines on board were saved the following day by the U.S.S. *Sabine*. Unfortunately, many medical supplies were jettisoned to lighten the ships during the storm and replacements would take months to reach the troops.

Cooper, George E., Surg., USA, at sea, en route to Pt. Royal, S.C.:

The storm, to which the expedition was exposed on the afternoon and night of November 1st, caused the destruction of the medical supplies belonging to the 48th New York and 50th Pennsylvania Volunteers, which, with other articles, were thrown overboard to assist in lightening the vessels. The men on board the transport *Winfield Scott*, were, for two days and nights, without cooked provisions, and were wet, worn-out, and prostrated by fatigue consequent upon bailing to keep the water from encroaching on the fires. The result of this fatigue and exposure was fever of a low grade, in several of the men....

November 4 (Monday)

Flag Officer DuPont's fleet assembled off Pt. Royal, S.C., preparatory to entering the harbor. The troops were still fairly healthy, the usual communicable diseases hadn't yet taken hold. These troops, at least some of them, had been exposed to the filthy conditions at Meridian Hill in Washington, and carried the seeds of sickness with them.

Today an inspection of the hospital at Camp Franklin, Va., was made by Gen. H. W. Slocum, the brigade commander. After the inspection, the conversation, as reported, was:

"How is it, Dr. Brickett, that your boys are so much more comfortable than those of other Regiments in the Brigade?"

"O," said the doctor, "we have got a Maine woman here who understands how to take care of the sick. She has drawn these things from the Sanitary Commission, and has arranged the whole thing with some of the nurses' assistance."

"I can't have any partiality in my Brigade," said the General, "give my compliments to Miss Bradley, and tell her I should be happy for her to take charge of the sick of the Brigade. I will take the Powell House and the Octagon House, that are empty a short distance from here where we will move them all, and tell her I would like her to go there and make a home for my 'boys.'"

The Octagon [Glebe] House still stands in Arlington, Va., and serves as a private residence.

November 6 (Wednesday)

After Gen. Albert Sydney Johnston took command of the Confederate armies in the west, he had trouble getting his commands moving because of disease. One command, Gen. Alcorn's at Hopkinsville, Ky., had 67 percent on the sick list. Gen. Lloyd Tilghman reported 750 sick, and the command lacked an officer well enough to command 100 men.

November 7 (Thursday)

At Pt. Royal, S.C., the fleet under the command of Flag Officer DuPont entered the Sound and engaged the Confederate squadron (meeting not much opposition) and Fts. Walker (located on Hilton Head) and Beauregard (located on Bay Point). The Confederate troops abandoned the forts readily enough under the accurate and withering fire of the Federal fleet. Gen. Thomas Sherman's Union troops were soon ashore and the occupation of Hilton Head and the Pt. Royal area began, and would last for the duration of the war. The season of sickness wasn't yet upon the Union forces; the full brunt would fall in the spring. Meanwhile, the various surgeons set up their hospitals where dry ground could be found, and began treating the usual array of diarrhea, measles, and mumps.

Cooper, George E., Surg., USA, Hilton Head, S.C.:

... after the capture of the fort on Hilton Head, a portion of the troops, some four regiments, were landed on the island, and in the course of five or six days the whole command was disembarked. The men landed in surfboats, and were wet from the waist down; no inconvenience seemed to follow this, though the men having no changes, retained their wet clothes during the night. But two wounded were found in the vicinity of the fort, and these were found in an old outhouse, where they had been left by the retreating Rebels. One of these had a wound in the back part of the head, caused by a piece of shell; the other had the thigh wounded, and the femur shattered at the neck by a piece of shell. The first case recovered after a tedious convalescence. The latter case was operated on at the hip joint, as I afterwards learned, and the patient soon died. Two men were found in the hospital building, who were prostrated by typhoid fever, and could not be moved; both of them recovered.

Brig. Gen. U. S. Grant fought his first battle, capturing a Confederate fortified position near Belmont, Mo., across the Mississippi from Columbus, Ky. Confederate Gen. Leonidas Polk sent troops across the river to counterattack, and Grant was forced to retreat. As a battle, Belmont amounted to little. Neither side gained an advantage, but Grant learned some lessons there that would hold him in good stead later.

Brinton, John H., Surg., Battle of Belmont, Mo.:

The expedition started from Cairo on the afternoon of the 6th of November, and proceeded down the Mississippi in transports. During the night the boats laid to on the Kentucky shore, eight or ten miles above Columbus.... Early the following morning the boats crossed to the Missouri side of the river, and the troops debarked at a point three miles distant from the enemy's camp at Belmont.... As soon as the light batteries were landed, the troops moved forward, skirmishers being thrown to the front to feel the enemy's position.

In a very few minutes, his pickets were driven in, and the engagement became general. The wounded shortly began to appear in the rear, and to gather around the hospital stations. The advance of the national troops was steadily pushed on, and the enemy were driven from tree to tree, from behind the bushes, and across the cornfields, until their camp at Belmont was reached, when they sought the cover of the riverbank. It was in dislodging the enemy from the rolling cornfields that the chief loss was sustained. The standing corn screened him perfectly from the observation of the national troops as they ascended the cleared slopes to the attack, whilst the latter presented a target against which every shot told: At the same time the enemy opened with fearful execution, from his batteries planted on the ridges....

As soon as the enemy were driven from their camp, it was immediately fired and destroyed, by order of Gen. Grant. Three of their guns were here captured ... During the conflagration of the camp, and when the scattered troops of the enemy had found shelter under the riverbank, the heavy guns mounted on the Kentucky bluffs above Columbus

opened their fire ... fortunately, the necessary depression of the guns was not obtained, and the shot and bursting shells passed high above the heads of the national troops, doing little or no damage.

...In the meantime, an attempt had been made by the enemy to land a large force [at the rear of] Gen. Grant's [army], and thus to cut him off from his boats. The backward path was, consequently, the scene of fierce conflict, but Gen. Grant finally succeeded in reaching his transports, which lay at the original landing, under the protection of the gunboats *Tyler* and *Lexington*....

Stearns, H. P., Surg., USV, Battle of Belmont, Mo.:

There were no hospital stores or ambulances. There was a sufficient supply of morphine, chloroform, instruments, and dressings. The wounded were attended to at a log house, about one mile in the rear of Belmont. All that were conveyed to this place were well cared for, and after their wounds were dressed, were immediately sent to the steamers. There was an abundance of water; no soup and no food except such as the men had in their knapsacks. When the troops left Belmont to again return ... some of the wounded were left upon the field and many of them remained till the next day when we removed them under a flag of truce. There was no rain, and the night was not cold. The wounded were removed from the field upon wagons, stretchers, and blankets fastened to poles and muskets....

With the withdrawal of the Union troops, both sides claimed a victory. The Union had suffered a total of 485 killed, wounded, and missing. When the troops returned to Cairo, both Mrs. Bickerdyke and Miss Safford were waiting on the dock. They had rounded up every empty wagon, buggy, handcart, or anything else that would carry wounded, to get the injured and wounded to the hospitals, inadequate as they were. The army, with its usual scorn for sick soldiers, had finally seen the light and decided that Cairo needed a more permanent place for the sick and wounded other than the tents they were now occupying.

November 8 (Friday)

The effect of locating camps in poor sites where drainage wasn't good, and where horses were present in large numbers, was described by Surg. Tripler.

Tripler, Charles S., Med. Dir., Army of the Potomac, Washington, D.C.:

... the surgeon of the 8th Illinois Cavalry reported to me that 200 of the men had received no overcoats from the United States; many of them were almost destitute of clothing. He had three hospital tents, floored, and furnished with stoves; his regiment was unusually healthy, no deaths had occurred in it in three months. The location of the regiment was afterwards changed; it was encamped in low ground that became intolerably muddy in the course of the winter; the part occupied by the horses was a perfect quagmire, never policed at all, the men became discouraged and careless, and, in January, 1862, there were 207 cases of typhoid fever among them....

November 9 (Saturday)

Once ashore at Hilton Head, S.C., the Union force now had to build fortifications in case the Confederates decided to revisit the island. The labor for this purpose took a dreadful toll on the troops, who were unused to the climate and terrain.

Cooper, George E., Surg., USA, Hilton Head, S.C.:

The labor of the troops from the time of landing was severe. Heavy fortifications to protect the land side of the island had to be erected, and all the supplies for the troops had to be brought on shore in lighters, and each and all of them had to be brought from the lighters on the shoulders of the men, or be placed by them in wagons from the boats. To do this, fatigue parties were compelled to be wet from the waist, and, at the same time, had an almost tropical sun beating upon their heads, and much sickness resulted from this necessary fatigue duty, which, oftentimes, was continued far into the night.

A bivouac building,... was made use of for a temporary hospital, and the sick were carried there for treatment, until the proper regimental hospitals were put in operation.... Some sixteen or twenty hospital tents had been brought by the quartermaster's department for the use of the expedition, but they could not be got at, as they had been placed in one of the ships, the exact one not known, and covered with other articles....

November 10 (Sunday)

At Cairo, Ill., following the battle at Belmont, a large, half-finished downtown hotel was commandeered for the military hospital and Bickerdyke became the unofficial supervisor of the building crew, pushing the carpenters for all they were worth.

November 11 (Monday)

On Hilton Head, Surg. Cooper noted the increase of sickness from malarial-type diseases within a few days after the expeditionary force landed.

Cooper, George E., Surg., USA, Hilton Head, S.C.:

Shortly after the troops were disembarked, the malarious fevers of the southern coast began to show themselves, principally among those encamped back on the island, at a distance from the sea beach, and who, at the same time, were on fatigue duty during the day.... The island of Hilton Head is low and sandy, and, where not under cultivation, covered with heavy pine forests, with thick undergrowth; on the side of the ocean are heavy ridges of sand, and back of these are, for some distance, freshwater swamps. Creeks are numerous through the island, and on the Pt. Royal harbor side is a large salt marsh. Water, soft and pleasant to the taste, can be procured in any part of the island, by sinking wells twelve or fifteen feet deep....

The fevers by which the men were attacked shortly after their arrival, were, in many cases, of the most malignant type, and in some cases the patients never reacted perfectly, but sank on the first chill. Men were brought into the hospital with what would be regarded as epileptic fits, but what, in reality, was the coast fever. These would froth at the mouth, have some convulsions, and, for a time, be perfectly demented. The chief complaints made by them were of severe headache, and of a burning skin, when in reality the surface was cold and covered with a clammy sweat. When reaction took place, the skin became excessively hot, the eyes bloodshot, the pulse bounding and corded. When the fever broke up the heavy sweat was of a most disagreeable odor. The only hope for the patient was in the exhibition of free doses of quinine....

November 13 (Wednesday)

The commandeered hotel in Cairo, Ill., was completed in record time and the patients from the tents were moved in. Along with them came Mrs. Bickerdyke, much to the chagrin of the surgeon-in-charge. Mrs. Bickerdyke was informed that her services weren't needed in any way and that she'd best vacate the premises.

Mrs. Bickerdyke didn't agree with this assessment, and went to see Gen. (then Col.) Grant, who was commanding the Cairo area. With no problem at all, Grant wrote a note to the surgeon-in-charge, saying that while he didn't want to tell the surgeon how to run his hospital, the General thought it would be a good idea to appoint Mrs. Bickerdyke as the matron of the hospital.

The surgeon, his ears smoking, made the appointment with the understanding that Bickerdyke's duties were confined to giving out supplies and running the laundry. She was to keep out of the kitchen because they had a chef, named Tom, from a Cairo restaurant, who was doing that task. Mrs. Bickerdyke agreed. She'd done enough cooking for awhile. She did, however, inform the surgeon that if the cooking wasn't to her satisfaction, she would give him plenty of trouble, and anyone else who didn't do right would also get trouble, which included surgeons.

November 14 (Thursday)

Cooper, George E., Surg., USA, Hilton Head, S.C.:

… measles broke out in the regiments from New England, and smallpox in that from Michigan. A variola hospital was established at a distance from the camps, and all attacked were transferred thither. The results of rubeola in the New Hampshire regiments were lamentable; many recovering from the disease were attacked with severe bronchitis, and tuberculous phthisis was rapidly developed in men of robust frames and apparently healthy bodies. This tendency to pulmonary disease was far more observable in the New Englanders than in the New Yorkers or Pennsylvanians.…

November 15 (Friday)

For ten days the hustle and bustle around the Powell and Octagon houses in Virginia made them resemble a beehive. Miss Amy M. Bradley, newly appointed Hospital Matron for the 7th Brigade, had been preparing for the movement of the brigade patients to new quarters. Seventy-five new iron cots and straw bed ticks had been obtained, as well as supplies from the U.S. Sanitary Commission such as quilts, blankets, sheets, pillowcases, shirts, socks, towels, etc., to make the patients as comfortable as possible. Soldiers had been detailed as nurses to help with the sick, and a Negro family was found living in a cabin to the rear of the Powell House who offered to obtain rations and protection. So, on this day, the patients arrived by ambulance from the various field hospitals to fill the beds and to be cared for in a more comfortable fashion. Miss Amy M. Bradley was in business.

November 16 (Saturday)

The arrangement for Mrs. Bickerdyke's duties didn't last long. For one thing, she wasn't supposed to go into the wards at all. If a ward master, who was usually a junior officer, came to her for an order from her stores, it was to be provided without question. Since the Sanitary Commission in Chicago sent their provisions to her personally at Cairo, these supplies were stored in her care at the hospital. The ward masters would bring requisitions for whiskey and the cooks would provide requests for preserved fruit and other delicacies from her storeroom, but she was forbidden to find out how the supplies were used.

Being Mary Ann Bickerdyke, it made no difference to her whether she was barred from the wards; she went there anyway. Once there, it took no time until she realized that the whiskey was going into the doctor's "lounge" for the benefit of the chief surgeon and his cronies. Other "goodies" were mostly being sold by the chief nurse. Tom, the cook, and many of his assistants, were waxing fat on the food from the Commission's donations, which were meant for the invalids in the hospital. The hospital seemed to be holding one big party, for everyone except the patients.

Mrs. Bickerdyke went to the chief surgeon and informed him that the Sanitary Commission supplies were being stolen. He, the surgeon, ordered her out of his hospital at once. Mrs. Livermore reports that Bickerdyke informed the surgeon:

Doctor, I'm here to stay as long as the men need me. If you put me out of one door, I'll come in at another. If you bar all the doors against me, I'll come in at the window, and the patients will help me in. If anybody goes from here it'll be you. I'm going straight to Gen. Grant. We'll see who gets put out of here.

The surgeon, seeing she was determined, backed down a bit and said that he might have been a little hasty, and that he'd see that the supplies weren't again abused, but, after all, she was only the matron and subject to his orders, and must show proper respect to his office.

Mrs. Livermore again reports the woman's reply:

I respect the office all right. I respect it so much I aim to see it filled the way it ought to be. All right, doctor, you see what you can do with that bunch of thieves you've got in here. I'll be watching, mind you.

November 18 (Monday)

Tripler, Charles S., Med. Dir., Army of the Potomac, Washington, D.C.:

I had long been solicitous to get possession of a few experienced regular medical officers to be employed as inspectors of the field hospitals.... This was accomplished at last. In the middle of November, 1861, two officers were assigned to me for that purpose; and, some weeks afterwards, a third. I prepared instructions for them, and set them at work at once....

November 19 (Tuesday)

Mrs. Bickerdyke kept a sharp eye on what was going on in the hospital at Cairo. One day, she went into a ward and found a young lieutenant, the ward master, talking to one of his friends before he completed his inspection, which completion was necessary before the noon meal could be served. Angry, Mrs. Bickerdyke approached the officer, whose uniform blouse was open, exposing his shirt. Something about the shirt seemed familiar, so Bickerdyke pulled open the officer's blouse and turned down the neck band on the shirt, where she found, clearly marked in indelible ink, the initials NWSC, which stood for the Northwestern Sanitary Commission. The young lieutenant was no match for the strong woman, who threw him to the floor, sat on his stomach, and removed the shirt, which she held up to the cheers of the patients. She then checked his trousers and found them to be his own. That wasn't true of his slippers and socks, which were also confiscated as NWSC property, for the use of patients only. Barefoot and shirtless, the officer completed his rounds, and that night applied for duty with a regiment leaving for the battle zone. He was never seen again.

November 20 (Wednesday)

Patients die for one reason or another, and such was the case of Amy M. Bradley's first patient, who finally succumbed to his illness.

My first patient, Charles G. Nichols, died of diphtheria. I feel very sad. I did not count on losing my boys, but alas! The best nursing cannot save them. His disease was too far advanced before he came to the Hospital. He suffered very much, and was loathe to have me leave him for a moment—he could not lie down at all. The night he died I talked with him about his coming dissolution. He'd been a professor of religion for some years. On inquiring of his friends I found his mother was a cousin to my own brother-in-law William Randelett, and that I had visited her with my sister and [her] husband the year before I came out. How strange that I should be the one to care to minister to him and be able to care for him, making his last hours as happy as possible. They have voted in our Regiment to raise money enough to send home the body of everyone who dies. We have our Charley packed in salt and saltpeter. There is a hothouse nearby, so I have purchased some delicate flowers and placed them around his pale face. How beautiful he looked asleep in Death! We shall meet again! Have telegraphed to his friends in Damariscotta, Maine, as I found a letter from them among his effects.

November 23 (Saturday)

At the hospital in Cairo, Ill., Mrs. Bickerdyke was still having trouble with Tom, the chief cook in the hospital kitchen. It seemed that the patients were still not receiving some of the food she'd issued to the cook, who was to use it for the more seriously ill patients. The cook's excuse was that the kitchen was always filled with people who had no particular function there, and maybe that was where the food went. Bickerdyke wouldn't accept this excuse.

Having recently received some dried peaches, Mrs. Bickerdyke had them brought into the kitchen and put them on to stew on one of the stoves, explaining to Tom that they could be used for dessert after supper for the patients. She admonished Tom not to let the peaches be eaten, because she wanted to supervise their distribution to the patients herself. Tom, acting offended, explained that she'd better quit accusing the kitchen staff of eating the Commission donations, or she was likely to get into serious trouble. Bickerdyke went back to her storeroom after placing the peaches in shallow pans to cool and putting them on a windowsill.

In her room, Bickerdyke watched the constant parade of doctors, ward masters, nurses, etc., going to the kitchen for their noon meal, or to get a drink of water. Soon the noise from there became such that she lay down her paperwork. She entered the kitchen, where she found the "visitors" and kitchen staff groaning and holding their stomachs. Bickerdyke's response was to explain to them that she'd added a large dose of tartar emetic to the peaches and that the visitors had trapped themselves when they'd eaten them, proving to one and all that they were indeed the thieves who took the food meant for the patients. She also told them that one night they might end up eating rat poison in the food if they persisted in stealing that which was meant for the patients.

November 27 (Wednesday)

When items continued to disappear from the hospital kitchen in Cairo, Mrs. Bickerdyke had a large refrigerator with a padlock sent down from Chicago. She had it installed in the kitchen for perishable food. She loaded the refrigerator and placed the key in her pocket. That night the lock was broken, and many of the delicacies were taken. This was the last straw.

Bickerdyke went to the Provost Marshal, and then both went to see Gen. Grant, who ordered an investigation. The result was that the chief surgeon and his officers were reprimanded and the enlisted men were transferred to out-bound regiments or returned to their own regiments. Tom, the cook, was also transferred after spending a few days in the

guardhouse. A new doctor took charge and won Mrs. Bickerdyke over immediately. She managed to select her own cooks and many of the nurses, which choice improved the health care immediately. The hospital shortly became widely known as a model for military hospitals.

November 28 (Thursday)

Having shipped the remains of Charles G. Nichols back to Maine for burial, and having written a letter to his family expressing her condolences on their loss, Amy M. Bradley received a letter from the family—the first, but certainly not the last, to be received from bereaved relatives.

Webb, Hannah C., cousin of Charles G. Nichols, New Castle, Me.:

> Your kind letter was received one week ago yesterday and it brought us very sad news. I have delayed writing until after the funeral, thinking you would like to hear that his remains arrived safely.… Yes, dear Cousin Charley is now laying beside his dear Father, Mother, and Sister, and we feel that they are better off—that we not ought to wish them back again to this world of trouble. Can we ever repay you for the kindness you manifested towards him? We are all very grateful and extend many warm and sincere thanks.…

November 29 (Friday)

Mrs. Livermore was travelling about the western states, raising money to equip the first of the river hospital boats. These boats would prove to be invaluable to move those wounded in the coming campaigns. Thousands of dollars were needed to procure these boats.

During her travels, she came to Cairo, Ill., to visit the Sanitary Commission agent in that city, the Rev. Folsom. While the most publicity had been given to Miss Mary Safford for her work at the hospitals, Rev. Folsom informed Mrs. Livermore that the real work behind the reputation of the Cairo hospital was Mrs. Bickerdyke, citing her industry, honesty, and inventiveness as a major resource for saving money and materials, while still providing the patients with a high standard of service. Livermore didn't have time to meet Bickerdyke on this trip, but she would in the very near future.

December 1 (Sunday)

Surg. R. N. Barr of the 36th Ohio reported that from September through this date the regiment had 1002 men on the sick list—only 49 of them having been wounded or injured. Twenty-seven men died during this period, two dying of hernias from marching through the hills of western Virginia. Most of the illness was diarrhea or catarrh, although measles was a close third. The sick list averaged 240 per day, and Barr began issuing two ounces of whiskey per day to the those considered "well," and to the nurses.

December 2 (Monday)

The winter campaign in western Virginia was beset with many cases of pneumonia caused by the rainy, chilly weather. This ailment was often compounded by other sicknesses, such as typhoid fever, smallpox, or measles. Except for the victims of smallpox, no effort was made to isolate those suffering from various other illnesses; consequently, the airborne germs were often spread among the other patients.

December 3 (Tuesday)

Typhoid fever, caused by contaminated food or drinking water, usually only spread among troops who'd been in camps for a long time, but this wasn't always the case. One commander asked for his troops to be sent to the field from their camp. He reported, "Typhoid fever is striking our men a heavy blow; 233 of my regiment are down, and dying daily.... We would rather die in battle than on a bed of fever."

December 5 (Thursday)

In Pt. Royal, S.C., the toehold gained by the capture of Hilton Head was to be expanded as rapidly as possible. Beaufort was occupied, and preparations for the assault on Ft. Pulaski were begun.

Cooper, George E., Surg., USA, Hilton Head, S.C.:

Some four weeks after the occupation of Hilton Head, the brigade of Gen. Stevens, composed of the 79th New York, the 50th and 100th Pennsylvania, and the 8th Michigan Volunteers, were directed to take post at Beaufort, South Carolina. The health of the troops composing the brigade was much improved by this change. The camping grounds and

hospital accommodations were much better than at Hilton Head, and they were enabled to procure many comforts and conveniences unattainable at any other place in the department....

December 6 (Friday)

The commander of the Army of the Potomac, Gen. McClellan, appointed a Board of Inquiry to investigate the cause of the fevers which ravaged his command near Washington. This was the second such board to be appointed (the first in October) and the results were about the same. No one recognized that most of the problems with typhus and typhoid were caused by unclean camp conditions, not necessarily the location of the camps. The reports claimed that the malarial fever resulted from the low-lying areas, which exuded noxious fumes, and that the typhoid was caused by overcrowding in the camp tents and overwork of the soldiers.

It was interesting that this board was appointed, not by a medically trained individual, but by Gen. McClellan, who knew so little of disease that when he came down with typhoid fever in mid-December he didn't know what it was, and he sent for a homeopath!

On this date, a group of Holy Cross Sisters, and other volunteers, from South Bend, Ind., departed for Cairo, Ill., and eventual duty at the Mound City Union hospital. Among these volunteers, but not a member of the Holy Cross order, was Margaret McCrea Durand, born in 1814 in County Tyrone, Ireland. She and her husband, William Durand, had three children, the last born in 1856. At the time of Margaret's departure for Cairo, only one child, the youngest, survived, and this child was left in the care of a friend, Mrs. Matilda Coquillard. Duties at the Mound City hospital were relatively light until April 1862.

December 7 (Saturday)

Cooper, George E., Surg., USA, Hilton Head, S.C.:

About the time that Beaufort was occupied, the 46th New York and a part of the 7th Connecticut were ordered to take post at Tybee Island, to hold the same, and commence operations for the siege of Ft. Pulaski. The work performed by this command was almost incredible. In order to transport artillery and material of war to the points required, it was necessary to make roads through morasses, which would bear up the heaviest classes of modern artillery. Sand hills had to be cut down, and hollows to be filled up. Everything, provisions, guns, ammunition, and all the numerous articles required for a siege, had to be brought ashore in boats, and that too in a dangerous roadstead, where the surf ran higher than in any place occupied by our forces on the southern coast....

The greater part of this work was done at night, as it was necessary to allow those in Ft. Pulaski to know nothing of the position of the batteries being erected. The heavy Columbiads, rifled siege guns, and thirteen-inch mortars were hauled to their positions, and there placed during the night....

December 9 (Monday)

One of Mrs. Bickerdyke's duties at the hospital in Cairo was unofficial. Being the only woman available, she was given the task of greeting and guiding visitors, mostly mothers and sisters of the patients, who descended upon the hospital to see how their relatives were being treated. Most of the visitors wanted to help, but this, obviously, was impossible, because so many of them would disrupt the routine of the patients. Bickerdyke's means of countering this, and also of using such help wisely, was to explain to the visitors that the food and clothing supplied by the Sanitary Commission were sent by individuals like themselves, working through their local Ladies' Aid Society. Their greatest contribution would be to help such an effort, which, in turn, would help their loved one and all the others as well. Bickerdyke's ideas gained quick response, and everyone benefitted.

December 11 (Wednesday)

After being in the hospital for fifteen days with a combination of typhoid fever and pneumonia, Walter H. Davis, Co. C, 5th Maine Regt., died. He was a favorite of Amy M. Bradley, matron of the 7th Brigade Hospital located at the Octagon and Powell houses, Alexandria, Va. Amy's natural maternal instincts were both a blessing to her patients and sometimes a curse to her own well-being. She wrote of Davis as if he were one of her children:

Bradley, Amy M., Matron, 7th Brigade Hospital, Alexandria, Va.:

He was a darling boy—so patient when he suffered so much! How his great blue eyes would brighten when I would open the door to enter his room! Once, I remember I had been gone all day to the Octagon House (where a large number from the 16th N.Y. are sick), and when I returned it was evening—I immediately went to see my sickest patients. When I asked [Davis] if they had taken good care of him in my absence, he answered, "Yes—but not as good care as you do." And when I said, "Why not?" he answered while a faint smile irradiated his heavenly countenance—"They don't love me as much as you do!" True, too true!... After having watched and cared for them so long, I love them as if they were my own children! Poor fellows! Why shouldn't I love them! Away from every fond heart—how they do yearn for sympathy and kind words! A soldier's life is a hard one—and woe be unto me if I do not strive to alleviate their suffering and make them feel that one heart is full of pity and love towards them.

December 13 (Friday)

The Army of the Potomac was preparing for the move to the York Peninsula and battling the problem of troops being absent sick at the same time. Many of the soldiers were now immune to measles, smallpox, chicken pox, mumps, etc., that had taken their toll earlier. They were, however walking carriers of many of the diseases which would rack that army in the coming months.

December 16 (Monday)

Steamships on the Mississippi were at a premium at this time. The Union Navy had scooped up most of the larger steamers and converted them to gunboats with iron outer shells. What was left were the smaller boats, but these would serve well for hospital evacuation transportation. From Chicago came Dr. Laurence Aigner, who leased the *City of Memphis, Hazel Dell, Franklin, War Eagle,* and *City of Louisiana* for the Sanitary Commission. These rentals nearly exhausted his funds for this project and the boats still had to be outfitted.

Fortunately, Mrs. Bickerdyke was on hand to help with the list of supplies needed for such boats and to help with the design of the interiors in order to be able to accommodate the most patients in a comfortable manner. Both Folsom and Aigner became fast and warm friends with Mrs. Bickerdyke, friendships that would last for the remainder of their lives. Those boats would be ready for the assault on Fts. Henry and Donelson in the coming year.

December 18 (Wednesday)

The sanitation about the various camps in the North needed tending to, to say the least. One frugal Yankee thought something could be done with the garbage and offal that smelled up the camps and made them unhealthy.

Day, D. L., Pvt., Co. B, 25th Mass. Vol. Infantry, near Annapolis, Md.:

I have been looking through the camp around here and am astonished at the amount of offal and swill that is buried up and lost instead of being turned into valuable account. An enterprising farmer could collect from these camps manure and swill to the value of $100 a day, costing nothing but simply carting it off, thus enriching his land and fattening hundreds of hogs and cattle; but this lack of energy and enterprise prevents these people from turning anything to account. They content themselves with sitting down and finding fault with the government and their more enterprising and energetic neighbors of the north.

December 20 (Friday)

Tripler, Charles S., Med. Dir., Army of the Potomac, Washington, D.C.:

It was the general understanding that the army wasn't to go into winter quarters ... but in December, 1861, learning that some of the regiments were excavating pits in the ground and covering them with their tents, I hastened to object strenuously to this plan. I suggested enclosures of rails or palisades, some three feet high, to be roofed over with the tents. The excavations could not be kept dry or well ventilated, and certainly would not be kept in good police; all of which objections would be obviated by the above-ground enclosure. This plan was adopted in a number of camps I visited, and they presented an air of comfort that was very gratifying....

December 23 (Monday)

In the early stages of the war the movement of troops to the battlefront was often a haphazard event (with the emphasis on *hazard*). The 6th New York Volunteer Cavalry was based on Staten Island, in New York Harbor, when its orders arrived to be ready to move on this date. The camp was dismantled, the tentage packed, and the men readied to embark on a steamer to go to Elizabethport, N.J., where they would take a train to York, Pa. The regiment assembled and stood in a cold, drizzling rain all day waiting for the steamer. At about dusk, the "steamer" arrived in the form of two open barges which had been decked over and were pulled by a tugboat. With soaked clothing, the troops were pulled to New Jersey on the open decks in a stiff December wind with the spray from the tug falling over them. They arrived at 3 A.M., after a journey of about eight hours. It was reported that 30 men died of exposure that night.

December 26 (Thursday)

Smallpox was still a problem within the armies, North and South. Surg. Tripler, in spite of all of his earlier precautions, wasn't entirely satisfied that everything possible had been done.

Tripler, Charles S., Med. Dir., Army of the Potomac, Washington, D.C.:

Not satisfied with what had been done, I asked for, and obtained, another order,... requiring division and brigade commanders to cause the brigade surgeons to again inspect all the men, vaccinating such as were still unprotected, and to report the results to me. At this late period, most of the brigades were found to have some men unprotected; in a few, the number was serious. In Slocum's brigade, there were fifteen hundred, in Blenker's, twelve hundred and fifty, and in Sickle's, seven hundred and fifty. Crusts were furnished, and the vaccination completed. As a result, smallpox, though rife in the community, never gained a foothold in the army.

Tripler's action on smallpox was carried on throughout the Union armies, but this wasn't true of the Southern armies. Gen. Lee caused an effective, ongoing program to be conducted in his Army of Northern Virginia, but the commanders of other armies didn't do so well. Many of the Confederate deaths in the Northern prison camps during 1864 were caused by Confederate inmates arriving infected with the disease and thus infecting others. In early 1864, 387 prisoners died in one month at Camp Douglas, Ill., having been infected with the disease from other prisoners.

December 28 (Saturday)

Late in the year, Surg. Tripler summarized the problems arising from the sanitary conditions in the camps around Washington of the Army of the Potomac.

Tripler, Charles S., Med. Dir., Army of the Potomac, Washington, D.C.:

I have observed some regiments, after arriving here in wretched sanitary condition, that have steadily improved, until their sick lists would compare favorably with the rest. This might be accounted for by acclimation; by improvement in discipline and police; by acquaintance with the wants of a soldier in camp. But other troops, and those, too, from particular sections of the country, have not improved. The Vermont regiments in Gen. Brooks's brigade are examples of this. They give us the largest ratio of sick of all the troops in this army, and that ratio has not essentially varied for the last three months. They suffered in the first place from measles, sharing the lot of all irregular troops. Since then, they have been the subjects of remittent and typhoid fevers. Surg. C. C. Keeney, USA, reports the police, clothing and tents of all these regiments as good, with the exception of those of the 2d and 3d regiments, which, strange to say, are in decidedly the best sanitary condition.

The camping ground of the 3d Vermont Volunteers is bad. The soil is clay, the face of the country rolling; but presenting many plains sufficiently exten-

sive for camps.... We are now called upon to guard against the diseases of winter and spring. The principal diseases we have to fear are typhus and typhoid fevers and pneumonia. These diseases prevail in this district during the present and approaching season. Already a number of cases have occurred. These diseases arise from foul air, bad clothing, imperfect shelter, exposure to cold and wet, and imperfectly drained and badly policed camps....

December 30 (Monday)

Tripler, Charles S., Med. Dir., Army of the Potomac, Washington, D.C.:

During the months of October, November and December, 3930 men were discharged from the Army of the Potomac upon certificates of disability; of these, 2881 were for disabilities that existed at the time the men were enlisted. These men cost the Government not less than $200 each, making nearly $200,000 a month, out of which the people had been defrauded.... It seemed as if the army called out to defend the life of the nation had been made use of as a grand eleemosynary institution for the reception of the aged and infirm, the blind, the lame, and the deaf, where they might be housed, fed, paid, clothed, and pensioned, and their townships relieved of the burden of their support....

December 31 (Tuesday)

Gen. A. S. Johnston, CSA, reported that of an assigned strength of 91,988, only 54,004 were present for duty—the remaining 37,984 being absent sick.

In Washington things weren't going at all well for Lincoln. In addition to McClellan in the east, he had to deal with Don Carlos Buell and Henry W. Halleck in the west, neither of whom was willing to do any joint planning. Lincoln was burdened by *prima donna* incompetents!

(Above) The wounded being transported by cacolets. (Below) Ambulance at City Point, Va.

Clara Barton

Mary Safford, "The Angel of Cairo"

The wounded at Fredericksburg, Va.

Surg. Charles S. Tripler, Med. Dir., Army of the Potomac, 1861–1862

Surg. Thomas A. McParlin, Army of the Potomac, 1864

Surg. Jonathan Letterman, Med. Dir., Army of the Potomac, 1862–63

Asst. Surg. J. S. Billing, who founded the Library of Medicine after the war

C

Field hospital, City Point, Va.

The wounded being moved by horse litter. This method proved to be impractical.

D

Armory Square Hospital, Washington, D.C.

E

Field hospital at Antietam (Sharpsburg), Md.

Douglas Hospital, Washington, D.C.

Hospital at Antietam (Sharpsburg), Md.

H

1862

January 1 (Wednesday)

With the dawn of the new year, activity around Pt. Royal, S.C., began to accelerate. Ft. Pulaski was still in Confederate hands, and had to be reduced before the area could really be called secure. The Union forces moved to accomplish the reduction.

Cooper, George E., Surg., USA, Hilton Head, S.C.:

On the 1st of January, 1862, the troops under Gen. Stevens, in conjunction with the gunboats, made a demonstration against Pt. Royal ferry, where the Rebels were erecting a battery which commanded the ferry. Our troops crossed over and had a skirmish which resulted in the destruction of the works, the capture of the guns, and the retreat of the Confederates. Our losses were slight, some six or eight wounded; all flesh wounds, with one exception, a fractured thigh by a conical ball. The patient was reported as having died from the effects of the wound, in some seventy-two hours after the skirmish....

In the Shenandoah Valley, Confederate Gen. Thomas J. Jackson began his movement towards Romney in western Virginia. His target was the Baltimore and Ohio Railroad and the locks of the Chesapeake and Ohio Canal—an attempt to cut the Federals' communications with the west. The Stonewall Brigade began the march in fairly nice weather for January, but as the day progressed the weather turned windy and cold and then the snow and ice came, a thoroughly miserable day for marching. Only 8 miles were covered this day.

January 2 (Thursday)

The Stonewall Brigade made another 8 miles today, as far as Unger's Store. They were travelling over very rough mountain roads in extreme weather.

January 3 (Friday)

The diseases that ravaged many of the new camps, North and South, left few untouched. It wasn't uncommon for a company that began with 100, or more, men to lose 20 or more to disease, accident or disability during the first few months of camp life. Statistics were to show that during the first year and half of the war, the Union would lose 2.01 percent of its forces from disease and sickness. The figures for the Confederate forces were higher, at 3.81 percent; nearly half again as many Rebels died of diarrhea and dysentery as did Yanks. Nearly five times as many Rebels died of pulmonary diseases.

After recovering from his bout with typhoid pneumonia, Dr. E. A. Craighill was assigned to the Confederate Receiving Hospital at Gordonsville, Va. This town, located at the crossing of two major railroads, the Virginia Central and the Orange and Alexandria, became a central point for the transfer of the wounded and sick in that region. The main hospital was located at the recently built Exchange

Hotel, which was situated within 200 feet of the railroad siding. The hotel, completed in 1860, was a three-story structure with a broad staircase in the front leading to the second story. The "inside" hospital was located in this building, which contained the operating room (2nd floor) and recovery wards (2nd and 3rd floors). The prepared food was brought from a separate building to the lower floor, where it was served to the staff, patients being served by a separate kitchen. Craighill was assigned to the "outside sick," those for whom there was no room in the hospital, or those who didn't require hospitalization. Craighill would be assigned to this place for over a year.

The Stonewall Brigade, en route to Romney, western Virginia, headed north and reached the area around the town of Bath (present-day Berkeley Springs), noted for its mineral water springs. Jackson hoped to surprise Union troops here, but a Union outpost discovered the Confederate force. The Brigade went into camp that night amid the snow, with little shelter.

January 4 (Saturday)

The Surgeon General of the Army of the Potomac today reported to Gen. McClellan that the health of the army was improving considerably, and left little to be desired. This was reported despite previous cases of disease and injury totalling more than 247,700 in the nine-month period preceding his report. This quarter-million figure included more than 40,000 cases of diarrhea and dysentery, over 10,000 cases of typhoid fever, nearly 6000 cases of measles, and nearly 47,000 cases of catarrh and bronchitis. Venereal disease wasn't absent—3545 cases of syphilis and nearly 4100 cases of gonorrhea were included in the totals. The childhood diseases of measles and mumps were also included, as were smallpox and chicken pox.

January 5 (Sunday)

Hospital facilities for the various regiments were, more often than not, wholly inadequate for the purpose, and usually makeshift. The 1st Maine Vol. Cavalry, at camp at the fairgrounds at Augusta, used the judge's stand as a hospital. Although the regiment was housed in tents, they weren't provided with stoves until the end of November 1861. The

regiment lost 200 men by death and disability during the winter, and reported over 260 on the sick list on January 28, 1862.

The men of the 3rd Ohio Vol. Cavalry slept on the bare ground in unheated tents through the severe winter of 1861-62 in northern Ohio. The result was several deaths from pneumonia and much sickness.

In northwestern New York, the 19th New York Vol. Cavalry used an old barn for a hospital during the first winter of the war, providing the sick only cornstalks for bedding.

This same winter, the 8th Illinois Vol. Cavalry housed their sick in a large tent. When a requisition for a stove was rejected, a pit about two feet square and one foot deep was dug, with a trench leading to the outside, where an empty barrel, with both ends removed, was placed over the trench. The trench was then planked over and the pit lined with rock. The draft of the trench-and-barrel combination was sufficient to draw out the smoke, and the tent stayed fairly warm, until the wind blew from the wrong direction.

January 7 (Tuesday)

On the morning of the 4th, Jackson captured Bath, chasing the Federals to the Potomac. The town of Hancock refused to surrender, and after giving time to remove the women and children, a few shells were lobbed into the town. The Arkansas troops with Jackson burned the railroad bridge over the Great Cacapon River in western Virginia. In addition, damage was done to a dam on the C&O Canal along the Potomac. More snow was falling, and the pickets almost froze.

Today, a severe ice storm developed, making the ground very dangerous walking for Jackson's column, now heading south. The column reached Unger's Store after a surprise skirmish at Hanging Rock Pass. The troops suffered horribly from the cold.

January 8 (Wednesday)

Jackson's men remained at Unger's Store for the day getting some rest and taking baths to try to thaw out. The sick list was very long.

Cooper, George E., Surg., USA, Hilton Head, S.C.:

In the early part of January, an expedition was organized to act on the coast south of Hilton Head.

These were embarked and proceeded to Warsaw Sound, where they awaited the movement of the gunboats. For some reason or other these were delayed much longer than was anticipated, and sickness broke out among the troops of the 6th Connecticut Vols., and several cases of spotted fever showed themselves on the transport where they were crowded. In consequence of this, these troops were ordered to return to Hilton Head and disembark. The rest of the expedition proceeded south and took possession of Fernandina, Jacksonville and St. Augustine [March 1862].

January 9 (Thursday)

A large body of troops were camped on Meridian Hill, near Washington, and this site became one of the major problems of disease for the Union Army. The site itself caused all the imaginable diseases and the troops carried these maladies to other locations when the men were relocated—thus infecting other bodies of troops. The 77th New York had complained to the local commanders about the odors around the camp, and the officer who was sent to inspect the site reported:

> ... the atmosphere is impregnated with a malarial odor, arising from the decomposition of animal matter just below in an open field, where a large number of dead horses are deposited upon the surface and allowed to remain and decompose. This, with the rather poor policing of the camp, has given rise to typhoid fever, from which, I regret to say, we have lost some ten or twelve men already.

In the west, a large body of Indians, accompanied by Confederate troops from Texas and Arkansas, had attacked Indian tribes loyal to the Union. The Federal force was comprised of three-fourths of the Creeks, two-thirds of the Seminoles, and an additional mixture of other tribes who'd remained loyal. The loyal Indians, led by Hopoeithleyohola, twice defeated the Confederate-led forces, but in a third battle the loyalists were defeated and forced to flee the Indian Nation (now Oklahoma), leaving behind everything that would impede their flight. The fleeing Indians scattered their dead and dying for more than 100 miles. Many of the Indians were barefoot and suffering from exposure. These Indians eventually settled in southern Kansas.

January 13 (Monday)

"Stonewall" Jackson's brigade resumed its march south after having remained at Unger's Store in western Virginia since January 7th. The day began sunny, again, but a storm developed in the late afternoon. The march continued towards Romney.

January 14 (Tuesday)

Jackson's men were on the road all day, marching in a rain-and-sleet storm, heading towards Romney. To date, this particular campaign had accomplished little except expose the Confederates to extreme cold and to incapacitate the unit.

January 15 (Wednesday)

Dalton, R. H., Surg., 11th Miss. Vols., Dumfries, Va.:

I was surgeon of the 11th Mississippi Regiment, and Dr. Estell of the 1st Tennessee Regiment. One morning we were both ordered to report at the quarters (two miles distant) of a captain of artillery for some professional service.... Dismounting near his tent, we observed the Captain sitting a few paces from the front of the tent, in company with a lady dressed in deep mourning, a black veil falling over her face. The Captain arose and met us, remarking that a youth was in the tent whom he wished us to examine in order to ascertain if he was diseased, and if so, whether it was organic and likely to have existed long, and then pointed us to the closed door. We entered and found a young man lying on a stretcher, with two soldiers armed and sitting on camp stools at his feet. The youth was quite delicate, well dressed and comely. After conversing with him in regard to his age, health, the origin and duration of his complaint, we made a careful physical examination. We found palpable organic affection of the heart, which had existed since his access to puberty, four years before that time. It was one of the clearest cases we had ever seen. Then approaching the couple as they sat in silence, I said, "Captain, the young man is certainly afflicted with organic disease of the heart of long duration, and he ought never to have been enlisted as a soldier." Instantly the lady sprang to her feet, screaming out, "God bless you, you have saved my only child!" and throwing her arms around me she wept with joy. Soon she rushed to the tent where her son lay.

It was a startling mystery to us, but the Captain explained. The boy had enlisted in '61, and from the battlefield at Manassas he had deserted and fled to his home. Late in the fall he had been arrested and returned to his command at Dumfries, where he had been tried and was condemned to be shot on the next day after our examination. In the meantime his mother, hearing the news, hastened to the army, and had arrived in time to plead for an examination to prove her son's real condition. The Captain showed us the General's order, which was, "Arrest the sentence and discharge him if the surgeons confirm the mother's statement."

January 16 (Thursday)

Jackson's brigade had reached Romney yesterday. Today, Jackson wanted to attack Cumberland, Md., which was a major terminus of the Baltimore and Ohio Railroad and to capture the storehouses there, but couldn't get enough men together for the attack, so it was deferred for the day. No record exists as to what he'd have done with the material in the storehouses, except perhaps to burn it. He couldn't even move his troops over the icy roads.

January 18 (Saturday)

Yesterday, Jackson ordered an attack on Cumberland, Md., again, but had to cancel for lack of troops. One of his companies had but 15 men able to walk. Jackson finally ordered his troops into winter quarters at Bath (Berkeley Springs) and Moorefield. Getting there meant another march. Loring's Brigade, a recent newcomer to Jackson's command, remained at Romney, which they referred to as a "pigpen." Loring, a former U.S. Army colonel of much experience, was seriously upset about the treatment his command had received.

January 19 (Sunday)

Today, the Battle of Mill Springs (known also by several other names) was fought near Somerset, Ky., between Union forces commanded by Brig. Gen. George H. Thomas and Confederate generals George B. Crittenden and Zollicoffer. As a battle it didn't really amount to much, but it left a crack in the Confederates' defense line in Kentucky that was wide enough to drive an army through, which is exactly what Thomas did. Casualties were light on both sides. The weather was rainy and the roads almost impassable. The medical after-action report to Surgeon General Finley in Washington pointed up some real problems in the care of the wounded.

Murray, Robert, Surg., USA, Medical Dir., Dept. of the Ohio, Battle of Mill Springs, Ky.:

The victory of Gen. Thomas was complete. Our loss was thirty-nine killed, and one hundred and twenty-seven wounded. That of the enemy was one hundred and fifteen killed, and one hundred and sixteen wounded. The wounded of the enemy, together with a large number of horses, wagons, guns, and stores, were captured. Gen. Thomas's command made a march of over one hundred miles over almost impassable roads, and were nearly destitute of ambulances. I have daily representations made to me from surgeons of regiments, brigades, and divisions of the absolute need of ambulances. I have made every effort to have them furnished by the quartermasters here, but they cannot procure them. Would not a representation from you [Finley] induce the quartermaster general to send them from Washington, or some eastern city? At least one hundred four-wheeled ambulances are needed. The two-wheeled are not strong enough for the rough country and bad roads here. Our army, of nearly one hundred thousand men, is a moving army, and the demand for transportation for the sick is imperative. We have much sickness, principally measles, typhoid fever, and diseases of the lungs. The average of men excused from duty is thirteen and a half percent....

January 27 (Monday)

Activity in the Pt. Royal, S.C., area had been especially difficult for the Union forces trying to block the river on the approaches to Ft. Pulaski. The area in which Union guns were to be placed was formed of islands consisting of a deposit of thick blue mud, overgrown with reeds. Nothing seemed stable for too long. With gigantic efforts, Union guns were moved into position, and river traffic sealed off from the mainland. Pulaski was now isolated between the Federal gunboats and the Union troops. Meanwhile, Surg. Cooper was looking towards the future.

Cooper, George E., Surg., USA, Hilton Head, S.C.:

As there was no hospital building at Hilton Head for the sick who might be brought there, it was thought proper to have a building erected with the capacity of three hundred and fifty beds, but which, in an emergency could be increased to four hundred and more. At first it was intended to have erected it in the pavilion style, but in consequence of the severe storms, which, at times occur in the region, it was decided that the hollow square was stronger and less liable to be blown down; and this form, too, could have porticos placed around it, which, in the southern country, is an absolute requisite. In order that ventilation might not be interfered with, the building was placed on piers, from one and a half to three feet in height,… so that a free circulation of air might be afforded from beneath the building, to the hollow square which it enclosed. The building inside and outside is surrounded by nine-foot porticos. Windows of large size are placed as close to each other as the strength of the structure would permit of. Large folding doors, too, aid in ventilating.

The wards are covered with a ceiling of boards, above which is an air chamber formed by the roof, which is rather flat, but over three feet from the ceiling at the apex. In this ceiling are large doors which open and shut by means of ropes running through pulleys. The air in this air-chamber escapes when heated by the sun's rays beating on the roof, through ventilators placed at convenient distances on the roof. These ventilators are furnished with blinds to prevent the ingress of the rain, but afford no obstacle to the egress of the heated air.…

The kitchens, bathrooms, wash- and storerooms, are in a series of buildings placed in the center of the square, equidistant from all parts of the hospital. From these buildings an underground drain has been opened, by means of which all the slops are carried off to the sea beach. The water for the use of the hospital is procured from wells in the square, of which some ten have been sunk.… The sinks for the hospital are on the beach. Piles have been driven below high-water mark, and the privies are placed thereon. A covered way, built on piles, leads to the sinks. The advantage of this position is the absence of all disagreeable effluvia, inasmuch as the rising of the tide, twice in every twenty-four hours, washes away

all the excrement that may have collected.… The hospital is built near to the sea beach and is exposed to all the winds from the north, east and south, and partially to those from the west.… The square inclosed by the hospital buildings is one of three hundred and twenty-five feet.…

Surg. Cooper would remain at Hilton Head until after the surrender of Ft. Pulaski on April 11, 1862. Cooper left Hilton Head on April 18th for Philadelphia, and a much-earned leave of 20 days, following which he reported to the Surgeon General in Washington.

January 29 (Wednesday)

On January 23, 1862, Surg. David P. Smith reported to Louisville, Ky., for his new assignment as Brigade Surgeon. Brig. Gen. Buell immediately sent him to Brig. Gen. George H. Thomas at Somerset, Ky., where the Battle of Mill Springs had taken place on the 19th. The roads were so bad that Smith didn't reach Somerset until this date.

Smith, David P., Surg., USA, aftermath of the Battle of Mill Springs, Somerset, Ky.:

Purchasing strong horses, I essayed the mud embargo. From Lebanon, the railroad terminus, to Somerset, Kentucky, where I found the General, the road to be traversed by all supplies for the General's division was of a most atrocious character. It spoke volumes for the hardihood of the men who could get, not only infantry, but artillery and supply trains, over it. Although but seventy-five miles, a wagon was often a fortnight on the road.

Reaching Somerset on the 29th, I found the little village crowded with sick and wounded. Churches and the townhouse had been pressed into the service. The wounded belonged to the 10th Indiana, 4th Kentucky, 2nd Minnesota, and 9th Ohio Volunteers. Going out to the battleground, ten miles distant, to see if all the wounded had been brought in, I became aware of the terrible trial it had been to the sufferers to be brought in by wagons. The roads were of such a wretched description that, taking into account the continual rain, it was wonderful that transportation of them to Somerset had been effected.

Returning thither, I commenced service with the wounded. With the exception of a few primary amputations, no operations had been done, and none seemed thought of. The chief medical officer was sick; and the others, new in the contemplation of the ravages of a conical ball, maintained the most heterodox and opposite theories....

The dreadful roads over which all of the wounded had been brought had induced profuse suppuration. All the food that could be procured was beef, pork, and hard bread. Shortly after my arrival, I saw one man die from the irritation produced by fragments of the upper jaw; which, although split in every direction by the passage of a minié ball, had been left without excision. The same state of things existed also in the case of a fractured lower jaw, and was followed by the same result. Two cases of gunshot wounds of knee-joint, in which amputation had not been performed, also came to a rapidly fatal termination. In four cases of gunshot fracture of the humerus, reported to me as doing well, I found such complete comminution that in two cases I excised large portions of the shaft, and, in the remaining two, the head of the bone....

January 30 (Thursday)

Jackson had sent most of his command back towards Winchester and Berkeley Springs to winter quarters, leaving Loring's command in Romney since January 15th. Today, Loring and his officers signed a petition asking for relief and movement from the severe weather. This petition was sent "over Jackson's head" directly to the Confederate Secretary of War, Judah Benjamin, because Loring believed he could get no satisfaction from Jackson directly. Benjamin immediately sent a directive to Jackson to remove Loring's command from Romney to Winchester. This ended one of the toughest campaigns attempted during the war by either army, but created much ill will between Jackson and Loring. Because of this campaign, many of the men in Jackson's command would have their health ruined, and would be discharged from the service.

February 1 (Saturday)

In Tennessee, the operations against Fts. Henry and Donelson were getting started. The Navy would send four armored gunboats upriver tomorrow.

Tripler, Charles S., Surg., Army of the Potomac, Washington, D.C.:

About the 1st of February, 1862, my attention was called by Gen. Seth Williams, A.A.G., to the condition of Gen. Lauder's division at Cumberland [Md.]. This was the first intimation I had that there were any troops there. I sent one of my inspectors immediately to examine into the facts, with authority to provide at once for their necessities, to hire buildings, or to put up hospital huts, if required....

February 3 (Monday)

Brig. Gen. Grant loaded his regiments on large steamer transports at Cairo, Ill., on this date and moved up the Ohio to the Tennessee River junction at Paducah, Ky.

February 4 (Tuesday)

Joined by Brig. Gen. C. F. Smith with ten regiments, Grant moved the entire force up the Tennessee towards Ft. Henry. The naval gunboats were already in place, having used the unusual flooding of the river to pass over the torpedoes placed by the Confederates near Ft. Henry.

February 5 (Wednesday)

Grant's combined force disembarked about ten miles from the targeted fort and prepared to move on Ft. Henry. Brig. Gen. McClernand was sent with ten regiments of Illinois infantry and one of cavalry to the Dover road to attack the fort from the rear. The remaining force was to move upriver along the bank.

Tripler, Charles S., Surg., Army of the Potomac, Washington, D.C.:

On the 5th of February, Brigade Surg. Suckley was assigned to Lauder's division, and instructed to use every exertion to put things in order. He was informed that the condition of the sick in that division was represented as scandalous, and that no effort must be spared to reform it....

February 6 (Thursday)

The Commissioner of Indian Affairs was informed today by Gen. Hunter that provisions for the nearly 8000 Indians currently in southern

Kansas would be exhausted by February 15th. These Indians had fled the Indian Nation in January, after their defeat by a combined force of Confederates and other Indians. The numbers of the Indians from the Nation had increased as more reached the safety of Kansas, and the total was expected to reach 10,000, or more. An amount of $10,000 had been spent to provide blankets and other clothing to the desperate refugees, but more was needed. The Indians expressed a desire to return to the Nation at the earliest possible time so that they could arrange for the planting of crops for the coming season. A report from Ft. Leavenworth, Kan., indicated that in the vicinity of Belmont and Ft. Roe there were about 4500 Indians, chiefly Creeks and Seminoles. Many of these were destitute of clothing, shelter, fuel, horses, cooking utensils, and food. The Federal government provided the necessary items to the Indians until such time as they could return to their homes.

At Ft. Henry, on the Tennessee River, most of the Confederate troops had been removed and sent across the neck of land between the Tennessee and Cumberland rivers to Ft. Donelson, leaving a token force in what was a flooded area. More rain had come last night to add to the misery. And then this morning, the gunboats cut loose, and within an hour the fort surrendered to the Navy. The fort was then turned over to Grant, who immediately began organizing the move on Ft. Donelson while the Ft. Henry prisoners were being collected.

Brinton, John H., Surg., USV, Med. Dir., Army of the Tennessee, Ft. Henry, Tenn.:

After the fall of Ft. Henry, the major part of the U.S. forces encamped on the hills overlooking the fort. A few companies were placed within the work and on the low ground in its immediate vicinity. A small garrison was subsequently stationed here. These troops occupied the log huts of the enemy, and were sufficiently protected from the inclemency of the weather. They suffered much, nevertheless, from disease, especially typhoid pneumonia and typhoid fever....

February 8 (Saturday)

Tripler, Charles S., Surg., Army of the Potomac, Washington, D.C.:

On the 8th, I received the report of the inspector; and it confirmed all that had been reported as to the shocking state of affairs. The regiments comprising the command were scattered in all directions for some forty miles over the hills; the sick, numbering twelve hundred, were abandoned to the city of Cumberland, and were in wretched condition. They were "quartered in close, compact, ill-ventilated rooms, where the police is bad, food badly cooked and improperly served out, men of different regiments reeling and staggering through the streets with fevers, seeking shelter and medical attendance." The inspector had succeeded in getting comfortable and roomy quarters for five hundred of the sick at the time of his report; had employed a number of women in making bed sacks, and had contracted for several hundred bunks.

Today, 7500 Union troops, under the command of Gen. Ambrose E. Burnside, landed on Roanoke Island, N.C., and assaulted the nearly 2000 Confederates under command of Gen. Henry A. Wise, meeting resistance which was quickly overcome. A brigade surgeon wrote Gen. Burnside an after-action report on the battle.

Church, W. H., Brigade Surg., USV, Roanoke Island, N.C.:

... upon the advance of Gen. J. G. Foster, the few houses and outhouses at Ashby's Landing were at once prepared for the reception of the wounded and placed in charge of Surg. M. Storrs, 8th Connecticut Volunteers, his regiment having been ordered there to protect the landing of our forces and to hold the position. Brigade Surg. J. H. Thompson now advanced with the troops, to take charge of the wounded on the field of battle, where he remained until the battery was taken, assisting in the care of the wounded, and sending them ... to the field hospital.... Finding that there was not sufficient room in these buildings to receive the wounded, we immediately took possession of Ashby's house, a short distance from the first, and quite as convenient to the field of action.... Surg. David Minis, Jr., 48th Pennsylvania Volunteers, who, after the drowning at Hatteras Inlet of Surg. F. S. Weller, 9th New Jersey Volunteers, was detailed to serve with the 9th New Jersey, was soon placed in charge of this temporary hospital, where there was sufficient room to receive all the wounded not provided for. During the action of this day, Col. Charles L. Russell, of the 10th Connecticut Volunteers, was shot through the lung and died almost immediately. Lt. Col. Vigiuer de Monteuil, of the 53d New York Volunteers, was also killed, by a ball passing through his brain.... Surg. J. Marcus Rice, of the 25th Mass. Volunteers, was wounded in the midst of his very arduous duties. The ball grazed his side, fortunately without inflicting a severe wound. We have found three large, commodious, and well ventilated buildings erected upon the island for hospital purposes, which will afford ample accommodation for our sick and wounded. The largest hospital, at the north end of the island, I have placed in charge of Surg. S. A. Green, of the 24th Mass. Volunteers, and Surg. George A. Otis, of the 27th Mass. Volunteers, has the management of the two hospitals near the fort at the centre of the island. I would respectfully ask your attention to the fact that the wounded of the enemy have received the same care and attention from the surgeons as our own wounded....

February 11 (Tuesday)

All of the wounded, North and South, had been collected at Ft. Henry and were sent North on the hospital steamer *City of Memphis*, which was under lease to the Sanitary Commission, on this date.

Tripler, Charles S., Surg., Army of the Potomac, Washington, D.C.:

Dr. Suckley was in position on the 7th; on the 9th, he'd collected ten hundred and seventy-nine of the sick; on the 11th, he had fourteen hundred. He found affairs in the town in a wretched condition; no discipline, no system; the commissary had no funds. There were nineteen regiments of infantry, besides cavalry and artillery, in the division....

February 12 (Wednesday)

Grant started moving his regiments across towards Ft. Donelson, sending a part of them overland and the remainder down the Tennessee and then up the Cumberland to a landing about three miles below Donelson. The regiments moving overland made contact with Rebel pickets late in the day.

February 13 (Thursday)

Grant had taken his army overland from Henry to Donelson, and by this date had nearly invested the fort. Commander Henry Walke, USN, commanded the river flotilla and the gunboat *Carondelet* during the action.

Walke, Henry, Cmdr., USN, U.S.S. *Carondelet*, on the Cumberland River, Tenn.:

... at 9:05, with the *Carondelet* alone and under cover of a heavily wooded point, fired 139 70-pound and 64-pound shells at the fort. We received in return the fire of all the enemy's guns that could be brought to bear on the *Carondelet*, which sustained but little damage, except from two shots. One, a 128-pound solid, at 11:30 struck the corner of our port broadside casemate, passed through it, and in its progress toward the center of our boilers glanced over the temporary barricade in front of the boilers. It then passed over the steam-drum, struck the beams of the upper deck, carried away the railing around the engine-room and burst the steam-heater, and, glancing back into the engine-room, "seemed to bound after the men," as one of the engineers said, "like a wild beast pursuing its prey...." When it burst through the side of the *Carondelet*, it knocked down and wounded a dozen men, seven of them severely. An immense quantity of splinters was blown through the vessel. Some of them, as fine as needles, shot through the clothes of the men like arrows. Several of the wounded were so much excited by the suddenness of the event and the sufferings of their comrades, that they were not aware that they themselves had been struck until they felt the blood running into their shoes.... After dinner we sent the wounded on board the *Alps*, repaired damages, and,... resumed ... and bombarded the fort until dusk....

February 14 (Friday)

Late the night of the 13th, Flag Officer Foote arrived near Ft. Donelson with three Union ironclads and two wooden gunboats. This morning all the ships in the flotilla readied their guns to continue the battle. At about 3:30 P.M. the Union gunboats were about one and one-half miles below the fort when the Confederate gunners opened fire and a general exchange of shot developed. Cmdr. Walke continues his description of the action on the *Carondelet*.

Walke, Henry, Cmdr., USN, U.S.S. *Carondelet*, on the Cumberland River, Tenn.:

As we drew nearer, the enemy's fire greatly increased in force and effect.... Soon a 128-pounder struck our anchor, smashed it into flying bolts, and bounded over the vessel, taking away a part of our smokestack.... Another ripped up the iron plating and glanced over;... another struck the pilothouse, knocked the plating to pieces, and sent fragments of iron and splinters into the pilots, one of whom fell mortally wounded, and was taken below; another shot took away the remaining boat-davits and the boat with them; and still they came, harder and faster, taking flagstaffs and smokestacks, and tearing off the side armor as lightning tears the bark from a tree.... One of the crew, in his account ... said: "I was serving the gun with shell. When it exploded it knocked us all down, killing none, but wounding over a dozen men.... When I found out that I was more scared than hurt, although suffering from the gunpowder which I had inhaled, I looked forward and saw our gun lying on the deck in three pieces. Then the cry ran through the boat that we were on fire, and my duty as pump-man called me to the pumps. While I was there, two shots entered our bow-ports and killed four men and wounded several others. They were borne past me, three with their heads off. The sight almost sickened me, and I turned my head away.... The carpenter and his men extinguished the flames." The *Carondelet* was the first in and the last out of the fight, and was more damaged than any of the other gunboats.... She fired more shot and shell into Ft. Donelson than any other gunboat, and was struck fifty-four times....

February 15 (Saturday)

The toll of wounded and dead aboard the Union flotilla was tremendous, including the wounding of Flag Officer Foote. An enormous amount of ordnance was expended by the flotilla with little effect on the Confederate emplacements. Capt. B. G. Bidwell, CSA, who was involved in manning the Confederate guns, reported:

... They must have fired near two thousand shot and shell at us. Our Columbiad fired about 27 times, the rifled gun very few times, and the 32-pounders about 45 or 50 rounds each.... Not a man of ours was hurt, notwithstanding they threw grape at us. Their fire was more destructive to our works at 2 miles than at 200 yards. They over-fired us from that distance.

Walke, Henry, Cmdr., USN, U.S.S. *Carondelet*, on the Cumberland River, Tenn.:

The 15th was employed in the burial of our slain comrades. I read the Episcopal service on board the *Carondelet*, under our flag at half-mast; and the sailors bore their late companions to a lonely field within the shadows of the hills. When they were about to lower the first coffin, a Roman Catholic priest appeared, and his services being accepted, he read the prayers for the dead. As the last service was ended, the sound of the battle being waged by Gen. Grant, like the rumbling of distant thunder, was the only requiem for our departed shipmates....

The gunboats were pouring fire into the fort, but the Rebels were ready to try something else. Confederate Gen. Pillow organized an assault on McClernand's line, aided by Gen. Buckner's troops. McClernand's line broke, and the road to Nashville was open, but briefly. An argument developed, and Pillow ordered the troops back into the fort. McClernand, with the help of Gen. Lew Wallace, advanced and the troops occupied their old positions by nightfall. After a council meeting, Confederate Gen. Floyd, commanding the fort, decided to surrender. He took the opportunity to flee the fort, turning his command over to Pillow. Pillow followed Floyd, leaving the command to Gen. Buckner.

Brinton, John H., Surg., USV, Med. Dir., Army of the Tennessee, Ft. Henry, Tenn.:

The theater of the bloody drama was almost a wilderness. Towns and villages were comparatively few, and the region, to a great extent, was uncultivated. Farmhouses were encountered only at intervals, and the country had been impoverished and drained of its resources by the enemy.... At no time ... were the conveniences for the establishment of large general hospitals to be found; in fact, the drugs, medicines, and hospital stores absolutely essential for the field were with difficulty obtained.... Usually every regiment possessed one or two two-wheeled ambulances ... and one, or sometimes two, four-wheeled ambulance wagons. The former vehicles proved, practically, failures; they were too light in their construction, unsuited to the rough, miry roads of the country, and were easily broken. They accommodated but two or three invalids, and, especially in rainy weather, required two horses to draw them. The four-wheeled spring ambulance fulfilled its purpose better....

The number of hospital tents did not exceed two to a regiment.... Of hand-litters or stretchers, two or three were usually carried. The very great degree of dampness and cold during the commencement of this campaign rendered some permanent means of warmth necessary for the comfort of the sick and wounded in the hospital tents. The stove usually adopted was the ordinary funnel-shaped one of sheet iron, open at the bottom, and placed directly on the ground. It answered the purposes of heating a small tent ... but was too small for the larger tents....

All of the ambulances ... were collected together for the formation of the ambulance trains. Each one of these trains was placed under the charge of a non-commissioned officer, whose business it was to see that a continuous line of wagons should ply between the scene of conflict and the general hospitals ... as a result, the majority of the wounded on the field were ... transported to points where every surgical attention could be rendered....

The exposure of the troops during the siege was very great. The weather was, at first, excessively cold; a light fall of snow, degenerating into a sleet, then occurred. The troops, resting on their arms during the night ... were, of course, unprotected by tents. But their greatest suffering arose from the total absence of fires during the night.... Each morning, at sunrise, the firing recommenced, and it was with the greatest difficulty that provisions could be prepared. The suffering of the wounded during this protracted battle ... was not to be prevented....

The unavoidable exposure sustained by the troops at Ft. Donelson resulted, ultimately, in grave diseases, which materially thinned the ranks of the army. Diarrhea, dysentery, and pneumonia of a typhoid type became fearfully prevalent, and thousands of soldiers were broken-down, and were then sent down the river to the general hospitals....

Stearns, H. P., Surg., USV, Ft. Donelson, Tenn.:

Early on Saturday, February 15th, the enemy attacked the right of Gen. Grant's forces.... The supplies of medicine were abundant, but hospital stores were exceedingly limited. Most of the regiments had one or two ambulances, and two or three common wall tents to be used as hospital tents. The wounded were conveyed to three farmhouses in the rear of the army. The most distant was about two and a half miles from Ft. Donelson.... There was an abundant supply of water; but the supplies of food were such as the surgeons could get from the surrounding country. Some young beef cattle were found and killed, and soups were prepared for the wounded. The weather was very cold during most of the time, and a severe snowstorm occurred, so that it was impossible to provide comfortable quarters for the wounded. They must have suffered exceedingly, many of them. The wounded were moved upon stretchers and ambulances to the field hospitals, and were thence sent to general hospitals....

The First Brigade suffered from the want of blankets and rations for thirty-six hours; the Second Brigade was without blankets, rations, or knapsacks for thirty hours. The Third Brigade was, during part of the march, destitute of blankets, rations, and overcoats. In the First Brigade, 144 cases of frostbite were reported; in the Second, 23 by name, and a large number not designated by military description; in the Third, only two cases were reported.

Goodbrake, C., Surg., 29th Illinois, USV, Ft. Donelson, Tenn.:

On the 15th, I took possession of the house of Mrs. Rollins for hospital purposes. The wounded soon began to arrive, and we had between one hundred and fifty and two hundred brought to our hospital. It was a well chosen place, a large double house, with several outhouses, and a large shed, which sheltered many. We provided an abundance of excellent soup from veal and poultry which we found on the premises. An excellent spring supplied us plentifully with water....

The steamers outfitted as hospital ships were sent to Ft. Donelson as soon as the word came that the battle had taken place. Mary Livermore reported the part played by Mrs. Bickerdyke in this exercise:

Livermore, Mary, Chicago, Ill.:

After the battle of Donelson, Mother Bickerdyke went from Cairo in the first hospital boat, and assisted in the removal of the wounded to Cairo, St. Louis, and Louisville, and in nursing those too badly wounded to be moved. The Sanitary Commission had established a depot of stores at Cairo, and on these she was allowed to make drafts *ad libitum*: for she was famous for her economical use of sanitary stores as she had been before the war for her notable housewifery. The hospital boats at that time were poorly equipped for the sad work of transporting the wounded. But this thoughtful woman, who made five of the terrible trips from the battlefield of Donelson to the hospital, put on board the boat with which she was connected, before it started from Cairo, an abundance of necessities. There was hardly a want expressed for which she could not furnish some sort of relief.

On the way to the battlefield, she systematized matters perfectly. The beds were ready for the occupants, tea, coffee, soup and gruel, milk punch and ice water were prepared in large quantities, under her supervision, and sometimes by her own hand. When the wounded were brought on board, mangled almost out of human shape; the frozen ground from which they had been cut adhering to them; chilled with the intense cold in which some had lain for twenty-four hours; faint with loss of blood, physical agony, and lack of nourishment; racked with a terrible five-mile ride over frozen roads, in ambulances, or common Tennessee farm wagons, without springs; burning with fever; raving in delirium, or in the faintness of death, Mother Bickerdyke's boat was in readiness for them.

"I never saw anybody like her," said a volunteer surgeon who came on the boat with her. "There was really nothing for us surgeons to do but dress wounds and administer medicines. She drew out clean shirts or drawers from some corner, whenever they were needed. Nourishment was ready for every man as soon as he was brought on board Everyone was sponged from blood and frozen mire of the battlefield, as far as his condition allowed. His blood-stiffened, and sometimes horribly filthy uniform, was exchanged for soft and clean hospital garments. Incessant cries of 'Mother! Mother! Mother!' rang through the boat, in every note of beseeching and anguish. And to every man she turned with a heavenly tenderness, as if he were indeed her son. She moved about with a decisive air, and gave directions in such decided, clarion tones as to ensure prompt obedience. We all had an impression that she held a commission from the Secretary of War, or at least

from the Gov. of Illinois. To every surgeon, who was superior, she held herself subordinate, and was as good at obeying as at commanding." And yet, at that time, she held no position whatever, and was receiving no compensation for her services; not even the beggarly pittance of thirteen dollars per month allowed by government to army nurses.

At last it was believed that all the wounded had been removed from the field, and the relief parties discontinued their work. Looking from his tent at midnight, "Black Jack" Logan, then a colonel, observed a faint light flitting hither and thither on the abandoned battlefield, and, and after puzzling over it for some time, decided it was someone robbing the dead. He sent his orderly to bring the rascal in. It was Mother Bickerdyke, with a lantern, groping among the dead. Stooping down, and turning their cold faces toward her, she scrutinized them searchingly, uneasy lest some might be left to die uncared for. She couldn't rest while she thought any were overlooked who were yet living.

This was to be Mrs. Bickerdyke's first meeting with John Logan, but certainly not her last. Logan, a former Congressman from Illinois, was a plain-talking, sensible, and very intelligent individual who recognized quality when he saw it. Mrs. Bickerdyke normally didn't like officers, because she considered them too pompous. There were some exceptions — notably Grant and Sherman, whom she considered *plain people*. Mrs. Bickerdyke's estimate of John Logan put him immediately into the same class. They developed a trust that was never to be shaken. Bickerdyke spent many days riding with Logan in the lead of his Fifteenth Corps during the dusty campaigns heading towards Atlanta. But that was far in the future.

February 16 (Sunday)

Gen. Simon B. Buckner in Ft. Donelson asked Grant for terms for surrender. Grant gave his now famous reply, "No terms except unconditional and immediate surrender can be accepted. I propose to move immediately upon your works." Buckner believed and accepted. The door to Nashville, and all of Tennessee, was wide open. With this surrender, Grant became the caretaker of more than 15,000 prisoners, including all the wounded.

February 17 (Monday)

South of Nashville, Tenn., John S. Jackman was witness to a rough scene concerning the handling of the Confederate wounded at Franklin. Jackman eight horses himself was a patient, but not immobile.

Jackman, John S., Pvt., "The Orphan Brigade," in hospital, Franklin, Tenn.:

Just before daylight the next morning a fire broke out on main street on the public square and caused a great deal of confusion. Walls were battered down by using artillery to stop the spreading flames.

That morning after daylight all the sick were moved to the Depot to be loaded on the cars. I hope never to witness another scene such as was presented there that day. Men at the lowest stage of sickness were not half attended and were thrown around like the commonest freight. Many died from want of attention. There was no official present to direct the removal of the sick—every man for himself. Capt. G. and myself were able to walk about and we had to give all of our attention to the two boys named, also to another of the company very sick. They all had the typhoid fever. We got into a passenger car and it was noon before we moved off. When all the troops had left and the Federal soldiers were near. About sundown we got to Franklin.

February 18 (Tuesday)

Although Lucius W. Barber arrived too late for the Battle of Ft. Donelson, he was in time to assist in the collection of the wounded from the battlefield.

Barber, Lucius W., Pvt., Co. D, 15th Ill. Vol. Infantry, Ft. Donelson, Tenn.:

Toward evening we disembarked and went into camp. Volunteers were called for to help attend to the wounded and place them on transports. In company with several others from Company D, I offered my services which were accepted. It was nearly midnight before our task was done.

It was a pitiful and sickening sight to see such a mass of mangled limbs and mutilated bodies, but the patience with which they bore their injuries excited our admiration. Of the twenty which I helped carry on the boat, not one uttered a complaint, even though a leg or an arm were missing. The next day

we took a stroll over the battlefield. We saw sights that fairly froze the blood in our veins. The dead lay as they had fallen, in every conceivable shape, some grasping their guns as though they were in the act of firing, while others, with a cartridge in their icy grasp, were in the act of loading. Some of the countenances wore a peaceful, glad smile, while on others rested a fiendish look of hate. It looked as though each countenance was the exact counterpart of the thoughts that were passing through the mind when the death messenger laid them low. Perhaps that noble looking youth, with his smiling upturned face, with his glossy ringlets matted with his own lifeblood, felt a mother's prayer stealing over his senses as his young life went out. Near him lay a young husband with a prayer for his wife and little one yet lingering on his lips. Youth and age, virtue and evil, were represented on those ghastly countenances. Before us lay the charred and blackened remains of some who had been burnt alive. They were wounded too badly to move and the fierce elements consumed them. We now came to where the Rebels made their last desperate effort to break our lines, and in a small cleared field the dead were piled up, friend and foe alike in death struggle.

Jackman, John S., Pvt., "The Orphan Brigade," in hospital, en route to Gallatin, Tenn.:

… daylight the next morning we were on the road to Gallatin. The weather turned cold that night and a snow two or three inches deep fell. The train was so heavy, the engineer said, that he could not pull it. I believe he wanted it captured. I did not sleep a moment that night. The car was crowded to overflowing with sick and I had to stand up a great deal of the time.

February 19 (Wednesday)

Following the Battle of Ft. Donelson, Tenn., Union Brig. Gen. G. W. Cullum in Cairo, Ill., had been busily supervising the transportation of the sick, wounded and Confederate prisoners of war to sites in the North. Most of this movement had been by river steamer, some steamers specially fitted for the movement of the infirm. This activity had been going on for nearly two weeks and Cullum was getting weary, as indicated in his telegram to Maj. Gen. Halleck in St. Louis:

My Dear General: It is mighty hard to play everything from corporal to general and to perform the functions of several staff departments almost unaided as I have done the past two weeks.… We have provided for all the sick and wounded thus far without sending any to Cincinnati, for which we have no steamer to spare. There are 1400 at Paducah and 1200 at Mound City and but few here. Volunteer surgeons and nurses have supplied all my wants and many more are constantly offering. Hordes of brothers, fathers, mothers, sisters, cousins, &c., have reached here to find the dead and see the wounded, but I have had to refuse passes to all, as they would fill all our steamers, eat our rations, and be of no service to the wounded.… I am completely fagged out, and being among the little hours of the morning I must say good night.

Gen. Grant, at Ft. Donelson, wired Brig. Gen. Cullum in Cairo, concerning the sick and wounded from the battle:

General: … As soon as I got possession of Ft. Donelson I commenced sending the sick and wounded to Paducah, as seems to have been the desire of Gen. Halleck. No distinction has been made between Federal and Confederate sick and wounded. Generally the prisoners have been treated with great kindness and I believe they appreciate it. Great numbers of Union people have come in to see us and express great hope for the future. They say secessionists are in great trepidation, some leaving the country, others expressing anxiety to be assured that they will not be molested if they will come in and take the oath.

Jackman, John S., Pvt., "The Orphan Brigade," in hospital, Gallatin, Tenn.:

At daylight we got to Gallatin and Capt. G. and I went to a hotel and got our breakfast. We brought the boys something to eat. All day long the train was trying to make it over a grade running up from the depot. In the evening late, the engineer and his fireman got drunk and were arrested by the military. Capt. G. took the three boys off the train and moved them to a private house. There N.O. died.

I remained on the train and at sundown a new engine was hitched on and we went flying to Nashville. I could scarcely walk to the hospital nearby. There were several of us together and all the bunks being occupied, we had to sleep on the floor by the stove. There were 150 sick men in that room,

their bunks all arranged in rows. A cold chill ran over me at seeing so many pale faces by gaslight.

February 20 (Thursday)

Jackman, John S., Pvt., "The Orphan Brigade," in hospital, Nashville, Tenn.:

The next day looking in all the hospitals for brother Jo, but did not find him. That morning, or the next, I have forgotten which, the news came of the fall of Ft. Donelson, and the whole city was thrown into consternation. Excited crowds collected on the corners and were harangued by prominent citizens. Commissary and Quartermaster Depots were thrown open to the populace, citizens commenced packing up and moving off; and the hospital rats commenced bundling up and "shoving out"—in fact, there was great confusion. The evening of the same day the startling news came, my regiment passed through in the march and I slung my knapsack, shouldered my gun, and fell into ranks. I could scarcely walk though. We camped four or five miles from town that night.

In Cumberland, Md., Dr. Suckley, acting on behalf of Surg. Tripler, made some inroads on the problem of the sick from Lauder's division.

Tripler, Charles S., Surg., Army of the Potomac, Washington, D.C.:

On the 18th, he [Suckley] asked for authority to build two pavilions to contain fifty patients each. This was immediately granted. I applied to the Commissary-General to place funds in the hands of the Commissary [at Cumberland]. On the 19th, Col. Taylor informed me that he had sent $5000. On the 20th, he [Suckley] had succeeded in making things more comfortable; and procured eight Sisters of Charity for nurses; had classified his patients, and had provided proper medical attention. He reported, also, that the mortality and gravity of diseases was diminishing. I ordered a supply of ambulances to be forwarded, loaded with bedding, from Baltimore.…

February 21 (Friday)

With the evacuation of the wounded in full swing, the "do-gooders" descended by the boatload upon the landing at Donelson. Most of these people had good intentions, but they had no idea about what they were getting into, never having seen the aftermath of battle before. Many of these people had come down on the Sanitary Commission boats, and when these were filled up, the wealthier ones chartered steamers that brought even more people to the action arena. The *City of Memphis* was heading downriver to the hospitals, and Mrs. Bickerdyke was still at the landing at Donelson cleaning the wounded and making them as comfortable as possible with what she had.

Then the horde of angels arrived. These ladies and gentlemen of refinement and grace were appalled at the stacks of arms and legs lying around, the bloody patients who hadn't yet been treated, and the lack of supplies and support personnel. For many of the "visitors," it was just too much. They vied for space on the next returning boat to "civilization." The ones who remained were the stalwarts who rolled up their sleeves and went to work under the direction of Mrs. Bickerdyke and the surgeons.

Among those who remained was Mrs. Bickerdyke's old helpmate, Mary Safford. She talked to the men, wrote letters for them, held their hands, and listened to their dying wishes. The strain was too much for Safford, and she became ill. After the last of the wounded had been moved, Bickerdyke ordered her to return North, where Safford suffered a nervous breakdown.

In Nashville, the remaining Confederate government officials were having a hard time dealing with reality. The city, loaded with mountains of supplies awaiting shipment east to the troops in Georgia and Virginia, would be quite a prize for the Union troops then en route. The military could only carry so much on its marches, and the railroads were jammed with fleeing citizens. The solution was to destroy the supplies rather than give them out to the local population, who might be able to use them. Orders were sent out for the guards to prevent citizens from taking any of the food from the warehouses, etc., for their personal use—after all, it *was* government property and the common citizen had no right to it.

Some, including one Col. Nathan Bedford Forrest, took exception to this policy and assisted the citizens in loading the food in wagons at the depots. There were entirely too few citizens, too few wagons, and too much food, so most of it was destroyed. Approximately 30,000 pounds of bacon and ham would be set ablaze, creating a river of grease and a fantastic odor that would last for days.

The fall of Donelson and the evacuation of Nashville had far-reaching effects on other areas also. The Quartermaster of Transportation at Chattanooga, Tenn., had a problem, as well.

Anderson, Charles W., Maj., CSA, Chattanooga, Tenn.:

The seats and aisles of all the cars arriving at Chattanooga were… packed with refugees; the platforms were crowded also, and numbers were seated on the steps, clinging to the hand railings for safety. The weather was cold, and all cars from over the mountain were covered with frozen snow.

Amid the excitement that such news and the advent of so many fleeing refugees was likely to produce, my consternation may be imagined on receiving another telegram, which informed me to be prepared to receive some thousand or twelve hundred sick and convalescent soldiers from the hospitals at Nashville.

At this time there was not an organized body of troops of any kind at Chattanooga, nor a man or officer there whose services I had a right to command. More than all, there was not a dollar of Government funds at the Post. Under such circumstances, to care for so great a number of men seemed to me an utter impossibility. Calling to my assistance some old citizens of Chattanooga, the work was begun at once.

Three large buildings were taken possession of and a force of negro men and women put to work cleaning them up. Two bakeries were contracted with for bread, and coffee, sugar and other supplies were purchased. Fuel was provided at all the buildings, and arrangements made for conveying to the hospitals all soldiers unable to walk, and a special contract was made with a reliable man to put up temporary stands at the depot and serve each soldier with hot coffee and fresh bread as the trains arrived.

When the first train arrived with some three hundred on board, they were in a most pitiable condition. They had been stowed away in box and cattle cars for eighteen hours, without fire, and without any attention other than such as they were able to render to each other. Tears filled the eyes of many at the depot when these poor fellows were taken from the cars, so chilled and benumbed that a majority of them were helpless. Two other trains came the following day with men in the same condition. Three soldiers were found dead in the cars, one died in the depot before removal, and another died on the way to the hospital.

The removal of these soldiers from the hospitals at Nashville was a military necessity; but why they were sent, unaccompanied or preceded by a proper corps of surgeons, medical supplies, and hospital attendants, I never knew. It was eight days after their arrival in Chattanooga before I was relieved of responsibility for them. In that time, six more were buried, and the number of deaths would have been far greater, but for the attendance of Chattanooga physicians, among whom I specially remember, Dr. P. D. Sims and Dr. Milce Smith. It was not until Gen. Floyd's Division reached Chattanooga that the hospitals were taken charge of by army surgeons.

Getting those men from the cars into warm, comfortable rooms was a great improvement in their condition, but they were without beds and were compelled to lie on the bare hospital floors. Carpenters were set to work making cot frames, and every bale of brown cotton cloth in Chattanooga was purchased. How the cots were to be covered and the bed sacks made was a matter that greatly troubled me, as sewing machines were rare and costly. It was then that Mrs. Helm came to my assistance, and to the relief of those poor sufferers. To her were they largely indebted for a speedy transfer from bare hospital floors to clean comfortable beds.

February 22 (Saturday)

Livermore, Mary, Chicago, Ill.:

Up to this time, no attempt had been made to save the clothing and bedding used by the wounded men on the transports and in the temporary hospitals. Saturated with blood, and the discharges of healing wounds, and sometimes with vermin, it had been collected, and burned or buried. But this involved much waste; and as these articles were in constant need, Mother Bickerdyke conceived the idea of saving them. She sent to the Commission in Chicago for washing machines, portable kettles, and mangles, and caused all this offensive clothing to be collected. She then obtained from the authorities a full detail of contrabands, and super-

intended the laundering of all these hideously foul garments. Packed in boxes, it all came again into use at the next battle.… How much she saved to the government, and to the Sanitary Commission, may be inferred from the fact that it was no unusual thing for three or four thousand pieces to pass through her extemporized laundry in a day.

With most of the work done at Donelson, and the patients all sent on north to hospitals, Bickerdyke obtained a pass from Grant, and attached herself and her boxes and bales to the 21st Indiana Vols., who were on the gunboat *Fanny Bullet*. She'd stay with the army for a long time.

February 23 (Sunday)

In Nashville, Tenn., panic and chaos reigned as the citizens tried to leave the city ahead of the arrival of the Union troops. In Washington, Pres. Lincoln named Andrew Johnson, a native of Knoxville, as military governor of Tennessee.

February 24 (Monday)

In Tennessee, Grant sent part of this troops to Clarksville, and ordered Nelson's division to Nashville. Nelson's troops were loaded on steamer transports and sent upriver, arriving at the docks in Nashville at about the same time that Buell arrived on the opposite bank. With the Army of the Ohio reunited, Nashville was occupied at the same time that Forrest was withdrawing his cavalry on the road to Murfreesboro.

February 25 (Tuesday)

Today, Union troops, commanded by Gen. Don Carlos Buell, occupied Nashville.

John S. Jackman had left Nashville just ahead of the Federal occupation and was now in Murfreesboro, Tenn., in a tent back at the Brigade.

Jackman, John S., Pvt., "The Orphan Brigade," Murfreesboro, Tenn.:

The day following, raining hard all day long. I lay in the tent with a high fever. Dr. P. came to see me and gave me medicine. That evening Col. H. gave me a pass, approved by Gen. Breckinridge, to go to a private house—I objected going to hospital. I got into an ambulance to be taken to town but it got stuck in the mud and I slept in it all night.

February 26 (Wednesday)

Jackman finally got to his "private" accommodations, and although they were a little crowded for a while, they were probably better than those in the hospital.

Jackman, John S., Pvt., "The Orphan Brigade," Murfreesboro, Tenn.:

Next morning "Capt. G." placed me in a large wagon and we were nearly all day finding a place to stop. At last "Prof" François took me to a family where he was staying. The accommodations were poor, but it was the best we could do. I had to sleep on the floor the first night, after that though had a bed provided. The "Pro" staid with me and was very kind. I was out of my head a great deal—bad off. Dr. P. and G. visited me daily.

March 3 (Monday)

Grant concentrated his forces at Ft. Henry, leaving a small force at Donelson. The river was still flooding the fortifications at Henry, and the army camped on the high ground around the perimeter.

Halleck, his pride wounded because his subordinate, Grant, was the hero of Donelson, ordered Grant to remain at Ft. Henry and to send Grant's troops under the command of Brig. Gen. C. F. Smith upriver to Savannah, a few miles south of Pittsburg Landing.

March 4 (Tuesday)

Brinton, John H., Surg., USV, Med. Dir. Army of the Tennessee, Pittsburg Landing, Tenn.:

The distance from Ft. Henry to Savannah is about one hundred and twenty miles. On the arrival of the expedition at this place, the debarkation of the troops was effected, although but slowly. For military reasons the troops were kept for several days closely packed on the transports. Many of these steamers carried a thousand men, and some few even more, together with the accompanying equipage and animals. Sufficient accommodation hadn't been provided for the troops on the boats; and, as the result of the overcrowding and exposure to the night air, the same disastrous sickness and mortality, which had prevailed below, accompanied them here. An epidemic typhoid fever of the most aggravated form

appeared, and the daily deaths were numerous. To add to the difficulties of the situation, the supplies of drugs and medical comforts ran short, while sufficient shelter and accommodation could not be provided for the sick. The town of Savannah became one vast hospital, and nearly every dwelling was occupied by invalids. Hospital tents, so badly needed, could not be procured, and the transportation by the boats at the disposal of the medical department, was sadly inadequate. In fact, but one steamer, the *City of Memphis*, was available for this purpose....

Craighill, E. A., Surg., CSA, Gordonsville, Va.:

There were a great many sick and very sick, particularly among the green men who had experienced none of the hardships of camp life....

This was particularly the case with Lawton's brigade of Georgians, said to be five thousand strong.... They camped in a field nearby, and very soon after they arrived measles broke out among them, which few had ever had, and to add to their discomfort, a steady cold rain set in, which lasted for days. We had no comforts or hospital accommodations for the poor fellows, not even tents, and their suffering was intense. The usual sequel of measles from exposure set in, and many of them were down with Pneumonia and Diarrhea. The mortality was frightful. I believe it is no exaggeration to say that out of the five thousand at least fifteen hundred were sick, and the number who died was appalling. There were no quarters to take the sick to, no hospitals had then been built, and I have many times seen these suffering ill men lying out of doors in the rain with Pneumonia. How many of them died the good Lord only knows, I do not.

March 5 (Wednesday)

Grant, back in command after Gen. C. F. Smith was injured, ordered part of the troops from Savannah to Pittsburg Landing, near Shiloh Church.

Nashville, now in Union hands, was visited by the medical director of the Dept. of the Ohio on March 2nd. His report to the Surgeon General of the Army, C. A. Finley, in Washington, covered several problem areas.

Murray, Robert, Surg., USA, Med. Dir., Dept. of the Ohio, Nashville, Tenn.:

I found that ample accommodations had been prepared here by the Confederates for their sick. The hospitals which were, and had been occupied would hold thirty-five hundred men. Many of the buildings, however, were not suitable for hospitals as they were warm houses with low ceilings, and long ill-ventilated rooms. On the hill, near the town, the university barracks, blind asylum, and high school, all in the same neighborhood, with a new and commodious factory building, will make the most admirable hospitals, and all have been used as such....

My experience in Louisville has satisfied me that warm houses cannot be made available for large hospitals with any regard for the lives of the patients. I have recommended frame buildings with single wards in each, and good ventilation, as these hospitals will be used mostly in summer.

The troops made a forced march from Green River to this place, and many of the regiments left their supplies behind them. They have been sent across the river also, without tents, and are exposed at night to rain, without shelter. We have to look after over twelve percent of sick from the command in Kentucky, and the men here are fast falling sick. It is evident, from the preparations for the sick made in this city and at Bowling Green, and from the accounts we have received, that the sickness in the Confederate Army has been greater than ours, and that much of it was produced by the same epidemic, that is, by measles. In an army which never exceeded forty thousand men, they must have had six thousand in the hospitals as an average, and they lost at least seven thousand by death....

There is a great scarcity of medical officers. The average is about three medical officers to two regiments, many surgeons being absent sick, or having resigned.... I find sick men left in such miserable condition, as I follow the rear of the army, that I have determined to give supplies to each division in the hands of a division medical purveyor to fit up hospitals. The transportation of the army is very limited, and one wagon only is allowed a regiment, and but two ambulances; so that the sick cannot be carried along, and must be left in every village that is passed. The regimental surgeons cannot spare bedding, or even medicines, from their small supply, and the men are sometimes found on the floor with no medicines, bedding, or any other comforts. The army is still encumbered with soldiers who will never

be fit for duty. I have recommended to Gen. Buell to appoint a commission, consisting of the medical director, an adjutant general, and a paymaster, to visit each regiment, and at once discharge and pay off all those presented by the regimental surgeons, and found to be proper cases for discharge.

Medical support problems also existed within the prisoner-of-war system. Today, Col. William Hoffman, Federal Commissary-General of Prisoners, visited the prison for Confederate soldiers outside Indianapolis, Ind. A problem existed with the care of the sick and wounded prisoners—these being mostly captured after the fall of Ft. Donelson in February. In his report to Maj. Gen. Montgomery C. Meigs, Quartermaster General of the Army, Hoffman stated:

I visited the prisoners at Camp Morton today and found them as well cared for as could be expected under the circumstances.

I have approved of the construction of some further accommodations for them suggested by Capt. Ekin, assistant quartermaster, and some few improvements to promote the health and comfort, all of which can [be] done at trifling expense. By this means the prisoners at Terre Haute will be provided for.

There are a great many sick among the prisoners and many are being sent to the hospital every day. They were much exposed to inclement weather before their capture which, with much unavoidable exposure since, is now resulting in very general sickness. Three to six die daily.

This state of things has rendered it necessary to provide hospitals for them in the city. The city hospital is occupied exclusively by sick volunteers and prisoners of war, and I have consented, if you approve it, that while so occupied the necessary expenses, which amount to [?] per week, be borne by the Government. It is under the charge of the physicians employed by the State to attend the sick at Camp Morton. One other building which will accommodate 300 sick, has been rented for $104 per month, and another, which will provide for 125, has been rented for $60 per month. The latter building I propose to give up as soon as the number of sick is sufficiently reduced to admit of it.

The expenses of the two hospitals will amount to $225 each per month, independent of the rent, viz: Attending physician, $100; steward, $40; two matrons, $30; apothecary, $25. Ward masters and attendants will be detailed from the prisoners.

To make more convenient and permanent provision for the sick than can be had here now it is suggested that an addition be made to the city hospital capable of holding 300 patients. The hospital contains all the necessary convenience of dispensary, kitchen, &c., and 300 more patients would only require a few more attendants and nurses, with some enlargement of the cooking apparatus. The addition could probably be put up for $2500, and as many expect there will be a great many sick and wounded of our own troops to be provided for even long after the close of the war, this expenditure would perhaps be good economy in the end. The city authorities give their consent to the arrangement and place the building entirely at the control of the Government, and I refer the matter to you.

The expenses incurred in providing for the sick prisoners will, I presume, be paid by the Quartermaster General.

A bake house at Camp Morton would provide a fund with which many necessaries for the troops and prisoners there might be purchased that must now be furnished by the Government, and I recommend that one be built immediately. At present the flour is given to the baker, who returns only 20 ounces of bread for 22 ounces of flour....

March 7 (Friday)

Gugin, D. S., Surg., 3d Iowa Cavalry, Battle of Pea Ridge, Ark.:

Our commissary trains from Rolla [Mo.] were sometimes waylaid and seized by squads of the enemy, so that very little reached us. Thus we were compelled to subsist, each day rapidly diminishing the supplies until the 6th of March, which was the first day of battle.... On the morning of the 7th of March he [the enemy] showed himself in strong force at Elkhorn Tavern, upon the road ... but as soon as it was found that the enemy had appeared in our rear, the front was changed.... It was very clear that the surgeons would soon be called upon.... There was, however, no medical head, for Surg. Otterson hadn't yet returned. Moreover, the medical supplies for which he had gone to St. Louis had not yet arrived....

A charge was made by a portion of our cavalry and a battery of light artillery, who were repulsed

with considerable loss.... The cavalry [was] pursued by mounted Indians and Texan cavalry armed with a formidable weapon, a short, heavy, and sharp sabre, made from heavy sawmill files by their own mechanics. One blow with this rude weapon would crash through the integument, bony structure, and into the brain, or make deep gashes upon the body. Our forces however rallied and drove the enemy. Before the enemy's cavalry sallied out upon our forces, their infantry concealed in the underbrush, fired a volley from squirrel- and shot-guns of all calibers, killing and wounding many....

I ordered out two ambulances, and with surgical appliances ... proceeded after them as speedily as possible. Before arriving at the village, the rapid discharge of cannon and small arms proclaimed the beginning of the conflict. On the way and while ascending the hill from the deep ravine,... we were met by about forty horses in the wildest and most furious stampede, with saddles, blankets and other cavalry equipment in disorder. They belonged to the cavalry who had been unhorsed by ball and sabre in the charge....

At Leetown I was soon engaged with Surg. D. W. Young, 36th Illinois, and several other medical officers in attending the wounded, in a building formerly occupied as a small store. It was one story and a half high, about thirty feet long, and twenty feet wide. Hospital tents were erected upon the grounds around, and the wounded were brought in more rapidly than there was room for their reception.... The wounded lay upon their blankets or on the naked floors. Water was scarce, and those who had lost largely of blood, suffered for want of it. The wounds were mainly produced by rifle balls and by the sabre already described....

In Wheeling, Va., Union Brig. Gen. Rosecrans sent an inspector to Cumberland, Md., to inspect the sanitation and hospitals in the area. Dr. William A. Hammond, Asst. Surg., U.S. Army, was detailed for this duty, which he performed on this date. His report indicated the problems facing the medical service.

Dr. Hammond found a new convalescent hospital being located at Clarysville, a small place of only 10 buildings, which was situated on the National Road and the railroad to Frostburg, Md., to the west. The village was located on a narrow plateau, 1570 feet above sea level and 1000 feet above Cumberland. There was a stream of water that was polluted from mining operations and contained too much sulphur to drink. Abundant springwater was available in the area and was remarkably pure. The entire village had been hired at thirty dollars a month.

The main building was brick, two stories high, with an attic. It had verandahs to both floors, front and rear. The verandahs to the back of the building were to be used as mess rooms and it was proposed that they be boarded up to keep off the weather. This, however, would cut the light from the wards facing the verandah. On the first floor, a wide hall ran through the building with two rooms on each side. Each of the rooms [was] 24×20×11 feet (5280 cubic feet). The front corner rooms had four windows, the rear rooms two each. The rooms were overcrowded at the time of the visit, fifteen men occupying each room. The air in the rooms was foul and offensive.

A kitchen was located in the back building. The room was of ample size, contained a good cooking stove and a large fireplace, although the walls were black with smoke and dirt.

On the second floor, there were seven rooms with a wide hall like the one on the first floor. One room was large—24×20×10 feet—with four windows, and contained 15 patients. Four rooms were 20×20×10 feet, one with three windows, the others two each. Each room contained ten patients. There were two rooms opening onto the verandah in the rear, each 20×20×10 feet, both with adequate windows, each containing eleven patients.

The attic of the building wasn't occupied but had the same large hall and three rooms which would serve for nurses and cooks.

In order to take advantage of light and ventilation, the calculation used for space per patient was 1200 cubic feet. The patients in this building had less than 364 cubic feet, only half that required for well men in barracks.

There were adequate facilities for 81 patients at the Clarysville hospital and the current patient population was 175. There were, however, two large barns which, with repairs, could accommodate 50

men each. In addition to those to be used primarily as wards, there were several outbuildings which were available for use as a surgery, guardhouse, privy, etc.

The hospital was placed under the care of a Dr. Townsend, a civilian physician who lived in the area, with a ward master living on the premises. Dr. Hammond found the nurses to be inexperienced, the ward master energetic but uneducated, and the local apothecary intelligent.

The food was pronounced tolerable. The bread was good, it coming from a bakery in Cumberland. The food provided was good in both quality and quantity, no attention being paid to the dietary needs of the patients.

Bedding was wholly deficient. There were no blankets, sheets, or coverlets; no pillows, nor pillowticks, nor cases; no bunks; nothing, in fact, but bed sacks filled with straw and the men's blankets.

Tripler, Charles S., Surg., Army of the Potomac, Washington, D.C.:

> Early in March, the sick were removed from the field to the general hospitals. Convalescents were left in the camps, that they might the more readily be returned to duty when well, and that they might form a part of the garrison of the works when the army was put in motion.…

March 8 (Saturday)

Dr. Hammond continued his inspection tour, this time of the fifteen buildings used as hospitals located in Cumberland, Md. The report of the inspection of the first building in Cumberland presents the worst-case scenario for hospitals. The remaining hospitals there, while deficient in many aspects, didn't match the first in squalor. Dr. Hammond reported:

> This is a three-story brick building, formerly used as a hotel (Barnum's), on Baltimore Street. It is badly placed for ventilation, and the surroundings are filthy in the extreme.
>
> The first floor main hall is large, but in a shocking state of police. Two large rooms on this floor are used as surgery and office. In addition, there are several other large rooms.
>
> Ward 1 is a good room, 36×18×11 feet. It has recently been occupied by 27 men, lying on the

floor as thickly as they could be packed, each man having about *23 square feet* of space. It is in a horrible condition…

Ward 2 is also empty at present. On the day before my inspection it contained 25 men.… Each patient has had … 18 square feet of space.… Is filthy in the extreme.

Ward 3 is 48×24×11 feet; has six windows and three doors, good light and ventilation … It has recently been occupied by 100 men who had each *11.5 square feet* of space. This room is now full of old straw, which has been used for bedding.

The night after the inspection, these rooms were again filled by a fresh arrival of patients, without having been cleaned in the meantime.

The mess room joins Ward 3.… Is in a filthy condition. The kitchen joins this room … is a good room for the purpose.… Is stinking and filthy in the extreme.

The condition of the yard of this building defies description. It is simply disgusting. The outhouses are filled with dirty clothes, such as sheets, bed sacks, shirts, &c., which have been soiled by discharges from sick men. The privy is fifty yards from the house, and is filthy and offensive, *ad nauseam*. It consists of a shed built over two trenches. No seats; simply a pole, passing along each trench, for the men to sit on.

On the second floor, Ward 9 is 15×12×9 feet. Has three windows. Light good; contains five men; police bad; stench from the room stifling.

Ward 10. Same sized room as preceding—contains six men; police very bad.…

The other rooms on this floor, in this, the main part of the building, are occupied by medical officers, and male and female nurses. One of these rooms, occupied by a male nurse, is worse than a pigsty. The floor is soiled with excrement and almost every other imaginable kind of filth.

The back building of this story consists of a corridor, with rooms opening on it at each side.… The rooms are nine in number … have each one window.… No attention whatever appears to be paid to ventilation or cleanliness.

The third floor in the main building.… These rooms form no exception to the others, as regards police, ventilation, &c. They are so much crowded that it is impossible well men could exist in them, and preserve their healthy condition.

The back building of this story contains ten rooms, similar in size, number of windows, &c., to those of the story below.… Ventilation is entirely disregarded, and the police deplorably bad. Bedpans and chamber pots, containing urine and excrement, were standing in many of the rooms out on the floor, uncovered. The stairs crowded with chamber pots, slop buckets, and other utensils.

… 9[3] inmates are reported. On the morning of my visit, the morning report of this hospital stated that there were 159 patients and 47 attendants. 113 inmates are therefore unaccounted for. Some [attendants] slept in offices, but the great majority must have slept on the floors of the rooms used as wards.…

I do not hesitate to say, that such condition of affairs *does not exist in any other hospital in the civilized world*; and that this hospital is altogether worse than any which were such *approbria* to the allies in the Crimean War.…

Dr. Hammond recommended that all but two of the hospitals in Cumberland be closed and moved to other quarters, preferably to new facilities to be built. He also recommended that the physician in charge of the hospital in the Barnum Hotel be relieved of duty. The source document indicates that the recommendations of Dr. Hammond were carried out and that new buildings were erected, each to house no more than 50 patients, and an additional group of tents were erected for use by convalescents. The facilities were retained at Clarysville and used to the end of the war.

Jackman, John S., Pvt., "The Orphan Brigade," to hospital in Atlanta, Ga.:

The night we were on the train for Atlanta was very disagreeable. The water gave out and I sat by a window and caught the rain in a cup drop-by-drop as it fell off the car. I was glad of its raining that night.

The train arrived at Atlanta about daylight and we were taken to the old City Hotel which was being fitted up for a hospital. So many sick were being brought to the city that they could be but poorly accommodated. We had to lie down on the hard floor. A doctor came to me just in the nick of time and had mustard plasters put on my chest. I was in great pain.

March 9 (Sunday)

The battle at Pea Ridge, Ark., continued through the 9th until about 11 o'clock in the morning, when the Confederate force withdrew.

Gugin, D. S., Surg., 3d Iowa Cavalry, Battle of Pea Ridge, Ark.:

Our killed and wounded were not as numerous as the day previous; but the character of the wounds [was] as serious, most of them having been received at short range. The wounded received prompt attention, and by noon all were cared for....

The next day our wounded were ordered to be removed to Cassville, and the work was begun with the ambulances and wagons. The distance was about twenty miles, and the road passing through a broken country, was rough and uneven. It required three or four days to complete this task.... In this engagement we had thirteen officers and one hundred and ninety privates killed, and fifty-two officers and nine hundred and sixteen men wounded. Total, two hundred and three killed, and nine hundred and sixty-eight wounded.

March 10 (Monday)

The 55th Ohio Vol. Regiment, a new regiment with only five months in service, had been sent to Grafton, western Virginia, where they arrived on February 17th and set up camp on a knoll located on the south side of the river. The Asst. Surgeon General, William A. Hammond, visited the Grafton site for an inspection of the sanitation of the camp and the medical facilities. Dr. Hammond's report describes a typical situation:

The soil and subsoil [in the camp] are clay, which is bad, on account of its retaining moisture a long time. At present, the mud is six or eight inches deep all over the campground. The tents are in a very bad state of police, and, for a permanent camp, overcrowded. They contain from ten to fourteen men each. The effluvia from them, on entering, was stifling. The straw is changed once a week. The tents have not been struck since the regiment has been at Grafton.... They are partly floored; the boards are not placed on joists, but directly on the ground.

The camp sink is located between the tents and the river. It is covered with fresh earth about twice a week, when the medical officer specially sees to it. The men, however, generally make use of the ground in the vicinity.

It can scarcely be expected that proper sanitary measures will be enforced in this camp, so long as the field officers do not reside in it, and experience the discomfort which arises from their neglect. The Colonel, Lieutenant Colonel, and Major occupy a house in a high, airy situation, half a mile from the camp.

I find the medical officer in charge active and energetic in the discharge of his duties, which are onerous in the extreme. The Surgeon is absent, sick, and the whole medical care of a large number of sick falls upon the Asst. Surgeon, Dr. Spooner.

The measles appeared in this regiment on the 13th of February. At that time 165 men of the command had never had that disease; of this number, 100 have since had it.... Unless something is done to arrest its progress, the remaining 65 will have it. There has also been a good deal of other sickness, consisting principally of chest affections, diarrhea, and dysentery. At present, there are, as near as can be ascertained, 120 sick; which, in a force of 950 men is excessive. One-seventh of the command is thus unfit for duty.

Of the sick, the greater portion are scattered about the town, in private houses. The hospital embraces five hospital tents and two frame houses. The tents contain 18 men, mostly cases of measles. They are in a tolerably good state of police, and the men would be comfortable but for the lamentable deficiency of bedding. There are bunks, badly made, and straw alone. No bedsacks, nor any other articles of bedding, have been received from the United States, except 40 blankets.

House "A" has four rooms occupied by the sick. One is of 672 cubic feet, about half the quantity of space requisite for one patient, and yet there are eight men in this horrible den; each man has, therefore, *eighty-four cubic feet* of space. Can it be wondered that men die of measles (a relatively mild disease) when crowded in this manner? The stench from this room was sickening. There were but two windows, and they were closed.

On the same floor is another room ... 840 cubic feet, with three windows. It contained six men. It is a dark dismal room, the windows being closed, and covered with India rubber cloth to keep out the light, and to retain the moisture as much as possible.

On the second floor are two rooms; one is ... 840 cubic feet, has four windows, and contains four men. The other is ... 1575 cubic feet. It has four windows and contains six men....

The police is very bad. No bedding but straw, bunks, and the men's own blankets, with such odds and ends as have been furnished by the Sanitary Commission and individuals.

House "B" is a small two-story frame structure, with two rooms as wards, and a kitchen. The latter is very dirty. One of the wards is ... 1372 cubic feet,... has three windows, and contains seven patients. The other is the same size, has two windows, and contains five men. In this building there are accommodations for two men. It contains twelve....

Only 44 of the 120 sick are in hospital. The others are scattered about the town in private houses. Since the regiment has been at this place, ten men have died; one of typhoid fever, one of pneumonia, and eight of measles. The probability (almost amounting to a certainty) is, that, had these last named been properly supplied with bedding and air, their lives would have been saved....

I have to suggest the following means for improving the sanitary conditions of this regiment:

1st. That the commanding officer be directed to move his camp, if only to a distance of a few hundred yards, and to spread his encampment over a larger area....

2d. That his attention be called to the filthy state of police which prevails, and that he be directed to strike his tents and change their location a few feet every week.

3rd. That a shed capable of accommodating properly fifty patients be built as soon as possible, upon the plan specified in my report on the condition of the Cumberland Hospitals.

4th. That the houses now used as hospitals be immediately abandoned, and the sick placed temporarily in floored hospital tents.

5th. That additional medical aid be supplied as soon as possible.

I believe it would be better to remove the 55th entirely from Grafton....

If something is not done soon to lessen the sanitary evils under which this regiment now labors, the

heat and moisture of spring will undoubtedly increase the amount of sickness and mortality.

March 12 (Wednesday)

The first Soldier's Home in St. Louis was established on this date at 29 S. Fourth St. by the Western Sanitary Commission and placed in the charge of the Rev. Charles Peabody. The Home had accommodations for from 60 to 100 persons, and would average about 30 per day. Rations were furnished by the Government, with supplemental food provided by the Sanitary Commission. Between this date and June 30, 1863, 16,886 soldiers would lodge there, and a total of 52,942 meals would be served.

March 14 (Friday)

The 3rd Michigan Vols., en route to the Peninsula, were embarked on a steamer which lay in the Potomac between Alexandria and Washington for nearly 36 hours awaiting further movement. The regimental surgeon noted the conditions in the river and their effect on the troops, which resulted in 150 on the sick list:

The water of the Potomac, always muddy and dirty, is at this point pretty well mixed with the drainings of sewers and filth of every kind from Washington, which at the present time, between citizens and other civilians and soldiers, must have a population of over 100,000. This was the only water our men had to drink from the time we embarked, and in less than twelve hours it began to show its effect in diarrhea and dysentery.

Tripler, Charles S., Surg., Army of the Potomac, Washington, D.C.:

On the 11th day of March, it [the Army of the Potomac] was put in motion for Fairfax C.H. The enemy having disappeared from our front, a return to Alexandria was ordered.... I left Fairfax C.H. for Washington at nightfall of the 14th of March. In the meantime, orders had been issued in Washington limiting [McClellan's] command to the Army of the Potomac in the field and organizing that army into corps. The latter order so changed the organization as to make it necessary and expedient to assign an experienced medical officer to each corps as a medical director.... Here, I intended to bring in the senior medical officers of the army, in the hospitals at

Washington, as medical directors. I intended to distribute them, to break up the Washington arrangements, to send purveyor, as well as hospital surgeon into the field; in short, to transfer everything in Washington to Ft. Monroe...

On my arrival in Washington, the Surgeon General informed me that he had resumed the control of hospitals and purveyor; that I must use my inspectors for medical directors and appoint another purveyor, as the one in Washington could not be spared. I was further informed that I could not strip Washington of supplies; that I could take part of what was there, and that the remainder of what I wanted would be ordered from New York, to meet me at Ft. Monroe. I was obliged to acquiesce.

A medical purveyor was appointed, and ordered to report to me from Baltimore. This officer promptly obeyed, but was in too feeble health to undertake the duty. I then substituted Asst. Surg. R. H. Alexander, of the army, who entered upon and continued to discharge the duty....

March 16 (Sunday)

The divisions of Sherman and Hurlbut arrived at the landing docks of Pittsburg Landing on the Tennessee River. Maj. Gen. Don Carlos Buell was ordered from Nashville to the area around Savannah, Tenn., which was close by. Halleck, on one of his better days, dismissed the rather superficial charges against Grant and restored him to command in Tennessee. Grant replaced Gen. C. F. Smith, who'd injured his leg getting into a boat. Forces continued concentrating around Pittsburg Landing.

March 17 (Monday)

Grant arrived at Pittsburg Landing and assumed command, placing his headquarters at Savannah, north of the Landing. At this same location was Mary Ann Bickerdyke, who'd arrived two days previously. Savannah, Tenn., wasn't a lovely place. There were a couple of hotels, some boardinghouses, and other public buildings, but not much else. Bickerdyke obtained a room and had her boxes and bales unloaded in the backyard, where, shortly after, the landlady complained that the boxes stank and she wanted them removed. Bickerdyke agreed to comply shortly.

The army, in one of its worse moves, refused the assistance of the Sanitary Commission and their hospital boats for this operation, deciding that they could handle the problem themselves. The only outside help they had was Mother Bickerdyke, and the doctors were very cool towards her and snubbed her assistance.

McClellan was preparing for the move to the Peninsula and his surgeon, Charles S. Tripler, was still having problems getting ambulances collected for so vast an army.

Tripler, Charles S., Surg., Army of the Potomac, Washington, D.C.:

On the 17th of March, I saw Gen. Van Vliet in Washington in reference to ambulances. He told me that thirty-six four-wheeled were then in transit from Perryville [Ky.] for Ft. Monroe; that he would send eighty-six more from Washington, and one hundred and forty two-wheeled, in addition to those then in possession of the regiments. Those from Perryville reached Ft. Monroe in good season, and were distributed by Capt. Sawtelle; the others did not arrive until from April 9th to May 1st. March 29th, the headquarters were transferred to the steamer *Commodore*, at Alexandria.

March 18 (Tuesday)

Getting settled in her room, Bickerdyke's next visit was to the local quartermaster, to obtain a team and wagon, and some strong backs. She got the wagon, but not the backs. The best she could do was some contrabands [runaway slaves] who'd followed Union troops in that area. She took these and put them to work moving her boxes and bales to a spot back in the woods, stopping on the way to pick up a large iron kettle and some pitchforks at one house and a large supply of lye soap at another—all paid for using Sanitary Commission tea.

Having arrived at the place she wanted, the wagon was unloaded of its smelly cargo, the kettle was filled with water from a nearby stream, a fire built, and the operation began. The bales were opened, much to the disgust of the workers, and the bloody clothing of the patients from the battle of Donelson was ready to be cleaned.

Into the pots they went, to be stirred with long sticks and pitchforks until clean. Then they were rinsed thoroughly and draped on the bushes to dry. The next day they were collected and offered to the

Medical Officer at Savannah's hospital—where they were refused, and the prospective donor told that her services weren't needed. Undismayed, Bickerdyke took the next couple of weeks to teach the troops how to cook and do their laundry. She made many new friends during this period, her fame at Cairo having preceded her.

March 23 (Sunday)

Today was fought the first battle of Kernstown, a few miles south of Winchester, Va., in the Shenandoah Valley. "Stonewall" Jackson's foot cavalry, comprising about 3500 men, drove against a force of Union troops numbering nearly 9000, commanded by Gen. James Shields. Jackson lost 718 killed, wounded, and missing, while the Federals lost only 590. Jackson moved south, *up* the Valley. Surg. W. S. King later reported on the battle.

King, W. S., Surg., USA, Med. Dir., near Kernstown, Va.:

When the battle terminated, therefore, we found the supplies inadequate for the occasion, and the medical force not so large as desirable in consequence of the number of officers being, from necessity, on duty with their regiments in pursuit of the enemy.

As soon as the action became severe, which was not till half-past four in the afternoon, the ambulances were sent to the front and commenced the work of removing the wounded to a place of shelter. As Winchester was nearby, and the night fast approaching, it was thought best to remove them to that place without delay. Camp fires were made on the field, the wounded collected around and directed to remain near them until the wagons could pick them up. After making these arrangements, about eight o'clock P.M., I returned to Winchester and spent most of the night providing for their accommodation and attending such cases as required immediate attention. As the medical officers were mostly inexperienced, and some confusion, inseparable to such an occasion, existed, I remained a day in Winchester after the command had advanced until things appeared to be working well, when I left to join headquarters, it being reported that an action was going on near Strasburg.

Complaints of inattention to the wounded having reached me, I again proceeded to Winchester, and found the arrangements not as satisfactory as I could wish, which was owing chiefly to a want of cooperation on the part of the quartermaster and commissary departments, arising from a want of knowledge or a want of disposition to perform their duties. From a consideration of the circumstances I believe that much of the discomfort of the wounded has been owing to the circumstances beyond the control of the medical officers. I mention these details in explanation of the difficulties known to exist in providing immediately for four hundred wounded soldiers suddenly thrown upon us without the means and appliances sufficient to accommodate them....

March 25 (Tuesday)

Mrs. Bickerdyke came to the conclusion that no matter what else happened, war produced tons of laundry in the hospitals, and that someone had to handle it. The key was to do the laundry in the hospital as quickly as possible, so that the stains didn't "set," making them impossible to remove. After thinking about this for a while, she notified the Sanitary Commission in Chicago that she wanted washing machines, tubs, kettles, irons, and mangles to do the laundry where necessary. While these items were costly, the savings in material alone would pay for them in no time at all. She gave the letter to Dr. Aigner, who passed it on to Mrs. Livermore, who immediately let it get lost in the shuffle of the bureaucracy. Meanwhile, Mrs. Bickerdyke taught the troops how to cook.

April 1 (Tuesday)

The last units of the Army of the Potomac were slowly consolidating with the main body of the army. The medical department, including Surg. Tripler's staff, was finally arriving. The headquarters left Alexandria, and arrived at Ft. Monroe on the 2nd, at 6 P.M.

Brinton, J. H., Surg., USV, before Shiloh, Tenn.:

About the first of April, the main body of the army moved to a point on the opposite, or left bank of the river, known as "Pittsburg Landing," shortly to become the scene of one of the most desperate conflicts of the war, the battle of Shiloh Chapel. The physical condition of the men about to engage in this severe action was unpromising in the extreme. Many of them had been for weeks suffering from the diarrhea peculiar to the Tennessee River. This is said to result from the large amount of animal decomposition which takes place on the mussel beds or shoals, a few miles above Pittsburg Landing....

April 2 (Wednesday)

Asst. Surg. D. C. Peters, USA, late of Camp Davis, and having been paroled in San Antonio, Tex., reached Richmond, Va., after a rather arduous journey. In Richmond, he was given a very strict parole and sent North via Nashville, Tenn. After reporting in to the U.S. Army authorities, he finally got his exchange and was then assigned further duties as an assistant surgeon in the Union Army.

Peters, D. C., Asst. Surg., USA, en route to Ft. Pickens, Pensacola, Fla.:

I was next ordered to Ft. Pickens, Fla., and started for that place on April 2, 1862. I went by Havana and Key West, in the first conveyance that offered, and reached Ft. Pickens, without delay, about the 15th of the same month.

April 4 (Friday)

Surg. J. B. Brown was a medical officer of the Regular Army who'd returned from a six-year period of service in Washington Territory and Oregon. He was assigned to the Army of the Potomac, and further assigned to the artillery reserve. This assignment lasted until March 26th, when he was assigned as the medical director for the Fourth Army Corps. Brown spent the next few weeks getting ready and deploying to the Peninsula with the corps. When McClellan ordered the advance up the Peninsula, things began to get interesting.

Brown, J. B., Med. Dir., Fourth Army Corps, Army of the Potomac, Peninsula, Va.:

At Young's Mills the pickets of the enemy were first encountered, and skirmished, in falling back, with the advance of the second division. The position at Young's Mills was a very strong one. It had been occupied by Gen. Cummings' Confederate brigade all winter. Very neatly constructed tents, with glass windows, were here found. The largest and best ventilated of these were policed and converted into hospitals, and two surgeons were detailed to remain with a number of sick and the wounded men....

Jackman, John S., Pvt., "The Orphan Brigade," en route to Shiloh, Tenn:

Had reveille at 4 and marched at daylight. Nearly all the baggage was sent to Corinth by direct road. We had to strike tents and load baggage in a pelting rain. Being weak and debilitated and feeling like a "snort," I picked up a bottle in which I thought was whiskey, but upon turning it up and taking a "big horn," I found it to be alcohol and camphor mixed—medicine for the "Prof's" inflammation. I thought the stuff would burn me up—it cut blood out of my throat. That taught me a lesson.

At the outset our road led through a swamp where, in some places, the mud and water was knee-deep every step. The rain continued to pour down all the forenoon. I soon regretted that I had started. For a time I kept up but soon the column commenced continuing past me. While the troops would be resting, I would be walking to overtake them. About noon our road led over piney ridges and the sun came out very hot. Once I stopped off on the side of the road at a spring to rest.... When I got back on the road I found the division, commanded by Gen. Breckinridge, the only troops on that road, had all past and the wagon trains moving by. I gave up walking any farther and got into our surgeon's wagon. At sundown we passed through Farmington, 4 miles of Corinth. Night soon overtook us and as the road often led over creeks, which were swampy, the train had to stop before coming up with the columns. That night it rained and James H. and I slept in a wagon. I had a high fever that night.

April 5 (Saturday)

McClellan, now in front of Yorktown, Va., believed that he was outnumbered. "Prince John" Magruder had been marching his men around in circles, letting the Federals see the long columns of troops through a gap in the fortifications. Meanwhile, Joe Johnston shifted his troops as rapidly as possible to support Magruder.

Jackman, John S., Pvt., "The Orphan Brigade," en route to Shiloh, Tenn.:

This morning felt completely broken-down. The wagon was so heavily loaded and behind too. I had to try it afoot again. The train rolled past me and I was left a complete straggler. A staff officer in charge of the rear ordered me back to Corinth but as soon as he was gone, I kept ahead. The next house I came to I stopped. The lady gave me some milk and bread to eat. I felt so bad I thought I would go no farther. Soldiers were straggling along all day. That evening, there was some artillery firing towards Shiloh. Again had fever that night.

April 6 (Sunday)

Early in the morning hours of this day Confederate Gen. Albert Sidney Johnston finally got all his troops together and sent them screaming into the still unsuspecting Union lines around Shiloh Church. As the picket firing increased dramatically, some Union troops reacted, but most didn't, and they were unprepared for the charge that burst upon them. Grant, at his headquarters in Savannah, Tenn., several miles north, was alerted, and immediately went to Pittsburg Landing. He also ordered Maj. Gen. Lew Wallace at Crump's Landing to march immediately to Shiloh Church. The first units of Maj. Gen. Don Carlos Buell's army were at Savannah, under Brig. Gen. William Nelson, with most of Buell's troops still en route.

Brinton, J. H., Surg., USV, Battle of Shiloh, Tenn:

On the morning of Sunday, April 6th, 1862, the national forces commanded by Maj. Gen. Grant were attacked by the enemy, led by Gens. A. Sidney Johnston and Beauregard.... The assault, fierce and impetuous, commenced on Gen. Grant's right, and rapidly extended along his entire front.... By noon, the front and middle lines of the Federal force, throughout their whole extent, were pushed back on the rear lines in the vicinity of the landing.... In the meantime,... by half-past four o'clock in the afternoon the first regiments of Nelson's division crossed and advanced to the support of the heavy battery. At the same moment, the guns of the *Lexington* and *Tyler*, wooden gunboats, opened on the enemy, who incautiously approached too near the river on the left. Darkness coming on, the attacking columns withdrew for a short distance ... fresh troops ... were constantly arriving from Savannah and rapidly passing to the front. Every moment of

this night was spent in preparation for the coming contest of the morrow....

The only building on the field which could be taken for a hospital was a single log hut, fifteen by thirty feet, near the landing, which had been originally used as headquarters.... The removal of the wounded was a matter of very great difficulty.... On the afternoon of the Sunday's action, the shot of the enemy, also, fell freely among the writhing masses of wounded, whose further removal or protection was impossible. During the latter part of the same day, large numbers of the injured were conveyed by boats, and especially by the hospital transport *City of Memphis*, to the town of Savannah, seven miles below....

Grant, U. S., Maj. Gen., USA, Battle of Shiloh, Tenn.:

During the night rain fell in torrents, and our troops were exposed to the storm without shelter. I made my headquarters under a tree a few hundred yards back from the riverbank. My ankle was so much swollen from the fall of my horse the Friday night preceding, and the bruise was so painful, that I could get no rest. The drenching rain would have precluded the possibility of sleep, without this additional cause. Some time after midnight, growing restive under the storm and the continuous pain, I moved back to the log-house on the bank. This had been taken as a hospital, and all night wounded men were brought in, their wounds dressed, a leg or an arm amputated, as the case might require, and everything done to save life or alleviate suffering. The sight was more unendurable than encountering the enemy's fire, and I returned to my tree in the rain....

Murray, Robert, Med. Dir., Union Army of the Ohio, Savannah, Tenn.:

On the morning of the 6th, I was at Savannah, and being ordered to remain there, I occupied myself in procuring all the hospital accommodations available in that small village, and in directing the preparation of bunks and other conveniences for wounded. In the afternoon, the wounded were brought down in large numbers, and I then superintended their removal to hospitals....

When the wounded began to arrive at Savannah, Mrs. Bickerdyke was there at the dock to receive them, regardless of what the army wanted. An army surgeon who was present described the scene:

> She was wrapped in a gray overcoat of a Rebel officer, for she had disposed of her blanket shawl to some poor fellow who needed it. She was wearing a soft slouch hat, having lost her inevitable Shaker bonnet. Her kettles had been set up, the fire kindled underneath, and she was dispensing hot soup, tea, crackers, panado, whiskey and water to the shivering, fainting, wounded men.
>
> "Where did you get these articles?" the surgeon inquired; "and under whose authority are you at work?"
>
> She paid no heed to his interrogatories, and indeed did not hear them, so completely absorbed was she in her work of compassion. Watching her with admiration for her skill, administrative ability, and intelligence—for she not only fed the wounded men, but temporarily dressed their wounds in some cases—he approached her again.
>
> "Madam, you seem to combine in yourself a sick diet kitchen and a medical staff. May I inquire under whose authority you are working?"
>
> Without pausing in her work, she answered him, "I have received my authority from the Lord God Almighty. Have you anything that ranks higher than that?"

When asked about the incident years later, Bickerdyke commented only, "And *that* shut him up all right!"

Jackman, John S., Pvt., "The Orphan Brigade," Shiloh, Tenn.:

> Soon after the sun had risen, the firing of artillery became so general and the roar of musketry could be heard as distinctly.... I wished to be on the field but was not able to walk so far. The gentleman with whom I was staying had his only remaining horse caught which I mounted.... The gentleman walked and kept up. Four miles brought us to Monterry and just beyond we met some of the wounded on foot with arms and heads bound up in bloody bandages and I felt then that I was getting in the vicinity of warfare. Soon we met ambulances and wagons loaded with wounded and could hear the poor fellows groaning and shrieking as they were being jolted over the rough road. Met a man on horseback with a stand of captured colors. We

> were now in proximity of the fighting and we met crowds of men, some crippling along wounded in the legs or about the body, others no blood could be seen about them yet all seemed bent on getting away. I now "dismounted" and started on foot.... Being in so much excitement, I became stronger....
>
> While passing a hospital in the roadside, I happened to see one of our company lying by a tent wounded. I went out to see him and there found the brigade hospital established. There were heaps of wounded lying about, many of them I knew and first one then another would ask me to give him water or some other favor for him. While thus occupied, Dr. P. told me to stay with him, that I was not able to go on the field, that I would be captured. There was no one to help him and I turned surgeon, *pro tempore*. I was not able to do much but rendered all the assistance in my power. Part of my duties was to put patients under the influence of chloroform. I kept my handkerchief saturated all the time and was often dizzy from the effects of it myself. It was about one o'clock in the day when I got there.
>
> All day long the battle raged.... All day long the ambulances continued to discharge their loads of wounded. At last, night set in and the musketry ceased, but the Federal gunboats continued shelling a while after dusk. Nearly midnight when we got through with the wounded. A heavy rain set in. I was tired, sick and all covered with blood. But I was in far better fix than many that were there. I sat on a medicine chest in the surgeon's tent and "nodded" the long night through.

At about 3 o'clock in the afternoon, Confederate Gen. Albert S. Johnston was wounded in the leg. At first the wound didn't seem serious, and he continued to direct the battle, but he slowly bled to death, his boot filling with blood. Fallen from his horse, he died shortly thereafter, and the command of the troops passed to Gen. Pierre G. T. Beauregard, who attempted to gather the scattered army and get it into some fighting shape, but time was against him, and he would have to wait for the next day.

Livermore, Mary, Western Sanitary Commission, Chicago, Ill.:

> The battle occurred unexpectedly, and was a surprise to our men, who nearly suffered defeat, and again there was utter destitution and incredible suffering.

Derby, N. R., Surg., U.S. Vol., hospital boat, Shiloh, Tenn.:

On April 2d, I was detailed on the hospital steamer *City of Memphis*, and, in this capacity, passed through the battles of the 6th and 7th of April. With the assistance of a corps of surgeons, I took charge of, and cared for, over fifteen hundred of the wounded from the bloody field of Shiloh.…

On April 6th, the steamer *City of Memphis* was lying at Pittsburg Landing. Early on that morning firing was heard. At ten, the wounded began to arrive from the field in ambulances. By four, several hundred had been received, which crowded the boat very much; and shells from the enemy's right beginning to fall in the water nearby, the hospital transport was ordered to proceed to Savannah, seven miles below, and to leave the wounded at the general hospital at that place.…

During the battle, Henry M. Doak, Adjutant of the 19th Tennessee, was crossing a creek on horseback when a minié ball struck his left hand as he reached to move the branch of a tree out of his way. Although he retained the hand, it remained in a permanent twisted condition for the remainder of his life, eventually, by a twist of fate, leading to his death. Doak left the Army and was appointed a lieutenant in the C.S. Navy, where he served for the remainder of the war, surrendering with the Naval Brigade at Appomattox C.H. with Gen. Lee's forces. Doak, an accomplished musician before the war, was unable to ever play "fiddle" again, a loss which he deeply regretted. In 1928, while exiting a streetcar in Nashville, his disfigured hand became caught in the dismount bar and he fell, fracturing his hip. He succumbed shortly thereafter at the age of 87. An inglorious ending for a gallant fighter.

The 20th Tennessee was also present at Shiloh, where it took heavy casualties and acquitted itself well. William G. Ewin, a member of Co. A of the regiment, was elected captain during the reorganization following the battle, when the Confederates retreated to Corinth, Miss. Ewin would remain as commander of the company during the hard campaigns of Murfreesboro, Chattanooga, and Chickamauga, and would be a part of the

withdrawal towards Atlanta during Sherman's advance in May 1864.

April 7 (Monday)

This morning, Gen. Lew Wallace's division arrived at Pittsburg Landing after a wearying march. Gen. Don Carlos Buell also arrived with the remainder of his troops. Grant now had the hammer to beat the Confederate anvil, and so assaulted early, and quickly regained his old camps and most of the ground lost on the previous day.

Brinton, J. H., Surg., USV, Battle of Shiloh, Tenn:

Early in the morning, the united forces under Gens. Grant and Buell, the former reinforced by the division of Gen. Lewis Wallace, which arrived in the evening, moved forward to the attack. The enemy, obstinately disputing the ground, slowly retreated.… By four o'clock, on Monday afternoon, the enemy had been driven from the field, and was in full retreat on Corinth, abandoning his dead and very many of his wounded.… The capture of the camps had stripped the regimental officers of all their medical supplies and instruments, which were carried off by the enemy in their retreat. The stores which had been forwarded from St. Louis hadn't yet arrived. The number of medical officers was scanty, and very many of them, who remained at their posts in local hospitals, had been captured during Sunday's fight.

The mass of the wounded in Sunday's fight, who received the attentions of the surgeons, had dragged themselves, as best they might, to the high bluffs between the middle and the hospital landings. Here, in the vicinity of the log hut previously mentioned, such tents as were procurable had been pitched, and such dispositions as the circumstances admitted were made. A limited quantity of hay had been obtained from the transports, and this, littered on the earth, served as a bed for those most grievously hurt. All others lay on the soaked ground. To feed the sufferers, bullocks were killed, and soups prepared with great difficulty, for neither cooking utensils nor hospital furniture could be obtained. The weather was terrible, the rain incessant, and the mud almost knee-deep.… To add to the terrors of the situation, it must be stated, that even the plateau occupied by the wounded had become a thoroughfare, and was swept over by the retreating masses of our troops, many of whom, a panic-stricken mob, sought the shelter of the cliffs to escape the fire of the enemy....

On the following morning ... the advance of our troops and the retreat of the enemy commenced. During this forward movement, vast numbers of wounded were brought in to the main hospital depot. These were not only those who had been hit on that day, but also our own and many of the enemy's wounded from Sunday's fight.... By the authority of Gen. Grant, all tents that could be found were at once pitched, and the hospital shelter was extended to its utmost.... A separate hospital for three hundred men was improvised by Asst. Surg. B. J. D. Irwin, USA, who, by prompt seizure of tents, camp kettles, cooking utensils, etc., from a camp adjacent to the fighting ground of his division, was enabled to place it in admirable working order.

The Army hospital ship *R. C. Wood*, under charter by the Army and previously named *City of Louisiana*, had been outfitted by the Western Sanitary Commission at a cost in excess of $3000. The ship was furnished with assistant surgeons, an apothecary, and male and female nurses, as well as necessary sanitary stores. The *R. C. Wood* would transport 3389 patients from Pittsburg Landing and other points on the river after the Battle of Shiloh. The ship was later released from the charter (summer of 1862) and then purchased by the government for use as a hospital ship. The ship was fast, and large. The staterooms were removed and the entire upper deck was converted into one large ward with provisions for bathrooms, hot and cold water, cooking facilities, nurse's stations, etc.

Murray, Robert, Med. Dir., Army of the Ohio, Savannah, Tenn.:

I left Savannah by the first boat on Monday morning, and arrived at Pittsburg Landing at 10 A.M. I found the main depot for the wounded established at a small log house near the river, about half a mile from the line of battle.... The wounded were being brought in very rapidly and in large numbers. I found Brigade Surg. Goldsmith,... endeavoring to provide sufficient accommodations for them. This was a matter of great difficulty, for, as our army advanced, not only the wounded of that day, but those of the day before, both of our own army and

the Confederates, were found on the field and were transported to the rear by hundreds....

The thick woods and undergrowth in every part of the field rendered it difficult and almost impossible to ascertain definitely the position of any of the troops. During the remainder of the day and night of Monday, I was occupied in providing sufficient accommodations for the wounded....

Derby, N. R., Surg., USV, hospital boat, Shiloh, Tenn.:

As early as possible on the 7th, the boat was again at Pittsburg, receiving the wounded. During the 7th and 8th, over eight hundred were placed on board.... Large numbers of those received during the 7th and 8th had been wounded on the 6th and had lain on the field held by the enemy since the morning of that day.... Many of the medical attendants doing duty on the hospital steamer during these three days were volunteers, and, as they had come down to operate, and were greatly desirous of doing so, I found it necessary to dedicate some portion of my time to the preservation of limbs that were about to be unnecessarily placed under the knife....

Jackman, John S., Pvt., "The Orphan Brigade," Shiloh, Tenn.:

With the dawn came the roar of battle.... Early, all the wounded that could walk were given passes to go to the rear, and those not able to walk were placed in wagons and started for Corinth. Many poor fellows were not able to be moved at all. Once that morning a body of Federal cavalry came close enough to fire on us, tearing up the tents but fortunately hurting no one. Dr. P. and I were standing close together talking when a ball passed between our noses which instantly stopped our conversation. We soon hung up strips of red flannel to prevent further accidents of the kind.... A line was being formed in the rear of us and we had to move. Jim B. and I put the only remaining wounded of our regiment who could be moved into a large spring wagon and started back. We had to leave some that it would have been death to put them in wagons. We hated to do so, but we could not do otherwise. The wagon was heavy, the horses were balky, and the roads were rough and muddy— besides the driver was inexperienced—all combined, we came near not getting out. B. was strong and would tug at the wheels—I would plan, abuse the driver, and try to [stir up] up the horses. At last we came up with brother Jo, who was slightly wounded, and he assisted us. I believe if it had not been for him, we never would have gotten out. Night overtook us before we got far and we drove off to the side of the road to wait till morning. As luck would have it, a tent fly was in the wagon and we cut bows and stretched it over the wagon bed. I crept in and with my feet propt up managed to sleep a little.

Island No. 10, the "key" to the Mississippi, surrendered to the naval forces of Flag Officer Foote. Four steamers were captured when the Confederate defenses surrendered. One of these, the *Red Rover*, a steamer, had been damaged by mortar fire. This ship was moved to Cairo and converted into the navy's first hospital ship. By June 10th she'd been outfitted by the navy and the Western Sanitary Commission and was back in service and, shortly thereafter, received her first patients. Sisters of the Holy Cross volunteered and served as nurses aboard the ship—pioneers of the U.S. Navy Nurse Corps.

Tripler, Charles S., Surg., Army of the Potomac, Peninsular Campaign, Va.:

On the 4th, we marched to Great Bethel; and, on the 5th, through a heavy rain, to a cluster of huts, some five miles from Yorktown. On the 6th, I visited Heintzelman's position, in front of Yorktown, inspected the hospital department, and found that his medical director, Milhau, had made excellent arrangements for his field hospitals in case of battle.... On the 7th, I went to Ship Point, and inspected the Rebel huts there. We had then three large clusters of huts, most of them nearly new and in good condition; one at Ship Point, one about four miles from there on the road to Yorktown, and the third at our own camp, near the road to Ft. Monroe.... The accommodations afforded by these buildings, it was evident, would not be adequate for our wants, even with the one thousand provided for at Ft. Monroe, in case of a severe action at Yorktown. The country, also, from Warwick Courthouse to the York River, at our position, was but a succession of swamps, that in warm weather would be too prolific of malarial poisons to admit of our establishing military hospitals there. I, therefore, determined to arrange, if possible,... for the reception of all wounded in excess of the one thousand, at some of the hospitals north.... April 26th, I received a reply from Surg. Wood, acceding to my proposal.... I had at that time made arrangements to keep a hospital steamer constantly at Chessman's Landing, for the reception of wounded only....

April 8 (Tuesday)

Shiloh, the bloodiest battle fought to date, had losses that were staggering. Union forces lost 13,047, of whom 1754 were killed. Rebel losses were 10,694, a total of 1723 killed. Combined, nearly 24,000 Americans had been killed, wounded, or were missing after those two days. This total was larger than the population of most cities of that era in Indiana or Illinois. There were more casualties here than there were at the Battle of Waterloo.

Although the fighting was mostly over at Shiloh, the cleanup of the battlefield was just getting off to a good start. The Federal forces now had to contend with their own wounded as well as with the Confederates'. Beauregard, unable, or unwilling, to take the offensive, began his retreat towards Corinth, Miss., where he'd sit and await developments.

Brinton, J. H., Surg., USV, Battle of Shiloh, Tenn.:

The regular hospital boat, the *City of Memphis*, under charge of Asst. Surg. Turner, 1st Illinois Artillery, was immediately laden with seven hundred wounded, who were transported to Mound City hospital. The steamers *Hiawatha*, *J. J. Roe*, *War Eagle*, and *Crescent City* [steamers leased and outfitted by the Sanitary Commission; little credit was given to the Commission's foresight in this, or other matters] were turned over to the medical departments. These boats were at once fitted up, as well as the circumstances would permit, and on Tuesday, Wednesday, and Thursday following the battle were filled to their utmost capacity and dispatched down the river.... Towards the end of the week, other boats arrived: the government hospital boats *Louisiana*, *D. A. January*, *Empress*, and *Imperial*, all of which left full of wounded for the hospitals of the great western cities. The able president of the Western Sanitary Commission, Mr. Yeatman, and Dr. Douglass, of the United States Sanitary Commission, soon arrived, and by the distribution of the stores at their command, contributed much to assist the efforts of the medical officers.

In addition to the civil aid thus rendered, volunteer boats from a distance shortly made their appearance. The one from Louisville deserves special mention. The officers of this vessel cooperated in the most satisfactory manner with the medical director, receiving and caring for the wounded of their own and other states, and also wounded Confederate prisoners.

It is to be regretted that this same liberal spirit did not animate all of the volunteer and aid societies who hurried to this scene of carnage. It unfortunately,... happened that, in some cases, boats fitted out by the governors of states, and by local sanitary committees, endeavored to distinguish between the wounded of their own and other states, in favor of the former, and refused to receive, or received unwillingly, those who, in the estimation of these charitable philanthropists, were not entitled to their aid. In short, so greatly did this illiberal conduct conflict with, and prejudice the action of, the medical department, that it became necessary for the director authoritatively to declare that, as regarded the wounded, all state distinctions should be ignored and that the helpless soldier, friend or foe, should alike be cared for.... By the expiration of the week of the battle, all the injured were sent away to permanent city hospitals.

The wounded were collected and removed for treatment. The dead were identified, where possible, and buried where they fell. Medical supplies and equipment were at a premium. The Sanitary Commission began bringing in supplies for the relief of the wounded, and before the last man was removed from the battle area, they would have dispensed over 11,400 shirts; nearly 3700 pairs of drawers; almost 3600 pairs of socks; about 2800 bedding kits; 543 pillows; nearly 1100 bottles of brandy, whiskey and wine; 800 bottles of porter; about 950 lemons; over ten tons of dried fruit; almost 7600 cans of fruit; and over seven tons of farinaceous food (ground corn for making mush).

Sister Anthony, a member of the Sisters of Charity in Cincinnati, Ohio, went to the Shiloh battlefield aboard a steamer, accompanied by several medical personnel. Her experience was recorded shortly after her return to Cincinnati.

Sister Anthony, Sisters of Charity, Shiloh Battlefield:

At Shiloh we ministered to the men on board what were popularly known as the floating hospitals. We were often obliged to move farther up the river, being unable to bear the terrific stench from the bodies of the dead on the battlefield. This was bad enough, but what we endured on the field of battle while gathering up the wounded is simply beyond description. At one time there were 700 of the poor soldiers crowded in one boat. Many were sent to our hospital in Cincinnati. Others were so far restored to health as to return to the scene of war. Many died good, holy deaths.... The soldiers were remarkably kind to one another. They went around the battlefield giving what assistance they could, placing the wounded in comfortable places.... I remember one poor soldier whose nose had been shot off, who had almost bled to death and would have been missed had we not discovered him a pen, where some kind comrade had placed him before he left the field, every other place of refuge being occupied. His removal from the pen caused great pain, loss of blood, etc. The blood ran down his shirt and coat sleeves, down his pantaloons and into his very boots. He was very patient in the boat up the river....

Murray, Robert, Med. Dir., Army of the Ohio, Shiloh, Tenn.:

Early the next morning ... many of the wounded had been put on board the quartermaster and commissary storeships at the Landing, and in the confusion, numbers had found their way, or had been carried without authority on board small steamers, and it was no easy task to find all these and to provide for them medical attendance, food, and nursing.

The hospital boat *City of Memphis*, after taking two loads of wounded to Savannah, was sent off with seven hundred more to Mound City. The *Minnehaha, Commodore Perry, John J. Roe, War Eagle, Crescent City*, and *Hiawatha* were turned over to us on Tuesday, Wednesday, and Thursday. They were fitted up as well and rapidly as possible, filled to their utmost capacity with wounded and sent to the general hospitals at St. Louis, Evansville, Louisville, New Albany, and Cincinnati....

On the Peninsula in Virginia, the Army of the Potomac was slowly entering into the battle of Williamsburg. Casualties up to this point were very light.

Brown, J. B., Med. Dir., Fourth Army Corps, Army of the Potomac, Peninsula, Va.:

On April 5th, the enemy were encountered in force by Gen. Smith's advance, about two miles beyond Warwick Courthouse, and a sharp skirmish of pickets ensued....

On April 8th, two men were wounded by fragments of shells; one receiving a fracture of cranium, and the other, of both bones of the leg, which was amputated primarily. A hospital was established at Warwick Courthouse under charge of Surg. Wheaton, 2d Rhode Island Volunteers....

April 9 (Wednesday)

Brinton, J. H., Surg., USV, Battle of Shiloh, Tenn.:

As has been already remarked, the supplies of medicines and hospital stores ... were but scanty, and most of the regiments lost all ... at the time of capture of their camps. The sufferings of our wounded, when carried to the rear, were necessarily much aggravated by this existing destitution.... Imagine thousands of human beings, who had been wounded and lacerated in every conceivable manner, on the ground, under a pelting rain, without shelter, without bedding, without straw to lay upon, and with but little food. The situation of a hale man, stricken down by violence is at all times pitiful in the extreme, even when surrounded by those who sympathize and render the aid they can. But the circumstances attending the battle of Shiloh were fearful, and the agonies of the wounded were beyond all description.... The difficulty, at all events,... lay in the absence of supplies.... Requisition after requisition had been made for the very stores, medicines, and hospital tents, the want of which proved so disastrous upon the 6th and 7th of April. Unfortunately, at this time the medical department of the United States Army had not yet freed itself from that system of blind routine which, serving well the wants of a small army, in time of peace, yet failed utterly to meet the necessities of a gigantic war....

The nature of the wounds caused by the fire to which the troops were subjected ... was of the most varied kind ... a large proportion of our wounded were hit in the lower extremities. The killed were mostly shot through the head and abdomen.... But

very few bayonet or sabre wounds presented themselves.... The exposure of the men immediately following the receipt of their injuries, the absence of proper nourishment, the scarcity of medical supplies, and the prolonged transportation in overcrowded boats, all tended so to depress the vital powers as to favor, to a marked degree, the development of pyaemia, and death from exhaustion.... The ground, too, on which the army was encamped was the field of battle. On this, and in its close vicinity, thousands of men and animals had been buried, and in certain portions of the plain the effluvia were most disagreeably perceptible to the passerby. As the result of these combined causes, the sick list of every regiment was rapidly increasing....

In Washington, Lincoln was trying to explain to McClellan that McDowell's Corps had been held behind for the defense of the city. McClellan was turning a deaf ear and calling for more men. Lincoln was also beginning to wonder about the rather large "discrepancy" between the count of the enemy as stated by McClellan and the count of the intelligence gathered by other sources.

The Confederate evacuation to Corinth was still in progress. The mixup of units had been so great that some weren't united for several days after the battle.

April 10 (Thursday)

Murray, Robert, Med. Dir., Army of the Ohio, Shiloh, Tenn.:

About the latter part of the week ... the hospital boats D. A. January, Louisiana, Empress, and Imperial arrived, and, also, several boats fitted up by state or local sanitary commissions from different cities....

Some of the volunteer boats, especially the one under the control of the United States Sanitary Commission and the one from Louisville, gave us satisfactory assistance, taking, with equal readiness, the sick and wounded, both National and Confederate. But those fitted out by governors of states and by some of the local sanitary committees caused much irregularity. They sought eagerly for wounded from their own states, received very reluctantly, or declined to receive, wounded from other states or Confederate wounded, no matter how uncomfortable they were on shore. Notice would be sent to regiments that a boat was at the Landing ready to receive and take to their homes the wounded or sick of a particular state. This, of course, would bring down many who were not sufficiently sick to be sent to hospital, or who were very slightly wounded, and many of this class succeeded in getting off without detection. Even were none carried away but proper hospital cases, much irregularity and unnecessary cost to the government will arise from this system. The wounded are not left by the state authorities at regularly established military hospitals, but are, in most instances, put in private hospitals or houses at a much greater cost to the Government, and are separated entirely from the army, probably never to return to duty....

By the sad experience of this battle, I am confirmed in the opinion of the absolute necessity of the addition to the medical department of a sufficient corps of medical purveyors, who, in addition to furnishing medical supplies, shall act as quartermasters and commissaries to the medical department in furnishing quarters, transportation, furniture, provisions, etc., for the sick and wounded. And, also, that there should be a large number of enlisted hospital attendants attached to the medical department. They should have no other duty but to nurse and attend to the sick, should have a distinctive uniform, and be thoroughly instructed in their duties. This would obviate much of the confusion and difficulty in providing for the wounded after a battle, and the enlisted attendants having, as part of their duty, to remove the wounded from the field, the great evil of half-a-dozen men leaving the ranks to remove even one slightly wounded man would be avoided....

Nearly one thousand of the Confederate wounded fell into our hands, and I am happy to say that our medical officers and men showed them the same attention that they did our own....

Barber, Lucius W., Pvt., Co. D, 15th Ill. Vol. Infantry, Shiloh, Tenn.:

Now we turned our attention to the Rebel dead.... It took two days to bury all of them. I will not attempt to give much of a description of this battlefield. It was Ft. Donelson on a larger scale.... On one spot of ground, where we generally had our reviews, an artillery duel was fought and the ground was so thickly strewed with dead horses that you could walk nearly all over it on the carcasses.... Our loss footed up two hundred and fifty-two, killed and wounded, and there was only one man but what was not accounted for. We had in our camp about thirty

wounded prisoners, and they received every attention from us that we could bestow. They were Louisiana troops and gloried in the name of "Louisiana Tigers." Judging from their looks and the arms they carried, they did not belie the name.

The Confederate medical department opened another hospital adjacent to the Chimborazo in Richmond on this date. Called the Winder Hospital, it was somewhat smaller in scope but equipped much the same as its larger neighbor. It had the most modern facilities, including Russian, steam, plunge, and shower baths, water closets, a bakery, icehouse, a 16-acre garden tended by convalescents, and 69 cows.

April 11 (Friday)

At Pittsburg Landing, Tenn., Union Maj. Gen. Henry W. Halleck arrived to assume direct command of the troops. This relegated Grant to number-two position. Tongues wagged about Grant's supposed "drinking problem." Grant considered resigning. Halleck called for Gen. Pope's army to join the forces at Shiloh in preparation for the Federal drive on Corinth.

The "Angel of Cairo," Mary Safford, went to Shiloh on the hospital boats and made several trips from Savannah to the Northern hospitals. The strain and stress were, however, too much for her, and she was carried back home to Cairo. There her brother sent her on a long vacation to Europe, where she remained for some years after the war.

Mary Bickerdyke wasn't without company, however. On one of the Sanitary Commission steamers came Mrs. Eliza Chappell Porter, who headed the Chicago office of the Commission, and who'd come down to see how the Commission's efforts were being used. The diminutive Mrs. Porter, the wife of a clergyman, at age 54 weighed less than 100 pounds, but she was packed with energy, common sense, and an unusual piety. She and Bickerdyke had met briefly in Cairo some time before, and it was she who'd answered Bickerdyke's blunt letters for "more soap and less marmalade" with soothing responses. In refinement and grace, she surpassed even Mary Livermore and Mary Safford.

Mrs. Porter, accompanied by her husband, wasn't the least squeamish when it came to dealing with the wounded. Mother of nine children, she was used to handling sick ones, and she shifted that knowledge over to adult patients. There were the problems of the supplies sent down and what more was needed. Mrs. Porter pointed out that the local butcher had given her husband a bill for fifty pounds of beef that he'd furnished Mrs. Bickerdyke, the latter saying that the Commission would pay for it. Bickerdyke confirmed that the beef had indeed been supplied and she fully expected the Commission to pay for whatever was used, knowing that the army wouldn't pay for it. Bickerdyke went on to explain that the Commission people in Chicago didn't seem to understand the problems. When the wounded arrived, they most likely had been lying in the rain, or cold, all night and needed immediate nourishment if they were to survive. The army stocks contained mostly salt beef with maggots. The beef could have been "requisitioned" without any problem if she wanted to do it that way, but that didn't seem right, even if the butcher was a Rebel.

The result of the meeting was that Mrs. Bickerdyke was authorized to draw on any Sanitary Commission stores—and would she please fill out a requisition so they could be accounted for? Mrs. Porter, in Chicago, then announced that she'd be leaving to return to Savannah and become a nurse working with Mrs. Bickerdyke. This caused consternation in Chicago, but even more in Savannah, where Bickerdyke agonized over how this small, frail lady could possibly last when Mary Safford, who was much younger, had suffered a nervous breakdown.

Livermore, Mary, Chicago, Ill.:

During a large part of her army life, Mrs. Bickerdyke was associated with, and most efficiently supplemented by, Mrs. Eliza Porter, wife of a Congregationalist clergyman from Chicago. She entered the service in the beginning, as did her associate, and turned not from work until the war ended. Together they worked in the hospitals, enduring cold and hunger, dwelling amid constant alarms, breathing the tainted air of wounds and sickness, and foregoing every species of enjoyment save that which comes from the consciousness of duties well done. Unlike in all respects, they harmonized admirably; and each helped the other. Mrs. Bickerdyke came less fre-

quently into collision with officials when in company with Mrs. Porter; and the obstacles in the way of the latter were more readily overcome when the energy of Mrs. Bickerdyke opposed them. Mrs. Porter patiently won her way, and urged her claims mildly but persistently. Mrs. Bickerdyke was heedless of opposition, which only nerved her to a more invincible energy; and she took what she claimed, no matter who opposed. Both were very dear to the soldiers, from each of whom they expected sympathy and pity, as well as courage and help.

April 12 (Saturday)

With Mrs. Porter came a letter appointing Mrs. Bickerdyke as an agent of the Sanitary Commission, a very valuable document since it gave her immediate access to all Commission stores *and* paid her $50 per month! Initially, Bickerdyke refused the money but then she had second thoughts; part of the money could be used to pay for the support of her two boys, who'd been left with neighbors in Galesburg, Ill.

Mrs. Porter had come fully expecting to work. For this she'd brought sensible clothing and an iron will to do what was necessary. The experience gained from nine children and living in the backwoods with her minister husband now stood her in good stead. Under Bickerdyke's tutelage, she soon learned how to deal with large numbers of patients. The two made an unbeatable team, and Mrs. Bickerdyke became extremely fond of her "little wren."

April 13 (Sunday)

Around Yorktown, Va., McClellan was still digging. Magruder was getting more troops; he now had about 30,000 to match Little Mac's 100,000. McClellan complained, still, about McDowell's Corps being left at Washington and asked for reinforcements.

April 14 (Monday)

Tripler, Charles S., Surg., Army of the Potomac, Peninsular Campaign, Va.:

I have already stated that the army was well supplied with medical stores ... before it was put in motion. What was my surprise, then, as soon as we were in position before Yorktown, to find my office flooded with requisitions for more. Upon inquiry, I found that, in many instances, these things had been left by the troops in their old camps. Spirits had very generally disappeared. Various excuses were rendered that were not satisfactory.... Many days passed before I could remedy this unwise improvidence. My storeship, after having reached Ft. Monroe, was detained there by a storm.... I succeeded, finally, in getting her a berth at Chessman's Creek.... The first of the large supply reached Ft. Monroe on April 14th; the last ... the 1st of May....

April 15 (Tuesday)

Peters, D. C., Asst. Surg., USA, en route to Ft. Pickens, Pensacola, Fla.:

By Surg. John Campbell, USA, senior medical officer at Santa Rosa Island, I was assigned to duty in the post hospital, and had charge of the sick and wounded of a regular artillery battalion; the numerical strength was in the neighborhood of eight hundred men, with fifteen officers.... The health of all these soldiers was far above the usual standard in garrisons more favorably located. The men suffered from scurvy, intermittent fever and diarrhea, which sickness was caused, in a great measure, by the sameness of their diet, the impossibility of obtaining fresh vegetables, and the inferior quality of the fresh meat, which had unavoidably become damaged in transit. Each volunteer regiment had its own hospital, and was well supplied with the substantials necessary for field service. Besides these three hospitals, there was, at a distance of one and three-quarter miles above the fort, a general hospital for use of our worst cases....

April 16 (Wednesday)

At Shiloh, Maj. Gen. Henry W. Halleck, had taken command of the Union forces, putting Grant into the background. Grant had now upstaged Halleck twice within three months and Halleck wasn't happy with that situation. Halleck started moving his forces creepingly towards the Confederates at Corinth.

April 17 (Thursday)

Tripler, Charles S., Surg., Army of the Potomac, Peninsular Campaign, Va.:

Soon after our arrival in front of Yorktown, malarial and typhoid fevers again appeared, though not with any alarming rapidity.... Desirous of keeping the army as little encumbered as possible with sick,... I took

measures to send to the north those too ill to move with us. On the 17th of April, three hundred and fifteen such patients were reported to me, a very small number, considering the strength of the army, the wretched weather, and the character of the country. The transport *Massachusetts* was prepared for them, and on the 26th, was despatched for Annapolis.

Boulware, J., Hospital Steward, 6th S.C. Vols., en route to the Peninsula:

Thursday we left our camp three miles from Richmond and had a warm dirty road to the city. We marched through the city direct to Rocket's Landing and embarked for the Peninsula on board the steamer *Curtis Pick* at half-past 11 o'clock A.M. and landed at King's Landing at 6 P.M., having travelled about 80 miles. Had quite a smooth ride, though much crowded. Nothing of interest was observed, except some fine-looking residences, &c. We marched six miles that night and when the brigade stopped (about 1 o'clock) more than half of the boys had dropped out by the way and taken up quarters for the night. I kept up with the command, but Butler Alston and I had just laid down when a night attack took place. It seemed terrible to us (not being accustomed to such sound). We were called to our arms but were permitted to lie down again. We slept with accoutrements all on, yet I slept soundly.

April 18 (Friday)

Boulware, J., Hospital Steward, 6th S.C. Vols., on the Peninsula:

We were marched to and fro, got requisite number of cartridges, 40 rounds, cleaned our guns and rested for the evening.

April 19 (Saturday)

Tripler, Charles S., Surg., Army of the Potomac, Peninsular Campaign, Va.:

On the 13th, six civilian surgeons ... arrived in camp and offered their services.... On the 19th, Professor Henry H. Smith, Surgeon General of Pennsylvania, arrived with the steamer *William Whilden*, completely fitted up with bedding, stores, instruments, a corps of eighteen surgeons and dressers, and a large number of Sisters of Charity for nurses. He brought with him, also, the means of embalming the bodies of the dead; which kind office he cheerfully performed for numbers of men from various states.… Soon after his arrival, the steamer *Commodore* was assigned to me by the quartermaster's department. Dr. Smith took charge of her equipment, and in a short time, had her ready to receive nine hundred wounded. This vessel and the *William Whilden* then became our receiving ships, one of which was to be constantly in position to receive the wounded.

Boulware, J., Hospital Steward, 6th S.C. Vols., on the Peninsula:

The men who had not reenlisted were put in different commands and had officers appointed over them. I ran the blockade and got a canteen of good whiskey. I have been detailed hospital steward to assist Dr. Gaston in his duties. I made my breakfast and dinner on crackers alone and ate heartily. Rations came by night and supper was something else. Had inspection this evening.

April 20 (Sunday)

Boulware, J., Hospital Steward, 6th S.C. Vols., on the Peninsula:

Rested well last night and arose quite refreshed and glad to see a quiet beautiful Sabbath day. But everything was soon astir, for we had to move a mile farther towards Yorktown. I was left at the old camp with several sick who were unable to walk. Skirmishing took place in the night, the enemy endeavoring to take a dam we held which inundated a large extent of land greatly strengthening our position. A good many were killed on both sides. Our forces filled the water with their dead bodies.

April 21 (Monday)

Boulware, J., Hospital Steward, 6th S.C. Vols., on the Peninsula:

The brigade took position three-quarters of a mile from the breastworks. I had to walk one mile this morning, fill out prescriptions of Dr. G. for the Regiment, get medicine for my own sick and go back and cook for them. Had to fry meat in a tin plate, work up flour on the head of a barrel and cook it on boards like Johnny Cake. It is raining very hard and seems likely to continue to rain.

April 23 (Wednesday)

Boulware, J., Hospital Steward, 6th S.C. Vols., on the Peninsula:

Rain continues. I have moved up to the regiment with my sick men. There is continual firing from the gunboats.

Smith, A. H., Asst. Surg., USA, 6th Maine Vols., Peninsula, Va.:

I was detailed as assistant in the field hospital of the brigade, a mile in the rear. This consisted of four tents and four flies, capable of accommodating sixty-four patients. Rude bunks were constructed with poles resting on crotches. We had about twenty bed sacks, which were used for the worst cases.… But few wounded were received. After the evacuation of Yorktown, I was left alone, and the number of sick increased to one hundred and twenty-five, the greater portion of them sleeping in shelter tents. We had a large cooking stove and two good cooks, and, as there was an abundance of fresh beef and flour, beef tea and flour gruel were furnished to the sick. A few days subsequently, I was ordered to remove my sick to Yorktown. The distance was ten miles, much of it over a corduroy road, and the weather was very sultry. A quantity of hay was placed in the wagons, and about forty of the most feeble patients were placed upon it. One man, with a gunshot fracture of both bones of the leg, was carried the whole distance on a stretcher; while another, shot through the lung, ten days before, rode my horse, with a man walking on each side to hold him on. Both recovered. The remainder walked, some of them not reaching Yorktown until the third day, but all eventually reported in safely.…

Jackman, John S., Pvt., "The Orphan Brigade," Castillian Springs, Miss.:

Early went out in town, a small village, and looking cadaverous, a lady called me in and gave me a nice breakfast of milk and bread. While out in this expedition, many ladies had assembled at the cars with provisions for the sick and wounded. The Springs are three miles from town and the soldiers were brought out in carriages. About the middle of the forenoon, J. H., D. P. and myself came out in a carriage.

The building is a two-story frame with "wings," "ells," etc., and is accommodating nearly three hundred sick and wounded—nearly all Kentuckians. The grounds are tastefully arranged about the springs and the scenery in the vicinity is romantic.

April 24 (Thursday)

Jackman, John S., Pvt., "The Orphan Brigade," Castillian Springs, Miss.:

When I got up in the morning I walked out on the upper gallery and could look down on the preparations for breakfast, the tables being set out in the yard. I did not like the appearance of the bacon and corn bread—my appetite did not crave such delicacies (?)—so I proposed ... to walk out a short distance in the country and get breakfast. I craved milk. My constitution was wasted and about all I needed was proper diet. In about a half a mile we came to quite a humble-looking residence; but on stopping at the gate, we were invited in and were treated with great hospitality. The lady's husband was in the army and she thought it very strange we did not know him. The old pipe-smoking grandmother was in the corner and she held up her hands in wonder when informed that we had never met her sons who were in the Virginia army. The rosy-cheeked daughter in the meantime had prepared us breakfast. I did justice to the buttermilk. No pay would be accepted, but we made arrangements to have milk sent us daily to the hospital for which we were to reimburse them.

April 28 (Monday)

McDougall, Charles, Med. Dir., Union Army of the Tennessee, Hamburgh, Tenn.:

On being assigned to duty on April 28th,... I found the purveying storehouses almost destitute of hospital supplies, especially of bedding, so much needed, and without which we were helpless providing for the comfort of the sick.... Orders were issued to establish a convalescent hospital at Hamburgh, four miles above Pittsburg Landing, with sixty-five hospital tents, two hundred bedsacks, and two hundred and forty cots.

Before the medical officers and attendants arrived at Hamburgh, the sick were pouring in from all quarters, and the hospital boats on the river were fast filling up. Orders had been given for a forward movement. For five days, from morning to until night, the unfortunate sick were thrown on the bank of the river, in parties of from two to fifty, and, in most instances, without any report in their cases, other than they were sick. Three or four assistants and myself were engaged during the five days in attentions to them, and distributing them to the floating and convalescent hospitals. Two thousand were sent off to hospitals in Missouri, Indiana, Kentucky, and Ohio, and two thousand five hundred, to the convalescent hospital at Hamburgh. Half of the latter were without shelter, for want of tents.... [During] the last six days, about three thousand sick and wounded have been sent to the different hospitals in the western country....

From careful inquiry, I find that at least one-half of the sick are cases of chronic diarrhea, which should have been discharged for disability or sent to general hospitals. The great majority of such cases cannot get well in camp or in this climate. Remaining in the immediate proximity of the army, such patients only retard its operations, and divert the services of the regimental surgeons and assistant surgeons from their special duties in the field....

April 29 (Tuesday)

Maj. Gen. Halleck, with over 100,000 men, prepared to attack Beauregard's nearly 65,000 now in Corinth, Miss. Halleck would march from Pittsburg Landing for Corinth. Grant, named second-in-command, was very upset at what he considered to be a demotion. In all events, Halleck wasn't looking for a hero who'd outshine him in the coming campaign, Grant had already done that twice.

April 30 (Wednesday)

The Union hospital at Mound City had been the scene of feverish activity since April 8th, when the first of the wounded from the Battle of Shiloh began to arrive. Within the past three weeks, more than 2000 wounded had been received. Many had died of their wounds, while others had been transferred to locations closer to their homes. Mrs. Margaret McCrea Durand was assigned as a nurse-matron on one of the wards of the hospital and found that the work was too strenuous. Margaret fell ill and was sent home to recover. She never returned to work as a nurse during the war, being too ill to participate. In 1891, the U.S. Congress passed an Act which placed personnel such as Margaret on a pension of

$12 per month. She didn't enjoy too much of that pension; she died in 1893, at age 79.

May 1 (Thursday)

Siege guns were being mounted opposite the Confederate fortifications at Yorktown, Va., thereby increasing the pressure against Gen. Joseph Johnston. If Yorktown was evacuated, the city of Norfolk, the Norfolk Navy Yard, and other peninsular assets would be abandoned. Pres. Lincoln was concerned that McClellan hadn't yet attacked Johnston, but seemed instead to be preparing for a lengthy siege.

Tripler, Charles S., Surg., Army of the Potomac, Peninsular Campaign, Va.:

On May 1st, Mr. Olmsted, the secretary of one association, had a boat, the *Daniel Webster, No. 1* in his possession; a steamer on which he could carry two hundred and fifty patients. At his request, I procured the *Ocean Queen*, a steamer of the larger class of seagoing ships, and turned her over to him. He agreed to fit her up in forty-eight hours after getting possession of her. It took rather longer than that, however, and then she carried but three-fifths of the number she should have carried.

May 2 (Friday)

The Sanitary Commission held the inauguration of the Ladies' Home for Sick and Wounded Soldiers, at the corner of Lexington Avenue and 51st Street in New York. National airs were performed by the Band of the Eighth Co., National Guard. An address was given by the Mayor of New York in which he pointed out that:

The ladies, ever foremost in good works, have fitted up this spacious building for the reception and treatment of disabled soldiers.... The building itself is a model of its class, and admirably adapted to the purpose to which it is now to be applied. The wards are large and well ventilated. They have been thoroughly cleansed, and fitted up with appropriate furniture and excellent bedding. The surgical and medical staff embraces the best professional skill in the city. The nurses will also be the best of their class, and, better than all, the ladies themselves, or at least a portion of them, will be in constant attendance, to infuse into the hearts of others a share of that devotion with which

they apply themselves to beneficent work. Their efforts could not be employed in a nobler cause....

May 3 (Saturday)

Confederate forces around Yorktown, Va., withdrew before McClellan started his bombardment. Richmond was alarmed about rumors that Norfolk and the Portsmouth areas were to be abandoned. Confederate forces numbered about 55,000, versus Union forces of over 100,000. McClellan was still calling for more manpower, even as the Rebels retreated.

There was minor skirmishing in the Corinth area between Beauregard's and Halleck's forces.

May 4 (Sunday)

The Army of the Potomac entered Yorktown, Va., and continued towards Williamsburg. Advance Union units clashed with Confederate Gens. Longstreet's and D. H. Hill's troops outside of town.

Tripler, Charles S., Surg., Army of the Potomac, Peninsular Campaign, Va.:

May 2d, I telegraphed to the medical director of Keye's Corps to break up his hospital at Young's Mills; and on the 4th, to concentrate his sick, with a suitable allowance of medical officers, nurses, and subsistence, and to keep his transportation well in hand for any further movement. The same day, I inquired for how many men he would want accommodation. The next morning, the officer left in charge of the sick at Warwick Courthouse reported two hundred and thirty-two men; before night the number increased to eight hundred. I then sent an assistant to see to the matter, and before his task was completed, more than twelve hundred were collected in the woods and elsewhere from that corps alone.... The boats of the Sanitary Commission were employed in transferring some of the sick to the north, and, by the 9th of May, they had relieved me of nine hundred fifty. We then had two thousand in hospital at Yorktown....

Ingram, Alexander, Asst. Surg., Army of the Potomac, Peninsula, Va.:

We proceeded immediately to Williamsburg, where I found four or five hundred wounded, almost exclusively Confederates.... A number of Confederate surgeons had been sent back from Gen. Longstreet's division, but being found on the streets without credentials, they had been picked up by guards and confined as prisoners. The facts being made known, they were at once released, and, with the few Union surgeons in the town, proceeded to make the wounded as comfortable as possible with our scanty means. The Confederate surgeons were entirely unprovided with instruments and stores, but the necessary instruments and a few essentials, such as chloroform, stimulants, and morphia, that had been carried on saddles were provided by us. Beef was soon obtained and distributed, which, with contributions from the residents, nourished the wounded until the following day, when our trains began to come in. The wounded were sheltered in churches and other buildings, and did not suffer from exposure. A number of amputations and a few extractions of balls were performed, the Union and Confederate surgeons working very amicably together....

In Mississippi, there was skirmishing around Farmington, the next location of the Union hospital supporting Grant and Halleck's drive towards Corinth.

Hatchitt, J. G., Surg., USV, en route to Corinth, Miss.:

About the 4th of May, 1862, this brigade commenced the march to Corinth, it still raining almost incessantly, and roads nearly impassable. Camp diarrhea prevailed to an alarming extent. Indeed it was hardly possible to find one not afflicted with it. Every few days the ambulances were filled with patients for Pittsburg or Hamburg landing, to be sent north....

May 5 (Monday)

Heavy fighting around Williamsburg, the old capital of Virginia, as McClellan's forces collided with those of Joseph Johnston. Longstreet and D. H. Hill fought their Confederates well in the rearguard action that brought on more casualties than would have been expected for this type of engagement. Johnston continued his retreat towards Richmond.

Boulware, J., Hospital Steward, 6th S.C. Vols., on the Peninsula:

At half past six o'clock the battle commenced. I was about to drink a cup of tea made in one of the houses built for winter quarters when the bullets began to

fall around us. I was with the surgeon. Dr. Post was hit on the head, rendering him unfit for duty that day. We carried him to a house in the rear where the wounded were taken. The artillery soon opened and our quarters being in direct range we were soon shelled from there. It commenced to rain, but the firing increased and by noon it was terrible. We soon drove the enemy back on our right wing. They came again and were again driven back. We took hundreds of prisoners and three pieces of artillery. Our regiment, 6th S.C., being on the left [was] not engaged until late in the afternoon. A rifle company was sent out as skirmishers, and at the first fire of the enemy's artillery, Hugh Smith and Lt. Campbell were cut down. We were forced to fall back, and on regaining the ground, alas! poor Smith was dead and Lieut. Campbell soon after died. Night came leaving us in possession of the field. We were busily engaged in carrying off the wounded and administering to their comfort until 2 o'clock that night....

The rain had been coming down all day and we had to go on ground where thousands of infantry, artillery, wagons and ambulances had been running. To no one who had not the same experience can form a faint idea of the place.

Charles S. Wainwright entered the Union Army as a major of artillery in October, 1861, in New York, at age 34. He was a member of an old New York farming family, and was an active member of the State Agricultural Society. Very well educated, he'd served in the militia artillery units and had travelled to Europe, where he'd visited several French artillery units. Very much "the gentleman," he expected all officers to conform to the "gentleman's code," and was a stern, but fair, disciplinarian. The First New York Artillery was assigned to the Army of the Potomac in late 1861, where it remained for the duration of the war. In the spring of 1862, McClellan took his army to the Virginia Peninsula to attempt capturing Richmond from that direction—an ill-fated enterprise. Wainwright's artillery was involved in the Battle of Williamsburg.

Wainwright, Charles S., Maj., N.Y. Artillery, Williamsburg, Va.:

My own men were very tired, some of them completely broken-down; they were all unaccustomed to fighting and doubtless worked harder than was necessary.... Some three hundred to four hundred yards back in the woods I pass[ed] our field hospitals where the wounded were receiving their first dressing, and then sent back in ambulances about a mile or so to where the main hospital was established in and around a fine large house.... Our little Dr. Goddard remained all day at the front, and gave his first care to our wounded almost among the guns where they fell. The road was now awful; my horse sank to his knees at almost every step. Ammunition and hospital wagons were stuck all along....

May 6 (Tuesday)

In Tennessee, Halleck's advance towards Corinth proceeded at a snail's pace. Halleck wasn't the most aggressive general in the world, but still he wasn't as bad as McClellan.

Federal troops occupied Williamsburg, Va., on the heels of the retreating Confederates. Joe Johnston continued his retreat towards Richmond.

Tripler, Charles S., Surg., Army of the Potomac, Peninsular Campaign, Va.:

The next day the battle of Williamsburg took place. In the night I was directed to send transportation to Queen's Creek for three hundred wounded. The *Commodore* was immediately despatched in charge of one of my assistants. At noon, of the 6th, she returned to Yorktown, having been unable to effect a landing on account of shoal water. I procured a lighter from Col. Ingalls, and taking charge of the *Commodore* myself, proceeded with her to Queen's Creek.... The water was so shallow the steamer could get no nearer to the landing than two miles. Lt. Reamy, of the Navy, boarded us, and courteously offered to land us in his boat. Leaving orders for the lighter to follow up the creek as soon as she came up, Dr. Smith and myself went ashore, set the ambulances in motion, and collected from the depots one hundred of our wounded and got them comfortably aboard the *Commodore* by 3 A.M. One hundred wounded prisoners were collected in one of the fieldworks near the landing. The next morning, having organized the ambulance train, I left Dr. Smith to embark the rest of the wounded,... and hastened back to Yorktown....

Boulware, J., Hospital Steward, 6th S.C. Vols., on the Peninsula:

Our men having had no rest for three nights were forced to lie down in the mud on their arms. Just before day they began the retreat leaving all of our wounded to fall in the hands of the enemy. The retreat was well executed, but the mud was awful, for remember we were the rear of Johnston's army. When the march began everyone felt he could not go five miles, but strange to say, we went sixteen miles without stopping for the night. We had nothing to eat except what we had put in our haversacks four days before. The enemy took possession of the vacated field early next morning, and followed pretty close in our rear; our cavalry, though, kept them at a respectful distance. Several surgeons of our division went back to wait on our wounded.

May 7 (Wednesday)

Wainwright, Charles S., Maj., N.Y. Artillery, Williamsburg, Va.:

Fighting a battle, I find, is the smallest part of a campaign. The repairing of damages, writing reports, and getting ready to go at it again is infinitely more fatiguing.... I took a look at several of the redoubts this afternoon.... I found Bailey camped with his command about half a mile north of Ft. Magruder. They all appeared really sorry that they did not get into the fight. Our men are still at work burying the dead. Our own are pretty much all interred. They say that they lay very thick in the slashing, and that a number had evidently been bayonetted by the Rebels, after they were shot down. I cannot think that there were many such cases. The Rebel wounded in our hands, and our prisoners generally, express much surprise at receiving such kind treatment: they had been told by their leaders that they would all be murdered. I saw several hundred Rebel prisoners in Williamsburg. They were a seedy-looking lot, most of them in grey or butternut clothes, and all sorts of slouch hats; you could hardly call it a uniform at all.

Tripler, Charles S., Surg., Army of the Potomac, Peninsular Campaign, Va.:

Here I was met by an order to hasten to Williamsburg, to care for the wounded there. Having despatched the Pennsylvania steamer *Whilden* to Queen's Creek,... I hastened to Williamsburg. Here I was joined by a party of able and distinguished surgeons.... All the wounded in Williamsburg, comprising about seven hundred of our own men and three hundred and thirty-three of the enemy, had the benefit of their care. The remainder of the wounded were attended to in the field depots near the James and York rivers. The whole number of killed in that conflict, reported to me, was four hundred and sixty, and, of wounded, one thousand four hundred and seventy-four. Four hundred and thirty-three wounded prisoners were left upon our hands.... Eight hundred of our men and one hundred prisoners were sent to Ft. Monroe on the *Commodore*, and four hundred and twenty-seven of our men and two hundred and seventy-three prisoners on the *William Whilden* and other transports. The *Whilden* sailed direct for Philadelphia. On the 11th of May, the embarkation of our own wounded was completed....

May 8 (Thursday)

In western Virginia's Shenandoah Valley, the Battle of McDowell took place, as Jackson's 10,000 men were attacked by about 6000 from Frémont's command under Gen. Schenck. The Federals retreated towards Franklin, and Jackson pursued.

Hart, Samuel, Asst. Surg., USV, Battle of McDowell, western Virginia:

In skirmishing with the enemy at Monterey, we had several wounded, one having a compound comminuted fracture at the knee, requiring amputation at the lower third of femur. After many ambulance journeys, and many escapes from hemorrhage, etc., the patient recovered with an excellent stump. Twelve miles south of McDowell, we were met by the enemy, and obliged to fall back to that town, where a stand was made to secure time. The engagement which followed was one of unusual sharpness. Our killed and wounded were all secured. The latter were removed to houses in town for operations; thence to the rear, during the night, the entire command following.

My regimental loss was six killed and twenty-five wounded. One man died on the march, after an amputation of leg. The other wounded suffered much in transportation over the very stony and corduroyed road to Franklin. When two wheels of a vehicle, either the forward or hinder, strike at once upon an obstacle, as in corduroyed roads, the shock seems more than double that of the striking of one wheel; and it sometimes happens that the successive

impingement upon the logs, and the vibration or swaying of the ambulance so synchronize as to produce violent concussion and straining of the springs and timbers, while the groans and outcries of the riders attest the severity of the trial of the already wounded muscles and fractured bones. The wounded from the battle of McDowell were removed to Franklin, and treated there two or three weeks, when those unfit for transportation fell into the hands of the enemy. Fifteen of my cases were left, eight of whom died....

May 9 (Friday)

In Florida's panhandle, the Confederate forces decided to evacuate Pensacola, not being able to use the port for blockade-running, since the Union held Ft. Pickens. To set the evacuation off in a "blaze of glory," the Confederate commander fired the facilities to deny their use by the Union.

Peters, D. C., Asst. Surg., USA, Ft. Pickens, Pensacola, Fla.:

... the enemy fired Fts. McRae and Barrancas, and also the marine hospital, the town of Warrington, their barracks, and the United States Navy Yard. The conflagration was a fearfully grand spectacle. Our heavy artillery immediately opened with the object of driving away the incendiaries, and, in a measure, succeeded. The firing commenced early in the evening and continued all night, and was heard many miles at sea....

May 10 (Saturday)

Gen. I. G. Arnold, USV, commanding the garrison at Ft. Pickens, had a strong desire to cross the channel to the western side and capture what remained of Ft. Barrancas and the other facilities. The problem was that he'd no means to cross the channel. Commodore Porter solved the problem by furnishing his own flagship for Arnold to cross the troops. Today, 600 regular U.S. troops were put ashore and began the assault on the empty, and smoldering facilities. Asst. Surg. Peters went along:

Peters, D. C., Asst. Surg., USA, Ft. Pickens, Pensacola, Fla.:

I was ordered to accompany this expedition. We landed without opposition, and at Ft. Barrancas arrested the fire, and took several cannon and other trophies. The *Harriet Lane* brought us reinforcements, and, when all was ready, we marched on to the town of Pensacola, which the enemy had vacated as we entered it.… The citizens remaining at Pensacola were found to be in a destitute condition. The city itself was filthy, and most of the wealthy people had deserted it.… Our lines had become extensive, and we required more troops to make the place tenable.… A request was sent to Key West for reinforcements, and the 91st New York Volunteer Regiment was dispatched to our aid.…

The Confederates set fire to the Norfolk Navy Yard before evacuating it, and moved west towards Richmond. Union troops under Maj. Gen. Wool crossed Hampton Roads and occupied Norfolk. While much of the supplies and materials were destroyed, much remained. The loss of the naval base was a great blow to the Confederacy, and left the C.S.S. *Virginia* without a home. In Richmond the departure of Pres. Davis's family for Raleigh, along with the departure of the families of most of the Confederate Cabinet's members, was reported.

May 11 (Sunday)

Boulware, J., Hospital Steward, 6th S.C. Vols., retreat from Williamsburg:

We are moving slowly on. Passed a beautiful residence that I admired above all I have seen. Moses Arledge was sick and died on the roadside today.

May 12 (Monday)

Tripler, Charles S., Surg., Army of the Potomac, Peninsular Campaign, Va.:

A drenching rain began in the night of the 5th, and continued the next day. I was informed that many of the regiments had left their camps with nothing in their haversacks. They had no shelter from the rain, and nothing to eat. The roads were shocking; it seemed almost impossible to get supplies to them. Their privations were consequently extreme. As a natural result, when the columns were again put in motion, a large number of men were thrown on my hands; some of them sick; most of them tired and exhausted. They came straggling in from the rear of the army, without reports, nurses, or subsistence. It was impossible to create hospitals for all these men at Williamsburg. I, therefore, caused a selection to be made for transportation to the rear, and ordered up one of the boats in charge of the Sanitary Commission, from Yorktown, to receive them. This boat, the *Elm City*, reached me during the afternoon of the 12th. I directed her, after she was filled up, to proceed to Washington.…

May 13 (Tuesday)

Mrs. Bickerdyke, along with all her Sanitary Commission stores, was en route to Farmington, Miss., in forty army wagons loaned her by Grant. Bickerdyke rode in her Commission ambulance along with two female nurses, who'd arrived just as she was leaving Savannah. Mrs. Porter had gone North for a short time to visit and rest up, having departed with Mrs. Bickerdyke's admonition ringing in her ears to "put on twenty pounds."

May 14 (Wednesday)

Tripler, Charles S., Surg., Army of the Potomac, Peninsular Campaign, Va., in a letter to Gen. McClellan:

Matters being arranged at Williamsburg, I moved, on the evening of the 13th, to rejoin headquarters. Bivouacking at night on the road, I reached Cumberland at noon on the 14th. Here I found a number of sick reported as unable to go on. It was raining hard, and the roads were almost impracticable. It was necessary to make some provision for the sick. I took a steam tug at night, and went down the river until I reached the steamer *Commodore*. The master of the vessel refused to go up the river without a pilot, as it would vitiate his insurance. I applied to the provost marshal at Eltham for a pilot. He knew of none. Chancing to hear of the mate of a brig about [to sail] for home, who was said to know the river, I sent him an order in your [McClellan's] name, to repair on board the *Commodore* immediately to pilot her up. I succeeded in getting her to Cumberland, and thus provided a hospital. Leaving her in position, on the 16th, I moved with the headquarters to White House.…

Around Corinth, Miss., the skirmishing was fairly light. Halleck was extremely slow during this campaign. It would prove to be the only time he commanded a force in battle, which wouldn't prevent him believing himself an expert in the science.

Jackman, John S., Pvt., "The Orphan Brigade," Castillian Springs, Miss.:

Brown died in our room this morning. How little feeling soldiers have sometimes! While willing to help a comrade while living, when dead, there is never much shedding of tears for them. We were all standing around Brown's bed and when he drew his last breath one of the boys bent over him, observed him for a moment, and said: "He never will draw another breath *so long as he lives.*" This was said so simply the whole room rang out in laughter. We buried B. in the evening. Many are dying here. Intend to go to the front in a few days.

May 15 (Thursday)

Gen. Joseph E. Johnston's Confederate Army withdrew across the Chickahominy to within three miles of Richmond.

Brinton, J. H., Surg., USV, Corinth, Tenn.:

The hospital of the Army of the Mississippi was … located at Monterry, five miles in the rear of Corinth. This hospital was composed of several hundred tents, situated on the slopes of two hills, in the vicinity of a running stream.… One object in the establishment of these field hospitals wasn't only to provide for the reception of future wounded, but also to furnish accommodation for the numerous sick of the command. The number of the latter was, at this time, very large, amounting to thousands. The medical director, in his report … computes the number sent at that time from Pittsburg Landing to be not less than eleven thousand. It was desirable to check this exodus of troops; for it had been found that, of the vast numbers who left, but few returned. This pernicious custom of leaving the command on the plea of sickness was becoming too prevalent, and had been much encouraged by the presence of boats fitted out by the governors of states and by volunteer commissions. When it was once understood by any command that a boat from their own state lay at the Landing for the reception of the state's sick, it was found impossible to prevent the flocking on board of many whose only complaint was nostalgia. The really sick were left behind, and the convalescent, and often the malingerer, was sent away. When, however, the large hospitals had been once established, these difficulties were remedied. The sick from the regiments were at once received into general hospital, and, when perfectly convalescent, they were returned to duty.…

May 16 (Friday)

In Richmond the panic eased and the citizens breathed a little easier. McClellan made his headquarters at White House, one of the old Lee family dwellings.

Tripler, Charles S., Surg., Army of the Potomac, Peninsular Campaign, Va.:

This being the new base of operations, it was necessary to establish a general hospital there. There were no buildings at all fit for the purpose, so, to meet present necessities, I resorted to the use of tents. A detail of soldiers was ordered to pitch them. It was furnished reluctantly, and was most inefficient. Under the superintendence of Brigade Surg. J. H. Baxter, with one hundred and fifty men, I learned that, after two days' work, there were but thirty-four tents pitched. At the end of four days, one hundred were ready; all that we could command. Cooking cauldrons were got in readiness, subsistence was procured, and bed sacks filled, without delay. The army being again in motion, more sick and a multitude of stragglers rushed in upon us. Our storeships and the hospital transports being up, I detailed the *Daniel Webster, No. 1* to convey a party of the worst cases to Boston.… Two hundred and sixty was the number to be received. Before one-half this number was sent from the hospital, the ship was reported full. Stragglers had rushed on board without authority and had taken possession. I sent a brigade surgeon to expel them but without avail. I then determined to send no more men from the Peninsula on account of sickness, if there were any means of avoiding it.… I am sure that hundreds of malingerers succeeded in deserting their colors on the hospital transports, in spite of every effort of mine to prevent it.… After the two hundred and sixty had left on the *Daniel Webster*, I found ten hundred and twenty in the hospital tents, and of these, nine hundred were reported to me by the medical officers in charge as men with such trifling ailments that they should never have been permitted to fall to the rear.

In the vicinity of Corinth, skirmishes occurred all along the line, with many pickets out on both sides.

May 17 (Saturday)

The 91st New York Vols. finally arrived at Ft. Pickens, Fla., to reinforce the garrison, which held both the major forts and the city of Pensacola.

Peters, D. C., Asst. Surg., USA, Ft. Pickens, Pensacola, Fla.:

On its arrival, the 91st New York Volunteers was in miserable health, but it was gradually improved by attending to the ordinary laws of hygiene and through discipline.... Pensacola is nearly encircled by a swamp, and as the hot weather advances, this marsh, if neglected, dries up, and then commences a bad miasma from decayed animal and vegetable matter. That this might be prevented, measures were taken to dam up the outlets, and only let the water escape gradually. In this manner the health of the city was in a great measure preserved. The principal diseases we had to contend against were intermittent, remittent, and continued fevers, also diarrhea and dysentery; yet, but few cases terminated unfavorably....

May 18 (Sunday)

Boulware, J., Hospital Steward, 6th S.C. Vols., near Richmond:

Have moved along at a slow rate—five miles a day—and lying over two or three days at a time. We are now five miles from Richmond at Laurel Church. I no longer have the sick squad under my care, and glad I am, for no one knows the trouble I have had with it. Capt. Jim Phinney has come to us; also Capt. Lyles of Buckhead. We came to camp very hungry, managed to buy a hen, made a good stew; late at night drew rations. This morning heard an excellent sermon from our chaplain, W. E. Boggs. It was chiefly on the similarity of our contest and that between David and Goliath—the hosts of Israel and the hosts of the Philistine. He exhorted us to rely as David did on the Lord of Hosts.

Mr. Ellison started home this evening. We have just received the mail after being without for several weeks, and I am sad to find no letter for me.

John G. Perry, a Boston native, entered Harvard College in 1858 intending to complete his medical training and become a doctor. Changes in plan required that Harvard be abandoned and the Scientific School be considered, which offered shorter terms and additional areas of study. This course was pursued until the spring of 1862, when the Federal government issued a call for contract surgeons to serve in the hospitals, thus freeing the commissioned military surgeons for duty on the battlefield. In May 1862, Perry left Boston for Ft. Monroe, where he was to report to Surg. Gen. Cuyler for duty.

Perry, John G., Asst. Surg., USV, Chesapeake Hospital, Ft. Monroe, Va.:

I am sitting on the bed of a wounded Confederate, and using paper he kindly offered me.... On our arrival I reported to the brigade surgeon, who promptly said there was neither room for me nor need for my services; still, he would do his best to find me work, and so politely bowed me to the door.... I wandered aimlessly about, conscious, however, that in my pocket were official credentials which entitled me to the position of a government contract assistant surgeon; but there seemed so much red tape to unfold I could hardly find the right end to begin on.

Seeing the door of a cottage ajar, I entered, and found myself in the presence of a surgeon who was hard at work at the operating table, with a number of assistants in attendance. I watched them, the surgeon now and then eyeing me, as if to say, "What the devil are you doing here?" until in the first spare moment he asked my business. I gave him my name, told him what I had come for, and of the rebuff I had just received. At that he laughed, saying, "Never mind, you are just the man needed; we are overloaded with work and help is absolutely necessary; you shall share my quarters, and I will see that you are all right."

This hospital is situated a short distance from the fort and on the Hampton Road. From where I am writing I see many ships of war riding at anchor in the stream, and also the very spot where the battle between the *Merrimac* and the *Monitor* took place. The building holds about seven hundred patients, and is now full; beside it is a cottage, and also some twenty tents, all occupied by sick and wounded Confederates. Dr. Cushing and I have entire charge of these men, who seem in good spirits and are finer looking fellows than our own men here. I hear that the surgeon who served before me, while dressing a soldier's wound, laid the knife down for a moment on the bed. The man seized it and made a lunge at the doctor, but instead of killing him, as he had intended, only ran it into his arm; whereupon the doctor instantly shot him....

May 19 (Monday)

Far up the Shenandoah Valley, at the town of Lynchburg, Va., population of just over 6800, the people of the town met to appoint a committee to "provide for the troops of Lynchburg who may be wounded" during the coming battles. Like many "committees," it accomplished little, being condemned two months later in July, and again in August for its neglect of the wounded after the Battle of Second Manassas.

Boulware, J., Hospital Steward, 6th S.C. Vols., near Richmond:

Slept well last night and began the duties of the day, but it soon began to rain. I dislike rainy weather for we have no tents, and while marching and carrying wet blankets we slip back almost as far as we advance.

May 20 (Tuesday)

Hatchitt, J. G., Surg., USV, Army of the Tennessee, Corinth, Miss.:

May 19th, we had advanced to within three miles of Corinth. A heavy picket firing and a brisk artillery duel commenced....

On May 20th, the medical director of the army of the Tennessee ... ordered me to establish a hospital in the rear of the right wing of the Army of the Mississippi, to accommodate five hundred wounded. I succeeded in getting a supply of medicines, blankets and bed sacks, but not a hospital tent or cooking utensil, except one mess chest, could be had in the department. Twenty old Sibley tents were all that could be obtained for shelter. Nearly a week was consumed in getting the supplies transported to a farmhouse selected for the hospital. Acting Asst. Surgs. W. H. Martin of Indiana, Deforest of Ohio, and Belote of Pine Bluff, Ark., a steward and a cook were detailed to assist me. It so happened that, though frequent details of nurses were made, none ever found their way to the hospital, they, in every instance, being made from parts of the

army two or three miles distant; after wandering a few days through the woods in search of the hospital, they would find their way back to their regiments. The consequence was that on May 31st,... I had three hundred sick delivered at the hospital within a couple of hours without a nurse....

May 21 (Wednesday)

Boulware, J., Hospital Steward, 6th S.C. Vols., near Richmond:

Have just returned from Richmond where I went to find my negro boy, whom I sent from Yorktown side. Got no tidings of him. Found everything very high. Ran the blockade. Paid 75 cents for 1 lb. coffee, 37 cents for sugar, 75 cents quart for molasses, 50 cents for thin cotton socks, $4.50 for a trifling shirt, $1 for a cotton handkerchief, and $2.50 for my dinner.

Tripler, Charles S., Surg., Army of the Potomac, Peninsular Campaign, Va.:

While still at White House, I received a telegram from the front that scurvy had appeared in two brigades of the army, one of which were the regular troops.... Having set the hospital at White House in motion ... I loaded three wagons with hospital supplies, and, on May 21st, started once more in pursuit of the army. I found headquarters at Tunstall's Station.... Here I investigated the report with regard to scurvy, and found it to be erroneous. I, however, requested the Adj. General to compel the men to use desiccated vegetables, and to make and use soup daily, unless that were rendered impossible by reason of being actually on the march....

May 23 (Friday)

Wainwright, Charles S., Maj., N.Y. Artillery, near Bottom's Bridge, Va.:

A damp, cold day, with drizzling rain in the afternoon. We moved up here, some four miles, getting our tents pitched shortly before dark, close to a great tumbledown old house,... which looks as if it might have been a tavern at one time. The house is now used as a hospital by some of Casey's division. Every abandoned house we have come across during the last ten days we have found occupied in this way.... There is a great deal of sickness in the army ... owing to the wetness of the ground, cold rains, and the fact that none of the men are seasoned, or know how to take care of themselves. In fact, the surgeons themselves know little more; many (most of them) being poor hands at their trade and pretty much all treading on new ground....

May 24 (Saturday)

Boulware, J., Hospital Steward, 6th S.C. Vols., near Richmond:

We commenced a hospital in the regiment; John Feaster and Peter Brown detailed as cooks; Pierson, Co. K, as nurse. Dr. Nye came to camp and reported for duty. Raining hard at this time. Have just got hospital affairs working smoothly and hear we are ordered to move tomorrow.

Tripler, Charles S., Surg., Army of the Potomac, Peninsular Campaign, Va.:

On the 23d, I returned to White House, and the next day proceeded to Yorktown to inspect the hospitals there. I found them in want of some articles of clothing and bedding, but generally in good order and well managed. One of these, in the Nelson House, with Miss Dix for housekeeper, was very neat. On my return, I inspected the hospital ships, made arrangements for completing their equipments, and directed the Sanitary Commission to send one thousand shirts, three hundred wrappers, three hundred pairs of slippers, and one thousand sheets to the Yorktown hospital.... I found stragglers still coming into the hospital, some really sick, who said they had been sent by their surgeons. On my return to headquarters, I met one hundred and twenty-five just coming in to Despatch Station to take the train, sent down in ambulances in direct violation of the standing orders of the army. I inspected these men on the spot, and sent a number of them back to their regiments....

May 25 (Sunday)

Boulware, J., Hospital Steward, 6th S.C. Vols., near Drewry's Bluff, Va.:

Camp near Drewry's Bluff. Moved today about two miles; fixed the hospital tents and heard a good sermon from Billy Boggs. He draws vast crowds to hear

him and is worthy of such a crowd. He will certainly do much good, for all seem anxious to hear him. We have a choir and have fine singing.

May 26 (Monday)

Boulware, J., Hospital Steward, 6th S.C. Vols., near Drewry's Bluff, Va.:

Fixed up to visit Drewry's Bluff but a soldier can count on nothing. The rumor is we are again to move, probably around Richmond.

May 27 (Tuesday)

Boulware, J., Hospital Steward, 6th S.C. Vols., on 9-Mile Road, near Richmond, Va.:

Moved camp again this morning to right of city on 9-Mile Road. Day very warm. Several soldiers gave out but came up next day. Our route led by a cemetery—Oak Grove—where mostly South Carolinians and Georgians are buried. The situation is well chosen and beautifully laid out and planted with trees of various kinds. It covers ten or twelve acres. Most of the graves seem fresh. Very few have marble headstones, yet all have boards with name, company, regiment and state. So by referring to the keeper's book, anyone may find the grave of relative or friend. I could not but think as I passed: "Here lies buried the hopes of many a dear friend."

Wainwright, Charles S., Maj., N.Y. Artillery, near Bottom's Bridge, Va.:

The worst is the awful amount of sickness in the army, amounting to a full quarter of our total force.... We have but 68,000 effective men now, Keye's whole corps not reaching 12,000. It is not nearly so bad in my own batteries, not more than one in ten being reported sick....

Tripler, Charles S., Surg., Army of the Potomac, Peninsular Campaign, Va.:

May 27th, Gen. F. J. Porter fought and defeated the enemy at Hanover Courthouse.... Ambulances were promptly sent for the wounded, and hospitals prepared for them in William Gaines's and Hogan's houses and outhouses. Hogan's house being under fire, I was afterwards obliged to remove the wounded prisoners to Dr. Gaines's buildings.... I requested Col. Ingalls to order the steamer *Knickerbocker* to be in readiness to receive them on May 30th. I also directed the *Elm City* to carry four hundred sick from White House to Yorktown. These boats were in possession of the Sanitary Commission and neither of them [was] ready. I then directed our own boat, the *Commodore*, to be placed in condition to receive the wounded, and requested Surg. H. H. Smith to take the general direction of affairs at that point. I then substituted the *Daniel Webster, No. 2,* for the *Elm City* to convey the sick....

May 28 (Wednesday)

Perry, John G., Asst. Surg., USV, Chesapeake Hospital, Ft. Monroe, Va.:

On one of the beds there lies, fast asleep, a Confederate surgeon, a thoroughbred South Carolinian, who had never, before the war, crossed beyond his own state's lines. He was captured with a number of others in the last engagement before Richmond, and as most of these men were wounded, he was detailed to care for them. Dressed entirely in Alabama homespun, which is the ugliest snuff-colored stuff imaginable, a broad-brimmed planter's hat covering his head, and stained with mud and blood from head to foot, the appearance of this officer when he first arrived was strange enough; but his face was bright and intelligent.

His greeting was unexpected: "I am delighted to meet men from Massachusetts, for I know I shall find in them intelligence and hospitality"; and he certainly did find the latter, for we furnished him throughout with clothes. He enjoys reading the Boston newspapers, and we have many pleasant chats together, for I find he is anxious to discover for himself the true state of affairs at the North, and whether the Yankee hordes are such bloodhounds as he has been taught to consider them....

About sundown last night I was walking on the beach quietly smoking my pipe, when I saw something which proved to be the body of a man floating on the water just at the edge of the shore. I pulled it upon the beach, covered it with seaweed, and then reported the incident.... The provost marshal ... recognized the body as that of one of the unfortunates who was drowned when the *Cumberland* was sunk by the *Merrimac*."

May 29 (Thursday)

After all the waiting and watching at Corinth, nothing happened! Beauregard decided to quit the bout before the first bell rang, and ordered a pullout. To cover the withdrawal, he had the frontline troops make loud noises to keep the Federals occupied.

Boulware, J., Hospital Steward, 6th S.C. Vols., on 9-Mile Road, near Richmond, Va.:

Went to Richmond today looking for brother Frank's boy, whom we sent off sick from Yorktown a month ago. Found him in the African hospital in an unfrequented part of the city. He was recovering from an attack of typhoid fever and [he] rejoiced to see me.

May 30 (Friday)

Halleck, positioned a few miles north of Corinth, was completely oblivious to the fact that Beauregard had moved his entire army towards Tupelo, and that there was only a thin screen between the Union and the retreating Confederates. Halleck proclaimed it a victory, others didn't.

May 31 (Saturday)

McClellan had one corps north of the Chickahominy and two south of that river. Joe Johnston's Confederates attacked the two corps at Fair Oaks (or Seven Pines). Several mistakes caused delays, and the attack didn't pick up momentum until 1 P.M., and even then the contact was spotty. The Rebel drive got stopped when Gen. Sumner, not waiting for McClellan's order, moved his corps into the battle. At this point a chance bullet changed the way the war would be fought from this time forward in the eastern theatre.

Gen. Joseph Eggleston Johnston was wounded, and Robert E. Lee was given command of the Army of Northern Virginia the next day (June 1st). During the night the Federals brought in more troops and strengthened their positions.

Boulware, J., Hospital Steward, 6th S.C. Vols., Battle of Fair Oaks, Va.:

Last night we had as hard a rain as I ever heard fall. The water flooded nearly every bed in camp. Aroused early this morning and ordered to pack up for a march, leaving most of the baggage behind. We had no idea where we were going, but after travelling a mile or two we guessed our destination. We entered the battle about two o'clock. Our boys soon began to fall and were brought to the rear. Those who were able came themselves. 'Twas a sad sight for so many of our bosom friends were brought horribly mutilated.

5 o'clock P.M. Our brigade has gone more than a mile driving the enemy before them. Night came and with it came silence, except groans of the wounded and cries for help. The wounded were not all brought in until late at night. I closed my eyes for only one hour that night.

Brown, H. E., Surg., USA, Hooker's Div., Battle of Seven Pines (Fair Oaks), Va.:

At the commencement of this engagement, the general depot for wounded of the division was established at a house directly in the rear of the field, where the action commenced on Sunday.... The wounded were brought in first on stretchers, but afterwards, as the tide of battle receded, in ambulances. The want of a properly instructed ambulance corps was severely felt here, as well as at all subsequent engagements which came under my notice. The regular hospital attendants were needed as cooks and assistants at the general depot, and the bands of the various regiments proved to be worthless in bringing off the wounded, behaving with the utmost cowardice, and required more persons to watch and see that they did their duty than their services were worth. As a natural consequence of this, whenever a man fell out of the line wounded, four, and sometimes six of his comrades, would fall out for the purpose of carrying him away, thus seriously depleting the ranks, and affording opportunity to the skulkers and cowards to sneak away.

The supplies for the wounded were abundant and the arrangements were excellent. A fine well on the spot furnished water, an outhouse was converted into a kitchen and supply store, and a competent man was placed in charge. Soup, coffee, and crackers were ready at all hours for such as needed them.... The only articles deficient were chloroform and ether; and that, I think, was not due to any neglect, but to the fact of the unusually large number of wounded....

There was one case of bayonet wound, and this man had two wounds from gunshot and five bayonet

wounds; and these last, he asserted, he received while lying on the field after being wounded.... The wounded after being attended to, were placed in ambulances and removed to Savage's Station, to be sent thence, by railroad, to White House, for transportation north....

Tripler, Charles S., Surg., Army of the Potomac, Peninsular Campaign, Va.:

It was intended to remove the remainder of the wounded the next day, but a heavy rain coming on, we were obliged to defer it. That day, at 2 P.M., the enemy attacked our left flank at Fair Oaks. The action lasted till nightfall.

Hammond, J. F., Surg., Second Army Corps, Army of the Potomac, Fair Oaks, Va.:

At the battle of Fair Oaks the Second Corps numbered more than twenty-two thousand men. The primary dressings were applied by the medical officers who accompanied the troops into the fight.... The wounded were thence transported to the houses nearest the battlefield, where, after filling the rooms, they were placed upon the ground outside of the houses, and bowers were built over them. Here those who had not been dressed where they fell, had their wounds cared for, and, in other cases, dressings were reapplied or readjusted. The attention they received was all that could be rendered them by the medical officers of the corps. Without exception, the latter were incessant in their efforts to relieve the wounded, and no body of men whatever could be more faithful in the discharge of their duties.

The supply of water was sufficient and good. Food was scarce, as we had left camp with but two days' rations in the haversacks, and wagons were not allowed to accompany the troops, and all supplies were cut off by the freshet in the Chickahominy, the loss of the bridges, and the state of the roads. The supply of canned soups was inadequate, and I found it necessary to give orders, with the approval of Gen. Sumner, to slaughter horses for soup for the wounded. The weather was cool at night and warm at midday, and much rain fell before the wounded were removed to White House.

All the ambulances of the corps were absent, detached by orders from general headquarters, before we crossed the Chickahominy, to transport the wounded of Gen. Porter's battle at Hanover Court-house. The medical director of the Army of the Potomac sent a medical officer to assure me that transportation by the railroad would be afforded the next day. It was agreed that the cars should arrive at the near-station at noon, the following day, prepared to take all of my wounded at once, and I was required to have them all at the station at that time. The removal of them was commenced at daylight, and they were at the railroad at the appointed hour; but the destruction of a part of the railroad by the rain, which fell in torrents, and the timidity of the conductors prevented the cars from taking the wounded for more than forty-eight hours after the time appointed.... Most of the wounded went on foot from the field to the field hospitals; the balance were all transported on hand litters. They were removed from the field hospitals to the cars, a mile or more, on foot or in ambulances, a few of which had then arrived, on hand litters and on horse litters. The horse litters, which permitted the recumbent position, served admirably for transporting the most painfully wounded....

O'Leary, Charles, Surg., USV, Brigade Surg., Army of the Potomac, Peninsula, Va.:

On May 31st, 1862, the battle of Seven Pines, the bloodiest I have witnessed during the war, was fought.... The utterly demoralized condition of Gen. Casey's troops, who straggled from the field and crowded every place wearing the appearance of a hospital was another difficulty. Better organization of the medical corps would have, as it has since, prevented most of these evils.... The wounds were generally of a slight character, being chiefly of round ball and buckshot.... During the two days subsequent to the action, many medical men from civil life flocked to the ground, and, owing to the absence of any hospital organization in the corps, went to work as they thought proper. The abuse of the authority they had obtained was more apparent than in any battle I have seen. Amputations were performed recklessly, by irresponsible persons, without any thought bestowed as to the subsequent treatment of the patient. It was chance, or accident, frequently, that the wounded man whose limb had been amputated obtained either an opiate or stimulant. Some, exhausted by lying on the field wounded from twelve to thirty-six hours, died on the table; some within a few hours after the

operation. I was placed in charge by Surg. F. H. Hamilton, but received no authority from him to stop a course that seemed to him and to me reckless and unjustifiable. His impression was that these men were there by order of the War Dept.... The last of the wounded of the Fourth Corps, amounting to about eleven hundred, were removed to White House four days after the battle.

Hatchitt, J. G., Surg., USV, Army of the Tennessee, Corinth, Miss.:

The regimental surgeons, supposing the hospital was in readiness, ordered their ambulances to take the sick to me. When the ambulances arrived, the surgeons and all who could help were several miles distant with their regiments. However, bed sacks were soon filled with hay, camp kettles from deserted camps, and every species of pot, etc., from the Rebel fortifications, some two miles distant, were gathered up, and nourishment, as good as army rations could make, was provided.... Water became very scarce.... Diarrhea and dysentery were the prevailing diseases. All being under malarial influences, it was necessary to administer quinine and whiskey freely....

June 1 (Sunday)

East of Richmond, near the Chickahominy the last day of the Battle of Seven Pines (Fair Oaks) was being fought. Lee was in charge, effective this morning, and by 3 P.M. had decided to have his troops withdraw to their original lines, having gained nothing except to increase the casualty list on both sides. The South had sustained more than 6000 new casualties, which was about 1000 more than the North had suffered. Both sides decided to wait.

Boulware, J., Hospital Steward, 6th S.C. Vols., Battle of Fair Oaks, Va.:

When the sun arose we had begun our work of getting off the wounded to York River Railroad. In two hours this work was done and we betook ourselves to the battleground where occasional firing was going on. Soon all was quiet and remained so all day.

The day was quite warm. I lost a great many of my friends in the engagement. Poor Jimmy Weir! I was sorry to lose him. In J. W. Phinney our regiment lost one of its best captains and the company lost its all.

Tripler, Charles S., Surg., Army of the Potomac, Peninsular Campaign, Va.:

It [the fighting] was resumed the next morning, and continued till 11 A.M. Immediately after the commencement of the battle, the boats at White House were ordered to be in readiness.... The transportation of the wounded was begun that night and kept up steadily until completed.... The whole number sent from White House by the steamers was three thousand five hundred and eighty. Of these, one hundred and sixty-seven were conveyed to Philadelphia by the *William Whilden*.

Edmonds, S. Emma E., Union field nurse, Battle of Fair Oaks, Va.:

On the evening of the same day in which the victory was won I visited what was then, and is still called, the "hospital tree," near Fair Oaks. It was an immense tree under whose shady, extended branches the wounded were carried and laid down to await the stimulant, the opiate, or the amputating knife, as the case might require. The ground around that tree for several acres in extent was literally drenched with human blood, and the men were laid so close together that there was no such thing as passing between them; but each one was removed in their turn as the surgeons could attend to them.... Those wounded, but not mortally—how nobly they bore the necessary probings and needed amputations ...!

Jones, John B., Rebel War Clerk, Confederate War Dept., Richmond, Va.:

The ambulances are now bringing in the enemy's wounded as well as our own. It is the prompting of humanity. They seem truly grateful for this magnanimity, as they call it, a sentiment hitherto unknown to them.

All day the wounded were borne past our boardinghouse in Third Street, to the general hospital; and hundreds, with shattered arms and slight flesh wounds, came in on foot. I saw a boy, not more than fifteen years old (from South Carolina), with his hand in a sling. He showed me his wound. A ball had entered between the fingers of his left hand and lodged near the wrist, where the flesh was much swollen. He said, smiling, "I'm going to the hospital just to have the ball cut out, and will then return to the battlefield. I can fight with my right hand...."

To the west, in the Shenandoah Valley, there was activity around Winchester, Va. Since early May, this area had gone from one side to the other. Surg. J. B. Peale, USV, had organized a hospital in the Union Hotel within the town on the 4th of May, and business had been brisk since then.

Peale, J. B., Surg., USV, hospital in Winchester, Va.:

On the 20th, I had but twelve patients remaining, all others having been sent to New Creek Station. On May 23d, some wounded were brought from Front Royal. On the evening of the 24th, two hundred and thirty patients were brought in from Strasburg, but nearly all started off early next morning, alarmed by the near approach of the enemy.

At eight o'clock A.M., on the 25th, the retreat of Gen. Banks's forces commenced. The quartermaster's storehouse, opposite the hospital, was fired, and the danger to the hospital was imminent. I had the patients placed in the yard. The Rebels, taking possession of the town, placed a guard over the hospital. Great praise is due the nurses for their determination to remain with the sick. Surg. Black, acting medical director of the Confederate force, called on me to say that I should continue unmolested in the care of the sick. On the 25th, thirty-three wounded were admitted to the hospital, and thirty-eight more on the 26th. On the 27th, Surg. Black instructed me that I should remain in charge of the hospital as surgeon-in-chief, with Surg. E. L. Bissell, 5th Connecticut Volunteers as assistant. Patients continued to come in all day, and the aggregate, at last, numbered three hundred and thirty. Surg. Black permitted me to detail sixty-four attendants from the prisoners, and [to obtain] Confederate commissary-issued provisions on my requisitions, so that all went on well to May 31st, except that I had no means to procure milk, eggs, or other delicacies for the wounded.

On the 31st, the Rebel provost marshal sent an officer to parole the patients in the hospital, who, with the attendants, signed a paper, a copy of which is forwarded. The Rebels then evacuated the town, removing the guard from the hospital and leaving no provisions. On June 1st, a small guerrilla party made us all prisoners again, and placed us in close confinement. There were nine deaths among the patients in hospital. The medical officers present were Surg. F. Leland, 2d

Mass. Volunteers, Surg. T. E. Mitchell, 1st Maryland Volunteers, Asst. Surg. P. Adolphus, USA, Asst. Surg. L. R. Stone, Asst. Surg. J. F. Day, Asst. Surg. E. L. Bissell, all of whom lent all the aid in their power.

June 2 (Monday)

At Fair Oaks, east of Richmond, the cleanup of the battlefield began with the burial of the dead and the gathering of scattered equipment.

Boulware, J., Hospital Steward, 6th S.C. Vols., Battle of Fair Oaks, Va.:

Returned to camp well worn-out and having little to eat. I wrote five letters today, of course, short, as I wished to give my correspondents a sketch of what had been done in the fight.

Brown, H. E., Surg., USA, Hooker's Div., aftermath of the Battle of Seven Pines (Fair Oaks), Va.:

On Monday, June 2d, the enemy having been driven from the battlefield, the general depot was moved two miles farther in front, and many of the wounded who had lain forty-eight hours on the field were here attended to. These poor unfortunates were in a most pitiable condition, weak and faint from loss of blood and want of food, and nearly dead of the horrible thirst which their wounds and the hot sun had produced; and to add to their misery, maggots appeared in large numbers in their wounds. These men were tenderly cared for, as far as means would allow, and forwarded, like the rest, to White House....

June 3 (Tuesday)

Spencer Glasgow Welch was born in Newberry Co., S.C., on March 12, 1834. He was educated at Furman University and graduated from Jefferson Medical College in Philadelphia. He married Cordelia Strother, a graduate of Old Barham Girls School, Columbia, S.C., on February 13, 1861, at "Fruit Hill," the Strother family home in Edgefield (now Saluda) Co., S.C. He arrived in Virginia with the 20th South Carolina Volunteer Regiment and was sent to Fredericksburg, Va., with his brigade.

Welch, S. G., Surg., 20th S.C. Vols., Battle of Ellyson's Mills, Va.:

Our army whipped the Yankees so badly on Saturday and Sunday (May 28-29) that there was no fighting

yesterday.... On Sunday I was sent to Richmond to look after our sick and did not return until late yesterday afternoon. While there I had an opportunity to observe the shocking results of battle.... Our casualties were certainly very great, for every house which could be had was being filled with the wounded. Even the depots were being filled with them and they came pouring into the hospitals by the wagon loads. Nearly all were covered with mud, as they had fought in a swamp most of the time and lay out all night after being wounded. Many of them were but slightly wounded, many others severely, large numbers mortally, and some would die on the road from the battlefield. In every direction the slightly wounded were seen with their arms in slings, their heads tied up, or limping about. One man appeared as if he had been entirely immersed in blood, yet he could walk. Those in the hospitals had received severe flesh wounds or had bones broken, or some vital part penetrated. They did not seem to suffer much and but a few ever groaned, but they will suffer when the reaction takes place. I saw one little fellow whose thigh was broken. He was a mere child, but was very cheerful....

Boulware, J., Hospital Steward, 6th S.C. Vols., Battle of Fair Oaks, Va.:

Again ordered to march [carrying] two days' rations, and thought we were in for another battle, but halted on Charles City Road and lay all night in drenching rain. I had the good fortune to occupy a place in an ambulance and kept dry. Next day was cloudy and we remained in the same position.

Wainwright, Charles S., Maj., N.Y. Artillery, near Savage's Station, Va.:

I was about used up when we got back to camp last night, and today am what I suppose is called absolutely sick.... Have turned over my command to Capt. de Russy of the Fourth Artillery....

I went back to the station to spend the day with Dr. Evarts, who has his tent pitched there. Found the doctor as miserable as myself, but as he had nothing to do we managed to work through the day. He has been hard at it night and day ever since Saturday noon. Near 1100 wounded men passed through his tent in twenty-four hours; some four or five civilian surgeons aided him. The medical director of Casey's division seems to be quite worthless, so that Evarts had to go on his own hook entirely....

June 4 (Wednesday)

Federal authorities sent a telegram to the Sisters of Charity Central House in Emmitsburg, Md., requesting nurses be sent to Frederick City (now Frederick), Md., to assist in the hospital. Unfortunately, there were only three Sisters available at Emmitsburg at the time, but seven more were assembled from the various Catholic schools and academies around Baltimore. Upon arrival at Frederick, they found their quarters had been established in an old stone barracks used during the Revolutionary War. The room contained ten beds so closely placed together that little space was left for walking. An old, rickety table and three chairs completed the furniture in the quarters. Their rations were issued by the military and [were] served on broken dishes. Their utensils were rusty knives and forks—the same utensils used by the patients who often joked that they got their daily dose of iron in that manner. The Sisters set to work cleaning up the patients and tending to their needs.

June 5 (Thursday)

Tripler, Charles S., Surg., Army of the Potomac, Peninsular Campaign, Va.:

A very large number of Rebels, killed at Fair Oaks, were interred by our troops; yet many more were left unburied. They had fallen in the woods, or had been carried thither, and escaped observation. In the course of time, the remains were so offensive as to seriously discommode our camps. Disinfectants were sent to be strewn over the grounds, and every exertion was made to abate this evil. Still it had not entirely ceased when we left the vicinity.

June 6 (Friday)

Earlier in this year, Wilmington, N.C., had begun a fund to pay for an ironclad to defend the city from the Union fleet, which had taken up the blockade of the port. Salisbury, a city in the western part of the state, raised some money for this purpose. However, it was decided in this month to use the money to provide and equip a "wayside hospital" near the local railroad station to serve the Confederate wounded who passed through on their way home to heal from wounds or sickness. The passing soldiers could receive meals and obtain overnight lodging, if needed. Medical treatment was available to a limited degree. Within a year, by May of 1863, more than 1500 soldiers would have been guests at this facility.

Memphis, Tenn., fell to the Union on this date. The Federal fleet under command of Commodore Charles Davis sailed down the Mississippi and engaged the Confederate ships below the bluffs of the city, which were lined with citizens from Memphis who'd come to watch the Federals be defeated. The fight became a free-for-all, with gunboats and rams going in every direction, either running or attacking. After an initial assault by the rams, the gunboats took over the action and blasted the Confederate ships, few of which escaped. The Confederates also lost five large transports and other vessels in the process of being built. The battle lasted only two hours and was completed by 7:30 A.M. Most of the spectators lining the bluff went home, many in tears. At 11 A.M., the mayor surrendered the city. Federal troops that had been a part of the flotilla occupied the city and mounted guards. The Mississippi was now open all the way to Vicksburg, Miss.

June 8 (Sunday)

Charles Wainwright had taken ill with dysentery, which debilitated and weakened him, as well as causing a marked weight loss.

Wainwright, Charles S., Maj., N.Y. Artillery, in hospital on the Peninsula:

On Wednesday Dr. Simm, our medical director, advised me to go apply for a sick leave, and gave me a certificate; but I thought then I should get better after a little while. In that I have been mistaken, as I have grown very weak, and worse each day. Today I have sent up my application and hope to get a leave by tomorrow....

June 10 (Tuesday)

The hot weather had created much discomfort in the panhandle of Florida, and the diseases which were prevalent at that time of the year appeared.

Peters, D. C., Asst. Surg., USA, Ft. Pickens, Pensacola, Fla.:

… the Dengue or breakbone fever made its appearance, and was a troublesome complaint during the remainder of the season. As it is considered a precursor of the yellow fever, every precaution was now taken to prevent that terrible scourge from making its appearance. The medical director issued stringent quarantine laws, which were faithfully carried out; and thus our garrison escaped to a certain extent, although, accidentally, the fever came near being forced upon us.

At Mobile, the disease was reported to be raging at a fearful rate, having been introduced there, it was said, by a Rebel steamer called the *Oreto*, afterwards the *Florida*, which ran the blockade, and brought the disease from Havana. At Key West, yellow fever was causing sad havoc, and a naval officer, on his way to join Admiral Farragut's fleet, touched there, contracted the seeds of the disease, and on reporting on board the flagship *Hartford*, at the Pensacola navy yard, was taken down with it, and soon died. Others were soon affected, and several of these cases, I understood, terminated fatally. The close proximity of the navy yard to our forces rendered our danger extreme, yet we escaped with the loss of only one man.

He was a regular soldier, and was seized with symptoms of the fever early in the morning, and died in the hospital under my charge the same day. I made a postmortem, and found pathological conditions which satisfied me of the man's true complaint. For reasons of policy, knowing that the fear of disease predisposes men to it, I kept my own counsel, destroyed the man's clothing, used antiseptics freely, and, in fine, employed every means in my power to prevent the fever spreading.… Before closing the subject of yellow fever, I would here state that the island of Santa Rosa could be rendered available to troops serving in the Dept. of the Gulf, as a place of safe refuge, in case they either have or are threatened with this terrible epidemic. There is no spot on the western coast of Florida more favorable for establishing a large general hospital.…

June 12 (Thursday)

Wainwright, Charles S., Maj., N.Y. Artillery, Baltimore, Md.:

My leave came on Monday afternoon, and as Dickenson sent over an ambulance with [the leave] we left at once for Savage's Station. After remaining there … for several hours, we got down to "White House" by a return train, and there went on board one of the hospital boats for the night.… It commenced to rain before we got down to White House, and rained all night and the next day; indeed, it has done little else than rain ever since this month commenced.… There were a lot of volunteer women nurses on board, ladies I suppose I ought to call them, who no doubt wanted to be very kind, but I would rather they had left me alone. In the afternoon, however, Mrs. Joe Howland came over from another boat to see me, and did me a world of good. I wonder whether most of the sick men appreciate the difference between a real lady and one so called.…

June 14 (Saturday)

Availability of qualified medical officers was always a problem, both North and South. Both sides used contract physicians to fill in the gaps where possible, especially in stationary hospitals. At this stage of the war, however, the patriotic zeal of some of the doctors led them to contract with the field armies, where they found that amputating limbs and plugging bullet holes wasn't quite like treating nine-year-old Alice Smith's running nose. Surg. Tripler found many of the contract physicians leaving the army for more genial climes.

Tripler, Charles S., Surg., Army of the Potomac, Peninsular Campaign, Va.:

… scurvy was again reported as having appeared in Sumner's corps. I sent an able medical officer to investigate it, who found six cases in the 19th and 20th Mass. regiments, and several others.…

At this time, I found it necessary to ask that [the section] of General Orders 102, March 19th, 1862, [which] authorized commanders of corps to grant leaves of absence for fifteen days to medical officers should be rescinded. Fifteen days would take them home, but it was a rare thing to find them at their posts at the expiration of it. Notwithstanding we had under contract nearly a hundred civilian physicians, the regiments were scarcely much better provided that when we began to fill vacancies in this way. Several of the contract physicians themselves soon repented of their bargains and begged to be relieved. As their contracts could be determined at their own pleasure, I could only refuse to terminate them myself, but could not prevent their doing so. To obviate this inconvenience for a reasonable time at least, I wrote to the Surgeon General to request him, for the future, to stipulate with these gentlemen that they should not terminate their contracts in less than three months. My suggestion was adopted, and we were thus enabled to retain several who would otherwise have left us.

June 15 (Sunday)

Perry, John G., Asst. Surg., USV, Chesapeake Hospital, Ft. Monroe, Va.:

This afternoon I collected all my convalescents in the kitchen of the cottage, placed them about a blazing fire, for it was chilly and raining hard outside—and started the singing of Methodist hymns. The music caught like an epidemic, and soon from every side came doctors, nurses, patients, negroes, until we had a rousing chorus. All of them sang with their whole souls, each one asking for his favorite hymn, and the concert ended with "Old Hundred." How I did enjoy it!

Hatchitt, J. G., Surg., USV, Army of the Tennessee, Corinth, Miss.:

On June 15th, I was ordered to move this hospital into Corono Female College building at Corinth … the most pleasant locality in that vicinity. At this place, with the help of convalescents, we erected a bakery that supplied an excellent article of bread for five hundred patients. There were over eight hundred in this hospital during the month of June.…

June 16 (Monday)

Tripler, Charles S., Surg., Army of the Potomac, Peninsular Campaign, Va.:

June 12th, the headquarters were removed to the right bank of the Chickahominy, near Dr. Trent's house.… On the 13th, the enemy made a raid to our rear, doing but little harm; our railway communications were not interrupted. On the 15th, the roads [being dry enough], I succeeded in transferring the remainder of the Hanover wounded to the floating hospitals at White House. June 16th, I took measures for providing a receiving hospital for the wounded at Savage's Station.…

June 17 (Tuesday)

In the west, Gen. Braxton Bragg, Sherman's old friend, was named to command the Confederates now facing Grant and Buell. Beauregard left the army ill and feeling mistreated.

June 19 (Thursday)

Tripler, Charles S., Surg., Army of the Potomac, Peninsular Campaign, Va.:

June 19th, I authorized Mr. F. L. Olmsted to fill the steamer *Daniel Webster, No. 1* and the steamer *Spaulding* from White House and Yorktown hospitals and to proceed with them to New York.

Jonathan Letterman, surgeon in the U.S. Army, was assigned as the Medical Director of the Army of the Potomac, succeeding Surg. Charles Tripler, USA, who'd been nominated as the Medical Inspector-General of the United States Army.

Letterman was born in Canonsburg, Washington County, Pa., on December 11, 1824. His father was a surgeon and practitioner of medicine in western Pennsylvania and trained his son in medicine until the young man entered Jefferson College in 1842. Letterman entered Jefferson Medical College in Philadelphia in March 1849. That same year he passed the Army Medical Board in New York and was appointed an assistant surgeon in the army, as of June 29, 1849.

Letterman served in several posts during the next several years, including duty against the Seminole Indians in Florida, duty on the frontier in Minnesota, a long march from Ft. Leavenworth, Kansas, to New Mexico for duty at Ft. Defiance, and action against the Gila Apaches with Col. W. W. Loring (later a general in the Confederate Army). He returned east on a leave of absence after four years on the frontier. In 1859 he was at Ft. Monroe, Va., and 1860 found him in California with the expedition against the Paiute Indians. In 1861 he returned to New York and was assigned as Medical Director of the Dept. of western Virginia in May 1862, serving there until June 19.

June 20 (Friday)

Gen. James Longstreet of Lee's Army of Northern Virginia wrote to the governor of Virginia that Longstreet's command had 23 Virginia regiments, one battalion, and 17 batteries with an assigned strength of 32,000 men, but only 20,000 were on the morning rolls. Of the latter, about 7000 were absent, leaving only 13,000 of the 32,000. The largest regiment contained only 691 men and the smallest less than 100 present for duty. The toll of dead and wounded, as well as the sick list, following the Battle of Fair Oaks had severely depleted the Confederate command.

Tripler, Charles S., Surg., Army of the Potomac, Peninsular Campaign, Va.:

On the 20th, I visited White House again and inspected the arrangements. I met there Mr. Brunot, of Pittsburgh, Pa., who had come on with a party of well qualified nurses, to offer their services. No more devoted band; none, perhaps, so devoted, had ever presented themselves. I quartered them temporarily upon the hospital steamer *Louisiana*. At the right time, they repaired to Savage's Station, performed ever memorable service, and crowned their self-sacrifice by cheerfully remaining with the wounded we were obliged to leave in the hands of the enemy when we retired to [the] James River.

June 21 (Saturday)

Tripler, Charles S., Surg., Army of the Potomac, Peninsular Campaign, Va.:

Returning to headquarters on June 21st,... I sent an order to the purveyor at White House to send a large quantity of supplies to Savage's Station. By telegraph, I received the reply that all was packed up and [that] the boat [had been] ordered to fall back to West Point. This was exceedingly vexatious. We were tolerably well supplied, and I had,... a reserve of three wagon loads in my own camp; nevertheless, this misunderstanding was a great disappointment, and caused me much anxiety. In a few days the boat returned. As soon as I heard of this, I repeated my order of June 21st, and telegraphed to the Sanitary Commission to send up supplies. The effort was made, but too late....

June 23 (Monday)

With the evacuation of Pensacola went most of the professional personnel—doctors, lawyers, city administrators, etc., This left a large void which had to be filled somehow.

Peters, D. C., Asst. Surg., USA, Ft. Pickens, Pensacola, Fla.:

In addition to the regular duties devolving upon me, in attending to the regular battalion at Pensacola, I was directed ... to give my professional service to the citizens of the city, and supply them with all necessary medicines. The physicians belonging to the city had taken their departure, and some were serving in the Rebel army. In giving my services to these poor people, mostly women and children, I found them ever grateful, and it was a source of satisfaction to me to aid in alleviating their sufferings. The number of cases treated by me, among the citizens, far exceeded the same among the soldiery, and my time, especially at night, was fully occupied. I found intermittent, bilious, and remittent fevers were more common in this locality than I had supposed, as my opinions had been formed on this subject from medical works....

June 25 (Wednesday)

The Seven Days' Battle began today when McClellan ordered his forward units to advance on his left flank, which, he said, was to be a general movement forward. The Federal troops of Gen. Samuel Heintzelman's corps clashed with the Confederates of Gen. Ben Huger, and a smart little fight began.

Brown, H. E., Surg., USA, Hooker's Div., Battle of Seven Days, Va.:

Until June 25th, I was engaged with the duties of the regiment, encamped on the battlefield of May 31st.... A more horrible place for a camp could not be conceived. Over three thousand dead had been buried there; the ground was covered with the remains of clothing and commissary stores. Dead horses, which had been insufficiently buried or burnt, filled the air with a noxious effluvium, and the only water was that obtained from the surface by digging down a few feet, and this infiltrated with the decaying animal matter of the battlefield. The duties of the men were very laborious, enough to break down a strong man under the most favorable circumstances.... It is not to be wondered that sickness broke out in the command. So far as my observation went, it took chiefly the form of a low typhoid diarrhea or dysentery, which did not yield in the least to ordinary remedies for these diseases. The prescription which I found of most value was a powder composed of five grains of the mercury and chalk of the pharmacopoeia, six grains of Dover's powder, and two grains of sulphate of quina, administered several times a day, according to circumstances....

On June 25th ... a severe engagement took place, which lasted about six hours.... Our depot for the wounded in this engagement was placed at Peach Orchard Station, on the railroad, and about half a mile in the rear of the field of battle.... During the engagement I took two hundred wounded to the White House on railcars. On my return, the battle of Gaines' Mill had been fought and lost, and the order for retreat was in contemplation. The enemy had appeared at Bottom's Bridge, threatening the hospitals in that vicinity. I was detailed by Gen. Hooker to proceed thither, and to break up the hospital of his division, and to proceed with such of the men as could travel to the nearest point on the James River, and to await further orders....

Leadbetter, M. T., Pvt., Co. C, 5th Alabama Battalion, Gaines' Mill, Va.:

On the evening of June 25, 1862, near sunset, our brigade received orders to cook rations and be ready to march at a moment's warning. On that order we boys began to hustle, for we believed that a big battle was upon us.... Before we had time to start fires even, we received orders to "fall in!" "fall in!".... We were directed also to relieve ourselves of all baggage....

The "god of day" was now setting behind the western horizon. All nature seemed to be draped in mourning. It was indeed a solemn time.... We marched all night slowly, occasionally halting. The entire army seemed to be on the move.... We continued our march until about noon the next day, when we halted and laid down by the roadside. I dropped down by my flag, and was so worn-out that I was soon sound asleep. Oh, I was sleeping so good! Suddenly I was awakened from my sweet rest by some of the boys "pounding" me in the side. "Get up! Get up! there is a big battle raging and we are

getting ready to go into it." We moved off in the direction of heavy firing. Cannons were booming and small arms could be heard distinctly.... The casualties of my old battalion were very heavy.... Many of the boys were killed in trying to get through. I had to wrap my flag around the staff while crawling through this abatis.

My flag was riddled in this battle, having been pierced with ten bullet holes through its folds, while a splinter was torn out of the staff, about six inches above my head, I came out, though, with a [just a] "scratch." When the firing ceased, our lines fell back a short distance, in a thick woods, and [we] huddled around talking over the various incidents of the battle. I soon went to sleep and knew nothing more until morning....

June 26 (Thursday)

The second day of the Seven Days' Battle began with sharp fighting around Mechanicsville, when Gen. A. P. Hill attacked at 3 P.M. after waiting for Jackson to come up. Hill's troops pushed through Mechanicsville, and the Federals fell back into strong prepared positions. Hill threw his men at the position and the attack failed. Jackson was still not on the field. During the night the Federals withdrew to other prepared positions around Gaines' Mill and McClellan ordered supplies moved to the James in the vicinity of Harrison's Landing. McClellan asked for more troops.

Leadbetter, M. T., Pvt., Co. C, 5th Alabama Battalion, Gaines' Mill, Va.:

Early that morning the enemy shelled the woods we were in furiously, cutting the branches of trees off over our heads.... They kept up this terrific cannonade about one hour.... About nine o'clock we moved out,... going over a considerable portion of the battlefield. I well remember passing over that part of the field, near Meadow Bridge, where it was said Gen. Lee led a charge in person. I saw many of our soldiers near this famous bridge stuck in the bog up to their knees and dead. We passed over this bridge and pursued the enemy on to Gaines' Mill. Here we found them strongly protected behind triple lines of heavy earthworks, with head logs to protect them.... The little knoll afforded very little protection, but we used it for all it was worth.... Finally a courier galloped up to Gen. Archer, delivered a message and then galloped off. Then the general walked in front of us and gave the command, "Attention!" At this command the whole line arose. The next command was "Forward, march." We moved out in regular line of battle towards the enemy's impregnable lines of breastworks.... An incessant fire was being poured into our lines.... Gen. Archer waved his sword over his head and gave the command, "Follow me!" That command was ringing in my ears when I was shot.

I moved on—my color guard was near me—until within about fifteen or twenty paces of their front line, when I looked back to see if the boys were coming; just then I was shot through my right hip. I did not know how badly I was wounded; I only knew that I was shot down.... I determined to make the effort to get away. I got up, but I found I could not walk, and if I made the trip at all I would have to drag my leg. I grasped my wounded leg with my right hand and started. Just then I saw four of the boys lying down, but I could not tell whether they were all dead or not. I made my way back, dragging my leg, under galling fire, when a minnie ball struck my left wrist and tore it up and took off my thumb at the same time. I mended my gait a little toward a deep gully. Before I reached it I looked back to see if the "Yanks" were coming, and just at that moment a ball drew a little from under my chin. A few more hops and I tumbled down into the deep gully. I wanted to stay there, but the boys insisted that as I was badly wounded I had better try and get to the rear or I would be captured. That scared me up.... So I did not remain in the deep gully but a minute or so....

I now had about six hundred yards to go before I could reach the deep cut road near the mill. I knew if I could make it there that I would be pretty safe. My route was strewn with the dead and wounded. They lay so thick that it was with very great difficulty, under the withering fire of grape and canister, that I made it back to the deep cut road. Over this entire route I dragged my helpless leg. I took shelter behind a large oak tree that stood by the roadside, in sight of Gaines' Mill. I lay down and felt pretty safe, although the shells were bursting all around me. I lay here an hour or more, watching the great number of reinforcements that were passing by, going into the battle that was raging furiously....

I was anxious to be removed further to the rear, and I was now in a helpless condition, and it seemed

I was dying, dying of thirst. I would have freely given the whole world for a drink of water. Finally four of our litter bearers came along making their way back to the field. I halted them. They had lost their litter in the charge and were using as a makeshift a big U.S. blanket. They spread this blanket down and placed me on it. About this time Sgt. Mattison, of Company "B," came along, wounded in the foot by a piece of shell. He gave them orders to carry me clear out of all danger. They did so. In the darkness of the night they missed their way, and I was carried to a North Carolina battlefield hospital, and on that account I failed to received the attention that I should have had. I remained at this battlefield hospital ... until about 4 o'clock Sunday evening, when I was placed in an ambulance, with a Dutchman, who had his leg cut off. He died that night....

Welch, S. G., Surg., 20th S.C. Vols., camped near Richmond, Va.:

Our brigade was ordered away last night with two days' rations, but I am left behind with the sick. There are a great many sick men in the hospitals and they are dying by the thousands. Our regiment has lost about one hundred men since we came to Virginia.... Since I began writing this letter I hear a terrific cannonading on the left wing of our army, and I believe the battle has opened....

Boulware, J., Hospital Steward, 6th S.C. Vols., Seven Days' Battle, Va.:

Everything has been quiet for a week or so, but now we are marching with three days' rations. Passed Oak Grove Cemetery and took down the Mechanicsville road. Lay all day long where we can hear the battle going on across the Chickahominy. After dark we moved down and crossed the river—no sleep at all that night.

Hannah Anderson Chandler Ropes was an unusual woman for her time. Born in New Gloucester, Me., on June 13, 1809, she was 53 at the time she went to the Union Hospital in Georgetown in Washington, D.C., to become a nurse. The daughter of a prominent Maine lawyer and the seventh of ten children, she was raised in a family of activists and those who were early into the abolitionist movement. She married William Henry Ropes, a Waterville College graduate and an educator, in February

1834. She bore four children, two of whom, Edward, called Ned, and Alice, lived to adulthood. In 1847, William left the family. Hannah became involved in the movement to settle Kansas with abolitionists, and moved there in 1855. The hostilities surrounding the Kansas-Nebraska Act and the border warfare sent her to Massachusetts in 1856, where she wrote a tract entitled *Six Months in Kansas: By a Lady*. This brought her recognition and the acquaintance and friendship of many notables, including Charles Sumner, Senator from Massachusetts. She also had contact with Nathaniel Banks, then a Senator from Massachusetts, and later one of the first political generals to be appointed. Her novel *Cranston House: A Novel*, which was published in 1859, was based primarily on her experiences in Kansas, and the book was a decided success. Her decision to volunteer as a nurse was a logical outgrowth of her previous experiences and her desire to aid and comfort.

Ropes, Hannah, Nurse, Union Hospital, Georgetown, Washington, D.C.:

Dear Alice: ... we arrived here at noon ... Miss Stevenson gave us a most cordial welcome, and the rooms at this house till we are rested and our work is arranged.... Yesterday after dinner I went into the Senate chamber and heard an animated discussion.... While waiting to receive my summons today I shall sit in the House and study some more faces. Washington is decidedly the ugliest and dirtiest city I ever saw. One finds nothing pleasant until you mount the Capitol and look off over the open beautiful country....

June 27 (Friday)

The third day of the Seven Days' Battle began with Fitz John Porter holding at Gaines' Mill, and the Confederates attacking about 3 P.M. Jackson wasn't up again. After dark, the Confederates under Gens. John Bell Hood and George Pickett broke the lines at Gaines' Mill, but the drive wasn't sustained and the Rebels fell back. Porter, amid the confusion, did a brilliant job of withdrawing his battered corps across the river and back into the folds of the Army of the Potomac. For the day, Porter lost about 6800 men to Lee's 8700. McClellan began his withdrawal to the James.

Boulware, J., Hospital Steward, 6th S.C. Vols., Seven Days' Battle, Va.:

Early this morning the fight began but was soon hushed. We then marched on for several miles following the enemy closely until noon, when we halted, and in a few hours the fight began in earnest. I was in the rear at the brigade hospital. Back went the enemy and back came to us our wounded men. The battle was dreadful, but not more so than the battle of Seven Pines. The enemy were driven back along the whole line with but little cessation, until night put a stop to all firing. Now came the busiest times for the surgeons. Ambulance after ambulance came up with its load until a two-acre lot was filled completely. We had few men killed or wounded in the 6th, but the rest of the brigade suffered very much. In the loss of Capt. Moore that company (F) has suffered greatly. I was up all night, as was Dr. Gaston, dressing wounds of men from South Carolina, Georgia, Mississippi, and Texas.

Brown, H. E., Surg., USA, Hooker's Div., Seven Days' Battle, Va.:

At three o'clock A.M. on June 27th, I removed about two hundred and fifty of the slight cases, leaving behind seventy-five very sick men in charge of Acting Asst. Surg. J. W. Powell and Asst. Surg. McAllister, 71st New York Volunteers. All of them, including the medical officers, were made prisoners.

After the abortive attack on Charleston, S.C., by Brig. Gen. Henry W. Benham on June 16th, Maj. Gen. David Hunter decided to abandon James Island near Charleston because of the sickness within the command. On this date he wrote:

Hearing from Washington that there is no probability of our receiving reinforcements, and it being all-important to provide for the health of the command in the sickly season approaching, I have determined to abandon James Island, in order that the troops may be placed where, in so far as practicable, in this climate, they may be out of the way of malarious influences....

By the 10th of July, Hunter notified Secretary of War Stanton that:

No epidemic fevers have yet appeared in any portion of the command, though the great numbers of men prostrated on James Island by bilious and low typhoid fevers and the increasing sick list ... give warning of what might be expected....

June 28 (Saturday)

The fourth day of the Seven Days' Battle was fairly quiet. The long lines of wagons moving towards the James marked the progress of McClellan's retreat. Lee reorganized his forces for yet another attack. McClellan sent a telegram to Lincoln saying that the battle was lost, because his force was too small, blaming the President for a failure that was really the general's fault.

In the midst of the Seven Days' Battle, Surg. Jonathan Letterman arrived at White House, on the Peninsula, to assume his duties as Medical Director for the Army of the Potomac. He found much confusion and lack of direction in the medical services being rendered. He was unable to report to Gen. McClellan for another four days.

Boulware, J., Hospital Steward, 6th S.C. Vols., Seven Days' Battle, Va.:

By sunrise Dr. Gaston was called up and we found that there were quite a number of wounded from other brigades who had received no attention as yet. I worked for hours upon them and afterwards assisted Dr. Gaston in seven operations. During the previous night I had cut out two grapeshot one and a half inches in diameter. We made coffee (Yankee) and gave our wounded some and others also. The fields were rich in coffee, sugar, rice, crackers, (superior) medicines, blankets, oil, cloths, canteens, clothes and in fact everything necessary for comfort....

Brown, H. E., Surg., USA, Hooker's Div., Seven Days' Battle, Va.:

I proceeded, with my command, across White Oak Swamp bridge, reaching the estate of Hill Carter, opposite City Point, Virginia, about six A.M. on June 28th, and reported to Maj. Pleasanton, USA, in charge of that point. Large numbers of sick and wounded from other points coming in during the day, and there being no order or discipline in regard to them, many large bodies being without any medical officer whatever, I was detailed by Maj. Pleasanton as local medical director, with instructions to organize the men, and separate them into their appropriate corps, and to provide

food for them; a work of great difficulty, but which, with the valuable assistance of Chaplain W. H. Cudworth, 1st Mass. Volunteers, I at length succeeded in doing, issuing about seven thousand rations, which I obtained from the steamer *Spaulding*, which opportunely arrived at this time. Here I remained until the evening of June 31st, when, our army having all passed by during the night, Maj. Pleasanton directed me to send my men to Harrison's Landing, five miles below.

Tripler, Charles S., Surg., Army of the Potomac, Peninsular Campaign, Va.:

On the 25th, we had a smart skirmish on our left. The wounded, who were very few, were sent to White House. On the 26th, Gen. McCall fought at Mechanicsville.... The sick were sent into the camp at headquarters without notice, without a report, a nurse, or a crust of bread. I was obliged to send them to Savage's Station to occupy room I wanted for wounded men.

On the 27th, Gen. Porter fought at Gaines' Mill. Ambulances were sent, and his wounded were brought in to Savage's Station. The cars were kept in motion, and as many as could be sent down were sent to the floating hospitals....

A large train was loaded at 10 A.M. on the 28th, when we found that the railway was in possession of the enemy, and I was reluctantly compelled to take the men back to the hospital. All this time, the services of everyone that could be commanded were employed in attending to the wounded. There were about thirteen hundred in the tents, buildings, and on the lawn.... In the afternoon I received orders to leave all that could not walk, with a supply of surgeons, nurses, subsistence, and hospital stores, to fall into the hands of the enemy. I caused the wounded to be carefully examined, and six hundred and fifty were reported to me as unable to move. A number of these, however, did contrive to get off and to march to James River in safety.

I then called for volunteers to remain with the wounded, and, to the credit of the medical gentlemen, be it said, all that I wanted immediately expressed their readiness to undertake the duty. Dr. Swinburne having had the organization of the hospitals, I constituted him chief of the party, and furnished him with a letter to the Confederate Commander, in these words:

To the Commanding General of the Confederate Forces, or Commanding Officer:

Dr. Swinburne, a volunteer surgeon, with a number of other surgeons, nurses, and attendants, have been left in charge of the sick and wounded of this army who could not be removed. Their humane occupation commends itself, under the law of nations, to the kind consideration of the opposing forces. It is requested that they may be free to return as soon as the discharge of their duties with the sick and wounded will permit, and that the same consideration shown to the Confederate sick, wounded, and medical officers, that have been captured by our forces may be extended to them. A large amount of clothing, bedding, medical stores, &c., have been left, both at Savage's Station and Dr. Trent's house.

Brumley, J. D., Surg., USV, Peninsular Campaign, Savage's Station, Va.:

The point where the wounded were taken first was about one and a half miles from Savage's Station, to which place they were all carried afterwards.... I was detailed by Surg. J. F. Hammond, USA, medical director of the Second Corps, to remain at a house on the field where the battle had been fought near the Williamsburg road, and about three-fourths of a mile from Savage's Station, in charge of about one hundred and sixty wounded men that had been collected there. No food or medical supplies of any kind was left. I remained here about four days, when I succeeded in getting the men removed to Savage's Station, where a considerable amount of medical and hospital supplies had been left. The only transportation I could possibly obtain was the common army wagon, without springs, and only for such as could not possibly get there themselves. The men exhibited great energy and perseverance in hobbling along on such rude crutches as we could make for them. We remained about two weeks at Savage's Station, until the supplies were nearly exhausted, and then were taken on freight and platform cars to Richmond, where the men were distributed to the different prisons. All of these that I visited were greatly crowded and very filthy. The diet, issued uniformly to all, consisted of fresh beef and soft bread. There was, apparently, a great destitution of all kinds of medical supplies and surgical appliances. I remained about four days in Libby prison, attending the sick and wounded prisoners, when I was permitted to leave

with them, and again joined the Army of the Potomac at Harrison's Landing.

June 29 (Sunday)

Tripler, Charles S., Surg., Army of the Potomac, Peninsular Campaign, Va.:

The fifth day of the Seven Days' Battle found Confederate forces closely following, and attacking, McClellan's retreating columns. The Federal rear guard was constantly in action and withstood the repeated assaults. Jackson was late again. Although the Federals safely withdrew, they left more than 2500 sick and wounded at Savage's Station on the Richmond and York Railroad.

Welch, S. G., Surg., 20th S.C. Vols., in a letter to his wife, while camped near Richmond, Va.:

I was correct in my last letter to you when I predicted that the great battle had commenced. The conflict raged with great fury after I finished writing, and it lasted from three o'clock until ten that night.... Next morning (28th) the battle began anew, but there was not nearly so much cannonading, because our men rushed upon the Yankees and took their cannon. The musketry, though, was terrific. It reminded me of myriads of hailstones falling on a housetop.... Our regiment had eight killed and forty wounded.... I was on the ground yesterday where some of the hardest fighting took place. The dead were lying everywhere and were very thick in some places. One of our regiments had camped in some woods there and the men were lying among the dead Yankees and seemed unconcerned.

The most saddening sight was the wounded at the hospitals, which were in various places on the battlefield. Not only are the houses full, even the yards are covered with them. There are so many that most of them are much neglected. The people of Richmond are hauling them away as fast as possible. At one place I saw the Yankee wounded and their own surgeons attending to them.... On my way to the battlefield I met a negro who recognized me and told me that your brother Edwin was wounded in the breast and had gone to Richmond. I fear there is some truth in it.

Leadbetter, M. T., Pvt., Co. C, 5th Alabama Battalion, in hospital, Richmond, Va.:

We arrived in Richmond about midnight. The hospitals in the city were all full. We were hauled around the city from hospital to hospital, and failing to find any room, we were then carried out to Chimborazo, a suburban hospital. Here I found a resting place in ward No. 32.

Schell, H. S., Asst. Surg., USA, Gaines' Mill, Peninsular Campaign, Va.:

We camped at Gaines' Mill until June 26th, and then marched to Mechanicsville, but did not participate in the engagement. We returned to Gaines' Mill during the night, and were attacked the next day.... I remained, during the falling-back of our forces from the battleground of Gaines' Mill, at a house used as a hospital, and situated very near the centre of our lines during the action. In consequence of this position, the hospital was surrounded by dead bodies of men and horses, and, together with its outhouses, was filled to overflowing with wounded. Among the cases, numbering in all one hundred and twenty, there was a large portion of very severe ones, so that nearly, if not full three-fourths of them were unable to move without assistance. These comprised four cases of fracture of the skull, ten cases of wounds of the abdomen, twenty of the chest, six of the pelvis, nine of the larger joints, and thirty-nine cases of fracture of the long bones. For five days after the engagement, we had but three assistants; scarcely enough to carry water; and, in consequence, [we were] obliged to use every man who was but slightly wounded only in an arm as a nurse.

At the termination of the above-named period, we succeeded in obtaining six prisoners, who were paroled not to escape. These men were detailed for nurses, but a more worthless half-dozen it would have been difficult to find. The ration furnished for the patient by the Confederate authorities consisted of flour and bacon, with a small proportion of beans, salt beef, and salt. The quantity was exceedingly small, and many of the poor wretches forgot the pain of their injuries in the more terrible pangs of hunger.

But while food was scarce, maggots were abundant, crowding and rolling in every wound, and searching beneath the dressings to fasten upon every excoriation. Oil of turpentine and infusion of tobacco and of the flowers of the elderberry were tried, for the purpose of getting rid of this pest; but the most effectual means was found to be dressing forceps; and

to keep the wound clean, it required to be examined every two or three hours. A solution of camphor in oil is an excellent remedy, if applied directly to the bodies of the intruders, the secretions of the wound having previously been removed by a piece of sponge. It seems to me that the maggot actually does damage in a wound; although not by attacking the living tissues, but only by the annoyance created by the continual sensation of crawling and irritation which it occasions, and of which the patient often complains bitterly. In certain states of the system, the nervous excitement or irritability thus engendered must react injuriously upon the parts.

The large number of severe cases rendered some crowding necessary, although the men were kept as much in the open air as possible. The fierce rays of a July sun soon started the usual series of changes in the dead bodies of horses and half-buried men, which strewed the earth for a mile around the house. Every hot breath of wind, as it swept over the field, came saturated with the disgusting odor of putrescent animal matter. All night, when the air was quiet, it became, on this account, peculiarly oppressive.

In a few days, a feeling of languor and debility seized upon the surgeons, assistants, and patients. Every fractured leg, or other part of the body that required to be kept in one position, excoriated and sloughed wherever it touched a point of support. Many of the wounds began to look badly; typhous symptoms rapidly developed; operative cases showed little or no disposition to heal; three or four cases of pure typhus occurred, and one half of the whole number of these unfortunate men died during the month....

June 30 (Monday)

On the sixth day of the Seven Days' Battle, at White Oak Swamp, Lee's Army of Northern Virginia tried to attack McClellan across the marsh. McClellan successfully countered the attack and Longstreet couldn't break the lines. By nightfall, McClellan had drawn his lines in around Malvern Hill, where the finale would occur the next day.

Boulware, J., Hospital Steward, 6th S.C. Vols., Seven Days' Battle, Va.:

On arriving at camp last night I found all quiet. The regiment had only stopped for a short time allowing the boys, tired as they were, time to cook dinner and [they] were marched down the Darbytown road six miles. After getting some sleep at camp I set out early to find the brigade. I had scarcely caught up when we received orders for a march further down the road. Dr. Owens who had charge of the ambulance train being absent, I was put in charge and conducted the train for miles down the road until we caught up with the retreating Yankees. Our brigade was in advance. We halted and the 6th regiment was displayed as skirmishers. About 2 o'clock the fight began, artillery opening the ball as usual. We soon found that we were fighting the same division that we drove from their fortifications a few days before on the other side of the Chickahominy, viz. Porter's Division. The enemy had 21 pieces of artillery posted on a rising ground in front of us and all seemed to be let loose on us at once for it was far more dreadful than any of the preceding fights. In the course of half an hour our brave boys had pressed on and taken the batteries—every one—but in a few minutes they were overpowered by the enemy and reinforcements failing to come up in time they were forced to give back, the enemy taking possession of the ground and recovering the artillery. Our forces meeting reinforcements 150 yards back, turned again upon the enemy, drove them back in confusion, retaking everything again and driving the enemy before them for two miles. Night soon came and closed all noises except that of getting off the wounded, which work took us until midnight. Tommy Boggs fell dead close to the cannon he had just assisted in taking from the enemy; Color-bearer J. W. Rabb fell dead just before him along with a host of other noble boys. It was my business to conduct the train of ambulances to and from the field of battle, which kept us busy until late at night. Among the number I came across my intimate friend Jimmy Matthews. Poor fellow, I watched over him that night as much as my business would allow me.

Wainwright, Charles S., Maj., N.Y. Artillery, New York, N.Y.:

At last I am getting on my legs again; have been pretty sick they say: still I managed to get downstairs every day. The first time I was able to walk so far, I went in to a grocer's and got weighed; just turned 106 lbs! Now I am so much better that I expect to go up home tomorrow or next day....

Leadbetter, M. T., Pvt., Co. C, 5th Alabama Battalion, in hospital, Richmond, Va.:

It was now about 2 o'clock A.M. Monday. I was very hungry by this time, having eaten nothing since I was shot Friday. I called a servant to my "bunk" and told him I wanted something to eat, that I was starving to death. He said "I am sorry for you, but you will have to do without until regular breakfast." I then called for the ward master. I made an earnest appeal to him, but without any success. He said, "It is positively against the rules, etc." I told him that it was hard, but I guessed I could stand it.

Breakfast came about 7 o'clock. The servants waited on me nicely, and brought me in plenty to eat. My ward master was a whole-souled and jolly kind of a fellow. I became very much attached to him....

In June, the Lincoln administration became worried about the safety of Washington—McClellan's Army of the Potomac being on the Peninsula—and decided to organize another army to stand between Lee and the Federal capital. To do this, the corps of Gens. Frémont, Banks, and McDowell were to be assigned to the newly formed Army of Virginia, and the command of that army was to go to Maj. Gen. John Pope. These three corps were designated the First, Second, and Third Army Corps. Some troops from the defenses of Washington and the Dept. of Western Virginia were also added and integrated into the assigned corps. The whole consisted of about 90 regiments, six batteries of artillery, and six cavalry companies, but they were scattered over a wide area, and command problems existed.

McParlin, Thomas A., Surg., USA, Med. Dir., Army of Virginia, Winchester, Va.:

On the 30th of June, 1862, I was assigned as Medical Director of the army of Virginia, and entered upon duty a few days thereafter.... I invited, by circular, information from medical directors of corps as to their condition.... Two inspectors-general were sent to ascertain and report on the military supplies and condition of the corps. From the many rapid and forced movements for months previous, the First and Second Corps were greatly deficient in all kinds of medical and hospital supplies and means of transportation. Reports were irregular and unfrequent.... For weeks I was occupied in ascertaining and directing by telegraph where supplies were to be sent; when and where sent for. Many consignments, put months before and sent by railroad, had not been received....

A large number of ambulances were ordered.... They were all, at my request, of one kind only; two-horse, four-wheeled ambulances to be made of seasoned timber, with wide-set tires and strong wheels, heavily ironed, to obviate known defects....

July 1 (Tuesday)

The seventh day of the Seven Days' Battle found Lee hoping to destroy the Federals entrenched on Malvern Hill. His artillery proved no match for the Union artillery and, although he tried several assaults, he couldn't get very far. This was one of Lee's costliest mistakes during the war. He'd make another exactly a year from this date, at Gettysburg. Due to poor coordination, his attacks were largely disjointed, and his men were cut to pieces by Federal gunners and riflemen. In many cases the Confederate casualties were very heavy, as in a South Carolina regiment that began piling up their dead to serve as breastworks to resist the attack of a Union brigade containing the 83rd Regiment Pennsylvania Vols. The Rebel regiment lost its colors in the fracas to Sgt. W. J. Whittrick.

Surg. Jonathan Letterman reported to Gen. McClellan at Harrison's Landing on the Peninsula and took up his duties as Medical Director on July 4th.

Boulware, J., Hospital Steward, 6th S.C. Vols., Battle at Malvern Hill, Va.:

Next day I saw him [Jimmy Matthews] die, and for the first time in the war I shed tears of sorrow. Tommy Boggs was brought back by his brother a corpse. I also carefully watched John Stevenson and saw him die, shot like Jimmy, through the abdomen. Late in the afternoon of July 1st the battle began on Malvern Hill. I was assisting Dr. Gaston to amputate a leg when the shells began to fall very near. My mind was occupied and I scarcely knew any shells had fallen until I was shown them afterwards. Dr. Gaston made six amputations that day. Generally the stragglers congregated about the different hospitals, but when the shelling began they put out in every direction, so we were not pestered by them any more that day or

the next. Our brigade was held in reserve that day and did not participate in the fight, but were directly under the fire. The fight at this place (Malvern Hill) is said to have been more destructive to our men than most of the other fights. I will relate an incident: While the heaviest fighting was going on, one of our former Congressmen was lying sound asleep on the table, or rather the scaffold we had been amputating on, *drunk*.

Ellis, F. P., Co. I, 13th Miss. Regt., Battle at Malvern Hill, Va.:

As the roar of musketry, the boom of cannon, the bursting of shells and hissing grapeshot slowly subsided, the shrieks of the wounded could be heard on every hand. Fervent prayers, bitter swearing, pitiful calls for water and for comrades by name or company were among the cries distinguishable. As the dense smoke, which had obscured everything, slowly lifted, the setting sun as red as blood could be seen, and the surface of the earth as far as I could see appeared to be covered with a mass of wriggling, writhing men, some vainly endeavoring to regain their feet, others seeking less painful positions. Intermixed with the wounded everywhere lay the silent forms of the dead, men of the gray and of the blue.

The Federals had yielded the ground only after desperately contesting every foot of it; and both armies, having fought to exhaustion, slowly withdrew from the central part of the field and had placed their vedettes. Those of us on the ground could outline the shadowy forms of these vigilant sentinels as they kept watch while their worn-out comrades slept on their arms. Night had now spread her mantle over the horrid scene. The last spiteful rifle crack had ceased, the sky became overcast, and soon a gentle rain was falling as if nature were weeping because of human slaughter. The louder cries of the wounded had either been silenced by death or had given place to the low moaning of the helpless sufferer as the feeling of chilly numbness came over one who had bled profusely and was now wet to the skin by the falling rain. We had no means of determining the hour.

Far in the night I [saw] outlined against the sky the form of a half-stooped man who was gliding silently and swiftly about the field, halting a moment here and there. I became very much interested; but when he stopped he stooped below my line of vision, and I did not learn his object until he came quite close to me, when I discovered that he was robbing the dead, turning pockets wrong-side out and stripping the rings from cold and stiffened fingers. Turning my eyes from him after several minutes, I saw four others similarly engaged. I was satisfied that they were soldiers, but for the life of me, I could not tell to which army they belonged.

A feeling of utter loneliness overcame me as I lay there unable to lift my head, an eighteen-year-old boy more than a thousand miles from home. My comrades who were near me were either dead or as helpless as myself. My command was gone, I knew not where, and I in the midst of a band of thieves!

After a seemingly interminable time I saw a dim light at quite a distance in the direction from which we had come on the field. I greeted this light as the shepherds of old did the star of Bethlehem. I saw that it moved, and I knew it was the light of the litter bearers gathering the wounded and conveying them to the field hospital. O how I watched that light, and how impatient I became at their apparent deliberation! Then I remembered that this was the seventh day's battle, and every night and part of every day for a week those litter bearers had been on duty. The light now appeared closer and then farther off, so that my hope for relief rose and fell accordingly.

Finally gray dawn came, and as daylight appeared both lines of outpost pickets quietly retired and the robbers, like wolves, slunk out of sight. I now had quite a clear view of my surroundings. I was on top of Malvern Hill in an open field and could see quite a distance in nearly every direction. There was a much greater number of dead on the field than I thought, and from the number of wounded between where I lay and where the litter bearers were at work, I calculated that it would be two o'clock that evening before they reached me, and subsequent events proved its correctness.

Perry, John G., Asst. Surg., USV, Chesapeake Hospital, Ft. Monroe, Va.:

A new contingent today of sick and wounded; in fact, the men arrived in such numbers that we laid them on the grass and dressed their wounds there. I was obliged to perform an operation on one man and cut off two of his fingers. He sat perfectly straight and did not wince a particle. I called him a "man," for he truly deserved the title, though he, poor fellow, was a mere boy of eighteen years.

Dr. Cushing, whom I assisted, has gone home, and I have entire charge of the cottage. The Surgeon General says he shall place the worst cases here, as it is the healthiest place there is. Think of the experience I shall gain!

July 2 (Wednesday)

On Virginia's James River, McClellan was retreating from Malvern Hill to Harrison's Landing in a driving rain. The Landing had been chosen by Commander Rodgers because it was so situated that gunboats could protect both flanks of the army.

The 4th Ohio Regiment arrived at Harrison's Landing on the Peninsula on this date with over 800 troops. Diarrhea caused the regiment to be reduced to less than 200 "present for duty" within six weeks, and by November the number of effectives was further reduced to less than 120, with only one soldier killed in action and about ten wounded.

Boulware, J., Hospital Steward, 6th S.C. Vols., aftermath of Malvern Hill, Va.:

We got off the last of our wounded today. There were two wounded prisoners brought to our hospital—Col. Timmons of the 9th Regulars and Capt. Diddle, adjutant to Gen. McCall. Col. Timmons died soon after he was brought in. Capt. Diddle was sent to Richmond with our wounded. Both were fine-looking officers and seem to be gentlemen at home.

July 3 (Thursday)

McClellan, safely entrenched at Harrison's Landing, was protected by both his artillery and the Federal gunboats. Lee was probing for a hole to drive his troops through, and on both sides the finger-pointing was getting into full gear as nearly everyone searched for scapegoats. McClellan chose Lincoln and Congress; after all, they hadn't given him the troops he'd asked for (despite the fact that he outnumbered Lee by 30,000). Lee was silent and was reorganizing his army while thinking of what could be done to John Pope, who was posturing near Manassas.

Tripler, Charles S., Surg., Army of the Potomac, Peninsular Campaign, Va.:

On the morning of June 29th, the headquarters moved in the direction of James River, and arrived at

Haxall's Landing the next day. The actions at Savage's Station, White Oak Swamp, and Malvern Hill occurred in quick succession. So far as circumstances would admit, the wounded were conducted, or found their way, to this point, to Carter's, and to Harrison's Bar. [To t]he latter position, the headquarters were transferred in the night of July 1st. The next day a heavy rain fell, deluging our wounded, many of whom had no shelter. Some of our hospital ships having reached Harrison's Bar at that time, I procured a lighter from the quartermaster, and commenced shipping the wounded; but I was obliged to suspend this operation by orders ... as the wharf was absolutely necessary for landing subsistence stores. Everything possible, however, was done for the comfort of the wounded; tea, coffee, soup, and stimulants were being constantly prepared and issued.... On July 3d, my successor, Dr. Letterman, having reported, I turned over the department to him.

Hammond, J. F., Surg., Second Army Corps, Army of the Potomac, Fair Oaks, Va.:

From the 28th June until the 3d of July, we did not see our wagons or ambulances. They were sent in advance of the column, filled with sick and wounded. Litters were borne by the attendants with the troops. At Allan's farm, the Second Corps were engaged generally for about five hours.... The wounded were taken to Savage's Station. But one wounded man was abandoned there to the enemy; he was wounded in the head; the brain was protruding, and he was insensible, though still living....

Ropes, Hannah, Nurse, Union Hospital, Georgetown, Washington, D.C.:

Dear Alice: It is almost dark, but I will begin a note to you, though I have heard nothing from you. Washington was never so sad as today! The news from Richmond is so fearfully bloody.... It is astonishing to see the *Boston Journal* jubilant over a "victory" which leaves twenty thousand of our men on the field, dead or wounded. I have been to the hospitals and seen some of the "first" who told me that our friends were unhurt up to Thursday. But the fight has been so severe since that we must prepare for the worst....

Perry, John G., Asst. Surg., USV, Chesapeake Hospital, Ft. Monroe, Va.:

A thousand wounded men arrived at the fort tonight, and tomorrow we shall probably have five hundred more. The work is endless.

Last night the heat was intense, and it seemed to me that a puff of pure air, free from the atmosphere of hospital wards, would be worth a kingdom; so, finding a few spare moments, I drew a mattress out on the cottage piazza, upon which I threw myself. The situation of our hospital is quite at the edge of the bluff over the water, so that we have the beautiful bay almost beneath us. The sun was just setting; sky and water were aglow with color, and ... below a large force of transports loaded with soldiers whom I knew were commanded by Gen. Burnside....

I have a plantation full of negroes under my charge across the river. Twenty are down with measles and twenty more with fever and ague. They are so confoundedly black that at first I found it difficult to discriminate the measles, but now I can see even the dirt. They always have very nice berry pies for me, and you may smile, but I really believe these berry pies will make a new man of me.

The pundits in Richmond had explanations as to why Lee should have done this or that, although they were safely in the rear when the battle raged. In Richmond, the more gory side of the battle was arriving.

Jones, John B., Rebel War Clerk, Confederate War Dept., Richmond, Va.:

Our wounded are now coming in fast, under the direction of the Ambulance Committee. I give passports to no one not having legitimate business on the field to pass the pickets of the army.

So great is the demand for vehicles that the brother of a North Carolina major, reported mortally wounded, paid $100 for a hack to bring his brother into the city. He returned with him a few hours after, and, fortunately, found him to be not even dangerously wounded.

I suffer no physicians not belonging to the army to go upon the battlefield without taking amputating instruments with them, and no private vehicle without binding drivers to bring in two or more of the wounded.

There are fifty hospitals in the city, fast filling with the sick and wounded. I have seen men in my office and walking in the streets whose arms have been amputated within the last three days. The realization of a great victory seems to give them strength.

Mrs. Sally Putnam, a resident of Richmond, wrote:

The month of July of 1862 can never be forgotten in Richmond. We lived in one immense hospital, and breathed the vapors of the charnel house.... Every family received the bodies of the wounded or dead of their friends, and every house was a house of mourning or a private hospital.... Sickening odors filled the atmosphere, and soldiers' funerals were passing at every moment.... Our best and brightest young men were passing away.

On the York Peninsula, the battlefield was strewn with wounded and dead. The Confederate forces, now under Gen. Lee, collected the wounded, both Union and Confederate, and began an almost hopeless task of tending them. Through a flag-of-truce, the Union had been requested to provide rations and medical supplies to treat their wounded. Since no cartel yet existed for the exchange of prisoners, the Union surgeon suggested a means of surmounting that problem.

Guild, L., Surg., CSA, to Maj. R. G. Cole, Asst. Commissary Off., USA, Crew's Farm, Va.:

Major: I am instructed by Gen. Lee to give you such information as will enable you to issue the special supplies requisite for the Federal sick and wounded within our lines. There are 400 at Mrs. Watts' house, near Gaines' Mill. They are entirely unprovided for and will need a full supply. This place is most accessible from some point on the York River railroad, at or near Savage Depot, being distant therefrom about three miles. About 3000 are at Savage Depot, on the York River railroad. They were provided to some extent with hard bread, prepared vegetables, coffee, &c., but are without meat of any kind. There are 500 in the vicinity of the battlefield of Monday, June 30, 1862, immediately on the Charles City road. They are entirely without subsistence. One thousand more will be found just beyond the battlefield of Tuesday, July 1, at Pitt's house, and at another house nearby. I would respectfully suggest that an intelligent agent be sent with each supply that there may be no mistake in the distribution.

Swinburne, John, Acting Surg., USA, to Gen. R. E. Lee, CSA, Crew's Farm, Va.:

Sir: I am left here by order of Gen. McClellan to look after the welfare of the sick and wounded, and since there are numbers of them placed in temporary hospitals extending from Gaines's house to this place, an area of twelve to fifteen miles, and inasmuch as it is impossible for me to oversee and insure proper attention as to medication, nursing, and food, I would therefore propose that some suitable arrangement be made either for condensing them at Savage's Station, that these ends might be attained, or, what would be still more agreeable to the demands on humanity, viz, the unconditional parole of these sufferers. From what I have seen and know of you and your ideas of humanity I feel assured that this application will meet with favor, even if the Federal Government does not recognize the principle of mutual exchange of prisoners. I trust that this rule ought not to be extended to the unfortunate sick and wounded. The real prisoners of war should be treated as belligerents, while humanity shudders at the idea of placing the wounded on the same footing. Your surgeons have performed miracles in the way of kind attention both to us surgeons as well as the wounded. If this proposition does not meet with favor I will, with your approbation, communicate with the Federal Government that some basis of transfer may be arrived at. The majority, in fact all medical directors in your army with whom I have conferred, fully agree with me as to the humanity of carrying out this proposition.

July 4 (Friday)

On the York Peninsula, Gen. Lee recommended to Richmond that the Federal wounded be consolidated as early as possible and that they be released on parole at the earliest possible moment.

Lee, R. E., Gen., Army of Northern Virginia, to Surg. Swinburne, J., USA, York Peninsula, Va.:

Sir: I regret to hear of the extreme suffering of the sick and wounded Federal prisoners who have fallen into our hands. I will do all that lies within my power to alleviate their sufferings. I will have steps taken to give you every facility in transporting them to Savage's Station. I am willing to release the sick and wounded on their parole not to bear arms....

Randolph, Geo. W., Secy. of War, C.S.A., to Gen. R. E. Lee, York Peninsula, Va.:

General: I have already ordered an examination into the condition of the sick and wounded of the enemy at Gaines's farm and Savage's, and on a report made this morning I directed them to be all collected at Savage's, where they can be properly attended. Lt.-Col. Shields, under Gen. Winder's orders, has been charged with this duty and I think that you need give yourself no further trouble about it. The sick and wounded of the enemy at the points mentioned are reported to be about 1700....

The Federal hospital at Frederick, Md., received nearly 400 patients on this day—most of whom were left outside in the broiling sun because there was no provision for them in the hospital wards nor any tentage to provide cover. The Sisters of Charity from Emmitsburg, Md., who were serving in the hospital as nurses diluted wine with water and circulated among the patients outside, giving them some relief. It was several days before all were cleared and placed under cover.

July 6 (Sunday)

Ropes, Hannah, Nurse, Union Hospital, Georgetown, Washington, D.C.:

… Found this great castle of a hotel in charge of a very handsome, tall, dark-eyed young surgeon from Maryland. He was gracious, took me over the establishment, and talked very pleasantly. He thought I should be better off to go back to Washington House … the sergeant, come to say the wounded were on their way, and we must get ready. Some of the nurses were away, and the way I took shirts, drawers, and stockings out of the boxes, the young doctor, tearing off the covers, was up to the top of my speed. Nurses drifted in and caught the piles of unwashed cotton and we laid out a piece of each upon every bed until the end of our supply, then sent to the church across the street for enough to make up 150 pieces. Only six patients arrived that night, and we went to bed expecting to be called every moment....

… there came a quick step over our private stairs in the wing of the "castle," and a voice—"all of the nurses report at the office of the surgeon." When we ran down the main hall stairs, such a sight met our eyes as I hope you will never wit-

ness. From the broad open entrance into the hall, to the base of the staircase, there, bent, clung, and stood, in dumb silence, fifty soldiers, grim, dirty, muddy, and wounded....

Miss Stevenson ran to the kitchen for the warm tea. I stood by the doctor as he took the name of each and handed each his bed with a ticket. They were led or lifted up over the great staircase, winding along, some to the ballroom, others to the banqueting room. When all were up, we each took our portion and commenced to wash them. We were four hours. Everything they had was stripped off—and, weak, helpless as babes, they sank upon us to care for them. With broken arms and wounded feet, thighs, and fingers, it was no easy job to do gently. One quite old man, sick every way, and bullet hole through his right hand, called me "good mother" when I laid his head on his pillow and soon he slept as though he had come to the end of war, unto a haven of rest. That was the experience of one day—5th of July, 1862....

In Richmond, John Jones recorded:

Thousands of fathers, brothers, mothers, and sisters of the wounded are arriving in the city to attend their suffering relations, and to recover the remains of those who were slain.

July 7 (Monday)

Near Charleston, S.C., the Union forces were contending with hordes of insects. Common houseflies swarmed and clouds of mosquitoes joined the attacks of sand fleas, lice, and gnats. Little peace was available for men without netting to protect them at night and no peace during the day from the bites of the millions of sand fleas. "Yellow jaundice" in epidemic dimensions struck the 6th Connecticut Vols. near Beaufort, south of Charleston. This disease, while debilitating, was not as deadly as yellow fever, which struck later. The incidence of jaundice increased from 8 cases in November 1861, to a reported 260 during this month.

July 9 (Wednesday)

Mrs. Bickerdyke arrived at the Farmington (Monterry) site to find that the army had placed the tents on a ridge where the drainage was good and fresh air was abundant, which was fortunate in this hot, steamy climate of northern Mississippi.

Kitchens had been established for each ward (or group of tents) in which food of a questionable nature was being cooked. In all, some 1400 patients were being cared for at this location. Mrs. Bickerdyke looked around and then decided what to do to get organized.

July 10 (Thursday)

Boulware, J., Hospital Steward, 6th S.C. Vols., on the Peninsula, Va.:

Our brigade is again back in camp after being on the go for fifteen days. We had no change of clothes and were of course dirty and *alive*, as to our condition in regard to Confederates. I washed, shaved, had my hair trimmed and put on clean clothes and fancied I would feel much better, but took an aching through my bones and suffered very much. I attributed it to excessive fatigue and exhaustion during the last battle and more than all to the rapid march all night of the 9th last.

July 11 (Friday)

After assuming his duties as Medical Director for the Army of the Potomac and taking an inspection tour, Jonathan Letterman issued a series of instruction designed to reduce the incidence of disease and to provide better care for the wounded. Thousands of men had taken ill and had been shipped by steamer to Northern hospitals, creating a serious drain on the army. Among Letterman's instructions were those to dig wells where possible to provide fresh water (impossible in some areas of the Peninsula); that fresh vegetables be issued and that cooking be done at the company level instead of the squad level (this would have been an improvement at any time); that tent flaps be opened daily and that tents be moved weekly; that the men bathe at least weekly (a real innovation); and that sinks (latrines) be dug and their use enforced, in addition to adding six inches of dirt to the latrine every day (this was an excellent idea but it left the trenches exposed to flies for nearly 12 hours); that kitchen and slaughterhouse refuse be buried as well as the manure from the horse and mule pens (this would have been a large job considering the number of animals with the army). No instructions were issued at this time concerning either the sterilization of water or eating

utensils. Such negligence was a major factor contributing to disease.

Confederate hospitals located at Charlottesville, Gordonsville, and Lynchburg were having severe problems in the intake of wounded. Part of the problem, as in Lynchburg, was that most of their young men were already in the Confederate Army, leaving only the older men and boys to support the women and slaves, who did most of the work. Still, there were cases where the wounded were sorely neglected.

Lynchburg Virginian, Lynchburg, Va.:

A Plea for Humanity—we have heard [stories of] our poor wounded soldiers … arriving here at night [and being compelled] to lie over until morning.

July 13 (Sunday)

Boulware, J., Hospital Steward, 6th S.C. Vols., on Darbytown Road, Peninsula, Va.:

Moved camp over on Darbytown Road about two miles. I lay in tent all day feeling badly and late in the afternoon Jimmy Richmond and I resolved to go out and pick a mess of huckleberries. We had a stew and made them into a tart for supper. This exercise I believe kept me from having a spell of typhoid fever, for I had the symptoms. I poured in the antiperiodic and baffled the attack.…

Ropes, Hannah, Nurse, Union hospital, Georgetown, Washington, D.C.:

Dear Alice: The healing process is very slow. When they first come they appear to gain because we feed them and tend so well their wounds, but soon the suppuration takes place, lead has to be probed for, and then they get sad and lose their appetite. Our men are fine specimens. Miss Stevenson, who has been in the army a year, says the heroes are in the ranks.… I have learned now how to take care of a shoulder wound. They are slow to cure and must have many dressings a day. Indeed, I had no idea it was such a slow and painful process—the uncertainty about what is in the wound, the waiting for the indications suppuration alone furnishes. We have one man with a shoulder wound who has just been put under the influence of ether and not only a bullet was dug out under his shoulder blade but a piece of his coat. Since that he has discharged at least a pint a day. We put *three* clean dressings and a shirt upon him daily, cutting the shirt open on the shoulder, down in front, and taking out the left sleeve. All of these shirts and bandages have to be thrown away, they are so offensive....

At Helena, Ark., the Western Sanitary Commission established an agency with Mr. A. W. Plattenburg in charge. The agency was stocked with adequate supplies of sanitary stores and served the army elements under Maj. Gen. Curtis. During the coming fall and winter, the agency would provide support to the local hospital during a wave of sickness and a large influx of refugees from the state.

With the support of the military, a large hospital was fitted for the aid and comfort of the refugees, greatly relieving their suffering. A new camp was established and schools opened for the indigents coming to the city and garden plots were established. Many of the refugees were to be given their initial treatment at Helena and then sent farther north to St. Louis, where they were processed and provided access to job opportunities or sent on to relatives.

July 15 (Tuesday)

Letterman, Jonathan, Med. Dir., Army of the Potomac, Peninsula, Va.:

On the 15th of July, about seven thousand had been sent to Ft. Monroe or to Northern hospitals. A large number remained, and, during the first week while the shipment was in progress, the troops that remained by the colors were suffering seriously from the effects of the late campaign. The deadly malarial poison was producing its full effects, and, with the want of proper food, and exposure to the rain, and fatigue, was now being fully manifested in the prevalence of malarial fevers of a typhoid type, diarrheas, and scurvy.

In a letter sent to Illinois, from Farmington, Miss., Mrs. Bickerdyke related an experience:

One day a coffin was brought in the ambulance [along] with a sick man. I said, "What have you got that thing for?" The driver replied, "Oh, we had it on hand, and as he is so nearly dead we thought we'd bring it along." "Well, you take care of your coffin

and I'll take care of the man," I said. And Frank—good fellow that he was, he could swear a little on occasion as well as pray—said "I'll split that thing up for kindling wood, and d—n the fellow who'd put a man in a coffin before he is dead!" And he was as good as his word.

July 17 (Thursday)

The hospital at Farmington was almost as bad as the one at Cairo had been the first time Bickerdyke had seen it. With her usual efficiency, she and her crew waded in and started scrubbing and washing the patients in a ruthless manner. Bickerdyke had brought two new female nurses with her. Her manner didn't sit well with the local army medical personnel, although the chief surgeon was amiable and reasonable enough. Those who didn't conform to Mrs. Bickerdyke's ideas on cleanliness quickly got the sharp edge of her tongue. Within a short time, the chief surgeon was bragging about "his" hospital being the best in the area.

July 19 (Saturday)

The campaign in the Shenandoah Valley caused many casualties, who were sent to the Federal hospital at Frederick, Md. Among these were many German-born soldiers who weren't proficient in English. This presented a problem for all concerned—including the Sisters of Charity, who were serving as nurses in the hospital. The Mother Superior of the order, at Emmitsburg, Md., located a German Sister and sent her to the hospital to act as a nurse and interpreter and also located a German-speaking priest to conduct services for those patients.

July 21 (Monday)

McParlin, Thomas A., Surg., USA, Med. Dir., Army of Virginia, Warrenton, Va.:

I found it advisable, July 21st, to break up the purveying depot at Frederick, Md.... I therefore moved the supplies to Alexandria, and made that the more important source of supply ... via the Orange and Alexandria railroad. Supplies were ordered to be kept there capable of supplying twenty thousand men.... I soon found, however, that a small movable depot would be necessary to furnish battlefield supplies, such as stimulants and anaesthetic, concentrated nourishment, cooking utensils, articles for temporary hospital service, instruments, dressings, blankets, bedding, and hospital tents....

The line of the Orange and Alexandria railroad made our communication easy and speedy with Alexandria, where supplies were placed. I proposed to use the railroad for transportation of wounded from depots near the field to hospitals in Alexandria, or, if necessary, to Washington and Georgetown.... I had entertained the hope of locating a large establishment at the Sulphur Springs, near Warrenton, Fauquier County, Virginia, the hotel and buildings there being well adapted for it. The commanding general would not approve of a guard for its protection, and its distance from the railroad made it too dangerous a site for the sick and wounded,... I had to content myself with establishing a temporary set of hospitals in and near the town of Warrenton, to which a branch railroad extended, seven miles from the Orange and Alexandria railroad. [The hospitals were] ultimately abandoned, and the sick and means of accommodation moved to Falls Church and Alexandria....

Boulware, J., Hospital Steward, 6th S.C. Vols., Surgeon General's Office, Richmond, Va.:

Dr. Nye went to Richmond today and got [an] appointment in Chimborazo Hospital as a contract surgeon, getting I suppose eighty dollars per month. He came out and told quite an amusing tale of the conversation between the Surgeon General and himself. The recommendation he got from Dr. Gaston was not at all enticing. I went also on the same business and strange to say we kept our secrets pretty much to ourselves, not meeting each other the whole day. I went to [the] Surgeon General's office and remained for some time. There was quite a crowd rushing to get in. I became designated, so I left and went down to Lieut. Clark's hospital to see Butler Alston, and then put out for our camp, having accomplished nothing, and thinking I would not go any more, for I abhor office-seeking above all else. Yet as I was doing the duty of assistant surgeon, I thought I might as well have the office as to do duty without the office.

July 23 (Wednesday)

The Confederate forces in South Carolina weren't immune to disease, although many of the troops were native to the area. Lt. Col. John G. Pressley of the 25th South Carolina wrote:

The health of the regiment is growing worse. Our medical staff were kept very busy, and we heard of the death of several of our comrades in the general hospital in Charleston. The regimental hospital was constantly full. It was distressing to see the shortened line of the regiment on dress parade. Some of the companies had scarcely a platoon of men fit for duty.

At Farmington, Miss., Mrs. Bickerdyke had been operating somewhat at a handicap, since she didn't have a good, large-scale cooking range for her diet-kitchen. Before leaving Savannah, Tenn., she'd tried to buy the range she used there, but the woman who owned it wouldn't part with it. Bickerdyke called on her friends in Chicago for help, and on this day a large shipment of Sanitary Commission supplies arrived at Corinth by rail, including a huge stove that had been made for a Chicago hotel. It had an immense cooking surface, a vast oven, and a water tank that kept water warm from the heat of the stove.

Perry, John G., Asst. Surg., USV, Chesapeake Hospital, Ft. Monroe, Va.:

I have many curious cases under my care. Some of the patients have been prisoners in Richmond, but although almost starved and their wounds dressed only by having water poured over them, they are all doing finely. One of them had a ball enter the very apex, or tip end, of his nose, and pass through his head, but he has not had a bad symptom and is now nearly well. Another man was struck by a ball in the forehead, whence it passed directly round his head under the skin, down and around his neck, making its exit close to the jugular vein and carotid artery. Two others were shot through the lungs, and yet all these fellows are doing finely. I account for it from the very fact of their enforced low diet.

July 24 (Thursday)

Boulware, J., Asst. Surg., 6th S.C. Vols., camped near Richmond, Va.:

Went to Richmond today and had an interview with Surgeon General S. P. Moore and was appointed assistant surgeon and ordered to duty in the 6th

Regiment—the place I desired to go. I found the Surgeon General quite a pleasant talking gentleman, yet he spoke to the point freely. Dr. Thompson was ordered to duty in the 6th Regiment and reported accordingly. The regiment started down the road in one of the hardest rains I ever saw fall, but slackened about noon. Came back that evening. We thought a fight was imminent, but found they only had to throw up breastworks about three miles from camp. The entire brigade would be marched down, but one regiment would work at a time. It was good exercise for the men, but it was hard work to make them go out—the difficulty being our lieutenant colonel would make them go when they were not excused by the surgeon. The next day we moved camp about one-half mile, got better water—better situation every way. We have just been paid off for four months. I was paid $94 and paid $26.50 for a pair of pants and $27 for a sound jacket. Immense gambling is going on all over the camp, and pie and chicken wagons throng the neighboring roads, always having large crowds with them, and asking double prices for what they have to sell. The soldiers (I am told) steal from them a great deal when the crowd is large.

July 25 (Friday)

Perry, John G., Asst. Surg., USV, Chesapeake Hospital, Ft. Monroe, Va.:

Released prisoners say that a pestilence is feared in Richmond, where almost every house is turned into a hospital. If a man dies of fever his body is rolled in tar and smoked before burial. Corpses are buried without coffins and scarcely covered with earth. No names mark the grave, but simply the number that one grave contains: "Sixty-five Confederates," "Twenty Federals," or "Yankees," etc.

July 26 (Saturday)

On the Peninsula of Virginia, the wounded and sick from the Seven Days' campaign were still being moved around. Most notably, the wounded prisoners from Richmond were being picked up and sent North.

Letterman, Jonathan, Med. Dir., Army of the Potomac, Peninsula, Va.:

From July 15th, the transports for the sick were chiefly employed in bringing our wounded and sick exchanged prisoners from Richmond, and carrying them to the Northern cities; principally to Baltimore, Philadelphia, and New York. They were almost wholly occupied on this duty until August 3d, when the last exchanges were made at City Point.

Shortly after communication was opened with the Confederate authorities, large supplies of fresh lemons, brandy, lint, and other necessities were … sent to City Point, to be turned over to the Confederate authorities for the use of the wounded, but would not be receipted by them, and were returned.…

Three thousand eight hundred and forty-five sick and wounded were thus transported. After this time, a portion of these transports, which had been while North taken from their legitimate use, were occupied in carrying exchanged Confederate prisoners from the North to City Point. On the return of these boats from this service to Harrison's Landing, they were found to be excessively filthy, and required a great deal of labor to render them again suitable for the transportation of the sick. The use of these vessels in this way embarrassed me.…

July 27 (Sunday)

Letterman, Jonathan, Med. Dir., Army of the Potomac, Peninsula, Va.:

There are always numbers of skulkers and worthless men in an army, who are on the watch for an opportunity to escape duty, and these always furnish the cases which require the most careful examination, and the men who raise the cry of inhumanity, want of attention, and cruelty of surgeons, so frequently taken up and re-echoed from one end of the country to the other. Out of three thousand cases examined, upon arrival at Ft. Monroe, six hundred were fit for duty, and ordered to their regiments.…

July 29 (Tuesday)

Jonathan Letterman, medical director of the Army of the Potomac, was an astute observer of the organization of things. He'd long thought about a system for an ambulance corps in which this service would become a part of the medical service, thus interlocking the vital functions of transport with the treatment of the wounded. While on the Peninsula, he wrote:

The subject of the ambulance, after the health of the troops, became a matter of importance. Medical officers and quartermasters had charge of them, and, as a natural consequence, little care was exercised over them, and they couldn't be depended upon during an action or upon a march. It became necessary to institute some system for their management, such that they should not be under the immediate control of medical officers, whose duties, especially on the day of battle, prevented any supervision, when supervision was, more than at any other time, required. It seemed to me necessary, that whilst medical officers should not have the care of the horses, harness, etc., belonging to the ambulances, the system should be such as to enable them, at all times, to procure them with facility when wanted ... and to be kept under the general control of the medical department. Neither the kind nor the number of ambulances required were in the army ... but it nevertheless was necessary to devise a system that would render as available as possible the material upon the spot, particularly as the army might move at any time, and it was not considered advisable to wait for the arrival of such as had been asked for, only a portion of which ever came....

The "ambulance corps" which was systematized within the Army of the Potomac by Surg. Letterman, and approved by Maj. Gen. George B. McClellan, wouldn't be formally adopted by the U.S. Army until it was approved by an Act of Congress on April 12, 1864. At that time, the institution of the Ambulance Corps was mandated for all army units. The official implementation of the system within the Army of the Potomac in April 1864 was merely a formality, since the system had been in place since July 1862.

July 31 (Thursday)

Wainwright, Charles S., Col., N.Y. Artillery, at home, The Meadows, N.Y.:

Another whole month at home; and yet hardly fit to go back to camp. I started a fortnight ago, but got a relapse from overexertion in New York, and had to ask for a further extension of twenty days.... Have been up to Albany to see about my commissions ... got a certificate of my promotion to lieutenant-colonel April 30th, and colonel June 1st....

August 1 (Friday)

Surg. Jonathan Letterman took the opportunity to visit the hospitals at Point Lookout, Md., Ft. Monroe, Va., Portsmouth, Va., and Newport News, Va., during the early part of this month. Many of the wounded and sick from the Army of the Potomac had been evacuated to these places, and Letterman was interested in the quality of treatment being afforded. On this date, there were 1820 patients in the hospitals visited, and during the month they would receive 5191 additional patients. Of these, 716 returned to duty, 101 were discharged, 4 went on furlough, 9 deserted, and 84 died. The month would close with 5879 patients on the wards.

Perry, John G., Asst. Surg., USV, Chesapeake Hospital, Ft. Monroe, Va.:

I have been up to the army, the Army of the Potomac, and returned last night on the hospital boat with released prisoners. The trip was very interesting, though full of hard work.... On my arrival at headquarters, at Harrison's Landing, after seeing all I could of camps and such matters, I stumbled into a hospital tent and there remained, sleeping that night under an ambulance, with my blanket for a pillow....

August 2 (Saturday)

Perry, John G., Asst. Surg., USV, Chesapeake Hospital, Ft. Monroe, Va.:

The next morning orders came to start the released prisoners for Chesapeake Hospital and leave the worst cases there. I went on board the transport and, finding the men in a most pitiable condition, offered my services, which were immediately accepted. Some were almost naked; others without a rag on them. Poor fellows! Their wounds had not been dressed at all, and many were so weak from starvation they could barely walk. We were fifteen hours on board that boat without a morsel of food, and I could have almost eaten my tobacco. Yet not a word of complaint had been breathed by one of those brave men; the fact that they were released seemed sufficient compensation for all their suffering. We were finally transferred from the hospital boat to a tugboat, which was loaded with bread.

August 3 (Sunday)

Maj. Gen. Halleck ordered the Army of the Potomac from the Peninsula to the area of Aquia Creek and Alexandria, Va. The evacuation from Harrison's Landing began almost immediately.

Letterman, Jonathan, Med. Dir., Army of the Potomac, Peninsula, Va.:

The army had to be transported northward, by water, from this place. All the vessels that could be obtained, the transports fitted up for the sick, as well as others, were required ... for this object. It appeared that it was necessary to have the troops transported with rapidity, as they were sent with scarcely any baggage. It resulted, that the ambulances and all their appurtenances were left behind, to be sent up as vessels could be spared for the purpose. Some of the vessels never arrived. A large portion of the medical supplies were also left behind, in some cases everything but the hospital knapsack, by orders of colonels of regiments, regimental quartermasters, and others; in some cases, without the knowledge of the medical officers; in others, notwithstanding their protest. For such acts as these, medical officers have been severely censured, and they were censured afterwards for not having the very supplies which had been left behind....

Ropes, Hannah, Nurse, Union Hospital, Georgetown, Washington, D.C.:

My Dear Alice: It is my opinion you would be vastly happier to pass the winter with the Barnards than to open a school.... If you were in a school, or I needed you here, it would be hard for you to break up, but if you were there a telegraph could send you on. Now, it would not do for you to be here. It is no place for young girls. The surgeons are young and look upon nurses as their natural prey.... Wounded men are exposed from head to foot before the nurses and they object to anybody but an "old mother."

August 4 (Monday)

Perry, John G., Asst. Surg., USV, Chesapeake Hospital, Ft. Monroe, Va.:

Something is going on near the army, for gunboats have been moving up and down the river all day, and the big Union gun at the fort is booming throughout

the surrounding country every half hour, making the very earth quake. The sound stirs in me an intense enthusiasm which I have instantly to stifle and suppress, for it is impossible to do more than I am now doing without my medical degree, which I must have before continuing the work much longer. The brigade surgeon says I must stay here, but the necessities of my future career force me back to my studies; although this surgical practice is of great value.... My cottage is full, in fact the whole hospital is crowded, and I am tired out, having no relief whatever from steady, close confinement....

Asst. Surg. John G. Perry was exhausted from his steady work since his arrival in May. He became ill and returned home to convalesce. On March 18, 1863, he was married to Miss Martha Derby after successfully passing his final examination for his degree at the Boston Medical School. Perry was commissioned as an assistant surgeon in the 20th Mass. Volunteers on the day of his marriage. He left Boston to return to the Army of the Potomac on April 11, 1863.

McParlin, Thomas A., Surg., USA, Med. Dir., Army of Virginia, Northern Virginia:

The hospitals were in use until August 4th, when I ordered the tents to Falls Church and Alexandria on account of the insecurity of sick and stores at Warrenton. Falls Church hospital,... was distant a few miles from Alexandria. At a later season of the year, it would have been an unhealthy and inconvenient position. The hospitals in Alexandria, where I had authority to send sick, were filled late in July....

Before the troops moved from the Shenandoah, while in preparation for march, not a few malingerers and convalescents, for want of proper medical inspection, were sent from the army to Harpers Ferry and Baltimore. Prompt attention was called to this neglect of duty on the part of medical officers, and officers were sent to bring back to Warrenton the able-bodied absentees. I will here add, however, that, with every care and fulfillment of duty by medical officers, vagrant soldiers will collect about every depot for reception of wounded and sick men, as occurred at Culpeper and Bealton station. In the absence of a military force, and in defiance of the efforts of the medical and transport departments, these skulkers intermingle with the sick, or mount the roofs of cars, especially in retreat, and go off. Unless there is a cordial cooperation on the part of the railroad agents with the medical officers, it has happened that, upon cars being changed at a station, the roof passengers speedily obtain comfortable places, while the wounded, being moved slowly, with difficulty find accommodation....

August 5 (Tuesday)

In Lynchburg, Va., the ladies of the town were having difficulties working in the local hospitals. This was caused by the perception that "ladies" wouldn't be "useful" in the crowded hospitals among strange men. This was further compounded by the clash with the military doctors, who somewhat resented the "interference" of civilians. The Lynchburg women were unlike today's nurses. Initially, they came to the hospitals dressed very modestly, carrying their baskets of "goodies" for the sick and wounded, and they provided color to an otherwise drab scene. They wrote letters for the men, did their shopping for necessities, and generally made themselves useful. Later in the war, they would be assigned more medical duties and the tension between the ladies and the medical staff would largely disappear.

On this date, the 21st Indiana went into the battle of Baton Rouge with 585 men, all that was left of the original 1000. Surg. Ezra Read reported on the action.

Read, Ezra, Surg., 21st Indiana Vols., Battle of Baton Rouge, La.:

As the regiment occupied the centre, it was exposed to a constant fire during the action, and for a short time received a heavy cross fire from the enemy's right flank. No regiment suffered so much in killed and wounded. Twenty-four men were killed on the field and ninety-seven wounded. Every field officer was killed or wounded. The projectiles from the enemy's small arms were oblong and inflicted injuries of the most serious character....

August 7 (Thursday)

In Virginia, Lee was moving out of Culpeper C.H.; the Battle of Cedar Mountain would take place in two days. Not all the Confederate troops would be present for the battle.

Bradwell, I. G., Pvt., CSA, near Gordonsville, Va.:

On the morning of the 7th of August, when the command marched away, I was too sick with that dreadful disease, typhoid dysentery, to stand on my feet, and they left me there to die. After they had been gone some time a teamster came along to pick up whatever baggage had been left to haul to Gordonsville. This kind-hearted man found a place for me on top of his load of all kinds of army plunder and hauled me over a rough country road to town. The jolting almost killed me before we got there.

He spread my blanket on the railroad platform and put me on it, then told me he had to follow the army, but he would see if he could get me into the hospital. After some time he returned to me with Lt. Floyd, who was there among the sick, and they told me that the doctor in charge of that institution had refused to take any more sick soldiers in, as it was already overcrowded. The whole town was full of sick men. The hotel nearby and other houses were converted into hospitals, and still there was not room enough. Floyd stood in silence a while looking at me and walked away, saying he would try again. Again he and the driver came back and reported their failure to get me in, the doctor absolutely refusing to take another man.

Floyd stood looking at me in silence and pity, then exclaimed angrily as he turned to go away: "It's a shame for you to die here on the platform for want of attention. They *shall* take you." After he had been gone some time, litter bearers came and took me to the hotel, where they spread my blanket on the floor near the foot of a stairway, then brought me a pill of opium and a little water and later two batter cakes and some clover tea. That night I slept soundly....

August 8 (Friday)

The hospital census of the Confederate Receiving Hospital at Gordonsville, Va., peaked this month. The hospital records show a record of 8139 patients, 31 of whom died. Nine hundred fifty-nine cases of diarrhea; 114 cases of measles; and 119 cases of pneumonia. The dietary problems seemed, as usual, to cause the greatest sickness.

Bradwell, I. G., Pvt., CSA, near Gordonsville, Va.:

... but the next morning I was very sick. I was then taken up and put in a freight car crowded with sick soldiers for Greenwood, a place on the rocky side of a mountain. It seemed as if we would never get to our destination. When we reached that place I was put in a tent stretched over a rock that occupied half the ground and many more much smaller. Among these stones I lay down and remained for several days with little or no attention....

August 9 (Saturday)

Union Gen. John Pope was in the vicinity of Culpeper, Va., advancing towards Orange C.H. and the Gordonsville area. Jackson's corps of troops were just south of Culpeper, on the north bank of the Rapidan, waiting to attack Pope. However, Gen. Nathaniel Banks attacked first, striking two of Jackson's divisions, and was besting the Confederates when A. P. Hill piled into the fracas in a counterattack. Banks pulled back, still with his force intact.

McParlin, Thomas A., Surg., USA, Med. Dir., Army of Virginia, Cedar Mountain, Va.:

On the 8th day of August, general headquarters were advanced to Culpeper.... Intelligence reached us, and artillery firing in the extreme front indicated, during the day, the approach of the enemy. Banks's Corps was ordered up from Hazel creek, and Sigel's from Sperryville to Culpeper. Banks arrived at night, and advanced the next morning in the direction of Cedar Mountain, seven miles. He found the enemy moving forward.... In the afternoon, a general advance and a severe engagement took place, near Culver's Tavern, which lasted several hours. During the evening, and through the night, the wounded continued to arrive in Culpeper and were temporarily quartered in hotels, churches, etc., receiving such dressing and surgical attention as was required. As soon as I was aware of the engagement in front, I applied ... for a train of cars, which was promptly held in readiness to convey the wounded.... A medical officer of rank was dispatched to Culpeper, with authority to secure transportation ... and directed to have the wounded sent at once to hospitals in Alexandria by railroad....

August 10 (Sunday)

Skirmishing around Cedar Run near Culpeper,

Va., went on all day. Jackson's and Pope's men were too close not to clash occasionally.

McParlin, Thomas A., Surg., USA, Med. Dir., Army of Virginia, Cedar Mountain, Va.:

The casualties of the past day were large, and every building convertible into shelter had a full complement of wounded in and around it. The unemployed ambulances were collected together and dispatched to remove them to the rear.... The most important duty on the 10th was to bring the wounded from the extreme front and the advance depots near the lines, which was done as rapidly as the ambulance force could effect it.... Great numbers were sent in to Culpeper, and so occupied the medical force there that the primary object—sending them rapidly to Alexandria—was overlooked, and, though the train was waiting, building after building was occupied and filled. Orders were reiterated by express to have the wounded forwarded by the train. Hours afterward, I ascertained no action had been taken. Anticipating the difficulty, with the limited means at hand, and knowing the delay incident to getting the wounded out of buildings extemporized into hospitals, I returned to Culpeper, changed the organization, and dispatched the first train of cars with wounded to Alexandria.... Each train of wounded had medical attendance, water, subsistence, straw, and necessary bedding supplied....

August 11 (Monday)

There was considerable skirmishing around Cedar Mountain yesterday. Today Jackson withdrew for a time from Cedar Run to south of the Rapidan, near Gordonsville.

McParlin, Thomas A., Surg., USA, Med. Dir., Army of Virginia, Culpeper, Va.:

The enemy retired under Jackson on the 11th and 12th, and our lines were advanced beyond the lately contested field, and occupied a position near Cedar Mountain. The casualties of the battle of the 9th and 10th were large.... The action on the 9th was in the vicinity of Culver's Tavern. The woods and ground on the right were the scene of the sharpest contest. About six hundred wounded were received ... that evening and night.... From an analysis of a list of four hundred and eighty-three wounded in the action, made at the railroad depot at Culpeper, I find the regions wounded in this proportion: of the head, twenty; face, nineteen; neck, seven; chest, eleven; of the upper extremities, two hundred and eight; lower extremities, one hundred and eighty-seven; abdomen, three; back and spine, eleven; of the perineum or genitals, two; of the large joints, fifteen....

Ropes, Hannah, Nurse, Union Hospital, Georgetown, Washington, D.C.:

My Dear Alice: ... I am sitting by Larh, who lost his hand. He never kept still a moment, I believe, and it is awful hard to keep such a mercurial temperament from opening afresh the wound, and if it does again, the doctor says he must bleed to death. I have just told him I am a mind to throw him out of the window, and he says he wishes I would! Our doctors are young but fine fellows. Close on the other side is a man who has lost his foot. We have got them both on to water beds, and it is a great rest to them. The army is astir, and you may expect news. We look for patients every hour.

Organization for the care of the wounded in Virginia was still in its formative stage. In many cases they arrived at the railway stations and were literally "dumped" onto the streets to be picked up later. A Virginia newspaper reported:

Lynchburg Virginian:

"THE WAY THE SOLDIERS ARE NEGLECTED—Yesterday morning early a number of soldiers [wounded] were lying about the streets of the city. In response to their inquiry respecting their treatment by the enemy they said that 'it was bad enough but it is worse here.'"

August 12 (Tuesday)

Things were quiet around Cedar Run in Virginia. Both Pope and Jackson awaited Lee's arrival from the Peninsula. McClellan was withdrawing from the Peninsula towards Alexandria and Aquia, Va.

Welch, S. G., Surg., 20th S.C. Vols., with Jackson near Orange C.H., Va.:

We have been moving about continuously since I wrote to you.... Most of our hard marching has been during the night, but much of it has been in the heat

of the day. We have had nothing to eat but crackers and bacon, and not nearly enough of that.

We first marched up into Culpeper County, and were within two miles of the battlefield [Cedar Mountain].... Last night we began falling back. I suppose it was some strategic move and that we will continue these operations until a decisive fight takes place....

Bradwell, I. G., Pvt., CSA, near Gordonsville, Va.:

At last one day, to my joy, I saw a rough young fellow, whom I recognized as a member of my regiment, passing my tent. I called him. I asked if he could write, then begged him to write a letter to my father, which he did at my dictation. I told father that when he received that letter I probably would be dead, but I wanted him to come to Virginia and take my body back to Georgia and bury it beside my mother's grave back of the house. Before he got this letter the authorities took a notion to move all the sick to Nelson Courthouse, a village three miles from the nearest railroad station, and when we arrived there we were put into tents in a field near the depot. Here we remained for several days, while I lingered between life and death, and I awaited the time when I should be released from my suffering....

August 15 (Friday)

During the winter of 1861-62, a Confederate soldier from Farmville, Va., Henry W. Edmonds, was wounded in the chest. He was evacuated to the Receiving Hospital at Gordonsville, Va., for treatment. His surgeon was Dr. E. A. Craighill, who recorded this unusual case:

I thought he could live only a few hours, possibly days.... For weeks, his life just hung by a thread, and I would not have been surprised any minute to see him die. Acute (traumatic) pneumonia set in, with very profuse suppuration, but the hole through him was so large, the lung could be kept well drained of the accumulation. He was wounded in the winter, and he had on at the time a flannel shirt, a well padded undercoat and overcoat, in the pocket of his vest and coats there was a rubber comb, a lead pencil, a tintype of his best girl, whose name he gave me, and possibly other things, all of which were carried through him with the ball, and during the progress of the case in dressing the posterior wound, I removed at least a large teacup full of scraps of comb, pencil, tintype, coat wadding, etc. After weeks, which lengthened into months, this man got well enough to be sent to his home....

Edmonds recovered and married his best girl, but didn't return to the Confederate Army. After the war, Craighill heard from him occasionally, but didn't see him until some time in 1905 when Edmonds visited Craighill's pharmacy in Lynchburg, Va., forty-three years after he left the hospital at Gordonsville.

Letterman, Jonathan, Med. Dir., Army of the Potomac, Peninsula, Va.:

Col. R. Ingalls, Quartermaster, USA, made every effort in his power to aid me in removing the sick, and placed at different times temporarily at my disposal,... ten steamers. Some of these could make but one trip, others made more, and carried, in all, from the 9th to the night of the 15th of August, five thousand nine hundred and forty-five men. One thousand nine hundred and eight men were sent away before the 9th on the regular transports. The total number sent away, consequent upon the movement of the army, was fourteen thousand one hundred and fifty-nine. The largest number of boats was obtained on the 13th, and on that day and night five thousand six hundred and twenty-nine were sent away....

August 16 (Saturday)

McClellan, now in Washington, was finally free of the Peninsula, and many of his troops were now at Alexandria and Aquia Creek. He was supposed to reinforce Pope's Army of Virginia, which was now heading into a major clash with Lee near Manassas, but his pride wouldn't allow him to be subordinate to Pope.

Lee's army, now consolidated, was moving north from Gordonsville towards Culpeper and Manassas.

McParlin, Thomas A., Surg., USA, Med. Dir., Army of Virginia, Culpeper, Va.:

On the 16th, Medical Director Rauch reports: "I have removed all the wounded that will bear transportation; so far, have lost none. Sent, also, sixty-one of the sick. Have just been applied to for ambulances for a portion of Burnside's command. They also need medical supplies. Have issued what was on hand to whomsoever

has applied. The candidates for Alexandria are innumerable." The troops referred to were those of Gen. Reno, reinforcing us from Fredericksburg with eight thousand men. The ambulances had now been in constant use for many days; forage was scarce; the animals were becoming poor and weak; while brigade commanders and surgeons were anxious to have them return from Culpeper and general service to their commands, to rest and [recoup]. Had there been an ambulance corps organization, much, if not all this trouble, would have been averted....

August 17 (Sunday)

McParlin, Thomas A., Surg., USA, Med. Dir., Army of Virginia, Culpeper, Va.:

About this period, I received from Alexandria six, out of thirty-three, Autenrieth medical wagons, filled with supplies, which I had applied for on the 1st of July. In coming from Culpeper to the field, only seven miles, over a rough road, three were damaged badly. One of them upset, being top-heavy and narrow, and having no brakes. For these defects, medical officers declined accepting them, for the reason that they would be unavoidably broken to pieces and abandoned. They were sent to the quartermaster's depot, and brakes ordered....

Bradwell, I. G., Pvt., CSA, near Gordonsville, Va.:

But again the authorities moved us, this time to the village, and I was put in a jury room of the little courthouse. Words cannot describe the misery and suffering in that place. Wheat straw was put on the floor for us to lie on, and this and the walls were soon alive with vermin, and little attention of any kind was given us.

When my father got my letter his private and public engagements were such that he could not leave home, and he sent my brother-in-law, B. C. Scott, who could find no record of me at Greenwood. He then went to Richmond and searched the hospitals there and then to other places without success. Finally he came to Nelson Courthouse, but there was no record there. He had just turned his back on the place and was returning to Georgia, supposing me dead, when he was seen by one of my comrades who had that day heard where I was. So he came to the jury room and looked in on the scene of misery, then called to me to stand up, as he could not recognize me. When I did so he exclaimed, "My God!" and turned away. Soon an ambulance drove up to the courthouse door, and they took me to the hotel, where I was bathed, put on new clothes, and given something to eat.

Scott took me before the doctor in charge of all the sick at that place and asked him to give me a discharge. But the doctor held an official paper in his hand and told him he had just received instructions not to discharge anyone, even if he had lost a limb; but he said he would give me a discharge from the hospital and Scott could take me home if he wished to assume the responsibility. This Scott agreed to do; but when we got to Charlottesville I was too unwell to make the trip to Georgia, and he got me into the house of a very nice family, who treated me with as much consideration as if I had been a son. When I was able to walk about I fortunately located our captain, who was on sick leave in the country at North Garden Station. He took me out with him, where the kind treatment of the good people and the fresh mountain air soon restored me to health.

Bradwell rejoined his regiment in November following the Battle of Antietam.

August 18 (Monday)

Pope, now being pressed by Lee's advance, withdrew north of the Rappahannock and waited for reinforcements from McClellan. It would be a long wait.

McParlin, Thomas A., Surg., USA, Med. Dir., Army of Virginia, Cedar Mountain, Va.:

From the 10th to the 18th, the wounded and sick were accommodated in Culpeper in the Episcopal, Baptist, Methodist, and Presbyterian churches, in the Piedmont, Virginia, and Depot hotels, Masonic hall, tobacco factory, Commerce street hospitals, and the hospital encampment near the railroad. The wounded were frequently sent by train, certain cases, too dangerous to move, being left behind. Sick were daily sent from the front....

This position was maintained until the 18th, when, the rapid approach of the enemy under Gen. Lee being manifest.... Immediate steps were taken to remove the sick, and all proper cases among the wounded, with food and attendance, from Culpeper,

by railroad. In a few hours, one train of cars had left for Alexandria, and others followed during the night. Surgeons were detailed to remain with cases it would be fatal to move, and subsistence and medical stores were left for them. The purveying stores and tents were packed in six cars, their numbers taken, and, with the purveyor ... sent down the road to await orders at Warrenton Junction. All night, our trains and troops were passing Culpeper.... Medical Director Rauch, with several assistants,... left with the last train before night on the 19th....

August 19 (Tuesday)

Sisters of Charity, hospitals, Washington, D.C.:

Every Union soldier wore a belt with the initials "USA"—United States Army. When a wounded man was brought to the hospital, notice was given to the Sister and she would at once prepare to dress the wound. One day a man was brought in on a litter, pale and unconscious, and the Sister rushed to give him attention. By degrees he became conscious, and the Sister asked him where he was wounded. He seemed bewildered at first, but gradually his mind returned. Again the Sister asked him where he was wounded. A smile spread over his face. "It is all right, Sister," he said; "don't disturb yourself." "Oh, no," she said, "tell me where you were shot." "Yes," he answered, "I was shot, but shot in the USA" The Sister understood at once the bullet had struck the initials on his belt, and they had saved his life.

August 20 (Wednesday)

Skirmishing between Pope and Lee was becoming more frequent and widespread. As Lee advanced, Pope withdrew, still waiting for reinforcements (that would never come) from McClellan's idle thousands.

McParlin, Thomas A., Surg., USA, Med. Dir., Army of Virginia, Manassas, Va.:

The enemy's cavalry advanced on the morning of the 20th ... and continued to threaten our troops on the west side.... After due examinations ... I selected Bealeton station as the depot for wounded and supplies.... The cars containing ... supplies were ordered from Warrenton Junction to Bealeton....

August 21 (Thursday)

McParlin, Thomas A., Surg., USA, Med. Dir., Army of Virginia, Manassas, Va.:

During the 20th, 21st and 22d, the enemy attacked us at various points, to force a passage of the river, and we were constantly engaged at one or more positions. The wounded from our front and entrenched positions on the west were brought over the bridge, dressed in the field depot, and thence, with other wounded, sent by empty cars or ambulances to Bealeton station. Houses, at convenient points in rear, were used as field hospitals by the corps directors and surgeons. To them, litter bearers and ambulances bore the wounded of the corps, and thence to Bealeton by empty railroad trains from Rappahannock station....

The difficulty of striking and packing tents, purveying stores, and other property into cars,... had so occupied my time at Culpeper that I determined,... to keep supplies packed in cars. Delay might endanger the loss of the entire amount. I therefore ordered the supplies at Bealeton to be kept in the cars, and had the switch lengthened so as to permit the cars to remain out of the way of trains. I also telegraphed orders ... to have two cars arranged with shelving and fixtures convenient for making issues, and to fill them.... They were ready on the 23d....

At the Confederate Receiving Hospital, Gordonsville, Va., one of Dr. E. A. Craighill's duties was the hospital "pesthouse."

Craighill, E. A., Surg., CSA, hospital in Gordonsville, Va.:

We then had a shanty, which eventually grew to be quite a house, in a retired place in the woods, for the treatment of smallpox patients exclusively, the dread disease having broken out among the soldiers. One of my duties was to visit this pesthouse every morning, and in addition, whenever called upon. This was not infrequent as the other surgeons did not go, and I was the only surgeon who did, and once I had under treatment eighty-four patients in all the stages of this horrible disease. No one can know how horrible it is unless they experience what I did, not the least being the disgusting and unmistakable odor that attends particularly bad cases, and I had some of the worst. I had no dread of the disease, but vaccinated myself every morning and thought I was protected.... Of course, I always changed my outer garments when I went to the hospital, and when I left, keeping my smallpox clothes in the woods in the open air when not in service....

August 22 (Friday)

In Mississippi, Confederate Van Dorn threatened the area of Corinth, causing the evacuation of the hospital at Farmington to the town of Corinth, where it would be better sheltered. All was packed and moved, including Mrs. Bickerdyke's new stove.

Still more skirmishing along the Rappahannock between Lee and Pope, as there had been for several days. McClellan still sat in Alexandria and gave excuses for his inaction. Pope was a little embarrassed when Jeb Stuart raided Catlett's Station and captured all of Pope's baggage and papers. Now Pope had neither clean shirts nor reinforcements.

McParlin, Thomas A., Surg., USA, Med. Dir., Army of Virginia, Manassas, Va.:

The enemy demonstrated on the various fords, but a large force, which had been detached to cross at the upper ford, passed on our right.... Their cavalry passed to our rear at Catlett's, and destroyed much personal and headquarters baggage. My office records were scattered about, several valuable papers and maps were lost, and my servant, horse and bedding disappeared. My cook, mess-chest and other baggage were not interfered with. One servant, however, returned, after a detour as prisoner to Richmond.... Pvt. Upham, of the general escort, faithfully followed me thereafter....

August 25 (Monday)

At Farmington, Miss., the word was that the Confederates were near and an assault was expected on Corinth at any time. Directions were given to evacuate the hospital and move the patients into Corinth for safety. This was ordered in such haste that the Union officers directed that any excess or "nonessential" supplies be left behind. This seemed such a waste to Mother Bickerdyke that she had two army wagons "lost" in the nearby woods until all the patients were moved, then the wagons were loaded with cooking utensils, spare bedding, soiled linens, which were to be cleaned, along with the pots in which to boil them, *and* the huge cooking range Bickerdyke had acquired in July. All magically appeared at the new hospital in Corinth.

McParlin, Thomas A., Surg., USA, Med. Dir., Army of Virginia, Warrenton, Va.:

> On the 24th and 25th, a rapid rise of the river threatened to carry away all communication across, and our force on the heights was brought over.... The freshet, and the presence of a force on our right and rear, the former holding the enemy in check, the latter demanding immediate attention, made it necessary … to move our forces in the direction of Warrenton.... The wounded from the lines and the sick, surgical supplies, tents, cooking department, surgical staff, purveying cars, etc., were ordered … to Warrenton Junction.... The wounded were sent by ambulances to Warrenton, where they were … lodged in public buildings,… until a train arrived from the Junction with supplies, and returning, took them to the depot … at Warrenton....
>
> No general engagement occurred at Warrenton.... Headquarters were transferred to the Junction. I found there the new medical purveying cars, well stocked with battlefield supplies, arranged conveniently for issue, and a cargo of ice. The wounded were in tents. Water was brought in tubs and barrels.... There was a goodly supply of food and comforts. Ice was abundant, but the water supply was scanty. Large caldrons were used for making soup and coffee, and cooks were as numerous as could be desired....

August 26 (Tuesday)

Today, Lee and Pope were to began the battle which would be known as either the Second Battle of Bull Run, or as Second Manassas. The opening action was taken by cavalry under Fitzhugh Lee, one of Robert E. Lee's sons, when he entered Manassas Junction and captured the rail depot, cutting the communication line to Washington. Jackson, on the move since the previous day, came through the Bull Run Mts. at Thoroughfare Gap and positioned himself at Bristoe Station. The Confederates captured tons of supplies at the Manassas Junction rail depot and begin moving much of it south. Meanwhile, Pope didn't know where Jackson, Lee, or anyone was at the moment. Pope did know where

McClellan was, sitting at Alexandria "awaiting the remainder of his army from the Peninsula."

Welch, S. G., Surg., 20th S.C. Vols., Battle of Second Manassas, Va.:

> We marched fast all day Monday and all day Tuesday and until late Tuesday night, when we bivouacked in a field of tall grass near Bristoe Station. Bob Land spread his wet horse blanket on a bare spot, and we lay on it and covered with his blanket and went to sleep without supper. The country was a waste, and I heard no sound of a chicken, cow or dog during the night.

Mother Bickerdyke's new hospital at Corinth was nearly perfect. A former young ladies' seminary, it had wide dormitories, large rooms, and airy places for the patients. In addition, it had a full kitchen and laundry in separate buildings, although both were poorly equipped for use by a hospital.

August 27 (Wednesday)

Pope, already outflanked by Jackson, left his lines and moved north towards the old Manassas battlefield. Jackson, at the Manassas Junction rail depot, was destroying everything that couldn't be carried off. Longstreet was coming up in support of Jackson. Pope was in deep trouble.

Welch, S. G., Surg., 20th S.C. Vols., Battle of Second Manassas, Va.:

> The next morning we got up before day and marched fast to Manassas Junction, and almost kept up with the cavalry. We found sutlers' stores and trainloads of flour and meat, and we captured a few prisoners. I went into a sutler's tent and got three days' rations of ham, crackers and salt. Before noon we started towards Washington, and after marching three or four miles we marched back to Manassas Junction again late that afternoon and found many prisoners and negroes there, who were all sent away towards Groveton. We staid there that night, and all the cars and everything were set on fire about the same time....

McParlin, Thomas A., Surg., USA, Med. Dir., Army of Virginia, Warrenton, Va.:

> After the 27th, orders were sent to Warrenton,… to break up the temporary hospitals at once, and to

remove the sick and wounded by railroad, with food and medical attendance.... Meanwhile, the inmates of our hospital encampment at Warrenton Junction were to be sent to Alexandria, and when that was done, the purveying cars, with the medical officers and cooking department were to be in readiness to move. General headquarters preceded me some hours on the march, while I was arranging for bringing off our wounded and supplies. Extensive fires appeared eastward in our rear, and it was rumored that the railroad was cut by the enemy. The expected reinforcements had not arrived at Centreville or Manassas to guard these places. Thoroughfare Gap was unoccupied, and the enemy had found an easy entrance.... The railroad bridge at Kettle Run was destroyed, and the flames of an extensive fire could be plainly seen on the high plains in the distance towards Manassas....

Ropes, Hannah, Nurse, Union Hospital, Georgetown, Washington, D.C.:

Dear Alice: ... We are in the receipt of men from every division in the army and are expecting a rush of wounded today from Pope. We have gone through twenty frights about Washington, and got so used to expecting to be taken prisoners that I think I am rather disappointed.... We have just cleaned and dressed over a hundred men from the Harrison's Landing—poor worn fellows! The most of them are in the church opposite, which is under our supervision. Last week the Directors of Hospitals sent a committee out here to spy us out and take notes, because no other hospital had supported itself on government allowance. The Doctor took them into the kitchen and told the cook to tell them what we had for dinner and breakfast that day. Then, upstairs, they questioned patients in every ward, and were told they had everything they wanted. You may imagine the surprise of the committee at this, but you can't when we assured them that we had over four hundred dollars over of ration money at the end of each month from which we bought some water beds, subscribed for twenty daily papers, the two monthlies, and placed the rest in the hospital fund...!

In Kentucky, Confederate Gen. Kirby Smith had invaded the state and was in the vicinity of Richmond. Union Gen. W. Nelson had been sent to that area to oppose Smith. Asst. Surg. B. J. D. Irwin,

USA, was assigned as medical director for Nelson's force. At this point, Irwin had no idea what frustration he was in for.

Irwin, B. J. D., Asst. Surg., USA, Med. Dir., action at Richmond, Ky.:

During the night of August 15th, Maj. Gen. W. Nelson,... received a telegram from Gen. Buell, directing him to proceed at once to Kentucky.... In obedience to this order, Gen. Nelson left next morning ... taking all the members of his staff. We arrived at Lexington, Ky., on the 26th, and I was announced as medical director of the army of Kentucky.

Next day, we proceeded to Richmond, Ky., and I lost no time in informing myself of the condition and wants of the eight new regiments, just concentrated, from Indiana and Ohio.... They had been only from fourteen to twenty days in the field, and had but few medical officers, who had neither medicines, instruments, ambulances, tents, or camp equipage, to enable them to perform their duties. With three exceptions, the medical officers were inexperienced in service and had but vague ideas as to the extent or sphere of their duties. I immediately despatched two of the most intelligent of them to Louisville and Cincinnati, to procure ambulances and medical supplies for the several regiments....

August 28 (Thursday)

Noon at Manassas, Pope arrived to find Jackson had withdrawn. Pope had no idea where the Confederate had gone. Jackson, meanwhile, was sitting along the Warrenton Turnpike just west of the old Bull Run battlefield. Pope, hurrying towards Centreville, where he thought Jackson would be, slammed unwittingly into the Rebel force at Brawner's Farm. Intelligence reports in this battle were very poor. At any rate, Longstreet and Lee proceeded through Thoroughfare Gap and passed undetected to the north of Pope. The stage was set for a Union defeat.

McParlin, Thomas A., Surg., USA, Med. Dir., Army of Virginia, Manassas, Va.:

... on the afternoon of the 28th a severe action ensued. The wounded from Gibbon's and Doubleday's brigades were brought to Manassas where [they were] ... promptly provided for.... An Autenrieth wagon furnished the amputating table, and every facility for surgical attention. I spent some hours there and on the road.... Many wounded officers were received at the depot.... The bridge beyond Manassas, towards Fairfax Station was burned. I had to locate the depot near the bridge or ford north of Bull Run,... the purveying depot took position in the yard. Tents were pitched, and the purveying wagons arranged. There were no supplies destroyed or left at Kettle Run, all being used ... or brought forward by Dr. Rauch to his depot....

Welch, S. G., Surg., 20th S.C. Vols., Battle of Second Manassas, Va.:

Thursday morning we marched nearly to Centreville, and from there towards Groveton, and Ewell's command got into a fight late that afternoon on our right. We remained there and bivouacked in the oak forest where our brigade fought next day....

August 29 (Friday)

At Manassas, Pope was trying to make sense of the tactical situation. He believed Jackson was trapped and ordered an assault against the Rebel positions. Jackson, in a strong position in a railroad cut at Sudley Springs, held without a problem. Meanwhile, Longstreet and Lee arrived about noon and took positions near the old Confederate line of July 1861.

As night settled, the fighting quieted down, as everyone waited for the next day. Halleck, in Washington, was urging McClellan to send troops immediately to support Pope. McClellan, having a strong dislike for Pope, "tried his best" to comply, but little was done. Many believed that "Little Mac's" ego wouldn't stand having to play second fiddle to anyone, let alone John Pope.

McParlin, Thomas A., Surg., USA, Med. Dir., Army of Virginia, Manassas, Va.:

Our army was engaged on the 29th.... Wounded were brought in from the front, and received the attention of the brigade and corps medical officers that night. The view from headquarters embraced a most extended country, filled with troops, the line of camp fires stretching for miles away towards Thoroughfare Gap.... The wounded from the day's action were numerous. I informed the Surgeon General of our condition and prospects, requesting surgeons, battlefield supplies and ambulances to be sent from Washington to meet the contingencies of a severe engagement. This by courier to the nearest telegraph station.

As the turnpike to Centreville was very rough, several bridges destroyed and our general depot was near the bridge, I instituted inquiries and found a short road running from the Centreville turnpike, near the battlefield, directly to the general depot. I sent circulars to the corps directors, informing them where the wounded should be sent, and stationed some mounted men on the pike, to direct the ambulances and wounded properly....

Welch, S. G., Surg., 20th S.C. Vols., Battle of Second Manassas, Va.:

Next morning we had breakfast, and I ate with Adj. Goggans. Our command took position in the woods near the cut of an unfinished railroad and sent out skirmishers, who soon retreated and fell back on the main line. The Yankee line came up quite near and fired into us from our right, and Goggans was shot through the body.... I looked at him as he was gasping his last, and he died at once. Then the wounded who could walk began to come back, and those who could not were brought to me on litters. I did all I could for them until the ambulances could carry them to the field infirmary and this continued until late in the afternoon....

Col. McGowan came limping back, shot through the thigh, but he refused to ride, and said: "Take men who are worse hurt than I am." Col. Marshall and Lt.-Col. Leadbetter were brought back mortally wounded.

Shells came over to us occasionally as if thrown at our reserves.... An occasional spent ball fell nearby and one knocked up the dust close to me, but the trees were thick and stopped most of the bullets short of us. The Yankees charged us seven times during the day and were driven back every time....

Our brigade was not relieved until about four o'clock. They had been fighting all day and their losses were very heavy ... [I] went back to the field infirmary, where I saw large numbers of wounded lying on the ground as thick as a drove of hogs in a lot. They were groaning and crying out with pain, and those shot in the bowels were crying for water. Jake Fellers had his arm amputated without chloroform. I held the artery and Dr. Huot cut it off by candlelight. We continued to operate until late at night and attended to all our wounded. I was very tired and slept on the ground.

Soldiers of the 7th New Hampshire Vols. arrived at Hilton Head Island from Key West carrying the dreaded yellow fever, causing an outbreak among the Union forces on this date. The spread was immediate and deadly, although generally confined to that island.

August 30 (Saturday)

At Manassas, Pope believed the Confederates had retreated, so he attacked Jackson's line, which was the Confederate left flank. Longstreet attacked the Union left flank and rolled up Pope's army, sending the Federals into retreat towards Centreville. Pope had been beaten, but the army didn't panic and go into a rout, as it had at First Manassas. Lee won the battle, but he didn't destroy the Union Army on the field.

When it was finally over, there was enough glory (Confederate) and blame (Federal) to share. Pope had been humiliated and would be sent west to command an administrative district and fight Indians. McClellan, as usual, would deny any blame for not reinforcing Pope, and Halleck had proven, once again, that he wasn't forceful enough for a crisis. The Union suffered over 16,000 casualties and the South over 9000.

McParlin, Thomas A., Surg., USA, Med. Dir., Army of Virginia, Centreville, Va.:

All day on the 30th, the ambulances were employed conveying wounded to this depot, where they were received and cared for. Col. Vollum informed me early in the day that the cooking arrangements were ample, and everything getting ready for their reception. Three wagons had been sent back to the railroad for supplies.... Our provisions and forage at this time were scanty. It became a constant care to find and obtain provisions for the wounded. The supply trains were with Banks, in the rear; the railroad was inoperative, and little was received by wagons from Alexandria....

... the battle was renewed on our right and continued for some hours. The enemy was arriving in the direction of Thoroughfare Gap, and seemed to be moving to our extreme left and on Manassas. The engagement became warmer hour by hour.... The ambulances had been busy all day conveying wounded to Bull Run hospital depot.... I joined general headquarters about four o'clock P.M., observing meanwhile the ambulance and litter service around me.

The field, for miles away, with moving troops, volleys, explosions and dust of shell and shot, were all in clear view from the high crest which we occupied. The dust of the enemy's main army train on the left, the advance of our regiments and the long line of the enemy's artillery fire, from the crest of the Manassas Gap railroad, were very conspicuous. Shot and shell were now flying near the ambulances of Patrick's brigade of the Third Corps. Surg. C. H. Wilcox, in charge, was soon under fire, and I apprehended each moment injury to the ambulance animals before they could be sent back loaded behind the hill....

The tide of battle swept backward and forward The crackling of musketry seemed almost continuous. The fury and onslaught, however, slackened at dusk, a determined resistance having checked the enemy's advance. Late in the evening, it was determined to retire to Centreville....

Welch, S. G., Surg., 20th S.C. Vols., Battle of Second Manassas, Va.:

We did nothing Saturday morning. There were several thousand prisoners nearby, and I went where they were and talked with some of them. Dr. Evans, the brigade surgeon, went to see Gen. Lee, and Gen. Lee told him the battle would begin that morning about ten o'clock and would cease in about two hours, which occurred exactly as he said. Our brigade was not engaged, and we spent the day sending the wounded to Richmond.

Irwin, B. J. D., Asst. Surg., USA, Med. Dir., action at Richmond, Ky.:

On the 29th, I was ordered, and went to Lancaster, twenty-five miles from Richmond, with the headquarters of the army; but hearing that the enemy was menacing our troops at Richmond, I returned next morning, and arrived on the field at eleven o'clock, and found that our forces, after having fought three hours and a half against superior numbers, had been obliged to fall back about two miles from the battleground, leaving our killed and wounded in the possession of the enemy, but under care of some five or six of our medical officers.... I was gratified to find that I had received a dozen ambulances, and supplies of medicine and stimulants for four of the regiments.... I had previously taken possession of the courthouse, and a seminary building for hospital purposes, and thither our wounded were conveyed.... The contest was renewed three times during the day in new positions, and terminated at dark, in a complete defeat and rout of our whole force. Gen. Nelson arrived on the field during the evening, and was shortly afterward severely wounded in the left groin. I rode from the field with him some distance to attend to his wound, but I was obliged to throw myself into the hands of a party of the enemy's cavalry, thereby securing his escape....

August 31 (Sunday)

At Manassas, the wounded were gathered for evacuation, the dead were buried, and the discarded equipment recovered for later use. A little late, two corps from McClellan's Army of the Potomac arrived to reinforce Pope. Lee, based on information gathered by Stuart's cavalry scouts, readied to attack Pope again by turning the Union right flank. He moved Jackson to a position just west of Chantilly, with Longstreet following along. The game wasn't over just yet.

McParlin, Thomas A., Surg., USA, Med. Dir., Army of Virginia, Manassas, Va.:

Early on the morning of the 31st, Med. Inspector R. H. Coolidge, USA, arrived at headquarters, assigned to duty as principal medical officer of all the troops serving west of the Potomac. The affairs of the transport service and of the medical and hospital department were afterwards directed by him at Centreville. On the 31st of August and 1st of September, supplies, ambulances, hacks, surgeons and citizens came out from Washington. The wounded from all directions, the surgical staff, purveyor's supplies and the cooking corps were collected as far as possible and moved on to Fairfax Courthouse....

Welch, S. G., Surg., 20th S.C. Vols., Battle of Second Manassas, Va.:

Early Sunday morning we started away, and I passed by where Goggan's body lay. Near him lay the body of Capt. Smith of Spartanburg. Both were greatly swollen and had been robbed of their trousers and

shoes by our own soldiers, who were ragged and barefoot, and did it from necessity. We passed on over the battlefield where the dead and wounded Yankees lay. They had fallen between the lines and had remained there without attention since Friday. We marched all day on the road northward and traveled about twelve miles.

Irwin, B. J. D., Asst. Surg., USA, Med. Dir., action at Richmond, Ky.:

Next morning, I was turned over to the Confederate commander, who, after placing certain restrictions on my movements, acceded to my request to be permitted to go to superintend the treatment of our wounded. Upon arriving at the hospital buildings, I found the rooms, corridors, and balconies densely crowded with men, wounded and mutilated in every conceivable way. Everything that our meager means would allow was being done for their speedy relief, but as the enemy had captured all our hospital stores, ambulances, etc., I was reduced to the utmost straits for means to meet the wants of so large a number of sufferers.... I was fortunate in being able to purchase some four hundred dollars' worth of medicines, dressings, stimulants, muslin, etc., from a druggist, and in borrowing instruments from some of the civil practitioners of medicine in the town. With commendable zeal and generosity, the loyal citizens brought in abundance of subsistence, fresh meats, soup, milk, fruit, light bread, etc. The ladies of Richmond and vicinity, for ten or fifteen miles around, came daily to the hospital, and with untiring devotion lent their valuable assistance in dressing and assisting our suffering soldiers.... Those detailed from among the prisoners of war deserted their posts, despite all our efforts, at the first opportunity. Being recruits, they possessed no feeling of sympathy for their wounded comrades, such as old soldiers are wont to evince for each other....

September 1 (Monday)

Following Manassas, Lee wasn't yet finished. He sent Jackson around the Federal right, where Stonewall ran into Federal Gens. I. I. Stevens and P. Kearny. In the midst of a heavy rainstorm, the fighting swirled around Chantilly until evening, and during this time both Stevens and Kearny were killed. Pope resisted mightily and withdrew towards

Centreville, pressured by Lee. As night fell, Washington was still safe, but Lee was very close.

McParlin, Thomas A., Surg., USA, Med. Dir., Army of Virginia, Centreville, Va.:

On the 1st of September,... I took charge of a flag of truce and a numerous corps of surgeons, attendants and volunteer assistants, with what ambulances could be found, and some wagons with supplies, having an escort ... and went to the battlefield. I selected a central point as rendezvous for the party, detailed surgeons, assistants and litter-bearers, and assigned sections of the field over which to collect wounded in small depots, to be brought thence by ambulances. There were many wounded in buildings along the road, but I deemed it more important to collect those left scattered helpless and exposed. For this purpose, I passed the ambulances far to the front and there loaded them. Medical Director L. Guild, of Gen. Lee's army, joined me, with assistants, and arrangements were made for paroling. The paroled wounded were sent to Centreville, using for the purpose all the wagons and ambulances, except two at the rendezvous. Subsistence and forage were sent for by courier to our lines, and urgent application made for ambulances to continue the work. These were scarce. One party was occupied in distributing the stores to depots of wounded from a stock scantily supplied from the medical storehouse in Centreville. A number of operations were performed at the rendezvous, and dressings were supplied from the Autenrieth medical wagon and ambulances.... Paroling was continued, and subsistence and medical supplies distributed....

Welch, S. G., Surg., 20th S.C. Vols., Battle of Second Manassas, Va.:

The next morning we continued our march towards Fairfax C.H., and had a battle late that afternoon at Ox Hill during a violent thunderstorm. Shell were thrown at us and one struck in the road and burst within three or four feet of me.... There were flashes and keen cracks of lightning nearby and hard showers of rain fell.... I went into a horse lot and established a field infirmary, and saw an old lady and her daughter fleeing from a cottage and crossing the lot in the rain. The old lady could not keep up and the daughter kept stopping and urging her mother to hurry. The bullets were striking all about the yard of their house.

Lt. Leopard from Lexington was brought back to me with both his legs torn off below the knees by a shell, and another man with part of his arm torn off, but neither Dr. Kennedy, Dr. Kilgore, nor our medical wagon was with us, and I had nothing with me to give them but morphine. They both died during the night. The battle continued till night came on and stopped it. We filled the carriage house, barn and stable with our wounded, but I could do but little for them....

After doing all I could for the wounded, my brother, my servant Wilson, and myself went into the orchard and took pine poles from a fence and spread them on the wet ground to sleep on. I discovered a small chicken roosting in a peach tree and caught it, and Wilson skinned it and broiled it, and it was all we three had to eat that day. Wilson got two good blankets off the battlefield with "U.S." on them, and we spread one on the poles and covered with the other.

September 2 (Tuesday)

South of Washington, Pope, pulling back into the entrenchments around the city, was being pressured by Lee with skirmishing at Fairfax C.H., Vienna, Falls Church, and Flint Hill. Lincoln, reluctantly, returned McClellan to command of all the armies in northern Virginia, a move hotly opposed by Secretaries Stanton and Chase. Pope was now without a command. Lee gathered his army near Chantilly and rested the men while he thought of what to do next. The Federals evacuated Winchester, much to the delight of Richmond, leaving enough ordnance stores for a campaign.

Welch, S. G., Surg., 20th S.C. Vols., Battle of Second Manassas, Va.:

The next morning the Yankees were gone. Their general, Kearny, was killed and some of their wounded fell into our hands. The two other doctors with our medical supplies did not get there until morning, and many of our wounded died during the night. I found one helpless man lying under a blanket between two men who were dead.

We drew two days' rations of crackers and bacon about ten o'clock, and I ate them all and was still very hungry. I walked over on the hill and saw a few dead

Yankees. They had become stiff, and one was lying on his back with an arm held up. I picked up a good musket and carried it back with me to the house and gave it to the young lady I saw running away the day before. She thanked me for it, and seemed very much pleased to have it as a memento of the battle.

Late that afternoon we drew rations again, and I ate everything without satisfying my hunger. A soldier came from another command and said he heard I had some salt, and he offered me a shoulder of fresh pork for some. Wilson cooked it and I ate it without crackers, but was still hungry....

Following the Battle of Second Manassas, as many as 7627 Confederate wounded were evacuated by train to the Receiving Hospital at Gordonsville, Va., where they were given immediate treatment. Those who could travel were sent on to hospitals at Lynchburg, Charlottesville, and Richmond. The flood of wounded into Lynchburg created major problems in the housing and care of the men. Large numbers had died during transport, being laid on bare floors in railway cars with no attendants to provide food or water. Trains arriving in the middle of the night or late evening weren't met by medical attendants and the wounded lay at the depot all night without care. This situation would improve, albeit slowly.

Letterman, Jonathan, Med. Dir., Army of the Potomac, Washington, D.C.:

From the date of the embarkation of the troops at Ft. Monroe, up to the time when the general was placed in command of the defenses of Washington, I know personally but little of the medical department of the Army of the Potomac. It was not under my control. On the 2d of September,... it came once more under my control, and I found it in a most deplorable condition. The officers were worn down by the labors they had ... undergone; a large portion of their supplies,... had been left at Ft. Monroe, and even much of that which they had brought with them was thrown on the roadside, I have been informed ... on the way to join Gen. Pope....

September 3 (Wednesday)

Irwin, B. J. D., Asst. Surg., USA, Med. Dir., action at Richmond, Ky.:

I obtained permission to send, under a flag of truce, to Lexington for clothing and medical supplies, and had the gratification to receive a wagon load of underclothes, dressings, sheets, etc., on the 2d instant; and on the 6th a supply of medical stores. The Confederate post surgeon, Dr. Tucker, evinced a sincere desire to share with me his limited supply of underclothing, cooking, and mess utensils, by which I was enabled to relieve the condition of those patients whose wants were most urgent. The number of wounded amounted to some seven hundred, the killed from two hundred and fifty to three hundred.... For want of transportation, I was obliged to leave some one hundred and sixty patients at Rogersville, six miles south of Richmond, the scene of the first engagement....

From the fact that the Confederate authorities had no suitable commissary supplies to furnish for the support of our wounded, and from the fear the supplies furnished to us by the generous-hearted citizens would become exhausted, I determined to proceed to Lexington, and to obtain permission from the Confederate commander to allow me to pass through his lines to Ohio to procure transportation for such of the wounded as would bear removing. Already some two hundred of them, whose wounds were slight and did not interfere with locomotion, were paroled and sent forward to our lines....

I left for Lexington on the 6th, when, after ten days' delay, I was permitted to go to Cincinnati to have the necessary transportation, nurses and subsistence, sent back to Richmond. Several volunteers accompanied the expedition which left here on the 9th.

Lee withdrew to around Leesburg, Va., but there was still skirmishing around Falls Church, Fairfax C.H., and other points in northern Virginia. Lee was now close to the ferries crossing the Potomac, and there were actions west of Washington, near Harpers Ferry. Confederate Gen. Richard Ewell had his leg amputated and would be absent from the army for nearly a year.

Pope, now without a command, wrote his report for Gen. Halleck, in which he accused Gen. Porter with disobeying orders in the face of the enemy, and Gen. McClellan with not sending troops in a timely fashion. He was right in McClellan's case.

McParlin, Thomas A., Surg., USA, Med. Dir., Army of Virginia, Centreville, Va.:

September 3d, I received orders to join general head-quarters, army of Virginia, and I went to Centreville, leaving Surg. Page, USA, in charge. Medical Director Guild, and Drs. Cullen and Maury accompanied me. Our army had retired from Centreville....

Welch, S. G., Surg., 20th S.C. Vols., Battle of Second Manassas, Va.:

During the night I became very sick from overeating, and next morning when the regiment left I was too sick to march. Billie, Mose Cappock, Billy Caldwell and myself all got sick from the same cause. We are all sleeping in the carriage house, and I have sent Wilson out into the country to get something for us to eat. We hope to be able to go on and catch up with the regiment in a day or two. It has gone in the direction of Harpers Ferry.

September 4 (Thursday)

The South's position in the international scene wasn't promising. Neither France nor England had recognized the Confederacy as a country separate from the United States, nor had any other nation. The Southerners needed to prove that the Confederacy was a viable force, deserving of standing in the community of nations. Lee felt that he had such a solution. An invasion of the North would prove that the Confederacy had sufficient strength to stand on its own feet. With this in mind, and with the approval of Richmond, Lee headed his troops to the crossings of the Potomac, and into Maryland, where he hoped the people would rise for the South. The movement into Maryland caused fighting at all the major fords of the Potomac. Federals evacuated Frederick, Md., just a few miles north.

The plight of the wounded left at Centreville seemed to be forgotten by the Union generals, who left and returned to Washington. There were, however, some medical personnel still working on the problem.

McParlin, Thomas A., Surg., USA, Med. Dir., Army of Virginia, Centreville, Va.:

So great was our need for ambulances, forage and food, that Medical Inspector Coolidge addressed,...

a communication to the Surgeon General, sent through Gen. Lee's headquarters, for the purpose of informing him of our situation, and requesting urgently that food, forage, and three hundred ambulances might be sent to the battlefield. Only one ambulance had come from the army to Centreville since it left that place....

Letterman, Jonathan, Med. Dir., Army of the Potomac, Washington, D.C.:

The labor expended at Harrison's Landing in rendering it [the medical service] efficient for active service seemed to have been expended in vain, and before it could be in a condition to render such service again it was necessary that it should be completely refitted. The circumstances under which the army was then placed made this simply impossible; there was not time to do it, for as soon as the troops reached the defenses of Washington, they were marched into Maryland, and no time could be allowed for medical officers again to equip themselves with the medicines, instruments, dressings, and stores necessary for the campaign in that state....

September 5 (Friday)

Stonewall Jackson's grey columns approached Frederick, Md., which he'd enter on the 6th. The Federal hospital at Frederick was staffed with ten Sister of Charity nurses from Emmitsburg, Md. The drums startled the Sisters in late evening and the surgeon announced the evacuation of all Federals who could be moved and the destruction of all military stores which couldn't be evacuated. The Sisters spent the remainder of the night tending to the patients who were too ill to be moved.

McParlin, Thomas A., Surg., USA, Med. Dir., Army of Virginia, Centreville, Va.:

Our supplies in Centreville were, of course, captured. The Confederate officers, however, shared with us, and on the morning of the 5th of September, our portion was sent out to the field.... Our wounded were suffering for food. The supplies brought were distributed. Dr. Coolidge secured from Dr. Guild other supplies, and some beef cattle were purchased. I am happy to say that the Confederate officers and soldiers shared with our wounded their scanty store....

September 6 (Saturday)

This day dawned on a scene of desolation at the military hospital in Frederick, Md., where the remaining patients were tended by four doctors and the Sisters of Charity. At about 9 A.M. the first of the Confederate scouts entered the area and demanded the surrender of the Federals remaining at the hospital. This was done and then a flood of nearly 400 sick Confederates were brought into the hospital for treatment. Not having too much in the way of rations to feed these new patients, the Sisters called for help from the townspeople, who responded quickly, providing food and assistance for the sick.

McParlin, Thomas A., Surg., USA, Med. Dir., Army of Virginia, Centreville, Va.:

On the 6th a train of ambulances came out. No information of our situation had reached the Surgeon General when it left. I was directed by Medical Inspector Coolidge to proceed to Washington, and report to him [the Surgeon General] in person the condition of affairs. I did so. Orders were issued that night for every available vehicle to be sent out, in addition to several weeks' supplies already on the way thither. The removal of the wounded went on under the supervision and direction of Inspector Coolidge. On my way to Washington, I saw ambulances were on the road with wounded from Chantilly, the last battlefield.... The day after my arrival in Washington, I was assigned to the charge of the general hospital in Annapolis....

September 8 (Monday)

Troops were needed in New Orleans and its environs at this time and the Regular Army troops at Pensacola were sent there to bolster the garrison, accompanied by Asst. Surg. Peters.

Peters, D. C., Asst. Surg., USA, Ft. Pickens, Pensacola, Fla.:

... the companies of regulars stationed at Pensacola were ordered to New Orleans, and I was directed to accompany them. On arriving in New Orleans, we were encamped first in Annunciation Square, and afterwards were moved to the Metairie racecourse, where our command used the visitors' stand for quarters. A portion of the stand was appropriated for a hospital; I remained in charge of this hospital, and,... was

detailed as acting inspector of the department. In this capacity I was employed in visiting hospitals, examining men who had been recommended for discharge by their regimental surgeons, and in rendering such other assistance as lay in my power. All officers applying for furloughs, or who contemplated resigning on the plea of ill health, had to be examined and have their certificates made out by me before [such certificates] were presented to the medical director.

The buildings used for hospitals in the city and its environs were generally judiciously selected, and were the most suitable buildings that could be obtained; the extensive experience of our worthy medical director, in treating diseases in this locality, enabled him to make some very important and beneficial improvements in them. The two largest hospitals were styled the St. James, formerly a hotel, and the Marine, a government building, which being erected upon "made" ground, was unhealthy....

The greater part of the soldiers under Maj. Gen. B. F. Butler were from the eastern states, and were unused to the malaria and the heat of this section of the country. Prior to occupying New Orleans, their health had been much undermined by service on Ship Island, in the Gulf.... The quarantine laws instituted by Gen. Butler, as after experience verified, had the effect of keeping the yellow fever from the city; although cases of the disease were quite numerous at the quarantine station, which was located at a safe distance below the city, and on the Mississippi River. At the racecourse, the regular battalion, both officers and men, suffered severely from intermittent fever, and it finally became necessary to change their positions to a more eligible locality, where the disease abated toward the latter part of November, 1862.

I was relieved from duty in this department, and received orders to take charge of Brig. Gen. L. G. Arnold, USV, who was laboring under general paralysis, the result of a *coup de soleil*, received while reviewing the brigade under Gen. Weitzel, in the streets of New Orleans, and to accompany him to his home in Boston, Mass. Our voyage was without incident, and was of great benefit to the general, whom I left among his relatives, and then reported myself at Washington.

September 9 (Tuesday)

Letterman, Jonathan, Med. Dir., Army of the Potomac, en route to Antietam, Md.:

Before leaving Washington, I had ordered a number of hospital wagons from Alexandria, Va., which reached me at Rockville, in Maryland, whence they were distributed to the different corps. While at this place, I directed the medical purveyor in Baltimore to put up certain supplies, and have them ready to send to such a point as I should direct....

September 10 (Wednesday)

In the area of Maryland west of Washington, McClellan learned that Lee had evacuated Frederick, Md. McClellan hastened his long blue lines to the northwest.

September 11 (Thursday)

The Sisters of Charity at Frederick, Md., sent two of their number to the Central House in Emmitsburg, Md., after obtaining the necessary passports from Gen. Robert E. Lee. The two Sisters reported on the conditions of the hospital and the remainder of the Sisters to the Mother Superior and prepared to return to Frederick.

Lee's men were in Hagerstown, Md. There were more skirmishes as the armies drew closer together. Lee's exact whereabouts or intentions were still unknown to McClellan.

September 12 (Friday)

The two Sisters of Charity returned to Frederick, to find that the entire Confederate Army had left the previous night, leaving only those men who were too sick to travel. Their services would be severely taxed within a period of eight days after the Battle of Sharpsburg (Antietam). At the end of the month, all ten of these brave women would be recalled to their Central House at Emmitsburg and wouldn't return to Frederick.

McClellan's men moved into Frederick, as Jackson was converging on Harpers Ferry. In Richmond, a debate went on about the advisability of invading the North. Harrisburg, the capital of Pennsylvania, had moved the public records, and Philadelphia was in an uproar.

September 13 (Saturday)

The Union Army was entering Frederick, Md., almost as soon as the Confederates left the other side of town. In the Federal ranks of the 27th Indiana

Vol. Regiment, Barton W. Mitchell found three cigars wrapped in paper lying in a fence corner. Being a frugal sort, and not having had a good smoke in a while, Mitchell picked up the packet and discovered that he had Gen. Robert E. Lee's Special Order No. 191 in his hand. This order contained all the details of the Confederate invasion. The order was rapidly transmitted to Gen. George B. McClellan, who was jubilant over the discovery. By evening, McClellan had his long blue columns hurrying west of Frederick towards South Mountain, a long hogback. Jeb Stuart and his cavalry awaited them.

Letterman, Jonathan, Med. Dir., Army of the Potomac, en route to Antietam, Md.:

> Upon our arrival at Frederick,... directions were given for the establishment of hospitals at that place, for the reception of wounded in the anticipated battle, and additional supplies,... were ordered to be sent from Baltimore at once. The Confederate troops had been in this city but the day before our arrival, and almost all the medical supplies had been destroyed, or had been taken by them. Just previous to our arrival in Frederick, two hundred ambulances were received from Washington, which I distributed to the corps.... The failure of the railroad company to forward the supplies caused serious annoyance. The railroad bridge over the Monocacy creek, between Frederick and Baltimore, having been destroyed by the Confederate troops, made it necessary to have all the supplies ... removed at that point.
>
> A great deal of confusion and delay was the consequence, which seriously embarrassed the medical department; and not from this cause alone, but from the fact that the cars loaded with supplies for its use were on some occasions switched off and left on the side of the road, to make way for other stores; and some of the supplies,... never left Baltimore....

In Shepherdstown, Va., just across the Potomac from Maryland, Mary Bedinger Mitchell was an eyewitness to the march of the Confederate forces on their way to Antietam.

Mitchell, Mary B., civilian, Shepherdstown, Va.:

> ... suddenly, on Saturday, the 13th of September, early in the morning, we found ourselves surrounded by a hungry horde of lean and dusty tatterdemalions, who seemed to rise from the ground at our feet. I did

not know where they came from, or to whose command they belonged; I have since been informed that Gen. Jackson recrossed into Virginia at Williamsport, and hastened to Harpers Ferry by the shortest roads.... They were stragglers, at all events—professional, some of them, but some worn-out by the incessant strain of that summer. When I say that they were hungry, I convey no impression of the gaunt starvation that looked from their cavernous eyes. All day they crowded to the doors of our houses, with always the same drawling complaint: "I've been a-marchin' an' a-fightin' for six weeks stiddy, and I ain't had n-a-r-thin' to eat 'cept green apples an' green cawn, an' I wish you'd please gimme a bite to eat."

Their looks bore out their statements, and when they told us they had "clean gin out," we believed them, and went to get what we had. They could be seen afterward asleep in every fence corner, and under every tree, but after a night's rest they "pulled themselves together" somehow and disappeared as suddenly as they had come....

September 14 (Sunday)

A whole series of blunders began today. Union Maj. Gen. William B. Franklin had been sent with his corps to reinforce Harpers Ferry, which was lightly held by a Federal force. He went through Crampton's Gap easily, brushing aside the troops of Confederate Lafayette McLaws, but then he got nervous and decided he was outnumbered and dug in. McLaws, keeping part of his troops to hold Franklin, sent the rest to Jackson, who was approaching Harpers Ferry and would attack that place in the evening.

Meanwhile, the Federal cavalry, under Gen. Pleasanton, engaged the troops of D. H. Hill at Fox's Gap and Turner's Gap, which provided passes through South Mountain. By evening, Hill's men had been outflanked, and the passes were in Federal hands.

Letterman, Jonathan, Med. Dir., Army of the Potomac, South Mountain, Md.:

The village of Middletown, about four miles in rear of the scene of action, was ... examined before the battle began, to ascertain its adaptability for the care of the wounded. Churches and other buildings were taken, as far as was considered necessary.... Houses and barns, the latter large and commodious, were selected in the most sheltered places.... The battle lasted until some time after dark, and as soon as the firing ceased I returned to Middletown and visited all the hospitals....

The battle of Crampton's Gap took place also on September 14.... The hospitals for the wounded were located at Burketsville, about a mile in the rear of our troops. As in the village of Middletown, churches and other buildings were appropriated for hospital purposes.... The most reliable reports ... show one thousand two hundred and fourteen wounded in these two engagements....

Mitchell, Mary B., civilian, Shepherdstown, Va.:

... the next morning—it was Sunday, September 14th—we were awakened by heavy firing at two points on the mountains. We were expecting the bombardment of Harpers Ferry, and knew that Jackson was before it. Many of our friends were with him, and our interest there was so intense that we sat watching the bellowing and smoking Heights, for a long time, before we became aware that the same phenomena were to be noticed in the north....

September 15 (Monday)

Harpers Ferry fell into the hands of "Stonewall" Jackson today. This wasn't the first time he'd been here. He'd stripped the arsenal of weapons-making machinery over a year ago and had sent it South.

With his army so scattered, Lee now became alarmed by McClellan's movements. Lee began to concentrate his forces at Sharpsburg, thinking seriously about withdrawing across the Potomac, just a few miles south. However, with the troops from South Mountain and Harpers Ferry in hand, he decided to stay at Sharpsburg and see what McClellan would do. McClellan was bringing his troops forward as fast as possible.

Letterman, Jonathan, Med. Dir., Army of the Potomac, South Mountain, Md.:

The army pushed on rapidly, and passing through the village of Boonsboro' on the ... 15th, it was examined, to ascertain what accommodation it afforded for hospital purposes.... Later in the evening, we passed through the village of Keedysville, a few miles beyond, which was also subjected to a similar inspection. Passing beyond this village, we came in sight, late in the evening, of what afterwards proved to be the battlefield of Antietam....

Mitchell, Mary B., civilian, Shepherdstown, Va.:

Monday afternoon, about 2 or 3 o'clock, when we were sitting about in disconsolate fashion, distracted by the contradictory rumors, our negro cook rushed into the room with eyes shining and face working with excitement. She had been down in "de ten-acre lot to pick a few years ob cawn," and she had seen a long train of wagons coming up from the ford, and "dey is full ob wounded men, and de blood running outen dem dat deep," measuring on her outstretched arm to the shoulder. This horrible picture sent us flying to town, where we found the streets already crowded, the people all astir, and the foremost wagons, of what seemed an endless line, discharging their piteous burdens. The scene speedily became ghastly, but fortunately we could not stay to look at it. There were no preparations, no accommodations—the men could not be left in the street—what was to be done?

... It would have been possible at this time, one would think, to send a courier back to inform the town and bespeak what comforts it could provide for the approaching wounded; but here they were, unannounced, on the brick pavements, and the first thing was to find roof to cover them. Men ran for keys and opened the shops, long empty, and the unused rooms; other people got brooms and stirred up the dust of ages; then swarms of children began to appear with bundles of hay and straw, taken from anybody's stable. These were hastily disposed in heaps and covered with blankets—the soldier's own, or blankets begged or borrowed. On these improvised beds the sufferers were placed, and the next question was how to properly dress their wounds. No surgeons were to be seen. A few men, detailed as nurses, had come, but they were incompetent, of course. Our women set bravely to work and washed away the blood or stanched it as well as they could, where the jolting of the long rough ride had disarranged the hasty binding done upon the battlefield. But what did they know of wounds beyond a cut finger, or a boil? Yet they bandaged and bathed, with a devotion that went far to make up for their inexperience. Then there was the hunt for bandages. Every housekeeper ransacked

her stores and brought forth things new and old. I saw one girl, in despair for a strip of cloth, look about helplessly, and then rip off the hem of her white petticoat. The doctors came up, by and by, or I suppose they did, for some amputing was done—rough surgery, you may be sure. The women helped, holding instruments and the basins, and trying to soothe or strengthen. They stood to their work nobly; the emergency brought out all their strength to meet it.

One girl who had been working very hard helping the men on the sidewalks, and dressing wounds afterward in a close, hot room, told me that at one time the sights and smells (these last were fearful) so overcame her that she could only stagger to the staircase, where she hung, half conscious, over the bannisters, saying to herself, "Oh, I hope if I faint someone will kick me into a corner and let me lie there!" She did not faint, but went back to her work in a few moments.... We worked far into the night that Monday, went to bed late, and rose early next morning....

September 16 (Tuesday)

In the pre-battle lull in Pleasant Valley, Md., Jonathan Letterman, Medical Director of the Army of the Potomac, continued riding the local area looking for hospital sites. Sites at Boonsboro; Keedysville; Hoffman; the Samuel Poffenberger farm where Clara Barton worked; the Pry farm; the barn on Henry Rohrbach's farm; the buildings at the Jacob Miller farm; the Grove farm; and the Smoketown Hospital were all selected and readied for the coming slaughter. Most of the civilians had abandoned the area and had left their homes and possessions to the less-than-tender mercies of the opposing armies.

Many problems remained for Letterman. There was a shortage of medical supplies, many having been captured or destroyed during the recently completed campaign on the Peninsula. Many of the ambulances for the army had been left at Ft. Monroe near Norfolk, Va., due to lack of transportation and lack of time to move them. A severe shortage of hospital tents created further problems. A good many men would die in the next two weeks because of lack of treatment.

Lee was gathering his troops at Sharpsburg, leaving Gen. A. P. Hill at Harpers Ferry, but bringing Jackson and the rest of his corps to Antietam.

McClellan was moving cautiously, as usual, and lost a good opportunity to crush Lee while Lee's army was still somewhat scattered.

Mitchell, Mary B., civilian, Shepherdstown, Va.:

Tuesday brought fresh wagon loads of wounded, and would have brought despair, except that they were accompanied by an apology for a commissariat. Soon more reliable sources of supply were organized among our country friends. Some doctors arrived, who—with a few honorable exceptions—might as well have staid away. The remembrance of that worthless body of officials stirs me to wrath. Two or three worked conscientiously and hard, and they did all the medical work, except what was done by our own town physicians. In strong contrast was the conduct of the common men detailed as nurses. They were as gentle as they knew how to be, and very obliging and untiring. Of course they were uncouth and often rough, but with the wounded dying about us every day, and with the necessity that we were under for the first few days, of removing those who had died at once that others not yet quite dead might take their places, there was no time to be fastidious; it required all our efforts to be simply decent, and we sometimes failed in that.

We fed our men as well as we could from every available source, and often had some difficulty in feeding ourselves. The townspeople were very hospitable, and we were invited here and there, but could not always go, or hesitated, knowing every house was full. I remember once, that having breakfasted upon a single roll and having worked hard among sickening [nauseous] details, about 4 o'clock I turned wolfishly ravenous and ran to a friend's house down the street. When I got there I was almost too faint to speak, but my friend looked at me and disappeared in silence, coming back in a moment with a plate of hot soup. What luxury! I sat down then and there on the front doorstep and devoured the soup as if I had been without food for a week.

It was known on Tuesday that Harpers Ferry had been taken, but it was growing evident that South Mountain had not been a victory.... As night drew nearer, whispers of a great battle to be fought the next day grew louder, and we shuddered at the prospect, for battle had come to mean to us, as [it] never had before, blood, wounds, and death....

September 17 (Wednesday)

The day dawned foggy and misty at Sharpsburg, Md. Dawn found the Army of Northern Virginia nearly assembled and ready for battle, outnumbered two to one. McClellan, as usual, delayed the attack for some hours until about 6 A.M., awaiting the alignment of his troops. Jackson and Stuart were on the left of the Rebel forces, with Longstreet's corps holding the right wing. A. P. Hill was not yet up from Harpers Ferry.

Color Sgt. George E. Bailey, carrying the national colors, was to lead the 11th Connecticut Volunteers in storming the stone bridge, forever after known as the Burnside Bridge. Another sergeant, carrying the state colors, refused to advance without a full color guard An officer slashed Bailey's arm for refusing to advance, whereupon Cpl. Henry A. Eastman took the colors from Bailey, and carried them into battle. Cpl. Eastman would survive the battle, later being promoted to captain. The 11th would lose 181 men during this battle.

The regiment suffering the most casualties of either army on this day was the 15th Massachusetts.

Sgt. Jonathan Stowe, Co. G, 15th Mass., wrote on this day:

Battle Oh horrid battle. What sights I have seen. I am wounded! And am afraid shall be again as shells fly past me every few seconds carrying away limbs from the trees.... Am in severe pain. How the shells fly. I do sincerely hope I shall not be wounded again.

As evening shadows filled the hollows throughout the battlefield, cries of the wounded could be heard The few women left in the area went to the fields looking for the soldiers, Yank and Reb, who needed aid and comfort. The stretcher-bearers continued their gruesome task of carrying the wounded to the aid stations and hospitals. The hospitals had become carnage houses where the wounded were treated on doors ripped from their hinges, or on window shutters which happened to be nearby. Hot water was readied to sluice the "operating table" after each operation but, in the heat of the activity, the fires were neglected, the water became merely warm, not hot, and finally even the washing was forgotten. The surgeons had no time to wash their hands or instruments; the coats of the orderlies and doctors become smeared, then caked, with blood from too many men. As the daylight faded, candles were stuck in bottles or musket barrels to provide a feeble light to amputate arms and legs. Little was available to alleviate pain. The shrieks of the patients filled the air.

Where did they put the wounded? An after-action report by a member of the Sanitary Commission stated:

> Indeed there is not a barn, or farmhouse, or store or church, or schoolhouse, between Boonesville [Boonsboro], Sharpsburg, and Smoketown that is not gorged with wounded—Rebel and Union. Even the corncribs, and in many cases the cow stable, and in one place the mangers were filled. Several thousands lie in open air upon straw, and all are receiving the kind services of farmers' families and the surgeons.

Letterman, Jonathan, Med. Dir., Army of the Potomac, South Mountain, Md.:

> The battle commenced on the evening of September 16th, and continued until dark; it was renewed in the morning of the 17th, and lasted until night…. After night, I visited all the hospitals in Keedysville…. The subject of supplies, always a source of serious consideration, was here peculiarly so. The condition of affairs at Monocacy Creek remained as heretofore described…. On the close of the battle, supplies of medicines, stimulants, dressings, and stores were sent for and brought from Frederick in ambulances, and were distributed…. I visited, after the battle, every hospital in the rear of our lines, and in no instances did I find any undue suffering for lack of medical supplies…. Not only were the wounded of our own army supplied, but all the Confederate wounded, which fell into our hands, were furnished with all the medicines,… required for their use…. An order was procured from Col. Ingalls for twelve wagons to bring up from Frederick supplies of medicines and food. These wagons could not be obtained. Two were then procured from the chief quartermaster … and I sent them in command of a medical officer, who brought up supplies of coffee, sugar and bread….

Mitchell, Mary B., civilian, Shepherdstown, Va.:

On the 17th of September cloudy skies looked down upon the two armies facing each other on the fields of Maryland. It seems to me now that the roar of that day began with the light, and all through its long and dragging hours its thunder formed a background to our pain and terror. If we had been in doubt as to our friends' whereabouts on Sunday, there was no room for doubt now. There was no sitting at the windows now and counting discharges of guns, or watching the curling smoke. We went about our work with pale faces and trembling hands, yet trying to appear composed for the sake of our patients, who were much excited. We could hear the incessant explosions of artillery, the shrieking of whistles of the shells, and the sharper, deadlier, more thrilling roll of musketry; where every now and then the echo of some charging cheer would come, borne by the wind, as the human voice pierced that demoniacal clangor we would catch our breath and listen, and try not to sob, and turn back to the forlorn hospitals, to the suffering at our feet and before our eyes, while imagination fainted at thought of those other scenes hidden from us beyond the Potomac.

When night came we could still hear the sullen guns and hoarse, indefinite murmurs that succeeded the day's turmoil. That night was dark and lowering and the air heavy and dull. Across the river innumerable camp fires were blazing, and we could but too well imagine the scenes that they were lighting. We sat in silence, looking into each other's tired faces. There were no impatient words, few tears; only silence, and a drawing close together, as if for comfort. We were almost hopeless, yet clung with desperation to the thought that we were hoping. But in our hearts we could not believe that anything human could have escaped from that appalling fire….

Confederate Veteran, April 1909, in an article about Sharpsburg (Antietam), Md.:

The 1st Minnesota Regiment was in the thick of the fight all day. It was located on the extreme right. Sam Bloomer was the color-bearer of the regiment, and early in the forenoon while he was resting the flagstaff on a fence in from of him, a minié ball struck his right leg below the kneecap, passing straight through. At the place of egress the bullet left a ghastly wound. About that time our line was broken, leaving its faithful color-bearer to his fate.

Sam crawled to the foot of a big oak tree for protection against the Confederate fire; but as our men fell back and the Confederates occupied the place, he found a change of base desirable. He crawled painfully and slowly around the tree to avoid the fire from his friends. Sam had ripped away his clothing, dressed his wound as best he could, and kept it bathed with water from his canteen, and then bound his leg above the knee with a strip from his blanket to prevent a fatal loss of blood....

"Not far from noon," says Sam, "a Confederate soldier, whom long afterward I learned was W. H. Andrews, first sergeant of Company M, 1st Regiment Georgia Regulars, came up; and learning my condition and the fact that I was between two fires, he and some of his comrades piled cordwood around me to protect me from the shots. I have no doubt that more than a hundred bullets struck that barricade during the day. Early in the evening Stonewall Jackson came riding by. He halted a moment, spoke kindly to me, asked to what regiment I belonged, and ordered the men who had charge of a lot of Union prisoners to supply my wants and make me as comfortable as possible. A captain of a North Carolina regiment a little later stopped and chatted with me, gave me a drink from his canteen, and spoke kindly and encouragingly. He rode away, but returned during the night and replenished my canteen with cool water. Previous to this a Confederate officer appeared whose conduct was unlike that of Gen. Jackson and the North Carolina captain. He reviled me with bitter words, called me a nigger thief, etc. I had a revolver and a short sword under my rubber blanket on which I lay, and in my rage I attempted to get at the revolver, intending to shoot the fellow; but he had eyes on me and shouted: 'Disarm that man!' The soldiers of course obeyed, although with a show of reluctance, and all that I could do was to protest indignantly.... "

On this day 23,110 Americans would be reported as killed, wounded, or missing in action—12,410 Union and 10,700 Confederates. The soldiers fell at the rate of about 2000 per hour, or about 35 per minute, for the period 6 A.M. to 6 P.M. If laid end to end, the dead and wounded would have lined a road for 25 miles. This was the bloodiest single day in American history.

September 18 (Thursday)

With dawn on this day thousands of dead and wounded were still lying in the fields and along the fencerows. Nearly 12,000 lay in Miller's cornfield. The Bloody Lane was filled with Confederate dead, in some places 4 deep. Lee's army regrouped and awaited McClellan's next action. "Little Mac" was, as usual, loath to act. The wounded suffered and the dead awaited burial.

Stowe, Jonathan, Sgt., Co. G, 15th Mass., hospital at Sharpsburg (Antietam), Md.:

Misery acute, painful misery. How I suffered last night. It was the most painful of anything have ever experienced. My leg must be broken for I cannot help myself scarcely any. I remember talking and groaning all night. Many died in calling for help.... Sgt. Johnson who lies on the other side of the log is calling for water.

Carried off the field at 10 A.M. by the Rebs who show much kindness but devote much time to plundering the dead bodies of our men.... Water very short. We suffer very much.

Confederate Veteran, April 1909, in an article about Sharpsburg (Antietam), Md.:

Sam [Bloomer] lay ... on the ground until the evening of Thursday, the 18th, when the Confederates carried him on a stretcher to a little barn surrounded by straw stacks, where he lay another night. He was not alone, for there were more than one hundred other prisoners in the hands of the Confederates, whom it was their intention to parole.

Mitchell, Mary B., civilian, Shepherdstown, Va.:

On Thursday the two armies lay idly facing each other, but we could not be idle. The wounded continued to arrive until the town was quite unable to hold all the disabled and suffering. They filled every building and overflowed into the country round, into farmhouses, barns, corncribs, cabins—wherever four walls and a roof were found together. Those able to travel were sent on to Winchester and other towns back from the river, but their departure seemed to make no appreciable difference. There were six churches, and they were all full; the Odd Fellows Hall, the Freemason's, the little Town Council room, the barnlike place known as the Drill Room, all the private houses after their capacity, the shops and empty buildings, the schoolhouses—every inch of space, and yet the cry was for more room.

The unfinished Town Hall had stood in naked ugliness for many a long day. Somebody threw a few rough boards across the beams, placed piles of straw over them, laid down single planks to walk upon, and lo, it was a hospital at once. The stone warehouses down in the ravine and by the river had been passed by, because low and damp and undesirable as sanitariums, but now their doors and windows were thrown wide, and, with barely time allowed to sweep them, they were all occupied—even the "old blue factory," an antiquated, crazy, dismal building of blue stucco that peeled off in great blotches, which had been shut up for years, and was in the last stages of dilapidation....

Alpheus S. Williams, born in Connecticut on September 20, 1810, graduated from Yale in 1831; later he studied law. He migrated to Detroit, Mich., in 1836, after travels through the United States and an extensive visit to Europe. He set up a law practice in Detroit, and by 1840 he was a probate judge in Wayne County. He was later the postmaster of Detroit for a period of four years. In 1836 Williams joined the Brady Guards, and by 1846 had been successively elected lieutenant, and then captain of the company. He went to Mexico, but arrived too late to participate in the fighting. By 1850 the Brady Guards had disbanded and were replaced by the Grayson Guards, who, in turn, were replaced by the Detroit Light Guard. By 1859 Williams headed a battalion of two companies, with the rank of major. His military education was extensive and, based on that, he was appointed a Brig. Gen. of Volunteers by Pres. Lincoln in August 1861. He'd serve in both the Army of the Potomac and Sherman's western armies with distinction—in many cases commanding corps during battle. Williams survived the war and returned to Detroit, later moving to Washington, D.C., where he died on December 21, 1878.

Williams, Alpheus S., Brig. Gen., USV, Antietam Battlefield, Md.:

It was understood that we were to attack again at daylight on the 19th, but as our troops moved up it was found the Rebels had departed. Some of the troops followed, but we lay under arms all day, waiting orders. I took the delay to ride over the field of battle. The Rebel dead, even in the woods last occupied by them, was very great. In one place, in front of the posi-

tion of my corps, apparently a whole regiment had been cut down in line. They lay in two ranks, as straightly aligned as on a dress parade. There must have been a brigade, as part of the line on the left had been buried. I counted what appeared to be a single regiment and found 149 dead in the line and about 70 in front and rear, making over 200 dead in one Rebel regiment.... In one place for nearly a mile they lay as thick as autumn leaves along a narrow lane cut below the natural surface, into which they seemed to have tumbled.... The cornfield beyond was dotted all over with those killed in retreat....

September 19 (Friday)

At Sharpsburg, Lee began his retreat across the Potomac and McClellan started to crow about his victory, although he had gone through the battle without committing over 30,000 of his soldiers. Such a commitment could have caused the overwhelming defeat of the Confederate force. He allowed Lee to disengage and escape without pursuit.

Mitchell, Mary B., civilian, Shepherdstown, Va.:

On Thursday night we heard more than usual sound of disturbance and movement, and in the morning we found the Confederate Army in full retreat. Gen. Lee crossed the Potomac under cover of darkness, and when the day broke the greater part of his force—or the more orderly portion of it—had gone on toward Kearneysville and Leetown. Gen. McClellan followed to the river, and without crossing got a battery in position on Douglas's Hill, and began to shell the retreating army and, in consequence, the town. What before was confusion grew worse; the retreat became a stampede....

Someone suggested that yellow was the hospital color, and immediately everybody who could lay hands upon a yellow rag hoisted it over the house. The whole town was a hospital; there was scarcely a building that could not with truth seek protection under that plea.... When this specific failed, the excitement grew wild and ungovernable. It would have been ludicrous had it not produced so much suffering.... Enough shells fell short to convince the terrified citizens that their homes were about to be battered down over their ears. The better people kept some outward coolness, with perhaps a feeling of *noblesse oblige;* but the poorer classes acted as if the town were already in a blaze, and rushed from their houses with their families and household goods to make their way into the country. The road was thronged, the streets blocked; men were vociferating, women crying, children screaming; wagons, ambulances, guns, caissons, horsemen, footmen, all mingled—nay, even wedged and jammed together—one struggling, shouting mass. The negroes were the worst, and with faces of a ghastly ash-color, and staring eyes, they swarmed into the fields, carrying their babies, their clothes, their pots and kettles, fleeing from the wrath behind them. The comparison to a hornet's nest attacked by boys is not a good one, for there was no "fight" shown; but a disturbed anthill is altogether inadequate. They fled widely and camped out of range, nor would they venture back for days.

Had this been all, we could afford to laugh now, but there was another side to the picture that lent it an intensely painful aspect. It was the hurrying crowds of wounded. Ah me! Those maimed and bleeding fugitives! When the firing commenced the hospitals began to empty. All who were able to pull one foot after another, or could bribe or beg comrades to carry them, left in haste. In vain we implored them to stay; in vain we showed them the folly, the suicide, of the attempt; in vain we argued, cajoled, threatened, ridiculed; pointed out that we were remaining and that there was less danger here than on the road. There is no sense or reason in a panic. The cannon were bellowing upon Douglas's Hill, the shells whistling and shrieking, the air full of shouts and cries; we had to scream to make ourselves heard. The men replied that the "Yankees" were crossing; that the town was to be burned; that *we* could not be made prisoners, but they could; that, anyhow, they were going as far as they could walk, or be carried. And go they did. Men with cloths about their heads went hatless in the sun, men with cloths about their feet limped shoeless on the stony road; men with arms in slings, without arms, with one leg, with bandaged sides and backs; men in ambulances, wagons, carts, wheelbarrows, men carried on stretchers or supported on the shoulder of some self-denying comrade—all who could crawl went, and went to almost certain death. They could not go far, they dropped off into the country houses, where they were received with as much kindness as it was possible to ask for; but their wounds had

become inflamed, their frames were weakened by fright and overexertion; erysipelas, mortification, gangrene set in; and long rows of nameless graves still bear witness to the results....

The wounded on the battlefield had mostly been picked up and given some attention. Sgt. Stowe wrote in his diary about his treatment by the Rebels:

Stowe, Jonathan, Sgt., Co. G, 15th Mass., hospital at Sharpsburg (Antietam), Md.:

Rained only a little. I had a rubber blanket & overcoat. Rebs retreat. Another painful night.

Oh good good a whole line of our skirmishers are coming.... There are lots of us here lain out.... By and by our boys come along. What lots of the 15th. Captain comes down to get the names and has coffee furnished us—'Twas the best cup I ever tasted. Dr. looks at my wound and calls it [a] doubtful case. Get me on ambulance at 3 P.M. but do not get to hospital till nearly dark. Plenty of water which gives us a chance to take down inflammation. Nurses worn-out by fatigue. Placed on straw near the barn.

Confederate Veteran, April 1909, in an article about Sharpsburg (Antietam), Md.:

Sam [Bloomer] sent word to the officers of his company by Minnesota troops telling of his sad condition. He and three others of the wounded were conveyed in an ambulance to the Hoffman barn. Sam was obliged to sleep on the ground another night, as there were hundreds of others ahead of him awaiting treatment by the surgeons.

... The next day Dr. Pugsley amputated the injured leg.... When the injured leg was amputated that strip [of blanket] was out of sight, enveloped in the swollen flesh on either side.

Charles Wainwright missed the Battle of Antietam, arriving from South Mountain in time to hear of Lee's escape across the Potomac.

Wainwright, Charles S., Col., N.Y. Artillery, near Sharpsburg (Antietam), Md.:

Orders soon came for us to move down to near Sharpsburg, which we did by the small byroad near the river which I was on yesterday, and pitched our camp about three-fourths of a mile from the town.... I did not go off to see the carnage in the worst places, but saw enough of it to satisfy me. In one place, even on the back road by which we marched, the corps had to halt until it was cleared of dead. The Rebs had buried none, and only carried off those of rank enough to warrant their bodies being sent home. We found sixteen of their wounded left in a house by the river, with a surgeon and two attendants in charge, but the other doctors had carried off all the medicines and surgical instruments....

The Sanitary Commission reacted to the carnage of Antietam by bringing in supplies and materials, as well as food, to treat the wounded of both sides. Before the last hospital was closed and the last wounded man sent from the area, the Commission would have distributed over 28,700 pieces of dry goods, shirts, towels, bed ticks, pillows, etc.; 30 barrels of old linen, bandages, and lint for dressing of wounds; nearly 3200 pounds of farina; over 2600 pounds of condensed milk; over 5000 pounds of beef-stock and canned meats; over 4000 sets of hospital clothing; 3000 bottles of wine and cordials; several tons of lemons and other fruit; crackers, tea, sugar, coffee, rubber cloths, tin cups, chloroform, opiates, surgical instruments, etc. All of these supplies were donated by volunteers in the Northern communities or bought with donated money.

The Confederates under Sterling Price had moved to Iuka, Miss., earlier, where they awaited Grant's response. They had only a short time to wait before Grant and Rosecrans drove towards Price, Rosecrans leading the way. It was hardly a contest, although the fighting was sharp for a while. Rosecrans forced Price to withdraw south.

Mother Bickerdyke was on hand at Iuka for ten days, during which time she worked at the temporary hospital, located in one of the town's resort hotels. The hotel was quite elegant, and Bickerdyke had no qualms about stripping it of its soft mattresses and pillows to send the wounded back to Corinth in comfort.

Grant and Rosecrans were attempting a pincer movement to capture the army of Confederate Gen. Sterling Price near Iuka. Surg. A. B. Campbell, USV, was assigned as Medical Director of the Army of the Mississippi.

Campbell, A. B., Surg., USV, Battle of Iuka, Miss.:

The battle of Iuka was fought on the afternoon and evening of September 19, 1862.... The battle commenced about half-past four in the afternoon, and raged until seven, with more or less firing till ten o'clock. The volleys by regiments were continuous and uninterrupted. But four cannon were used. We had only eight pieces, and the enemy not more, and the lines of the armies were so close together that when once engaged artillery could not be used. The enemy outnumbered us at least two to one.... They were chiefly armed with smoothbore muskets, firing the ball with three buckshot. Their range was but little over one hundred yards, and sometimes less.... The battle was fought so close to the hospital that the men detailed as bearers could go to the field and return at very short intervals. The moment a man fell, he was taken up, and in three minutes his wounds were being dressed.... No anaesthetics were used, and not a groan or sign of pain was heard. The firing continued long after dark, and the wounded were occasionally brought in until ten o'clock P.M.

During the night the enemy retreated. The hospital was established at Rix's house, near a good supply of water, and about seven hundred yards from our line.... At nine o'clock an order was received to remove the wounded, and,... the last load left before daylight for the new depot, two and a half miles in the rear.... Before the last ambulance was unloaded at the new depot, an order was received from Gen. Rosecrans to remove the wounded to the town of Iuka, and before noon their removal was completed....

September 20 (Saturday)

Lee moved his divisions across the Potomac unopposed. This was a major blunder on McClellan's part, for he could have trapped Lee's army against the flooding river, where he could have done serious damage to the Confederates. Instead, McClellan sent his cavalry to harass the grey columns and sat in Antietam. This was to be McClellan's last battle.

Throughout the countryside around Sharpsburg the wounded lay in the open, having no place to be sheltered. The weather so far had been reasonably mild, but this was September, and fall comes early in this northern latitude. Those who could be evacuated were moving. The more seriously wounded awaited their fate.

Stowe, Jonathan, Sgt., Co. G, 15th Mass., hospital at Sharpsburg (Antietam), Md.:

Fearful it will rain. How cheerful the boys appear. Many must lose their arms or legs but they do not murmur.... Leg amputated about noon. What sensations—used chloroform hope to have no bad effects. There are some dozen or more stumps near me. Placed in barn beside J. Hughes....

Wainwright, Charles S., Col., N.Y. Artillery, near Sharpsburg (Antietam), Md.:

The whole road from Sharpsburg to the river was lined with abandoned guns, caissons and wagons; while every house, barn and shed was filled with Rebel wounded, and many more lay under trees, or wretched apologies for tents. Sharpsburg itself is a small place, with very comfortless looking houses, though most of them are stone or brick; a few have holes through them, made by stray cannon balls, and all are crowded with Rebel wounded.

Mitchell, Mary B., civilian, Shepherdstown, Va.:

Saturday morning there was a fight at the ford The negroes were still encamped in the fields, though some, finding that the town was yet standing, ventured back on various errands during the day. What we feared were the stragglers and hangers-on and non-descripts that circle round an army like the great buzzards we shuddered to see wheeling silently over us. The people were still excited, anticipating the Federal crossing and dreading a repetition of the bombardment or an encounter in the streets. Some parties of Confederate cavalry rode through, and it is possible that a body of infantry remained drawn up in readiness on the hills during the morning, but I remember no large force of troops at any time on that day.

About noon, or a little after, we were told that Gen. McClellan's advance had been checked, and that it was not believed he'd attempt to cross the river at once—a surmise that proved to be correct. The country grew more composed....

September 21 (Sunday)

More wounded were leaving Antietam today. Slowly, ever so slowly, the dead were buried and the dying given their final solace. Many wounded, especially amputees, would die from infections caused

by the unsanitary "operating room" conditions.

McClellan sat while Lee withdrew into Virginia.

Stowe, Jonathan, Sgt., Co. G, 15th Mass., hospital at Sharpsburg (Antietam), Md.:

Very weak and sore.... Hot weather by day cool at night. Hard to get nurses. Men come in and stare at us but detailed men clear out & leave us. How piteously do they beg for water. People come in from all parts of the country. Stare at us but do not find time to do anything.

Letterman, Jonathan, Med. Dir., Army of the Potomac, Antietam, Md.:

The removal of so large a body of wounded was no small task. The journey to Frederick in ambulances was tedious and tiresome, and often painful to wounded men. It was necessary that they should halt at Middletown for food, and to take rest; that food should always be provided at this place at the proper time, and for the proper number; that the hospitals at Frederick should not be overcrowded; that the ambulances should not arrive too soon for the trains of cars at the depot at Frederick, the bridge over Monocacy Creek having been rebuilt; and that the ambulance horses should not be broken-down by the constant labor required of them.... The hospitals in Frederick were soon established....

Mitchell, Mary B., civilian, Shepherdstown, Va.:

On Sunday we were able to have some short church services for our wounded, cut still shorter, I regret to say, by reports that the "Yankees" were crossing. Such reports continued to harass us, especially as we feared the capture of our friends, who would often ride down to see us during the day, but who seldom ventured to spend a night so near the river. We presently passed into debatable land, when we were in the Confederacy in the morning, in the Union after dinner, and on neutral ground at night.... This Saturday came to an end, the most trying and tempestuous week of the war for Shepherdstown was over.

September 22 (Monday)

Federal troops returned to Harpers Ferry after the Confederates had departed south with Lee's columns. At Antietam, the wounded were still dying at a tremendous rate.

Stowe, Jonathan, Sgt., Co. G, 15th Mass., hospital at Sharpsburg (Antietam), Md.:

Two men died last night…. How painful my stump is. I did not know I was capable of enduring so much pain. How very meager are accommodations—no chamber pots & nobody to find or rig up one. How ludicrous for 2 score amputated men to help themselves with diarrhea.

Ropes, Hannah, Nurse, Union Hospital, Georgetown, Washington, D.C.:

My Dear Mother: … I have not found time to answer any letters for the past two weeks. The house has been full of suffering of such a complicated nature as you can hardly conceive. We have been up from six in the morning till one at night, and then laid down ready to jump at a moment's warning.

The young man who was shot through the lungs, to our surprise and, as the surgeons say, contrary to all "science," lived till last night, or rather this morning. We considered him the greatest sufferer in the house, as every breath was a pang. I laid down last night and got asleep, when I was roused by hearing him cry, very loud, "Mother! Mother! Mother!" I was out of bed and into my dressing gown very quickly, and by his side. The pressure of blood from the unequal circulation had affected the brain slightly, and, as they all are, he was on the battlefield, struggling to get away from the enemy. I promised him that nobody should touch him, and that in a few moments he would be free from all pain. He believed me, and, fixing his beautiful eyes on my face, he never turned them away; resistance, the resistance of a strong natural will, yielded; his breathing grew more gentle, ending softly as an infants. He was a brave soldier and a truthful boy.

Last Sunday I left him for an hour to go into the church opposite and hear the service…. The church was full of beds, the chaplain stood near the entrance between the beds, and a few singers sat on stools behind him. The nurses were fanning the sickest patients; and near one bed sat the mother of the sick man. I think they all felt better for the services…. Outside, the rumble of army wagons made almost indistinct the words of the speaker….

I don't know how long we shall be able to hold out…. Our house is one of constant death now.

Every day someone drops off the corruption of a torn and wounded body. It is more from the worn condition of the soldier before the wound, and the torture of exposure on the field, added to the forced removal in the heavy wagons to the hospitals, than to the dangerous nature of the wounds.…

In Richmond, the chairman of the committee supervising the [Confederate] Army Medical Dept., Augustus R. Wright, wrote a letter to the Secretary of War, G. W. Randolph, describing the committee's visit to a prisoner-of-war hospital in Richmond:

Mr. Secretary: You will find enclosed a resolution passed this morning at a session of the committee on the medical department. In the discharge of our duties we visited the hospital of the sick and wounded of our enemies now in our custody. All of the wards are in a wretched condition. The upper ward was such as to drive the committee out of it almost instantly. The honor of our country will not permit us to bring the matter to the attention of Congress, thereby making the matter public.

We attach no blame to the Secretary of War. We know that in his almost overwhelming labors this matter has escaped his attention. We address you in the full confidence that you will have this condition of things altered at once. We think that the hospital for prisoners ought to be on average at least with those of our own soldiers.

September 23 (Tuesday)

The fields of Antietam were being cleared of the wounded, more wounded had been evacuated, and the Sanitary Commission was active in providing supplies and aid to the wounded. Surg. Letterman described the operations:

Immediately after the retreat of the enemy … measures were taken to have all the Confederate wounded gathered in from the field over which they laid scattered in all directions, and from the houses and barns in the rear of their lines, and placed … at such points as would enable their removal … to Frederick, and thence to Baltimore and Ft. Monroe to their own lines. They were removed as rapidly as their recovery would permit…. A sufficient number of ambulances and supplies having been placed at the disposal of Surgeon Ranch, these wounded were collected in convenient places, and everything done to alleviate their sufferings.... Humanity teaches us that a wounded and prostrate foe is not then our enemy.

There were many patients whose wounds were so serious that their lives would have been endangered by removal; and to have every opportunity afforded them for recovery, the Antietam hospital, consisting of hospital tents, and capable of comfortably accommodating nearly six hundred patients was established at a place called Smoketown, near Keedysville,... and a similar hospital, less capacious, the Locust Spring hospital, was established in the rear of Fifth Corps....

Immediately after the battle, a great many citizens came within our lines, in order to remove their relatives or friends who had been injured, and in a great many instances when the life of the man depended upon his remaining at rest. It was impossible to make them understand that they were better where they were, and that a removal would probably involve the sacrifice of life. Their minds seem bent on having their friends in houses. All would, in their opinion, be well if that could be accomplished. No greater mistake could exist.... Within a few yards, a marked contrast could be seen between the wounded in houses, barns, and in the open air. Those in houses progress less favorably than those in the barns, those in the barns less favorably than those in the open air....

The surgery of these battlefields has been pronounced by some journals butchery; gross misrepresentations of the conduct of medical officers have been ... broadcast over the country, causing deep anxiety to those who had relatives in the army. It is not to be supposed that there are no incompetent surgeons in the army; but these sweeping denunciations against a class of men ... because of the incompetency of a few, are wrong....

Stowe, Jonathan, Sgt., Co. G, 15th Mass., hospital at Sharpsburg (Antietam), Md.:

Oh what long fearful horrid nights. What difficulties we have to contend [with].... Relief can hardly be found. I have at length got my limb dressed by a volunteer surgeon. But never was so nearly exhausted for want of refreshment.

In Mississippi, Mother Bickerdyke had returned to Corinth and the hospital in the former seminary. Due to the fighting at Iuka and the amount of sickness, the seminary hospital had overflowed and patients were now housed in tents on the lawns. The amount of soiled linens, bedclothes, etc., was enormous. Bickerdyke reported that in one day 1532 undershirts, 200 shirts, 175 pairs of drawers, 400 handkerchiefs, 6 pairs of pants, 600 towels, 32 blankets, 80 quilts, 478 pillowcases, 22 feather pillows, and 70 bed sacks were processed through the laundry outside of the town in a woods. This was a total of 3595 pieces of laundry done using only normal-size washtubs filled with water heated in iron kettles, the water being dipped from a nearby stream, the articles hand-scrubbed, rinsed, wrung out, and hung to dry on bushes. The work was done by contrabands from the area, the men cutting the wood and tending the fires, the women doing the laundry work. An incredible amount of work had to be done, using primitive tools.

September 24 (Wednesday)

Stowe, Jonathan, Sgt., Co. G, 15th Mass., hospital at Sharpsburg (Antietam), Md.:

One week today fought and wounded. Such a week. Suffering all around.... Showers this A.M. and all look for the barn.

Surg. Spencer G. Welch remained in the vicinity of Manassas Junction for a period of time, recovering from an illness brought on by overeating undercooked pork. He finally rejoined his regiment, the 20th South Carolina Volunteers, the day after the Battle of Sharpsburg (Antietam). The wounded were evacuated across the Potomac at Shepherdstown and taken by wagon train to hospitals around Charles Town and Halltown, in western Virginia.

Welch, S. G., Surg., 20th S.C. Vols., in a letter to his wife, after Antietam, from Charles Town, western Virginia:

I have not written to you in three or four weeks, because there has been no mail between us and Richmond. I have seen sights since then, I assure you. If I should tell you what our army has endured recently you could hardly believe it. Thousands of the men now have almost no clothes and no sign of a blanket nor any prospect of getting one, either. Thousands have had no shoes at all, and their feet are now entirely bare. Most of our marches were on graveled turnpike roads, which were very severe on the barefoot men and cut up their feet horribly. When the poor fellows could get rags they would tie them around their feet for protection. I have seen the men rob the dead of their shoes and clothing, but I cannot blame a man for doing a thing which is almost necessary in order to preserve his own life.... Doubtless you have learned how our regiment suffered in the battle, and it is useless for me to tell you of the shocking scenes I have witnessed. Billie was in the battle at Shepherdstown. Our men put it right into the Yankees there, when they had them in the river....

I am now here at a hospital with our wounded, and will remain until they are well enough to be moved away. The Yankees came near enough the other day to throw several shells into the town, but they did no harm except to wound a little boy....

September 25 (Thursday)

Stowe, Jonathan, Sgt., Co. G, 15th Mass., hospital at Sharpsburg (Antietam), Md.:

Such nights! Why they seem infinitely longer than days. The nervous pains are killing 2 or 3 every night. All sorts of groans & pleadings.... Many patients are leaving daily. Some have gone today to H. Ferry. I watch over J. Hughes nightly. Has had fever. Very cold last night & we are very short for clothing. Sundown, just Recd. Blankets and beds.

Edmonds, S. Emma E., Union field nurse, Antietam Battlefield, Md.:

The only amusing incident after a battle is the crowd of spectators from Washington and other places. If they are in carriages, their vehicles are sure to get smashed, and then the trouble arises, what are they to do with their baggage? Carry it, of course, or leave it behind. Even the wounded soldiers cannot help laughing at their sorry plight, gesticulations, and absurd questions.

Among this class of individuals, there are none to be compared with government clerks for [self-]importance and absurdity. On one of these occasions I remember a number of those pompous creatures being distressed beyond measure, because they could not return to Washington on a train which was crowded beyond description with the wounded. After the cars moved off ... said one, "I came here by invitation of the Secretary of War, and now I must return on foot, or remain here." One of the soldiers contemptuously surveyed him from head to foot, as he stood there with kid gloves, white bosom, standing collar, etc., in all the glory and finery of a brainless fop, starched up for display. "Well," said the soldier, "we don't know any such individual as the Secretary of War out here, but I guess we can find you something to do; perhaps you would take a fancy to one of these muskets," laying his hand on a pile beside him.

The clerk turned away in disgust, and disdaining to reply to the soldier, he inquired, "But where shall I sleep tonight?" The soldier replied, "Just where you please, chummy; there is lots of room all around here," pointing to a spot of ground which was not occupied by the wounded. A chaplain stepped up to him, and said, "If you wish to sleep, there is some hay you can have"; and went on to give him a brief lecture upon the impropriety of a young man, in perfect health, just fresh from the city, talking about comfortable lodgings, and a place to sleep, when so many wounded and dying lay all around him. He was horrified, and disappeared immediately....

September 26 (Friday)

Stowe, Jonathan, Sgt., Co. G, 15th Mass., hospital at Sharpsburg (Antietam), Md.:

Very cold last night. J. Hughes had shakes again last night.... This cold weather may all come for best, certainly maggots do not trouble so much and air is some purer.

4 P.M. J. Hughes died.

P.M. more [of a] system day by day.... O there comes Mrs. Gray with refreshments. Such a treat ... I got tomatoes ... just what I wanted. Have since forgotten my stump's first hemorrhage—It was very copious and tho I had stoutly affirmed that I would not use Brandy was now plainly told that if not should be dead in 3 days.

It was about this time that a new being entered the life of Mary Ann Bickerdyke, one who'd share her life for the remainder of the war.

Having often remarked that she needed a saddle horse to get around on because it was a bother to have to always hitch up the ambulance buggy to go anywhere, her "boys" kept this in mind, and after the fracas at Iuka, they presented her with a captured horse which she dubbed "Old Whitey." At the time of presentation, Old Whitey was a rather sorry-looking sack of bones. The Confederates had used him to do common pulling and they hadn't taken good care of him. Bickerdyke said he needed a "little feeding up" to get him back into shape. With her usual skill with man or beast, it wasn't long before Old Whitey was looking pretty trim, and all his harness sores had healed. From somewhere an "extra" cavalry saddle appeared, and Bickerdyke used both horse and saddle for the remainder of the war. She could never quite get used to the idea of riding astride the horse, so she rode sidesaddle in the regular saddle, a position that must have been awkward At the end of the war, Old Whitey proudly carried Mother Bickerdyke in the Grand March, only this time he wore a proper sidesaddle that had been "liberated" from a plantation in Georgia during Sherman's March to the Sea.

September 27 (Saturday)

Stowe, Jonathan, Sgt., Co. G, 15th Mass., hospital at Sharpsburg (Antietam), Md.:

Commence taking brandy none too soon. Dr. tells me I am dangerously ill and must take his prescription in order to change condition of blood. He is earnest & too good a man. Mr. L. Sloan a kindhearted chaplain telegraphs for me. Suffer continuously from position in bed. Have to elevate my stump to prevent bleeding and be very still....

September 28 (Sunday)

Stowe, Jonathan, Sgt., Co. G, 15th Mass., hospital at Sharpsburg (Antietam), Md.:

Oh what lengths to the nights. The horrid smell from mortifying limbs is nearly as bad as the whole we have to contend [with]. Mrs. Lee and another lady are here daily dispensing cooked broths.... They seem to employ their whole time for us. Move outdoors in P.M. Excessively hot.

September 29 (Monday)

Stowe, Jonathan, Sgt., Co. G, 15th Mass., hospital at Sharpsburg (Antietam), Md.:

Slept little more comfortable last night. Got nice soups and nice light biscuit and tart also nice butter from Mrs. Lee. Also she gets me milk again this morning.

How the quinine keeps me parched for water and so sleepy and foolish. Am much better off here than in barn. 10 A.M. my comrade died from 18th Minn. Regt. I recd 4 letters from friends at home but am so boozy it takes the whole A.M. to read them. Mr. Dr. Kelsey dressed my stump admirably and am quite comfortable if the quinine does not choke me to death. It is far more quiet here but begins to rain.

At 7:54 this evening, Stowe had a telegram sent to J. W. Stowe as follows: "Dangerously wounded at Hoffman's Hospital near Sharpsburg. Come instantly."

On October 1st, Stowe died of his wounds and the amputation. He'd lain on the battlefield for a day without food or water and then was taken to the Nicodemus farm by the Rebels and remained there without treatment for 24 hours. The cumulative effects had been too much.

The news of the results of the battle at Antietam were slow to reach Richmond. Some of the wounded from that conflict reached hospitals in Winchester, Gordonsville, and Lynchburg—a few went to Richmond.

Jones, John B., Rebel War Clerk, Confederate War Dept., Richmond, Va.:

Hitherto 100,000 sick and wounded patients have been admitted into the army hospitals of this city. Of these, about 10,000 have been furloughed, 3000 discharged from the service, and only 7600 have died. At present there are 10,000 in the hospitals. This is not so much sickness this year as there was last, nor is it near so fatal....

September 30 (Tuesday)

John B. Jones, the Rebel War Clerk, recorded in his diary, with no further explanation:

"... the yellow fever is raging at Wilmington, N.C."

October 1 (Wednesday)

For Richmond, the starving time was approaching. This coming winter would be very severe for the inhabitants, the local troops, the patients in the hospitals, and the Union prisoners in Libby and on Belle Isle. There was much food available throughout the countryside, but no means at hand to transport it in large quantities. John B. Jones recorded:

… How shall we subsist this winter? There is not a supply of wood or coal in the city—and it is said that there are not adequate means of transporting it hither. Flour at $16 per barrel, and bacon at 75 cts. per pound, threaten a famine.…

October 2 (Thursday)

John B. Jones recorded that the yellow fever was worse in Wilmington, N.C.

October 3 (Friday)

At Corinth, Miss., the Confederates, led by Van Dorn and Sterling Price, attacked Rosecrans's lines and drove the the Federals in towards the town. Mother Bickerdyke's hospital was within the perimeter at Corinth, and the incoming shells landed perilously close to her patients.

Campbell, A. B., Surg., USV, Medical Dir., Army of the Mississippi, Corinth, Miss.:

In anticipation of an engagement with the enemy on October 3d,… I selected the large building recently constructed for a commissary department, as the place best protected by the nature of the ground and the safest for hospital purposes. The men furnished by the quartermaster worked expeditiously, and everything was prepared, medicines, instruments, cots and buckets of water were ready before the first wounded man was brought in. It became evident, in a short time, that the building, although a very large one, would be altogether too small for their accommodation. I then took posesession of the Tishomingo Hotel and of the Corinth House.…

All of the surgeons worked diligently … and by six o'clock the wounded were all comfortably disposed of and their wounds dressed.…

At Antietam, Md., Lincoln visited the headquarters of the Army of the Potomac. McClellan regaled Lincoln with parades and demonstrations put on by what Lincoln called "Gen. McClellan's bodyguard."

October 4 (Saturday)

Letterman, cogitating on the shortcomings of the medical service, thought out a new system to be tried which could, possibly, improve the way supplies were issued and used.

Letterman, Jonathan, Med. Dir., Army of the Potomac, Antietam, Md.:

Hitherto large amounts of medical supplies had been lost, and in various ways wasted, and, not infrequently, all the supplies for a regiment had been thrown away for want of transportation, and, of course, were not on hand when wanted. It was necessary that this should be remedied, and, in order to do so, it was necessary to diminish the amount that was furnished a regiment at one time, which would affect the whole existing system, and make the change a radical one. The objects … were to reduce the waste,… to have a supply given them, small, but sufficient,… and to have these supplies easily attainable, and replenished without difficulty.… It was necessary, also, that they should be transported with facility,… and yet, at the same, to preserve a proper degree of accountability. To accomplish this, a system of supplying by brigades was adopted on the 4th of October, 1862.…

Before the adoption of this system, one, and sometimes two wagons were required to transport the medical supplies of a regiment, and another wagon was required to transport cooking utensils, hospital tents, and baggage of the medical officers. With the new system, one wagon sufficed for the medical department of a regiment; one wagon was added to a brigade, and the essential medicines and supplies were in such shape as permitted them to be carried on a horse, if necessary, and not abandoned and lost as heretofore.…

On the second day near Corinth, Van Dorn renewed his attacks on Rosecrans. The battle swung back and forth, attack and counterattack, until midafternoon, when Van Dorn retreated to the northwest around the town of Chewalla. The Union lost about 2500 and the Confederates a few more than 4200. The battle ended in a draw, with the rail center of Corinth still in Federal hands.

Because of the artillery firing into the perimeter at Corinth, the patients in the hospital there were removed to a grove of trees beyond the range of fire. Here Bickerdyke received the newly wounded soldiers, both blue and grey, to add to her already burgeoning flock. At night confusion reigned. One story had it that Bickerdyke was handing out coffee to the men by firelight when one of the local ladies reached for a cup of the brew. Bickerdyke's sharp reply was that the lady should make herself useful taking care of the wounded Confederates, who needed the coffee more than the lady did.

Campbell, A. B., Surg., USV, Medical Dir., Army of the Mississippi, Corinth, Miss.:

At three o'clock next morning I was ordered to remove all the wounded to Camp Corral, and by six o'clock they were all collected into the new hospital. The ambulances then went to the scene of the action to bring off those recently fallen.... I found upon the railroad platform a large number of tents, which I took and used. The battle ceased just before noon, and by night all the wounded were under shelter, provided with cots, and their wounds dressed....

I have to state that there was neglect on the part of the Rebel surgeons for their wounded. The surgeon placed by Gen. Van Dorn in charge of over one hundred wounded at Ripley, neglected to make out a requisition, although repeatedly urged to so, with the assurance from myself, that all he needed should be delivered to him within forty-eight hours....

October 5 (Sunday)

Confederate Gen. Van Dorn, retreating, was ambushed by Federal troops under Gen. E. O. C. Ord at the Hatchie River, where a sharp, stiff fight took place. When the Federals paused to regroup, the Rebels beat a fast track towards Holly Springs, ending a campaign that accomplished little except to increase casualties.

It was now time to move the hospital back into Corinth from Kincaid's Grove. The Corinth facility, already full, was now overflowing with new casualties. Tents were set up where possible and new kitchens established. A major problem was bedding for the patients. No hay or straw was available, or so it seemed. The quartermaster professed to have neither cots nor blankets for issue.

Again, it was Bickerdyke to the rescue! Taking wagons to the depot, she directed her workers to load bales of cotton and hay that were there on the wagons and to go back to the hospital. The quartermaster protested, but Bickerdyke overcame his objections, since she had no time to get his requisition forms filled out. The wagons left loaded and the patients were kept from the hard ground for a while.

October 6 (Monday)

Lincoln, having returned to Washington on the 4th, now directed McClellan to take some action.

He sent a message through Gen. Halleck: "The President directs that you cross the Potomac and give battle to the enemy or drive him south. Your army must move while the roads are good." No response from McClellan, as usual.

In Kentucky, Bragg's main Confederate force was withdrawing towards Harrodsburg, as Buell entered Bardstown. Neither side was moving too quickly.

Ropes, Hannah, Nurse, Union Hospital, Georgetown, Washington, D.C.:

Dear Alice: ... I have got up to attend to a man who has just had his leg taken off—he is reduced in strength, and it always is a good deal of a job to bring a weak man safe out from the effect of the chloroform. The doctors say give all the brandy they will take, but be sure and keep them awake.

Today we send off fifty men. Not half of them are able to go, but that is of no account to one head surgeon, who cares no more for a private than a dog.... We upon the whole have had goodish men to rule over us. Still, between surgeons, stewards, nurses and waiters, the poor men in all the hospitals barely escape with life or clothes or money.

The wars on the James River [are] nothing compared with the fights I have with the stewards. We now have our fourth, as big a villain as ever walked unhung. I have entered a complaint to the Surgeon Gen. but I don't suppose it will do any good at all. But at any rate I shall have nothing to do with him. I ordered him out of my room, and don't speak to him now. The men have not had enough to eat for a week—this morning, one slice of bread to each man! As soon as I found it out, I took a half-bushel of apples and went into the court and told the men if I could have my way they should have more than enough, and I hoped the steward would go hungry sometime. They gathered round me as thick as chickens and [ate] their apples....

October 7 (Tuesday)

At Corinth, Miss., the hospital was slowly emptied as the patients were loaded on trains and sent North. Special railcars, provided by the Sanitary Commission, contained fixed cots on their floors, with hammocks slung above them. This was a vast improvement over earlier methods of merely loading the patients into boxcars and cattle cars.

In Kentucky, Bragg's Confederates were moving on two different roads and were therefore divided. Buell, hoping to take advantage of this, approached the column near Perryville, hoping to defeat that Confederate column before the other could come up.

October 8 (Wednesday)

Welch, S. G., Surg., 20th S.C. Vols., Berkeley County, Va.:

When I left Charles Town yesterday morning the weather was delightful and I felt so buoyant and fresh that it caused me to walk too fast, and today I am very sore and stiff.... There is smallpox in Winchester, and Gen. Lee has ordered the entire army vaccinated....

The clash between Maj. Gen. Don Carlos Buell's Union forces and Gen. Braxton Bragg's Confederates at Perryville was the only major battle fought in Kentucky. Bragg's force was divided and outnumbered by more than two to one. The Federals lost 845 killed, 2851 wounded, and 515 reported missing out of a force of about 37,000. Confederate losses (over 20 percent) were 519 killed, 2635 wounded, and 251 reported missing from a force of about 16,000. It was a partial victory for the North—and in some ways a total victory, in that no major invasion was attempted again by the South in the western theatre of operations.

There were many problems encountered in treating the wounded, North and South, after the battle, not the least of which was the water supply. Before the battle, the town of Perryville contained 300 inhabitants, and now, after one occupation by Confederates, and two by Union forces, it contained over 3000. The wells in the town had run dry, and water was brought from two springs located about a mile from the town. Food was also a problem. The armies had consumed most of the available supply, and fresh milk, eggs, etc., weren't to be had at any price.

Perhaps the major problem was the lack of medical supplies and equipment, especially in the Union Army, which, having been left in possession of the field, had to care for the enemy's sick and wounded as well as for its own. J. S. Newberry of the United States Sanitary Commission took great exception to the state of readiness of the medical departments before and after the battle. The Union forces were wholly unprepared for the action, having little or no medical supplies and equipment on hand at Perryville. Newberry, in his report of October 23, 1862, pulled no punches:

Who, then, is responsible for the facts, that at the battles of Ft. Donelson, Shiloh, and Perryville, no adequate provision was made beforehand for the care of the wounded; that proper supplies of medicine and hospital stores and an abundance of appropriate food were not on hand or within easy reach? Whose fault is it that there were so few surgeons and trained assistants; so few ambulances, and ambulance attendants, that men must lie two, three, four days, on the battlefield before they could be taken up, sheltered from the sun, the frost, the rain, their hunger and thirst assuaged, and their wounds dressed?.... To anyone acquainted with the theory of our military organization, and familiar with the *personnel* of our army, the question need not be a difficult one. The fault is, for the most part, incident to the workings of a defective system, in special instances aggravated by individual incompetency. The defect in our military system ... is this—that the Medical Dept., on which the responsibility and the care of the sick repose, [has] no part of the functions of the Quartermaster and Commissary Dept. [which] are independently entrusted. As a consequence, the sick, having no official representative in these departments, are constantly the victims of the caprices or necessities of those whose duty is first to their own work, and then attend to them if they can....

Shumard, G. G., Surg., USV, Perryville, Ky.:

It is proper here to remark that previous to starting from Louisville, the different surgeons of the army were directed by Surg. R. Murray, USA, medical director, to procure full supplies ... but no sooner were the supplies procured that they were *ordered to be left behind by Gen. Buell*, who directed that only one wagon should be furnished to each brigade for ... medical and hospital stores.... No hospital had been previously established anywhere along the route travelled by the army. To add to this difficulty, no tents of any character were allowed the troops. As the marches were long and fatiguing, while the nights were cool and disagreeable, the army suffered severely from diseases, and by the time it arrived at Perryville, the number of sick was unusually large....

The battle ... was fought on October 8, 1862.... Most of the wounds inflicted were from conical balls, and were large and severe, *the balls appearing to have entered the body sideways, revolving....* [Italics added.]

October 9 (Thursday)

Ropes, Hannah, Nurse, Union Hospital, Georgetown, Washington, D.C.:

... we turn away with saddened eyes from the long list of those whose last sleep has fallen upon them in this hospital. Fifteen have died within the month just ended, some of them so worn with fatigue and fasting as to be wholly unable to rally, others kept along with wounded limbs until too exhausted to bear amputation, and thus died.... Apothecary and medicine chest might be dispensed with if an equal amount of genuine sympathy could be brought home to our stricken men and the rations converted into more delicate food. Not more than eight cents per day is the cost actually dealt out by the steward! Our men have been saved only by the best of nurses and the kind and constant help from friends at home; and to those good people we turn our eyes....

The steward I think will prove the climax of unfaithful servants. Indeed they are a strange race of mortals, so far as I have watched them; and, as we have had four during our hospital life of three months, perhaps I am as well prepared to judge them as the others. Our first was ... round faced, [with] beady eyes, black hair and short of stature. He would talk so sweet to me, and rob me of a bottle of wine, a shirt or pretty pocket handkerchief at the very moment I was looking at him to reply! [He was by] the kind will of providence ... sent to the Peninsula, after ushering into his place a gentle, well disposed Pennsylvanian, who knew about as much of the world and society as his neighboring Dutch farmers, or the present President. [The second] soon tired of the annoyances of his position and was transferred. Number 3 was from Virginia, young, compact, becoming his uniform remarkably well; but his features all turned up and his manner suggested to me the nature of a porcupine.... I kept out of his way till he came to my premises. Then we had a pitched battle over the rights of the soldiers, lasting a good hour. At the close, he hauled down his colors, took a cup of

hot tea from my hand, and we laid some plans for bettering the diet of the patients....

Our next and last, a French Canadian, came in with the doubtful, dreary sphere of a raven or a bat. Dressed in his dark blue suit of pants and close fitting jacket, with a wide, bright green stripe down the side, and making a cuff to the sleeve above the elbow, a stiff linen collar up under the ears, both hands thrust down into his pockets, we felt that this man was the opener of a new epoch.

October 10 (Friday)

After learning of the battle of Perryville, Ky., the Sanitary Commission swung into action as quickly as possible to send supplies and agents to the area.

Read, A. N., M.D., U.S. Sanitary Commission, Perryville, Ky.:

Immediately on the reception of the news of the late battle, I took such measures as were in my power for the performance of our duty in the relief of the wounded.... I obtained at once three Government wagons, and the promise of 21 ambulances, to be ready the day following. The wagons were loaded with stores ... and started the same evening for Perryville. I myself hired a buggy, and ... pushed on as rapidly as possible.

We found the first hospital for the wounded at Maxville. This was a tavern, with sixteen rooms, containing 150 wounded and 30 sick, mostly from a Wisconsin regiment. Twenty-five were on cots; some on straw; the others on the floor with blankets.... Flour was very scarce; cornmeal, beef, mutton, and chickens, plenty. The cooking was all done at a fireplace, with two camp kettles and a few stew pans. The ladies of the town, however, were taking articles home and cooking them there, thus giving great assistance.

From this place to Perryville, some ten miles, nearly every house was a hospital. At one log cabin we found 20 of the 10th Ohio, including the major and two captains. At another house were several of the 92d Ohio; and the occupants were very poor, but doing all in their power for those in their charge. The mother of the family promised to continue to do so, but said, with tears in her eyes, she feared that she and her children must starve when the winter came....

On our arrival [at Perryville] we learned that we were the first to bring relief where help was needed more than tongue can tell. Instead of 700, as first reported, at least 2500 Union and Rebel soldiers were at that time lying in great suffering and destitution about Perryville and Harrodsburg.... There had been almost no preparation for the care of the wounded at Perryville.... For this state of things, however, the surgeons are not to blame.... The fault lies higher than they—with the superior military authorities, who withheld from the surgeons the information and denied them the resources which alone would have enabled them to meet the emergencies of the case....

October 11 (Saturday)

Ropes, Hannah, Nurse, Union Hospital, Georgetown, Washington, D.C.:

The new steward has been in to my room to talk about the washing. I show him how badly the clothes are washed. I did not know till after he left the room that he kept back a part of the ration of soap. I think the hardest thing for me to comprehend is such meanness.

He seemed to be trying to buy me, and I was involuntarily getting at the quality of his mind; he spoke rather contemptuously of the privates. I fired up at that and told him, "they were really the heroes of the war, that there were privates in the house who were independent as far as money makes men so, and they know what their rights are as privates." He said, with a sneer, he was not of the benevolent kind, that he was here to make all the money he could out of the hospital, adding triumphantly that the power was in his hands, that he had sent away three loads of their clothes now!...

As the true life of this steward gleamed upon me, astonishment took the place of all other emotions. When I first began to think, standing there before him I found I had received from him the impression that we could work together in the game of peculation! Then I said, "You may go, I think I have your measure now." In the space of an hour he came back to the door and knocked.... He made a most gracious bow; I stepped onto the threshold and said, "No farther sir! Neither now nor at any other time—go your way and I mine, they are wide apart."

Every day the inmates of the house bring charges against him to me; I have been to the head

surgeon but it makes not the slightest impression upon him....

Read, A. N., M.D., U.S. Sanitary Commission, Perryville, Ky.:

In the morning [I] secured ... two rooms, which were put in order, the three loads of goods taken in and opened, and a U.S. San. Com. sign placed over the door. Soon after the twenty-one ambulances arrived, loaded with our stores.... Surgeons were then notified that stores could be had, and they were rapidly given out. There were, at this time, some 1800 wounded in and about Perryville. They were all very dirty, few had straw or other bedding, some were without blankets, others had no shirts, and even now, five days after the battle, some were being brought in from the temporary places of shelter whose wounds had not yet been dressed. Every house was a hospital, all crowded, with very little to eat....

October 12 (Sunday)

Read, A. N., M.D., U.S. Sanitary Commission, Perryville, Ky.:

Leaving Dr. Goddard to superintend ... I went with Mr. Thomasson to Danville. We here found the wants of the sick as urgent as those of the wounded at Perryville. The Courthouse was literally packed; many had eaten nothing during the day, most of them nothing since morning. I inquired if soup could be made here. The surgeons thought not, but kindly gave me authority to get it if I could.... It was now 5 o'clock P.M. There was no beef in the city, but the butcher agreed to bring in an animal, kill it, and have it ready in two hours. There was no water in the town—the wells were all dry—but the same good butcher sent and hauled water in barrels. Then there were no kettles for sale, all having been taken by the Rebels; but at last one was found in a private family; another was discovered two miles out of the city, owned by Mr. John J. Craig; he sent that in, saying that he should not want it until hog-killing time, and would lend it. No pails were to be had for love nor money, but I bought ... a washtub and spade, then dug trenches and laid stones with my own hands, and thus set both kettles. I made a fire of some old boards found in the Courthouse yard, sent a soldier for some pepper and salt, and at half past 10 o'clock I had the satisfaction of seeing two 32-gallon kettles of nutritious and palatable soup ready for distribution. This was given out at once, but by other hands than mine, as by this time I was completely exhausted....

October 15 (Wednesday)

Read, A. N., M.D., U.S. Sanitary Commission, Perryville, Ky.:

On the 15th, having with much difficulty obtained horses and saddles, we rode on to the advance of the army, then at Crab Orchard, reaching Gen. Mitchell's Division ... after dark. On making a hasty inspection of the condition of the troops, I found that the new regiments had suffered much from the severity of the service they had performed, and the exposure to which they had been subjected. The men had made long marches, were without tents, had only one blanket or an overcoat each—some one, some the other—their food, hard bread and bacon; beef occasionally; no vegetables. For new recruits, this had proved rather trying, and over ten percent had been disabled by it. I found several of the regimental surgeons with no medicines whatever, and they informed me that they had received strict orders not to take any. Some of them told me they had a few medicines which they carried on their persons. The spirit of the army is not what it should be. Through distrust of the Commanding General [Don Carlos Buell, who was later replaced by Rosecrans], they are seriously demoralized.

On my return to Danville, I found the number of sick considerably increased. As there were many who were without shelter, I looked around to find some building where they might be carried, and, at least, have a roof over their heads. After some search, a carriage shop was found which would answer the purpose. This belonged to Mr. J. W. Welch. At my solicitation he opened it, had the carriages removed, and placed it at my disposal. I then procured two loads of straw, which was spread on the floor, and two hundred men were brought in and laid upon it.... On the 18th I returned to Louisville....

October 16 (Thursday)

The aftermath of the Battle of Perryville, Ky., was particularly gruesome due to the lack of medical supplies. Surg. Shumard continues his report from October 8th:

I continued with this corps until October 16th. By this time the sick had accumulated so rapidly that it was found necessary to establish large hospital depots for their accommodation. Perryville and Harrodsburg were already crowded with the wounded, [and] besides these, large numbers of sick and wounded were scattered about the country in houses, barns, stables, sheds, or wherever they could obtain shelter sufficient to protect them from the weather. As the army marched through Danville, all the remaining sick were ordered to be left, which increased the number of sick and wounded in the district from both armies, the Rebels during their retreat having left most of their sick and wounded behind, to nearly eight thousand.... In two days the number of sick at this point [Danville] was increased to two thousand five hundred....

October 20 (Monday)

At the hospital in Corinth, Miss., Mother Bickerdyke went on a tour of supposedly empty tents to see if anyone had been overlooked. Mary Livermore wrote of Bickerdyke's findings:

Orders had been given to bring the wounded lying in tents into her large hospital, as fast as there was room for them. At last she was informed that the tents were all vacated. With her habit of seeing for herself if the work was done, she went from tent to tent, examining them. Turning from one, she thought she saw movement under a heap of blankets in a corner. She raised the nauseous, fly-covered blanket, and there lay a man, still breathing, but hardly alive. He had been shot through both cheeks, a part of his tongue had been cut off, which was swollen to bursting in his mouth, and the left shoulder and leg were broken. How long he had been forgotten, no one could tell; but the flies had rioted in his wounds, and he was in a most lamentable condition.

He was brought on a stretcher immediately to her hospital, when she devoted herself to his restoration, fighting grim death inch by inch, hour by hour, until she came off conqueror, and the man recovered. He is living today, and is proud to call Mother Bickerdyke his savior. It was something to witness the tempest that burst over the heads of the men who had been commissioned to remove the wounded, and had passed by this poor fellow. Mother Bickerdyke was merciless on such an occasion, and flashed such lightnings of wrath on the offenders as to astonish them into speechlessness....

October 26 (Sunday)

McClellan's Army of the Potomac began crossing that river into Virginia, its first major move in more than two months. This movement wasn't rapid.

November 1 (Saturday)

Ropes, Hannah, Nurse, Union Hospital, Georgetown, Washington, D.C.:

Today the steward's reign reaches a culminating point. I had said yesterday to Dr. Ottman, in his room, "Do you know a *dark hole* has been parted off in the cellar, said to be for any patient the steward chooses to incarcerate therein?" The chaplain was in the room at the time, a gentle refugee from Virginia and a professor in some college there. Peaceful, retired citizens both, neither answered directly. The question was incidental, after I had closed the object of my call. I rose from my chair to leave, but turned, placing my hands on the back of the chair, looking askingly at them both. I said, "You men may have fears too strong to allow you to act, I have no office to lose or gain. I am free to do right, and if any patient in this house is put into that black hole I will go to Washington and stay till I gain the 'open sesame' to that door. How can you let this hospital be turned into a prison?" It was eleven o'clock and the stir for dinner preparation began as I finished my rounds and slumped into my chair to look at the morning paper.... Hardly was I seated with spectacles on my nose before Fanny appeared, pale and trembling, holding by the door. "Mrs. Ropes! Julius is in that awful place!" "What! In the cellar?" "Yes, what shall we do?" "Do?" Off went the glasses, down went the paper, away broke my prospective rest of half-an-hour in my easy chair; and when I had tumbled noisily out of that chair, another figure appeared in the door by Fanny's side—our little mite of a Miss Kendall.... I caught sight of her quivering face, her earnest, sad eyes, glistening with tears that drift and float there always, and ... I said, "Come, will you go with me?"

Our bonnets were soon on and we in the car. Our first call was at General Banks' headquarters: He

had gone to New York! ... We took a car back to the Surgeon General's office. Three chairs lined the side of the public entrance; two strong men held up, respectively, the side of the door and the rail of the stairs. I asked audience of the Surgeon General; the man at the doorpost said, "It is three o'clock, and he is never here after that time." As he spoke, the Surgeon walked in and, passing us ... vanished behind the opening door of his inner office.... The man at the staircase followed his master, then came back to ask if I could send in my message. "No, it must be given in by myself." He returned only to say we could see the Asst. Surg., but at his door in the rear of the entry we were met with the notice that we must wait, he was engaged.

Two rebuffs seemed about enough for a woman of half a century to accept without compromising her own dignity, and [these rebuffs were] sufficient spur to take us to the Secretary of War['s] office. Here the tone of things was very much more genial; we were welcomed at least as having a right to sit in a nice room, and received the promise of seeing the Secretary as soon as he came to his room. Ten minutes passed ... a large man with dark beard, bald head, and legal brow walked into the room, stationing himself in front of a desk. The gentleman who had so kindly greeted us when we came, told me who it was. I went to the end of the desk and, without introducing myself at all, stated in the fewest words possible the facts about Julius. Secretary Stanton's eyes gleamed with the fire of a purpose. "Call the Provost Marshal" was all he said, and went on writing. Before we got hold of the importance of the order, that functionary appeared. Stanton lifted the pen from the paper and, looking at him, said, "Go to the Union Hospital with this lady, take the boy out of that black hole, go into it yourself so as to be able to tell me all about it, then arrest the steward and take him to a cell in the Old Capitol Prison, to await further orders!"

Very soberly he said it, and as soberly he said to me, "I am very much obliged to you, very much, for giving me this information...." The same car that brought us out, brought the men to take away our ogre, the steward. It was a frightfully grand scene to see the [a]maze[ment] of the steward, the joy of the men, and pale terror of the head surgeon....

November 3 (Monday)

The Union forces in the South Carolina campaign reported nearly 25 percent, on the average, of their strength on the sick list for the period November 1861 through October 1862. By far the greatest culprit was diarrhea and dysentery (12,284 cases), out of a total of 52,178 wounds and disease cases. Malaria was second with 3,866 cases, followed by remittent fever and others. Deaths were recorded at 724 for all causes.

November 4 (Tuesday)

Ropes, Hannah, Nurse, Union Hospital, Georgetown, Washington, D.C.:

A whole lifetime has been crowded into the past four days. Straps and buttons have been hurrying through the halls; wise-looking men in long boots have stood about; and legal people have been into my room to take testimony. Above everything else, the head surgeon has been spirited off and locked in the Old Capitol Prison.... On Saturday the Medical Inspector came to look about.... This man I had seen here with Gov. Andrew.... He came in and sat down by the men in a fatherly way, and I could have told him everything I ever did without a doubt of justice at his hands. First he asked me about the steward, and I stated all I could remember of his conversations.... Then he asked me about the Doctor. I replied truthfully, but also with a leaning towards pity.... I said, "He is a nervous, irritable person; the work here has been new to him, and he is young, too young for the place; beside, his past life has given him no general knowledge of society.... They [the majesty of his shoulder straps] seem to have conveyed to his mind a sense of irresponsible power." "But," said the Inspector, "you believe him unjust to the patients." "Yes indeed, always harsh and unsympathizing, but you can see as well as I that it will not mend the matter to punish him any more than he has been."

He looked upon the floor without speaking for awhile; then, as if he had made up his mind from a process of reasoning, said, "I think he best remain in prison over the Sabbath."

November 5 (Wednesday)

Things brightened for Mrs. Hannah Ropes at the Union Hospital for a few days while Dr. Clark resided in the Old Capitol Prison. Clark eventually did return to the hospital and attempted to dismiss Ropes, but he was thwarted by Stanton's order that she was *not* to be dismissed. After several days of trials and tribulations, Clark was removed from the hospital and the army medical service.

In what would be a shock to McClellan, Pres. Lincoln assigned Maj. Gen. Ambrose E. Burnside as the commander of the Army of the Potomac. Burnside, an able general at some levels, realized his own capabilities, and Burnside told Lincoln that he didn't want the command, and was unfit for it.

McClellan's military career ended, and his removal created much controversy in the ranks of the Army of the Potomac, whose soldiers venerated him. He'd been their father and protector almost since the army had been formed. At the same time, Maj. Gen. Fitz John Porter was relieved of his command, and was replaced by Maj. Gen. Joseph Hooker. Porter was McClellan's man, through and through, but Hooker was Hooker's man, first and last.

November 7 (Friday)

In Chicago, Mrs. Bickerdyke, directed to take a break, was on a well-deserved rest from the army. She had arrived at Mrs. Livermore's home exhausted from her 18 months of continuous labor. Shortly after Bickerdyke's arrival, Mrs. Livermore was to attend a wedding and invited Bickerdyke to go with her.

The wedding was long and tedious; Mrs. Bickerdyke slept through the entire proceedings. When it was finally over, she asked to be introduced to the bride. After the introduction, she informed the bride that if her new husband, a major, were ever to be hurt, Bickerdyke would try to take good care of him. At this point the groom exclaimed:

Why, Mother Bickerdyke! God Bless You! I am glad to see you! You have already taken care of me. After the battle of Donelson I was brought up on one of the boats filled with wounded men, and you took care of me, as you did of the rest, like a mother. Don't you remember a lieutenant who had a minié-ball in his leg; and the doctors wanted to amputate the leg, and he fought against their doing it, and how you helped him to keep it? I am the man. Here's the old leg, good as new. I have been promoted since.

November 10 (Monday)

Edmonds, S. Emma E., Union field nurse, Warrenton, Va.:

The new commander marched the army immediately to Falmouth, opposite Fredericksburg.... I went to Washington, and from thence to Aquia Creek by water.

I did not return to Washington on the cars, but rode on horseback, and made a two days' trip of it, visiting all the old places as I went. The battleground of the first and second Bull Run battles, Centreville, Fairfax C.H., and Chentilla.

But how shall I describe the sights which I saw and the impressions which I had as I rode over those fields! There were men and horses thrown together in heaps above ground; others lay where they had fallen, their limbs bleaching in the sun without the appearance of burial. There was one in particular—a cavalryman; he and his horse both lay together, nothing but the bones and clothing remained; but one of his arms stood straight up, or rather the bones and the coatsleeve, his hand had dropped off at the wrist and lay on the ground; not a finger or joint was separated, but the hand was perfect. I dismounted twice for the purpose of bringing away that hand, but did not do so after all.... I looked in vain for the old "brush heap" which had once screened me from the Rebel cavalry; the fire had consumed it. But the remains of the Stone Church at Centreville was an object of deep interest to me....

November 12 (Wednesday)

Mrs. Bickerdyke didn't long remain idle in Chicago. After a few days' rest, she began attending meetings around the Chicago area and raising funds for the Sanitary Commission. Until the end of the year she'd be twisting arms and browbeating bankers and the rich for donations, and doing it very successfully.

November 13 (Thursday)

Welch, S. G., Surg., 20th S.C. Vols., Berryville, Va.:

Our brigade is now camped in the suburbs of Berryville and is doing picket duty; however, in three days more another brigade will relieve us....

The weather is quite cold, but the health of the brigade remains good.... We have plenty to eat. For breakfast this morning we had biscuit (and they were shortened too), fried bacon and fried cabbage. For dinner he had boiled beef and dumplings, with biscuit and boiled eggs. Dr. Kilgore and I dined in Berryville yesterday with a Dr. Counsellor. The dinner was fine and the table was graced by his charming wife....

November 19 (Wednesday)

With the possibility of battle looming at Fredericksburg, Va., refugees were leaving that city in large numbers for Richmond.

Jones, John B., Rebel War Clerk, Confederate War Dept., Richmond, Va.:

The cars this afternoon from the vicinity of Fredericksburg were crowded with negroes, having bundles of clothing, etc., their owners sending them hither to escape the enemy. A frightened Jew, who came in the train, said there was an army of 100,000 near Fredericksburg, and we should hear more in a few days. I doubt it not.

Salt sold yesterday at auction for $1.10 per pound. Boots are now bringing $50 per pair; candles (tallow) 75 cts. per pound; butter $2.00 per pound. Clothing is almost unattainable. We are all looking shabby enough....

Lt. Gen. James Longstreet brought his Confederate corps onto Marye's Heights near Fredericksburg today after a march from Culpeper. Burnside arrived at Falmouth, across the river.

Letterman, Jonathan, Med. Dir., Army of the Potomac, Fredericksburg, Va.:

Maj. Gen. A. E. Burnside assumed command of this army on the 9th day of November, 1862, at Warrenton. On the 17th ... we left that place for Fredericksburg, and arrived opposite that city on the 19th.... It was generally believed that, upon our arrival there, we would at once cross the Rappahannock and take possession of the city. This was not done, and it soon became apparent that, if we attempted to do so, a battle would ensue....

It became necessary to see that everything in the medical department should be ready for any emergency which might arise. The principal objects to be accomplished were, that an extra amount of supplies for such an occasion should be at hand.... Ample supplies of medicines, instruments, stimulants, and anesthetics were ordered from New York and Washington.... In addition to these supplies, large quantities, over and above what were required for issue, of beef stock, stimulants, dressings, milk, coffee, tea, blankets, and underclothing were ordered and kept on hand.... All the hospital Autenrieth wagons that could be procured were distributed.... The requirements ... of field hospitals were to be attended to.... The ambulance corps in each army corps was examined.... Horses, harness, stretchers, lanterns, and all that was necessary for putting the trains in serviceable order were procured, and officers were assigned, and men detailed to complete and render effective the organization.... Five hundred hospital tents were ... ordered ... and kept at the depot, ready....

November 21 (Friday)

On the Rappahannock, Burnside asked that the city of Fredericksburg surrender, which demand was refused. The bombardment of the town was threatened, the Mayor requested time to remove the sick, wounded, women, and children. Jackson was hurrying from the Shenandoah Valley.

Ropes, Hannah, Nurse, Union Hospital, Georgetown, Washington, D.C.:

The nurse came and asked me to go in and see [a patient]; he lay sleeping quietly, under cover of which the angels were loosing him from the clay prison, the hospital life so painfully distasteful to him, and making ready for him a home for which he pined in silence, for which he was so eminently fitted. I was glad he was unconscious, for he had a wife and two pretty children; their likeness lay under the pillow where his head rested, with the death damp dripping like tears onto the case so precious to him! Above his head was his Bible, presented by his wife, with her name on the flyleaf....

Hannah Anderson Chandler Ropes, venerable matron of Union Hospital, fell ill in late December, 1862, of typhoid pneumonia. She lingered until January 20, 1863, when she died. Her remains were returned to Massachusetts for burial. She'd been a brave, unselfish, and dedicated woman.

November 24 (Monday)

Refugees from the Fredericksburg, Va., area were coming to Richmond in ever-increasing numbers. This meant more mouths to feed on already skimpy rations.

November 29 (Saturday)

Mrs. Phoebe Yates (Levy) Pember was born in Charleston, S.C., on August 18, 1823. Her father, a prosperous and well-educated man, had married Fanny Yates, a native of England. Phoebe was their fourth child. In 1850 the family moved to Savannah, Ga. At some point before 1861, Phoebe married Thomas Pember, a native of Boston, and they moved to Aiken, S.C., where Thomas died on July 9, 1861, age 36. Phoebe went back to Savannah to her parents. Early in 1862, the family left Savannah for Marietta, Ga., because of the threat of a Federal invasion of the coast.

Mrs. Pember was an acquaintance of Mrs. G. W. Randolph, the wife of the Confederate Secretary of War. Pember also moved in the same social circles as Mary Chesnut and other socially prominent Southern women. Mrs. Randolph convinced Phoebe that she should apply for a position as matron of one of the Confederate hospitals in the Richmond area. On this date, Phoebe wrote her sister that she was going to Richmond to become a matron at Chimborazo Hospital. She was the first matron to be appointed to that facility.

December 1 (Monday)

Near Fredericksburg, Jackson arrived from the Shenandoah Valley, with his corps ready for a fight. Longstreet was dug in on Marye's Heights. Lee awaited Burnside's actions.

December 2 (Tuesday)

Minor skirmishing took place along the Rappahannock between Lee and Burnside's forces. The civilians evacuated Fredericksburg as fast as they could, many taking trains to Richmond. Many sent their slaves to points south to prevent them from either escaping into the Federal lines or being freed by the Federals.

December 4 (Thursday)

Welch, S. G., Surg., 20th S.C. Vols., near Fredericksburg, Va.:

We traveled 175 miles from the Valley to this place in twelve days, and are now encamped upon precisely the same spot we were occupying when we left this region last spring....

We have an enormous force concentrated here now. Nearly all the men are well clothed, but some few are not. We still have a few barefoot men because their feet are too large for the government shoes. The health of the troops continues fine....

Allen, Julius D., Pvt., Co. K, 1st Battalion, 10th Illinois Cavalry, St. Louis, Mo., in a letter to his parents:

It has been so long since I wrote ... that you probably think I am no longer in the land of the living. After I wrote to you in August, my health improved very much and I became quite hearty, but I went to the hospital of the 33rd Illinois at Old Town and remained until the fever had broken. I then lay in camp for some time without proper food or medical attendance. I was then sent up the river in a boat to this hospital. I have now been here two months. When I came here my system was so out of order that I recovered my health and strength slowly. With the best of treatment which I have had all the time at this hospital, I am happy to inform you that I am now quite restored to health again and will return to my Company soon.

This hospital is about five miles west of the city. The building is a large, three-story one, built of brick, and is warmed up with heaters, which make the rooms quite comfortable in the coldest of weather. There are about 900 sick and wounded men here. Many are quite well and are going to their Regiments all the time but newcomers fill their places as fast as they leave. We have good physicians and nurses here, and get plenty of good wholesome food. Many a poor soldier is restored to health here who would die if left in the camp. I believe that I would never have recovered if I had been left in camp.

Although I have encountered many dangers and hardships and have had a hard spell of sickness since I enlisted, I am not tired of the service, and feel as ready and willing to serve my country and aid in putting down the wicked rebellion as I did on the day I enlisted. I hope that our armies will accomplish much this winter, and that the rebellion will be crushed in a few months more. I believe it could have been done before now if things had been managed right, and the war had been prosecuted with vigor from the first.

The sickly season down in Arkansas is now over, and a letter from one of our Company received a few days ago states that the health of the men is much improved. The place where I was taken sick—Old Town Landing—is the meanest, sickliest place I have ever been in my travels. Nearly all the boys were sick, but few of them died.... I wish I could spend the Christmas holidays with you; but it cannot be, so I will not think about it....

December 5 (Friday)

Mrs. Phoebe Pember reported to duty at Chimborazo Hospital No. 2 and settled in fairly rapidly. After her first "indoctrination" by the chief surgeon of the hospital, Phoebe was shown her working quarters, which were less than adequate. Her first task was to prepare the food for the special diets, as prescribed by the doctors. She had a small stove, "very small, very rusty, and fit only for a family of six. There were then about six hundred men upon the matron's diet list...." She also discovered the power of the "requisition." Using this newfound power, she requested two chickens, which were promptly supplied, dressed, and ready for cooking. Then, for the first time in her life, she "... cut up with averted eyes a raw bird, and the Rubicon was passed." After she'd prepared the soup, she added parsley sprigs and took some of it to one of the patients. The patient, after due consideration, whined, "My mammy's soup wasn't like that, but I might worry a little down if it war'n't for them weeds a-floating round." Next time, the parsley was omitted.

December 7 (Sunday)

The weather in Virginia turned even colder, causing bitter discomfort to soldier and civilian alike. Rebel War Clerk Jones's house was cold, but how much colder were the wounded prisoners without blankets or living in canvas tents in the field hospitals?

Jones, John B., Rebel War Clerk, Confederate War Dept., Richmond, Va.:

Last night was bitter cold.... Is this the "sunny South" the North is fighting to possess? How much suffering must be in the armies now encamped in Virginia? I suppose there are not less than 250,000 men in arms on the plains of Virginia and many of them who survive the war will have cause to remember last night. Some must have perished, and thousands, no doubt, had frozen limbs. It is terrible, and few are aware that the greatest destruction of life, in such a war as this, is not produced by wounds received in battle, but by disease, contracted from exposure, etc., in inclement seasons.

 ... A friend just returned from the battlefield of June, near the city, whither he repaired to recover the remains of a relative, says the scene is still one of horror. So great was the slaughter (27th June) that we were unable to bury our own dead for several days, for the battle raged a whole week, and when the work was completed, the weather having been extremely hot, it was too late to inter the enemy effectually, so the earth was merely thrown over them, forming mounds, which the rains and the wind have since leveled. And now the ground is thickly strewn with the bleaching bones of the invaders. The flesh is gone, but their garments remain. He says he passed through a wood, not a tree of which escaped the missiles of the contending hosts. Most of the trees left standing are dead, being often perforated by scores of Minié-balls, but thousands were prostrated by cannonballs and shells. It will long remain a scene of desolation, a monument to the folly and wickedness of man....

About 12 miles outside Fayetteville, Ark., two evenly matched armies got into a fight in freezing weather in what later became known as the Battle of Prairie Grove. Gen. Thomas C. Hindman's 10,000 Confederates attacked the combined Union force of 10,000 men of Gens. James Blunt and Francis J. Herron. Herron, coming to Blunt's support, arrived in time to thwart Hindman, who'd hoped to fight the Federals piecemeal. During the night the Rebels withdrew and sought shelter. The casualties were about even too, 1251 Federals and 1317 Confederates.

Hubbard, George H., Surg., USV, Battle of Prairie Grove, Ark.:

[The Union troops] marched about ninety-five miles after Thursday morning, December 4th, and went into action, without resting, at noon of Sunday December 7th. They were of course very much fatigued, but in the highest moral condition. Many of the regiments had been in service for more than a year without having been in action, and all made the march.... Supplies of medical and hospital stores were abundant. By my express order each regiment marched with sixty days' supply of all essential articles, and I took with me an abundance of everything needed after an engagement. Ambulances were plenty and were promptly at hand when wanted....

 The battlefield was Crawford's Prairie, bounded on the east by Illinois creek, which was easily fordable for ambulances and by stepping-stones, for men on foot. The medical officers were stationed near this ford, thus enabling them to examine each man as he came off the field. The ambulances took all who could not walk from this place to the small buildings in the rear....

 The battle ceased at dark, and the ambulances went over the whole field bringing away every man not previously removed, so that before morning every wounded man had been placed in a comfortable situation and properly attended to. Water was abundant and pure; but little food except hard bread was to be obtained till Monday, when soups were prepared for all. I will here remark that I believe more harm is done from too much food and too free use of stimulants with wounded men than from the want of an adequate supply. I believe that many lives were lost after the battle from this cause, while I have no reason to believe that anyone died from a want of these articles....

December 8 (Monday)

Hubbard, George H., Surg., USV, Battle of Prairie Grove, Ark.:

On Monday I ordered all the wounded to be sent to Fayetteville, ten miles distant, as fast as possible, where I proceeded to establish a general hospital, to which all were conveyed within three days. Primary amputations were performed as fast as it was possible to reach the cases; but the number wounded in so short a time rendered it impossible, with the limited number of medical officers, to prevent too great delay in many cases. The earlier the operations were performed, the better the results. Chloroform was the anaesthetic with no accidents from its use.... About the 25th of December, the general hospital was placed in charge of Surg. Ira Russell, USV, and I afterwards had little more than a nominal direction of its affairs.

The reported lack of coal and wood to heat the hospitals in western Virginia and the upper Shenandoah Valley caused suffering among patients as well as staff. This was especially true in Lynchburg, Va., where the winter weather was very cold, and snow was usually present during that season.

December 9 (Tuesday)

At Falmouth, just across the river from Fredericksburg, Va., Burnside gave orders for his Grand Division commanders to issue 60 rounds per man, prepare three days' cooked rations, and be prepared for an assault on the Rebels across the river. Pontoon bridges were coming up to span the Rappahannock for the crossing.

December 11 (Thursday)

Today, a Union expedition force departed New Bern, N.C., for Goldsboro, N.C., under the command of Maj. Gen. John G. Foster. The force was accompanied by Surg. B. B. Breed, U.S. Vols., who was assigned as medical purveyor for the expedition.

Breed, B. B., Surg., Med. Purveyor, Goldsboro expedition, N.C.:

The column was composed of eighteen infantry regiments, four batteries, and one regiment of cavalry. They were all well equipped. Each regiment was furnished with a hospital wagon, panniers, a hospital knapsack, and a proper allowance of hospital stores. No hospital tents were carried. The ambulances were of the two-wheeled Coolidge pattern. They were insufficient in number, and nearly worn-out. In all ... engagements the wounded were attended in houses on or near the battlefield. Good water was generally accessible, and sufficient supplies of soups, bread, and farinaceous food and stimulants were provided from the stores in my possession. The wounded were removed from the fields of action to the field hospitals by detachments of men selected by the regimental surgeons. The

ambulances for each brigade were under the charge of the senior surgeons of brigade....

At 4:45 A.M., the Confederates were alerted that the Yankees were building their bridges for the assault. The Confederates went to their positions, with Barksdale's Mississippians placed in the brick buildings whose blank rear walls faced the river to the west. Loop-holes were knocked from the brick, and firing posts, looking directly out on the bridges, were assigned.

At daylight, the firing began and it became dangerous to be on the bridges. The engineers left their positions to scamper back out of the fire only to be driven back to work by their officers. Finally, at 10 A.M., Burnside had had enough of this. He ordered his artillery to demolish those brick buildings, which they certainly did. Over 140 guns poured nearly 5000 rounds of heavy artillery into the city, blowing things sky-high. Barksdale's men came back, however, and shot a few more of the engineers. Eventually, a bridgehead was established, and the Yanks poured over the bridges and into the city. The Confederates withdrew and it was nearly 7:30 P.M. by the time the last of the Mississippians were back into their own lines. It would be a long night for everyone.

Letterman, Jonathan, Med. Dir., Army of the Potomac, Fredericksburg, Va.:

On the morning of December 11th, an attempt was made to throw the pontoons across the river. Gen. Hunter's reserve artillery opened upon the enemy's works beyond the city, and upon that portion of the town which skirted the river, where the riflemen of the enemy [were] pouring deadly fire upon the engineers.... In the afternoon, the fire was tremendous.... Under its effect, the enemy, who were but few in number, were, late in the day, driven from the cellars and other places of concealment along the bank of the river, and the bridges were constructed....

December 12 (Friday)

Midst a dense fog that limited visibility, Burnside's men came to the bridges, crossed and headed for the heights above the town, where Lee's formidable entrenchments were waiting. Lee's artillery had been sited and fields of fire had been laid for the Confederate infantry. The fog didn't lift until noon, however, and by then it was too late to organize the assault, which would have to wait until the next day. Lee sent for Jackson's two divisions to come up from downriver, where they were covering Skinker's Neck crossing....

Letterman, Jonathan, Med. Dir., Army of the Potomac, Fredericksburg, Va.:

On the afternoon of the 11th and on the 12th, the troops crossed.... Those who were wounded previous to the night of the 12th were promptly and properly cared for in the hospitals prepared on the north side of the river. In passing through the city on the afternoon of the 12th, for the purpose of examining that part of it ... to its adaptability for hospital purposes, I found desolation everywhere visible from the effects of the bombardment.... Some houses were shattered, others in ruins, and others burned. The courthouse, several churches, and such other buildings as were deemed suitable, were selected.... As many hospital wagons as were required were sent over, and the organization of each hospital was commenced....

December 13 (Saturday)

Sunrise was at 7:17 A.M. at Fredericksburg, Va., but the fog was so thick you couldn't see the sun. Longstreet, on the Confederate left flank, waited in his entrenchments. Jackson held the right of the main line. Stuart was to Jackson's right, covering the right flank. All was ready.

At ten o'clock the fog thinned and the artillery began to roar. On Marye's Heights, the Confederates watched as the Federals aligned their ranks and prepared for the charge up the hill. It finally came at 11:30 A.M., when the Yankees assaulted Longstreet's men, who were positioned uphill behind a stone wall. It was slaughter of the worst kind. Wave after wave of blue-clad troops lined up and went up the hill, only to be shot down. This lasted until nearly 3:30 P.M., when a lull occurred.

An assessment was made, and the assault resumed. Five charges had been made by sunset, about 4:15 P.M., and all had been repulsed. A sixth was ordered and went dutifully forward, only to meet the fate of the first five. By 6 P.M., the fighting was over in the darkness. Burnside would recross the river in the early hours of the 14th. It had been a futile exercise that killed nearly 1300 Union troops, wounded about 9600, and left almost 1800 as prisoners. The South lost about 600 killed, 4100 wounded, and 650 missing.

Letterman, Jonathan, Med. Dir., Army of the Potomac, Fredericksburg, Va.:

... before the action began on December 13th, the hospitals were in readiness.... Mattresses and beds were procured from the dwellings.... The wounded, who, on the north side, had been ... attended to, were left in charge of a sufficient medical officers.... All the tents were left standing, and others on hand, ready for use, should they be wanted....

On the morning of December 13th, the battle continued.... The wounded, who were rapidly brought in by the stretcher-bearers throughout the day and evening, were promptly and efficiently treated. The labor of the medical officers did not, of course, cease with the close of the day. The ambulances now commenced their legitimate duties.... As night closed in, the firing slackened, and shortly after altogether ceasing,... began gathering in the wounded who yet remained upon the field. The night was very dark, and the difficulty great in finding the objects of their search. The lanterns could not be used, as the glimmering of a candle invariably drew the fire of the enemy;... before dawn, all the wounded who were inside our lines had been taken to the hospitals.... Here, throughout the night, the medical officers ... engaged in attendance upon them, as they were brought in, blankets being fastened over the windows and every aperture to conceal the lights, every appearance of which drew a shot from the enemy's guns planted on Marye's Heights. During the day, the hospitals were not infrequently struck by shot and shell from these guns, but, fortunately, no one was injured....

Reed, Wm. H., Union Nurse, aftermath of battle, Fredericksburg, Va.:

Even the entries of this old mansion were crowded with the sick and dying men. No available space was left unoccupied. The poor fellows just arrived had not had their clothes off since they were wounded, and were sleeping in blood and filth, and were swarming with vermin. They lay as close as they could be packed, the contaminated air growing worse every hour. The openings in the torn and tattered walls assisted somewhat in ventilation; but were needed and welcome breathing holes. And so from room to room, from entry to entry, all was still, and dark, and ghastly. Pallid faces, or bronzed faces, with eager eyes, looked up in melting thankfulness, sometimes turning, in their unrest, to change a position which was wearing them to the bone, and to pray for a sleeping powder, which for this night at least should give them relief in unconsciousness.... Here side by side they lay, through long days and longer nights of suffering, with no sound but the clock, the stifled moan, or the delirious muttering. The air was so close and nauseating that we often reeled with faintness at our work, while these poor fellows waited and bore all their burden in a brave endurance that was like a miracle....

December 14 (Sunday)

Burnside considered ordering another assault, but was dissuaded by his commanders. Lee declined to leave his prepared positions and attack Burnside. He had no pontoons to cross the river and, besides, there was a mighty array of cannon to face. The cleanup of the battlefield began with the search for the wounded and the burial of the dead.

December 15 (Monday)

While the rest of the Union force withdrew to the north side of the Rappahannock, the recriminations began. Hooker would be one of the most vocal of Burnside's critics, a fact that Lincoln would remembered in days to come.

Letterman, Jonathan, Med. Dir., Army of the Potomac, Fredericksburg, Va.:

On December 14th, the troops remained on the field.... Late at night, orders were given to have the wounded removed to the north side of the river.

On December 15th, and early next morning, the removal began. On the left, a number had been removed on the 13th, whilst the action was taking place.... Early in the morning, it was understood that no ambulances would be permitted to cross the river on the right, orders regarding them having been partially misunderstood. This created ... some delay and confusion at the upper bridge, which I soon remedied, and directed them to be crossed over on the lower bridge.... After the last ambulance had left

the city, it was thoroughly inspected and policed by my direction, and not one wounded or sick man was found.... It rained very heavily during the night ... but no suffering was occasioned by the storm....

In Richmond, the casualties from the Battle of Fredericksburg, Va., arrived by train from the north. War Clerk Jones recorded:

Yesterday evening several trains laden with wounded arrived in the city. The remains of Brig. Gen. T. R. R. Cobb, of Georgia, were brought down. Brig. Gen. Gregg of South Carolina is said to be mortally wounded. It is now believed that Maj. Gen. Hood, of Texas, did not fall. The number of our killed and wounded is estimated, by a surgeon who came with the wounded, to be not over a thousand.

Today, stragglers from the battlefield say that our loss in killed and wounded is 3000. It is all conjecture....

December 16 (Tuesday)

Louisa May Alcott was already an established writer at the beginning of the Civil War. Like many other public figures, she had a desire to serve in some capacity to aid the war effort. She'd earlier volunteered to become a nurse and was assigned to the Union Hospital at Georgetown, Washington, D.C., where she came in contact with Mrs. Hannah Ropes, another New Englander, who was matron of that hospital. Alcott's *Hospital Sketches*, published in 1869, provide an insight into the work of the female nurse, written in the words of an excellent and very articulate observer. The casualties from the Battle of Fredericksburg, Va., fought on December 13th and 14th, were now reaching the hospitals at Washington:

Alcott, Louisa M., Volunteer Nurse, Union Hospital, Georgetown, Washington, D.C.:

"They've come! they've come! hurry up, ladies— you're wanted." "Who have come? the Rebels?" This sudden summons in the gray dawn was somewhat startling.... "Bless you, no child; it's the wounded from Fredericksburg; forty ambulances are at the door, and we shall have our hands full in fifteen minutes." "What shall we have to do?" "Wash, dress, feed, warm and nurse them for the next three months, I dare say. Eighty beds are ready, and we were getting impatient for the men to come....

Come to me in the ballroom when you are ready...."

The first thing I met was a regiment of the vilest odors that ever assaulted the human nose, and took it by storm. Cologne, with its seven and seventy evil savors, was a posy-bed to it.... Having been run over by three excited surgeons, bumped against by migratory coal-hods, water pails, and small boys, nearly scalded by an avalanche of newly filled teapots ... I progressed by slow stages upstairs and down till the main hall was reached.... There they were!

In they came, some on stretchers, some in men's arms, some feebly staggering along propped on rude crutches, and one lay stark and still with covered face, as a comrade gave his name to be recorded before they carried him to the dead house. All was hurry and confusion....

Presently, Miss Blank tore me from my refuge behind piles of one-sleeved shirts, odd socks, bandages and lint; put basin, sponge, towels, and a block of brown soap into my hands, with these appalling directions: "Come, my dear, begin to wash as fast as you can. Tell them to take off socks, coats and shirts, scrub them well, put on clean shirts, and the attendants will finish them off, and lay them in bed...."

Hav[e] done up our human wash, and laid it out to dry.... Great trays of bread, meat, soup and coffee appeared; and both nurses and attendants turned waiters.... Very welcome seemed the generous meal, after a week of suffering, exposure, and short commons; soon the brown faces begin to smile, as food, warmth, and rest, did their pleasant work....

All having eaten, drunk, and rested, the surgeons began their rounds; and I took my first lesson in the art of dressing wounds.... The amputations were reserved till the morrow....

December 17 (Wednesday)

Union Gen. John G. Foster's expedition to Goldsboro, N.C., captured Kinston on the 14th, and continued on towards White Hall, N.C., where a brief battle was fought on the 15th. There was additional skirmishing at Mt. Olive Station and Goshen Swamp before arriving at Goldsboro on this date. After burning a bridge near Goldsboro, Foster withdrew to New Bern, arriving there on the 20th.

Breed, B. B., Surg., USA, Med. Purveyor, Goldsboro expedition, N.C.:

The wounded at Kinston and White Hall were left at the field hospitals, under charge of surgeons detailed for the purpose, until the return of the column from Goldsboro'. Nearly one-half of the wounded, numbering in all, five hundred, were carried to New Bern in ambulances or army wagons. The others were taken below Kinston, on the Neuse River, on board of a stern-wheel, flat-bottomed steamer, and on a scow towed by the steamer. The wounded were much crowded on these boats. The facilities for cooking were very limited. Only by constant exertion were we able to furnish the necessary supplies. In the narrow and crooked river, the steamer, encumbered by the scow, was nearly unmanageable, and we were twenty-nine hours in accomplishing the voyage of sixty miles. The nights were excessively cold, but the men were well provided with extra blankets. The wounded were all placed in hospital at New Bern. Almost all the operations were primary, and were performed at the field hospitals. Chloroform was almost invariably employed as an anaesthetic, and without bad effects in any case.

On this expedition the following articles were taken by me on two large army wagons: eighty bed sacks, two hundred blankets, forty pounds of tea, fifty pounds of candles, forty-eight pounds of ether, ten ounces of sulphate of morphia, ten pounds of simple cerate, one hundred dozen bandages, twelve dozen bottles of whiskey, twelve pounds of tow, forty strips of pasteboard, forty-eight ounces of tincture of opium, ten pounds of Dover's powder, one hundred dozen opium pills, fifty yards of adhesive plaster, two sets of assorted splints, ten ounces of sulphate of iron, one pound of liquor of ammonia, ten pounds of lint, twenty-five gutta-percha bed covers, one hundred dozen quinine pills, twenty ounces sulphate of quina, one hundred dozen compound cathartic pills, fifteen pounds of flaxseed meal, one set of horse panniers, one hospital knapsack, six basins, two bed pans, one hospital mess chest, two lanterns.

At the commencement of an engagement, these wagons, which, on the march, were placed in rear of the ambulance train, and in front of the supply train, were brought to the houses selected for the field hospitals, and such articles as were of immediate use issued to the surgeons in charge. The bed sacks were filled with corn husks, and, with the army blankets, furnished clean and comfortable beds for the wounded, as they were brought in from the field. There was a deficiency of cooking utensils, which will be obviated as soon as the new medicine wagons, already ordered, shall be furnished to the department. I am convinced that extra stores thus provided, can be of great benefit in case of an engagement....

December 19 (Friday)

This year, 1862, saw the peak of the epidemic diseases in both the armies. In the South, there were 226,828 cases of diarrhea reported, with 3354 deaths from that disease during the year.

December 27 (Saturday)

The 96th Ohio, at full strength of 1000 officers and men, arrived on the levee near Vicksburg, Miss., and were placed in camp in a flooded cotton field. Disease rapidly depleted the ranks, and filled the regimental hospital. When they departed on March 12, 1863, they left 196 graves on the levee. The regimental surgeon recorded:

No abatement of the rain, no abatement of the diseases that did their fearful work; our hearts sank within us as we saw our feeble comrades bearing the uncoffined dead to their graves. The row of little mounds on the levee day by day became longer; our members, day by day, less; eyes more sunken, steps more feeble, souls more spiritless.

Rosecrans's army moved slowly towards Bragg at Murfreesboro, Tenn. Contact was reported by Surg. A. J. Phelps, USV.

On December 27th, our forces had a brisk skirmish with the enemy at Lavergne, losing, in killed, two; wounded, thirty-two. The wounded were held at Lavergne under charge of a medical officer....

December 30 (Tuesday)

At Murfreesboro, a major battle was taking place. Fighting began with unexpected contact and an assault on the Federal lines, the Confederates driving them back through the woods. Fortunately, Maj. Gen. Philip Sheridan was there with his division. He held, although he lost his three brigade commanders before the day was over. At night the firing faded and the commanders, on both sides, prohibited the troops from building fires to warm themselves. In the bitter cold, everyone had a miserable night.

Phelps, A. J., Surg., USV, 14th Corps, Battle of Murfreesboro, Tenn.:

On the evening of the 29th, we came upon the enemy in force two and three-quarter miles from Murfreesboro'.

On December 30th, while our forces were being placed in position, I established one field hospital for each division on the left wing under the charge of their several medical directors.... To these points were brought the hospital wagons, ambulances, etc., of each division, and also the reserve supply of hospital stores....

December 31 (Wednesday)

At Murfreesboro, Hardee's corps made an attack in a wheeling motion and the Federals retreated, also in a wheeling motion, a sort of *danse macabre*. Finally, Rosecrans's troops were pinned against Stones River and went no farther. The Confederates assaulted the Union line until late afternoon with no results. The Confederates had won the day, but at a very heavy cost, their casualties being in excess of 9000. With a few more victories such as this, Bragg would have no army.

Phelps, A. J., Surg., USV, 14th Corps, Battle of Murfreesboro, Tenn.:

Thus affairs stood on the 31st. Soon after the battle opened, when the right wing gave way, the Rebel cavalry swung around and captured one hospital, and began to drive off our supplies, and even despoiled some of our medical officers of their personal property, but it was only a brief period before the hospital and property were recaptured by a dash of our own cavalry. As the battle progressed it became necessary for us to accommodate a very large number of wounded from the centre and right, whose temporary hospitals, and some of whose surgeons, fell into the lines of the enemy. Our accommodations becoming speedily exhausted, we were fortunate in getting control of a large proportion of the hospital tents that were so wisely brought in the rear train from Nashville. These were pitched, and long sheds were formed from their flies; by all these means it was estimated that we accommodated at these three hospitals not less than four thousand five hundred wounded....

Barrell, H. C., Asst. Surg., USV, 27th Ill. Vols., Murfreesboro, Tenn.:

I left Nashville on Tuesday night, December 30th, with eleven wagon-loads of supplies. Gen. Mitchell sent with the train the 10th Michigan Volunteers, and on Wednesday afternoon at two o'clock we arrived within a few miles of the scene of action.... The road was completely blocked by wagons returning to Nashville, and among them a great many ambulances, which the drivers, either through misapprehension of orders or through cowardice, had turned in that direction, thus depriving the wounded of their much needed services. A great many of these wagons were burned, and in many of them all of the three-months' medical supply of a regiment. Nearly all the stores of the medical purveyor of the right wing had fallen into the hands of the enemy, and my arrival was most opportune....

1863

January 1 (Thursday)

Barrell, H. C., Asst. Surg., USV, 27th Ill. Vols., Murfreesboro, Tenn.:

At Lavergne, a small town halfway between Nashville and Murfreesboro', many of the subsistence trains were destroyed, and the army was suffering severely in consequence. The scarcity of food was so great that during the battle, in some of the regiments, the men ate the flesh of mules slain in action…. Thursday morning I commenced issuing medicines and stores; but as the hospital at which I was stationed was not considered perfectly safe from the enemy's attacks, it was deemed prudent not to remove anything from the wagons, and in fact it was necessary twice during the day to retire farther within the lines. In the evening the supplies were unloaded.…

January 2 (Friday)

Barrell, H. C., Asst. Surg., USV, 27th Ill. Vols., Murfreesboro, Tenn.:

The amount of nourishment for the wounded was limited. The concentrated beef was used very largely, and was much sought after. The supply of milk was chiefly that known as solidified or granulated, as prepared in Dutchess County, N.Y., and wasn't much liked. The concentrated milk prepared by Borden was much preferred by medical officers.

On arriving in Murfreesboro' we found the public and many of the private houses occupied by the enemy's wounded, which, in their hasty retreat, they were compelled to leave. They were almost destitute of medicines, and to keep them supplied I drew very largely upon our stores. There was a great scarcity of stimulants among them, and it was necessary to issue a great amount from our depot. The town being so crowded, it was found necessary to transport a great number of the wounded to Nashville.…

This was the month when the "cyclone in calico" hit Memphis, Tenn. Mrs. Mary Ann Bickerdyke, hospital matron *extraordinaire*, arrived and reported to the Medical Director for the area. Huge hospitals had been organized at Memphis because of that city's proximity to the river and transportation. Bickerdyke first tackled the Adams Block Hospital, and within a short time it was in good running order, even though some of the personnel still had their ears ringing from Bickerdyke's scolding. Most were happy to see her leave for Ft. Pickering, Tenn., and the "Smallpox Hospital," although they were happy also with the results of her visit.

January 5 (Monday)

Mr. Plattenburg of the Western Sanitary Commission agency at Helena, Ark., went south on the Mississippi to where Gen. Sherman's army was attacking Vicksburg. The large quantity of supplies taken there was distributed to the sick and wounded on land, as well as on the hospital steamers. Later, in March, when Grant moved his major force below

Vicksburg, the Sanitary Commission moved to Milliken's Bend, where supplies were given to the sick and wounded. The work at the agency at Helena was transferred to another office for administration.

January 7 (Wednesday)

In Washington, the government gave permission for 450 women and children (Southern refugees) to leave for Petersburg, Va. Their final destination would be the Richmond area....

January 8 (Thursday)

Mrs. Bickerdyke, knowing the necessity of a good laundry service to the hospitals, began organizing such a service at the first opportunity. After finding a central location, she ordered the washing machines, wringers, tubs, kettles, mangles, soap, and all the other items to be sent to her from Chicago. While this was perking, she went on to the "pesthouse" at Ft. Pickering.

January 9 (Friday)

At the town of Gordonsville, Va., the Exchange Hotel had been taken over by the Confederate government to serve as a receiving hospital for the sick and wounded. Those who couldn't be accommodated inside were placed in tents to the rear of the building, or left outside in the elements. After initial processing, the patients were sent farther to hospitals at Charlottesville, Lynchburg, Danville, or Richmond. During quiet periods, the flow of patients would be sporadic and would increase as the campaigns in the Shenandoah Valley and other points in Virginia filled the pipeline.

January 10 (Saturday)

The 450 women and children who left Washington on the 7th arrived in Petersburg, Va., on the 10th.

Alcott, Louisa M., Nurse, Union Hospital, Georgetown, Washington, D.C.:

"My dear girl, we shall have you sick in your bed, unless you keep yourself warm and quiet for a few days...." This advice was delivered, in a paternal manner, by the youngest surgeon in the hospital, a kind-hearted little gentleman, who seemed to consider me a frail young blossom, that needed much cher-

ishing, instead of a stout spinster, who had been knocking about the world for thirty years.... He discovered me sitting on the stairs ... while I enjoyed a fit of coughing, which caused my head to spin ... as I waited for the frolicsome wind to restore the breath I'd lost.... My head felt like a cannonball ... the walls at times undulated in a most disagreeable manner; people looked unnaturally big ... I resolved to retire gracefully....

For the benefit of any ardent damsel whose patriotic fancy may have surrounded hospital life with a halo of charms, I will briefly describe the bower to which I retired, in a somewhat ruinous condition. It was well ventilated, for five panes of glass had suffered compound fractures, which all the surgeons and nurses failed to heal; the two windows were draped with sheets.... A bare floor supported two narrow iron beds, spread with thin mattresses like plasters, furnished with pillows in the last stages of consumption. In a fireplace, guiltless of shovel, tongs, andirons, or grate, burned a log, inch by inch, being too long to go on all at once; so, while the fire blazed away at one end, I did the same at the other, as I tripped over it a dozen times a day, and flew up to pike it a dozen times a night. A mirror (let us be elegant!) of the dimensions of a muffin, and about as reflective, hung over a tin basin, blue pitcher, and a brace of yellow mugs. Two invalid tables, ditto chairs, wandered here and there, and the closet contained a varied collection of bonnets, bottles, bags, boots, bread and butter, boxes, and bugs.... Two arks, commonly called trunks, lurked behind the door, containing the worldly goods of the twain who laughed and cried, slept and scrambled, in this refuge; while from the white-washed walls above either bed, looked down the pictured faces of those whose memory could make for us—"One little room an everywhere."

January 11 (Sunday)

Alcott, Louisa M., Nurse, Union Hospital, Georgetown, Washington, D.C.:

For a day or two I managed to appear at meals; for the human grub must eat till the butterfly is ready to break loose, and no one had time to come up two flights while it was possible for me to come down. Far be it from me to add another affliction or reproach to that enduring man, the steward; for, compared with his predecessor, he was a horn of plenty; but—I put it to any candid mind—is not the following bill of fare susceptible of improvement, without plunging the nation madly into debt? The three meals were "pretty much of a muchness," and consisted of beef, evidently put down for the men of '76; pork, just in from the street; army bread, composed of sawdust and saleratus; butter, salt as if churned by Lot's wife; stewed blackberries, so much like preserved cockroaches, that only those devoid of imagination could partake thereof with relish; coffee, mild and muddy; tea, three dried huckleberry leaves to a quart of water—flavored with lime—also animated and unconscious of any approach to clearness. Variety being the spice of life, a small pinch of the article would have been appreciated by the hungry, hardworking sisterhood, one of whom, though accustomed to plain fare, soon found herself reduced to bread and water; having an inborn repugnance to the fat of the land, and the salt of the earth....

January 13 (Tuesday)

At Ft. Pickering, the arrival of Mrs. Bickerdyke caused quite a stir. Mrs. Livermore reported the event:

There had been great neglect here; and the loathsome place had been left uncared for until it was fouler and more noisome than an Augean stable. But Mother Bickerdyke was just the Hercules to cleanse it. She raised such a hurricane about the ears of the officials whose neglect had caused its terrible condition, as took the heads from some of them, and sent back to their regiments several privates, soldiers who had been detailed as nurses.

The storm she raised left the atmosphere and premises sweeter than she found them. The walls were whitewashed, the kitchens regenerated, so that the patients could have the diet necessary to them, and both they and their beds were supplied with fresh clothing. Disinfectants were used with a lavish hand, and then, leaving a matron in charge who was an abridged edition of herself, she went to Gayoso Hospital, to organize and take charge of that.

January 14 (Wednesday)

Miss Alcott, using some of her free time during convalescence, visited one of the other Washington area hospitals:

Alcott, Louisa M., Nurse, Union Hospital, Georgetown, Washington, D.C.:

Very soon after leaving the care of my ward, I discovered that I had no appetite, and cut the bread and butter interests almost entirely, trying the exercise and sun cure instead.... Every morning I took a brisk run in one direction or another; for the January days were as mild as spring.... One of these trips was to the Armory Hospital, the neatness, comfort, and convenience of which makes it an honor to its presiding genius, and arouses all the covetous propensities of such nurses as come from other hospitals to visit it.

The long, clean, warm, and airy wards, built barrack-fashion, with the nurse's room at the end, were fully appreciated by Nurse Periwinkle, whose ward and private bower were cold, dirty, inconvenient, upstairs and downstairs, and in everybody's chamber. At the Armory, in ward K, I found a cheery, bright-eyed, white-aproned little lady, reading at her post near the stove; matting under her feet; a draft of fresh air flowing in above her head; a table full of trays, glasses, and such matters, on one side, a large, well-stocked medicine chest on the other; and all her duty seemed to be going about now and then to give doses, issue orders, which well-trained attendants executed, and pet, advise, or comfort Tom, Dick or Harry.... As I watched the proceedings, I recalled my own tribulations, and contrasted the two hospitals in a way that would have caused my summary dismissal, could it have been reported at headquarters. Here, order, method, common sense and liberality seemed to rule in a style that did one's heart good to see; at the Hurly burly Hotel, disorder, discomfort, bad management, and no visible head, reduced things to a condition which I despair of describing....

January 17 (Saturday)

The springlike weather of January departed and was replaced by the cold rain and wind that was more usual in Washington during that month. Miss Alcott, still convalescing, returned to her room at Union Hospital:

Alcott, Louisa M., Nurse, Union Hospital, Georgetown, Washington, D.C.:

Shut up in my room, with no voice, spirits, or books, that week was not a holiday, by any means. Finding meals a humbug, I stopped away altogether.... Like a flock of friendly ravens, my sister nurses fed me, not only with food for the body, but kind words for the mind; and soon, from being half-starved, I found myself so beteased and betoasted, petted and served, that I was nearly killed with kindness, in spite of cough, headache, a painful consciousness of my pleura, and a realizing sense of bones in the human frame. From the pleasant house on the hill, the home in the heart of Washington, and the Willard caravansary, came friends new and old, with bottles, baskets, carriages and invitations for the invalid; and daily our Florence Nightingale climbed the steep stairs, stealing a moment from her busy life, to watch over the stranger, of whom she was as thoughtfully tender as any mother....

January 18 (Sunday)

Alcott, Louisa M., Nurse, Union Hospital, Georgetown, Washington, D.C.:

Being forbidden to meddle with fleshly arms and legs, I solaced myself by mending cotton ones, and, as I sat sewing at my window, watched the moving panorama that passed below; amusing myself with taking notes of the most striking figures in it. Long trains of army wagons kept up a perpetual rumble from morning till night; ambulances rattled to and fro with busy surgeons, nurses taking an airing, or convalescents going in parties to be fitted to artificial limbs. Strings of sorry-looking horses passed, saying as plainly as dumb creatures could, "Why, in a city full of them, is there no *horsepital* for us?" Often a cart came by, with several rough coffins in it, and no mourners following; barouches, with invalid officers, rolled around the corner, and carriage loads of pretty children, with black coachmen, footmen, and maids. The women who took their walks abroad, were so extinguished in three-story bonnets, with overhanging balconies of flowers, that their charms were obscured; and all I can say of them is, that they dressed in the worst possible taste, and walked like ducks.

The men did the picturesque, and did it so well that Washington looked like a mammoth masquerade. Spanish hats, scarlet-lined riding cloaks, swords and sashes, high boots and bright spurs, beards and mustaches, which made plain faces comely, and comely faces heroic; these vanities of the flesh transformed our butchers, bakers, and candlestick makers into gallant riders of caparisoned horses, much handsomer than themselves; and dozens of such figures were constantly prancing by, with private prickings of spurs, for the benefit of the perambulating flowerbed. Some of these gentlemen affected painfully tight uniforms, and little caps, kept on by some new law of gravitation, as they covered only the bridge of the nose, yet never fell off; the men looked like stuffed fowls, and rode as if the safety of the nation depended on their speed alone. The fattest, greyest officers dressed most, and ambled stately along, with orderlies behind, trying to look as if they didn't know the stout party in front, and doing much caracoling on their own account....

January 21 (Wednesday)

The Memphis area hospitals often contained tens of thousands of patients who required care and a healthy atmosphere in which to recover. A major contribution to this atmosphere was the magnificent laundry that had been devised and operated by Mrs. Bickerdyke for the hospitals. Literally unnumbered thousands of items were processed by the laundry during a single day, all being returned to the hospital from which they came, or, if no identification was possible, held at the laundry storeroom for issue as required. The operation required the services of nearly 70 contrabands who were furnished and paid by the army. Had it been a for-profit business, Bickerdyke could have made a fortune.

A major advantage Mrs. Bickerdyke had was the trust placed in her by Gen. U. S. Grant. Grant had given Mrs. Bickerdyke a pass to go anywhere she wanted in his area of control without hindrance. Further, she had his authority to visit any hospital, camp, or facility that she felt was necessary to accomplish her work. She also had Grant's authority to draw any item of equipment or food she wanted from any quartermaster in the general's operational area. As Grant's area of operations expanded, so did Mrs. Bickerdyke's access to what she wanted.

The Sanitary Commission also authorized her to draw any supplies from its depots at Memphis, Cairo, Chicago, Indianapolis, Cincinnati, or St. Louis. With this power, Bickerdyke became one to be dealt with gingerly in Memphis, but there was never a single recorded case where Mrs. Bickerdyke abused the trust placed in her by either Grant or the Commission.

January 24 (Saturday)

Louisa May Alcott's illness with typhoid finally got the better of her after a three-month stint as a nurse in Union Hospital. She'd delayed returning home, although counseled to do so by her doctors, until finally her father came to Washington and took her back to New England, where the road to recovery was swift and sure. She kept contact with many of the people she'd worked with and met during her tenure at "Hurly burly Hotel," and later wrote some of her impressions. One such impression presents a typical doctor/patient relationship:

Alcott, Louisa M., Nurse, Union Hospital, Georgetown, Washington, D.C.:

… must not lead anyone to suppose that the surgeons were willfully hard or cruel, though one of them remorsefully confided in me that he feared his profession blunted his sensibilities, and perhaps, rendered him indifferent to the sight of pain.

I am inclined to think that in some cases it does; for, though a capital surgeon and a kindly man, Dr. P., through long acquaintance with many of the ills flesh is heir to, had acquired a somewhat trying habit of regarding a man and his wound as separate institutions, and seemed rather annoyed that the former should express any opinion upon the latter, or claim any right to it, while under his care. He had a way of twitching off a bandage, and giving a limb a comprehensive sort of clutch, which, though no doubt entirely scientific, was rather startling than soothing, and highly objectionable as a means of preparing nerves for any fresh trial. He also expected the patient to assist in small operations, as he considered them, and to restrain all demonstrations during the process.

"Here, my man, just hold it this way, while I look into it a bit," he said one day to Fitz G., putting a wounded arm into the keeping of a sound one, and proceeding to poke about among bits of bone and visible muscles, in a red-and-black chasm made by some infernal machine of the shot or shell description. Poor Fitz held on like grim Death, ashamed to show fear before a woman, till it grew more than he could bear in silence; and, after a few smothered groans, he looked at me imploringly, as if he said, "I wouldn't, ma'am, if I could help it," and fainted quietly away.

Dr. P. looked up, gave a compassionate sort of cluck, and poked away more busily than ever, with a nod at me and a brief—"Never mind; be so good as to hold this till I finish.…"

February 4 (Wednesday)

Mrs. Mary Ann Bickerdyke was still in Memphis, visiting the hospitals and supervising the laundry, but having a little trouble with the medical director of Memphis. It seemed that this officer was fairly young and full of his own importance, so much so that he decided that Mrs. Bickerdyke should "revolve in an orbit he marked out for her." Bickerdyke was to refrain from going outside his authority to see anyone to ask for assistance. As a result, he was soon at loggerheads with this woman who normally did things her own way, regardless of what someone else wanted. Mrs. Livermore reported one clash between the two protagonists:

Mrs. Bickerdyke cared little for what he said or thought, if he did not meddle with her; for she was no more in love with the medical director than he was with her. He inspected her hospital regularly, and never found fault with it; for its perfect management defied criticism. Once in passing through a ward, he espied some half-dozen eggs under a sick man's pillow. The man was recovering from a fever, and had a great craving for food, that could not be allowed him in his weak condition. Especially, he coveted boiled eggs; and, as the poor fellow was very babyish, Mrs. Bickerdyke had petted him in her motherly way, and tucked a half-dozen hard-boiled eggs under the pillow, telling him he should have them to eat when he was well enough. The sick man found a vast deal of comfort in fondling the eggs with his hands. I have seen men in hospitals handling half a dozen potatoes under their pillows in the same way. The medical director espied the eggs, and ordered them to the kitchen, declaring "he would have no hens' nests under the pillows." The man was just weak enough to cry miserably over his loss; and the nurse in charge hastened to report the story to Mother Bickerdyke.… Catching up a large pail filled with eggs, she strode into the ward, her blue eyes blazing, her cheeks glowing: "Dr. ——
——, will you tell me what harm it does to humor a sick man in an innocent fancy? Let this boy have the eggs where he can see them. There, John, there's a whole pailful of eggs," pushing them under his bed;

"and you may keep them there until they hatch, if you've a mind to." And she strode out again. The doctor chose not to hear, and the boy's eggs were not meddled with again.

February 5 (Thursday)

Mrs. Phoebe Pember, the matron at Chimborazo Hospital No. 2 in Richmond, Va., dealt primarily with patients who were common soldiers of the Confederacy. These men, mostly unlettered, weren't sophisticated, and often had difficulty expressing themselves. On one occasion, a rather rough Kentuckian complimented her on her small feet with the words, "You will wear them little feet away running around so much. They ar'nt' much to boast of anyway." On another occasion, a burly Texan gave her a minute inspection and then remarked: "… Why, you's as pretty as a pair of red shoes with green strings."

February 11 (Wednesday)

In Memphis, Tenn., there had been somewhat of an armed truce between Mrs. Bickerdyke and the area medical director since their last set-to about the boiled eggs. He had far from given up, however. He was firmly determined to get Bickerdyke's contrabands, who worked in the laundry, back to the camps and out of his hospitals. He started his wrestling match with an alligator.

One day when Bickerdyke returned from her usual trip to the Smallpox Hospital, she found that the medical director had written an order directing that all of the contrabands be sent back to their camps not later than 9 A.M. the following day. The weather was stormy and her mules were tired, so she told her assistant to have something to eat and get ready to go to see Gen. Hurlbut at his headquarters, even though it was late. Soon thereafter, she and Mrs. Livermore departed to find the general, albeit over Mrs. Livermore's objections. The mission was finally accomplished when they found the general, who'd gone to bed, and got him to sign an order that the contrabands could remain in the laundry. Back went the two heroines through the slashing rain, happy and triumphant.

At 9 A.M. the medical director made his appearance at the hospital expecting to see the Negroes gone. Instead, all were at work as if it were a normal day. Furious, he went to the kitchen, where Mrs. Bickerdyke was making soup, and asked for an explanation: "Did she, or did she not, receive an order to remove all the contrabands?" "Yes, she certainly did," she replied after tasting the soup she was making. "Then, why was the order not obeyed?" asked the medical director. "Because," said Mrs. Bickerdyke, "Gen. Hurlbut gave me an order permitting me to keep them," whereon she produced the order and handed it to the Medical Director.

The medical director wasn't happy. In fact, he was most unhappy and vented his anger for some time to the world. He even went so far as to tell Mrs. Bickerdyke "he wouldn't have her in Memphis, he would send her home before she was a week older." Mrs. Livermore describes what followed:

"But I sha'n't go doctor!" she answered. "I've come down here to stay, and I mean to stay until this thing is played out. I've enlisted for the war, as the boys have, and they want me and need me, and can't get on without me; and so I shall stay, doctor, and you'll have to make up your mind to get along with me the best way you can. It's of no use for you to try to tie me up with your red tape. There's too much to be done down here to stop for that. Nor is there any sense in your getting mad because I don't play second fiddle to you; for I tell you I haven't got time for it. And, doctor, I guess you hadn't better get into a row with me, for whenever anybody does one of us two always goes to the wall, and 'taint never me!"

February 13 (Friday)

On this date, the Western Sanitary Commission opened a Soldier's Home in Memphis, Tenn., in the buildings and grounds that were the former home of a Confederate officer. The grounds, containing about six acres, contained a large mansion which had a great hall, a front porch, a large piazza in the rear, many large rooms, and an excellent kitchen. Many large trees were on the grounds and nearly three acres were set aside for gardens. Only discharged and invalid soldiers were permitted to stay at the Home, which served as a way station. Because of so many of this category of soldier arriving by steamer, the Western Sanitary Commission in conjunction with the United States Sanitary Commission fitted a temporary "lodge" near the steamboat landing where arriving "guests" could be housed overnight before being transferred to the Home. The Home at Memphis had been donated at no cost to the government, nor to the Commission. The government furnished rations that were supplemented by the Commission. The Memphis Home was placed in charge of Mr. O. E. Waters, with Miss A. L. Ostram serving as Matron. In a three-month period (February-April), this facility furnished lodgings to 1976 "guests" and served over 4000 meals.

February 23 (Monday)

The Soldier's Home established at Columbus, Ky., by the Western Sanitary Commission, was located on the military post. It functioned as a way station for discharged and invalid soldiers who required overnight lodging and furnished them with "bag lunches" to take when they continued their journeys. During its first four and one-half months of operation, it received over 10,500 soldiers, served over 16,200 meals, and provided 1204 "take-out" lunches.

March 15 (Sunday)

The armies in Tennessee had gone into winter quarters in February, when the weather got too rough for further campaigning. At Murfreesboro, the Dept. of the Cumberland's medical director was busy.

Perin, G., Surg., USA, Med. Dir., Murfreesboro, Tenn.:

Soon after joining this army in February, 1863, my attention was directed first to the diet of the men, the method of cooking, etc., which resulted in the publication of Dept. General Order No. 76. The medical officers generally took a great deal of interest in this matter, and I may safely say the health of the command was much improved in consequence.

While this subject was receiving the attention it deserved, a large tent hospital was established near the railroad, on the bank of Stones River, of capacity sufficient to accommodate fifteen hundred patients. This hospital was provided, as far as practicable, with movable furniture, such as light cots of the Chicago pattern, bed sacks, camp kettles, etc. As soon as the tents were erected, patients were sent to that point instead of to the hospitals in the town of Murfreesboro'. A large garden was planted near the field hospital, which soon afforded an abundant supply of vegetables....

March 19 (Thursday)

Perin, G., Surg., USA, Med. Dir., Murfreesboro, Tenn.:

Ambulance trains were organized.... I will remark,... that the ambulance trains were generally well served in this organization; but there were grave defects, among which I may mention that the ambulance master was not a commissioned officer, and could not exercise the authority necessary to secure efficiency; next, there were no men detailed to assist in placing the wounded in or taking them out of the ambulances. The ambulances were receipted for and held under the control of the quartermaster's department. The regimental ambulances were found to be almost useless for general service in transporting wounded, because they were used as carriages and for transporting personal baggage and other freights, so that, when required for legitimate use, they were either out of order, or the animals were broken-down. So seriously were these defects experienced, that I recommended for adoption the plan of an ambulance corps ... arranged on the same basis as that ... of the Army of the Potomac....

March 29 (Sunday)

The Western Sanitary Commission was today authorized a government-furnished steamboat to provide transportation for Sanitary Commission materials. Maj. Gen. U. S. Grant, in Special Orders No. 88, Dept. of the Tennessee, directed:

I. The Quartermaster's Dept. will provide and furnish a suitable steamboat, to be called the "United States Sanitary Store Boat," and put the same in charge of the United States Sanitary Commission, to be used exclusively for the conveyance of goods calculated to prevent disease, and supplement the Government supply of Stores for the relief of the sick and wounded.

II. No person will be permitted to travel on said boat except officers of the Army and Navy (and they only on permits from their proper commanding officers), discharged soldiers and employees of the Sanitary Commission. No goods whatever, for trading or commercial purposes, will be carried on said steamer, and no goods will be taken for individuals, or with any conditions which will prevent their being delivered to those most needing them in the Army or Navy.

III.The contents of all packages to be shipped on said United States Sanitary Store Boat will be inspected before shipment, by an agent of the said Sanitary Commission, at the point of shipment....

Special Orders No. 88 inadvertently didn't include the *Western* Sanitary Commission in its authority. This oversight was immediately corrected by the issuance of Special Orders No. 101, same date, which included the *Western* Sanitary Commission and placed it on the same footing with the United States Sanitary Commission.

April 13 (Monday)

Asst. Surg. John G. Perry of Boston had returned to that city in August of last year to recover from a serious illness brought on extreme exhaustion. While in Boston, Perry completed his medical training and was graduated from Boston Medical School. On March 18, 1863, he was married, and he received his commission in the 20th Mass. Volunteer Regiment. He left Boston on April 11th for his regiment, which was located near Falmouth, Va.

Perry, John G., Asst. Surg., USV, 20th Mass. Vols., Washington, D.C.:

Of all the disagreeable soldier-loafing places I was ever in, this is the worst. The city is rambling, the streets are dusty, unclean, filled with army officers of every grade and with privates. Were it not for the necessity of procuring passes, I would be at this moment with my regiment. Vague rumors concerning army movements have been flying through the city, and I am anxious to be on duty. There is no surgeon with the Twentieth now, so I expect to have full charge.

April 15 (Wednesday)

Perry, John G., Asst. Surg., USV, 20th Mass. Vols., Falmouth, Va.:

I have felt dazed and benumbed since my arrival here, probably from the effort I made before leaving home to suppress all gathering emotions. On the Sound boat I gave way, and I confess to behaving as I did when a child for the first time away from home. I cried as I did then, all night long. I thought Harry Abbott in the berth above me was fast asleep, when suddenly he rolled over and looked down upon me. I felt for the moment thoroughly ashamed of myself,

but he said nothing and settled back into his place, and then I heard him crying also. We had talked things over a bit, and I knew the poor fellow felt that he had seen his home for the last time, and that he had passed safely through so many battles he could hardly escape unscathed again....

April 16 (Thursday)

At the hospitals in Memphis, a major problem existed in finding sufficient quantities of fresh milk and eggs for the kitchens. What was available was sold at very high prices and even then supplies were scarce. Milk sold for 50 cents per quart, and that price was in Union greenbacks.

Mrs. Bickerdyke conceived the idea of going back to Illinois and obtaining sufficient cows and chickens to satisfy the hospitals' need and have them shipped by rail to Memphis. When she approached the medical director with the plan, he scoffed, believing her to be a little mad. However, she finally persuaded him, and she went North for 30 days to try her luck. When she went North, she escorted several hundred amputees, who, if possible, were then placed in hospitals nearest their homes for further convalescence.

Once back in Illinois, she had little difficulty obtaining the cows she wanted. Jacob Stawn, of Jacksonville, Ill., and a few of his neighbors provided 100 cows within a very few days. These animals were sent to Springfield, where the governor promised to have them sent on to Memphis—usually in small herds of 15 to 20 animals with a drover to take care of their feeding and watering. The chickens were also obtained.

Livermore, Mary, Sanitary Commission, Chicago, Ill.:

The hens were sent to the rooms of the Commission in Chicago. In a week after the call, our building was transformed into a huge hennery, and all the workers therein were completely driven out. The din of crowing, cackling, and quarrelling was unbearable; and, as the weather was warm, the odor was yet more insupportable. The fowls were despatched to Memphis in four shipments, in coops containing about two dozen each.

Before her thirty-days' leave of absence was ended, Mother Bickerdyke was on the return route to her hospital, forming a part of a bizarre procession of over one hundred cows and one thousand hens, strung all along the road from Chicago to Memphis. She entered the city in triumph, amid immense lowing, crowing, and cackling. She informed the astonished Memphians: "These are *loyal* cows and hens; none of your miserable trash that give chalk and water for milk, and lay loud-smelling eggs."

Gen. Hurlbut, the local area commander, sent the cows and chickens to President's Island, in the Mississippi, along with sufficient contrabands to care for them. Mrs. Bickerdyke now had a sufficient supply of milk and eggs for "her boys." When the hospitals in Memphis emptied to a reasonable degree, Mrs. Bickerdyke moved on with the army. The chickens went into the stew pot and the cows went on the march—providing their own brand of "Bickerdyke" whiskey for the troops.

April 22 (Wednesday)

On April 17, Col. Benjamin Henry Grierson, U.S. Cavalry, left La Grange, Tenn., to raid through Mississippi with a force of over 1000 cavalry. He intended to distract the Confederate forces at Vicksburg so that Grant could make a landing to invest the city. Grierson's route was generally through the eastern part of the state in the beginning; he then swung southwest, towards Baton Rouge, La., which he entered on May 2nd, 16 days after his departure from La Grange. During the raid, much consternation was caused among the citizens and military units in the state. In the following situation, the wounded in a hospital were to be used to defend the town of Shuqualak, Miss.

Stevens, James A., Pvt., CSA, hospital at Shuqualak, Miss.:

... there was a large number of sick soldiers in the hospital at Shuqualak, Miss., many of them sent up from Vicksburg just before its investment by Gen. Grant.... While the men were convalescent the news came that the Federal Cavalryman Gen. Grierson, was coming on a certain day to raid the town.

The commandant of the post, Capt. H———, was a very ambitious officer and determined to fight, but could muster only his personal staff to win him

laurels. Then he bethought him of calling out the several hundred sick men, and he had a medical officer to visit the various wards and ascertain who were well enough to walk and carry a gun; in fact, he called for volunteers. Of course every man with any pride at all who could walk fell into line on the only street in town, about a hundred in number.

On such occasions there is always something to make one laugh. Just before leaving my cot as a volunteer, a big, brawny Irishman next to me called out lustily to the sawbones: "Docther, can't you give me something for me trouble?" Pat's size in painful contrast to his doleful request tickled me so that I almost forgot my own suffering and fell into line with something like a willing spirit. The Irish soldier is usually recklessly brave, but this one was an exception. He was scared.

Well, the farce of arming the squad, battalion, or whatever you would call it, was gone through with and suggested a line of propped-up cadavers more than Confederate soldiers.... Most of the poor fellows were not in the best humor from this being called to the field of carnage, and what made them madder was the sight of a number of able-bodied citizens of the town standing in front of the stores and laughing at us. Some of the boys swore they would rather turn their guns on these shirkers or exempts than on the hated Yankees.

April 27 (Monday)

At Falmouth, Va., the Army of the Potomac was on the move from its winter quarters. It marched up the Rappahannock, towards the fords. This move would place it at Lee's rear.

Billings, J. S., Asst. Surg., USA, Battle of Chancellorsville, Va.:

On the 27th of April, the division commenced the march across the Rappahannock.... But two ambulances were allowed to the division, and no stretchers or stretcher-bearers, nor did any medical supply or Autenrieth wagons accompany us across the river....

April 28 (Tuesday)

Upstream from Fredericksburg, Hooker's Army of the Potomac began crossing the fords of the

Rappahannock, leaving a major force commanded by Maj. Gen. "Uncle" John Sedgwick facing Lee. At Fredericksburg the bells of the Episcopal Church rang out an alarm for the Confederates.

April 29 (Wednesday)

The majority of Hooker's army was across the river at Kelly's and U.S. Ford, beyond the left flank of Lee's Army of Northern Virginia. Movement was made through the Wilderness area into the clearings around the Chancellor home.

April 30 (Thursday)

At Chancellorsville, Hooker, in his exuberance, prepared a message to be read to the troops on May 1st in which he informed his army that:

…the operations of the last three days have determined that our enemy must ingloriously fly, or come out from behind their defenses and give us battle on our ground, where certain destruction awaits him.

May 1 (Friday)

Hooker, with 70,000 men, crossed the Rappahannock fords and began the Battle of Chancellorsville. Lee withdrew most of his force, all but Jubal Early and 10,000 of Early's men. Lee left this small force to face Maj. Gen. Sedgwick's 40,000, and with 47,000 men Lee turned to face Hooker.

The Army of the Potomac moved forward, and then in the afternoon Hooker stunned his own officers *and* Lee by withdrawing and concentrating in a small area near Chancellorsville. With little or no fighting, "Fighting Joe" Hooker went on the defensive.

Tonight Lee and Jackson talked in the now-famous "cracker barrel" conference. Jackson would take 26,000 of the 47,000 available forces around the Confederate left flank to attack Hooker's Union right flank.

Billings, J. S., Asst. Surg., USA, Battle of Chancellorsville, Va.:

After a rapid march over muddy roads, the division reached the brick house of Dr. Chancellor on the evening of the 30th of April, and encamped in the woods about half a mile beyond, on the road leading from that place to Banks's Ford After marching about one mile, the enemy opened fire with rifled

shell from a section of artillery so posted as to sweep the road. The column immediately debouched to the left, forming a line of battle at right angles to the road, and advanced at double quick.

Soon after leaving the road, I received orders to repair to a small frame house on a little knoll nearby, which was to be used as a temporary hospital. On reaching it, I found several men with slight shell wounds. I had hardly dismounted, when the fire seemed to be concentrated on the spot; shell fell on all sides, one passing through the house; and, in five minutes, I was the only person left about the place. I then rode back about three hundred yards to another small frame house by the roadside, where I found my assistants, and was soon after joined by the other members of the staff of the hospital.…

The infantry being now engaged, the wounded began to come in very rapidly, and I proceeded to the relief of the more urgent cases, performing several amputations, among others, two at the shoulder joint, also, one execution of the same joint and one of the elbow. In about two hours, we were informed that our troops were falling back, and were ordered to remove the wounded to the brick house of Dr. Chancellor.…

On reaching the brick house, everything was found in confusion. All the large rooms in the house were locked and filled with furniture; the wounded were lying about in the verandah, in the halls, and wherever space could be found; while a crowd of teamsters, orderlies, contrabands and stragglers filled the kitchen and outbuildings. I immediately broke open the doors; had the furniture carried out, and the wounded taken into the parlors; cleared out the kitchen, and ordered a cook to prepare soup; after which, I resumed the care of the wounded.…

At this place, the most extensive shell wounds that I have ever seen came under my notice. In two instances, the abdominal walls were entirely carried away; and, from a third patient, I removed the entire head of a three-inch shell which had passed into the abdominal cavity, and was slightly impacted in the bodies of the lumbar vertebrae. This man suffered but little pain, was sensible of his desperate condition, but was very importunate to have the fragment removed, as he said it felt heavy and gave him the colic. After its removal, he expressed himself as much relieved; he lived forty-eight hours. In a fourth case, a large fragment of a three-inch shell had passed through the pelvis from one trochanter to the other. In another, the arm had been torn entirely off, and three inches of the brachial artery were hanging out of the wound and pulsating to within an inch of its extremity. I also observed four cases of wounds of the abdominal walls, with protrusion of unwounded intestines and omentum. In two of them, it was very difficult to return the protruded mass, which was as large as the fist, the muscles of the abdominal walls being strongly and spasmodical-ly contracted. At first I supposed that the difficulty was due to constriction at the base of the tumor, and enlarged the opening slightly with a probe-pointed bistoury, but the protrusion increased, and all attempts to replace the slippery mass were futile, as it glided out at one angle when pushed in at the oth-er, until I caused one attendant to lift the patient by his head, and another by his heels, the nates just touching the ground, thus relaxing the abdominal walls, while, with silver spatulas, I lifted the abdomi-nal walls away from and over the tumor. I then closed the wound by means of sutures and collodi-on. Our labors continued all night....

Perry, John G., Asst. Surg., USV, 20th Mass. Vols., Falmouth, Va.:

The sun has set, the moon is resplendent, and if orders should come tonight the march would be enjoyable. Everything is packed and my horse sad-dled, but the waiting is very trying. Today we have heard firing on all sides, and two hundred prisoners captured by our forces have just passed. There was a little excitement this afternoon, when a private who was crazy drunk rushed into our quarters, insulted us, and attempted to strike Harry Abbott, who hap-pened to be standing near. After a hard struggle we conquered him. He will be severely punished for such folly.

As Grant's forces gained the east side of the Mis-sissippi, they were pushed inland as rapidly as possi-ble by McClernand towards Pt. Gibson. Troops from the Confederate force at Grand Gulf, now having been outflanked, raced to head off McCler-nand's Federals; there was much skirmishing throughout the day. Gen. John S. Bowen's Confed-erates occupied Pt. Gibson briefly and then evacuat-ed the town.

May 2 (Saturday)

Early in the morning Jackson's corps moved deeper into the Wilderness. Moving rapidly past Catherine Furnace, the corps reached the Orange Turnpike late in the afternoon, and at 6 P.M. opened the assault against the unsuspecting Federals' right flank. The butternut columns crashed through the brush and second-growth timber, screaming the Rebel yell at the top of their lungs. On the Federal left flank, Lee opened fire against the Federal line to draw attention from Jackson. The Federal right flank fell into confu-sion and panic and rolled up like a carpet. Few of the units maintained integrity; most fled towards the main body of the army at Chancellorsville.

In the twilight, Jackson and some of his staff were riding between the lines when they were mistaken for Federals, and they were fired upon by their own troops. Jackson was struck twice in the left arm and once through the palm of the right hand and was taken to a nearby farmhouse, where his arm was amputated later that evening. Later in the evening, Hooker belatedly ordered Sedgwick to assault Lee from the Confederate rear, bringing on the Second Battle of Fredericksburg.

Billings, J. S., Asst. Surg., USA, Battle of Chan-cellorsville, Va.:

... we were ordered to remove our wounded and rejoin our division, then lying about a mile and a half to the rear. Dr. Hichborn was left at the Chancellor house to receive and care for such men as might be brought in from the field. He was killed the next day in attempting to escape from the house. On reaching the division, I found it preparing to march.... It was then about four in the afternoon, but it was dusk before the column got fairly in motion. A confused medley of wagons, artillery and stragglers blocked up the road; while, to add to the confusion, the First Corps, under Gen. Reynolds, was coming up at right angles to the line of march. The woods were full of stragglers, who were lighting fires in every direction, while a body of cavalry was attempting to drive them in and to extinguish the fires....

Welch, S. G., Surgeon, 20th S.C. Vols., Battle of Chancellorsville, Va.:

On Saturday morning I received an order to ship the wounded to Richmond, store our medical supplies and follow the wagon train to Chancellorsville.... We started late in the afternoon, and I marched with the wagon train all night. It was carrying rations and did not stop once....

Just before daylight I saw a dead Yankee lying close to the right of the road. I did not know until then that there had been any fighting.... I had heard no firing and knew nothing of what had taken place. Just as it was getting light the Yankees threw shells, which burst about the wagons ... the fighting then began just as soon as they could see.

I went on hunting for the field infirmary, and when I found it our wounded were coming back and a few had been brought back before I got there, and I at once went to work assisting in amputations, and continued at it all day and until late at night. Jackson's men came in from the rear on Saturday night and drove the Yankees from their breastworks and occupied them that morning....

In the confused fighting of this day, Frank O. Anderson, born in Green Co., Ky., on June 11, 1840, was wounded in the knee by a minié ball, something he'd carry for the rest of his life. Anderson, living in Clarksville, Tenn., at the time, had joined Co. A, 14th Tennessee Regiment, in May 1861, and went with the regiment to Virginia, where it remained for the rest of the war. Anderson had participated in the battles at Williamsburg, Richmond, and Fredericksburg before being wounded at Chancellorsville. Anderson was evacuated from a field hospital to the home of a relative near Richmond, where he remained for about four months recuperating before he was finally well enough to return to duty. However, his wound precluded him from service in the infantry, so he was assigned to a Tennessee regiment serving with John Hunt Morgan, operating from Tennessee. He next saw service during Morgan's raid into Kentucky in June 1864.

In the west, Grant's corps was moving rapidly eastward towards Jackson.

May 3 (Sunday)

At dawn, Stuart moved artillery to a low hill called Hazel Grove, from which he shelled the Federal emplacements. A shell struck the house where Hooker was headquartered and some falling debris struck him on the head, temporarily disabling him.

Hooker ordered a retreat and Maj. Gen. Darius Couch organized the rearward movement across the Rappahannock.

Sedgwick twice attacked Marye's Heights and drove Early off the Heights on the second attempt, but the Union suffered tremendous casualties. The Rebel line gave way and Early retreated. Lee, using some of the troops awaiting Hooker's assault, turned and stopped Sedgwick at Salem Church late in the afternoon.

Welch, S. G., Surg., 20th S.C. Vols., Battle of Chancellorsville, Va.:

The Yankees came back early and tried to retake [the breastworks], and I could hear them fighting furiously for several hours. We knew nothing of Stonewall Jackson's being shot the night before.

During the assault, Col. Edwards walked along on top of the works waving his sword to encourage his men, and was shot through the shoulder. When he was brought back I helped him out of the ambulance and expressed sympathy for him, which caused him to shed tears, but he said nothing. Col. James Perrin was brought back shot through the body and in great agony, and Gen. McGowan was struck below the knee while standing upon the works. I saw my brother once during the day bringing a wounded man back.

Capt. McFall and Lt. Mike Bowers came back looking for stragglers, and found four young men who were known to be cowards, but who were always braggarts after a battle was over. They all pretended to be sick, but I could see no indication of it, and they were marched off, but, before reaching the works, one of them slipped away, although the fighting had ended.

After all the wounded were attended to I was very tired and went to sleep late that night in a tent. I would wake up cold during the night and reach out for a jug of whiskey and take a swallow and go back to sleep again....

Curtis, Finley P., Pvt., Co. B, 1st N.C. Infantry, Chancellorsville, Va.:

At dawn of Sunday, May 3, the battle recommenced in earnest. The Federal army had entrenched during the night in and around Chancellorsville; and, to our great delight, Confederate artillery had arrived upon the waiting scene. It was a tense moment—nerves and muscles taut, hearts pounding wildly, guns loaded, yet no thought of death or fear—waiting impatiently for orders.

We moved forward. Our small command dropped for a moment behind a little hill; then, at the order "Charge!" we leaped to our feet and with a loud yell rushed toward the Federal trenches.... Our thin scattered line rush[ed] heedlessly into the jaws of death; the sharp, ceaseless staccato bark of a thousand rifles intermingled with the deep reverberating boom of cannon; the sibilant hiss of hail-dense flying lead; the terrible shrieks of bursting shells loosed from smoke-belching hells; the soul-nauseating impact of lead on flesh; the last dying farewell cries; the silent fall of men and horses; then the wild shout of victory as the dauntless decimated ranks leaped over into the trenches and routed the enemy.... I leaned for support against the captured breastworks, mental activity suspended, dizzy with exertion, gasping for breath, saturated with perspiration, black from biting cartridges, and stained with powder smoke, looking blankly around me.

A molten hail of lead hissed like pronged serpents' fangs about my ears, sang and hissed like maddened demons, rent the air, perforated the earthen mound, and filled the dead bodies everywhere strewn. I marveled that I stood on hostile ground alive in the midst of a death hurricane so withering, seeing, as in a dream, hundreds of collapsing forms. A spent ounce ball caught the concave palm of my upraised loading hand, faintly stinging. For a moment I held it thus, thinking nothing, then purposelessly threw it down. Again and again I wished I had kept it. It is strange that I had caught a bullet in my hand, but true.

Suddenly, almost imperceptibly a bullet (or was it a twig?) brushed my neck; another pierced my shoulder; another, severing my coat sleeve, seared my arm. They had found me at last, those hissing reptile tongues, and sought to devour me. My knapsack slipped silently to the ground. The Testament at my side followed simultaneously. But no pain tortured me. Where was my conscious mind? I could not think. Even the crimson stream of blood spouting painlessly from my neck as from the severed jugular of a hog—even that did neither frighten nor interest me. I grew sleepy; but I must not sleep! All my will could not resist its soothing influence, and I sank

gently down on my face. Night fell. I knew no more.

I was awakened—ages afterward—by the near rattle of musketry. Slowly I opened my eyes. Our own men came charging and firing at the fleeing enemy. I attempted to rise, but some heavy something forbade me. Mechanically I unbuttoned my shirt; and an eight- or ten-pound mass of congealed blood—my blood—as large as a gallon bucket, rolled out on the ground. I staggered weakly to my feet and leaned heavily on the breastworks for support. Dead covered the earth; and wounded, with eyes closed as in death, rested against trees. It was a horrible sight. Finally, having regained some of my strength, I began my tottering walk to the rear. I spoke to several of my stricken comrades, but the finger of death had ceased their speech. Weak and exhausted from the exertion, I reached the field hospital at last, and the ball was extracted from my shoulder....

Billings, J. S., Asst. Surg., USA, Battle of Chancellorsville, Va.:

At daybreak, I was ordered to establish a hospital in a hollow in the woods, on the road to Banks's Ford, about six hundred yards to the rear of our line of battle.... An old sawmill nearby furnished enough boards to make a shelter for about forty men, and this was extended by mans of evergreens and pieces of shelter tents, as far as was found necessary. Two hundred and fifty rations were obtained from the commissary of the corps, and, in the afternoon, the brigade medical supply wagons were brought up. While at this point, we received and treated about eighty wounded men, very few of whom, however, belonged to our corps. I excised the shoulder joint in two cases at this place. I operated, also, in three cases in which a ball had entered the cranium through the frontal bone, and penetrated the substance of the brain. In the first case, I merely removed the fragments and spiculae of bone which had been forced into the cerebral substance, the ball not being found by an examination which I deemed prudent to attempt. In the second case, I removed the ball, the fragments of bone and the letter of the man's cap, which had been forced into the anterior lobe of the brain. I may add that I saw this man, four weeks afterward, in the corps hospital. At that time, the wound had nearly healed, and no unfavorable symptoms of any kind had occurred. In the third case, a Confederate, I removed the ball and fragments of bone from the centre of the anterior lobe, and forty-eight hours after, when I left, the man was leaning against a tree, smoking a pipe and observing my proceedings with great interest. In none of these cases was there any disturbance of the mental faculties, after the first two hours, during the time that they remained under my care.

May 4 (Monday)

Union Maj. Gen. Joseph Hooker lost his nerve and the initiative, and ordered his Army of the Potomac back across the U.S. Ford on the Rappahannock, breaking contact with Lee's Army of Northern Virginia. Lee immediately pulled troops from his front and reinforced Early near Salem Church, where a late-afternoon attack failed to cut off Union Maj. Gen. "Uncle" John Sedgwick from Banks' Ford over the Rappahannock. Sedgwick's corps crossed the river during the night using pontoons.

Welch, S. G., Surg., 20th S.C. Vols., Battle of Chancellorsville, Va.:

The next morning we did nothing. Several handsome young Yankee surgeons in fine uniforms came over with a white flag, and I went to where they were attending their wounded. While there I talked with a wounded man from Ohio, and saw one of our soldiers cut a forked limb from a tree and make a crutch for a Yankee who was wounded in the foot. The unfed horses of a Yankee cavalry regiment had been hitched to the trees nearby and had gnawed off all the bark within their reach. We stayed there for three days until the Yankees crossed back over the Rappahannock River, and then we marched back to Moss Neck in the daytime in peace and found our tents standing where we left them.

May 5 (Tuesday)

The Battle of Chancellorsville was over, as was the Second Battle of Fredericksburg. The Union fielded nearly 134,000 men, suffering almost 17,300 casualties. Confederate losses were about 12,800 from an effective force of nearly 60,000— more than 20 percent—a loss that they could ill afford. But perhaps the greatest loss to the Confederacy in this battle was "Stonewall" Jackson— there was no replacement for him.

Billings, J. S., Asst. Surg., USA, Battle of Chancellorsville, Va.:

On the 5th of May,... I removed all the supplies from the brigade wagons, except about fifty blankets and a few bottles of whiskey, and sent them off with all the wounded belonging to our corps. I then had the wounded belonging to other corps transferred to their respective hospitals, leaving no patients except fifteen wounded Rebels. All the other medical supplies of the division, and about two hundred rations were left in charge of Asst. Surg. Bacon, USA. One hospital steward, one cook and one nurse were also detailed to remain. Before leaving, I suggested to Dr. Bacon the propriety of burying, or otherwise concealing, a box of whiskey and some chloroform and morphine. This was done, and I have since been informed by Dr. Bacon that it proved a very useful precaution, as the greater part of the stores not so concealed were appropriated for the Rebel wounded as soon as they came up.

On the morning of the 6th of May, we joined the division, which was then on its way towards the river, acting as rear guard, and crossed about nine o'clock. On the evening of the 6th of May, in a pouring rain, the division reached its old camp near Potomac creek.

Perry, John G., Asst. Surg., USV, 20th Mass. Vols., Falmouth, Va.:

Yesterday the regiment was in the city of Fredericksburg; today it is back in its old quarters at Falmouth, and I am in the same house and room. We have had two days of pretty hard fighting; the first day winning everything, the second losing all we had gained.

On Saturday night we broke camp and marched to the Lacy house, where we expected to cross the river by pontoon bridge. No bridge having been built, I managed to sleep very well in a gutter, forming a half-circle, with my head on one side and feet on the other. In the morning we crossed the bridge that had been finally put together during the night, and easily marched into Fredericksburg, which was not only deserted by the Confederate Army, but by most of the able-bodied inhabitants as well.

This attack on the city and its heights was a "blind" to hold the enemy in check while Gen. Hooker should cross the river above.... The Confederates made but little resistance, abandoning their entrenchments and retreating before our line until the order "Halt!" was given to our men.… The Twentieth Massachusetts was then detailed to occupy the city of Fredericksburg as a provost guard. Meantime I searched for my mare, "Bessie," and found her securely tethered with Macy's horse on the bank of the river, in charge of an orderly. Mounting, I rode into the city, and there saw the necessity of a provost guard, for the houses had been pillaged, and our men were masquerading through the streets in women's attire—nightcaps and gowns, silk dresses, etc.

I selected a nice brick house for my hospital. On entering the parlor … I was startled to see a Union officer, in rank a major, stretched upon the floor, and quite dead. How came he here before the arrival of his companions, and, if a spy, why that dress? I searched the body for a name, or for any sign that might give a clue to his fate, but in vain; everything was shrouded then, as now, in impenetrable mystery.…

… the next morning our men had the mortification of being driven back from the earthworks into the city, and losing that which they had so splendidly gained the day before. More than this, our force was so small that we could do nothing but fall back upon Falmouth without striking a blow.… I had to run the gauntlet many times, and on one of my expeditions heard a woman's piercing screams from a house by the way. I rushed in, and found an elderly woman of immense size in a violent fit of hysterics. She was seated in a rocking chair, swaying back and forth, evidently beside herself with terror, screaming, moaning, and crying. While I did what I could in the hurry of the moment to reassure the poor thing, a shell came whizzing through the air above, exploding as it fell into the square in front of us. Over went the old woman backwards, turning a complete somersault, chair and all. For a moment there was a convulsion of arms and legs, and then such shrieks that it seemed to me the din outside was nothing to that within. I gathered her together as quickly as I could—it was difficult to find any particular part to hold on to—and when she'd wit and breath enough to answer, asked for the other inmates of the house; vague and muffled sounds told me they were near, and when she pointed with her finger downwards, sure enough, I found them in the cellar huddled together, both whites and negroes. It seemed that the old woman was too large to manage the cellar stairs, and they, supposing from all the uproar that she was

killed, were every moment expecting a like fate for themselves.…

The long lines of springless wagons begin their trip to the rear, both North and South. The Union wounded would be taken to Aquia Creek, where they would be loaded on steamers for the hospitals in Washington. The Confederates would be taken by train from Fredericksburg to Richmond as they could be moved. In both cases, the agonizing trip from the battlefield to the hospital would cause many deaths and the cries of the wounded jolting over the rutted roads would stay with the survivors for as long as they had memory.

May 6 (Wednesday)

An anxious Lincoln got news of the defeat at Chancellorsville from Hooker *and* the Richmond newspapers, adding more to his sorrow.

Perry, John G., Asst. Surg., USV, 20th Mass. Vols., Falmouth, Va.:

Sad and discouraging news comes to us this morning. Gen. Hooker, who was behind Fredericksburg, expecting to fight the great battle there, has been flanked and driven back to the river, which he is now recrossing. The Confederates are pushing him hard, and he will find it difficult to save his whole army. I can distinctly hear the bursting of the enemy's shells as they pour upon him.…

May 7 (Thursday)

Sherman, now across the river from Milliken's Bend with his large corps, started moving towards Jackson, Miss., directly east of Vicksburg, to cut the rail lines of supply. In an early lesson on foraging, Grant's orders were to "live off the country," and this was exactly what the Federals did. Foragers fanned out daily to raid farms and plantations for their food. The countryside was soon stripped.

Curtis, Finley P., Pvt., Co. B, 1st N.C. Infantry, Chimborazo Hospital, Richmond, Va.:

I was removed to Chimborazo Hospital, in Richmond, where for a month I lay among hideous scenes of sick, wounded, and dying soldiers. Father came to take me home, but not until I was safe from relapse would the physicians allow me to depart. They feared that the exposed neck vein would inflame and burst. However, the wound healed rapidly, and I reached home at harvest time. But I was no means safe; for out in the field under the hot sun my neck began to sting and burn. It grew hot, and on the next day the wound inflamed and reopened. The doctors pronounced me once more a victim of typhoid fever and warned me to keep my bed until the crisis had passed.

However, as usual, ministered unto by my family and the kind old doctor, I recovered quickly. Twice now had I been in the clutch of this disease; but each time I had happily come forth free from any baleful mark of its ravage, free from its fearful aftermath....

May 8 (Friday)

At Pt. Hudson, La., the Union Mortar Flotilla, under Commander Charles H. B. Caldwell, and supported by the U.S.S. *Richmond*, Capt. Alden, opened the bombardment of the fortifications of that city.

In Memphis, Tenn., Mrs. Livermore was still with Mrs. Bickerdyke at the Gayoso Hospital, when about noon the ward master from the fourth floor came into the kitchen to tell Bickerdyke that the patients on the ward had not had breakfast because the surgeon for that ward had not come and prepared the special diet list, and the food hadn't been prepared. Lightning struck next.

Livermore, Mary, Gayoso Hospital, Memphis, Tenn.:

"Haven't had their breakfasts! Why didn't you tell me of this sooner? Here, stop! The poor fellows must be fed immediately." And filling enormous tin pails and trays with coffee, soup, gruel, toast, and other like food, she sent a half-dozen men ahead with them. Extending to me a six-gallon pail of hot soup, she bade me follow her, being freighted herself with a pail of similar size in each hand. I stood looking on at the distribution, when her clarion voice rang out to me in tones of authority; "Come, make yourself alive, Mary Livermore! Try to be useful! Help these men!" I never knew anyone who deliberately disregarded her orders—I had no thought but to obey—and so I sat down to feed a man who was too weak to help himself.

While we were all busy, the surgeon of the ward came in, looking as if he had just risen from sleeping off a night's debauch. Instantly there was a change in the tones of Mother Bickerdyke's voice, and in the expression of her face. She was no longer a tender, pitying, sympathizing mother....

"You miserable, drunken, heartless scalawag!" shaking her finger and head at him threateningly, "What do you mean by leaving these fainting, suffering men to go until noon with nothing to eat, and no attention? Not a word, sir!" as he undertook to make an explanation. "Off with your shoulder straps, and get out of this hospital! I'll have them off in three days, sir! This is your fourth spree in a month, and you shall go where you belong. Off with your shoulder straps, I tell you, for they've got to go."

She was as good as her threat, for in less than a week she had made such charges against him that he was dismissed [from] the service, and that by the very medical director with whom she had had weeks' wrangling. The dismissed surgeon went to Gen. Sherman to complain of the injustice done him. "He had been grossly belied, and foul charges had been made against him, which he could prove false," was his declaration. "Who was your accuser?" asked Gen. Sherman; "who made the charges?" "Why—why—I suppose," said the surgeon reluctantly, "it was that spiteful old woman, Mrs. Bickerdyke." "Oh, well then," said Sherman, "if it was she, I can't help you. She has more power than I—she ranks me."

May 9 (Saturday)

Grant, now at Utica, about 20 miles southwest of Jackson, Miss., was driving hard. Confederate Gen. Joseph E. Johnston was assigned overall command of all troops in Mississippi, but there was little he could do with his limited resources.

Mills, Madison, Surg., USA, Med. Dir., Army of the Tennessee, Utica, Miss.:

... May 9th joined the headquarters of Gen. Grant.... Shortly after assuming the duties of medical director in ... March, I had ordered all medical officers to make quarterly requisitions for supplies, commencing on April 1st. The system of making special requisitions having prevailed to a great extent in this army, I was determined to have the abuse corrected as far as it was in my power to do so, and no special requisitions were allowed to be made unless for extra issues, and accompanied with a proper certificate, explaining the necessity of the articles called for. My instructions on this important subject were obeyed fully in the Seventeenth Corps, only partially in the Thirteenth, and almost wholly disregarded in the Fifteenth....

The army moved rapidly, and with scanty transportation for a time. Some medical officers failed to carry their supplies, having been ordered by their commanding officers to leave them and give ammunition the preference; but I know that the commanding general intended that nothing pertaining to the medical department should be left. This interference on the part of generals commanding divisions might have resulted in serious trouble to my department, if I had not taken the precaution to hurry up the supplies....

May 10 (Sunday)

Perin, G., Surg., USA, Med. Dir., Murfreesboro, Tenn.:

During the month of May, the sick were sent to Nashville as fast as due regard to their welfare would permit.... By the time the army was ready to make the advance, there was enough room in the various hospitals at Murfreesboro' to accommodate all that could not march. The buildings used as hospitals in the town were vacated first that they might be thoroughly aired and purified by whitewashing. These buildings were not reoccupied until the wounded brought from the battlefields of the Gaps were placed in them....

May 12 (Tuesday)

Grant was at Raymond, Miss., barely 10 miles from Jackson, when Gen. John Logan's division of McPherson's corps ran into a brigade of Confederates commanded by Brig. Gen. John Gregg, causing a stiff fight. The outnumbered Rebels were forced to withdraw to Jackson. Meanwhile, Sherman and McClernand found they had skirmishers to their front. Grant decided to handle the city of Jackson first and then go to Vicksburg. Gen. Joe Johnston tried to encourage Pemberton to stiffen Vicksburg's resistance.

Mills, Madison, Surg., USA, Med. Dir., Army of the Tennessee, Raymond, Miss.:

... on May 12th,... one division of the Seventeenth Corps (McPherson's) engaged the enemy for several hours, and defeated him. They were driven off the field, leaving their dead and wounded. Our wounded, numbering two hundred and nineteen, were promptly attended to in field hospitals, and the next day removed to hospitals in Raymond, only a few miles distant. Medical officers and supplies were left with them. The wounds received by our men in this engagement were generally severe. The Rebels occupied two buildings in the town with their wounded....

Williams, Alpheus S., Brig. Gen., USV, Aquia Creek [Va.] Union Hospital:

All our wounded—700 or 800—were taken back to Aquia Creek and put in large hospital tents on the high hills overlooking the Potomac River. They were made as comfortable as the severely wounded (and none others were kept in hospital) could be. It took me all day to go through and I saw and talked with every man of my division. I need not say that they all seemed pleased to see me, but I had a terrible surfeit of looking at amputated legs and arms, and of all imaginable kinds of severe wounds. It was wonderful how men could survive some of them. Several had been shot through the lungs; one through both eyes and was stone blind; many had had several inches of bone cut out of legs and arms (ex-section) and were doing well. One poor fellow had had his leg amputated by the Rebs on the field and the flesh had sloughed off, leaving a long bone sticking out, and he was much reduced by secondary hemorrhage; but strange to say, with this one exception, all had healthful, and many cheerful faces, and talked to me cheerfully and happily. One poor fellow had been wounded through the hips, and his feet had lain in the water until they gangrened and more than half the flesh had fallen off, leaving the bones of the feet protruding fleshless, nothing but skeletons of toes and outer bones. I intended to have sent you [the U.S. Surgeon General] a full account of these terribly wounded [men] and of the heroic manner they bore up under these distressing injuries, but it is too late now. I was gratified after my visit to get repeated messages from the surgeons from the wounded that my visit had done them so much good and that they had said that the general's medicine was better than the doctor's. It was four or five miles from my camp or I should [have] gone often....

May 13 (Wednesday)

Grant sent Sherman and McPherson towards Jackson, Miss., and diverted McClernand north to Clinton, about 10 miles northwest of Jackson, and an important rail center. Johnston, with only about 12,000 men available, was trying his best to stall Grant until help could arrive.

May 14 (Thursday)

The Army of the Potomac rests in its old camps at Falmouth, Va., living with the shame of having retreated from Chancellorsville without having tried very hard. Most longed for McClellan's return.

Wainwright, Charles S., Col., N.Y. Artillery, Fredericksburg, Va.:

> A good sanitary order has been drawn up by Dr. Letterman, medical director for this army. I particularly like what he says against camping in the woods, and believe that it is cooler as well as more healthy on the open hilltops. Every item in the order is sound sense, except that requiring all sinks to be dug eight feet deep! The doctor probably does not know how much eight feet is, and has no idea of the labor of digging a hole to that depth....

Perry, John G., Asst. Surg., USV, 20th Mass. Vols., Falmouth, Va.:

> There is no sign of movement; the days pass, but nothing is done. The whole army cries for "Little Mac," who, if he returned today would be greeted with the heartiest cheers that ever filled the air. This is the opinion of every man in the regiment, and they have all served under him....

Sherman's and McPherson's corps neared Jackson, Miss., in midmorning. Sheets of rain were restricting visibility and making the march soggy. Joe Johnston, knowing he had little hope against Grant's superior force, evacuated as much of the vital supplies as he could and sent two brigades to delay the Yankees until he could get safely away with the remainder of his troops, taking all the wounded who could be transported with him. The two brigades were ineffective against the Union, and by midafternoon Union troops were in control of Jackson. Meanwhile, McClernand was solidly astride the railroad at Clinton, the only link to Vicksburg. Grant prepared to move west.

Mills, Madison, Surg., USA, Med. Dir., Army of the Tennessee, Jackson, Miss.:

> On May 14th the city of Jackson, Miss., was attacked at two points by our forces, the Fifteenth (Sherman's) and Seventeenth Corps, and after three hours' fighting the place was captured. The heaviest fighting was by the Seventeenth Corps, in which we had one hundred and sixty-six men wounded. The Fifteenth Corps engaged on the right and lost but few, and had only twelve wounded..... Ample hospital accommodations were found in the city, and appropriated. The Rebels had hospitals established which contained the wounded unable to escape. Medical and other supplies were readily obtained from the drug stores, and our men were made as comfortable as possible....

May 15 (Friday)

Recognizing that the food cooked by the individual messes, usually comprised of a squad of men, was detrimental to the health of the command, the Army of the Potomac today issued General Orders No. 52, requiring that all cooking be done at the company level. This order, which would be largely ignored by the end of the year, certainly saved many men from ulcers and diarrhea.

At Chimborazo Hospital No. 2 in Richmond, Phoebe Yates Pember, the hospital matron, was giving brandy to a patient, when a youth of about 18 years old caught her attention. The young man was obviously dying, and his only wish was "I want Perry." Perry, it turned out, was his friend and tentmate from his unit in the Confederate Army. Mrs. Pember took an ambulance and searched the other hospitals in Richmond until she came to Camp Jackson, where she found Perry in one of the wards. When they returned to Hospital No. 2 with Perry, they found the young soldier asleep. A bed was prepared for Perry next to the young man and Perry lay on it to await the young soldier's awakening. At last, the young man awoke and realized that Perry had indeed come to him. Mrs. Pember described the scene:

> As he recognized his comrade the wan expressionless lips curved into the happiest smile—the angel of death had brought the light of summer skies to that pale face. "Perry," he cried, "Perry," and not another word, but with one last effort he threw himself into

his friend's arms, the radiant eyes closed, but the smile still remained—he was dead.

Leaving Sherman in Jackson to dismantle the place, Grant moved in several columns to about 15 miles east of Clinton to Edward's Station, where Pemberton's main Confederate force was located. By nightfall, Grant was within four miles of Pemberton.

May 16 (Saturday)

Grant, moving fast towards Edward's Station, blocked a move by Pemberton to join Johnston, and Grant and the Confederate forces collided at Champion's Hill. By midafternoon the hill had changed hands three times, and the Confederates had had enough, beginning their withdrawal towards Vicksburg and towards the bridge crossing the Big Black River. They had lost about 3850 men at Champion's Hill, as opposed to 2440 Union men lost. Pemberton couldn't afford such losses for long. Johnston never got into the fight.

Mills, Madison, Surg., USA, Med. Dir., Army of the Tennessee, Champion's Hill, Miss.:

... the Thirteenth and Seventeenth corps engaged the enemy under Gen. Pemberton. This bloody battle was hotly contested for nine hours, and finally resulted in a complete victory for our arms. We had one thousand five hundred and sixty-three wounded, who were attended to in three division hospitals organized in such dwellings as could be conveniently appropriated for the purpose. Our men, with a few exceptions, were removed from the field the morning following before daylight....

Our troops were now getting short of hardbread, and it was difficult to obtain a sufficiency for the hospitals. Beef was plenty and ... soups were readily made, together with corn bread, so that our men subsisted fairly enough until a full supply of rations were sent to them. Hospitals for the enemy's wounded were also established and attended to by our medical officers as well as their own. We also found Rebel hospitals on the field which had been established previous to the battle. They were destitute of provisions as well as medical supplies....

I remained on the battlefield three days, and on May 19th had all cases that could be moved transferred to the front, leaving a sufficient number of medical officers to look after those remaining.

On May 20th five wagon loads of supplies, consisting of medicines, stores, and blankets reached them, and ... thirty thousand rations for our wounded there, as well as at Jackson and Raymond, were sent to the rear by a flag of truce, and reached their destination about May 25th.

May 17 (Sunday)

The Confederates under Pemberton had their backs to the Big Black River and, with some misgivings, they were facing Grant's Union corps. Grant attacked and the Rebels retreated across the bridge and burned it. Grant was stopped temporarily, and Pemberton went into Vicksburg—minus about 1700 prisoners. Starting with about 20,000 men, in two days Pemberton had lost nearly 5550. Grant, stymied, began building bridges to cross the Big Black.

DeGraw, C. S., Asst. Surg., USA, 15th Corps, siege of Vicksburg, Miss.:

Our crossing of the Black River at Bridgeport was delayed by a small force left there by the enemy. We succeeded after a time in dislodging the enemy, and crossed the same evening, May 17th, by means of a pontoon bridge.

Early on the morning of the 18th we were on the march, reaching Walnut Hills, in the rear of Vicksburg, that afternoon. The battalion was ordered forward as skirmishers, the enemy's skirmishers falling back. By that evening we were established upon the hills....

May 18 (Monday)

Today, Grant invested Vicksburg. The fortifications were completely surrounded on the land side, and the gunboats were on the river. No escape now for Pemberton's army.

The number of Union wounded during the siege of Vicksburg totaled only 2988 for the period May 18th through July 4th, the day of the city's surrender. The Army of the Tennessee had established hospitals complete with steel cots, ice, and other niceties. The Confederates inside Vicksburg suffered badly due to lack of food and medical supplies.

May 19 (Tuesday)

At Vicksburg, Grant made his first assault on the entrenchments, sending Sherman, McPherson, and

McClernand against the Confederates in a quick rush he hoped would gain a quick victory. This was not to be. The Union forces were repulsed. The Union fleet of mortar boats began their deadly barrages, supported by the gunboats on the flanks of the city.

DeGraw, C. S., Asst. Surg., USA, 15th Corps, siege of Vicksburg, Miss.:

On the 19th an assault was ordered to be made at two o'clock P.M. on the enemy's works. The nature of the ground rendered this task most difficult, being a succession of ravines choked with brush and trees felled to obstruct our progress; and all directly under the fire of the enemy's musketry and artillery.... The 1st battalion went into action on the 19th about two hundred strong; next morning, eighty-three were reported killed, wounded or missing; a few of the missing made their appearance during the day. Of the twelve officers seven received marks of bullets....

In the assault of the 19th the wounded received immediate temporary attention, and were then conveyed by means of ambulances to the division hospital, distant about a mile.... At the hospital, water was readily obtained from cisterns, there being no wells and very few springs; food and soup were supplied plentifully.... As early as convenient many of the wounded were transferred by boat to hospitals north.... The assault of the 19th having failed, another was ordered for the 22d.... This assault also failed.... After the failure of the second assault a siege was determined upon, which terminated in the capitulation of Vicksburg, July 4th....

May 22 (Friday)

At Vicksburg, Grant lost almost 3200 of his total force of 45,000 in a second attack on the Confederate defenses. The attack began at 10 A.M. and extended over a three-mile segment of the line. The Confederate losses were less than 500. Sherman's troops briefly held the top of one trench line but were beaten back. Grant went into siege operations.

May 23 (Saturday)

Craighill, E. A., Surg., CSA, Lynchburg, Va.:

I arrived in Lynchburg, after spending the night with my old friend, Willie Alexander of Charles Town,

who had charge of the "Ladies Relief" Hospital at the corner of Main and 6th Streets....

May 24 (Sunday)

Craighill, E. A., Surg., CSA, Lynchburg, Va.:

... next morning I reported to surgeon William Otway Owen, who had charge of all the hospitals at the post. He assigned me to ... College Hospital, my old friend, Dr. T. H. Fisher being in charge.... The college building was L-shaped, the foot of the L fronting on Floyd Street, probably covering half the space between 11th and 10th Streets, while the body of the L occupied nearly all the space on 11th between Floyd and Wise Streets. The building ... had a tower, probably 80 or 90 feet high, from which much of the surrounding country could be seen, a really magnificent view. The Floyd Street front was then three stories, the 11th Street part but two. It was the neatest and best hospital in town, indeed the best I ever saw....

May 27 (Wednesday)

Maj. Gen. Nathaniel Banks today launched an attack on Pt. Hudson, La., with little result other than nearly 2000 were killed, wounded, or missing out of a force of 13,000. The attack, poorly coordinated, was made through terrain that was heavily wooded and cut with deep ravines. This rough topography caused troop alignment problems.

Sanger, Eugene F., Surg., USV, Chief Med. Off., 19th Corps, Pt. Hudson, La.:

Pt. Hudson was completely invested May 24th, and the assault was made on the 27th. The action commenced at six hundred yards with a murderous fire of minié balls, grape and canister, and approached within one hundred yards. Total killed: sixty-one; total wounded, four hundred and twenty-five. Number of amputations, thirty.... I am satisfied that too many limbs were amputated, and if greater efforts were put forth in constructing good roads and easy transportation from the division hospitals to landing places, and comfortable and well-ventilated general hospitals, the ratio of deaths would be smaller and the percentage of amputations much less. The distance from the battlefield to division hospital was two and a half miles, over rough roads with poor ambulances. Distance from division hospital to Springfield Landing, eight miles, and thence to Baton Rouge by boat, eighteen miles....

June 1 (Monday)

The Western Sanitary Commission, originally established on September 10, 1861, in St. Louis, Mo., had by this date distributed more than 752,938 articles since November 1, 1861 (no records were kept during September and October, 1861). These articles, valued at $395,335.96, consisted of blankets, pillows, sheets, comforts, bed sacks, shirts and drawers, socks, slippers, towels, handkerchiefs, dried and canned fruits, jellies, pounds of butter, pounds of zwieback, pounds of crackers, packages of farina, bushels of vegetables, bottles of wine, brandy, and whiskey, etc.

The articles were provided as free gifts from the women and other agencies of the North and were distributed solely through the Sanitary Commission agents to hospitals in Illinois, Missouri, Kentucky, Tennessee, and Arkansas. The fleet of hospital ships wasn't neglected in this distribution. Supplies were also furnished to the *R. C. Wood, D. A. January, City of Memphis, Nashville, Empress, Imperial, City of Alton*, and the Navy's hospital ship *Red Rover*.

Since September 1861, in excess of 42,776 sick and wounded had been inmates of the hospitals of St. Louis and vicinity, and about 30,000 had been transported on the hospital steamers. This, in addition to the more than 75,000 sick and wounded, who also benefitted in the regimental hospitals from the Sanitary Commission largess, put the total number of men assisted to more than 150,000.

June 6 (Saturday)

Perry, John G., Asst. Surg., USV, 20th Mass. Vols., Falmouth, Va.:

Yesterday morning the Confederates disappeared from the heights of Fredericksburg, after having spent the night in burning their camps. In the afternoon, about three o'clock, we could see and hear tremendous firing on our left.... I ordered my horse and rode down there,... and found we had several batteries of fieldpieces sweeping the broad plain on the other side of the river.... On the rise where I was standing was planted a battery of very large guns;

while the Confederates were running through the chasm our men brought one of these guns to bear upon them, throwing a shell directly in their midst. The effect was horrible, and I turned away, unable to endure the sight....

June 8 (Monday)

In Tennessee, the opposing armies seemingly awoke and began taking potshots at each other today. The warm-up for the coming campaigns.

June 9 (Tuesday)

At Beverly and Kelly's Ford on the Rappahannock, west of Fredericksburg, Va., Union cavalry galloped across the fords, driving in the Confederate pickets, and went looking for information concerning where Lee had gone. Stuart, at Brandy Station, was caught by surprise, and rapidly engaged in the largest cavalry battle ever fought in North America. Almost 20,000 horsemen, evenly divided, swirled and clashed at Stevensburg and Fleetwood Hill for about 12 hours. The Confederates held the ground at the end of the day, but it had been a close battle indeed. Gen. Alfred Pleasanton's Federal cavalry had reversed the image of the North's cavalry arm and given Southern cavalry a bloody nose. Jokes about "Who ever saw a dead cavalryman?" would no longer be in vogue in either army. The disposition of the Union wounded was reported by Asst. Surg. B. Howard.

Howard, B., Asst. Surg., USA, aftermath of the Battle of Brandy Station, Va.:

... encountered the enemy at Brandy Station, when a brisk fight ensued, confined mainly to the cavalry on both sides. The wounded were brought to Kelly's and Rappahannock Fords as fast as possible. Those taken to the latter place were immediately placed on the cars for Alexandria; those arriving at Kelly's Ford were unprovided for. I immediately converted the Mt. Zion brick church near the ford into a hospital. All the wounds were properly dressed at once, and necessary operations performed. *The wounds were mainly sabre cuts; one man had five of these.* [Italics added.] The entire force recrossed the same evening. Next morning, all the patients were sent from Mt. Zion to Rappahannock Station by ambulance and shipped thence by railroad to Alexandria. The supplies were ample.

June 14 (Sunday)

After several false starts, which did much to destroy morale, Asst. Surg. Perry finally got his marching orders. The suspense for the past ten days had been wearing.

Perry, John G., Asst. Surg., USV, 20th Mass. Vols., Falmouth, Va.:

At last! Tomorrow we move—for what point I know not. Our brigade is to cover the rear, which is the post of honor, and, of course, we appreciate the compliment.

June 15 (Monday)

The Union forces left Falmouth and headed northwest. The 20th Mass., acting as rear guard, was subject to attacks from stray bands of Confederate cavalry and local partisan forces sent to harass the column. In an accident that happened while Perry was moving around some fallen trees, his horse became entangled in downed telegraph wires, and he was thrown from the saddle. In the resulting confusion, the horse kicked Perry in the leg and, to put it in his words: "Seeing the sole of my boot facing me, I knew what had happened." This accident provided an opportunity for Perry to ride in one of the ambulances being driven at breakneck speed to catch the column. This was to be an educational experience he'd remember.

Perry refused to have his leg amputated at the field hospital and was eventually placed aboard a train and sent to Washington, where he again refused to have his leg amputated. He then took unauthorized leave and went to New York, with the connivance of the Sanitary Commission. Once in New York, and reunited with his wife, the search was made for a doctor to set the leg. Most of those who saw the leg wanted to amputate. Finally, with the help of his wife and her brother, he set the leg himself. He was off-duty for a few months following this episode, and was present in New York during the draft riots of July 1863.

June 19 (Friday)

Earlier in the month, Maj. Gen. Joe Hooker finally got his army out of the camps at Falmouth, Va., and headed to some unknown point north, wherever Lee's army had gone. Surg. Jonathan Let-terman, the Medical Director of the Army since July 1862, took some obvious steps to cover his medical "bases."

Letterman, to this point, had systematized the medical department of the army and had it working fairly well, that is until now. On the 19th, the department's transportation was reduced to, on the average, only two wagons per brigade. This reduction was done despite Letterman's verbal and written protests. The reduction would cause great shortages of tents, etc., in the coming campaign.

June 21 (Sunday)

Welch, S. G., Surg., 20th S.C. Vols., en route to Gettysburg, Pa.:

We are in the Valley of Virginia again and are now within ten miles of Winchester. You cannot imagine how delighted the Valley people are at our appearance. The ladies wave their handkerchiefs from every little farmhouse we pass and cheer us onward....

We camped on the top of the mountains last night. The night before we did not go into camp until about ten o'clock, and then it began to rain furiously. We were in an open grass field and so we had to stand up and take it. It was a very heavy rain and the night was the worst I ever experienced. I sat up the entire night on a rock and kept dry with an oilcloth....

Our army is very large now, and if we get into Maryland or Pennsylvania and Hooker engages us, you may be certain that he will be severely whipped. Gen. Lee and his army are bent on it....

June 23 (Tuesday)

Lincoln finally bestirred Rosecrans enough to get him moving towards Braxton Bragg's Confederates at Tullahoma, Tenn. Rosecrans did well in this campaign, outflanking Bragg and forcing him to fall back towards Chattanooga, but this activity would be largely overshadowed by Gettysburg and Vicksburg, when the campaign for middle Tennessee ended in early July.

June 24 (Wednesday)

Rosecrans was doing well against Bragg in middle Tennessee. Bragg had his hands full, and Pres. Davis wanted Bragg to send troops to assist Gen. Joe

Johnston, who was trying to relieve Vicksburg. Bragg declined, citing his own problems.

June 26 (Friday)

The Western Sanitary Commission agent at Milliken's Bend, Mr. A. W. Plattenburg, heard of the battles being fought to the rear of Vicksburg between Gens. Grant and Pemberton. Plattenburg gathered together a large store of sanitary supplies and went down the Mississippi, past Vicksburg, accompanied by over 50 doctors and nurses, to assist in the care of the sick and wounded. The nurses' salaries and the cost of the stores were paid by the Sanitary Commission.

June 27 (Saturday)

Today, in Washington, Lincoln relieved "Fighting" Joe Hooker as commander of the Army of the Potomac, replacing him with Maj. Gen. George Gordon Meade, USA. The army was now located at Frederick, Md.

In Tennessee, Rosecrans was mixing it up with Bragg at Tullahoma, with heavy skirmishing at other points nearby.

Perin, G., Surg., USA, Med. Dir., Murfreesboro, Tenn.:

When the army marched from Murfreesboro' on June 24th, everything … was in readiness and as complete in appointment as could be desired. Skirmishing with the enemy was quite brisk at Hoover's and Liberty Gaps, June 25th and 26th. As a result of these encounters, together with the subsequent pursuit of the enemy … about four hundred wounded had to be provided for; these were mostly sent to Murfreesboro'. At Tullahoma a number of tents abandoned by the enemy were erected for men broken-down on the march, and a building constructed for a hotel, of capacity sufficient for one hundred beds, was opened as a hospital. Four hospital tents were erected in the hospital yard for wounded men. A few days after the occupancy of Tullahoma the railroad was repaired, and such of the sick and wounded as could bear removal were sent to the rear.…

June 28 (Sunday)

Three days ago, the 25th, Letterman sent Asst. Surg. Brinton, USA, to Washington to receive the supplies Letterman had ordered from the medical purveyor and await word on where to go. The next day, the 26th, Letterman wired Brinton to move his train of supplies to Frederick, Md., although no one knew if the army was headed in that direction. This was good guessing on Letterman's part.

Yesterday, the Army of the Potomac arrived in Frederick, and Brinton's twenty-five wagons arrived today. Brinton's supply train followed the headquarters until he reached Taneytown.

Welch, S. G., Surg., 20th S.C. Vols., Franklin County, Pa.:

We are in Yankeedom this time, for certain, and a beautiful and magnificent country it is too.… We are about fifteen miles over the Pennsylvania and Maryland line and within seven miles of Chambersburg. We are resting today and will get to Harrisburg in three more days if we go there.…

We are taking everything we need—horses, cattle, sheep, flour, groceries and goods of all kinds, and making as clean a sweep as possible. The people seem frightened almost out of their senses. They are nearly all agricultural people and have everything in abundance that administers to comfort. I have never yet seen any country in such a high state of cultivation. Such wheat I never dreamed of, and so much of it! I noticed yesterday that scarcely a horse or cow was to be seen. The free negroes are all gone, as well as thousands of the white people. My servant, Wilson, says he "don't like Pennsylvania at all," because he "sees no black folks.…"

My brother Billie is out today guarding a man's premises. He was also out last night and he told me this morning that they fed him splendidly. The reason houses are guarded is to prevent our troops plundering and robbing, which would demoralize them, thereby rendering them unfit for soldiers.…

June 29 (Monday)

Meade's army continued the march towards Gettysburg, still not knowing where Lee and his greyclad troops were. Meanwhile, Lee started to concentrate his forces at Gettysburg, recalling Gen. Jubal Early from York. At Gettysburg, Gen. Buford's cavalrymen were already in town, and more troops were coming up fast.

June 30 (Tuesday)

In Pennsylvania, Early's men left York for Gettysburg to join Lee. Gen. Meade ordered Gen. Reynolds to occupy Gettysburg. Buford's Union cavalry was scouting the area looking for Lee's main force. They were about to find it.

Welch, S. G., Surg., 20th S.C. Vols., en route to Gettysburg, Pa.:

On the night of the 29th of June we camped on the west side of the Blue Ridge Mountains, where they extend into Pennsylvania. On the morning of the next day we renewed our march. Shortly after starting it began raining, but the road was hard and well macadamized and the rain made the march rather agreeable than otherwise. On this same morning we passed where a splendid iron factory had been burned by Gen. Early.... It belonged to a very celebrated lawyer and politician of Pennsylvania by the name of Thaddeus Stevens....

During the day we wended our way up the mountains.... In the afternoon about one or two o'clock we halted and bivouacked among the mountains.... A while after we stopped I started off to one of these farmhouses for the purpose of getting my dinner.... On going to the house a very nice, smiling young girl met me at the door, and, upon my making known my wishes, she very pleasantly said she "guessed so"; but said they already had agreed to accommodate a good many and that they would do the best they could by us all if I would return about four o'clock.

This I did, and found Adj. Reedy of the Fourteenth Regiment and several others of my acquaintance. Reedy, being quite a young man, talked a good deal to the girl. I was hungry as a wolf.... It seemed that there was no end to everything that was good. We had nice fried ham, stewed chicken, excellent biscuit, lightbread, butter, buckwheat cakes that were most delicious, molasses, four or five different kinds of preserves and several other dishes. We also had plenty of good coffee and cold, rich milk to drink. None but a soldier who has experienced a hard campaign can conceive of how a gang of hungry men could appreciate such a meal.

After we had finished eating I felt ashamed to offer them Confederate money, but could do no better, and offered it with an apology. They very readily accepted it, and when I insisted that they should take a dollar they refused and would have only fifty cents. This house was guarded to prevent our men committing depredations such as they had been doing....

Upon returning to camp I found that an order had been received during my absence to cook one day's rations and have it in haversacks and be ready to march at five o'clock next morning....

The Confederates under Bragg evacuated Tullahoma, Tenn., today and withdrew towards Chattanooga, abandoning middle Tennessee to the Federals. There would be no large organized body of Confederates in the state again until mid-December, 1864.

July 1 (Wednesday)

Letterman's medical department was positioned outside the Gettysburg area, Meade decreeing that only ammunition wagons and ambulances would be allowed nearer. The medical trains were ordered to assemble between Union Mills and Westminster.

Welch, S. G., Surg., 20th S.C. Vols., Battle of Gettysburg, Pa.:

Next morning about five o'clock we began moving. We had not gone more than a mile and a half before our suspicions of the evening previous were fully verified and our expectations realized by the booming of cannon ahead of us in the direction of Gettysburg.... As we advanced the cannonading increased in fury. It was Heth's Division, ahead of ours, fighting. At last we arrived upon a hill where, upon another hill in front of us and about a half-mile distant, we could see Heth's cannon arranged and booming away at the Yankees, who were replying with considerable briskness, and we could also see the infantry of Heth's division advancing in line of battle. It was really a magnificent sight. The country was almost destitute of forest and was so open that it was easy to see all that was going on. Our division continued to keep within about a half-mile of Heth's. McGowan's brigade was at the right of the division and the Thirteenth Regiment at the right of the brigade. This being the case, I could see from one end of the division to the other as it moved forward in line of battle. It was nearly a mile in length. The scene was certainly grand, taking all the surroundings into consideration. After Heth had driven the enemy some distance, it became necessary for our division to go to his support. McGowan's South Carolina and Scales's North Carolina brigades were the first to relieve Heth. The hardest fighting did not begin until McGowan's and Scales's divisions went into it. Then such a rattle of musketry I never heard surpassed. It lasted for about two hours and a half without cessation; and how many brave fellows went down in death in this short period of time...! Most of the casualties of our brigade occurred this day. As the enemy were concealed, they killed a great many of our men before we could get at them. There were a good many dwellings in our path, to which the Yankees would resort for protection, and they would shoot from the doors and windows. As soon as our troops would drive them out, they would rush in, turn out the families and set the houses on fire. I think this was wrong, because the families could not prevent the Yankees seeking shelter in their houses. I saw some of the poor women who had been thus treated. They were greatly distressed, and it excited my sympathy very much.... I passed through a house from which everyone had fled except an extremely old man. A churn of excellent buttermilk had been left, and I with some other doctors helped ourselves. Someone nearby shot at us as we came out and barely missed us.

The fighting on the first day ceased about night.... I returned to the hospital.... When I arrived [there] my ears were greeted as usual at such time with the moans and cries of the wounded. I went to work and did not pretend to rest until next morning after daylight....

Wainwright, Charles S., Col., N.Y. Artillery, Gettysburg, Pa.:

The day had been a most unfortunate one for us, our greatest misfortune being the loss of Gen. Reynolds.... The loss of the corps today is put at 7000, some 3000 of them being found prisoners, captured at the last charge, and stragglers picked up in the town. All our wounded, and nearly all our surgeons, were prisoners in the town, including Heard and Bache, and my own little doctor. My own loss is four officers wounded, and about eighty men killed, wounded and prisoners—eleven of them prisoners.... The enemy's loss must have been quite considerable, for our fire on the Seminary Ridge was very severe. We also captured a thousand prisoners or more, for they evidently were not expecting a fight at this point any more than we were....

Plank, Elizabeth, civilian, Plank Farm, west of Gettysburg, Pa.:

... all kinds of rumors ... that soldiers were coming and a battle would be fought.... Sometime in the afternoon on June 30, 1863 ... looking west, saw a long dark fence, upon closer observance [I] saw the line move and small objects glittering in the sunlight. It really was the Confederate Army.

The next morning, the first excitement was the burning of the barn on the Fairfield Road, next a house near the Springs Hotel, and the farmers began leaving their homes with their horses ... going over the Mason & Dixon line to friends in Maryland.

[The farm was] about three miles west of Gettysburg, situated on the west bank of Willoughby's Run. The house was a large brick with two large halls, one on the first floor and one on the second, each opening into four large rooms with kitchen off.... Firing of guns was heard and the roar of cannon. Not long after this, an ambulance arrived at the farmhouse, and without ceremony, forced open the front door and carried in a wounded officer and placed him in the guest's room and the best bed in the house. Now, the family hearing the racket and thinking of the baby asleep upstairs, rushed up, where they were met by several [doctors'] orderlies.... While other men were driving a staple in the ceiling and with a rope and pulleys made a swing for the officer's wounded foot, tearing the sheets and linens into bandages for the emergency.

Now it was not long before all the beds were filled with wounded, and the floor covered with straw carried from the barn, all over the floors in the halls, on the porches, in the outbuilding, on the barn floor and every place were wounded—hauled there in ambulances, on wagons, gun machines and every way possible, and using the Garner Organ for surgical or operating room. Many limbs and arms were amputated and their wounds dressed, while the battle raged. As the horses tired out ... they were turned into the wheat and oats field near the house to rest and feed on the growing grain; unfortunately, two wounded horses died in the yard back of the house.

Now these horrible sights were too much for the family to bear so they were advised to leave their home for awhile.... Taking a few articles of clothing, they also went to their friends in Maryland.

The Plank farm was to remain as a hospital for some weeks after the battle was over. During the three days of Gettysburg, the farmhouse became the hospital for Confederate John Bell Hood's division. More than 1540 wounded were treated at that place, one of the outbuildings being used as a dead house. When Lee withdrew into Virginia, 515 Confederate wounded were left at the house for a period of about six weeks. When the family finally returned from Maryland, Plank described the scene:

Can you imagine the home it was? The yard and garden fence were gone, the flower and garden beds were as the mud roads, the poultry, hogs and cattle were consumed for food, the fences and part of the building were used for camp fires, the floors of the house were strewn with blood-soaked straw, also the flies and vermin of the dog days.

At Vicksburg, the end was clear for the Confederates: surrender or starve. Grant's army encircled the city with a death grip. Gen. Joseph E. Johnston's small Confederate force to the east around Clinton, Miss., was vastly outnumbered and had little, or no, means to transport itself beyond the railroad line that ran from Jackson to Vicksburg.

July 2 (Thursday)

During the second day's heavy fighting, Wainwright's artillery was stationed atop Cemetery Hill, immediately outside the town of Gettysburg. Longstreet was attacking the area on the Union left near the Big and Little Round Top, and Confederate Jubal Early was throwing his troops against the bend of the "fishhook" defensive line. Wainwright's gunners found themselves the target of heavy Confederate artillery fire.

Wainwright, Charles S., Col., N.Y. Artillery, Gettysburg, Pa.:

I saw during this artillery duel two instances of the destruction which can be caused by a single twenty-pounder shot: both of which happened within ten yards of me as I sat on the stone wall between Cooper's and Wiedrich's batteries, along with Gen. Ames. One of these shot struck in the centre of a line of infantry who were lying down behind the wall. Taking them lengthways, it literally ploughed up two or

three yards of men, killing and wounding a dozen or more. Fortunately it did not burst....

The other was a shell which burst directly under Cooper's left gun, killed one man outright, blew another all to pieces, so that he died in half an hour, and wounded the other three.... So soon as the shell burst I jumped from the wall and told Cooper to put on another detachment, that Gen. Ames would let some of his men carry off the wounded; not a murmur was uttered, but five other men at once took place over their dead and wounded comrades, and fired before they could be removed.... The man who was so badly blown to pieces lost his right hand, his left arm at the shoulder, and his ribs so broken open that you could see right into him....

Welch, S. G., Surg., 20th S.C. Vols., Battle of Gettysburg, Pa.:

I found that Longstreet had come and that McLaw's division of ... [Longstreet's] corps was encamped near the hospital. Kershaw's brigade was almost in the hospital grounds. On looking around I discovered many of my old friends from Laurens whom I had not seen since the war began. They all seemed surprised and glad to see me; but I had work to do and they had fighting, so we could not remain long together. They were all lively and jocose. Milton Bossardt was in a gay humor and left me as one going on some pleasant excursion, but before two o'clock of the same day he was a corpse. He was shocked to death by the bursting of a shell....

On the second day of the battle the fighting did not begin until about twelve or one o'clock, from which time until night it raged with great fury....

Pvt. W. C. Ward, writing in the third person, recounted his Gettysburg experience years later, in 1900, at a meeting of the Confederate veterans in Birmingham, Ala.

Ward, W. C., Pvt., Co. G, 4th Alabama Regt., Little Round Top, Gettysburg, Pa.:

Rushing up to the fence, dropping on the left knee, fixing bayonets, and springing over the wall, expecting to be riddled with bullets, was the act of a moment, not minutes. Looking around, this soldier saw his comrades quickly coming over the wall and forming into line of battle. The enemy had retreated up the sides of the mountain. The dead, fallen chestnut timber formed a natural abatis, through which passage was difficult. As soon as the line was formed,… the march through the abatis up the mountainside began at a quick step. There was a long line of boulders cropping out on the mountainside, forming a natural breastwork. Over and through this the line had to mount. The line had become broken because of the timber, and those of us in the front line, as soon as we were uncovered, received the first fire of the hidden Federals. A long line of us went down, three of us close together. There was a sharp, electric pain in the lower part of the body, and then a sinking sensation to the earth; and, falling, all things growing dark, the one and last idea passing through the mind was: "This is the last of earth."

Over their fallen comrades the men rushed up the mountainside, and soon struck the main line of the enemy, for there was a clash of musketry at close range. Minié balls were falling through the leaves like hail in a thunderstorm. Consciousness had returned. Dragging himself along the stony earth, as a wounded snake might have done, this soldier took shelter under a boulder four or five feet in height, and there he ascertained the character of the injury.…

Later the line of battle fell back to where the soldier was lying, and he heard one of his comrades say: "Halt here boys, and let us make a stand at this place!" Soon they came to him, placed him on a stretcher, and carried him to the rear, where he would be safe, comparatively, feeling certain the battle would be renewed. In the meantime the field surgeon had administered a stimulant and morphine. All night in agony he lay, until about 3 o'clock in the morning, when he, with two others, was placed in an ambulance and carried to the Plant Farm Hospital, just in rear of the line of battle.

Lokey, J. W., Pvt., Co. B, 20th Georgia Regt., Gettysburg, Pa.:

On the 2d of July, 1863, we made a forced march, reaching Gettysburg about 2 P.M. We formed on the extreme right, advancing across an open field, and came to some small timber, through which we passed, arriving at a small opening and hill, on top of which was a battery of three pieces. We drove back the enemy and captured this battery. The enemy was in a solid line to the rear and left of this [captured] battery in a piece of timber. After firing several shots

I became aware that about a dozen of us were in an exposed position and in advance of the regiment. So I dropped back down the hill a few yards; but finding that I couldn't do much good there, I advanced up the hill to the right. In ascending to the right I passed Col. Jack Jones, of my regiment, lying on his back with about half of his head shot off. I then passed one of Company K, of my regiment, lying flat on the ground, and he said to me: "You had better not go up there; you'll get shot." I passed on to the top of the hill, and, throwing up my old Enfield rifle, I was taking deliberate aim at a Yankee when a minié ball passed through my right thigh. I felt as if lightning had struck me. My gun fell, and I hobbled down the hill. Reaching the timber in the rear, I saw a Yankee sergeant running out in the same direction, being inside our lines. I called to him for help. Coming up, he said: "Put your arm around my neck and throw all your weight on me; don't be afraid of me. Hurry up; this is a dangerous place." The balls were striking the trees like hail all around us, and as we went back he said: "If you and I had this matter to settle, we would soon settle it, wouldn't we?" I replied that he was a prisoner and I was a wounded man, so I felt that we could come to terms pretty quick.

We had not gone far when a rear guard came running across the field and asked me where I was going. I told him I was wounded and was going to the rear, and I think he was glad to have an excuse to turn back. We soon reached a good spring and shade trees, and I lay down to rest. He took my prisoner, who was a sergeant belonging to the 4th Maine Regiment.… I lay on the field that night.…

With the battle raging at Gettysburg, Meade's major medical support was parked nearly twenty-five miles away near Westminster, effectively depriving the medical teams of much of the means of taking care of the wounded in a reasonable time. In the corps and division medical staffs, the wagons used for medicines, etc., moved with the troops so that immediate, basic, aid was available. The major items wouldn't be on the field until the 5th, although Brinton's supply wagons arrived the evening of the 4th.

At Vicksburg, the tension was almost unbearable. Surely the city couldn't hold much longer. Joe Johnston's Confederates awaited the outcome with dread, knowing that when Grant was finished with

Vicksburg, he'd turn on them. At Pt. Hudson, the bombardment continued.

July 3 (Friday)

Letterman, Jonathan, Surg., Med. Dir., Army of the Potomac, Gettysburg, Pa.:

I had an interview with the commanding general on the evening to the 3d of July, after the battle was over, to obtain permission to order up the wagons containing tents, etc. This request he did not think expedient to grant but in part, allowing one-half of the wagons to come to the front; the remainder were brought up as soon as it was considered by him proper to permit it....

Welch, S. G., Surg., 20th S.C. Vols., Battle of Gettysburg, Pa.:

On the third day the fighting began early in the morning and continued with the greatest imaginable fury all day; at one time, about three o'clock in the afternoon, with such a cannonading I never heard before. About 150 pieces of cannon on our side and as many or more on the side of the enemy kept up one incessant fire for several hours. It was truly terrifying and was like heavy skirmishing in the rapidity with which the volleys succeeded one another. The roar of the artillery, the rattle of the musketry and the wild terrific scream of the shells as they whizzed through the air was really the most appalling situation that could possibly be produced. Our troops charged the enemy's strong position, which they had now entrenched, but with no avail, although we slaughtered thousands of them.

On the night of the 3d, Gen. Lee withdrew the army nearly to its original position, hoping, I suppose, that the enemy would attack him; but they didn't dare come out of their strongholds, for well they knew what their fate would be if they met the Confederate Army of Virginia upon equal grounds.

Ward, W. C., Pvt., Co. G, 4th Alabama Regt., Little Round Top, Gettysburg, Pa.:

The wounded of the division were gathered there, those most severely wounded receiving surgical aid first. Under the influence of a powerful opiate, sleep came, and for a few hours there was forgetfulness. When he awoke, he felt the craving of hunger; and, feeling for his haversack, he found that it, with the

good rations prepared the day before, was gone. Some rascal, supposing him dead, had carried away the provisions he needed to save life.

Here his attention was arrested by a cannonading such as earth never before heard. The one hundred and twenty-five pieces of artillery of Lee's Army replied to one hundred twenty-five of the Federal Army. Shot and shell passed in midair, and there was elemental war such as could only be where an army of demons contended with an army of demons, shot and shell shrieking in midair as lost souls might shriek and as wildest animals might shriek when engaged in death battles.

Lying under this fearful war of shot and shell lay Pickett's Division prone on the earth, awaiting the dread command, nerves strung and minds intent. At last there was a pause in the dreadful artillery duel, and then rang out the clear bugle note, calling the men to attention. Then sprang to life from Mother Earth eight thousand Virginians. Better men never went to battle and to death. To make grander men, God must create a new world.

Down they descended into the valley of death, marching elbow to elbow as if on parade.... Over the earthworks went the brave Virginians, but they had attempted more than human bravery could accomplish. They were hurled back.... From the point where they started to the enemy's line the ground was strewn with the dead and dying.... They did not win the battle, but they had won immortality as soldiers, and, as a division, left to the survivors and to the loved ones at home a fame imperishable and undying....

I never hear the sound of martial music or see the brave array of men clothed in the habiliments of war that I do not say: "O that I were young again and in the long line, charging on the enemy's guns!" But it cannot be. The spirit of war still warms within me, but the chill of age has crept into my blood....

Lokey, J. W., Pvt., Co. B, 20th Georgia Regt., Gettysburg, Pa.:

The next day, July 3, about ten o'clock, I got to the field hospital. I served through the Virginia campaign and was in many hard-fought battles, but I never heard such cannonading as at that field hospital when Pickett was making his historic charge. I had never been a prisoner and had a horror of a Yankee prison. I saw no chance of getting back to Virginia. Every ambulance and empty ordnance wagon was loaded with wounded and sent back to the Potomac at Williamsport. When loading the last wagon they said there was room for another man if he could sit up and ride, and I told them I could. This wagon had four mules hitched to it, and there were four wounded men lying on their backs in the bed. Two planks were across the bed, with the wagon sheet tied up to the bows in the middle. Two men were on the front board and one on the right of the rear board. I took my place on the left. Being shot through the right thigh, I could not stand any pressure on my wound. So I had to hold my right leg with both hands locked below my knee, letting my left leg hang on the outside of the wagon. The road was [not] macadamized, and language would fail me should I try to tell what those poor wounded men suffered on this trip.

We left Gettysburg about two o'clock, and that night about two I told the men on my right that I must get out even if the Yankees got me. So I got out and went into an old schoolhouse.

The great Battle of Gettysburg was over, though both armies still lay on the field. The South had been badly battered, and Lee ordered a retreat. Gen. John Daniel Imboden, CSA, was given the task of guarding the retreat of the wounded from the scene of battle. His report follows:

When night closed upon the grand scene the Confederate Army was repulsed. Silence and gloom pervaded our camps. We knew that the day had gone against us, but the extent of the disaster was not known except in high quarters. The carnage of the day was reported to have been frightful.... Few camp fires enlivened the scene. It was a warm summer's night, and the weary soldiers were lying in groups on the luxuriant grass of the meadows we occupied, discussing the events of the day.... About eleven o'clock a horseman approached and delivered a message from Gen. Lee that he wished to see me immediately. I mounted at once.... And rode the two miles towards Gettysburg.... He invited me alone into his tent, where, as soon as we were seated, he remarked:

"We must return to Virginia. As many of our poor wounded as possible must be taken home. I have sent for you because your men are fresh, to guard the wagon trains back to Virginia.... I can spare you as much artillery as you require, but no other troops, as I shall need all I have.... All the transportation and all the care of the wounded will be intrusted to you. You

will recross the mountain by the Chambersburg road, and then proceed to Williamsport, Maryland, by any route you deem best, without halting...."

After a good deal of conversation [Lee] sent for his Chiefs of Staff and ordered them to have everything in readiness for me to take command the next morning....

On the Mississippi, early this morning in Vicksburg, the white flags of truce appeared on the defenses of the city. Gen. Pemberton had bowed to a superior force and six weeks of siege after nearly a year of Union operations against him. The two generals, Grant and Pemberton, met under an oak tree to discuss the terms of surrender which would take place the next day—the Fourth of July.

In Tennessee, near Tullahoma and Winchester, the Confederates under Bragg were forced back by Rosecrans's Union forces and withdrew farther towards Chattanooga.

July 4 (Saturday)

Today, at Vicksburg, Gen. John Pemberton and about 29,000 Confederates surrendered to Gen. Grant, laying down their arms and marching out of the battered city. Grant watched the flag-raising at the Court House and on the river the boats shrilled their whistles. The Mississippi was now open, save for Pt. Hudson, which couldn't hold out much longer. The citizens of Vicksburg wept with sorrow as the surrender was completed....

DeGraw, C. S., Asst. Surg., USA, 15th Corps, siege of Vicksburg, Miss.:

That same evening we received orders to prepare to march next day to join Gen. Sherman, who was in command of the forces at Black River, watching Johnston....

In Gettysburg, Lee had decided to retreat into Virginia. Late in the afternoon, in a heavy downpour, the wagons filled with wounded began their agonizing journey south, going ever so slowly. As the long wagon trains cleared the camps, they would be followed by the infantry and artillery, covered by Stuart's cavalry. Meade, left in possession of the field, had no plans to follow Lee, although he was urged to do so by Lincoln. This would be another opportunity lost to the Army of the Potomac.

Welch, S. G., Surg., 20th S.C. Vols., Battle of Gettysburg, Pa.:

On the 4th our army remained in line of battle, earnestly desiring the advance of the Yankees, but they did not come. During this day the rain fell in torrents, completely drenching the troops. A while after dark we began to leave, but took a different and nearer route to the Potomac than the one we had just passed over. Though nearer, it was very rough and not macadamized, and the passing of the wagons and artillery over it cut it up horribly and made it almost impassable. Yet over this road our large army had to pass. I was lucky enough to get into a medical wagon and rode until next morning....

Lokey, J. W., Pvt., Co. B, 20th Georgia Regt., Gettysburg, Pa.:

The next morning wagons were still passing. It was raining and every teamster told me he was loaded and couldn't take any more. After hobbling along two or three miles in the rain and mud, I was taken in a wagon belonging to the 11th Virginia Cavalry, which carried me to the Potomac. The river was up and booming. With a strong cable wire stretched across it, our men were putting across one ambulance and one wagon and about seventy-five men at a trip.... The nearest railroad was at Staunton, Va.; and as the wagon train went no farther, I had this distance to walk. The road was lined with wounded....

Wainwright, Charles S., Col., N.Y. Artillery, Gettysburg, Pa.:

As usual, we were up by daylight this morning, but it was not ushered in by a volley of cannon and musketry as it was yesterday. On the contrary, our pickets in the outskirts of the town soon reported that there was no enemy in their front.... All our severely wounded of the first day and those of the enemy were left in the town, as also all the surgeons of the First and Eleventh Corps, who were caught there on our falling back.... Every house was full of wounded.... On returning to the hill [Culp's] I got off a couple of notes home to say that I was alive and well, and then went all around the base of Culp's hill to see the effect of so much firing yesterday morning. All the trees on the northeast side of the hill were full of bullets way up to their tops, big branches actually cut off by them; it was apparent how wild the firing

had been. It had not all been thrown away, however, for I passed several hundred of the Rebel dead lying around among the rocks and boulders. In one place they lay really thick around....

I have no fondness for looking at dead men.... This, though, is the great battle of the war so far, nor is there likely to be one in which I shall get so good a chance again to see what slaughter is.... A short distance before reaching the right of the Second Corps, I found Capt. Fitzhugh with his battery. Here the dead of both sides began to lay quite thick, for the burial parties were only just beginning work. Indeed, so numerous had they been, the stretcher-bearers were still bringing in the wounded.... Outside the wall the enemy really lay in heaps; far more so at least than dead often do on the battlefield, for historians draw largely on the imagination when they talk of heaps of slain, and rivers of blood. There was about an acre or so of ground here where you could not walk without stepping over the bodies, and I saw perhaps a dozen cases where they were heaped one on top of the other. A captain lay thus across the body of a lieutenant-colonel. Both, especially the latter, were very handsome men....

The greater part of the wounded of both sides had been brought in, but there were a number of poor Rebels still out on the ground. One poor fellow, an officer, had been shot in the mouth; his lips were fairly glued together with the gore; another one begged me for some whiskey, but I had none; most of them asked if I could not have them moved. For this I was powerless, save to blow up some of the regimental surgeons who, when I spoke to them on the subject, objected that they did not belong to their regiment. I fear that I should be very hard on such fellows if I had the power. As a rule the wounded of both sides are treated alike by our surgeons.... At night I again slept in the gate house.

Imboden, John D., Gen., CSA, retreat of the wounded from Gettysburg, Pa.:

On the morning of the 4th of July my written instructions and the package for Mr. Davis were delivered to me. It was soon apparent that the wagons and ambulances and the wounded could not be ready to move till late in the afternoon. The general sent me four four-gun field batteries, which with my own gave me twenty-two guns to defend the trains.

Shortly after noon the very windows of heaven

seemed to have been opened. Rain fell in dashing torrents, and in a little while the whole face of the earth was covered with water. The meadows became small lakes; raging streams ran across the road in every depression of the ground; wagons, ambulances, and artillery-carriages filled the roads and fields in all directions. The storm increased in fury every moment. Canvas was no protection against it, and the poor wounded, lying upon the hard, naked boards of the wagon bodies, were drenched by the cold rain. Horses and mules were blinded and maddened by the storm, and became almost unmanageable. The roar of the winds and waters made it almost impossible to communicate orders. Night was rapidly approaching....

About four o'clock in the afternoon the head of the column was put in motion and began the ascent of the mountain. After dark I set out to gain the advance. The train was seventeen miles long when drawn out on the road. It was moving rapidly, and from every wagon issued wails of agony. For four hours I galloped along, passing to the front, and heard more—it was too dark to see—of the horrors of war than I had witnessed from the Battle of Bull Run up to that day. In the wagons were men wounded and mutilated in every conceivable way. Some had their legs shattered by a shell or minnie ball; some were shot through their bodies; others had arms torn to shreds; some had received a ball in the face, or a jagged piece of shell had lacerated their heads. Scarcely one in a hundred had received adequate surgical aid. Many of them had been without food for thirty-six hours. Their ragged, bloody, and dirty clothes, all clotted and hardened with blood, were rasping the tender, inflamed lips of their gaping wounds. Very few of the wagons had even straw in them, and all were without springs. The road was rough and rocky. The jolting was enough to have killed sound, strong men. From nearly every wagon, as the horses trotted on, such cries and shrieks as these greeted the ear:

"Oh God! Why can't I die?"
"My God! Will no one have mercy and kill me and end my misery?"
"Oh! Stop one minute and take me out, and leave me to die on the roadside."
"I am dying! I am dying! My poor wife, my dear children! What will become of you?"

Some were praying; others were uttering the most

fearful oaths and execrations that despair could wring from their agony. Occasionally a wagon would be passed from which only low, deep moans and sobs could be heard. No help could be rendered to any of the sufferers. On, on; we *must* move on. The storm continued and the darkness was fearful. There was no time even to fill a canteen with water for a dying man; for, except the drivers and guards disposed in compact bodies every half mile, all were wounded and helpless in that vast train of misery.... We knew that when day broke upon us we would be harassed by bands of cavalry hanging on our flanks. Therefore our aim was to go as far as possible under cover of night, and so we kept on. It was my sad lot to pass the whole distance from the rear to the head of the column, and no language can convey an idea of the horrors of that most horrible of all nights of our long and bloody war.

The route of the wagon train was over dirt roads and one such, called the "pine stump road," was aptly named. To alleviate congestion on the road and because the road was badly damaged by the heavy wagons driving through the mud, the wagons took to the fields, where possible, and presented a broad front nearly 1/2 mile wide moving slowly south. Though the pace was constant, the individual wagons stopped occasionally and removed the dead for burial, marking the graves where possible. The rain continued, further increasing the misery.

One farmer and his son, who lived near New Franklin, along the route north of Greencastle along the route, recalled the events:

Snyder, Jacob C., farmer, New Franklin, Pa.:

About ten or eleven o'clock on the night of Saturday, July 4th, 1863, we heard a great noise of horses' feet clattering and tramping along the road. It was at first supposed that another detachment was passing to Gettysburg. After a little the rumbling of wagons was heard. I at once arose, struck a light, opened the door and went out, and in less than fifteen minutes the large hall of my house and the yard in front were filled with wounded Confederate soldiers. They at once set up the clamor to my wife and other members of my family, *"Water! Water!! Give us water!!"* They also begged to have their wounds dressed. O, what a sight! I at once came to the conclusion that something unusual had taken place, and as the rain was falling in torrents, I put on my overcoat and walked out to the barnyard at the roadside with a staff in my hand. I there found that some cavalrymen were driving part of my young cattle out of my barnyard. I walked up to the gate and closed it to prevent any more from being driven out. The officer in charge, sitting on his horse and seeing the staff I carried, supposed it to be a gun and at once rode away.

Snyder, J. Milton, Rev., New Franklin, Pa.:

I can well remember when the Confederate train of wounded came from Gettysburg, by way of my father's residence and New Franklin. I was quite young at the time, and hence noticed many things that failed to attract the attention of older persons.

On Saturday evening, July 4th, 1863, whilst we were quietly seated in the house, my father heard a peculiar noise—like the approach of a heavy storm. This was, if I remember correctly, about ten o'clock on Saturday night. Father went out into the darkness to listen. A short time after a body of Confederate cavalry came down the road from Greenwood. They halted in front of my father's house and called him out. The night was very dark, and they asked to be directed to Greencastle. They seemed to be lost or bewildered.... About midnight the first of the train of wounded reached our place. The wagons kept the main road as much as possible, and on either side of the train a continual stream of wounded soldiers kept moving. Thus they continued coming and going the remainder of Saturday night, all day Sunday, and the last wagon passed by New Franklin Monday morning at nine o'clock.... Wounded Confederate soldiers were left all along the route of retreat. Many died and were buried by the roadside. I shall never forget those ghastly wounds, those thousands of faces dusky with powder, and that battery of black and horrid fieldpieces, which had sent, as could be seen, many charges of grape and canister into the bosoms of our brave men....

On this evening, citizens of Chambersburg, Pa., heard a low rumbling coming from the wagon train which was passing some six miles to the south of town during the storm.

July 5 (Sunday)

Welch, S. G., Surg., 20th S.C. Vols., retreat from Gettysburg, Pa.:

It rained nearly all night, and such a sight as our troops were the next day! They were all wet and many of them muddy all over from having fallen down during the night. Billie looked as if he had been wallowing in a mud hole, but was in perfectly good humor.

On this day we recrossed the Blue Ridge mountains.... We met no obstacle until we came to Hagerstown, Md., where we stopped on account of the Potomac's being too high to ford. While here the Yankees came up and our army was placed in line to meet them, but they did not dare to attack. In this situation we remained for several days....

Wainwright, Charles S., Col., N.Y. Artillery, Gettysburg, Pa.:

Early this morning the runaway inhabitants of Gettysburg began to return. Nine-tenths of the men had cleared out, leaving the women behind them, and gone off to look after their own safety. Now the danger was over, they came back; great strong able-looking fellows most of them, but not one had courage enough to take a musket in hand for defense of his own home. Hundreds from the country around too, came down in their wagons to see the sights, to stroll over the ground, and gaze and gape at the dead and wounded. But not one lifted a finger to help the tired soldiers remove the one or bury the other. Nor were any seen travelling over the ground with aught to relieve the poor fellows who had (some of them) been lying where they fell for three days and nights. One man was found selling pies at twenty-five cents to the poor fellows by Dr. Bache. Gettysburg may hereafter be classic ground, but its inhabitants have damned themselves with a disgrace than can never be washed out....

Instead of helping us, they were coming in shoals with their petty complaints of damages. One man wanted a dead horse removed out of his stable! Another demanded twenty dollars for bringing half-a-dozen wounded cavalrymen some seven miles. Fortunately the quartermaster to whom he applied was not weak, and instead of paying him the money took his horses for government use, and left him to walk home....

During the morning I rode out over the ground of the first day's fight. Very few of our dead were buried and some of their own even had been left lying where they fell. The bodies presented a ghastly sight, being swollen almost to the bursting with their clothes, and the faces perfectly black. Burying parties were out gathering all the dead, but the work of burying them was very ineffectually done, for twenty or more were put in a trench side by side, and covered with only a foot or two of earth....

Imboden, John D., Gen., CSA, with the retreat of the wounded from Gettysburg, Pa.:

Daybreak on the morning of July 5th found the head of our column at Greencastle, twelve or fifteen miles from the Potomac River at Williamsport, our point of crossing. Here our [perceived] troubles from the Federal cavalry began. From the fields and crossroads they attacked us in small bodies, striking the column where there were few or no guards, and creating great confusion.

... After a great deal of harassing and desultory fighting along the road, nearly the whole immense train reached Williamsport a little after the middle of the day. The town was taken possession of; all the churches, schoolhouses, etc., were converted into hospitals, and proving insufficient, many of the private homes were occupied. Straw was obtained on the neighboring farms; the wounded were removed from the wagons and housed; the citizens were all put to cooking, and the army surgeons to dressing wounds. The dead were selected from the train—for many had perished on the way—and were decently buried. All this had to be done because the tremendous rains had raised the river more than ten feet above the fording stage, and we could not possibly cross....

At Chambersburg, some Confederate wagons had become disoriented during the night and had arrived in the town looking for aid. The wagons were loaded with the wounded, who presented filthy wounds, with no dressings, and swarming with vermin. The wounded had neither been fed nor treated since they were stricken and were begging for food and water. These men were immediately taken into the hospital for treatment.

Snyder, Jacob C., farmer, New Franklin, Pa.:

At about one o'clock A.M. [a] man with a short leg rode up to the yard gate in company with five or six others. He very politely asked Mrs. Snyder for a drink of water. He seemed to be strapped to his horse. When riding away one of the men said he was

Gen. Ewell.... The long-wished-for daylight at length dawned, and revealed to the farmers along the road that their fences were torn down and that ambulances and wagons, together with hundreds of cavalry, were making a way through their fields, and that their wheat, corn, and grass were being ruined. The narrow road in many places was so badly cut up that the wagons could scarcely get on, and many had to take [to] the fields. Broken-down wagons and caissons, yet containing large amounts of ammunition, were strewn all along the route. O, what a sight! The groans of the wounded and shrieks of the dying beggar description....

At two o'clock P.M. a company with a battery of six brass pieces drew up in front of my barn and fed their horses. This battery was supported and accompanied by about one hundred cavalry and some infantry. The cavalry dismounted in a ten-acre field of prime wheat, all out in head. At the same time during the halt the men were slaughtering cattle at Mr. Jeremiah W. George's. At this place some of the men died and were buried....

Smith, J. C., Rev., Greencastle, Pa.:

Saturday, July 4th, 1863, closed in perfect quiet at Greencastle.... Four o'clock Sunday morning we awoke to hear the rumbling of wagons, the trampling of horses, the noise and racket attending an army in motion.... Hastily dressing and going out into the street, we were supremely happy at seeing the army heading the other direction. It was the army of wounded from the battlefield hastening on toward the Potomac to cross over to Virginia. No one, with any feelings of pity, will ever want to see such a sight even once in a lifetime. Here came the men who but eight or ten days before had passed through our town in the prime of health, boasting of the exploits they would do when they would have the happy chance of seeing the Union Army. A more crestfallen, woebegone mob may never have been seen. Hurry was the order of the day. They seemed almost to be pushing each other forward... No one counted the wounded. They could not be counted because hundreds of wagons loaded with them were a part of this train. All who were wounded in the low extremities were placed into these huge and rough-rolling army wagons. When passing over any part of the street where the wagons would jolt, they would yell and groan with pain. Many had received their hurt on Wednesday or Thursday before, with no attention paid to them by surgeons, the doctors having been kept busy with the graver cases. All who were wounded in the head, the arms, the shoulders, the nonvital parts of the body were compelled to walk through the mud ankle-deep, with no food save a little flour mixed with water and baked on a few coals. Those wounded in the arms or shoulders would tear away the garment and expose the wounded part. Such arms—swollen to twice or thrice their natural size—red and angry. When they came to a pump, one would place his wounded member under the spout while another would pump cold water on the sore. Then he would do a like service to his comrade. Thus the pumps were going all day. I will particularize one case; this will be a sample for probably five or six thousand similar ones. He was from North Carolina; was shot through the arm, between the shoulder and the elbow. The arm was swollen to the size of a man's thigh, very red and very much inflamed. Nothing had been done for him by the doctor save to press a wad of cotton into the wound in each side of the arm. He had received the injury on Wednesday.... We estimated the number of wounded that passed through our town at twelve to fifteen thousand. It was an easy matter to trace their route of flight. Dead horses, broken-down and abandoned wagons, cannons, carriages and caissons, new-made graves were everywhere to be seen. It was simply a road covered with wrecks.

After several days, the Potomac subsided and the wounded were moved down to Winchester, Va., where they were either placed in hospitals there or sent on to Lynchburg, Gordonsville, and Richmond for further treatment.

Ward, W. C., Pvt., Co. G, 4th Alabama Regt., Little Round Top, Gettysburg, Pa.:

On July 5 we heard the retreating tramp of comrades passing through the apple orchard where we lay holding our breath; and we knew that Gen. Lee had retreated, though in good order.... Then began a battle grim and great—Skeleton Death against Skeleton Soldier. The little we had to eat scarcely kept life in our emaciated bodies—broth from poor boiled beef, unsalted, and broth again from the same boiled beef, and then the same unsalted, twice-boiled beef; and when at last the Federal officers took knowledge of us, they gave us as delicacies, suited to pain-racked frames and fever-burned bodies, hardtack and pickled pork.

Great green flies in swarms of millions gathered in the camp, grown unnaturally large, fattened on human blood, and contended with us for the hardtack and pickled pork. Fever-smitten, pain-racked, there came to us another terror; we were to be devoured while living by maggots—creeping, doubling, crawling in among the nerves and devouring the soldier while yet alive. A comrade from Marion, Ala., who lay on his back on the ground until great sores had eaten into his body, discovered one day that he was bleeding very rapidly from the wound. A surgeon was summoned. The femoral artery had sloughed, and he was bleeding to death. To stay the bleeding, a tourniquet was placed over the artery, and this every movement of the body displaced.... For forty-eight hours this struggle went on, the one wounded man staying the flow of the life current of the other. The blood had accumulated in a pool from the point of his hip to his heel, and in that blood at the end of forty-eight hours the maggots were rioting in their gory feast and reveling in the poor fellow's wound. The noise they made, as they doubled and twisted, crept and crawled, was that of hogs eating corn.... The surgeons at last did something; they ligated the artery, and saved the man....

Vicksburg was in Federal hands, supplies came in for the relief of the citizens of the city, and troops occupied the public buildings. The work began on paroling the Confederates. Sherman stirred his men out of their entrenchments and prepared for an attack towards the city of Jackson, and Joe Johnston, to the east.

DeGraw, C. S., Asst. Surg., USA, 15th Corps, en route to Jackson, Miss.:

Accordingly on the morning of the 5th we marched, and reached Black River on the 6th; Johnston falling back toward Jackson. We followed him up closely and arrived in front of Jackson on the 10th. We found the place fortified and Johnston determined to make a stand. We proceeded to invest the place, and on the 17th the enemy evacuated....

July 6 (Monday)

Letterman, Jonathan, Surg., Med. Dir., Army of the Potomac, Gettysburg, Pa.:

Over six hundred and fifty medical officers are

reported as present for duty at that battle. These officers engaged assiduously, day and night, with little rest, until the 6th, and in the Second Corps, until the 7th of July, in attendance upon the wounded. The labor performed by these men was immense. Some of them fainted from exhaustion induced by overexertion, and others became ill from the same cause.... Thirteen of them were wounded; one of whom, Surg. W. S. Moore, 61st Ohio, Eleventh Corps, died on the 6th of July, from the effects of his wounds....

July 7 (Tuesday)

Letterman, Jonathan, Surg., Med. Dir., Army of the Potomac, Gettysburg, Pa.:

The ambulance corps ... acted in the most commendable manner during those days of severe labor. Notwithstanding the great number of wounded,... I know,... that not one wounded man of all that number was left on the field within our lines early on the morning of the 4th of July. A few were found after daylight beyond our farthest pickets, and these were brought in, although the ambulances were fired upon, when engaged in this duty, by the enemy, who were within easy range.... A number of horses were killed and wounded, and some ambulances injured.... I know of no battlefield from which wounded men have been so speedily and so carefully removed, and I have every reason to feel satisfied that their duties could not have been performed better or more fearlessly.

The number of our wounded,... amounted to fourteen thousand one hundred and ninety-three. The number of Confederate wounded who fell into our hands was six thousand eight hundred and two; making the total number of wounded thrown by that battle upon this department twenty thousand nine hundred and ninety-five. The wounded of the 1st of July fell into the hands of the enemy, and came under our control on the 4th.... Instruments and medical supplies belong[ing] to the First and Eleventh Corps were in some instances taken from the medical officers of those corps by the enemy....

Mrs. Bickerdyke was in Vicksburg organizing the hospitals and caring for the sick and wounded. Sherman was in the city at the time, getting ready for the drive on Jackson, Miss. William Tecumseh Sherman occupied a special place in the mind and heart of Mary Ann Bickerdyke. They were both Ohioans, born in adjoining counties there. Both were very practical and energetic when it came to getting a job done. Bickerdyke felt at home with "Billy," and trusted him implicitly. For his part, he knew that she had only the care of his men at heart and trusted her judgment without question. While she esteemed and admired Grant, and looked upon Hurlbut and "Black Jack" Logan with fondness and understanding, no one replaced Sherman in her eyes—he was *her* general. Because of this friendship, she attached herself to the Fifteenth Corps, which was the one that Sherman most often marched with, and the men of that corps adopted her as their own. Sudden disaster would befall anyone who said a word against Mother Bickerdyke within the hearing of a soldier from that organization.

July 8 (Wednesday)

Ward, W. C., Pvt., Co. G, 4th Alabama Regt., Little Round Top, Gettysburg, Pa.:

Notwithstanding these terrible dark days, some things occurred that meant light in the gloom. Not long after the retreat of Gen. Lee—one sad, terrible day as we lay under the tent fly—a shadow of a woman fell over us; and, looking up, we saw a handsome young woman, whose kind and intelligent face expressed gentleness and sympathy. She called to a sister, who was not far off and who rapidly came to where we lay. We soon knew them as Misses Mary and Sally Witherrow, whose home was in Gettysburg. They had heard that out in the fields, behind the line of battle, a large number of Confederate wounded were lying. Miss Mary Witherrow, with different young women at different times, came out to see us, sometimes bringing little delicacies; and one time she brought a bottle marked "Madeira Wine," and with it there was some cut-loaf sugar. When my comrade, Smith, had bled so nearly to death and looked like the pale marble of death, I gave him quite freely of that bottle of whiskey. Whatever else I may forget, I will remember that bottle marked, "Madeira Wine...."

At Gettysburg, the movement of the wounded from the battlefield to the general hospitals was still in slow progress. A major problem was the condition of the railroads. The Surgeon General in

Washington sent Medical Inspector E. P. Vollum from his office to help expedite the movements.

Vollum, E. P., Med. Insp., USA, Gettysburg, Pa.:

I was detained a few hours ... at Hanover, Pennsylvania, where I found about one hundred and fifty wounded, chiefly from Kilpatrick's cavalry.... They were comfortably situated in a schoolhouse and in dwellings. The inhabitants had furnished them with bunks, bedding, dressings, utensils and food in sufficient quantity, the people in each street in the town furnishing food, delicacies, nurses, etc., [for] two days at a time.

I arrived at Gettysburg about seven P.M. on the 8th, and, in consequence of some irregularity or delay in the railroad trains, there were about two thousand slightly wounded men collected at a point a mile from town (where the trains stopped), without food, shelter or attendants for the night. Fortunately, through the agents of the Sanitary Commission, these men were all fed, and some three hundred sheltered [for] the night. No system had as yet been adopted for the transportation of the wounded, nor had this been possible in the deranged condition of the railroad.... The railroad officials were perplexed, and deficient in [loco]motive power and rolling stock. The bridges put up since the Rebel raids proved too weak for the lightest engines, and some [bridges] for a second time were carried away in the floods. The telegraph wires were down, and the obstruction to transportation seemed insurmountable until Gen. Haupt arrived and assumed military control of the road to Hanover Junction. We then experienced no further delays till the 18th, when an important bridge on the road to Harrisburg gave way under a cattle train, thus diverting, for the following five days, the trains that were intended for New York to Baltimore and York, Pennsylvania....

In South Carolina, the Union forces were readying the assault on Ft. Wagner. The hospital staffs and surgeons prepared for the wounded.

Craven, J. J., Surg., USV, Folly Island, S.C.:

I proceeded to Folly Island on July 8, 1863. After making a survey of the field, I established a hospital by erecting several hospital tents upon the beach, or ocean shore, about half-a-mile from the point batteries. I chose the position for the purpose of securing good air,

and a good road for the transportation of the wounded from the front; the beach being as hard as a Macadamized road. This hospital being completely furnished, on the evening of the 9th was placed in charge of Surg. W. W. Brown, 7th New Hampshire Volunteers, Surg. C. M. Clark, 39th Illinois Volunteers, and Surg. M. S. Kittenger, 100th New York Volunteers. Surg. G. S. Burton, 3d Rhode Island Heavy Artillery, Asst. Surgs. W. D. Murray, 100th New York Volunteers, T. C. Brainerd, USA, and S. Bunton, 7th New Hampshire Volunteers, I placed in the batteries, well protected by splinter proofs, and furnished with litters, dressings, and restoratives.

July 10 (Friday)

Near Charleston Harbor, Federal troops landed on Morris Island for the assault on Ft. Wagner under cover of naval gunfire from the ironclads U.S.S. *Catskill*, Commander G. W. Rodgers; the *Montauk*, Commander Fairfax; *Nahant*, Commander Downes; and *Weehawken*, Commander Colhoun, all from the South Atlantic Blockading Squadron. During the landings, the enemy poured 60 shots into the *Catskill*, six into the *Nahant*, and two into the *Montauk*.

Craven, J. J., Surg., USV, Morris Island, S.C.:

At sunrise on the morning of the 10th, our batteries opened, ceasing fire at eight o'clock, when the ambulance train proceeded to the front, finding two men wounded, and one killed.

I had placed upon the beach, at a safe distance from the batteries, an ambulance loaded with all the necessary supplies for a field hospital. As soon as our forces had established a footing upon Morris Island, I hurried to Lighthouse Inlet, and placing my stores and ambulance upon a boat, I immediately embarked for Morris Island. Upon reaching the island, I reloaded my ambulances, and advanced to a secure place and established a field hospital, where I gathered the wounded, making them comfortable, and sending them to the inlet, thence by boat to Folly Island, where they were conveyed to the beach hospital. By midnight of the 10th, I had five ambulances on Morris Island, a ferry established to connect with the ambulance train on Folly Island, making the beach hospital on Folly Island but half-an-hour to the rear....

July 11 (Saturday)

Vollum, E. P., Med. Insp., USA, Gettysburg, Pa.:

Medical Inspector Cuyler arrived on the 11th,... and, by mutual arrangement, I continued in immediate charge of the transportation of the wounded, which confined me to the railroad depot and city of Gettysburg. Every train of wounded was placed in charge of a medical officer detailed by Surg. H. James. Instruments, dressings, stimulants, etc., were furnished him, and he was instructed to announce his coming by telegraph, if possible, and to report in person to the medical director of the place of his destination. Each car was filled with a sufficient quantity of hay, and, on the longer routes, watercoolers, tin cups, bed pans and urinals were placed in them, and guarded on the route by some agents of the Sanitary Commission. In some instances, these conveniences were furnished by the medical department, but the demand for them by the hospitals often exhausted the supplies at the purveyors. Before leaving, the wounded were fed and watered by the Sanitary Commission, and often hundreds of wounded laid over for a night or a part of a day, were attended and fed by the commission, whose agents placed them in the cars. At Hanover Junction, they were again refreshed and fed by the Christian Commission. At Baltimore, the agents of several benevolent societies distributed food bountifully to the wounded in the cars immediately on their arrival; and at Harrisburg, the Commissary Dept. had made arrangements for feeding any number likely to pass that way....

On Morris Island, Charleston Harbor, Brig. Gen. Quincy A. Gillmore's Union troops made a futile assault on Ft. Wagner; a larger force was needed to begin with.

Craven, J. J., Surg., USV, Ft. Wagner, Morris Island, S.C.:

... and by four o'clock on the morning of the 11th, the field was clear, except of a few Rebel wounded remaining in a hospital occupied by Surgs. Hapwood and Hannehan, of the Confederate Army. Flying the yellow flag, they were left with the hospital for the purpose of keeping the place, the point being within range of Ft. Sumter and the ground occupied by our troops.

On the morning of the 11th, an unsuccessful assault being made upon Ft. Wagner, I commenced removing the wounded to the boats, and forwarding them to Folly Island. Learning that the hospital steamer *Cosmopolitan* had reached Stone Inlet, and anchored at Pawnee Landing, on the opposite side of the island, less than one half of a mile from the beach hospital, I dispatched a communication directing Surg. Bontecou, USV, in charge of the *Cosmopolitan*, to commence the removal of the wounded from the beach to the [ship].... In the charge on the morning of the 11th, there were eleven killed, ninety-nine wounded, and one hundred missing....

July 12 (Sunday)

Craven, J. J., Surg., USV, Ft. Wagner, Morris Island, S.C.:

Finding the position occupied by the field hospital untenable on account of the fire from Ft. Sumter, I sent to Folly Island for the tents at the beach hospital, and selected a position upon the extreme point and ocean shore of Morris Island, where I caused to be erected a field hospital, and bringing over the remaining ambulances from Folly Island, I established a line of transportation along the outer beach, and under cover of the sand hills, to within half a mile of Ft. Wagner....

July 13 (Monday)

Welch, S. G., Surg., 20th S.C. Vols., retreat from Gettysburg, Pa.:

After a pontoon bridge was finished at Falling Waters and the river was sufficiently down to ford at Williamsport, we left the vicinity of Hagerstown. It was just after dark when we began leaving. It was a desperately dark night and such a rain I thought I never before knew to fall. I did not meet with such luck as the night we left Gettysburg, Pa., but had to walk all night, and such a road I think troops never before traveled over. It appeared to me that at least half of the road was a quagmire, coming in places nearly to the knee.

Hill's Corps went by Falling Waters and Longstreet's and Ewell's by Williamsport, where they had to wade the river, which was still very deep, coming up nearly to the shoulders. The pontoon bridge was at Falling Waters, where we crossed. Our division was in the rear at this place, and when we got within about a mile and a half of the river we halted to enable the wagons ahead to get out of the way. Being very tired, we all lay down and nearly everyone fell asleep, when suddenly the Yankee cavalry rushed upon us, firing and yelling at a furious rate. None of our guns were loaded and they were also in a bad fix from the wet of the previous night. They attacked Gen. Pettigrew's North Carolina Brigade first. Our brigade was lying down about fifty yards behind his. I was lying down between the two brigades near a spring. Gen. Pettigrew was killed here. I was close to him when he was killed. It was a serious loss to the service. We fought them for some time, when Gen. Hill sent an order to fall back across the river, and it was done in good order....

July 15 (Wednesday)

In Memphis, at about this time, Gen. W. T. Sherman sent for Mrs. Bickerdyke to report to his headquarters. When she arrived, she was told that the Fifteenth Corps would be taking on a hard campaign in the early fall and he wanted *all* his soldiers in good shape. That included Mrs. Bickerdyke, whom Sherman *ordered* to take a two-week leave to go home for a visit. He was probably the only one she'd accept an *order* from. So Bickerdyke packed up and went North.

July 16 (Thursday)

Vollum, E. P., Med. Insp., USA, Gettysburg, Pa.:

I endeavored to make up the deficiencies in medical supplies at Gettysburg by telegraphing to Surg. Simpson, USA, at Baltimore. In reply, he ordered liberal supplies of alcohol, solution chloride of soda, tincture of iron, creosote, nitric acid, permanganate of potassa, buckets, tin cups, stretchers, bed sacks and stationery of all kinds for ten thousand men in field hospitals. On the day after my arrival, the demand for stationery, disinfectants, iodine, tincture of iron and some other articles was so great and immediate that I purchased them in Gettysburg and sent the bills to the quartermaster there for payment.

July 17 (Friday)

Welch, S. G., Surg., 20th S.C. Vols., Jefferson County, Va.:

You will see by this letter that we have gotten back into "Old Virginia" again. It seems that our invasion of the North did not prove successful. We fought a dreadful battle at Gettysburg, Pa. It was the greatest battle of the war.... Gen. Lee had to fall back to keep them from getting the advantage. My brother was not hurt in the battle. Milton Bossard, Capt. Cromer, Burford Wallace, Mr. Daniel's two sons and many others from Newberry were killed; but it is better for us to be killed than conquered.

We have had some very disagreeable marching, as it has rained so much, but I have gotten hold of an old horse, which helps me along very much. We have plenty of beef and bread to eat. We gathered up thousands of beeves in Pennsylvania—enough to feed our army until cold weather....

My servant got lost in Maryland. I do not think it was his intention to leave, but he was negligent about keeping up and got in rear of the army and found it too late to cross the river....

We hear that Vicksburg has fallen. That is unfortunate....

July 18 (Saturday)

On Morris Island, Charleston, S.C., another Union assault was made on Ft. Wagner after a heavy pounding by Federal mortar boats and ironclads. The gunboats began their fire shortly after noon when the tide permitted them to get within 300 yards of the fort. This close-range firing effectively silenced the fort's guns and kept them from firing on the fleet. The night assault by Brig. Gen. Truman Seymour's men was led by the 54th Mass. Volunteer Infantry, one of the first of the Negro regiments to enter the war. Of the 6000 men in the assault, 1515 of them would be casualties, including Col. Robert Gould Shaw, who organized and commanded the 54th Massachusetts. He'd be buried in the trenches with his men. Later, when his father came to claim the body and asked where it was, he'd be told, "He is buried in the trench with his niggers."

Craven, J. J., Surg., USV, Ft. Wagner, Morris Island, S.C.:

On the night of the 18th, at dark, an attack was made upon Ft. Wagner. At nine o'clock, the firing stopped and the ambulance train advanced to the front, near the enemy's lines, and commenced the transportation of the wounded.... The island being exposed, and not knowing what advantage the enemy might take, while we were in a crippled condition, I thought it best to remove all the wounded from the island.... I had the steamer *Alice Price* moored to the shore, at the inlet opposite my hospital, and sent a courier to the steamer *Cosmopolitan* with an order directing [it] to proceed ... to the mouth of the Stono, and in smooth water, just inside the bar, anchor, and await the coming of the *Alice Price*, upon which steamer I ... placed two hundred and forty wounded men and she proceeded to Stono, where her load was transferred to the *Cosmopolitan* in two hours. The *Alice Price* was under charge of Surg. A. C. Barlow, 62d Ohio Volunteers, and Surg. Stone, 54th Mass. Volunteers. Knowing that the *Cosmopolitan* had as many as she could accommodate, I directed [the ship] to proceed to Hilton Head immediately.

The steamer *Mary Benton* was placed at my disposal, and [we] commenced loading her. I placed upon this ship two hundred and fifty-six wounded officers and men, making in all shipped during the night, four hundred and ninety-six men.

I directed that each man, as he passed on the boat, should be examined, and it was found necessary, upon search, occasionally to remove tourniquets and ligatures from limbs, placing a person in charge of each of these cases to watch for hemorrhage.... In most cases above mentioned the circulation was entirely controlled, and before morning would have jeopardized the safety of the limbs.

The failure of the assault on Ft. Wagner would cause a change in the Union plan of attack on Charleston from one of frontal assault to one of siege. For siege purposes, more heavy guns were brought up, including one monster called the "Swamp Angel," which threw a 200-lb. projectile. The Confederates also shifted guns from Sumter to other points on the Charleston defense perimeter.

July 20 (Monday)

The battle for Ft. Wagner over, the cleanup continued. Surg. Craven took steps to exchange the wounded as early as possible.

Craven, J. J., Surg., USV, Ft. Wagner, Morris Island, S.C.:

At sunrise on the 20th, the wounded, with the exception of six, were all removed from the island, and by

eight o'clock were on their way to the general hospitals at Hilton Head and Beaufort. At daylight, through the kindness of Fleet Surg. Clymer, USN, a number of naval surgeons reported to me, and offered their services. As I had no wounded upon the island, I accepted the services of but three: Asst. Surgs. Hazelton, Mann and MComber, USN. These gentlemen took charge of the steamer *Mary Benton*, and proceeded to Beaufort....

On the evening of the 20th, in company with Lt. Col. Hall of the New York Volunteer Engineers, Provost Marshal General, and by direction of Gen. Gillmore, I proceeded to the front, and, under a flag of truce, communicated with Gen. Hagood of the Confederate Army, commandant of Ft. Wagner, with whom we negotiated for the exchange of the wounded, naming the following Friday morning at ten o'clock, as the time when I would meet a Confederate steamer in Charleston harbor....

When Mrs. Bickerdyke notified the Sanitary Commission in Chicago that she was coming North, Mrs. Livermore asked that Bickerdyke stop at Cairo, Ill., to assist in the planning of a new Soldier's Home that was to erected there at government expense. Also involved in this planning effort was Bickerdyke's old friend Mrs. Porter, who'd recently been doing duty at the Smallpox Hospital near Memphis, and Mrs. A. F. Grant who'd been assigned as matron of the hospital at Cairo when Bickerdyke left that location. Between these four ladies and the large number of men from the Sanitary Commission involved in the project, a rather large structure was planned which, while paid for by the government, would be staffed and operated at Commission expense. After several days of planning, Bickerdyke and Livermore went to Chicago.

July 22 (Wednesday)

The work of removing the wounded from Gettysburg continued apace until this day. During the period July 7th through July 22nd, a total of 7608 Union and 3817 Confederate wounded were transferred to general hospitals via the railroad from Gettysburg. An additional 4000 were sent to Baltimore from the hospitals in Westminster and Littleton. Remaining at Gettysburg were 1995 Union and 2922 Confederate wounded. Vollum reported that the total wounded amounted to 20,342. This was equivalent to placing in hospital beds the population of almost any city of that era.

The arrival of such a famous personage as Mrs. Bickerdyke didn't go unnoticed in the Chicago press. Almost immediately Bickerdyke was swamped with so many invitations to speak at meetings, both in Chicago in and the surrounding states, that it would have been impossible for her to comply with all the requests.

Among Bickerdyke's first acts was to visit her two sons, who were in a boardinghouse in Chicago at the time. She found them well and thriving, although a little lonely for their mother.

July 24 (Friday)

Craven, J. J., Surg., USV, Ft. Wagner, Morris Island, S.C.:

I returned to Hilton Head, and placed all the Rebel wounded upon the *Cosmopolitan*, whence I returned to Charleston harbor, meeting at the appointed time the Confederate steamer *Alice*, and delivered to the officers in charge of the flag, thirty-nine wounded Confederates.... We received on board the *Cosmopolitan*, from the officers in charge of the *Alice*, one hundred and five wounded officers and men. The officers in charge of the *Alice* reported still remaining in hospitals at Charleston one hundred and eight officers and men, and dead in their hands fifty-one.... As soon as the transfer was made, the *Cosmopolitan* conveyed our wounded to Hilton Head....

July 25 (Saturday)

Perin, G., Surg., USA, Med. Dir., Dept. of the Cumberland, Cowan, Tenn.:

A division of the Twentieth Corps was pushed forward on the line of the railroad, the advance occupying Stevenson, about July 25th. In order to insure ample hospital accommodation, as well as to be prepared for a general advance, I directed that half of the field hospital at Murfreesboro' be brought to Cowan, a small town at the foot of the Cumberland Mountains. This was accomplished, and the hospital made ready for the reception of patients several days before the army crossed the mountain. As soon as the army took up its march for the valley of the Tennessee River, I directed the remainder of the Murfreesboro' field hospital to be transferred to

Stevenson, Alabama.... During these movements the hospital train was running regularly to Nashville.... The supplies for these hospitals were brought from Nashville ... leaving the reserve supplies for the corps almost untouched....

July 26 (Sunday)

Payment of the troops during the war was a haphazard process. Often, troops weren't paid for months on end, and, if they had no money to send home, the families suffered. No system of allotments was in effect, although eventually a makeshift one was started. One "service" that the Sanitary Commission started at about this time was to help soldiers get their back pay.

While in Chicago, Mrs. Bickerdyke took the opportunity to visit some of the families of the soldiers she'd left in the hospitals in the South. In one instance, the family was about to be evicted from its home because they owed six months' rent and the wife had received no money from her husband for ten months. Mrs. Livermore reported the outcome:

She found one of these families in great distress and poverty. The husband and father had been in positions for ten months that removed him beyond reach of the paymaster; and his family were in great need of the money which he failed to receive. They were owing six months' house rent; and the landlord, a hard man, had served a writ of ejectment upon them, and was preparing to put them summarily into the street. Mother Bickerdyke paid him a visit at his office, and sought to turn him from his purpose with all the peculiar eloquence of which she was mistress. He could not be moved, but scorned her and ordered her from his premises. She rose to go, and, taking a Bible from the shelf, which was never used except to give legality to oaths, she opened to the sixteenth chapter of Luke, and, straining to her full height, with a solemn and almost terrible face, she read these words before an audience of a dozen or more men:

"And it came to pass that the beggar died, and was carried by angels into Abraham's bosom. The rich man also died and was buried, and in *hell*—in HELL—in HELL," increasing the emphasis each time— "he lifted up his eyes, being in torments, and saw Abraham afar off, and Lazarus in his bosom. You see what you are coming to, sir," she added, "and the time may not be far off. May God have mercy on your mean soul! Goodbye."

Then the resolute woman sought another house for the soldier's family, and rested not in her humane work until she had raised the money to pay the rent six months in advance.

July 28 (Tuesday)

At about this time, the planning for the great Sanitary Commission Fair to be held in Chicago was begun. The idea, born in Mrs. Livermore's fertile mind, became an obsession with the entire staff in Chicago and they planned to surpass the efforts of their counterparts in New York. This effort would take months before the Fair opened on October 27, 1863, in Chicago.

July 30 (Thursday)

Mrs. Bickerdyke, her visit completed in Chicago, returned to Vicksburg, Miss., and continued her work in the hospitals in that area. It was to be a busy autumn.

July 31 (Friday)

The previous influx of refugees from Arkansas, Tennessee, Mississippi, Alabama, Louisiana, and Texas into St. Louis, Mo., began to increase early in August. Many of them were women and children, travelling without adult males, who were brought to the levees and unloaded from steamers usually poorly dressed, shoeless, and generally with no means of support. The fathers had been killed in the war or were in hiding from the Confederate conscription officers. Many of the men had been killed by guerrillas.

Initially, these refugees would be taken to the local police station (hardly the place for young children). After a period of time, these displaced persons would be taken to the Sanitary Commission's Refugee Home on Elm Street, where they would be taken in and cared for. Those who were in need of contacting relatives in other parts of the country were assisted in that way, while others were found employment in other parts of the area, or in the city, and sent on their way to a new life clothed, fed, and furnished a small amount of funds.

In late August, the President of the Sanitary Commission was called to an unfurnished room on the upper floor of the Pacific Hotel to determine what could be done with a refugee family. The family was seated on the floor of the room, clothed in rags, and dirty. The oldest of the six children was a boy of 12 who was taking care of his blind mother and the other children. The family had walked from Arkansas to Rolla, Mo., a distance of several hundred miles, the children leading their mother by the hand and the oldest boy providing what he could by begging. At Rolla, they were placed on the train and taken to St. Louis at the expense of the railroad.

The woman, a Mrs. Hargrave, was sent to the St. Louis Hospital, kept by the Sisters of Charity, and the children were adopted by Rev. Dr. Eliot and placed in the Mission School. At the hospital, the woman was cared for and when her health was sufficiently recovered, an operation was performed to remove the cataracts from her eyes. As soon as she could see, the children were brought to her for a joyous reunion. The unfortunate woman died of tuberculosis after her sight had been completely restored.

August 2 (Sunday)

In Richmond, the weather was warm and fair, but a gloomy pall seemed to hang in the air. The citizens were disheartened. After Gettysburg and Vicksburg came the loss of Pt. Hudson, and now there was a major threat to Charleston. The hospitals around the city were still full of the wounded from Gettysburg, and from the Peninsula operations. Food was still scarce and costly.

August 10 (Monday)

In the west, Grant's army was being broken up even more. Sherman's Fifteenth Corps was to be sent to Louisiana, where it would perform garrison duty. Neither Grant, Sherman, nor Bickerdyke were unhappy about the move.

Welch, S. G., Surg., 20th S.C. Vols., Orange C.H., Va.:

All is quiet here now. When two armies have a great battle both sides are so crippled up that neither is anxious to fight soon again.... I have seen letters from some of our wounded who were left at Gettysburg. They are now in New York, and all say they are treated well. I had a chance to remain with our wounded, and, had I preferred to do so, I might have had a very interesting experience....

Our army is in splendid health and spirits, and is being increased rapidly every day by conscription and by men returning from the hospitals. Last year when a soldier was sent to a hospital he was expected to die, but all who come from the hospitals in Richmond now are highly pleased with the treatment they received. The hospital sections set aside for officers are admirably kept....

August 14 (Friday)

Hand, D. W., Surg., USV, Med. Dir., New Bern, N.C.:

On August 14, 1863, I relieved Surg. F. G. Snelling, USV, as medical director of North Carolina. On assuming charge of the medical department, I found fourteen thousand troops in the district. Seven thousand of them were in and about New Bern. Most of them were encamped on the outskirts of the town, and between it and the extensive swamps everywhere surrounding New Bern. They were in either stockade tents or temporary barracks, and for the most part were in a good state of discipline. One regiment, the 27th Mass. Volunteers, was doing provost guard duty, and was quartered in large dwelling houses in the town. Extensive entrenchments had recently been thrown up around the city, ditches had been dug, and a belt of brush and timber about a mile wide had been cleared in front of the breastworks....

August 16 (Sunday)

In Tennessee, Rosecrans finally moved from Tullahoma towards Chattanooga, at about the same time that Burnside left Louisville for eastern Tennessee. Rosecrans (not unexpectedly) had delayed, citing the need to gather the crops into his commissary from the surrounding countryside before leaving.

August 17 (Monday)

The Chickamauga campaign opened today, with its first skirmish at Calfkiller Creek near Sparta, Tenn. Rosecrans moved slowly towards Chattanooga.

August 20 (Thursday)

Rosecrans's Army of the Cumberland reached the Tennessee east of Chattanooga, where Bragg had deployed and was awaiting action. Bragg, reluctant to go on the offensive, considered the 2.5-to-1 odds against him.

August 21 (Friday)

In Tennessee, Union troops were close enough to throw artillery shells into Chattanooga. There was also skirmishing between infantry forces near the city.

August 24 (Monday)

The monumental efforts of Surg. Jonathan Letterman in organizing and outfitting the new Ambulance Corps for the Army of the Potomac finally came to fruition when General Orders No. 85 of the Army of the Potomac was issued on this date formally establishing the corps.

The order provided for assignment of the Ambulance Corps to the Army Corps level of organization, providing a captain at corps level, one 1st lieutenant for each division, one 2nd lieutenant for each brigade, and one sergeant for each regiment.

Only two-horse ambulances would be used, and the allocation would be three ambulances to each infantry regiment, two to each cavalry regiment, and one to each battery of artillery—each ambulance to have two privates, one driver, and two stretchers. The ambulances would be permanently attached to the units being supported. Two army wagons to carry medical supplies were allocated to the Corps Headquarters and two to each division.

When in camp, the ambulances would be assembled at Army Corps level and be under the supervision of the captain. No ambulance was to be used for other than its designated purpose—carrying sick and wounded.

The General Order detailed the specific duties of the various members of the Ambulance Corps while in camp and in the field. To identify the enlisted personnel assigned to the corps, the caps of these men would be sewn with a one-and-one-quarter-inch green band. Sergeants would wear chevrons on each arm, above the elbow, the point towards the shoulder, of the same material. Privates would wear a single half-chevron of the same green material on each arm, above the elbow.

Obviously, this organization was sorely needed, but it fell far short of the real need to evacuate wounded during and after a battle. Three ambulances to support an infantry regiment of 1000 men is hardly adequate!

August 30 (Sunday)

Wainwright, Charles S., Col., N.Y. Artillery, Middleburg, Va.:

We have had a great deal of fun about a Mrs. Fogg, who is down as an agent of the Maine Sanitary Commission. We have but one Maine regiment in the corps and two batteries; still the woman seems to have taken them under special protection. Lt. Twitchell she has made a pet of, and brought him over here to Smith's house, where she herself was stopping. Our doctors curse the old woman up and down as a meddling pest, doing ten times the harm that she does good. Her bringing Twitchell over here at last excited the General's ire, so that yesterday he ordered her out of the corps. The sanitaries no doubt do some good—perhaps a great deal in the general hospitals and just after a big battle—but when they send women down to poke around the camps with an unlimited supply of jam and sweet cakes, they are mistaken in their zeal. When their agents go still farther than this and attempt to run against regulations, they become a nuisance not to be borne.

The overcrowding of the Sanitary Commission Refuge Home on Elm Street in St. Louis, Mo., became a more serious problem when another woman and two children appeared at the door of the commission headquarters on Fifth Street with no place to go and no resources. This woman's husband had been killed by guerrillas near Ft. Smith, Ark., and she'd made her way to Rolla, Mo., walking and riding on government wagons. At Rolla, she was put a train for St. Louis, where she was directed to the Sanitary Commission.

September 1 (Tuesday)

Following the arrival of the refugees from Ft. Smith, Ark., three women and children arrived at the Sanitary Commission's offices from Jackson, Tenn., in an equally destitute condition.

This was too much of a strain on the Home on Elm Street. Another house was rented at 39 Walnut Street to be used for the same purpose, and from September 1, 1863, to September 1, 1864, a total of 322 men, 679 women, and 1163 children—all white refugees—were sheltered and provided for at the Walnut Street Home. In most cases, the government paid for the services rendered, either in cash or in kind, but incidental expenses were paid for by the Sanitary Commission.

Welch, S. G., Surg., 20th S.C. Vols., Orange C.H., Va.:

We still remain quiet in our old camp, with no sign of an enemy anywhere. I see no indications of our leaving here soon, but there is no telling.... My new servant, Gabriel, arrived yesterday from South Carolina, and he seems well pleased so far.... Gabriel bought a watermelon in Richmond and brought it to us. It is the first one we have tasted in two years....

In eastern Tennessee, near Chattanooga, Rosecrans's Army of the Cumberland was crossing the Tennessee to prepare for the assault on Bragg's army.

September 2 (Wednesday)

Union Gen. Ambrose E. Burnside easily took Knoxville, Tenn., thus blocking any direct Confederate communication between Tennessee and Virginia. His presence in the area was in support of Rosecrans's operations against Chattanooga.

Perin, G., Surg., USA, Med. Dir., Dept. of the Cumberland, near Chattanooga, Tenn.:

By the 25th of August every preparation had been made for an advance upon Chattanooga. The field hospitals at Stevenson and Bridgeport were in readiness.... During the first days of September the army crossed the river, and passed over Sand Mountain into Lookout Valley.... After the passage of the Tennessee River, a collision with the enemy was to be looked for any day....

September 3 (Thursday)

Surg. Jonathan Letterman continued his organization of the medical support facilities for the Army of the Potomac by issuing a circular containing the *Supply Table for the Medical Dept. of the Army of the Potomac*. This circular, very detailed as to the content of each of the ambulances and medical-supply wagons, contained some very interesting concepts.

The allowance for a brigade for one month for active field service was one medicine wagon, filled; one medicine chest for each regiment, filled; one hospital knapsack for each regimental medical officer, filled; and a list of supplies to be carried in an ordinary army wagon. The list of supplies was very detailed, allocating medicines by the ounce, pound, or bottle. Hospital stores included canned beef stock (48 pounds to be carried in the army wagon), candles, farina, nutmeg, sugar, tea, and dried milk. A large assortment of instruments and dressings was also included. In addition to those articles described in the tabular listing, a box would be carried under each ambulance seat to contain such articles as bed sacks (3), beef stock in 2-lb. cans (6), leather buckets (1), hardtack (10 lbs.), camp kettles (3), lanterns and candles (3), tin plates (6), tablespoons (6), and tin tumblers (6). This box could only be opened by an appropriate medical officer during battle or during emergencies.

September 4 (Friday)

Bragg, at Chattanooga, now had Rosecrans's Army of the Cumberland forming for the assault across the Tennessee. Bragg now faced Union forces from two directions, since Burnside was en route from Knoxville.

September 5 (Saturday)

Coming out of northeastern Alabama, Rosecrans moved into the mountains of northwestern Georgia, driving against Bragg, who was in Chattanooga. Burnside was coming from Knoxville.

September 8 (Tuesday)

Pres. Davis's decision to send a corps to Bragg from Lee's army in Virginia resulted in Longstreet loading up his troops and heading towards Chattanooga. Meanwhile, the Chickamauga Campaign opened with fighting at Winston's Gap, Ala., and Alpine, Ga.

September 9 (Wednesday)

Rosecrans won an easy victory when he outflanked Confederate Gen. Bragg, causing the evacuation of Chattanooga, Tenn., without a struggle. Rosecrans's Union Army of the Cumberland imme-

diately occupied the city and Rosecrans sent part of his force probing into Georgia looking for Bragg. Rosecrans, with his army scattered over forty miles of mountain roads, rushed to get his troops collected, since Bragg was only a few miles away.

Longstreet, on his way to assist Bragg, was blocked by Burnside's occupation of Knoxville. Longstreet had to move his troops through the Carolinas to Atlanta and then to northwest Georgia. The South's lack of a good rail network had, yet again, created problems.

Perin, G., Surg., USA, Med. Dir., Dept. of the Cumberland, near Chattanooga, Tenn.:

> When the heads of our columns penetrated the gaps in Lookout Mountain, the enemy hastily evacuated Chattanooga, and, on September 9th, the Twenty-first Corps occupied it. As soon as I learned this fact, I made immediate disposition to have supplies forwarded, and such buildings as were suitable for hospitals prepared....

The major problems of camp sanitation weren't solved in some units for a long time, and the cause of malaria fever(s) was attributed to many things. Charles F. Adams, Jr., the son of the U.S. Minister in London, wrote his father:

> ... an army, any army, does poison the air. It is a city without sewerage, and policing only makes piles of offal to be buried or burned. Animals die as they do not in cities and,... animals are slaughtered for beef and so, what with fragments of food and scraps of decaying substances, all festering under a midsummer sun, an army soon breeds a malaria which engenders the most fatal of fevers.

September 13 (Sunday)

In Memphis, Grant was ordered to send all available troops to Rosecrans at Chattanooga. Grant's troops were to assist in the battle to come at Chickamauga. The skirmishing prior to battle was producing serious numbers of casualties on both sides.

Perin, G., Surg., USA, Med. Dir., Dept. of the Cumberland, Chattanooga, Tenn.:

> By the 13th, the army had crossed Lookout Mountain, and the advance had felt the enemy in several skirmishes. As the presence of the enemy in force was

well established, dispositions to concentrate our army were made. It was soon discovered that the main body of the enemy was moving down the valley of the Chickamauga toward Rossville. The ridge that divides the valley of Chickamauga from that of Chattanooga was traversed in several places by wagon roads. It was by these roads that our wounded must be conveyed to the rear. The wagon road down the Chickamauga Valley was near the base of this ridge, on the south side, where there were but few springs. As every indication pointed to a conflict on the north side of the creek, our wounded were to be provided for at these springs, or taken over Mission Ridge into Chattanooga Valley. After consultation ... I selected Crawfish Spring as the main depot for the wounded....

September 16 (Wednesday)

In Georgia, Rosecrans concentrated his troops near Lee and Gordon's Mills on the Chickamauga Creek, some 12 miles south of Chattanooga. The positions taken placed Crittenden at Gordon's Mill, Gen. Thomas to his right (farther south), and Gen. Alexander McDowell on the right flank, near Alpine, Ga. The battle was imminent.

Welch, S. G., Surg., 20th S.C. Vols., Orange C.H., Va.:

For two or three days we have been expecting another fight, and we had three days' rations cooked and were ready to move. It now appears that the Yankees have all gone back and that they sent only their cavalry forward...

Two men will be executed in our division next Saturday for desertion, and the entire division will be ordered out to witness it....

September 17 (Thursday)

Rosecrans now had his units in position where they could support each other. Bragg had missed his chance to attack the isolated units and beat them piecemeal. As usual, Bragg blamed his corps commanders for this lapse and they, of course, blamed him.

September 18 (Friday)

Confederate Gen. James Longstreet and his corps from the Army of Northern Virginia arrived at Bragg's location in Georgia early this morning, giving Bragg a numerical superiority of 7000 troops over Rosecrans. Bragg wasted no time, he drove all but three of his divisions across West Chickamauga Creek from Ringgold with a part of Longstreet's corps. Almost immediately, heavy fighting broke out with Rosecrans's cavalry at several points of contact near the fords and bridges.

Rosecrans moved Thomas's corps northeast around Crittenden to protect the Union flank on the left. Through the night the Union troops moved through near-freezing temperatures, down a dry, waterless road lined with fires to light the way and to provide a little heat at the halts. They wouldn't attain their new positions until dawn of the 19th, when Thomas reached the Kelly house.

Much of the area was a low growth of scrub oak, pine, cedar, and dogwood with an underbrush of honeysuckle, poison oak, briers, and other vines. Occasionally there was a clearing or large trees with little or no brush. Farms were dotted throughout the area, although most of them were of the bare-subsistence kind. Before the next day was over, these areas would be filled with wounded and dying men.

After the surrender of Vicksburg, Grant's army had been broken up into small units to garrison the delta areas of Mississippi and Louisiana. The remainder of his army had been put into camp between Vicksburg, the Yazoo River, and the Big Black River—an area of wet low ground. During the late summer the incidence of malaria, typhoid fever, and dysentery increased dramatically. Many regiments lost a major part of their strength during this period and orders were issued to discontinue the ritual of firing salutes over the graves because it had begun to sound like a major battle was occurring every day.

September 19 (Saturday)

With neither commander knowing exactly the disposition of the other's troops, Bragg and Rosecrans were like two boxers stumbling around the ring blindfolded. Thomas, on the Union left, guarding the route to Chattanooga, sent part of his corps up to find the Confederates, and the Union forces ran into Nathan Bedford Forrest's dismounted cavalry. The fighting became general, and by 2 P.M. raged on the entire three-mile front. Bragg attempted to cut the Union lines to Chattanooga, but couldn't make any progress. Casualties were heavy on both sides, and at dark the lines were about in their original locations. With darkness, the fighting ceased, and the troops on both sides went out looking for their wounded, for this was to be a cold night.

Perin, G., Surg., USA, Med. Dir., Dept. of the Cumberland, Battle of Chickamauga:

On the 19th, as the battle progressed, the army moved down the valley of the Chickamauga, so that when night closed it was about four miles distant from the hospitals, and the only road to the latter was … at the south base of Mission Ridge. This movement made the removal of the wounded a task of considerable magnitude, as our loss in wounded on Saturday afternoon was very severe, being,… about four thousand five hundred. The ambulance trains were worked very steadily until midnight, when almost all of the wounded accessible had been removed and placed in the hospitals.… Every effort was made to place them under shelter, but particularly to provide them with covering, as the night was cold. When this could not be done, the men were arranged in rows near each other, and lines of camp fires were built at their feet.…

September 20 (Sunday)

Bragg ordered a dawn attack by Polk against the Union right, Longstreet to hold the Confederate right. Dawn came but Polk didn't begin to move until almost 8 A.M. and the momentum of the attack didn't really get under way until about 9:30, when Breckinridge's division lunged forward with one of his brigades overlapping Thomas's exposed left flank, which was immediately corrected with the arrival of more Union troops. The Union left fell back somewhat, but held. Then about noon, Longstreet came up opposite the Federal center and found a hole in the line where the Union troops under Thomas J. Wood had been pulled out and shifted to the left, leaving a wide gap that Longstreet immediately filled with Confederates, sending them howling into the Union rear, where units fled in panic.

The only intact units remaining were controlled by Thomas, who formed a new line around a rise known locally as Snodgrass Hill, where he held throughout the afternoon, repelling assault upon assault by the Confederates. The "Rock of Chickamauga" earned his nickname this day, fighting for hours against desperate Confederates attacking his position. The Confederates, however, couldn't seem to bring enough troops to bear at any one time to take the hill. As darkness fell, the fighting ceased and the Confederates withdrew.

That night, Thomas, under orders, disengaged and withdrew towards Rossville, on the way to Chattanooga, where he set up new defensive lines. The casualty rate for both sides was high—about 28 percent of the forces engaged. The Union casualties were 16,170, the Confederate casualties slightly higher, at 18,454. Bragg had won the battle, but Rosecrans still held Chattanooga.

Jackman, John S., Pvt., "The Orphan Brigade," Battle of Chickamauga, Ga.:

Before daylight the division moved to take position in line of battle.… I had to pass over the ground where Cleburne had fought the evening before. The dead of both sides were lying thick over the ground. I saw where six Federal soldiers had been killed from behind one small tree and where eight horses were lying dead—harnessed to a Napoleon gun. Men and horses were lying so thick over the field one could hardly walk for them. I even saw a large black dog that had been mangled by grape.… The boys were lying in line of battle and cracking jokes as usual. Many of them I noticed to be in the finest spirits were a few minutes afterwards numbered with the slain. All the time, the skirmishers about two hundred yards in advance were very noisy.

About 10 o'clock A.M., Maj. Wilson rode up to Gen. Helm, who was sitting against a tree in rear of our regiment talking to Col. C. and gave him the verbal order from Breckinridge to advance in fifteen minutes.… I had intended to go along with the infirmary corps but as the drummers had not come up with the horses, Col. C. told me to go back and see if I could find them. I had not gone far before I came to a crowd of our boys that had been wounded on the skirmish line and as the shells were tearing up the ground about them, which makes a helpless man feel very uncomfortable, I helped put them in an ambulance and sent them to a hospital.…

I then started back for the regiment. The rattle

of musketry was kept up pretty lively.... When I got to the regiment it was just falling back under a heavy fire having charged three times unsuccessfully. The regiment was greatly reduced.... Out of our company my old friend J. H. had fallen with others and many had been wounded. Gen. Helm had received a mortal wound and had to be borne to the hospital on a litter. Our brigade hospital was more than a mile from the field, across the Chickamauga. The wounded I found scattered over a half-acre of ground—all out of our brigade too....

Perin, G., Surg., USA, Med. Dir., Dept. of the Cumberland, Battle of Chickamauga:

On the morning of the 20th, the movement of the army to the left continued. Our hospitals to the right becoming more distant,... it was deemed best to establish small depots immediately in rear of the left wing as soon as the right gave way. Communication with Crawfish Spring, the main hospital depot, was cut off; the position, too, was becoming unsafe, when Surg. Phelps ... appreciating the danger, availed [himself] of the empty supply trains parked at that point, to send the wounded across Mission Ridge and, by the Chattanooga Valley, to Chattanooga....

Although these officers labored faithfully to remove all the wounded from Crawfish Spring, it was found impracticable. Medical officers were, therefore, detailed to remain, and provisions were distributed in such manner as to insure them for the benefit of the patients during the confusion.... The wounded at the hospitals on the left were detained only long enough to perform such operations as admitted of no delay.... About one thousand five hundred of the graver cases were left on this part of the field. From the best information I can procure, I should estimate the total number of wounded left upon the field to be about two thousand five hundred....

In the retreat, every vehicle, baggage wagon, and supply train, as well as the ambulances, were filled with wounded. Great numbers who were able to walk found their way on foot to the north side of the Tennessee River, and continued their journey toward Bridgeport. The graver cases were removed from the ambulances and wagons and placed in hospitals at Chattanooga, while the others were taken to Bridgeport and Stevenson....

September 21 (Monday)

At dawn, Gen. Thomas was at Rossville in good defensive positions which he would hold all day, retiring to Chattanooga after dark. Rosecrans had occupied defensive positions around Chattanooga, and with Thomas inside the perimeter, the Union Army was safe, at least for the time. Bragg ordered a new offensive and then cancelled it, missing a chance to severely damage the Union forces.

The Union defeat had a sobering effect on the North, while the South celebrated—after Gettysburg and Vicksburg, it had been the only bright spot of the year!

September 22 (Tuesday)

The defeated Union force, safely within its entrenchments at Chattanooga, still faced a strong Confederate force on Missionary Ridge and Lookout Mountain. Hemmed in by mountains and the river, the Union position was uncertain.

Perin, G., Surg., USA, Med. Dir., Dept. of the Cumberland, Battle of Chickamauga:

A tent hospital sufficiently large for one thousand five hundred patients, was established on the 21st and 22d, at Stringer's Spring, on the north side of the river and about two miles distant. Ambulances were sent out on the Bridgeport road, to take up and bring back the wounded who had undertaken the journey to Bridgeport on foot, and had fallen by the wayside....

To provide Rosecrans with support, three divisions of the Fifteenth Corps of Grant's army at Vicksburg were entrained and shipped east as quickly as possible. Also entrained were Sherman and the redoubtable Mrs. Bickerdyke.

At Knoxville, Burnside had been ordered to go to Rosecrans's relief, but he was having a hard time holding his own positions and controlling the extremely mountainous terrain of east Tennessee.

September 23 (Wednesday)

In Washington, a council of war resulted in the decision to send the Eleventh and Twelfth Corps of the Army of the Potomac, commanded by Joseph Hooker, to Chattanooga immediately. By commandeering every railcar and engine on the lines, and moving with unheard-of speed, the move was accomplished in an incredibly short time. The first troops of the Eleventh Corps started moving on September 25th, and the last of them arrived in Chattanooga on October 2nd! For the first time in the history of warfare, large numbers of troops had been moved by rail for strategic purposes. Chattanooga would be held.

Perin, G., Surg., USA, Med. Dir., Dept. of the Cumberland, Battle of Chickamauga:

By the evening of the 23d, the wounded not sent to the rear were provided for.... It has been a cause of regret that, in the confusion of the retreat, primary operations could not be performed to the extent desired; thus many cases of injuries of the knee and ankle joints subsequently proved fatal that might have been saved....

As soon as the army had taken up its position in front of Chattanooga, and order was restored, the commanding general sent a flag of truce with propositions for the recovery of our wounded left upon the field. One thousand seven hundred and forty were thus restored to our care....

It may be mentioned here that upon the occupancy of the town, over two hundred bales of cotton were found secreted in various places, which were seized, carefully guarded, and reserved for mattresses. Had it not been for this fortunate circumstance the suffering of our wounded men would have been much greater.... About one hundred and fifty upholsterers, tailors, and saddlers were detailed to make mattresses, so that by the tenth day every severely wounded man was provided with a comfortable bed. The ambulance trains were busily employed transporting such cases as could bear transportation to Bridgeport until the autumnal rains rendered the roads impassable.... As the roads became more and more difficult by reason of the rains, only those subsistence stores that were absolutely essential could be brought, and even those were soon reduced in quantity far below the standard ration....

September 25 (Friday)

The last of Sherman's Fifteenth Corps left Vicksburg by boat for Memphis, where they would board railcars for Chattanooga. Mrs. Bickerdyke and her entourage were included in the shipment.

September 27 (Sunday)

Welch, S. G., Surg., 20th S.C. Vols., Orange C.H., Va.:

We had nine more military executions in our division yesterday.... We have been having some cavalry fighting recently. On the 23d the enemy threatened to flank us, and our division was moved about six miles up the Rapidan River, but we soon returned....

I must close, as a doctor has just come for me to go with him to assist in dissecting two of the men who were shot yesterday.

September 28 (Monday)

Looking for scapegoats for Chickamauga, Union Maj. Gens. Alexander McDowell McCook and T. L. Crittenden were relieved of their respective corps commands and ordered to Indianapolis, where a court of inquiry would be held on the conduct of the battle. Gen. Thomas escaped criticism.

Barber, Lucius W., Cpl., Co. D, 15th Illinois Vol. Infantry, Natchez, Miss.:

There were camped here about twenty thousand negroes. Their condition was distressing in the extreme. The smallpox broke out amongst them carrying off as many as one hundred daily. They just rolled in filth and rags, dependent upon the Government for support. A good many earned a little by washing clothes for the soldiers. Most of the able-bodied males enlisted and several regiments were formed here. Some of our boys went in as officers of companies.

October 1 (Thursday)

Asst. Surg. John G. Perry finally recovered from his broken leg and returned to duty in early September, rejoining the Army of the Potomac on the 27th of September. His leg was very stiff and he wasn't entirely mobile again, but he was anxious for duty. The weather was cool and the nights were very cold.

Perry, John G., Asst. Surg., USV, 20th Mass. Vols., Culpeper, Va.:

We had a drunken row in camp last night, owing to some villain's having sold whiskey to the men, and it was one o'clock before the noisy ones were secured and all became quiet. These conscripts, or rather substitutes, behave disgracefully, deserting at every possible chance, even to the enemy. Notwithstanding that two who belonged to our regiment were shot, thirty-four deserted immediately after. One fellow, having failed to escape in the direction of his home, attempted to go over to the enemy, but was prevented. He then shot his finger off, with the hope of being sent to the hospital, where the opportunities for desertion are greater, but the result is that he will serve with one finger less.

Last night the moon was brilliant, campfires blazed in every direction, and with our blankets spread around a huge mass of burning embers and our pipes lighted, we lay listening to music from the bands; I, for one, dreaming of matters and things far enough away from where I was....

October 3 (Saturday)

In Tennessee, Joe Wheeler's Confederate cavalry was creating havoc behind Rosecrans's lines. At Bridgeport, Ala., just south of Chattanooga on the Tennessee River, Gen. Hooker and 20,000 men arrived, having ridden the railroad for 1159 miles in seven days. The only road open to Chattanooga from Bridgeport was the mountainous trail over Walden's Ridge.

October 4 (Sunday)

In Memphis, Sherman's son Willy had died of typhoid fever, and on this day the U.S. Thirteenth Infantry Regiment carried the small body of their mascot aboard the *Gray Eagle* to be sent north with Sherman's wife and remaining children.

October 5 (Monday)

Early this morning, Sherman boarded the last train for Corinth, Miss., there to join the Fifteenth Corps, who'd gone on before. Around noon, the train was near Colliersville when it was attacked by Confederate militia. Sherman had the train backed to a station that had been reinforced as a blockhouse and prepared to hold out with the 600 men on the train, meanwhile telegraphing for help. The attacking force attempted to loot the train and destroy it, but were driven off again and again by the Thirteenth Regulars. Late in the afternoon, help arrived from Memphis and the attackers were driven off.

October 6 (Tuesday)

Confederate Joe Wheeler's cavalry burned an important railroad bridge near Murfreesboro, Tenn., causing an interruption in the flow of supplies and troops to Chattanooga. More Federal troops were being sent from Memphis towards Rosecrans, in addition to the two corps coming in with Hooker, and the Fifteenth Corps divisions from Grant's old army.

October 9 (Friday)

In Tennessee, Wheeler's cavalry continued raiding between Nashville and Chattanooga, as Union troops moved across the state in a steady stream to aid Rosecrans at Chattanooga.

In Virginia, Lee was on the move, across the Rapidan and heading west trying to get around Meade's right flank and threaten Washington. Meade, alerted days before, took immediate action to cover his flank.

Perry, John G., Asst. Surg., USV, 20th Mass. Vols., Culpeper, Va.:

We expect to move from here any hour. Stewart's cavalry annoys us greatly, and I fear some fine day, before we know it, a few hundred of us will be gobbled up. Once we heard horses' hoof thundering through the woods, the yells of their riders, and the cry from our men, "The cavalry, the cavalry!" followed by a sharp order to form a hollow square.... Just then there seemed no use for me, and afterward I remembered a moment's wish to make a hollow square of myself, then being amused at the thought that having but one front, the rest of me would be ridden down.... But it was all a false alarm, for though the enemy was close upon us, something turned them just in time to miss our whereabouts.

This army is so demoralized by substitutes and conscripts that it seems to me it is in critical condition. We have drunken rows and disturbances in the camps about us almost every night....

It is now eleven o'clock A.M., and at two P.M. a man in the division is to be shot. The execution is to take place by the side of our camp. All the regiments in the division are to be present and I expect to be detailed as one of the surgeons to examine the body after it falls. I feel too sad to write. I can bear to see hundreds shot in battle, but everything in me recoils from seeing a man shot in cold blood; and if these horrible scenes do not stop, my whole nature will change....

While on the march we halted near an old icehouse, the roofless cellar only remaining, its bottom filled with old straw. In this cellar a ladder leaned against one side, and, as most of these abandoned icehouses are homes for snakes, a fellow in the ranks offered to bet that no one would dare go down that ladder and trample the straw. Quiet reigned for a moment while each man thought the matter over, when a little ignorant recruit, about nineteen years old, accepted the bet and gallantly started down the ladder. Just as his face reached the level of the beam which had supported the roof, he saw lying under it a moccasin snake, its head only a few inches from his face. His eyes became fixed, his teeth chattered, and his whole body was so rigid that the men got frightened and hauled him up by the coat collar. It was some time before he was restored to consciousness, and, although unmercifully chaffed by the men, his legs were so weak that for the rest of the march they had to support him.

October 10 (Saturday)

Lee was pushing hard to get past Meade's right flank and behind the Union Army, but so far was having no luck. Union cavalry was probing, trying to find the main body of Lee's army. For once, the armies were well matched in strength. Heavy skirmishing took place at Russell's Ford, Germanna and Morton's Fords, and at other points on the Rapidan.

October 11 (Sunday)

The Fifteenth Corps, Sherman's command, reached Corinth and found the railroad had been destroyed by local guerrilla forces and Wheeler's cavalry. Sherman was ordered to repair the road as he came, which task was a major irritant. Progress was slow, and even slower in the rains which bogged down his wagon trains filled with rations and supplies for Chattanooga.

October 12 (Monday)

Perry, John G., Asst. Surg., USV, 20th Mass. Vols., Battle of Bristoe Station, Va.:

We are on the march.... We struck tents on Saturday, marched some three miles to the west of the town of Culpeper, and were formed in line of battle in the woods, where we remained through a terrible storm without shelter or fires, in momentary expectation of an attack.

At three o'clock in the morning we were ordered to move on. The night was of the blackest, the streams swollen.... In the dense growth of trees and underbrush the column broke, men became bewildered and demoralized, lost their way, stumbled over rocks and roots, plunged into ditches and then scrambled out as best they could, soaked with mud and water. Bonfires were lighted to extricate us from our dilemma, but instead set the woods on fire. Sparks flew in all directions, and soon tongues of fire were everywhere. The frightful heat, the dense smoke, and the mad rush of men to free themselves at any cost made "Hell." No other word can describe the scene. By daybreak, however, we ... joined the main column. At nine o'clock in the morning we halted for ten minutes to eat a little hardtack, and then pushed on until four o'clock P.M., when we ... again halted for rest and food, after a march of thirteen hours. Knapsacks were opened, and pork, hard bread, and coffee dealt out in abundance....

October 13 (Tuesday)

Meade had withdrawn to the vicinity of Manassas and Centreville, closely followed by Lee. The same Confederate tactic used at Second Bull Run (a wide flanking movement) was again successful.

Perry, John G., Asst. Surg., USV, 20th Mass. Vols., Battle of Bristoe Station, Va.:

We marched and countermarched, prepared for battle by day and made forced marches by night.... While on the march I suffered so much with my leg that it was impossible to keep up with the regiment, although extremely dangerous to fall behind.... There was no proper food for the men or horses; what hardtack we had was so full of maggots that it had to be baked, which hardened it still more. No pork, and no water, except what we got from the puddles by the roadside. Men became so exhausted that they fell asleep while marching, and I slept while sitting in my saddle. The nights were bitterly cold; the roads almost impassable from the furious rains. The enemy threatened us on all sides,... but we did not run foul of them until the 14th.

In the area of New Bern, N.C., the troops were settling in for the winter, although this didn't preclude the sickness caused by the swamps in which they dwelled. The local surgeons, and the medical director noticed that camp location affected the type and amount of sickness, especially from malaria, but they made no connection between the two.

Hand, D. W., Surg., USV, Med. Dir., New Bern, N.C.:

During September and October, it was found that the intermittent and remittent fevers prevailed extensively. The number of men daily off duty on account of sickness being from forty to one hundred and sixty-eight in each regiment. A number of cases of congestive fever occurred, producing death within from six to thirty hours after the attack. I have reason to believe that some of these cases were mistaken for cerebrospinal meningitis by the medical officers in attendance.... Each regiment had a hospital of its own, with a liberal supply of medicine and stores, and most of the medical officers were active and intelligent.

There were also in New Bern two general hospitals for the reception of such cases as the regimental surgeons saw fit to send to them. In October, these hospitals were united under the charge of Surg. J. Delamater, USV, and thereafter formed the Foster general hospital, with a capacity of five hundred beds. To this hospital were brought chronic and tedious cases from all parts of the district.

The regiment quartered in the city suffered little from malarial fevers, and all through the fall was remarkably healthy. It was also noticed that the 92d New York Volunteers, stationed at Ft. Anderson, on the east bank of the Neuse River, and where the prevailing southwest wind reached it only after passing over a two-mile stretch of water, was remarkably free from intermittent fever, and its sick list was very small. A number of fatal cases of congestive fever, however, occurred among these men....

October 14 (Wednesday)

Near Bristow Station, Va., Lt. Gen. A. P. Hill's Confederates struck Meade's rear guard, which included the 20th Mass. Volunteers, but with insufficient strength to dislodge the entrenched Yankees. Meade had time to prepare his lines around Centre-

ville near the old Manassas battlefields. The battle that ensued was fairly matched. Lee found no easy solution as he had at Second Manassas and Meade couldn't find a good opening for an attack. The Union forces kept falling back to prepared entrenchments, giving Lee no opportunity to break the Union lines.

Perry, John G., Asst. Surg., USV, 20th Mass. Vols., Battle of Bristoe Station, Va.:

Unknown to us, they had cut in and occupied the roads through which we were to march. When we reached a defile among the hills and were about to cross a broad stream, a sharp fire of musketry and artillery opened upon our brigade from Gen. Hill's corps. The corps immediately halted, formed into line of battle, and waited for the enemy's assault, which presently came in great force. The men stood firm as rocks and poured volley after volley into their ranks, but had a hard time of it....

Col. Morgan ordered our brigade forward as skirmishers to drive the Confederates from the woods and take their batteries, but our advance was much impeded by the stream which had first to be crossed directly under the enemy's fire. This stream was very deep and its banks steep and slippery. Men fell headlong into the water, horses rolled down the bank backwards, carrying their riders with them, and for a time utter chaos and confusion reigned. The new recruits crouched, and I even heard some of them scream with fear, while the older troops and officers drove them on at the point of sword and bayonet.

A line was finally formed on the opposite bank, a charge made, and the enemy driven back. The fight lasted about six hours. It was the enemy's cavalry only which took part in the engagement, or we should not have had such an easy victory.... We lay there, surrounded by the graves of the dead, and the stench from the battlefield was beyond expression. When we moved it was in a thick fog. Marching by the railroad track, we reached an open space, intersected here and there by low ridges, near Bristow Station. I was riding with Gen. Webb at the head of the column when, through the lifting mist, we dimly saw another column marching parallel to ours, and the prevailing color in the ranks being blue, we supposed it to be one of our own corps. Both columns stopped and stared in amazement at each other, but in a moment what had seemed a spectral host turned about-face and fired a tremendous volley into us. This was sufficient proof that we faced an enemy.

Our men were immediately filed into line behind an embankment, but still by the side of the railroad. The Confederates formed a straight and strong line of battle and advanced upon us.... Our men were largely conscripts, who had never seen an attacking force before. They were ordered not to fire until the enemy was close upon them.... On came the Confederates with such steady force and such perfect coolness that the raw recruits of the [?] New York regiment could not stand the strain, and rushed headlong, pell-mell, for the rear. Col. Mallon of that regiment, but who at the time commanded the brigade, was fortunately behind them, and, drawn sword in hand, succeeded in stopping the stampede.

The enemy still advanced without wavering. Suddenly the order "Fire!" rang along our lines. Hundreds of the Confederates dropped; others, bewildered, rushed back, some forward, while our fellows, with a wild cheer, fired volley after volley into them. Not a man seemed to be left standing, and they came into our lines as prisoners by fifties, wounded and bleeding. Another line, still stronger, still steadier, was formed by the enemy, but our batteries were now run out, and shell, solid shot, and canister were poured upon them with marked effect. They closed and closed, advancing in a solid mass. Our guns again were quiet, awaiting a nearer approach.

Col. Mallon was at [the] time with me in the rear ... and we were lying side by side, flat on the ground, so as to be out of range of the enemy's guns, when the colonel,... rose and was instantly shot through the abdomen. I dragged him to a little muddy stream—the only place of safety—where the poor fellow lay with the water almost running down his throat. He lived until the fight was almost over, and finally expired in my arms. He was just married.

The fight continued until dark, the enemy throwing out line after line up to that time. I was busy enough after the battle was over, and came within an ace of being taken prisoner.... The prisoners told us that, notwithstanding this success of ours, we could not escape,... but in spite of this on we marched, all through that night, without a halt, worn-out as we were. I cannot express the torture I endured in trying to keep my eyes open. I believe I rode for miles in a sound sleep.

October 15 (Thursday)

Near Bristow Station, both Lee and Meade were groping for weakness in the other's lines and they were both having poor results. This battle had about run its course.

Perry, John G., Asst. Surg., USV, 20th Mass. Vols., Battle of Bristoe Station, Va.:

At dawn we joined the main army in the fortifications here at Auburn, bordering the Bull Run River. The day's work had been a most signal victory, and our brigade had captured five guns and two colors.

October 16 (Friday)

Beginning on the this date, Lee begin to pull back to his old positions on the Rappahannock. For the next three days there would be skirmishing at several points, serving little except to add to the prisoner and casualty rate on both sides. Meade would be content to let Lee settle into his old camps on October 19th without further battle.

A new Military Division of the Mississippi had been created, placing Grant in command of the old Depts. of the Ohio, the Cumberland, and the Tennessee. Grant was en route from Vicksburg to Cairo, Ill., to confer with Secretary of War Stanton.

October 17 (Saturday)

Grant arrived at Cairo, Ill., and was ordered on to Louisville, Ky. At Indianapolis, he met Secretary Stanton, who was en route to Louisville to see Grant. Riding together on the train, Stanton gave Grant his orders, creating the new Military Division and placing Grant in command. Of the two versions offered, Grant selected the one that relieved Rosecrans of command and appointed Gen. George Thomas as commander of the troops at Chattanooga. Sherman was to remain in command, as well as Burnside.

Lt. Col. William S. Pierson, commanding the Federal prison camp at Johnson's Island, Ohio, notified Col. William Hoffman, Federal Commissary-General of Prisoners, that smallpox had been brought to Johnson's Island three times by incoming prisoners; twice from the prison at Alton, Ill. The disease was causing somewhat of a panic among the prisoners, although those sick were confined to the pesthouse.

October 18 (Sunday)

Today, Grant assumed command of all Union forces from the Mississippi east to the Cumberland Mountains. Rosecrans, relieved of his command at Chattanooga, went North, and Gen. George Thomas took command, with the admonition to hold Chattanooga at all costs. The roads west of Chattanooga were a mess; the rains had been heavy, and getting wagons over Walden's Ridge with supplies was a real problem.

October 20 (Tuesday)

Today, Grant left Louisville for Nashville, en route to Chattanooga and the Army of the Cumberland, which was facing Braxton Bragg in northern Georgia.

In northern Virginia, Jeb Stuart took the last of the Confederate forces back across the Rappahannock and into Lee's lines at Orange C.H., ending the campaign which had accomplished almost nothing for either side. Casualties were about equal—Confederate, 1381; Union, 1423.

Welch, S. G., Surg., 20th S.C. Vols., Culpeper County, Va.:

We have succeeded in maneuvering Meade entirely out of Virginia, as you must have already learned. The infantry did not have much fighting to do at any time on the entire trip, but the cavalry fought a large part of the time. Two North Carolina brigades became engaged with the enemy late one afternoon near Bristoe Station, and our side got rather the worst of it. It was all due to miserable management of Gen. Hill or Gen. Heth, or possibly both of them....

We have destroyed the railroad between Manassas and this place, so the Yankees cannot advance by that route again this winter, and I am sure the Army of Virginia will do no more fighting this year. Some part of it is sure to be sent somewhere soon, and our corps might go to Tennessee after resting a few days, or it might possibly be sent to Gen. Bragg.

The part of Virginia through which we have marched has been totally devastated. It is now nothing but one vast track of desolation, without a fence or planted field of any kind. I do not understand how the people exist, yet they do actually continue to live there. They are intensely hostile to the Yankees, and there is certainly no submission in them....

October 21 (Wednesday)

Grant and Rosecrans met in Stevenson, Ala., to discuss the situation at Chattanooga. Rosecrans, relieved of command, was going to Nashville and then on north, Grant on to Chattanooga. Grant's accident in New Orleans a few weeks before still had him on crutches, which made getting around in the mud (which was everywhere) a real chore.

October 23 (Friday)

After spending the day yesterday slipping, sliding, and slopping around in the mud, Grant arrived today, around dusk, at Thomas's headquarters in Chattanooga, where he was briefed immediately on the situation of the Army of the Cumberland and the defenses of the city.

October 24 (Saturday)

In central Tennessee, Sherman assumed command of the Army of the Tennessee, replacing Grant. Being able to operate in shallow water, two light-draft Union gunboats arrived at Eastport, Miss., to support Sherman's operations along the Tennessee River. At Chattanooga, Grant inspected the defenses of the city and the state of the troops. The famous "Cracker Line" was then ordered into effect.

This supply line had been suggested by the Army of the Cumberland's Chief Engineer, Maj. Gen. William F. Smith. Essentially, it involved gaining control of the Tennessee frontage (below Raccoon Mountain), which was held by the Confederates. This done, supplies could then be brought in by boat. The plan was set in motion.

October 25 (Sunday)

Arrangements for the expedition to set up the "Cracker Line" were in process. Troop units and equipment were being designated and readied for the mission.

Perry, John G., Asst. Surg., USV, 20th Mass. Vols., near Warrenton, Va.:

We do not stay long in one place, but go marching on. We have stopped here only temporarily; yesterday it rained so hard, and our supplies are so far gone, that we cannot move again for at least twenty-four hours, for the men have had literally almost nothing to eat. The supper last night for our own mess consisted of maggoty hard bread and brown sugar (*alias* sand). We are encamped on the slope of a hill, just under the Blue Ridge, surrounded by thick forests. The other regiments are encamped in the woods facing us, and the music of the bands, which play in every direction, just fills my soul.... Today I inspected the rations of the men, and have already condemned about a thousand pounds of hardtack.

October 26 (Monday)

Brig. Gen. Gilman Marston, commanding the prison at Point Lookout, Md., notified Col. William Hoffman, Federal Commissary-General of Prisoners:

Among every lot of prisoners sent from Ft. Delaware to this point there have been cases of smallpox. There were twenty-six in the last lot. So many cases create alarm here among the troops and the citizen employees of the Government. I trust no more will be sent here.

The Federal Surgeon General directed that no additional prisoners be transferred from Ft. Delaware until the smallpox had abated.

At 3 A.M., 24 pontoon boats were loaded with Brig. Gen. William B. Hazen's Ohioans and a detachment of the 1st Michigan Engineers. Using the current of the Tennessee River, they went around Moccasin Point, a dry neck of land opposite Confederate-held Raccoon Mountain, to Brown's Ferry, where they were joined by Brig. Gen. John Basil Turchin, who'd marched a brigade across Moccasin Point in the dark, undetected.

October 27 (Tuesday)

In Chicago, the long weeks of planning came to an end and the great Northwestern Sanitary Commission Fair opened amid fanfare and a three-mile-long parade. The mayor of Chicago had declared a holiday, and the streets were lined with thousands of people who'd come to watch the bands and floats. The Fair would run for two weeks, and at its end, the Commission would bank $100,000 in donations. This was quite a sum for the time, when a hotel room cost less than a dollar.

At Bridgeport, Ala., Gens. Hazen and Turchin threw a pontoon bridge across the Tennessee and secured both sides of the stream. Gen. Joseph Hook-

er's orders were to move his men up the Tennessee and secure the crossing at Brown's Ferry by cleaning out the Confederates at Raccoon Mountain who threatened the Union forces and their newly created bridgehead. Hooker moved, wasting no time. During the night he was attacked by Longstreet's men at Wauhatchie in Lookout Valley. The Confederates used larger numbers, but the Union force under Brig. Gen. John. W. Geary held, and by 4 A.M. the Confederates withdrew. The "Cracker Line" wasn't bothered again for the length of the campaign.

Perin, G., Surg., USA, Med. Dir., Dept. of the Cumberland, Chattanooga, Tenn.:

Partial relief from this condition [shortage of food] was afforded, after the battle of Wauhatchie, which opened a new and shorter route to the base of supply. A few days after this battle, the small steamer *Paint Rock* passed the enemy's batteries successfully, and we were enabled to resume the transfer of patients to the rear. At Kelly's Ferry, a point ten miles distant, where the boats discharged their freights, a few hospital tents were erected and other preparations made for the care of the wounded in transit. Patients were sent in ambulances from the hospitals in town, as well as Stringer's Spring, to this point as rapidly as circumstances would admit, the roads being bad, and the weather very rainy and cold.

The patients were also exposed while going from Kelly's Ferry to Bridgeport, for the boats were small, with open decks, having been hastily constructed for carrying freight only....

October 28 (Wednesday)

Welch, S. G., Surg., 20th S.C. Vols., Culpeper County, Va.:

There was a cavalry fight across the river yesterday, and I am told that we whipped them and took three hundred prisoners.... Old Jim Beauschelle, our chaplain, is out of prison and is back with us again. He was at Ft. Delaware a while, and was then sent to Johnson's Island in Lake Erie. He looks better than I ever saw him. He has a new hat, new shoes, and everything new, and looks like a new man. He speaks very highly of the Yankees and the way they treated him and of the good fare they gave him. He seems perfectly delighted with the North and the

Yankees. I am sorry they did not handle him rather roughly and cure him of his wonderfully good opinion of them....

I now feel quite sure that I shall be able to get home before much longer, but don't look for me until you see me walk in.

October 31 (Saturday)

Sherman's march to Chattanooga across northern Alabama was a nightmare. Mrs. Bickerdyke got little rest at the end of a dreary day's march, being constantly asked by the weary soldiers for help fixing their blistered feet. The army-issued shoes were falling apart in the rain and the damage to their feet was enormous.

November 1 (Sunday)

Skirmishing occurred in the vicinity of Eastport and Fayetteville, Tenn., on the outskirts of Grant's lines at Chattanooga. Few casualties were reported.

November 2 (Monday)

Before leaving the area of Murfreesboro, Tenn., the Union Army had created a hospital train by fitting two ordinary passenger railway cars with bunks, two cars without bunks, and one car for cooking. To lessen the jolting motion of the cars, additional cars had been fitted elsewhere with berths suspended from elastic rings.

About the middle of September, the latter cars were placed into service, moving the wounded and sick from the depot hospitals to Nashville and points north. This train was capable of moving sixty patients in reasonable comfort and was used extensively until the depot hospitals were largely emptied.

November 5 (Thursday)

In Chattanooga, Grant was inspecting the lines and waiting patiently for Sherman to arrive. Sherman wasn't making too much progress with his long wagon trains, which contained tons of rations for Grant's army. These rations, loaded before the "Cracker Line" had been opened, were somewhat redundant now, but Sherman couldn't just leave them in the wilderness. It took him 13 days to cover about 115 "air" miles—probably about 170 road miles.

November 6 (Friday)

At Point Lookout, Md., scurvy reared its ugly head. Brig. Gen. Gilman Marston, commanding the Union prison, wrote Col. William Hoffman, Federal Commissary-General of Prisoners:

The surgeon in charge of the Rebel camp informs me that most of the prisoners are afflicted with scurvy, and he advises that vegetables be furnished them. I have thought it might be advisable to purchase a schooner load of beets, carrots, turnips, cabbages, and the like and pay for the same out of the fund arising from the savings from food rations. It would probably not add to the actual cost of their food....

Considering the poor diet already furnished the prisoners—usually the same as the Union troops, which was bad enough—it isn't surprising that scurvy wasn't even more prevalent.

November 9 (Monday)

Col. William Hoffman, Federal Commissary-General of Prisoners, replied to Brig. Gen. Marston's request of November 6 concerning the purchase of vegetables for the Confederate prisoners to prevent scurvy. Col. Hoffman agreed that the vegetables were necessary, and that their purchase should be out of the "prisoners fund." Hoffman then expounded the view of a parsimonious bureaucrat by stating: "... *By the use of vegetables the savings of other parts of the ration will be increased, so that the cost will be to some extent refunded ...*" Hoffman further says that "*As the prisoners are bountifully supplied with provisions, I do not think it well to permit them to receive boxes of eatables from their friends ...*" [Italics added.]

There were probably 10,000 prisoners at Point Lookout who would contest Hoffman's concept of "bountiful" when it applied to their rations.

November 10 (Tuesday)

Mr. W. F. Swalm, a representative of the U.S. Sanitary Commission, today reported on his visit and inspection of the Hammond General Hospital at Point Lookout, Md.:

Visited and inspected the different wards, kitchen, dining rooms of the Hammond General Hospital, which is now mostly occupied by the Rebel sick, and in charge of Anthony Heger, surgeon, U.S. Army, who was very kind and courteous towards me and was glad that I had come to make an official visit to the hospital. He, in company with the officer of the day (Dr. Bidlack), visited with me every ward, kitchen,… &c., and showed me every attention in their power.

The hospital is arranged like the spokes of a wheel and has fifteen wards, together with one building used as the executive department, and containing also the sleeping apartments of the different surgeons, dispensary, linen room, &c. The capacity of the hospital, allowing 900 cubic feet per bed, is 1050 beds, or 70 beds to each ward. Including the convalescent ward and the wards for erysipelas and hospital gangrene, there are about 1400 beds. Ventilation good, high ceilings and plenty of good sea air. Number of patients at present in the hospital is 1277; of these 493 are Union men and 784 Rebels. The Union soldiers are all nearly convalescent, while the prevailing disease among the Rebels is chronic diarrhea. Of the 1208 sick in the hospital last week there were 46 deaths or 38.07 percent., and the mortality slightly on the increase. They receive on the average thirty per day from the hospital within the encampment and in the very worst condition. Some are moribund when they arrive at this hospital. At the postmortem examinations the doctor said nearly all of those who died of diarrhea had pneumonia. Did not show itself during life, probably from the extreme weak condition of the patient. From the 1st of March to the end of September, there were only twenty-eight deaths. Union soldiers then occupied the hospitals, and the sick report on the last day of July was 1192. The highest number was 1330, but the average for the six months was 1100. Diseases, typhoid fever, diarrhea, and typhoid pneumonia.

The wards were in very good condition, but there was a vast difference in the cleanliness of those occupied by our men; no spitting on the floor or lounging on the beds with clothes on, as was seen among the Rebels. Could do nothing with them; impose no punishment, for they were too weak. Every attention was paid them, and all possible care to keep the wards and bedding as clean as possible. In the half- and low-diet kitchen found the trays all ready to convey the food to the sick. The Rebels received the same as our own men; no distinction whatever. Potatoes, rice, cabbage, sweet milk, soft bread and butter, and farina of cornstarch being prepared in this kitchen; had female cooks. The full-diet kitchen was by the side of the dining room, with everything complete, ovens, boilers, &c. The dining room, capable of seating 1000 persons, was in splendid condition, with tables, floor, &c., in good order.

I shall not enter into the detail of these various apartments, but will speak of the rations, which to us now is of more interest. It was my fortune to enter the dining room as dinner was being placed upon the table, and found about 6 ounces of fresh beef, boiled; 3 potatoes, 2 thick slices of bread, butter, 1 pint of soup with vegetables, and the condiments of pepper, salt, vinegar, and mustard; and to this the Rebels sat down at the same time and in the same room with our own men. What could they wish more? And if there was any complaint at all it ought to come from us, that they received too much and are entirely too well treated.

Full diet: Breakfast—bread, 8 ounces; butter, 1 ounce; Indian meal, boiled, 2 ounces; molasses, 0.32 of a gill. Dinner—beef soup and vegetables, 1 pint; meat, 10 ounces; sweet potatoes, 7 ounces; bread, 4 ounces. Supper—coffee, 1 pint; bread, 5 ounces; cheese, 2 ounces; butter, 1 ounce. The diet is changed every day, when they also receive cabbage, tomatoes, macaroni, and on Sunday have both Irish and sweet potatoes, puddings, &c. The bread ration was formerly six ounces, but the doctor has cut it down one ounce breakfast and supper and two ounces dinner.

Bath, laundry, and engine rooms complete and in good order. The linen room and liquors are in the executive building and under the charge of Sisters of Charity; well supplied with everything.

In the afternoon visited the smallpox hospital, and [it] is about a quarter of a mile north of the encampment, among the pine bushes, under the charge of Dr. W. Broadbent, acting assistant surgeon. This hospital was opened two weeks ago, and up to today have received therein 133 patients, during which time thirty-three deaths have occurred. The sick are in wedge tents, three to a tent, lying on straw on the ground, with a blanket and a half to a man. Their ration is the same, and bean soup is given every day; to those not allowed it, coffee in its stead. The men are much more comfortable here than in the encampment, and those who are in attendance do not want to go back. I should also state that they occasionally get soft bread. No complaints at all; were getting along as well as they could expect.

Medicines very short; no cathartics at all. In connection with the smallpox, the majority have scurvy and scabies, and some are in horrid condition.

In the remarks that I have made concerning the prisoners, it is evident that with the facilities they now possess they could be made 10 percent more comfortable if they had someone to command them. That they are suffering from want of clothing and covering is true. Of their treatment they do not complain; their ration they do not deem quite sufficient; but of their filthy condition and habits more is attributable to their indolence and laziness, and they have the facilities at their disposal to correct this and they ought to be made to do it....

November 11 (Wednesday)

The Army of the Potomac, after much marching and many hardships, finally came to rest for the winter near Mountain Run, Va., at the foot of the Blue Ridge Mountains.

Perry, John G., Asst. Surg., USV, 20th Mass. Vols., near Mountain Run, Va.:

On the 9th we had quite a little snowstorm, and yesterday, when on the march, the snow-covered "Blue Hills" towered above us, their icy cliffs illuminated by the sun's rays into every enchanting color. We have ice now every night, and last night it froze nearly two inches thick.

I have been working hard today, pitching my tent upon a log foundation. It will be warmer, and will allow me to sit up. Tomorrow I shall build an underground fireplace, for the wind blows so hard here in the winter that it is impossible to keep warm by an outside fire, for while your front is warming your back is freezing, and if the fire is very near the tent, the smoke blows in and smothers you. My eyes are now almost put out by the smoke; my hands are covered with pitch from handling pine logs; my feet are soaking wet; and I am cross....

November 12 (Thursday)

At Chattanooga, Grant waited for Sherman to arrive. Grant's current problem was one of morale. The Army of the Cumberland he'd inherited was, he felt, badly demoralized by its defeat at Chickamauga. Grant also felt that Hooker's two corps from the

Army of the Potomac would perform poorly because they had never won a battle. What he wanted was a body of troops that was accustomed to winning and a commander to match them: Sherman and his Fifteenth Corps. Sherman was still two days away.

November 13 (Friday)

Mr. Frederick N. Knapp, Associate Secretary of the U.S. Sanitary Commission in Washington, today completed his inspection report on Point Lookout, Md., which was forwarded to Col. William Hoffman, Federal Commissary-General of Prisoners. The report, covering the survey of the prison hospital and camp, paints a rather grim picture of the life of the Confederate prisoners held there:

The accommodations here were much better than I expected to find them and much more comfortable, yet they had by no means the best of care. The hospital was situated in the southern part of the encampment and was composed of eighteen hospital tents, complete, arranged two together, end to end, and placed in two rows, a broad street intervening, with the cook and dining tent on the eastern end and facing the street. In these tents there were 100 patients, and all were lying on mattresses with at least one blanket for covering. Eight of their own men were detailed to take care of them, and although they were enlisted men, yet six were graduates from some medical school and the other two had been students. Four were graduates from the University of the City of New York; one of the school at New Orleans; one from the eclectic school, Cincinnati, and the other two were students in the University of Pennsylvania, seceders. Still, little or no attention did they give to their sick comrades, and, except in giving the necessary food and medicine, they scarcely even visited them. There is either a lack of sympathy or else indolence enters largely into their composition, and I am inclined to believe it is the latter, for, with the accommodations at their command, with good beds and shelter for the sick, if they had one particle of pride they could render them much more comfortable, especially as regards cleanliness. As it is, they are in a filthy condition; faces and hands apparently strangers to soap and water and hair seemingly uncombed for weeks.

No attention was given to the separating of different diseases. Wounded and erysipelas, fever and diarrhea, were lying side by side. (The wounded were two that were shot while trying to escape; two were killed.) Their being no stoves in the hospital, the men complain greatly of cold, and I must admit that for the poor emaciated creatures suffering from diarrhea a single blanket is not sufficient; yet as I told them, they had plenty of bricks and plenty of men; they could build fireplaces. One tent only had a board floor. Chronic diarrhea is the most prevalent disease, yet they have mild cases of remittent fever and some erysipelas. Mortality, none, for when any cases assume a dangerous character they are immediately removed to the general hospital, and they generally remove from twenty to thirty per day on an average, leaving in camp hospital eighty sick.

The dispensary is a poor apology for one, having little or nothing but a few empty bottles. Not a particle of oil or salts, in fact, a cathartic of no kind. About half a dram of opium, half pound of sulphether, half pound of simple cerate, and a few other things constitute the whole supply. Here also was shown the want of discipline and cleanliness; everything covered with dust, and what few articles they had were exposed to the air and placed indiscriminately along the counter and in the most perfect confusion; were going to arrange the bottles, &c. The books were extremely well kept,... and each day's report was copied in the report book as soon as returned from the surgeon in charge.

The rations are very good, both in quantity and quality; amply sufficient for any sick man; but there are exceptional cases where they need something more delicate than the regular army ration. But the majority are perfectly well satisfied, and very little complaint is made in this particular. I will here give the quantities they received in full, half, and low diet:

Full diet: Dinner—beef or pork, 4 ounces; potatoes, 4 ounces; hardtack, 3 ounces. Breakfast and tea—coffee or tea, 1 pint; rice, 2 gills; molasses, 1 ounce; hardtack, 3 ounces.
Half diet: Dinner—meat 2 ounces; potatoes, 3 ounces; hardtack, 2 ounces. Breakfast and tea—coffee or tea, 1 pint; rice, 1 gill; molasses, half an ounce; hardtack, 2 ounces.
Low diet: Dinner—no meat; potatoes, 2 ounces; hardtack, 1 ounce. Breakfast and tea—coffee or tea, 1 pint; rice, 1 gill; molasses, half an ounce; hardtack, 1 ounce.

Soup and soft bread is also given at least once a week. The cooking is done by their own men, and heard no complaint in this quarter, except they were poorly supplied with cooking utensils and were very much in want of tin cups, knives and forks. The patients were required generally to eat with their fingers. They had a large cooking stove, but they complained it was not sufficient for their purpose, as it kept them at work nearly all the time; the very reason that it should not be changed or another given them. The cooks' tent and stove were dirty (the peculiar characteristic), and the tent where the nurses and attendants dined was in the same plight although I am glad to say the table from which they ate was scoured and looked very clean, as also the plates and cups.

The grounds around the hospital have not, according to looks, been policed for a very long time. Filth is gradually accumulating, and the sinks are not at all thought of, requiring a little extra exertion to walk to them. They void their excrement in the most convenient place to them, regardless of the comfort of others.

The surgeon in charge of this hospital and of the whole Rebel encampment is Dr. Bunton, assistant surgeon Second New Hampshire Volunteers, assisted by Drs. Russell and Walton, acting assistant surgeons, the latter gentlemen having just entered upon their duties. I think a great amount of the misery experienced in the hospital and throughout the camp might be obviated if a little more energy was displayed by the surgeon in charge. There is lack of system and want of discipline, neither of which (with all due respect to the doctor) do I think he is possessed of. The assistants saw what was needed and were determined to entirely renovate and change the whole condition and aspect. If done, much suffering might be alleviated and less sickness would ensue.

It is in the quarters that we have the most complaint and suffering. Men of all ages and classes, descriptions and hues, with various colored clothing, all huddled together, forming a motley crew, which to be appreciated must be seen, and what the pen fails to describe the imagination must depict; yet I will endeavor to convey their exact condition, &c., and give as accurate description as possible.

They are ragged and dirty and very thinly clad;

that is, the very great majority. Occasionally you will find one of the fortunate possessor of an overcoat, either a citizen's or the light blue ones used by our infantry, and these serve as coverings for the rags beneath. Others, again, are well supplied as regards underclothing, especially those who are from Baltimore, being sent to them by friends. But the great mass are in a pitiable condition, destitute of nearly everything, which, with their filthy condition, makes them really objects of commiseration. Some are without shirts, or what were once shirts are now hanging in shreds from their shoulders. In others the entire back or front will be gone, while again in some you will see a futile attempt at patching. Their clothing is of all kinds and hues—the gray, butternut, the red of our zouaves and the light and dark blue of our infantry, all in a dilapidated condition.

Of their shelter there can be no possible complaint, for they all have good tents, such as wall, hospital, Sibley, wedge, shelter, hospital and wall tent flies. Majority are in the wedge tent. Average in a hospital tent, from 15 to 18 men; in wall tent, from 10 to 12; in shelter tent, 3; in Sibley tent, from 13 to 14…. The shelter tents, only a very few are excavated and boarded at the sides, and almost every tent throughout the camp has a fireplace and chimney built of brick made by them from the soil (which is clay) and sun baked. In a few of the Sibleys holes are dug, fire built, and covered at the top. Generally the tents are filled with smoke. Although they have fireplaces, wood is not issued to them, but they are allowed to go out in squads every day and gather such as may be found in the woods where trees have been cut down, but they are not allowed to cut down others. There are instances where they have completely dug around the root of a stump and taken all; for it is impossible in this way for them to get enough to keep them warm, and as they are poorly supplied with blankets they must have suffered severely from the cold, more so where they are, for it is a very bleak place.

On visiting the quarters, found them crowded around a few coals in their respective tents, some having good blankets thrown across the shoulders, others pieces of carpet, others a gum blanket, others a piece of oilcloth commonly used for the covering of the tables. Generally they have one blanket to three men, but a great many are entirely without. A great many of the tents have been pitched over old sinks

lightly covered. Complaints have been made, but nothing has been done to change them. The interior of the tents are in keeping with the inmates, filthy; pieces of cracker, meat, ashes, &c., are strewn around the tent, and in which they will lie. In preference to sitting on a stool they will sit upon the ground, and I even heard their own men say that they never saw such a dirty set in their lives, fully convincing me that it is their element, and they roll into it as a hog will wallow in the mire.

Concerning the rations, I heard a great deal of complaint that they did not get enough to eat. They wanted more meat. What they did get they spoke of in the highest terms. On questioning some of them which they would prefer an increase of the rations or blankets, all concluded that they could get along with the ration if they could get blankets. On being shown a ration, I do not think they receive half the amount of meat they are entitled to, but with the crackers, &c., given they cannot suffer at all from hunger. The ration to the well man is, pork, 3 ounces; salt or beef, 4 ounces; hardtack, 10 ounces; coffee, 1 pint; a day's ration. Soup is also given once a week; potatoes and beans every five days; soft bread once a week, and fresh meat had been issued to them once a week up to two weeks ago, when from some cause unable to find out it was stopped. Others, again, did not find fault with the ration, but the cooking; that it was not done well, and there ought to be changes made, &c., so visited the kitchens and dining rooms. These are in the northwest corner of the camp and composed of six wooden buildings, 160 feet in length, with twenty feet off for the kitchen. Only five of the buildings are in use. The kitchen arrangements are very good, each one containing four cauldrons, and in one five, each cauldron capable of containing from fifty to sixty gallons. Here the rations were cooked, and [I] was told that they served the meat ration all at dinner, not being enough to make two meals, and they were thus enabled to give them one good meal a day. Breakfast and supper they relied upon hardtack, tea or coffee; and, as I said before, there is no likelihood of their starving. The dining room contains three tables, and each house feeds 1529 men, 500 at a time. Seem to be well supplied with all necessary articles, both for kitchen and dining room. Will make allowance for the condition of the kitchen, as they were just through serving dinner, and were making preparations for cleaning up. Yet there was evidence of a want of care and cleanliness. Still, I found them in a much better condition than I expected. There was such a vast difference that I did not notice as much the number of bones thrown from kitchen on the outside. Still there were some.

The sick in quarters average from 160 to 200. Prevailing disease, scurvy. Yet a great many are troubled with the diarrhea, and as they gradually grow worse are admitted to the hospital to be sent to the general hospital. These men who are sick in quarters and who are unable to eat the ration given them have instead, vinegar, 3 ounces; potatoes, 5; rice, 1 gill; molasses, 1 gill; one day's rations. Each man cooks for himself. They are troubled greatly with the itch, and it is spreading throughout the camp, and until sulphur was sent them by the commission they had nothing for it. They have abundance of water in the camp, notwithstanding several of the wells are unfit for use. The waters of those not in use are strongly impregnated with iron and will stain white clothing yellow or light brown. Outside of these there is an abundance of good water, and no excuse whatever for being otherwise than clean, but they seem to abhor soap and water. At least their appearance so indicates.

A great many are employing their time making brick and have now a great quantity on hand. Others employ themselves in making rings, chains, seals, &c., from bone and gutta-percha, and notwithstanding the complaint that they do not get enough to eat, you will find them on the main street, which they call The Change, gambling both for money and rations. They have games at cards, keno, sweat cloth, &c. Also on this street they do their trading, hardtack for tobacco and tobacco for hardtack. It is here that you will find them in crowds, sitting or kneeling in the dirt, eagerly watching the different games, and see them arise dissatisfied at having lost their day's rations, and while thus engaged they are unmindful of the cold. The size of the encampment is a little over 1000 feet square, or about 16 acres, the whole surrounded by a board fence twelve feet high, with a platform on the outside for the sentinel, sufficiently high for him to look within the enclosure. With so many men and no one to take charge of them, it is not at all to be wondered at that the camp is in any but a desirable condition. The sinks, which should have special consideration, especially in a camp of this size, and where so many men are congregated, are entirely neglected, and it is a perfect mystery that

there is not more sickness than they have, and God knows they have enough, for they live, eat, and sleep in their own filth. Sinks have been prepared for them, but little or no attention is paid to them, unless they should be in close proximity when they desire to answer the calls of nature. The holes dug in getting out clay for bricks are used as sinks. You will find them by the side and in front of their tents, in various portions of the encampment, and are the receptacles of their filth. Refuse matter from the tents or whatnot right under their very noses, yet they heed them not. Others, again, have no particular place, but will void their excrement anywhere on the surface that is most convenient to them, heedless of the convenience of others.

Have no drainage around the tents, but there has been an attempt to drain the streets. Ditches were dug, but they are worse than useless, constantly filled with water, and afford another place to throw filth. With this state of affairs and so many men (by the by, over 1300 more came in the camp on the afternoon of November 10, making nearly 10,000 men) the camp would soon become in an impassable condition. The men themselves complain and hope that some severe punishment, even shooting, will be the penalty to anyone who will so outrage decency and lose respect due themselves. Some of the sinks are filled and [have] not been covered and not a particle of chloride of lime has been used in the encampment for a long time. After stating the above facts, giving the condition of the camp and its inmates, some might say that it is not our fault that they are in this condition. As far as clothing, it is not; but it is our fault when they neglect to enforce those sanitary rules which keep camps and inmates in a clean … condition, and this … to prevent disease. It is our fault when the officer in command fails to place in charge someone of good executive ability, capable of giving commands and seeing that they are enforced, one who will have the camp regularly policed and severely punish any offender of the sanitary rules. It is beneficial otherwise, for it will give employment to a certain number of men every day.

As regards medicine and clothing, they are sadly in want of both, and would suggest that the commission send them, place them in the hand of Mr. Fairchild, and I know they will be judiciously distributed. I know that they are our enemies, and bitter ones, and what we give them they will use against us, but now they are within our power and are suffering. Have no doubt that to compare their situation with that of our men words would hardly be adequate to express our indignation. I merely gave this suggestion because I think you would be doing right and it might prove beneficial to us.

November 14 (Saturday)

At Chattanooga, Sherman had finally arrived, leaving his wagon train at Bridgeport and rushing forward to see Grant. Immediately, Grant, Thomas, and he went for a tour of the lines to discuss strategy. What Sherman saw was a valley shaped like a huge amphitheatre, running northeast to southwest, with the prominence of Missionary Ridge about three miles distant to the northeast. To the southwest was Lookout Mountain, which towered over Chattanooga. The ridges provided a grand panorama filled with the tents and camps of the Confederate Army.

Bache, Dallas, Asst. Surg., USA, Chattanooga, Tenn.:

In the middle of November it became evident, from the nature of the preparations … that a movement against the enemy was intended.… Supplies, in addition to those already on hand, were ordered from Nashville, and such of the churches and available buildings as had been previously completed were again refitted for the occupation of the wounded.…

November 15 (Sunday)

Perry, John G., Asst. Surg., USV, 20th Mass. Vols., near Mountain Run, Va.:

I wrote you, I think, of the wet, boggy ground we are encamped on. Last night it rained in torrents, and in five minutes the bottom of my tent held one or two inches of water. My couch is made of leaves packed between two logs, and by nine o'clock the water became so deep that it ran over the logs into the bed, and on waking I found myself perfectly drenched and everything I owned in the same condition.…

November 16 (Monday)

Hand, D. W., Surg., USV, Med. Dir., New Bern, N.C.:

Plymouth, N.C., had a garrison of three thousand men, five regiments, and the commanding officer kept the troops in good spirits by occasional expeditions to points on the different rivers emptying into Albemarle Sound. As at Washington, the troops and the newly erected breastworks were close upon the town. Much slashing had been done. The Roanoke River is here very deep, and its current swift; but the shores are low, and opposite the town the water spreads out for miles among the cypress roots and tall rank grass. In September, October, and November, 1863, this command suffered severely from malarial fever. At times full one-half the men would be off duty on account of sickness, and all suffered more or less from intermittent fever. Few cases of congestive fever, howerer, occurred, and the mortality was not great. As cold weather came on, the health of the men improved.…

November 19 (Thursday)

In Gettysburg, Pa., Pres. Lincoln delivered the brief and eloquent Gettysburg Address.

Meanwhile in Chattanooga, Tenn., Grant and his generals continued to plan their next move. Bragg was sitting at Chickamauga Station arguing with his generals, as usual.

November 20 (Friday)

Mrs. Bickerdyke, having come into the Chattanooga area, set up her field hospital about five miles from the city on the edge of a forest near the Tennessee River. The weather was extremely cold, with freezing rain and sleet. Tents were blown down, fires drowned, and life was generally miserable.

The hospital had been arranged with the tents around a central fire of huge logs, in the hope that the heat would help each of the tents. Over this fire were several iron caldrons. One contained boiling water for the ever-present laundry; a second was always filled with simmering soup; the third was used for washing the patients. Bricks from an old chimney nearby became bed warmers for the patients when heated by the fire. In all there was little to work with. Mrs. Bickerdyke did, however, have on hand several jugs of prime Confederate moonshine appropriated from a "captured" still.

At the prison near Alton, Ill., across from St. Louis, a Confederate prisoner reported his treatment during a bout with smallpox.

Thomas, D. C., Texas Cavalry, prisoner, Alton, Ill.:

The winter was unusually severe, even for this climate, and our supply of provisions, coal, and wood was very limited. I was soon prostrated with a severe fever, and when Dr. Riley visited me he pronounced it a distinct case of smallpox, and told me that it was his imperative duty to report it to the authorities, and that I would be sent to the smallpox island. Imagine my feelings. The Mississippi River was now frozen over, so that wagons loaded with green wood and drawn by six mules were constantly crossing on the ice. Soon after Dr. Riley pronounced mine a case of smallpox, two men placed me on a litter and carried me to the river's edge, where I was rolled onto a sled and drawn over the ice to the island, where I was again placed on a litter, carried into a tent and rolled off onto the ground. I told Dr. Gray, a Confederate prisoner on detail service, that I was a special friend of Dr. Riley, and requested that I be furnished with a bed. Dr. Gray inquired of a nurse if he could furnish me a place to lie down. The nurse replied that a man had just died, and that as soon as he was removed I could have his place.

This smallpox island was in the Mississippi River, between the Missouri and Illinois shores, and the hospitals were cloth tents. After waiting for some time I was carried into the tent and tumbled off onto the dead man's bunk, the nurse remarking: "They have sent some dead men over here for us to bury."

On the bunk were two pairs of blankets: one pair to lie on, and the other to cover with. A nurse approached, and asked how many blankets I had. I replied that I had three pairs, but that one was my private property, that I had brought with me. With an oath he snatched my blankets, remarking that I was entitled to but two pairs of blankets, and should have no more. I was as weak as a child and had a burning fever, but my anathemas dumfounded him, and without a word he laid my blankets on another bunk and left the tent. A convalescent prisoner named Lane was a witness to what had occurred, and when the nurse left the tent he brought my blankets and spread them over me, and said that a detail had been over that day from the prison and had washed and hung out to dry some blankets, and that as soon as it grew dark I should have another pair. He was true to his promise, and also took the socks off my feet, washed and dried them, and did all in his power to render me more comfortable. That night a nurse came round and

placed on my bunk a tin cup filled with a white fluid, which he said was milk. There was also a hard lump of boiled cornmeal in the cup. This he called mush. Being thirsty, I drank the white fluid, but did not know how to manage the lump, as I had no spoon. My good friend, Robinson, hearing through a returned convalescent of my condition, bribed a passing guard, and sent me a spoon and an apple. That night a man called for a nurse to come with a light, saying that a man was on him in his bunk. When the nurse came, the delirious man had gotten off the bunk and was sitting on the ground at the foot of it, dead. All day and all night, day after day, night after night, the groans and prayers of the poor, suffering prisoners could be heard piteously begging for water or for some trivial attention from the cold-hearted nurses.

November 21 (Saturday)

After a couple of days of moving troops in the mud around Chattanooga, Sherman was again on the move, crossing the Tennessee at Brown's Ferry and heading northeast for the Confederate right flank around Missionary Ridge. Sherman was to attack the north end of the ridge, Thomas the center. Hooker was to attack the Confederate left flank. There were delays, even more than usual, because of the heavy rains, and the roads were quagmires.

Perry, John G., Asst. Surg., USV, 20th Mass. Vols., near Mountain Run, Va.:

We are perfectly deluged with rain, and my tent, raised on logs, has a deep pool of water around it.... Next Thursday will be Thanksgiving Day. How I wish our men could have something extra to eat, poor fellows! They have had potatoes only about a dozen times since last June, and are becoming badly run-down. We have received from one of our officers now at the North a quantity of raisins, flour, pickles, etc., for Thanksgiving dinner, and we also have permission to send to Washington for more supplies. We officers do not need these extras, as our pay enables us to buy pickles and such things to prevent scurvy, but the men have not the money for luxuries.

November 22 (Sunday)

On Missionary Ridge, Ga., Gen. Braxton Bragg detached Gen. Simon Bolivar Buckner from his

Army of Tennessee and sent Buckner to Knoxville, Tenn., to support Gen. James Longstreet, who was besieging Union forces under Gen. Ambrose E. Burnside. Bragg was unaware that a storm of blue was about to descend upon him in the form of Grant's army. Gen. George Thomas was to demonstrate in front of Missionary Ridge the following day.

November 23 (Monday)

At Chattanooga, George Thomas sent the divisions of Maj. Gen. Philip H. Sheridan and Brig. Gen. T. J. Wood forward to demonstrate against the Confederate lines. They moved to about a mile from the Rebel lines, taking Orchard Knob with light opposition before dark. After dark, Sherman sent a brigade across the Tennessee near South Chickamauga Creek to prepare a bridge.

Blair, W. W., Surg., 58th Indiana Vols., Battle of Missionary Ridge:

On November 23d, at three o'clock in the afternoon, the grandest military movement of the war took place,... giving us as a result, possession of the enemy's line of rifle pits, passing over the summit of Orchard Knob. The wounded were promptly removed from the field.... That night and the next day were spent in administering to the wants of the wounded.... During the assault on Missionary Ridge,... together with the advance upon Orchard Knob, we lost from the entire division one hundred and sixty killed, and eight hundred and seventy-three wounded....

November 24 (Tuesday)

Very early on this morning, the blue-clad troops of Gen. Joseph Hooker crossed Lookout Creek and began the climb up Lookout Mountain to what was to become known as the "Battle Above the Clouds," so named because the top of the mountain was shrouded in mist. Little opposition was met, because most of the Confederate troops had withdrawn to Missionary Ridge. Even then, by midafternoon the wounded were stumbling down Lookout Mountain and being carried by stretcher-bearers to Mrs. Bickerdyke's hospital. By night, the tents were half-full. When a lull in the fighting occurred, a flood of wounded arrived at the hospital to be laid on the frozen ground or propped up against trees when all the tents were full. Outside the operating tent, a pile of amputated limbs grew rapidly.

Menzies, S. G., Surg., USV, 1st Div., 4th Corps, Battle of Lookout Mountain, Tenn.:

By three o'clock on the morning of the 24th, orders came to ... move on the mountain, which was done.... I established a temporary field hospital at the foot of the mountain, and received the wounded as they were brought down, which was done with great difficulty. The ambulances could go but little way up the ascent, and the men had to be carried over a very rocky and almost precipitous surface....

In taking Lookout Mountain the troops ... bore a conspicuous part throughout the day, and deep into the night of the 24th, when they bivouacked on a slope under the jutting rock specially designated Lookout, near the White House. During this day and night Surg. Beach, of the 2d Brigade, with several assistant surgeons, was on the field, giving temporary relief to the sufferers, and sending them back to us in the bottom....

On the Confederate right, Sherman had captured what he thought was the north end of the ridge, only to find that he was on high ground but that a ravine separated him from the real ridge and Tunnel Hill, one of his main objectives. Things settled down for the night.

Moore, John, Surg., USA, Med. Dir., Army of the Tennessee, Chattanooga, Tenn.:

The hill was in our possession before four in the afternoon, with no other casualty than a severe flesh wound.... Up to this time it had not been decided whether the hospital should be established on the eastern or western side of the river. The great convenience of having them on the same side as the troops engaged was, of course, obvious.... But when we had possession of a portion of the ridge, and saw the range of the enemy's shot, it was decided to place hospitals in suitable positions near the bridge, about five miles above Chattanooga, and two in rear of our line of battle....

November 25 (Wednesday)

In the early dawn, Sherman's men moved against the north end of Missionary Ridge and Tunnel Hill, the latter being held by Gen. Patrick Cleburne's troops. Heavy fighting continued until about 2 P.M. with little or no progress being made. Hooker, on the Confederate left, was also having little luck. Grant then sent Thomas with four divisions against the center. The Union troops advanced rapidly from the base of the ridge, overwhelming the Confederate line and driving them up the steep slope. The Confederates on top couldn't fire for fear of hitting their own men, and it became a footrace up the steep slopes, the Federals reaching the top in some places before the Rebels. The Confederates then broke and ran down the back slope of the ridge towards Chickamauga Creek, where some waded through the icy water rather than going to the bridges. The continued Union assault up the ridge had been unplanned, and it seemed that the troops had taken it upon themselves to take the ridge. Sheridan's division pursued the Confederates, but Hardee's corps held them off and then the Rebels withdrew in the darkness.

The battle was over, the siege of Chattanooga was broken, and Bragg's army was beaten, but intact. Grant, with his typical aggressive style, issued orders for a follow-up at first light. The Federal troops, feeling avenged for the defeat at Chickamauga, screamed at the top of their lungs, "Chickamauga! Chickamauga!"

Bache, Dallas, Asst. Surg., USA, Chattanooga, Tenn.:

The wounded men were more readily and rapidly cared for than [after] any previous battle of that army. The ambulance trains moved rapidly from the town to the front, only a distance of two or three miles, and returned with their loads. In this way all were comfortably housed, except here and there some severely wounded man who had found his way to some house, and was unable to report his situation.... Here admirable opportunity was offered for the prompt exercise of surgical skill in primary operations, but the previous health of the men had been so much lowered by deficient food, that the success was in no wise flattering.... The hospitals were much overcrowded, as only those able to bear exposure and fatigue could be safely sent to the rear by the journey of boats and cars. Hospital gangrene now manifested itself, attacking with few exceptions ... the [amputees'] stumps.

Although the line of railroad was now entirely in our possession, it was not until the middle of January that the trains commenced their regular trips from Nashville, and the hospital train could be used to deplete the crowded hospitals. In the meantime, on account of the severe weather, it was impossible to send any more sick or wounded by the regular way, so that all were held in Chattanooga....

About four hundred Rebel wounded and thirteen of their medical officers fell into our hands at this battle. They were assigned to several buildings, and one of their number placed in charge of the whole. They kept their hospitals in the filth that seems necessary to their comfort, and showed a want of interest in the care of their patients, that was attended with the usual results....

Moore, John, Surg., USA, Med. Dir., Army of the Tennessee, Chattanooga, Tenn.:

About nine o'clock the following morning, portions of the corps were constantly engaged near the Rebel entrenched positions at Tunnel Hill, from this time until about four in the afternoon.... Great numbers were killed or wounded. As soon as the action commenced, the ambulances, of which there were two to a regiment, with their stretcher-bearers, were sent out to the front. Owing to the fact that the firing of the enemy was nearly parallel with the direction of the ridge, the ambulances came safely to the foot of it, thus getting much nearer than is usual during the ... engagement, and in this way greatly facilitated the removal of the wounded....

All the wounded were brought off before night, except a small number who fell so near the Rebel entrenchments that they could not be reached. But all these were brought off before ten o'clock that night, when it was found that the enemy had abandoned his position....

At Mrs. Bickerdyke's hospital, the men whose limbs had been amputated began the old plea, "Would someone make sure my arm (or leg) is properly buried?" Bickerdyke always assured them that the limb would receive proper burial, although they both knew that the limbs would be piled somewhere in a remote clearing, doused with kerosene, and burned. Whole bodies of the dead, both Union and Confederate, were given proper burial, but no one had time to provide that for amputated limbs.

Bickerdyke usually provided a ration of her favorite postoperative dish to patients after surgery. This dish she called *panado* and it was made of a mixture of whiskey, hot water, brown sugar, and crumbled hardtack prepared thick enough to eat with a spoon. Although a strong temperance supporter, the mixture of the whiskey with the other ingredients somehow endowed the mixture with medicinal properties not available as separate entities.

During the night a major storm arrived, bringing high winds and sleet. Men had been detailed to cut down trees to feed the fires of the hospital and at this point a good stock was on hand. Bickerdyke and her helpers were kept busy tending the wounded and feeding them soup from steaming caldrons. By this time there were nearly 2000 patients in their hospital.

Perry, John G., Asst. Surg., USV, 20th Mass. Vols., near Mountain Run, Va.:

Night before last, orders came to march at daylight. No fires could be lighted, and preparations were to be made in the strictest silence. A northeast storm was blowing, a drizzly rain falling, and everything was cold and cheerless. With the exception of one hour, when I took a hurried nap, I was up throughout the night preparing the sick and disabled for the move, and at five o'clock A.M., without coffee or anything to eat except wet hard bread, we started off. Rumor said we were bound for the Rapidan and Richmond.

It rained—oh, how it rained! We marched about half a mile through bog and mud, when we came upon a battery of artillery stuck fast. To go on seemed to all of us an impossibility, and while we halted, waiting to extricate the cannon, orders came to return to old quarters and again encamp. A cheer rose from every throat, and most fortunate it was, I think, that we did return, for the rain continued during the day and all of the following night. When re-reached the old camp I bailed out my little enclosure as one would bail out a leaky boat.

Asst. Surg. Perry would spend the remainder of 1863 and the early months of 1864 in the cold camps of the Army of the Potomac. While some activity would occur, little would happen until early May, 1864.

November 26 (Thursday)

The battle for Chattanooga was over. Sherman and Thomas drove Bragg's troops from Chickamauga Station towards Ringgold, Ga., without pause. Near Ringgold, Union troops clashed with Pat Cleburne's rear guard, and heavy fighting erupted. The Federals finally called a halt, and Bragg had a chance to regroup his army.

Moore, John, Surg., USA, Med. Dir., Army of the Tennessee, Chattanooga, Tenn.:

The cooking stoves and operating tables were at once put to important uses. A sufficient amount of beef essence, and all needed stimulants were on hand for use during the day, and, on the following day, a large supply of both these important articles, together with one thousand two hundred blankets, arrived from Nashville.... Straw was found in abundance in the neighborhood, and the tents being thickly littered with it made a comfortable bed, which was improved in all severely injured cases, by spreading a blanket or gutta-percha cloth over the straw....

In two of the divisions the tents were inadequate for the accommodation of their wounded, and temporary shelters, made of lumber taken from vacant buildings in the neighborhood, were improvised which answered the purpose. The weather for the first two or three days after the battle was warm and clear, and fires were not needed to make the hospitals comfortable. This time was improved to the utmost in extending and improving the appliances for cooking, by the erection of temporary kitchens out of poles, covering them with tent flies or boards, as well as collecting from houses in the neighborhood such large pots as were not essential for the use of the inhabitants. It should be added here that these articles were either returned to the owners or left [behind] on breaking up the hospitals....

Supplies composed of the ordinary soldier's ration were obtained from Chattanooga. This was varied and improved during the first ten days by additions in the way of mutton, chickens, and beef brought in by enterprising foraging parties from the surrounding country. These predatory excursions were then stopped by orders from the department commander....

About eight days after the battle, the weather became very cold, and as heating stoves were not to be had, other expedients for warming had to be resorted to. Where brick was obtainable it was used for the construction of chimneys or flues, and when this failed, chimneys were built of sticks and mud, or flues made through the tents by digging a small trench from the outside through the tent terminating from five to eight feet beyond the opposite side. This trench was then covered with flat stones, an inch or two of earth thrown over these, and a chimney or flue some eight or ten feet high erected at one end and a fire made in the other.... When properly covered with clay, this makes an admirable heating arrangement; the same flue then can be run through several tents....

In Washington, Col. William Hoffman, Federal Commissary-General of Prisoners, planned for the return of sick and wounded Union prisoners. Hoffman notified Surg. A. M. Clark:

You will proceed immediately to Fortress Monroe, Va., with a view to consult with Brig. Gen. S. A. Meredith, commissioner for the exchange of prisoners, in relation to making suitable provision on the flag of truce boat for the reception of sick Federal prisoners of war who may be delivered from time to time at City Point. Sufficient bedding should always be upon the boat when such deliveries are to be made, with a proper supply of such food as prisoners in their condition require, and ample accommodations for cooking. The boat should be prepared to deliver them at Annapolis and notice should be given to Col. Waite, commanding in that city, of the time of their arrival so that everything may be prepared for their reception in the general hospital or the hospital at Camp Parole....

November 27 (Friday)

At Chattanooga, the Confederates had withdrawn towards Ringgold Gap and Taylor's Ridge, closely followed by Grant's army. Now that the siege of Chattanooga was broken, Grant sent part of his troops to Knoxville to the relief of Burnside.

Moore, John, Surg., USA, Med. Dir., Army of the Tennessee, Chattanooga, Tenn.:

Two divisions were then ordered back to vicinity of Chattanooga; and the other two, in conjunction with the Eleventh Corps, under Gen. Howard, and part of the Fourth, under Gen. Gordon Granger, were ordered to ... Knoxville to relieve Gen. Burnside.... The distance was one hundred and twenty miles; the troops had but three days' rations, and the Eleventh and Fifteenth Corps were almost without tents or camp and garrison equipage of any kind. The weather turned very cold, and for several days the roads were frozen hard. The march was made. The siege was abandoned the day before our arrival, and on the following day the return march began....

Menzies, S. G., Surg., USV, 1st Div., 4th Corps, Battle of Lookout Mountain, Tenn.:

The 27th saw the soldiers bright and cheery, moving on Ringgold, which was reached at nine o'clock in the morning. Gen. Cruft's command formed the reserve. The divisions of Gens. Osterhaus and Geary attacked the enemy, who was posted in strong positions on the heights, and in a pass in the mountain. After a severe struggle of two hours, the Rebels retreated. Having no wounded of our own, I placed the surgeons' supplies, ambulances,... and rendered what assistance we could to their wounded.... After the battle ceased, many were taken into the town and placed in the Catoosa Hotel, the courthouse, and bank building....

November 28 (Saturday)

Sherman sent more troops, in addition to those sent with Gen. Granger, to relieve Burnside at Knoxville. Bragg, feeling despondent, was little at fault this time; he'd been defeated by overzealous Union soldiers who'd refused to stop at the bottom of Missionary Ridge.

Blair, W. W., Surg., 58th Indiana Vols., march to Knoxville, Tenn.:

On November 27th, the division was ordered to march to Knoxville, with all possible speed.... November 28th, we started our march. Owing to the very limited amount of clothing in the quartermaster's department, our troops were compelled to start upon this march of more than one hundred miles, in a very destitute condition, many men being barefoot and without underclothing of any kind. We marched with great rapidity, making from fifteen to twenty-five miles per day.... On the way up, knowing that many of our men were totally barefoot, I suggested that moccasins be made from the skins of the animals slaughtered on the march. This suggestion was extensively followed, adding at least something to the comfort of our men. Notwithstanding the limited clothing and shelter, the health of the command continued good, and in many instances, owing to the complete change in diet, for we were compelled to subsist upon food collected from the country,... there was a marked improvement in health....

Hand, D. W., Surg., USV, Med. Dir., New Bern, N.C.:

Around Beaufort harbor, doing garrison duty at Beaufort, Ft. Macon, Morehead City, and Newport, were stationed about two thousand two hundred men, who, during the fall of 1863 escaped the malarial fevers and were in excellent health. On the line of the railroad from New Bern to Morehead City were two stations, Croatan and Havelock, where, from fifty to one hundred men were constantly kept. These posts were in the midst of swamps, and the men suffered so much from intermittent fever, that they had to be relieved every ten days.

Farther down on the railroad, at Newport, Caroline City, and Morehead City, the prevailing winds came directly from the sea, and the troops at these points were free from malarial fever. Several regiments, much broken-down by sickness, near New Bern, were removed, on my recommendation, to these places with marked benefit.

November 29 (Sunday)

The snow and ice in and around Knoxville, Tenn., made travel, even walking, difficult. About dawn, Longstreet sent his Confederates against the defenses of Ft. Sanders, one of the forts guarding the city. After a valiant effort, the grey-clad troops held the parapet for a short period of time, but had to retreat. This was Longstreet's last attempt to take Knoxville. He would retreat, knowing that Grant had reinforcements on the way.

November 30 (Monday)

Bragg had offered his resignation after the defeat at Missionary Ridge, and today he received a telegram from the War Dept. in Richmond accepting his offer. He would turn the army over to Gen. Hardee, who'd act as caretaker until a new commander was appointed. The Army of Tennessee was

slowing being pulled together after its near-rout from Missionary Ridge. The troops began to settle in for the winter.

December 2 (Wednesday)

In Dalton, Ga., Bragg turned over command to Lt. Gen. William Hardee. Hardee would be commander only a short time before Gen. Joseph E. Johnston arrived to assume leadership.

December 3 (Thursday)

At Knoxville, Longstreet began moving his troops away from the city, northeast to Greeneville, Tenn., effectively ending the siege. Tennessee was now almost occupied by Union forces.

December 4 (Friday)

D. C. Thomas, the Confederate prisoner at Alton, Ill., who'd been shipped to the island in the Mississippi suffering from smallpox, returned to the prison today.

Thomas, D. C., Texas Cavalry, prisoner, Alton, Ill.:

After some two weeks, ten or fifteen of us were pronounced sufficiently recovered to return to prison, and each of us was furnished with a pair of old blue pants with a large hole cut in the seat and an old army overcoat with the tail bobbed off in an unshapely manner. These garments, which they compelled us to wear, they called the "Jeff Davis uniform."

The sun had shown out for several days, and the ice on the river was beginning to thaw. We were marched across the river, a distance of about a mile, sinking into the mush ice up to the top of our shoes at every step, and when we reached the city and were again incarcerated in the old penitentiary my feet were wet, half-frozen, and a ring of ice around each ankle. Why this trip did not kill us all is more than I can explain....

December 6 (Sunday)

Maj. Gen. W. T. Sherman and his staff entered Knoxville, Tenn., on this date, officially ending the siege. Parts of his old Fifteenth Corps were close behind and coming up fast.

The railroad between Chattanooga and Nashville wasn't only unsafe, it was unsteady. It was also filled with military cargo when the trains were running.

With this problem, the Sanitary Commission formed a huge mule-drawn wagon train and sent it to Mrs. Bickerdyke at Chattanooga. Most of the cargo was dressings, clothing, and medicine. Very little food was sent, except for Bickerdyke's requested supply of yeast.

Using an abandoned mill, she soon had flour for bread, but no ovens. This problem was solved by using bricks from the chimney of a burned-out house, barrels, mud, and a lot of ingenuity. Soon crusty loaves of bread were being delivered to the patients. When the yeast ran out, she used salt-rising bread using fermented cornmeal as a leavening. On a good day the ovens could turn out nearly 500 loaves. All this effort was sincerely appreciated.

December 7 (Monday)

Maj. Gen. Benjamin F. Butler, famed as the "Beast of New Orleans," was now commanding the Dept. of Virginia and North Carolina, with headquarters at Ft. Monroe, Va. Butler learned of an epidemic of smallpox among the Federal prisoners confined at Belle Isle in Richmond and those farther west in Lynchburg, Va. Butler communicated with Robert Ould, Confederate Commissioner of Exchange in Richmond:

Sir: I have been informed that the smallpox has unfortunately broken out among the prisoners of war now in the hands of the Confederate authorities, both at Belle Isle and at Lynchburg.

Anxious from obvious humane considerations to prevent the spread of this terrible disorder, I have taken leave to forward for their use, by Maj. Mulford, assistant agent of exchange, in behalf of the United States, a package of vaccine matter sufficient, as my medical director informs me, to vaccinate six thousand persons. May I ask that it shall be applied under the direction of the proper medical officer to the use intended.

Being uncertain how far I can interfere as a matter of official duty, I beg you to consider this note either official or unofficial as may best serve the purposes of alleviating the distresses of these unfortunate men....

No formal receipt is needed; a note acknowledging the receipt of this being all that can be desired.

If more vaccine matter is necessary, it will be furnished....

Blair, W. W., Surg., 58th Indiana Vols., Knoxville, Tenn.:

On December 7th, we arrived in the vicinity of Knoxville, where we remained in bivouac about eight days; very few men were so ill as to require hospital treatment. On December 16th, we were ordered to march at once to Blain's Cross Roads to assist in repelling what was supposed to be an advance of the enemy. This supposition proved to be without foundation, and we remained quietly in camp in the vicinity of Flat Creek, until about the middle of January, 1864.

December 9 (Wednesday)

Two days ago, Robert Ould received, via Federal Maj. Mulford, a shipment of the smallpox vaccine matter to be used for the Federal prisoners at the Belle Isle and Lynchburg, Va., prisons. Mr. Ould today responded:

Sir: The package of vaccine matter has been received and will be faithfully devoted to the purposes indicated in your letter. Permit me in response to the friendly tone of your letter to assure you that it is my most anxious desire and will be my constant effort to do everything in my power to alleviate the miseries that spring out of this terrible war....

At Knoxville, Tenn., Maj. Gen. John G. Foster replaced Maj. Gen. Ambrose E. Burnside as commander of the Dept. of the Ohio. This replacement was primarily due to Burnside's failure to defeat Longstreet.

December 12 (Saturday)

Hand, D. W., Surg., USV, Med. Dir., New Bern, N.C.:

At Morehead City, the Mansfield General Hospital was opened in September, 1863, with a capacity of three hundred beds. A general hospital, with a capacity of two hundred beds was already in operation at Beaufort, on the opposite side of the sound. To these hospitals the convalescents and slight fever cases were removed from the post and regimental hospitals at New Bern, Washington, and Plymouth, and the patients rapidly recovered. It was noticed, however, that very many men coming to the seashore from the interior would have chills developed at once, and others would have slight attacks, much aggravated at first. It was found to be the same with persons going north who had long been exposed to the malarial poison.

Washington, N.C., was garrisoned by a force of eighteen hundred men. This town is on the Tau River, and is nearly surrounded by swamps and low marshes. The pickets were close in. The entrenchments about the town were early thrown up and very circumscribed. Much slashing had been done in front of the breastworks and a fine grove of cedar trees on the riverbank, southwest of the town, had been foolishly cut down. In consequence, the malarial fevers this fall were very violent and prevailed to an alarming extent. Few men there escaped an attack of chills, and in October, cases of congestive fever were very frequent. Most of these at first proved fatal; but through the energy and promptness of the medical officers on duty there, these cases soon became manageable and nearly all recovered. It was noticed that the men were generally seized at night and often while on guard and finding that only the most vigorous and prompt treatment promised success, the medical officers arranged to have bathtubs and hot water constantly on hand at their hospitals and skilled attendants on duty there night and day. A hot bath, with internal stimulation and free doses of quinine was found to be the successful treatment.... I repeatedly noticed that the men recovering from this congestive form of fever had a peculiar appearance of the eyes for several weeks after, looking as though there had been some effusion on the brain.

December 16 (Wednesday)

Today Gen. Joseph Eggleston Johnston, CSA, was assigned to command the Army of Tennessee, replacing Lt. Gen. William Hardee. Johnston, at Brandon, Miss., left his current command to Lt. Gen. Leonidas Polk.

December 17 (Thursday)

Surg. Spencer G. Welch was granted a furlough in November to return to South Carolina for a period. During his stay, his son George died of a childhood illness. Welch stayed over his leave for a period of one week to console his devastated wife, and then left for Virginia.

Welch, S. G., Surg., 20th S.C. Vols., in a letter to his wife, returning from home in South Carolina to Richmond, Va.:

I was delayed about ten hours in Charlotte, N.C., and did not arrive in Richmond until seven o'clock this morning. The weather was very agreeable for traveling and I had no trouble with my trunks.

I ate but once out of my haversack the whole way here. My appetite was gone, for the death of our dear little George, together with the parting from you in such deep grief, made me sadder than I ever felt before in my life. The heaviest pang of sorrow came upon me when I entered the train to leave....

I visited both houses of the Confederate Congress today and saw Col. Orr and others from our State, and also the distinguished men from other States.... I shall go on to Orange C.H. tomorrow and will write you....

In the hospital at Chattanooga, Mrs. Bickerdyke endured storms of wind and rain, keeping her patients fed and as warm as possible. Today, around the huge fires, she and her contrabands broiled beef and mutton, made soup and coffee, and dispensed *panado* as necessary, regardless of the weather.

Bickerdyke, always in her calico dress, had a problem with the fires burning holes in it. Mrs. Livermore obtained one of these dresses and later described it "burned so full of holes that it would hardly hang together when held up. It looked as if grape and canister had played hide-and-seek through it."

December 20 (Sunday)

Moore, John, Surg., USA, Med. Dir., Army of the Tennessee, Chattanooga, Tenn.:

On December 20th, arrived at Chattanooga, after a continuous march of eighteen days. The three days' rations were made to answer for eighteen by being eked out from the forced contributions of the farmers in the fertile valleys of east Tennessee. On the return march several hundred men were entirely barefoot. The weather was cold and the roads frequently frozen during the forenoon....

December 25 (Friday)

Christmas Day at the hospital in Chattanooga was dismal. Many packages were awaiting transport from Nashville on the railroad, but didn't have priority for shipment. Mrs. Bickerdyke, not to let her beloved "boys" go without some Christmas cheer, made molasses taffy for all the patients, who spent a reasonably happy day sitting around the fire, pulling taffy and swapping lies.

December 27 (Sunday)

The winter seemed to be a bad time for smallpox among the troops and for the general populace, in whatever location, North or South. New Bern, N.C., was no exception.

Hand, D. W., Surg., USV, Med. Dir., New Bern, N.C.:

> During the winter of 1863 and 1864, smallpox prevailed extensively among the refugees and negroes congregated in and about New Bern. Every effort was made to protect the soldiers by vaccination; but twenty-seven of them had variola or varioloid and six died. *Sarracenia purpurea* was at this time extensively used in the treatment of smallpox; but without any beneficial result. The hospital accommodations for smallpox patients at New Bern are excellent....

December 31 (Thursday)

The weather turned vile with icy winds sweeping down the mountains and through the valleys around Chattanooga, blowing down tents in the hospitals and driving rain onto the recovering patients, where it froze where it touched. The patients, trying to get out of the weather, became still sicker from broken bones and cold-related diseases. The rain flooded the area, flowing from the mountains into the valleys where the tents were located, and the water drowned many of the men before they could be moved.

Mrs. Bickerdyke worked like a demon to save the patients under her care, piling the fires higher and higher with logs, hoping for enough warmth to keep the men from freezing. Before midnight the fuel supply gave out and Bickerdyke went to the surgeon in charge to have more brought in. He refused to send men out in such weather, saying "We must try and pull through until morning, for nothing can be done tonight."

Mrs. Bickerdyke, of course, could not accept this as a solution. She approached a company of the Pioneer Corps nearby and asked them to tear down the breastworks close by and use them for the fires. The breastworks were of no defensive value, having already served their purpose during the campaign. At first the men demurred, knowing that official orders were required to destroy such works. But, after having been plied with helpings of Bickerdyke's *panado*, they decided that the lives of the wounded were more important than the orders, and they tore apart the breastworks for the fires. Meanwhile, Bickerdyke had huge vats of coffee, soup, and other warming items prepared for the men who were working and she even provided large barrels of cornmeal mixed with hot water for the mules. Hot bricks were placed around the patients where possible, to help fight off the cold, while they were fed good soup and hot drinks.

From out of the rain and wind came 13 ambulances sent earlier from the hospital at Ringgold, Ga., carrying wounded men who'd been nearly 18 hours on the road. Mrs. Livermore described the scene:

> On opening the ambulances, what a spectacle met Mother Bickerdyke's eyes! They were filled with wounded men nearly chilled to death. The hands of one were frozen like marble. The feet of another, the face of another, the bowels of a fourth, who afterwards died. Every bandage had stiffened into ice. The kegs of water had become solid crystal; and the men, who were past complaining, almost past suffering, were dropping into the sleep that ends in death. The surgeons of the hospital were all at work through the night with Mrs. Bickerdyke, and came promptly to the relief of these poor men, hardly one of whom escaped amputation of frozen limbs from that night's fearful ride.

1864

January 1 (Friday)

Last night's ordeal wasn't over at Mrs. Bickerdyke's hospital at Chattanooga. The fires were still burning to keep the patients warm, and Bickerdyke was still working trying to save as many as possible. The troops supplying the firewood from the dismantled breastworks kept the supply coming until such time as the woodcutters could go out into the woods for more, which would be at full daylight.

Meanwhile, the officer in command of the area learned of Mrs. Bickerdyke's exploits and went down to investigate. There he found the breastwork in a state of dismemberment, and although he recognized the necessity for it, it was still against regulations. Seeking Mrs. Bickerdyke, he said to her, "Madam, consider yourself under arrest!" Her reply was, "All right, Major! I'm arrested! Only don't meddle with me till the weather moderates; for my men will freeze to death, if you do!" Then she continued carrying warm bricks and hot soup to the patients.

Later, there was a court of inquiry. They attempted to fault her for her actions, but she'd have none of it. Her response to the court was:

It's lucky for you, old fellows, that I did what I did. For if I hadn't, hundreds of men in the hospital tents would have frozen to death. No one at the North would have blamed *me*, but there would have been such a hullabaloo about your heads for allowing it to happen, that you would have lost them, whether or no.

In this aspect Bickerdyke was absolutely right, and the officers knew it. Had the patients frozen because no firewood was provided when a forest stood nearby, heads would have rolled because of the rage in the Northern press.

The men for whom she labored so long knew and appreciated her efforts. For some time afterwards she was greeted with three cheers when she appeared, until she demanded that they stop "such foolishness." Bickerdyke was tired and needed a rest badly.

Near Dalton, Ga., Gen. Joseph E. Johnston's Confederate Army also felt the cold.

January 2 (Saturday)

The medical authorities hadn't, as yet, made any connection with the real cause of the malaria among the troops in swampy areas. Surg. Hand, again, noted that where the wind blew from the sea, the presence of malaria decreased.

Hand, D. W., Surg., USV, Med. Dir., New Bern, N.C.:

Since the capture of Roanoke Island, about five hundred men have usually been kept there. The western part of the island, which is swampy, proved to be unhealthy, while the eastern and northern portions, being near the sea, were found to be nearly free from malarial fever. At Hatteras Inlet, one hundred and fifty men have done garrison duty since the capture of the forts there. They have always been free from epidemic or endemic disease.

January 3 (Sunday)

During this month, the 65th U.S. Colored Infantry would be organized and mustered into service. During the next 15 months, 755 of its 1000 men would die of disease, accident, or in Confederate prisons. *Yet the regiment suffered not one battle casualty!*

Welch, S. G., Surg., 20th S.C. Vols., in a letter to his wife, from Orange C.H., Va.:

The cars ran off the track below Gordonsville yesterday, consequently we have no mail today. You do not know how anxious I am to hear from you. Your letters relieve the distress of my mind like a soothing balm placed upon a painful wound. I am sure I could forget the loss of our dearest earthly object much sooner if I could only be with you; but time will blunt the keenest thorns of anguish....

Our weather remains intensely cold, but the wind has abated somewhat today. I think yesterday was the coldest day I ever experienced, and it was made worse by the strong biting wind which blew incessantly. It is most severe on the wagoners and others who are out and exposed so much....

I gave my old black coat to my brother. It fits him well and he is very much pleased with it. He has been keeping a chicken and it is now nearly grown, so we intend to have a big dinner soon, and will make a pot of dumplings and also have stewed corn and Irish potatoes....

January 5 (Tuesday)

Last month, December 1863, two agents of the Christian Commission had applied for transportation to Chattanooga from Nashville for themselves and a wagon load of religious tracts and Bibles. This was during the time of the nonmilitary-goods embargo on the rail line between the two points, and the agents met with Sherman's firm and final refusal: "Certainly not. There is more need of gunpowder and oats than any moral or religious instruction. Every regiment at the front has a chaplain."

The Christian Commission was a hybrid organization consisting of the Young Men's Christian Association (YMCA), the American Bible Society, and the American Tract Society. The Commission's purpose was clearly defined when its members first appealed for funds from the public:

The chaplains wish our aid, Christians in the army call for it; and the precious souls of thousands, daily exposed to death and yet unprepared, demand it of us, in the name of Him who died for us. It is a field white unto the harvest. The soldiers are ready to hear the Word of God spoken in love, and to receive the printed pages. Brethren, will you aid us?

In the east, the Christian Commission visited hospitals and camps, held services, gathered converts into the flock, and admonished the sinful and the backsliders. The Commission finally decided to expand into the western theatre of operations, but it wasn't necessarily prepared for the long distances and the hardships involved in following a western army.

Another problem was the Christian Commission's interaction with the U.S. Sanitary Commission, which operated in the east, and the Northwestern Sanitary Commission, which operated out of Chicago. All three organizations distributed religious tracts, counselled the wounded and dying, prayed for the sinful, etc., but the latecomers, the Christian Commission, didn't get a start on a large scale until late in the war, and it was only in this year, 1864, that its tentacles were reaching into the western theatre.

The Christian Commission agents, Protestant ministers J. F. Loyd and H. D. Lathrop, were from Cincinnati. Upon arriving in Chattanooga, they found their job in the hospitals, calling on the sick and dying, but this was too *tame* for them. They wished to go to the front among the battle casualties and do their good works, but their request was denied by Sherman. So they applied to Mrs. Bickerdyke, who got them the authority. The ministers didn't realize that Mrs. Bickerdyke wasn't above exacting her pound of flesh for favors given—if it benefitted her "boys." In the hospital, where she put the ministers to work bathing the patients, the Commission's agents wrestled the devil for the patients' souls.

January 9 (Saturday)

At Pilot Knob, Mo., the Superintendent of Refugees, Chaplain A. Wright, received large shipments of clothing and shoes, glazed window sash for new refugee buildings, axes for women to cut their own fuel, and medicines for the sick—all from the Western Sanitary Commission in St. Louis. These materials were distributed to, or used for, the benefit of the refugees during that cold winter.

Chaplain Wright wrote about the winter and the suffering of the people and animals during that season:

> The winter of 1863-64 will long be remembered by the inhabitants of southeast Missouri as one of unparalleled severity. Cattle and horse by hundreds died of starvation, and it was heartrending to see the poor beasts, that brought their miserable riders to the post of Pilot Knob for the rations allowed by the Government, gnaw the fences and boards where they were tied, in a vain attempt to appease their hunger. Many dropped down in the road, and died in a few minutes. Not a pound of forage for beast, or food for man, could be bought at any price for hundreds of miles from that post.

A boost came from Union Brig. Gen. Clinton B. Fisk, commander of the District of St. Louis, and his wife, who procured hundreds of dollars' worth of material for clothing as donations from the merchants of St. Louis. The clothing was taken to Pilot Knob for distribution.

January 11 (Monday)

An analysis of medical-department operations in the Army of the Potomac was conducted during the year 1864 by Asst. Surg. J. S. Billings, USA. Dr. Billings' report was presented late in the year to the Medical Director of the Army of the Potomac.

By December 1864, the Army of the Potomac had undergone some revolutionary changes in the organization of its medical services. The separation of ambulance drivers and attendants into a separate *Ambulance Corps* was now being organized, and was well on its way to completion. This concept would have far-reaching effects on medical organization within the entire army.

Billings, J. S., Asst. Surg., USA, Army of the Potomac, Va.:

> In the majority of instances, and especially in the case of the wounded, the patients have been sent to depot hospitals in the rear, within forty-eight hours after their entrance into the field hospitals. The primary treatment of the sick and wounded has been furnished almost exclusively in the division hospitals,

the regimental medical officers having been able to do but little for the serious cases. The organization of the medical staff of these hospitals has been essentially that prescribed by Dr. Letterman, viz:

> One surgeon in charge of the hospital, three operating surgeons, each with two or three assistants, one medical officer to provide food and shelter, and one to act as recorder, the last-named officer being usually assisted by the chaplains and by one or two hospital stewards.

> The corps of the army have almost always acted as units in the several battles, and the division hospitals of each corps have therefore been placed together, forming a sort of corps hospital, the location of which has usually been selected by the corps medical director and chief ambulance officer; thus removing one of the principal motives which formerly impelled the surgeon-in-chief of [a] division to remain at headquarters and ascertain the position of the line of battle of the division in order that he might place his hospital properly. Owing to the rapid and extensive movements of the army, necessitating prompt action in the disposal of the wounded, it was necessary that the corps medical directors should be able to find the surgeons-in-chief of divisions at any moment, which was best effected by having them all stationed at the point where his work was to be done, viz, the hospital.

> The presence of the surgeons-in-chief of divisions at their hospitals has undoubtedly been of great benefit to these institutions; but, on the other hand, there has been too little supervision of the medical officers at the advance depots near the line of battle, and complaints that no medical officer could be found near the front when an engagement was going on have been frequent, and in some cases well founded.

> During an engagement each division hospital is a general hospital, receiving wounded from all divisions and corps if necessary. The medical officers sent to the front with their regiments formed brigade depots in the Fifth and Sixth Corps; in the Second Corps they usually followed their regiments. In the Ninth Corps, *they were ordered by the corps medical director to remain within three hundred yards of the line of battle at all times, each being behind his own regiment, a position in which they were about as useless as they well could be.* [Italics added.]

January 14 (Thursday)

On this day, Surg. Thomas A. McParlin, U.S. Army, replaced Surg. Jonathan Letterman, U.S. Army, as Medical Director of the Army of the Potomac. Surg. McParlin reported to Maj. Gen. George G. Meade, then commanding the Army of the Potomac.

January 15 (Friday)

Perry, John G., Asst. Surg., USV, 20th Mass. Vols., near Stevensburg, Va.:

I am out on picket duty, as the surgeon detailed for the work is ill. Gen. Hancock has forbidden covers or fires at the outposts, and consequently half of the men from the picket line come back ill, as they are exposed to inclemency of the weather for three days at a time. There is nothing in the world to do here, and at night we have to lie on the snow and try to sleep, frozen almost to death. The cold has been most unusual this winter....

The refugee situation at Rolla, in southwestern Missouri, was very bad this winter. Chaplain A. H. Tucker wrote:

Refugees are constantly coming in from the southwest. There are now over two hundred destitute families here partly subsisted by Government. There is a great deal of sickness among them, and assistance by way of something nourishing for the sick to eat is much needed. The schoolbooks and clothing were duly received, and according to My. Yeatman's orders turned over to Dr. Hanson, and the Ladies' Refugee Society.

January 16 (Saturday)

Welch, S. G., Surg., 20th S.C. Vols., Orange C.H., Va.:

The army is filling up with conscripts, absentees and others, and if we get also the principals of the substitutes our army will soon be very formidable. Mose Cappock has returned, although his wound has not quite healed....

An officer in our regiment was cashiered for forging a furlough, sure enough. I feel very sorry for him and think he should go to the Yankees the first chance he gets, for he is ruined wherever this thing becomes known.

The winter has been unusually severe so far, but I am perfectly comfortable in every way, except that our diet is becoming anything else but bountiful or extravagant. We draw a little coffee and sugar occasionally. For breakfast this morning I had a cup of "Pure Rio," some ham, rice, biscuit and butter, but I have a hankering for such things as syrup, sweet potatoes, sauerkraut, and the like....

Edwin still has some of the good things to eat which he brought from home in his trunk. His servant, Tony, stole some of his syrup to give to a negro girl who lives near our camp, and Ed gave him a pretty thorough thrashing for it. He says Tony is too much of a thief to suit him and he intends to send him back home. I had to give Gabriel a little thrashing this morning for "jawing" me. I hate very much to raise a violent hand against a person as old as Gabriel, although he is black and a slave. He is too slow for me, and I intend to send him back [with] Billie when he goes home on furlough....

January 19 (Tuesday)

Billings, J. S., Asst. Surg., USA, Army of the Potomac, Va.:

The best and most complete system in all its parts was that adopted by Surg. J. J. Milhau, USA, medical director of the Fifth Corps. He proceeded on the principle that a medical officer is a general staff officer and a regimental officer only in name. The medical officers were collected in groups behind each division, as near the front as an ambulance could be brought, and two or three ambulances stood close by ready to move. *This was called the ambulance picket.* [Italics added.] Each medical officer had a pocket case and a hospital knapsack, or field companion. The position was protected from musketry fire, either by the nature of the ground, or by a small breastwork of logs and earth, thick enough to stop a rifle ball, and a small hospital flag was planted on the top. Further to the rear, in a position as secure as possible from shell and musketry, was the ambulance picket reserve, where eight or ten ambulances were kept in readiness. A medicine wagon was also on the spot when no engagement was going on or imminent. When one ambulance came in loaded, another passed out from the picket reserve to take its place.

During a battle, all the ambulances of the corps were at the reserve, with the exception of those on picket, or moving to the hospitals with wounded. In this way but few ambulances were under fire at any one time, and yet they were always ready. The labor of receiving, collecting, and transporting wounded from the front to the ambulance picket was performed by stretcher-bearers, under the direction of the officers of the ambulance corps.

January 26 (Tuesday)

McParlin, T. A., Surg., Med. Dir., Army of the Potomac, Culpeper, Va.:

The country, being elevated and undulating, afforded excellent sites for camps, which were generally well located, well drained and supplied with good springwater. The winter quarters of the troops were completed during the month of January, consisting for the most part of log huts about eight feet square, the walls four feet high, and roofed with shelter tents, each hut accommodating from three to five men. Much skill and taste was evinced in the arrangement of many of the camps. Those of the Maine regiments were especially noticeable for the neatness and comfort of their huts. The beds of the men were in all cases raised from the ground, and the huts were warmed by open fireplaces. The rations furnished ... were abundant in quantity, and of good quality and variety, the average weekly issue, including three days' rations of fresh beef, three-and-a-half of fresh bread, four-and-a-half of potatoes and two-and-a-third of other vegetables....

The clothing and bedding of the men were abundant and of good quality. The camp and personal police were,... well attended to. The *morale* of the troops was excellent....

January 28 (Thursday)

After getting settled in, Surg. McParlin inspected the medical departments of the Army of the Potomac to ascertain their combat readiness. The new Ambulance Corps, designed and implemented by his predecessor, Surg. Letterman, wasn't as yet in effect and working in all cases.

McParlin, T. A., Surg., Med. Dir., Army of the Potomac, Culpeper, Va.:

Frequent inspections were made to secure all wagons, harness, mules, camp and garrison equipage, clothing

and other quartermaster's property, and funds were drawn by the ambulance corps as required for the duties incident to the care and comfort of the sick and wounded. It was constantly necessary to preserve the division of responsibility and property between the medical and ambulance officers, that each should receive and account for what was proper to his own department. Neglect to make returns, followed by stoppage of pay, were otherwise to be expected in the new organization. Attempts were made to institute some system of ambulance service to meet the necessities of the artillery reserve, but without success, until the order promulgating the ambulance law was issued.

January 30 (Saturday)

Surg. Welch received a "box" from home. From the contents, it must have been quite large and heavy. It was a wonder that it survived the trip from South Carolina.

Welch, S. G., Surg., 20th S.C. Vols., Orange C.H., Va.:

The weather has been fine recently and there have been some indications of a move....

About ten days ago I succeeded in buying some turnips and cabbage, and I found them most delightful for a change until our box from home arrived. Everything in it was in excellent condition except the sweet potatoes. It contained ten gallons of kraut, ten of molasses, forty pounds of flour, twelve of butter, one-half bushel of Irish potatoes, one-half peck of onions, about one peck of sausage, one ham, one side of bacon and some cabbage....

January 31 (Sunday)

In Danville, Va., the Confederate government had established a prison stockade outside of the town and placed the prison hospital in the middle of town. Danville's residents were very concerned about this situation. They wrote the Confederate Secy. of War, James A. Seddon, on this date:

Your petitioners, the mayor and common council of Danville, would respectfully represent that we deem it our imperative duty earnestly to petition for the removal of the Yankee prisoners located among us to some other place, or at least outside the limits of the corporation of Danville. The reasons for this application, which are embodied in this petition are explained by the certificates hereto annexed.

The hospitals of the prisoners and sick are located in the very heart of the town, and are not all in one place, but scattered in the most public and business places, so as to infect the whole atmosphere of the town with smallpox and fever now raging within the limits of the corporation. Your petitioners fear mostly the increase of the number of cases of fever and the virulence of the same.

The stench from the hospitals even now (in winter) is almost insupportable, and is offensive at the distance of several hundred yards. We are advised by our medical advisers, the board of health, that they believe the great number of cases of fever now in Danville proceeds from the cause above indicated. Your petitioners believe that no police regulations, however efficient, can remove the evil from which they apprehend so much mischief, particularly in the summer months. The filth of the neighborhood of the hospitals runs down in small sluggish branches that run nearly through the breadth of the town, and it is permitted to remain until a rain partially removes it, the most of it finding a permanent lodgment in the drains. The town has no waterworks to cleanse its streets.

February 1 (Monday)

Hand, D. W., Surg., USV, Med. Dir., New Bern, N.C.:

... a Rebel force under command of Maj. Gen. Pickett attempted to capture New Bern. The troops on outpost duty were driven in, and the reinforcements sent to them were met by the enemy and badly beaten. Our loss was twenty killed and about eighty wounded. Three hundred men were taken prisoners. The wounded fell into the hands of the enemy. Ample preparations were made at the Foster hospital for the reception of the wounded at this time; but, after besieging the town two days, and making one unsuccessful assault, Gen. Pickett withdrew his troops....

February 4 (Thursday)

For the last month, the Union forces had been concentrating for an expedition on the area around Jacksonville, Fla., to devastate the area

and destroy, if possible, the Confederate military forces in that area. The Union Medical Director, Dept. of the South, was today notified to send his sick patients to the general hospital, turn in all excess medical supplies, and be ready to board steamers for the attack on Jacksonville. There were some problems.

Swift, E., Surg., USA, Med. Dir., preparing for the Jacksonville expedition, while in Hilton Head, S.C.:

I telegraphed to the assistant quartermaster at Beaufort, Capt. Moore, to send to Hilton Head, by the first boat, ten ambulances. In reply to this, Surg. M. Clymer, USV, telegraphed that Capt. Moore refused to let the ambulances be sent unless an order from Gen. Gillmore was given through the chief quartermaster. This difficulty was finally overcome by personal [contact with] ... Gen. Turner, Chief of Staff, who issued a positive order to the quartermaster, and, on the following day, six ambulances were forwarded, and sent to Florida. I also shipped in the steamer *Maple Leaf*, eight ambulances....

February 6 (Saturday)

McParlin seemed to use the tax on newspaper vendors and sutlers to a great advantage during this long winter on the Rapidan. The fund created by this tax was unique to the Army of the Potomac, the tax not being imposed in the western armies of Grant and Sherman.

McParlin, T. A., Surg., Med. Dir., Army of the Potomac, Culpeper, Va.:

The sick of the army were chiefly treated in regimental hospitals during the early part of the winter. Division hospitals, to which the more severe cases were sent, were organized during the month of February. These hospitals were floored with boards, and heated by means of open fireplaces, and their condition ... was in every way good. Jellies and canned fruits were kept on hand and issued by the medical purveyor and *from the fund created by the tax on newspaper vendors and sutlers,* [Italics added] which had been put at the disposal of the medical director of the army. Funds were turned over to the medical directors of [the] corps ... to be expended for oysters, and other delicacies required by the sick....

February 7 (Sunday)

Surg. Swift, determining what still was required for the expedition to Jacksonville, Fla., remained at Hilton Head, S.C., to wind things up, when he found that the general had taken his steamer.

Swift, E., Surg., USA, Med. Dir., preparing for the Jacksonville expedition, in Hilton Head S.C.:

Hourly expecting a hospital steamer from New York, I delayed embarking till her arrival, in order that I might make any additions which might be found necessary in her supply and equipment. The commanding general, meeting the steamer at the bar, embarked on her with his staff, for Florida. I received the following communication from the general: "Steamer *Fulton*, February 8 [actually the 7th], 1864, Off Hilton Head, S.C.: I met the *Cosmopolitan* coming in and must take her, so that the *Fulton* can go back to the Head and discharge. You will have to do the best you can, and send forward the extra medical supplies on the first transport...." Procuring the steamer *Peconic* the same day, the 7th, I put on board of her the supplies of seven regiments....

Perry, John G., Asst. Surg., USV, 20th Mass. Vols., near Stevensburg, Va.:

Harry Abbot returned last night from his furlough, and Wendell Holmes, Jr., with him. It seemed strange enough to hear them talk of Boston affairs, balls, and such like. Wendell is very blue, and sits over the fire shivering. It is an awful strain to jump from every comfort into this rough life. Last night we bundled him in buffaloes, blankets, overcoats, and tents; yet he suffered and could not sleep. Airtight houses and furnace heat unfits one for this sort of thing. It is, of course, much colder at the North than here, but it is the dampness of the cold in this locality which pierces to the very marrow.

February 8 (Monday)

Today, Brig. Gen. Truman Seymour's Union troops began moving from Jacksonville, farther inland, skirmishing near Point Washington, Fla., and vicinity.

Swift, E., Surg., USA, Med. Dir., Jacksonville, Fla.:

On the following day, I joined the major general commanding on the St. John's River, and arrived at Jacksonville that night. On my arrival, I learned there had been that day, the 8th, some skirmishing, by which we had drawn the enemy from his position, and seized his camp, his supplies, and much valuable property, with but small loss on our side, three killed and twelve wounded....

Welch, S. G., Surg., 20th S.C. Vols., in a letter to his wife, from Orange C.H., Va.:

The Yankees advanced to the Rapidan River yesterday and we were ordered off to meet them. After some little fighting, they retired....

Billie and I are enjoying our box immensely—especially the sauerkraut.... I am sending you the soldier's paper which I take, and you will find it interesting....

February 9 (Tuesday)

Swift, E., Surg., USA, Med. Dir., Jacksonville, Fla.:

The following day, I procured permission from the major general commanding to occupy, and fit up for a hospital, a block of brick buildings, known as the Hoag block, for the accommodation of three hundred sick; this, he informed me, would be more than sufficient for the number of troops that would be sent to this district. The corner storeroom in this block, I designed to reserve for the use of the assistant purveyor, and at once transferred to it, from the steamboat *Peconic*, my medical supplies, and a quantity of Sanitary Commission stores brought from New York on our hospital boat. These [the Commission stores] were subsequently removed, without my knowledge, by the personal order of M. M. Marsh, the agent of the Commission, after I had notified Gen. Seymour, by telegram that these articles were available for issue. They consisted chiefly of potatoes, onions, and apples, and were supposed, at that time, to be needed by troops at the front....

February 10 (Wednesday)

Swift, E., Surg., USA, Med. Dir., Jacksonville, Fla.:

On the 10th, I made a reconnaissance up the St. John's, for oranges and vegetables for the hospitals, and to examine the condition of the hotel buildings at Magnolia and Green Cove Springs, with a view to the establishment of a sanitarium or convalescent hospital at this delightful invalid's home.... One of these, a newly finished building, was admirably adapted to my purpose and would accommodate more than three hundred men. I reported this to the general commanding, but was informed by him he could not afford the necessary guard to protect a hospital in such an exposed situation. The buildings have since been destroyed by the enemy. The wounded now arriving from the scene of the recent engagement, thirty-five miles from Jacksonville, I ordered Surg. Majer, USV, by telegraph, to send them on at once, and to use his ambulances for that purpose....

The last sentence of Surg. Swift's account, above, is interesting. Note that messages are being sent by *telegraph* as Union forces move inland. This indicates either that telegraph lines already existed and were being repaired and used as the force moved, *or* that the Union force was stringing its own lines for communication. Either way, this technology was an innovation brought about by the war.

February 11 (Thursday)

The Union force west of Jacksonville, Fla., further advanced towards Lake City, skirmishing with the Confederate forces in their front.

February 13 (Saturday)

Three days ago, Surg. Swift had told Surg. Majer, who accompanied the troops inland, to send the wounded to Jacksonville by ambulance as soon as possible. Today, Majer arrived without the wounded, informing Swift that they would be sent by rail as soon as the railroad was repaired. Swift, having waited for a week, went back to Hilton Head, S.C., to obtain the necessary furniture and stores to establish the hospital at Jacksonville. At this time, no further inland movement was expected.

February 14 (Sunday)

Inland from Jacksonville, Fla., the Union troops of Brig. Gen. Truman Seymour were divided and a portion sent to Gainesville, Fla., which was captured after a brief skirmish. The remaining force continued inland.

February 15 (Monday)

After capturing Gainesville, Fla., the Union forces of Brig. Gen. Seymour continued on to Fernandina,

Woodstock, and King's Ferry Mills, destroying anything that looked useful, sending the sick and wounded to the rear as they moved.

Perry, John G., Asst. Surg., USV, 20th Mass. Vols., near Stevensburg, Va.:

You can have no idea of the bitter cold of the last few days. Even the pail of water for bathing, which I set in the fireplace freezes! The ink in my pen freezes as I write. Last night, beside being in my bag with a single blanket over me, I had outside of that two overcoats, haversacks, boots, and every variety of thing, yet was too cold to sleep. One of our officers had three of his toes frozen during the night, while in bed. I am all puckered up by this weather, but find it healthy.

February 16 (Tuesday)

Col. Charles S. Wainwright took advantage of the lull in field activity to return to New York to recruit for his artillery units, and for a meeting of the State Agricultural Society and, also, to take a short leave. Departing the camp near Middleburg, Va., with his party on the 5th, he arrived in New York on the 6th. After his visit to Albany, he went to his home at The Meadows for a visit and returned to Albany, where he met with Gov. Seymour. One of the subjects discussed was the recruitment that was in process at the time of the "heavy" artillery regiments. These were designed to be used in fortifications and not for field duty. As such, they were very popular with the recruits, who saw a chance to serve without the discomfort of living in the field and being shot at all the time. Many of the regiments of this type had a strength of over 2000 men—nearly twice the size of the regular regiments.

Wainwright recruited replacements for his New York units, but due to the bureaucracy, he'd receive no credit for their enlistments. The credit would go to the local provost-marshal, who had the responsibility for recruiting. Wainwright recorded how the recruits were handled at Poughkeepsie:

Wainwright, Charles S., Col., N.Y. Artillery, Poughkeepsie, N.Y.:

Provost-marshals are most of them politicians. Platt of the Poughkeepsie *Eagle* holds the position in our district, and according to Mr. Pudney's account is proving himself a great rascal. He has accepted scores of men as volunteers whom he rejected on the draft three months ago as overage or physically exempt; many of whom, Pudney says, will not be able to stand a week's service. Then he retains his recruits at Poughkeepsie as long as he can before sending them to the depots, as he gets so much for their rations and quarters, which of course he makes as poor as possible. He has a large empty warehouse where they are crowded together in a condition little better than the "Libby." Pudney told me that he went there the other day to see one of his recruits who was sick; he found him lying on a little straw on the floor, in a crowded room, for there was no provision to separate the sick from the others. When he returned home he found his arms covered with lice from the sick man's body!—and this man was a very respectable, well-to-do man before he enlisted. Such treatment will cause the loss of a great many men by sickness and death; still more by desertion. Nor can one blame a decent man who is driven to deserting from being shut up in such close companionship with the lowest dregs of society....

Charles Wainwright returned to the Army of the Potomac and the First New York Artillery to participate in the final campaigns of the war. He survived Grant's drive through the Wilderness and on to Petersburg, seeing heavy fighting along the way. He was in on the chase of Lee's fleeing legions after the fall of Richmond, and he was at Appomattox for the surrender. Returning to Washington, he marched in the Grand Review and left the army immediately thereafter. He travelled to Europe, lived in New York for a period, and in 1902 he applied for his pension, while living in Washington, D.C.. He'd lived in the capital for the last 18 years and was now totally blind and suffered from the effects of malaria. He died at George Washington University Hospital on September 13, 1911, at age 84. His body was returned to New York for burial.

February 20 (Saturday)

Union forces under Brig. Gen. Truman Seymour had landed at Jacksonville, Fla., and moved inland. There had been little resistance, but this was about to change.

On the march from Barber's Plantation towards Lake City, Fla., Seymour's men approached Olustee, Fla., where they were met by Confederate forces under Brig. Gen. Joseph Finnegan. The only major battle to be fought in Florida began with an attack on the 5500 Federals by about 5000 Confederates. Two of the Union regiments, the 7th New Hampshire and the 8th U.S. Colored Troops, broke in the confusion of the battle and fell back. The Confederates kept up the pressure until nightfall, when the Federals fell back and withdrew from the field. The retreat to Jacksonville began, the Federals taking with them 203 killed, 1152 wounded. An additional 506 Union troops were missing, presumed prisoners. The Confederate losses were lighter: 93 killed, and 841 wounded.

Majer, Adolph, Surg., USV, Battle of Olustee, Fla.:

It becomes my duty to report the engagement ... occurring at a place known as Olustee, Florida, and distant from Jacksonville some forty-five or fifty miles in a westerly direction.... On the evening of February 19, 1864, the general commanding ordered his command to be in readiness, with several days' cooked rations, for a forward movement from Barber's Station, thirty-two miles from Jacksonville, on the Florida Central railroad.

At daybreak, February 20th, the command took its line of march on the road to Sanderson.... Passing Sanderson, the general commanding was informed that we should meet the enemy in force, fifteen thousand strong, some miles this side of Lake City.... About five miles farther on, our advance reported some sixty or seventy skirmishers of the enemy falling slowly back on the north side of the railroad toward Lake City.... The general ordered a halt and directed shells to be thrown through the pine barrens. Hardly had the second shell been thrown, when a solid shot fell directly in front of the staff. A second one, following closely on the first, and a third one passing in close proximity to our heads.... The infantry line of battle was ... formed. Soon our artillery fire became hotter and hotter, and the musketry incessant.

Looking for a convenient ambulance depot, I rode on our right toward a couple of log houses, the only buildings within many miles; but I found that these houses were so much exposed, that while inspecting them even, I was in danger.... About two hundred yards in the rear of our left wing, observing a cluster of pine trees, I directed our ambulances, twelve in number, to be drawn up in line, the surgeons preparing their instruments and appliances to be in readiness.... Our wounded men began to arrive, part walking, some in litters, and others in open ambulance wagons; first singly then in a steady stream increasing from a single row to a double and treble, and finally in a mass. In half-an-hour from the commencement of the action, stray shots passing through the pines and breaking off the trunks like canes, admonished us to remove the depot farther to the rear. Within one mile we drew our ambulances up behind a small stream and guarded in front by marshy ground, and secured a sufficiency of water, yet not suitable protection against missiles from the rifled guns.

The battle had been raging for three hours when we heard cheers from the front, and the firing ceased abruptly. Our troops fell back about a mile, and I received an order to bring our wounded as far to the rear as we could get with our limited transportation. Ambulances, caissons, army wagons, litters, single horses, carts, in short, every conceivable mode of conveyance was made use of to secure the large number of our wounded; and with a readiness which deserves high commendation, everyone endeavored to execute the order.

Our troops fell back to Barber's Station under the protection of our cavalry brigade ... While passing Sanderson, I sent the following telegram: *"To the Surgeon in charge of field hospital at Barber's Station:* A large number of wounded. Prepare coffee, tea and beef soup."

We reached Barber's Station at midnight, and unhappily, some forty cases of wounded had to be left at the ambulance depot near the battlefield, under the charge of Asst. Surg. C. A. Devendorf, 48th New York Volunteers, and twenty-three more at Sanderson, badly wounded. Two companies of cavalry were dismounted and saved eighty more men. We had now to take care of and forward by cars and wagons, eight hundred and sixty wounded, two hundred and fifteen of whom were at once placed on the hospital ship *Cosmopolitan*, at the wharf at Jacksonville....

The expedition into Florida and its occupation, we believed to be ... a sanguinary undertaking....

February 21 (Sunday)

Seymour's Union force, retreating after the battle at Olustee, Fla., fought rearguard actions with Finnegan's Confederate soldiers. The Rebels kept up the pressure as they repaired the railroads that had previously been destroyed by the advancing Federals. The blue-clad columns continued towards Jacksonville, their train of wounded in the advance.

February 22 (Monday)

Brig. Gen. Truman Seymour's Union troops reached Jacksonville and the protection of the Union gunboats lying in the harbor. The Federals effectively stopped the advance of Brig. Gen. Joseph Finnegan's Confederate troops, who'd been pursuing them since the Battle of Olustee, two days before. The wounded were loaded on the hospital transports as rapidly as possible and sent to Hilton Head, S.C. Much property had been destroyed, 296 men had been killed and 1993 wounded, North and South, and little else was accomplished.

Surg. Swift had returned to Hilton Head, and was unaware that the battle had been fought. He was still organizing equipment for a hospital to be established in Jacksonville.

February 23 (Tuesday)

Swift, E., Surg., USA, Med. Dir., Jacksonville, Fla.:

Arriving at Hilton Head, I gave instructions to Surg. Craven, medical purveyor, to pack for shipment to Jacksonville hospital furniture, dressings, medicines, etc., for five hundred beds. These articles were all shipped on the *Maple Leaf* on the 22d, and left for St. John's River. The evening of the same day, I embarked on the *Charles Houton*, and ... on the 23d, arrived at Jacksonville. I found the wounded comfortable; in fact, generally able to walk about. These are they who were reported as having been obliged to remain on board the steamer all night at Beaufort, by the intelligent reporter of the *Tribune*, implying neglect on the part of the medical officers at that place. I need not say the *Cosmopolitan* is as complete, and, in organization, as perfect as can be found in any general hospital; that her patients were comfortable in bed, and as the nights were damp and chilly, inhumanity would seem to be on the side of removal under the circumstances....

Soon after arriving in Jacksonville, I procured the steamer *Dictator* from the quartermaster's department, and put on board of her more than two hundred wounded; and though the medical officers were instructed to send to the boat only their worst wounded, these were not to exceed a dozen patients who were not able to walk about and help themselves. From a suspicion of malingering, and to prevent persons who should not from entering the boat, officers were stationed at each gangway, to examine all those who seemed to be not much injured. Many of them should never have been permitted to leave their regiments. On the third day after the engagement, all the seriously, and many of the slightly, wounded had already been sent to general hospital at Beaufort or Hilton Head.... I sent to the rear all sick and wounded who would not probably be fit for duty in two weeks....

Besides the twenty days' supply of medicines, etc., ordered to be taken by the medical officers ... I had stored the three months' supply of seven regiments and a liberal amount of these articles on the steamer *Cosmopolitan*, which I directed to be issued freely to the hospitals when wanted. Notwithstanding the unexpected battle, and some regiments being obliged to abandon their supplies, to burn or destroy them, to prevent their falling into the hands of the enemy, yet,... in all necessary articles there was enough and to spare when I arrived on the evening of the 23d with an abundance of everything....

March 3 (Thursday)

In Chattanooga, Tenn., Sherman's army was passing the weary winter days and waiting for spring and a new campaign. Mrs. Bickerdyke, worn by the long months of labor for her "boys," went North for a rest. She went to Chicago to see Mary Livermore, who described Bickerdyke's visit:

Now for the first time, and the only time, Mother Bickerdyke broke down. The hardships through which she'd passed, her labors, her fasting, her anxieties, had been sufficient to kill a dozen women. She was greatly reduced by them; and as soon as her place could be supplied by another matron, she came North, a mere shadow of her former self.

The same efforts were made to honor her as on a previous visit; but, as before, she put aside all invitations. She had rendered great service to the Wisconsin regiments in the Western army; and the people of Milwaukee, who were just then holding a fair for the relief of the sick and wounded soldiers,

would not be denied the pleasure of a visit from her. I accompanied her, for she refused to go anywhere to be lionized unless someone was with her, "to bear the brunt of the nonsense," as she phrased it. She was overwhelmed with attentions. The Milwaukee Chamber of Commerce had made an appropriation of twelve hundred dollars a month for hospital relief, to be continued until the end of the war. And she was invited to their handsome hall, to receive from them a formal expression of gratitude....

A very felicitous address was made [to] her by the president of the Board of Trade, [on] behalf of the state of Wisconsin, and she was eloquently thanked for her patriotic labors, and informed of the recent pledge by the Board. A reply was expected of her, which I feared she would decline to make; but she answered briefly, simply, and with great power:

"I am much obliged to you, gentlemen, for the kind things you have said. I haven't done much, no more than I ought; neither have you. I am glad you are going to give twelve hundred dollars a month for the poor fellows in the hospitals; for it's no more than you ought to do, and it isn't half as much as the soldiers in the hospitals have given for you. Suppose, gentlemen, you had got to give tonight one thousand dollars or your right leg, would it take long to decide which to surrender? Two thousand dollars or your right arm; five thousand dollars or both your eyes; all that you are worth for your life?

But I have got eighteen hundred boys in my hospital at Chattanooga who have given one arm, and one leg, and some have given both; and yet they don't seem to think they have done a great deal for their country. And the graveyard behind the hospital, and the battlefield a little farther off, contain the bodies of thousands who have freely given their lives to save you and your homes and your country from ruin. Oh, gentlemen of Milwaukee, don't let *us* be telling of what *we* have given, and what *we* have done! *We* have done nothing, and given nothing, in comparison with *them*! And it's our duty to keep on giving and doing just as long as there's a soldier down South fighting and suffering for us."

March 8 (Tuesday)

At the Willard Hotel in Washington, a rather n ondescript major general, accompanied by a small boy, stepped up to the desk and asked if a room was available. The clerk, as befitting an employee of the best hotel in town, almost decided to deny the officer a room. However, he asked that the general sign the register. The clerk, reading the name, saw that the general had signed "U. S. Grant & Son—Galena, Illinois." The new Lieutenant General of the Armies of the United States had arrived in Washington.

The guests in the hotel's lobby were dumfounded to see this small man, who'd become such a hero. They were more accustomed to swaggering Joe Hooker and grand George McClellan than to the unassuming Grant. Lincoln, hearing that Grant had arrived, sent word that he was to attend the President in the White House that evening, without informing Grant that this was the day of the President's weekly reception, when anyone who was anyone visited the President's mansion. Grant, wearing his battered uniform, went the short distance to the White House, and was ushered into a hall filled with people dressed "to the nines." Lincoln greeted Grant warmly, and asked him to stand on a sofa in the East Room, so that everyone could see him. The crowd cheered, and Grant felt embarrassed, as did Lincoln. Yet, a feeling of mutual trust was almost immediate between the two, who'd suffer so much together.

March 9 (Wednesday)

Today, Grant was commissioned Lieutenant General, being officially handed the commission by Pres. Lincoln in the presence of the Cabinet. After the ceremony, Grant and Lincoln held private conversations before Grant left for the Army of the Potomac and a visit to Maj. Gen. Meade.

March 10 (Thursday)

The lessons that had been learned in 1861 regarding the examination of recruits *before* they were sworn in apparently had been forgotten. McParlin recorded the results.

McParlin, T. A., Surg., Med. Dir., Army of the Potomac, Culpeper, Va.:

A large number of recruits, substitutes and drafted men were sent to the army … and among them were many entirely unfit to perform the duties of a soldier. By a special report … it appears that of fifty-seven recruits sent to the 6th New York Heavy Artillery, seventeen were hopelessly disabled from causes which must have long existed, and, in some of the cases, from causes which must have been apparent, even to a nonprofessional man, such as curvature of the spine, loss of part of the right hand, double hernia, idiocy, etc.… It appears that among the recruits received by the Cavalry Corps, the number on sick report averaged thirty-two per centum; of permanently disabled men, eight per cent, and of deaths, one-half per centum.… Examining boards were appointed in each corps for the examination of recruits, and the objectionable eliminated, but there still remained a number of youths, from eighteen to twenty years of age,… who soon broke down in the long marches.…

March 11 (Friday)

On this date, Congress enacted a law that firmly established the Ambulance Corps. This was a great advancement in the removal and treatment of wounded men on the battlefield.

March 12 (Saturday)

In the east, Grant had spent two days with Meade near Culpeper, Va., and now returned to Washington only long enough to take a train to Nashville, where he'd meet Sherman, who was to command the western armies. Maj. Gen. Halleck, at his own request, was relieved as General-in-Chief and named Chief of Staff to Grant; Grant was assigned command of *all* the armies; Sherman was named as Grant's replacement in the west, with McPherson filling Sherman's vacancy.

March 14 (Monday)

Confederate Gen. Braxton Bragg, now acting as a senior advisor to Jefferson Davis, directed that Surg. T. G. Richardson conduct an inspection of the prison hospital facilities in Richmond. On this date Surg. Richardson forwarded his report to Gen. Bragg.

Richardson, T. G., Surg., CSA, Richmond, Va.:

The buildings are three in number, each of brick, three stories above ground. One is situated at the corner of Twenty-fifth and Carey streets, one at the corner of Main and Twenty-sixth streets, and the other at the corner of Franklin and Twenty-fifth streets. The last two seem to be well adapted for the purpose designed, being well ventilated and easily kept clean;

but the first, possessing neither of these conditions, is wholly unsuitable.

The three buildings can accommodate comfortably about five hundred (500) patients, allowing eight hundred (800) cubic feet per man.

On the 11th instant, there were present in hospital eleven hundred and twenty-seven (1127) sick and wounded. The wards contain, therefore, more than twice the number [of] patients prescribed by orders; and such is their crowded condition that in some instances two patients were found on a single bunk.

The evil consequences of this state of affairs are clearly manifested in the severe mortality exhibited by the reports of the surgeon in charge:

Ratio of deaths per 1000 in December 1864 188
Ratio of deaths per 1000 in February 240
Number of deaths in March,
      to date (eleven days) 244

Stated in another form, the average number of deaths per day during the month of January was 10; the average ... of February, 18; the average ... of March to date, 22; on the day previous to that of inspection, the number was 26.

The ratio, it will be observed, is rapidly increasing; and, compared with that of the hospital for our own sick and wounded, the mortality in which for the same period did not in any case exceed 20 per 1000, and in some did not reach 10 per thousand, is truly frightful.... In the month of February, of 337 cases of diarrhea admitted, 265 were fatal, a result ascribed, in part, by the medical officer, to the want of flour—cornmeal alone being furnished.

Of typhoid fever cases admitted during the three months preceding March 1st, 64^1/$_2$ percent. proved fatal.

Dr. Wilkins, the surgeon in charge until very recently,... made to the proper authorities a report dated November 21, 1863, setting forth the capacity of the hospital buildings, and the overcrowded state of his wards, and urging the necessity for further accommodations; but it seems that his request was not complied with. He again, in a communication dated December 16, 1863, called attention to the same subject; but so far as it appears, with no effect. He further reports ... that the medical purveyor does not furnish a sufficiency of medicines, and that the commissary does not provide for the sick requiring its use.

The kitchen and laundries of two of the buildings are tolerably well arranged, and well attended to. The latrines are badly located, but well cared for. From the crowded condition of the wards it is impossible to preserve them from offensive effluvia....

The ward at Libby Prison appropriated to sick and wounded Federal officers is also objectionable, being on the ground floor and not well ventilated; but the mortality has been very slight, owing in a measure,... to the fact that the patients generally have the means and privilege of purchasing better diet than can be furnished by the commissary. There are 40 sick in this ward, which is its full capacity.

The bedding of the hospital is, in the main, good, and, considering the limited facilities, well taken care of. The books and records are neatly kept....

March 17 (Thursday)

Grant, in Nashville, formally assumed command of all the armies of the United States. He and Sherman boarded a train for Cincinnati, O., to plan the future campaign. Sherman would remember forever after the details of what happened in that room—the plan to skin the Confederacy alive.

March 18 (Friday)

In Cincinnati, Grant and Sherman, in a hotel room covered with maps and thick with cigar smoke, plotted the destruction of the Confederacy. Sherman had now officially assumed command of the armies in the west.

The Sanitary Commission was holding a fair in Washington to raise funds, and Lincoln was present at the closing to make a few remarks. His comments included praise for the contribution of the women to the war, saying "... if all that has been said by orators and poets since the creation of the world in praise of woman applied to the women of America, it would not do them justice for their conduct during this war."

March 20 (Sunday)

At about this time, Mrs. Bickerdyke returned to Chattanooga, Tenn., using the blanket pass for transportation previously issued by Gen. Grant. Having rested and seen her sons, she was ready for the fray again. In Nashville, when she was passing through, the resident Sanitary Commission agents were very worried because the railroad refused to take any of the Commission's supplies to Chattanooga, and the hospitals there were getting somewhat desperate.

When told of this situation, Mrs. Bickerdyke went to the rail yards to see for herself. There she found army ambulances being loaded with stretchers and other medical materials before they were loaded on the flatcars headed southeast. Bickerdyke then solved part of the problem by having the spaces in and around the army supplies filled with supplies from the Sanitary Commission, thus filling the wasted space and getting some of the supplies shipped.

March 23 (Wednesday)

Grant left Cincinnati and returned to Washington. Sherman headed for Nashville to coordinate his movement into Georgia.

March 24 (Thursday)

One of the effects of Grant's promotion was the elimination of some of the layers of command within the Army of the Potomac. On this date, Maj. Gen. George G. Meade, commanding that army, issued General Orders No. 10, which consolidated the five corps of that army into three, which allowed both Grant and Meade to eliminate some of the less effective commanders and to send a number of generals "on leave" for an indefinite period.

March 26 (Saturday)

Grant had now returned to Virginia and established his permanent headquarters with the Army of the Potomac at Culpeper C.H.

March 29 (Tuesday)

Among the first things Sherman did when he arrived in Nashville was to restrict all rail cargo going to Chattanooga to military supplies, which excluded Sanitary Commission supplies and other hospital supplies. The thousands of tons of food, grain, hay, ammunition, rifles, horses, saddles, and the other supplies for the Atlanta campaign had to be moved as rapidly as possible.

Knowing that Sherman was the only one to solve the shipping problem for the Sanitary Commission supplies, Mrs. Bickerdyke headed for his headquarters. Mary Livermore reported the exchange at headquarters.

Livermore, Mary, Sanitary Commission, Chattanooga, Tenn.:

"Halloo! Why, how did you get down here?" asked one of the General's staff officers, as he saw her enter Sherman's headquarters.

"Came down in the cars, of course. There's no other way of getting down here that I know of," replied the matter-of-fact woman. "I want to see Gen. Sherman."

"He is in there, writing," said the officer, pointing to an inner room; "but I guess he won't see you."

"Guess he *will!*" and she pushed into the apartment. "Good morning, General! I want to speak to you a moment. May I come in?"

"I should think you had got in!" answered the General, barely looking up, in great annoyance. "What's up now?"

"Why, General," said the earnest matron, in a perfect torrent of words, "we can't stand this last order of yours, nohow. You'll have to change it, as sure as you live. We can get along without any more nurses and agents, but the supplies we *must* have. The sick and wounded men need them, and you'll have to give permission to bring them down. The fact is, General, after a man is unable to carry a gun, and drops out of the lines, you don't trouble yourself about him, but turn him over to the hospitals, expecting the doctors and nurses to get him well and put back again into the service as soon as possible. But how are we going to make bricks without straw? Tell me that if you can."

"Well, I'm busy today, and cannot attend to you. I will see you some other time." But though Sherman kept on writing, and did not look up, Mother Bickerdyke saw a smile lurking in the corner of his mouth, and knew she would carry her point. So she persisted.

"No, General! Don't send me away until you've fixed this thing as it ought to be fixed. You had me assigned to your corps, and told me that you expected me to look after the nursing of the men who needed it. But I should like to know how I can do this if I don't have anything to work with? Have some sense about it now, General!"

There was a hearty laugh at this, and a little badinage ensued, which Mother Bickerdyke ended in her brusque way, with, "Well, I can't stand fooling here all day. Now, General, write an order for two cars a day to be sent down from the Sanitary Commission at Nashville, and I'll be satisfied." The order was written, and for weeks all the sanitary stores sent from Nashville to Chattanooga, and the posts along that road, were sent directly or indirectly through Mother Bickerdyke's mediation.

April 7 (Thursday)

Maj. Gen. Nathaniel Banks' Red River campaign was still grinding along. The Union forces were near Mansfield, in the piney woods of upper Louisiana, when, in a little opening near a bayou, they engaged Confederates under Gen. Richard Taylor. The action, primarily cavalry, was close range and the wounds were severe. The wounded were removed to Pleasant Hill. When the Union Army advanced in the morning, the wounded were left at that point.

April 8 (Friday)

Sanger, Eugene F., Surg., USV, Chief Med. Off., 19th Corps, Sabine Cross Roads, La.:

April 8th, the battle of Sabine Cross Roads was fought at about five o'clock P.M., seventeen miles from Pleasant Hill, and about two-and-a-half miles from Mansfield.... I had just organized a division field hospital when the rout of the cavalry division and Thirteenth Corps became complete, and I was obliged to abandon the hospital. A portion of the wounded were rescued. Twenty ambulances were captured, and eight medical officers.... There were two hundred and ten wounded left in the hands of the enemy. The 1st division, Nineteenth Corps, checked the pursuit of the enemy, and repelled his charges with terrible slaughter. Night closed the scene, both armies resting on their arms within speaking distance.

I immediately organized a division field hospital ... and every exertion was made by the medical officers to collect our wounded in the thick woods and darkness, with a limited number of ambulances—most of the ambulances being blocked up in the rear, by the stampeded mass of wagons, artillery, infantry and cavalry. Our forces retired at twelve o'clock....

April 9 (Saturday)

Sanger, Eugene F., Surg., USV, Chief Med. Off., 19th Corps, Pleasant Hill, La.:

Arrived at Pleasant Hill at six o'clock A.M. Immediate orders were issued to send all transportation to Grand Ecore, forty miles to the rear. All my wounded were sent.... The battle of Pleasant Hill was fought on the 9th of April at five o'clock P.M.... The battleground was a large open field of three or four hundred acres, on an elevated piece of ground forming a beautiful plateau, completely surrounded by woods. A few houses and shops on the hill; no water excepting a few wells.... We repulsed the enemy at dark, and night only stopped our pursuit. I organized a large hospital in three or four of the largest dwellings on the hill.... Immediately after the battle was over, I obtained permission to send for my medical stores; but by a change of plans and orders, I discovered ...

.... at six o'clock A.M. of the 10th, after a hard night's labor with the wounded, that the infantry had retreated during the night, and a small squadron of cavalry was guarding the rear immediately in front of my hospitals. I had no other alternative than to put a medical officer in charge, leave him a very meager supply of medicines and follow the infantry, then five miles distant....

April 12 (Tuesday)

Sanger, Eugene F., Surg., USV, Chief Med. Off., 19th Corps, Grand Ecore, La.:

Arrived at Grand Ecore about noon April 11th, and on the 12th I obtained permission to take two loads of medical and hospital stores to our wounded at Pleasant Hill, under a flag of truce. I found them kindly treated, but suffering for medicines, bedding and hospital stores; all of which I was able to supply....

Today, at Culpeper, Va., Maj. Gen. George G. Meade issued Special Orders No. 197, which placed the medical department of the Army of the Potomac on the same level as the other staff corps. The order designated the surgeons-in-chief of brigades and divisions, thus rendering their positions to a great extent independent of the caprice of brigade and division commanders. A great leap forward.

McParlin, T. A., Surg., Med. Dir., Army of the Potomac, Culpeper, Va.:

As the provision of the ambulance law corresponded in all essential particulars to the system already instituted in the army by Surg. Letterman, no difficulty or delay occurred in its adoption. All of the ambulances were thoroughly repaired, painted and marked with the distinctive badge of their several corps, details of medical officers and men for the ambulance service were made, and the persons so selected carefully examined. As was to be expected, a large portion of those first detailed were rejected, regimental commanders having attempted to rid themselves of their weak and worthless men. The men attached to the ambulances were carefully and regularly drilled, minute inspections of everything connected with the ambulances and horses were made, and guidons and hospital flags were procured and distributed.

April 13 (Wednesday)

Perry, John G., Asst. Surg., USV, 20th Mass. Vols., near Stevensburg, Va.:

This morning I was awakened by feeling myself tightly held, seeing Hayward's face close to mine, and hearing him say in some agitation, "John, don't move for your life till I say 'three,' then seize my hands and spring to your feet. One, two, three!" Up I sprang, and never made a cleaner jump, but just in time to see a moccasin snake dive under my coat, which I had used for a pillow. Armed with sticks, we dragged the coat away, but saw only the hole into which the snake had glided. I was glad afterwards we missed killing him, for he had lain coiled almost under the back of my neck, and, as it proved, waited patiently for me to move and let him enter his hole; so I feel rather pleased that his patience was rewarded.

April 14 (Thursday)

Another major advantage of the order of April 12th was the reorganization of the hospitals within the Army of the Potomac.

McParlin, T. A., Surg., Med. Dir., Army of the Potomac, Culpeper, Va.:

The medical staff of these hospitals was the same as established by Surg. Letterman, viz: one surgeon in charge, one recorder, three operators, each with two or more assistants, and one medical officer to provide food and shelter. As a plan of the division hospitals … a brief sketch of the hospitals … will perhaps best illustrate.…

In the 1st division, Second Corps, twenty-two hospital tents, fourteen army wagons and four medicine wagons were allowed for medical purposes, the division containing four brigades, twenty-one regiments and eight thousand men. Six of the army wagons carried the regimental medical property; four, the brigade supplies; two, the hospital tents; one, the cooking utensils and three hundred rations, and one was loaded with blankets, beef-stock, whiskey, chloroform, bandages, lint, etc.

In pitching the hospital, no attention was paid to brigade organizations, except that an operating table was established for each brigade, the corresponding medicine wagon being drawn up beside it, and the surgeons-in-chief of brigades were *ex officio* the operators.

Thirty-six regular hospital attendants were employed in the preparation and distribution of food, dressing wounds, and care of the patients. These men wore on the left arm a half chevron, composed of a green and yellow stripe.

During a battle, or series of battles, the drum corps of the division, numbering three hundred and fifty men and boys, were put on duty in the hospital, being organized into five companies, commanded each by a sergeant, and the whole commanded by a lieutenant having an orderly sergeant as an assistant. From this corps, details were made, whenever called for by the surgeon in charge for pitching and striking tents, loading and unloading wounded, bringing water and wood, burying the dead and for police duty.…

Sanger, Eugene F., Surg., USV, Chief Med. Off., 19th Corps, Grand Ecore, La.:

On the 14th of April, I sent four loads of supplies and clothing to our wounded. They allowed one of our captured medical officers to come to our lines, but would not allow another medical officer to enter their lines.

April 15 (Friday)

In Chattanooga, Tenn., the hospitals were being emptied as rapidly as possible and the patients sent north by train to the General Hospitals in Nashville and Louisville and then further transferred to other points. Mrs. Bickerdyke and the agreeable Mrs. Porter, leaving the patients in Chattanooga in the hands of the two ministers from the Christian Commission, moved their hospital to Huntsville, Ala., to the former home of John C. Calhoun, the famous orator and statesman. When the women arrived, the house was still intact and full of expensive furniture and many historical artifacts. Mrs. Bickerdyke had all of the furniture stored in the wine cellar, along with the paintings, etc., to prevent theft. Mrs. Bickerdyke kept the key herself as long as she was in Huntsville. All the contents of the house were returned to the Calhoun family intact at the close of the war.

April 17 (Sunday)

McParlin, T. A., Surg., Med. Dir., Army of the Potomac, Culpeper, Va.:

The medical and hospital supplies of the army were carried in the brigade supply and medicine wagons, the regimental and division wagons, the ambulance boxes, hospital knapsacks and field companions, and in a reserve train of thirty-five army wagons which moved with the main trains of the army.... This supply was estimated as sufficient for the wants of the army until June 1, 1864, and for the necessities of twenty thousand wounded for eight days in addition....

April 19 (Tuesday)

Welch, S. G., Surg., 20th S.C. Vols., Orange C.H., Va.:

We are still in camp, but yesterday we received an order to send back all surplus baggage and be ready to move at any time....

Gen. Longstreet's army is at Charlottesville. He may come here or go to the peninsula.... The capture of Ft. Pillow by Forrest was excellent for us....

I was glad to hear that old Jim Beauschelle was at our home. My father is decidedly hostile to the preachers who stay at home and preach to the women and old men, but I know he treated Beauschelle like a prince. If you see a certain widow, you might take the liberty of teasing her a little about old Beauschelle. She sent him some nice warm articles of clothing recently.

I have just finished my breakfast. I had corn bread, meat, molasses and coffee. Such a meal is first-rate for soldiers, but if the same were offered me at home I should feel like turning up my nose at it.

April 22 (Friday)

At about this time, Mrs. Bickerdyke got into a flaming row with the Sanitary Commission headquarters in Nashville. The previous winter, the Union troops suffered terribly from scurvy (especially those in Chattanooga) before Grant opened the "Cracker Line." The cure for scurvy, of course, is vegetables and fruits. However, how do you supply these in large quantities in the dead of winter? The answer that the Sanitary Commission came up with was *vinegar*. Now, for the most part, those who supplied the Sanitary Commission with their products were women belonging to the various Ladies' Aid Societies. While they didn't know too much about scurvy, they did know how to pickle. The Sanitary Commission was flooded with thousands of barrels, kegs, jars, etc., filled with pickled cucumbers, beets, meats, vegetables, and anything else that would stand still long enough to get pickled. These were duly forwarded for use by the troops, whether the troops wanted them or not.

Before Mrs. Bickerdyke left Chattanooga, she and Gen. Sherman had agreed that the pickles weren't the answer, and Sherman wasn't going to use his too-few railcars to move pickles. Therefore, Mrs. Bickerdyke told Nashville not to send pickled products, but instead to send dressings and lint for bandages. The Sanitary Commission in Nashville was furious. In stepped Mrs. Porter, who calmed the waters by informing Mrs. Livermore in Chicago that there was no scurvy anymore, and that pickles wouldn't be needed.

April 23 (Saturday)

In late March, when Sherman closed the railroad lines between Nashville and east Tennessee to all but military traffic, there was a storm of protest from locals along the line who'd previously relied on the railroad for supplies from Nashville. Sherman's response was that they could drive their cattle over the mountains and move their supplies by wagon, the way it had been done before the railroad. "His" line was too important for such things.

A Pennsylvania Quaker, wishing to travel with food supplies to eastern Tennessee, pressured Washington to force Sherman to allow the trip. Sherman let the Quaker travel, but the supplies stayed in Nashville.

One of Sherman's major problems was the bureaucratic way in which the trainmen ran the railroads. In the beginning, only about 60 cars a day ran from Nashville southeast to Chattanooga, and Sherman saw the need to double that number. The general then proposed laying a double track on the route, but said that even with a double track, the trainmen were so used to timetables that they wouldn't be able to cope with the additional traffic. To increase the number of railcars, Sherman seized all freight cars arriving from Louisville, or other points north, and convinced James Guthrie of the L&N Railroad to seize all cars arriving in Louisville and send them to Nashville. With this pool of cars available, Sherman amazed the railroaders by having 130, then 150, and a maximum of 193 cars per day moving southeast to Chattanooga.

April 25 (Monday)

The capture of Vicksburg, Miss., and its occupation by Union forces led to a large influx of Southern refugees displaced by fighting to the east of the city. Many of these were Confederate deserters who'd been small farmers prior to the war and who'd reached the conclusion that there was no future in fighting further. These refugees needed only enough to get started again and to be left alone; the former could be provided by the Sanitary Commission in part, the latter was impossible outside Union lines.

The Sanitary Commission agent at Vicksburg reported to St. Louis concerning this "other" class of refugee:

The greatest distress prevails among a class known as "poor white trash," who knowing nothing, are responsible for nothing, but suffer all. Their condition is even more deplorable than the that of the negroes, for equally with them they have borne the curse of slavery without acquiring the habits of industry which the negroes have so severely learned. These are in a large proportion women and children, who have been literally driven by famine into our lines.… These people have crowded into every vacant hovel in town. I wish you could see a case which came to my notice yesterday.… I was called in

by the post surgeon to see a case of want. The foul air as I entered the door was sickening in the extreme, and there, crowded into two small rooms, were twenty persons. Of these, three were able to stand; one little child was dead, another dying, and the other fifteen sick upon the floor and one dirty bed! This morning the child, thank God! is dead, and another that was born there last night is dead also. All these poor creatures had to eat until yesterday was hard bread and bacon. In another room I found a man lying upon a vile cot perfectly helpless, apparently in the last stages of pneumonia.… I had him removed to the hospital, and the little boy we took to our "Home" where he is cared for. All this house of sufferers that death does not take, will be taken there as soon as they can be removed.…

April 27 (Wednesday)

McParlin, T. A., Surg., Med. Dir., Army of the Potomac, Culpeper, Va.:

During the last week in April, all the sick and wounded were sent to Washington, the hospitals were broken up, all the surplus property sent to the rear, and every preparation made for the immediate movement. The medical purveyor's depot at Brandy Station was broken up, and the surplus supplies sent to Alexandria.…

April 28 (Thursday)

In Georgia, Sherman's army was poised to move on Atlanta. Sickness in the army for the past four months had drained the overall strength of the regiments by over 26,000 men, who'd been sent back to general hospitals around Nashville and St. Louis. This figure represented only slightly over half of the sick reported during that time, the remaining 18,000 having been returned to their regiments or retained in local hospitals. Scurvy, a major problem during the winter, would largely disappear when the local corn crop could be eaten.

May 1 (Sunday)

The Army of the Potomac reported that the Ambulance Corps, as of April 30, had: 592 ambulances; 40 medicine wagons; 209 army wagons; 15 forges; 1871 horses and 1146 mules; 1214 stretchers; and 60 officers and 2275 enlisted men.

May 3 (Tuesday)

In the area of Brandy Station, Va., Grant directed Meade to move the Army of the Potomac out of winter quarters and to cross the Rapidan on the morning of the 4th. Sherman, now in Ringgold, Ga., was notified of the movement. The new offensive was ready.

McParlin, T. A., Surg., Med. Dir., Army of the Potomac, Culpeper, Va.:

On the 30th of April, the 2d division of the Cavalry Corps was withdrawn from Warrenton, and moved to Paoli mills. The movement of the army began at midnight the 3d of May.

May 4 (Wednesday)

Shortly after midnight, the long-dormant Army of the Potomac moved across the Rapidan and headed for the Wilderness crossroads. Grant's army had nearly 122,000 men, against Lee's 66,000. Grant moved around the Confederate right, forcing Lee to move from Orange C.H. and the Gordonsville area to meet him. Confederate Gen. Richard Ewell led the way towards the Wilderness, followed by A. P. Hill, and Longstreet bringing up the rear of the long columns.

Welch, S. G., Surg., 20th S.C. Vols., Orange C.H., Va.:

We are still in our old camp. It may be some time yet before we have a big fight, although it can't remain off a great while, for the weather is fine and the roads are good.

Dr. Tyler leaves this morning for Richmond, and Dr. Kilgore will not come; so I am alone. I have very little to do, as there is scarcely any sickness....

McParlin, T. A., Surg., Med. Dir., Army of the Potomac, Culpeper, Va.:

No opposition was made to the crossing, and as soon as the infantry had reached the river, the cavalry moved southward, the 2d division to the vicinity of Piney Branch church, and the 3d division to the vicinity of Old Wilderness Tavern. A small body of Confederates were found at Chancellorsville....

In Georgia, around Varnell's Station, there was light skirmishing between Sherman's and Johnston's forces.

May 5 (Thursday)

Near the Wilderness Crossroads in Virginia, Meade's Army of the Potomac collided with Lee's Army of Northern Virginia in the tangled, wooded area south of the Rapidan. By noon the armies were locked in full-scale combat. Grant wouldn't commit his forces piecemeal—Lee would have to fight the whole army. At the close of the day, both armies entrenched, started bringing in the wounded, and lay in their positions, awaiting tomorrow.

Welch, S. G., Surg., 20th S.C. Vols., Wilderness, Va.:

On the 5th we marched all day on the plank road from Orange C.H. to this place. We got into a hard fight on the left of the road rather late in the afternoon. The fighting was desperate for two or three hours, with the least cannonading I have ever heard in a battle....

After night Maj. Hammond rode up to where we doctors were and told us that about two miles to the rear there was a poor Yankee who was badly wounded. He insisted that someone of us go back to help him. I went, and found him paralyzed from a shot in the back. I gave him water and morphine, and made him comfortable as best I could. The poor fellow seemed very grateful.

After I returned to our lines the order came to move back with our medical stores to Orange C.H.. We marched nearly all night....

Perry, John G., Asst. Surg., USV, 20th Mass. Vols., Wilderness, Va.:

Hot firing opened at daybreak, and it seemed so near that when orders came to "fall in line," the new German recruits simply would not obey. They were so terrified that they lay like logs, and no amount of rough handling, even with bayonets, had any effect upon them whatever. The order to advance was given; still these fellows clung to the ground with faces buried in the grass, and, although some were shot by the officers, literally nothing moved them.... We pushed forward, and very quickly were walking over rows of dead bodies piled at times two and three deep, and they lay in lines, exactly as if mowed down, showing the havoc of yesterday's fight.... I noticed a man near me in the ranks at this time singing a hymn with all his might and main. His head was thrown back, his mouth wide open, and he seemed completely absorbed in the emotion called forth [by] the hymn, which made him oblivious of all surroundings. I watched him curiously, and understood that it was an instinctive impulse on his part to try to hold his senses together and to steady himself under the well-nigh unendurable strain....

The right of the Twentieth bore on the turnpike for about two miles, when we met the enemy and the fighting began. I stationed myself behind the regiment in the woods on the side of the road, and opened my hospital paraphernalia; then sent the stretcher-bearers over the field. Soon I was deep in work.

Meanwhile reserves were brought up, and among them I saw Gen. Bartlett at the head of his brigade; but we had time only for a passing salute. Shortly after that an orderly came towards me, leading a horse, with an officer in the saddle, back from the front. The man was bent far over the horse's neck, bleeding profusely from a wound in the head, and white as death. To my dismay, I saw it was Frank Bartlett, and I called his name again and again, but did not succeed in rousing him. Passing my finger into the wound before taking him from the saddle, I found the ball had not penetrated the bone, but had simply severed an artery in the scalp; so, pressing the artery till the steward brought a ligature, I shouted, "No harm done, old boy; this is only a flesh wound; you will be all right when I tie the artery and take a stitch or two"; and this good news seemed to bring him back to consciousness. I then laid him on the ground, and, after my work was finished, gave him a good horn of whiskey and very soon he rallied completely....

About the middle of the afternoon Gen. Hancock rode up and told me to stop work and send all my wounded to the rear, as our troops were to fall back. This was tough and hard work, but I gathered all I could find and fell back with the rest....

McParlin, T. A., Surg., Med. Dir., Army of the Potomac, Wilderness, Va.:

Early on the morning of the 5th of May, it was found that the enemy were advancing from Orange Courthouse.... The division hospitals of the corps were placed on a slope of open ground by a small creek which crosses the Fredericksburg pike one mile east of Old Wilderness tavern. Water for the hospitals was obtained from excellent springs in the vicinity. Tents were pitched, operating tables and kitchens

prepared, surgeons and attendants were at their posts, and everything was in readiness for the reception of the wounded an hour before the cases began to arrive. The advance depot for the ambulances was near the turnpike, about four hundred yards behind the line of battle.... The wounded began to come in about twelve P.M., and by nine o'clock P.M., twelve hundred and thirty-five men had been received, fed, dressed and sheltered.

The Sixth Corps was posted on the right of the Fifth, extending to the river, the second division moving during the day to the left of Fifth Corps. The hospitals of the first division of this corps were at the Spottswood house, one the Germania Ford turnpike; that of the second division, on the Old Wilderness Run, near Woodville Mine, and that of the third division near Old Wilderness Tavern. About one thousand wounded were brought in during the day....

May 6 (Friday)

In the early dawn hours, just as the soldiers could see the blooming dogwoods in the Wilderness, the Federals advanced and collided heavily with the Rebels. Longstreet's flank attack set the Federals back, but temporarily. In late afternoon Longstreet attacked again, only to be stopped short of the Union lines, and he was severely wounded.

McParlin, T. A., Surg., Med. Dir., Army of the Potomac, Wilderness, Va.:

During the 6th and 7th of May, the battle of the Wilderness continued.... It was a series of fierce attacks and repulses on either side, and the hostile lines swayed back and forth over a strip of ground two hundred yards to a mile in width, in which the severely wounded of both sides were scattered. This strip of woods was on fire in many places, and some of the wounded who were unable to escape were thus either suffocated or burned to death. The number who thus perished is unknown, but it is supposed to have been about two hundred. The stretcher-bearers of the ambulance corps followed the line of battle closely, and displayed great gallantry in their efforts to bring off the wounded lying between the lines, but with little success, it being almost impossible to find wounded men lying scattered through the dense thickets, and the enemy firing at every moving light or even at the slightest noise....

The hospitals of the Second Corps,... being but a short distance from the front, the influx of patients was so rapid, and their numbers so great, that it was not possible to record all of them. About one hundred and twenty of the enemy's wounded were brought in, chiefly to the hospitals of the Second Corps.... Number of wounded according to the classified returns ... fifteen thousand and four.... The proportion of officers wounded was very large, being one to every sixteen enlisted men.... As a somewhat interesting fact bearing upon the character of the conflict, it may be mentioned that *it is stated by the chief ordnance officer that but eleven rounds of ammunition per man were used by the army during the three days' fight.* [Italics added.]

... All the ambulances and hospital wagons were at the several hospitals by nine o'clock A.M., of May 6th. The labors of the ambulance corps during this battle were very severe. The ambulances of the Fifth and Sixth Corps travelled about fifty miles on the 6th of May. Every wounded man who could be reached by the stretcher-bearers was brought off the field, and about four thousand blankets and shelter tents were collected and brought to the hospitals.

Perry, John G., Asst. Surg., USV, 20th Mass. Vols., Wilderness, Va.:

Something happened to me in this retreat to the crossroads which Hayward says was a heatstroke, but there was no exposure to the sun, as I was sheltered by the woods. I remember nothing from the time Gen. Hancock ordered me back and the wounded were sent off, till I found myself lying under an apple tree, with "Uncle Nathan" sponging my head with cold water. My steward says that while on the retreat I talked incoherently, then ran and shouted, until he guided me to the Division Hospital, where I fell unconscious....

Welch, S. G., Surg., 20th S.C. Vols., Wilderness, Va.:

... just before day we were ordered back to the Wilderness again, and we reached there soon after sunrise. Longstreet came up about this time, having made a forced march all night. Then the fighting began in earnest—continuing fearful and desperate all day. The tremendous roar of artillery and the rattle of the musketry seemed to make the woods tremble.

Late in the afternoon of this day I went among the wounded of the Third Regiment South Carolina Volunteers and of the Yankees who had fallen into our hands. As usual on such occasions groans and cries met me from every side. I found Col. James Nance, my old schoolmate, and Col. Gaillard of Fairfield lying side by side in death. Near them lay Warren Peterson, with a shattered thighbone, and still others who were my friends. Many of the enemy were there. Not far from these was an old man, a Yankee officer, mortally wounded. I learned that he was Brig. Gen. Wadsworth, once governor of New York.

I picked up an excellent Yankee overcoat on the battlefield, but the cape is off. I will have a sack coat made of it. I also found an India-rubber cloth that is big enough for four men to lie on or to make a tent of. I have never seen a battlefield so strewn with overcoats, knapsacks, India-rubber cloths and everything else soldiers carry, except at Chancellorsville. The dead Yankees are everywhere. I have never before seen woods so completely riddled with bullets. At one place the battle raged among chinquapin bushes. All the bark was knocked off and the bushes literally torn to pieces....

In Georgia, Sherman's nearly 100,000 troops driving for Atlanta, moved out from Ringgold towards Joe Johnston's Confederates.

May 7 (Saturday)

Shortly after midnight of this day, the Army of the Potomac found that the new overall army commander intended to fight and maintain contact with the enemy. The long blue columns began moving from the right flank, behind the army, and to the southeast towards Richmond.

Perry, John G., Asst. Surg., USV, 20th Mass. Vols., Wilderness, Va.:

I am safe and well, but our losses have been fearful. Poor Abbott is dead; Macy has a slight wound in the leg, not dangerous; Bond is shot in the jaw, but doing well; Walcott in the shoulder and three others badly wounded.

During the first day's fight I was with the regiment, but now I am detailed to the hospital with Dr. Hayward, three miles in the rear. I have been operating all day, and really learned more in the way of experience than in all the time since joining the regiment.

McParlin, T. A., Surg., Med. Dir., Army of the Potomac, Wilderness, Va.:

On the morning of the 7th of May, Maj. Gen. Meade ordered that all the wounded should be sent to Rappahannock Station, by way of Ely's Ford, to be sent from thence to Washington. All the army wagons of the general and corps trains which could be emptied were turned over to the medical department during the day, and by six o'clock P.M., were being loaded with wounded. These wagons were thickly bedded with evergreen boughs, over which, shelter tents and blankets were spread, and were comparatively comfortable for the class of cases for which they were used.… Three hundred and twenty-five wagons and four hundred and eighty-eight ambulances were used for the wounded of the infantry corps, and it was found absolutely necessary to leave behind nine hundred and sixty of them for lack of transportation.… Two medical officers, one hospital steward, and ten attendants were detailed to every five hundred men, and rations, dressings and medical stores furnished for three days. Surg. E. B. Dalton, U.S. Volunteers, was placed in charge of the entire train, and a regiment of dismounted cavalry accompanied it as a guard.

On the evening of May 7th, it was determined to abandon the line of the Rapidan, and the army moved during the night to the vicinity of Spotsylvania C.H.. The train containing wounded was therefore ordered to accompany the trains of the army to Oldrich's, on the Fredericksburg plank road, two miles south of Chancellorsville.

Welch, S. G., Surg., 20th S.C. Vols., Battle of the Wilderness, Va.:

When I wrote … on the 7th instant I thought our fighting was over, for we had driven the Yankees off the field at the Wilderness and they had refused to attack us again; but we had another big fight with them the next day near this place.…

In Georgia, Sherman's army was on the move, and with it went Mrs. Bickerdyke and Mrs. Porter. Riding the ambulance stuffed with bandages, tea, whiskey, brown sugar, condensed milk, dried beef, and other necessities for treatment of the wounded, the two women awaited the first major set-to with Johnston.

May 8 (Sunday)

Grant moved southeast towards Spotsylvania C.H., trying to arrive there before Lee. It was a footrace Grant would lose. Early in the morning, the Federal Cavalry Corps attacked the Confederate lines at Spotsylvania C.H., causing about 250 Union casualties. Those wounded were quickly gathered, their wounds dressed, they were fed, and then placed in ambulances for the trip to Fredericksburg. The cavalry withdrew about 10 o'clock in the morning, only to be replaced by the Fifth Corps, which began a sharp fight about 11 o'clock, having been on the march all night.

The advance was somewhat sluggish in the heat, and there was much confusion. A skirmish line was formed in the rear to drive forward all stragglers, even those of the walking wounded, of whom there were many, but eventually the advance slowed and then stopped. Those wounded severely enough were gathered together along the roads and were slowly evacuated to the hospitals in the rear, located near Todd's Tavern and Spotsylvania C.H. Slightly wounded men straggled everywhere across the front. Even those who were more severely hurt would get an escort of three or four able-bodied men to take them to the rear. The effect was to bleed the units in the front of their manpower. The medicine wagons and other hospital equipment couldn't get forward because the roads were blocked with marching units, artillery, and quartermaster wagons. The ambulances having left for Fredericksburg, light transportation wasn't available to move the wounded. To compensate for the lack of transportation, Meade directed, at about 4 P.M., that spring wagons of any description should be turned over to the medical officers, along with any army wagons that could be emptied, for the transport of the wounded. While not many wagons were available, those few helped considerably.

Meanwhile, the wagon train of 813 vehicles, stretching about ten miles, was to follow in the wake of the army as far as the Fredericksburg plank road, which the train would then take to Fredericksburg. The wounded, at that time, had been loaded in the 325 army wagons for almost 24 hours. These wagons, primarily meant to haul cargo, had no springs. Each rut was felt as a jarring motion that ground fractured bones together, caused bandages to chafe raw wounds, and opened wounds which had been surgically closed. The roads, after being trod upon by cavalry, artillery, and infantry, were in abominable shape. The wounded cried for relief from the jolting, asking to be removed from the wagons so that they could die peacefully. In some cases, they pleaded to be shot rather than endure the agony of the jolting wagons and ambulances.

Surg. McParlin, knowing that the facilities at Fredericksburg were wholly inadequate to handle the number of wounded in the train, telegraphed Washington at ten o'clock in the morning to get medical personnel, hospital ships, and stores to Fredericksburg at the earliest possible moment.

Meanwhile, Meade ordered that a small regiment of infantry and cavalry be detailed to accompany the train to Fredericksburg. The ambulances were to be returned to the army for further operations, but the wagons would be retained for the transport of the wounded. In addition, a flag of truce would be arranged under which the wounded remaining on the battlefield were to be recovered.

Not only had the wounded lost the more comfortable ambulances, but there was to be a further delay in starting for Fredericksburg.

Perry, John G., Asst. Surg., USV, 20th Mass. Vols., Wilderness, Va.:

Exhaustion and confusion.... Although perfectly well, I am tired and hot, having slept only a couple of hours out of the last forty.... I now sit on the ground in the woods, leaning against a log and writing on my knee. I am surrounded by soldiers, bonfires, and kicking horses—but out of their reach,... my face is black with dirt and perspiration, clothes soiled and torn almost to pieces. I am too tired to sleep, too tired to stand.... Although we have been steadily banging away at each other for a week, neither side has gained much advantage....

McKenzie, Thomas G., Med. Purveyor, Army of the Potomac, Alexandria, Va.:

... April 9, 1864, I proceeded to Alexandria, Va., for the purpose of establishing a medical purveying depot at that place. Having obtained a suitable building, No. 43 Union street, I remained on duty there, receiving and storing medical supplies, and awaiting further orders.

On the morning of May 8th, I received orders from the Acting Surgeon General to despatch at once to Rappahannock Station, on the Orange and Alexandria railroad, a battlefield supply for three thousand wounded for seven days, including barrels for ice water, tin cups, buckets, etc., etc., for the use of the wounded on the train expected from the front. The supplies were sent forward immediately ... two cars having been loaded for a number of days previous with a battlefield supply....

Gen. Joseph Johnston occupied Rocky Face Ridge near Dalton, Ga., awaiting the arrival of Sherman's blue columns. It was to be a short wait indeed. Already Sherman was demonstrating against Johnston's lines, probing the Confederate defenses, while McPherson attempted to turn Johnston's left flank.

Foye, John W., Surg., USV, 20th Corps, Buzzard Roost, Ga.:

On the morning of May 8th, the left of the command became engaged with the enemy at Mill Creek Gap, on Taylor's Ridge, one of the series of ridges known collectively as Buzzard Roost, and after a brisk fight of about five hours, in which advantages were gained and lost, darkness closed the struggle and gave us an opportunity to care for and remove the wounded....

The supplies of stimulants and surgical appliances were abundant; but they did not reach the field until several hours after we became engaged, in consequence of the roads being occupied by the troops. Our panniers furnished the requisite dressings until the arrival of the wagons. A field hospital was established half a mile from the foot of the ridge and one mile from the enemy. Water was abundant, and our supplies of fresh beef and hospital stores were ample. Our wounded were removed from the summit to the base on blankets and shelter tents, and were thence conveyed in ambulances to the field hospital. The fire was principally from musketry at short range.... We lost forty-nine killed, and one hundred and eighty-four wounded men were treated in the field hospital, of whom seven died during the night. Eleven amputations and seven excisions were performed during the night....

May 9 (Monday)

Grant lost the footrace and now faced Lee at Spotsylvania C.H. After the fracas yesterday, the armies spent the day sizing each other up and adjusting lines. Burnside moved up closer with his Ninth Corps. Sheridan, drawing Stuart off, began a sixteen-day run around Lee and towards Richmond.

The wagon train of wounded, having left the Wilderness battlefield yesterday, arrived at Fredericksburg at 11 o'clock this morning, after a 16-hour agony-filled trip for the passengers.

McParlin, T. A., Surg., Med. Dir., Army of the Potomac, Spotsylvania C.H., Va.:

Early on the morning of the 9th, the hospitals of the Fifth Corps were established on a grassy lawn around Cossin's house,... a mile and a half to the rear of the line of battle. The hospitals of the Second Corps were ... near those of the Fifth Corps in open ground on the south branch of the Ny river. The Sixth Corps hospitals were placed in the pinewoods on the Courthouse and Piney Branch church road, half a mile north of the intersection of the Block-house road.

All the wounded were transferred to these points during the day by means of spring wagons and stretchers.... Large numbers of blankets and shelter tents, which had been dropped and abandoned in the woods by stragglers and wounded, were collected and brought to the hospitals by the attendants and the field music[ians], who, in some instances, were regularly deployed as skirmishers and sent through the woods for that purpose. About twenty-five thousand blankets and five hundred shelter tents were obtained in this manner. The only fighting during the day was between the pickets and sharpshooters, in which, however, we sustained a heavy loss in the death of Maj. Gen. Sedgwick,... who was killed by a sharpshooter about eleven o'clock A.M.....

The greater part of the ambulances sent to Fredericksburg returned during the night of May 9th. The horses were greatly exhausted by the severe and continuous labor ... and were badly in need of rest. All the hospital supplies in the ambulances had been removed at Fredericksburg.

McGill, George M., Asst. Surg., USA, Sheridan's Cavalry, raid on Richmond, Va.:

On the 9th of May, Surg. Pease being too sick for mounted duty, I was made acting medical director by Maj. Gen. Sheridan. The corps was, at that time, upon the march, and numbered about nine thousand mounted men. There was one ambulance at the headquarters of the corps, and the batteries of artillery had each an ambulance, in which however, the mess things of the artillery officers and their bedding were carried.... Thirty-one ammunition wagons were with the command, all heavily laden.... An engagement used up ammunition enough to make it possible to carry such of the wounded men as were cases to bring along.... Each medical officer had a field companion, and each regiment was provided with the field register. During the five days in which we had no communication, the medicines and dressings were used up, but a supply of dressings were obtained by a foraging party. The wounded were abundantly fed by foraging.... After a capture of three wagons and three ambulances, made upon the night of 9th of May, a corps ambulance train was organized.... As the number of our wounded increased, the battery ambulances, with such spring wagons as could be appropriated in the corps or taken from inhabitants of the country, were added to the train, which finally assumed formidable proportions.... The first engagement was on the telegraph road approaching Childsburg; an affair of the rear guard, in which, however, we lost heavily. Many of the wounded were captured by the enemy, but nineteen were saved and transported in the ammunition wagons. On the night of the 9th and morning of the 10th, we had twenty men and officers wounded in skirmishing....

McKenzie, Thomas G., Med. Purveyor, Army of the Potomac, Alexandria, Va.:

The supply arrived safely at its destination, where it remained until the morning of the 9th of May, and was then ordered back to Alexandria. Immediately on its arrival,... the stores were unloaded and conveyed on board the steamers *State of Maine* and *Connecticut*, they lying at the wharf. These stores were all placed under the charge of Surg. John H. Brinton, USV, who was ordered to proceed to Fredericksburg with them....

Sherman found the Confederate defenses of Rocky Face Ridge too strong for him and fumed because McPherson didn't complete the turning of Johnston's left flank. For the moment, there was a stalemate.

Foye, John W., Surg., USV, 20th Corps, Buzzard's Roost, Ga.:

At eleven o'clock on May 9th, the wounded were placed in ambulances and sent under the charge of three medical officers and a proper number of attendants to Ringgold, a distance of twenty-five miles. One death occurred on the route....

May 10 (Tuesday)

Late in the afternoon, Grant threw the three corps of the Army of the Potomac against the Confederate "mule shoe" positions at Spotsylvania C.H., with the heaviest attack made at about 6 P.M. This last attack temporarily breached the Confederate line, but fell back. Burnside repositioned and entrenched facing Early's corps.

Near Beaver Dam Station, Va., Sheridan and Stuart fought skirmishes along the North Anna River. Sheridan was now within 20 miles of Richmond. Stuart took a position between Sheridan and Richmond at a crossroads called Yellow Tavern.

McParlin, T. A., Surg., Med. Dir., Army of the Potomac, Spotsylvania C.H., Va.:

During the morning of May 10th, orders were issued ... to send to the rear the wounded in the field hospitals, using for that purpose the army wagons which had been emptied by the issue of rations and ammunition ... and were going to Fredericksburg for fresh supplies. No ambulances or spring wagons were sent, as a general engagement was going on at the time.... The train was organized at Silver's house, near which the main trains of the army were parked, and moved from that point at five o'clock P.M. The number of wounded sent in this train,... sixteen hundred and ninety-four wounded and two hundred and sixty-three wagons. To the above ... should be added about six hundred slightly wounded, who moved with the train, most of them from the day's engagement,... which would make a total number sent two thousand two hundred and ninety-four.

The wagons were bedded with straw and small evergreen boughs, covered with blankets and shelter tents, and carried from three to five men each, hard-bread boxes being used as seats for those who were able to sit up. Four thousand rations were sent with the train, and medical officers and attendants in the

same proportion as the first train from the Wilderness.... This train reached Fredericksburg ... at eleven o'clock P.M., having halted once on the road to furnish soup and coffee to the wounded....

Two general assaults were made on the enemy's line during the day, the principal one about four o'clock P.M. By nine o'clock P.M., there had been collected and brought to the field hospitals ... nineteen hundred [wounded]. A number of the wounded of the Second Corps fell into the hands of the enemy, when the corps withdrew in the evening to the north bank of the Po. The number so lost is estimated to have been three hundred.

The train of the medical purveyor was at this time at Silver's, only four miles from the hospitals, and large issues were made during the day, especially for the purpose of refilling the ambulance boxes which had been emptied at Fredericksburg. All the hospitals were supplied with ice, lemons, canned peaches, jellies, hospital clothing, etc., in addition to the hospital stores usually furnished....

McKenzie, Thomas G., Med. Purveyor, Army of the Potomac, Alexandria, Va.:

The steamers started early on the morning of the 10th of May for Belle Plain. Asst. Surg. George P. Jacquette, USA, having been placed in charge of the medical supply steamers *Hugh Jenkins* and *Farmer*, was also despatched to Belle Plain, where he arrived before any other vessel was in sight, and a day in advance of the arrival of the wounded from Fredericksburg at that point....

In Georgia, Sherman ordered a general movement around the Confederate left, and towards Resaca.

West of White Sulphur Springs and east of Charleston, W.Va., lies a stream called New River, which flows past Cloyd's Mountain. Overall, this is an insignificant place except to the soldiers, North and South, who fought there. Surg. G. M. Kellogg, USV, under Brig. Gen. Crook, described the action.

Kellogg, G. M., Surg., USV, Cloyd's Mountain, W.Va.:

... at Cloyd's Mountain, West Virginia, May 9, 1864, and at New River Bridge, on the 10th, the enemy fought behind breastworks; and, in assaulting their strong position at Cloyd's Mountain, our force suffered severely. Having been engaged for several hours in collecting our wounded from the field and attending to their wounds, I was ordered to follow the command with all the wounded I could transport. After three or four hours, I was able to follow with over two hundred of the wounded. I left others of our wounded at the field hospital, and still some on the field, with four of our best medical officers, and more than half of my medical and hospital supplies. A number of those left were mortally wounded and very many required amputation. The distance between Cloyd's Mountain and New River Bridge, which it was necessary to reach at once, was eleven miles, Gen. Averell's command being hotly pursued by the Rebel Gen. Morgan, who followed up toward New River, it was not thought possible to remove any more of our wounded, and our transportation was too limited to bring away more than we brought. As it was, our means of transportation were sorely tried in crossing two rivers, and over rough mountain roads, for the distance of two hundred miles. We had but thirty-eight ambulances in all, only twelve of which were in good condition. Of the wounded brought through, one died from erysipelas supervening upon a wound of the arm.

We arrived at Meadow Bluff on the 21st. I was ordered to remove the wounded at once to hospital at Charleston, West Virginia, and to Gallipolis, Ohio, which I accordingly did. No report has yet reached us of our wounded left behind, but I have every reason to believe them better off than is usual within enemy's lines.... I took one hundred and ninety-two wounded to hospital at Gallipolis ... and to Charleston,... all of which were cases of wounds of the arm, forearm, and feet, or flesh wounds of more-or-less grave character.

May 11 (Wednesday)

Sheridan's cavalry, now at Yellow Tavern, about 6 miles north of Richmond, was attacked by Jeb Stuart's. In a swirling fight of sabres and revolvers, a dismounted Federal cavalryman shot Stuart as he rode past, mortally wounding him. Stuart was taken from the field for treatment and later removed to Richmond.

McGill, George M., Asst. Surg., USA, Sheridan's Cavalry, raid on Richmond, Va.:

During the afternoon of the 11th, the battle of Yellow Tavern was fought, an engagement in which the whole corps was concerned. Our corps hospital was established half a mile to the rear of the centre; it was under fire part of the time, but there was no situation within our lines that was not. It was thoroughly organized with a surgeon in charge, operators, dressers and recorders. The night and day following this battle were extremely trying for the wounded, as the corps moved during the night to near Meadow bridge, within the outer defenses of Richmond, and fought all the day....

At Spotsylvania C.H., Grant and Lee still were still faced off, awaiting developments. Grant, obviously, had the next move. Lee couldn't afford to attack the larger army and hope to survive long. He couldn't afford the casualties.

McParlin, T. A., Surg., Med. Dir., Army of the Potomac, Spotsylvania C.H., Va.:

On the 11th ... another train of wounded was organized and sent to Fredericksburg ... Silver's again being the point of rendezvous. The number sent was ... two thousand four hundred and forty-seven, using two hundred and fifty-six ambulances and one hundred and sixty-four wagons.... This train was four miles long and had to be collected and organized in the midst of a heavy storm, which began about three o'clock P.M., and continued all night with but little cessation. It left Silver's about nine o'clock P.M., but when within four miles of Fredericksburg, was halted and compelled to wait four hours, until a guard could be sent, so that it did not reach its destination until six o'clock A.M. of the 12th. As the town was already crowded, only six hundred of the most serious cases were left, and the remainder moved on to Belle Plain, arriving there about noon. The train was then parked in sections, and the wounded fed, furnished with dry blankets, and made as comfortable as possible in the wagons. Early the next morning [the 13th], the train was moved to the landing and the whole day was consumed in shipping the wounded. The men in the train suffered severely from the wet and cold, and twenty died on the road.

About seven hundred wounded were brought in from the front on the eleventh.

In Georgia, Sherman was on a swing towards

Resaca, southeast and completely behind the Confederate Army now at Rocky Face Gap and Buzzard's Roost.

May 12 (Thursday)

At Spotsylvania C.H., wave after wave of Federals charged Lee's prepared lines in one of the costliest battles of the war. The "Bloody Angle" claimed about 6800 Union and 5000 Confederate casualties, in killed and wounded alone. Another 4000 Confederates were captured. The wounded were sent by ambulance to Aquia Harbor, north of Fredericksburg, to be loaded on hospital boats and taken to Point Lookout, Md., and Washington, D.C. Grant was accused of butchery. Lee now had nearly 10,000 fewer men in his army; he'd never recover from this loss.

McParlin, T. A., Surg., Med. Dir., Army of the Potomac, Spotsylvania C.H., Va.:

At daybreak on the 12th, the Second Corps attacked the enemy from [the Union's] ... new position on the left, and by eight o'clock A.M., the engagement had become general, and the wounded began to pour into the hospitals. The advance ambulance depot of the Second Corps was near the Landron house. The rain of the previous eighteen hours had made the roads very muddy, and, in some places, almost impassable for vehicles, and as nearly one-half of the ambulances were ... at Fredericksburg, the duties of those remaining were very arduous. The number of wounded in this day's battle was large, and the labor of collecting and bringing them in went on until midnight. The following numbers were received ... three thousand five hundred and sixty. The proportion of severe wounds was unusually large, not over one-fourth of the number being able to walk back to the hospitals. Two hundred and forty ambulances collected the remainder.... All of the wounded were fed and sheltered, and the majority dressed and operated upon during the day.... Fortunately the night was not cold....

McKenzie, Thomas G., Med. Purveyor, Army of the Potomac, Belle Plain, Va.:

Besides the supplies taken down by Surg. Brinton and Asst. Surg. Jacquette, I was ordered, May 11th, to proceed to Belle Plain with two barges loaded with medical and hospital stores, and arriving early on the morning of the 12th, I reported to Acting Medical Inspector Gen. Cuyler. On my arrival at Belle Plain, I found it impracticable for the steamers *Hugh Jenkins* and *Farmer* to lay alongside the wharf, on account of the shallowness of the water. There was, at that time, but one wharf, at which not only all the stores of the several departments were unloaded, but the troops arriving as reinforcements had to be disembarked. To add to the confusion, all the wounded were conveyed along this wharf to the transports, and hence it was an utter impossibility to work expeditiously or effectually.

Such being the case, it was thought best for the supply steamers to remain out in the stream, sending supplies ashore on a lighter as they were needed. Accordingly one was obtained from the quartermaster, together with a gang of negroes. The two barges under my immediate charge were brought up as near the wharf as possible, and such articles as could be furnished from them ... were conveyed across other barges, and loaded on the wagons as speedily as they came up....

McGill, George M., Asst. Surg., USA, Sheridan's Cavalry, raid on Richmond, Va.:

On the 12th, the corps was engaged on three sides. On the left, facing Richmond, the 3d division was engaged with one of the Rebel fortifications. On the right, the 2d division contended against a heavy force of infantry, while the 1st division built a bridge over the Chickahominy, and forced a passage in the face of the cavalry force defeated by the corps the day before. The wounded from these points were sent to the corps train after being carefully dressed. Most of the cases saved were brought off on horseback, as all our ambulances were already overloaded. Our loss was comparatively light, forty men in all being wounded in the 2d and 3d divisions. On the afternoon and evening of the same day, the corps fought at Mechanicsville, and during the two days following, marched to Haxall's landing, which was reached on the afternoon of the 14th. During these days, surgeons were detailed night and morning to dress and attend to the wounded....

Sherman's troops had passed Snake Creek Gap and were approaching Resaca, where Johnston's army lay in wait.

May 13 (Friday)

Grant, having failed to break Lee's lines at Spotsylvania C.H., moved around to his (Grant's) left with Warren's corps in the lead to the southeast. This sidestepping movement would characterize the campaign.

McParlin, T. A., Surg., Med. Dir., Army of the Potomac, Spotsylvania C.H., Va.:

On the 13th, another train of ambulances and army wagons, obtained from the supply train, was organized to convey wounded.... The number sent was ... three thousand one hundred and ninety-three, using one hundred and twenty-two ambulances and two hundred and forty-five wagons ... collected at Silver's, leaving that place at nine o'clock P.M., and reaching Fredericksburg early the following morning. The wounded on this train suffered very much; it rained all night, the men were wet and chilled, and it was impossible to supply them with hot food on the road. Fourteen men died during the trip.

The necessity of sending off as many as possible, however, was imperative, as the army moved during the night of the 13th, and the ground occupied by the hospitals was abandoned to the enemy. No more ambulances could be spared, as there were still some wounded lying on the field to be brought in .... Every wagon was obtained from the quartermaster's department which could possibly be emptied, but four hundred and twenty of the wounded of the Fifth Corps and two hundred of the Second Corps had to be left on account of lack of transportation. Tents, medical officers and attendants, dressings, medical supplies and three days' rations were left with them.

Welch, S. G., Surg., 20th S.C. Vols., in a letter to his wife, from a field hospital, Spotsylvania C.H., Va.:

... on the 10th another big fight here, and then one again yesterday that was the most terrific battle I have ever witnessed. The musketry and cannon continued from daybreak until night.... We were behind breastworks, but the Yankees charged into them in many places, fighting with the greatest determination, and it strained us to the utmost to hold our own.... It was an awful day, and it seemed to me as if all the "Furies of Darkness" had come together in combat. Everybody who was not firing was pale with anxiety, but our noble solders stood their ground, fighting with the utmost desperation.

The Yanks certainly tried their best yesterday, and they made us try our best too. It was the most desperate struggle of the war.... We have quiet today.

My brother passed through it all untouched. His company lost four killed, besides many wounded. John Landrum was killed and Scott Allen badly wounded. Gen. Abner Perrin was killed, Col. Brockman lost his arm, Capt. McFall his eye, and Gen. McGowan was severely wounded in the arm. This makes the fifth time he has been wounded.... I saw your brother Edwin yesterday. He was well....

Perry, John G., Asst. Surg., USV, 20th Mass. Vols., Spotsylvania C.H., Va.:

Fighting still—ten days of it without intermission. I am so exhausted and nervous it is difficult to express myself; am operating day and night. This thing cannot last much longer, for one side or the other must yield from sheer exhaustion. I am trying to gather together the Twentieth, but so far can find but two officers, no men, no colors. The only privates I have discovered are here in the hospital, and apparently there is almost nothing left of the dear old regiment.

At Resaca, Ga., Gen. Joe Johnston's army took up positions and awaited Sherman's arrival.

May 14 (Saturday)

In Georgia, Sherman arrived at Resaca and ordered probing attacks against Johnston's line, especially on the Confederate flanks.

In the rear of the Fifteenth Corps, Mrs. Bickerdyke and Mrs. Porter were riding their ambulance through the rugged, hilly terrain, awaiting developments. Late in the afternoon they begin to hear sounds of artillery firing in their front—and they knew a battle was pending. As dark approached, they found themselves with plenty of work to do. Mrs. Livermore wrote:

As they were pushing along in their ambulance on one occasion, packed with battle-stores, they heard the distant sounds of fierce cannonade—and knew that a battle was in progress ahead of them. On they went, the sounds becoming louder, clearer, and more distinct. Now [the sounds were] mingled with the crash of musketry, the calls of half a hundred bugles, the thundered commands of officers leading their men to the conflict, the yells of the infuriated soldiers as they hurled themselves on their antagonists with the shock of an avalanche—and sometimes, overtopping all, the awful cries of mortal agony, that came up from the battlefield, from men writhing in every form of ghastly wound. They were in the rear of the battle of Resaca. On one side were heaped the knapsacks, and other *impedimenta*, of which the men had stripped themselves for the fight—on the other the amputating tents of the surgeons, surrounded by an ever-increasing quantity of mangled and dissevered limbs. The field hospitals were in readiness for the wounded, who lay about under trees, and on the grass, awaiting their turn at the amputating table, or to have their wounds dressed.

In a short time both women were at work. Their portable kettles, with furnaces attached, were set up, their concentrated extract of beef was uncanned, and soon the fainting and famishing men were uttering their thanks for the great refreshment of a palatable soup. In the interim, [the women] dressed wounds, took down memoranda of last messages to be sent North to friends, received and labelled dying gifts to be distributed East, West, and North, encouraged the desponding, and sped the parting soul to Heaven with a brief verse of hymn, a quotation from the words of Christ, or a fervent and tender prayer. This arduous but blessed work they continued at Kingston, Alatoona, and Kennesaw Mountain, on to Atlanta.

Grinsted, W., Surg., USV, 3d Div., 20th Corps, advance on Atlanta, Ga.:

On May 8th we first encountered the enemy at Buzzard Roost, in two days' operations we had some ten men wounded. By a series of light marches we arrived at Snake Creek Gap, where we joined the Sixteenth Corps, and on the afternoon of May 14th, we had severe skirmishing with the enemy in which we had thirty-five men wounded. These were left at Barrett's farm, and the division advanced to Resaca.…

In Virginia, Grant was shifting to the Union left in the rain and mud; Lee followed as rapidly as possible. No major fighting, except with the elements, took place today. At the hospitals where the Union wounded had been left, the Confederates visited.

McParlin, T. A., Surg., Med. Dir., Army of the Potomac, Spotsylvania C.H., Va.:

On the evening of the 14th, a body of the enemy's cavalry,… entered the hospitals and removed all the Confederate wounded who could walk, about eighty in number, and also all stragglers and hospital attendants who wore no distinctive badge. The soldiers of the squadron carried off the greater part of the rations left for the wounded. As soon as these facts were reported, a regiment of the Second Corps was sent to drive off the marauders, who had gone, however, before our troops arrived. Surg. Thomas Jones, 8th Pennsylvania Reserves, who had been left with the wounded in the Fifth Corps hospital, was killed.… Additional rations were left with the wounded.…

McGill, George M., Asst. Surg., USA, Sheridan's Cavalry, Haxall's Landing, Va.:

… As soon as Medical Director McCormick heard of our arrival, he sent a transport well fitted up for the wounded. While lying at Haxall's, nearly three hundred men were sent to general hospital, two hundred and ten of whom were wounded. Much-needed medical supplies were here obtained for the corps. From Haxall's, we moved to White House, where fifty-seven sick and wounded were sent to general hospital.…

May 15 (Sunday)

At Resaca, Ga., Sherman decided that Johnston's positions were too strong for a frontal assault, so he started another flanking movement. There was heavy fighting along the Oostenaula River, south of Resaca, with Sherman sending both cavalry and infantry to force the decision. Johnston evacuated his positions during the night, burned the bridge over the Oostenaula, and withdrew towards Calhoun and Adairsville.

In the hospital at Resaca, both Mrs. Bickerdyke and Mrs. Porter worked day and night feeding and dressing the wounded from the previous day's battle. Mrs. Porter, from Wisconsin, often wiped the face of a wounded man and found a friend or acquaintance from the Wisconsin regiments. Porter was always fearful of finding her own son among the wounded, for he was with a Chicago artillery battery serving in Sherman's army.

Foye, John W., Surg., USV, 20th Corps, Resaca, Ga.:

On May 12, the command moved to the right, and, passing through Snake Creek Gap, came upon the enemy near Resaca, and after a series of manoeuvres, became engaged shortly after noon on May 15th.... The supplies were abundant and of good quality. The field hospital was located about a mile and a half in the rear, near a good supply of water. The wounded were conveyed from the field depots to the field hospital in ambulances, and their removal was completed about two o'clock on the morning after the battle. The fire was from artillery and musketry, the latter being at short range and very severe.... The wounded were transferred from the field hospitals to the general field hospital at the Department of the Cumberland, located at Resaca....

Grinsted, W., Surg., USV, 3d Div., 20th Corps, Resaca, Ga.:

Here the command suffered severely, losing fifty-five men killed and five hundred and eighty wounded.... The wounded were admitted and attended to rapidly, and the whole number dressed, operated on, and made comfortable by ten o'clock the next morning.... The wounded, with those left at Barrett's farm, remained nearly a week, and were then sent in ambulances to the field hospital at Resaca....

At Spotsylvania C.H., Va., Grant was still moving to the Union left, hoping to outflank Lee. The Federal regiment sent to chase off the guerrillas returned to the Fifth Corps, leaving the hospitals unprotected.

McParlin, T. A., Surg., Med. Dir., Army of the Potomac, Spotsylvania C.H., Va.:

... meantime, a series of depot hospitals had been organized at Fredericksburg,... on the 9th of May. All the churches, warehouses and convenient dwellings in the place were immediately occupied for hospital purposes, each corps organization being kept distinct as far as possible.... Supplies of all kinds arrived at Belle Plain on the 10th and 11th of May, and were brought to Fredericksburg.... The stores sent with the first train, and those contained in the ambulance boxes, served for the necessities of the wounded until supplies could be brought from Belle Plain. The wounded officers were at first billeted upon the inhabitants of the town, who, as a general rule, received them kindly and treated them well....

After the first week, an officer's hospital was established.... The greatest deficiency was in medical officers.... Fifty medical officers in all were sent from the front,... all that could be spared. A number of medical men (civilians) came down from Washington as volunteers....

A large number of the sick and slightly wounded, many of the latter self-mutilated, did not go to the field hospitals, nor accompany the regular trains, but straggled to Fredericksburg and thence to Belle Plain, relying upon the agents of the Sanitary Commission for food, and keeping as much as possible out of the way of medical officers. About five thousand of these men were in Fredericksburg at different times, and the tales invented by them ... gave rise to many of the false reports of suffering and destitution among the wounded which for a time were prevalent in the north. Nearly all the slightly wounded passed directly through ... to Washington as fast as the boats could be procured.... About six hundred malingerers and stragglers had also been received and turned over to the provost marshal.... After the first three days, all men were carefully examined by a medical officer before they were allowed to pass to the boats.

May 16 (Monday)

Outside of Resaca, Ga., the seemingly endless rains were making the hospital area a quagmire for Mrs. Bickerdyke and her co-workers. At daybreak, soldiers at the point of exhaustion would stumble into the hospital area, get a quick bowl of Bickerdyke's soup and a cup of scalding coffee, and go back to the front lines. The army wagons hauling rations for sick and well alike were nowhere to be seen this day, being far in the rear, trying to get up through the mud. Later in the day, about 10 A.M., Sherman's men marched into Resaca and wondered why there'd been such a fuss over such a dingy place.

At Spotsylvania C.H., Va., a train of two hundred ambulances was sent to pick up the wounded left at the Fifth Corps hospital. The Corps hospitals had begun to move earlier, and new hospitals were set up in the vicinity of the Beverly house, on the courthouse grounds, and near the Fredericksburg turnpike. They would remain in these positions until the 21st of the month.

McParlin, T. A., Surg., Med. Dir., Army of the Potomac, Spotsylvania C.H., Va.:

The obstacles to the removal of the more seriously wounded by way of Belle Plain were very great.… The road between that point and Fredericksburg was, to a considerable extent, corduroyed, very rough, and could not have been improved by any means then available. But one small wharf existed at Belle Plain, and at this all the supplies of the army had to be landed.… The light-draught steamers, with barges, were used to remove the wounded by the river, the larger hospital transports remaining below at Tappahannock, where the wounded were transferred to them. These hospital transports were the steamers *Connecticut* and *State of Maine*. They were completely fitted up with beds, cooking apparatus and everything pertaining to the care and comfort of the sick.…

May 17 (Tuesday)

After the Battle of Spotsylvania C.H., Grant cleared up the battlefield mess and his organization, and developed more plans for attack. Within the two weeks following the Battle of the Wilderness, several attempts were made to recover the wounded who'd fallen into Confederate hands. Several wounded were immediately turned over and transported to Fredericksburg. These wounded were collected primarily at Parker's store and Robertson's tavern in the Wilderness. This netted about three hundred wounded, the tents, etc., being left with those too badly injured to move.

About the 14th of May, the Confederates decided that they would transfer no more wounded unless the request came directly from Gen. Grant. On the 18th, a wagon train went out carrying a letter from Grant to the local commander concerning the wounded. The Confederates refused this letter because it wasn't directly addressed to Gen. Lee. The Confederates did, however, permit the supplies being carried to be sent on for the use of the wounded. Again on the 22nd an attempt was made with the same result, and, to add insult to injury, the surgeon in charge of the relief effort was stopped by guerrillas on his way back to the Union lines and was relieved of his horse, papers, and cash. An attempt was made again on the 27th, only this time Grant sent a strong force of cavalry with the surgeons, and 86 wounded

were recovered. When these men finally reached Fredericksburg, they were loaded directly onto a hospital ship and sent to Washington.

Welch, S. G., Surg., 20th S.C. Vols., in a letter to his wife, from a field hospital, Spotsylvania C.H., Va.:

We are still "in statu quo," the two armies confronting each other. I expect you know more about the situation—or more—than I do, for, although we are right here, we know nothing unless we see the newspapers. I sent a telegram to Father on the 7th inst. from Orange C.H. that my brother Billie had passed through the battle of the Wilderness safe.

We left there late that afternoon for Spotsylvania. I went over part of the battlefield as we were leaving, and saw that the Yankees had not taken time to bury their dead except behind their breastworks.… I understand that the dead are very thick on the battlefield near this place.

The weather cleared off yesterday, but it looks like rain again today. I never was more tired of rain. We all still have plenty to eat.

Perry, John G., Asst. Surg., USV, 20th Mass. Vols., Spotsylvania C.H., Va.:

Seventeen days since I have heard a word from the North. Not a single mail has been sent us since we left winter quarters.

We now find that six officers of the Twentieth are living (excluding Surg. Hayward and myself) out of twenty who started with us. I am at present detailed to run the Division Hospital with Dr. Divenell.… For ten days the battle raged each day, we being the assaulting party. We have been comparatively quiet the last two days, burying our dead.

On his withdrawal from Calhoun, Ga., Joe Johnston's Army of Tennessee held briefly at Adairsville, facing Union Gen. George Thomas at Johnston's front, and Union generals McPherson and Schofield coming around both Confederate flanks. Johnston hurried his retreat to escape the box.

Donoho, A. G., Surg., CSA, Calhoun, Ga.:

After the battle there were ten men, seriously wounded, for whom we had no transportation. They were left at the field hospital, with me in charge, to be captured next morning when the enemy came.

Two Irishmen were left with me to assist in attending to them. They were to leave as soon as the enemy approached. My papers were made out for me to be captured and sent around and exchanged. That did not suit me.

I had no desire in the world to make a trip North. I knew I would be of no service to the men nor see them any more after the enemy took charge of them, and the hard part of it was that the men were not of my brigade, but belonged to a Florida brigade in our division. My first effort was to get a wagon or wagons to move them. I went to every wagon I heard passing, the hospital being two or three hundred yards from the road; they were all loaded and could not help me. About midnight everything became still, and so still!—no more wagons, no more noise....

When Sherman's army moved from Resaca, the disposition of the wounded at that place became a problem. A problem, that is, until Mrs. Bickerdyke remembered her two Christian Commission ministers she'd left in Chattanooga—J. F. Loyd and H. D. Lathrop. These gentlemen were more than happy to come to Resaca and take over the treatment of the wounded from Mrs. Bickerdyke and Mrs. Porter. It gave the two another "field white unto the harvest."

May 18 (Wednesday)

Another attack on the new Confederate lines at Spotsylvania C.H. did little other than create more casualties. Grant moved farther south and east.

Roden, J. B., Pvt., CSA, Spotsylvania C.H., Va.:

I was wounded on the skirmish line near Spotsylvania C.H. on the morning of May 18, 1864. As the balls were flying thick my first concern was to know how to get to the rear. I made a start, and when approaching the regiment the boys began to quiz me: "O yes, don't play off that way; you just want a furlough." I passed to the hospital, where the doctor examined my wounds and told me he would have to preform an operation. When asked if amputation would be necessary, he said: "Not just now." The operating table was a barn door set on two trestles.

It was soon reported that Grant's army had turned our right flank and captured Guinea Station; consequently all the wounded were ordered to the rear. All who could walk were ordered to Milford Station, some thirty miles distant. I started alone about 2 P.M., and made twelve miles, stopping overnight at a farmhouse, where I was treated very kindly.

McParlin, T. A., Surg., Med. Dir., Army of the Potomac, Spotsylvania C.H., Va.:

On the morning of the 18th, the Second Corps ... attacked the enemy's works. Five hundred and fifty-two wounded were the result, and the character of the wounds was unusually severe, a large proportion being caused by shell and canister....

McGill, George M., Asst. Surg., USA, Sheridan's Cavalry, Haxall's Landing, Va.:

On the 18th, while lying at Baltimore stores, an expedition was made by Brig. Gen. Custer, who cut the Richmond and Fredericksburg railroad near Hanover Courthouse. In this expedition, two men were wounded, one of whom was lost. Crossing the Pamunkey river, the corps next marched to Dunkirk, on the Mattapony, thence to our wagon train, near Milford Station. In all there were about three hundred and eighty men wounded during the expedition, of whom about two hundred and eighty-five were secured.

The Union Army of the Tennessee followed Confederate Joe Johnston's Army of Tennessee from Adairsville to the Cassville-Kingston area, where fighting occurred as the Union forces converged.

Donoho, A. G., Surg., CSA, Calhoun, Ga.:

After midnight the cavalry skirmish line fell back, leaving me between them and the enemy. A few of them came to where I was and seemed sorry for me. I asked to what command they belonged and found it was Col. McKinley's Tennessee cavalry, whose headquarters were about one mile to the rear. I asked them to watch the men for me until I could see Col. McKinley and get some ambulances, which they cheerfully agreed to do. I went double-quick most of the way. The colonel treated me courteously and kindly, but had only one ambulance, and the hind wheel of that was broken-down; but he said that if I would write a note to Gen. Loring, who was about five miles to the rear, he would send a courier with it, and if Gen. Loring had any ambulances he would send them. I wrote the note, off went the courier with it, and I went back to the men after thanking him. I felt like hugging him for his kindness....

When I got back, my Irishmen were gone and two cavalrymen on guard. I waited and waited, O so long!—long enough for several nights to pass. I had confided to my cavalry friend my intention to stay until I could see the enemy approaching, then leave, for I could do no good after they had taken charge. He approved of my plan and agreed to let me ride behind him out of range of the enemy's guns.

Just as I could see the gray dawn in the east, three ambulances came. My cavalry friend assisted me in getting the men loaded in the ambulances, which occupied some time. Before we got them all in, we could see the enemy advancing, and just as we had the last one they saw us and opened fire. When the last man was in, the minié balls were cutting up the dust. The last man in, I caught on the hind end of the ambulance (there was no room inside), waved my hand to the Yankees, and trotted until within the lines.

After I got to the railroad station, I was fully compensated for all my long night of anxiety. One of the men, a lieutenant of a Florida regiment, looked up into my face with such an expression of gratitude as only a few times in life have I seen, with words of thanks to me for getting him within the lines so he could go home to his mother to die. I bade them all farewell and went in search of my regiment, which I soon found. They were all as glad to see me back as if I had been the lost babe in the woods. Col. Hale was pawing up the dirt that the surgeon of the division should have detailed me to stay with wounded men of another command.

May 19 (Thursday)

Lee sent Gen. Richard Ewell to the Confederate right, where Ewell brought on a severe fight with Union forces. The battle lasted most of the day, again accomplishing nothing but creating more casualties. Grant was moving towards the Po River to the southeast. For the several battles which made up the whole of Spotsylvania, the Federals lost about 17,500 out of nearly 110,000 engaged—about 17 percent. The South's losses were never accurately recorded but could be estimated roughly at 6000 from a total engaged of about 50,000—about 11 percent. Grant could afford the loss, Lee couldn't.

The wounded, of course, felt it worse than anyone. The dead no longer cared.

McParlin, T. A., Surg., Med. Dir., Army of the Potomac, Spotsylvania C.H., Va.:

During the evening of the 18th and the morning of the 19th, the corps hospitals were moved to the left, and established on the Massaponax church road, north of the Anderson house. This removal was fortunate, as the hospitals thus escaped from the confusion caused by the enemy's attack on the evening of the 19th. This attack was repulsed by heavy artillery regiments, armed as infantry, who had lately joined the army, and for many of whom it was the first battle. The total number of wounded from the affair was eleven hundred, most of whom were able to walk back to the field hospitals, being hit in the hands and arms. In many of these cases, the skin was so blackened with powder as to prove that the injury was self-inflicted, either by design or accident. Very many of the wounded came into the hospitals with extemporaneous tourniquets tightly applied, and their hands and forearms swollen and livid in consequence. Dread of hemorrhage is simply another proof of the inexperience of troops. No large trains of wounded were organized after the 13th; as the road to Fredericksburg was open and safe, the corps medical directors sent their wounded off as fast as they were received.... This was the last of the series of battles about Spotsylvania Courthouse, the army moving on the 21th towards the North Anna....

Reed, Wm. H., Nurse, Union hospital, Fredericksburg, Va.:

The fearful and undecided battles of the Wilderness and of Spotsylvania, the decimated regiments, and the prospects of continued operations ... made the call for reinforcements imperative. The fortifications of Washington were left comparatively undefended, and [the capital's] garrisons were transferred to active duty in the field. A column of sixteen thousand [Union] men moved down to join the [main body of the] Army [of the Potomac]. We had received the news of the success and capture of prisoners and artillery at Spotsylvania, who were actually passing to the rear, while this body of fresh troops was marching through Fredericksburg for the front. They were full of fire, and their enthusiasm was kindled afresh at the sight of these captured guns and other trophies of that bloody field....

Within twenty-four hours five hundred men were brought back bleeding, wounded, dead, or dying.... Ewell's Corps, detached from its main army to make a detour of our rear to capture our wagon trains, was met, fought, and repulsed within six miles of where we were; and now the ambulances were returning over the very ground upon which these men had moved with steps so firm and hearts so light but a few hours before.... As the train must halt for the night, it was parked in an open, ploughed field, directly at the foot of Marie's Heights....

The camp for the night was settled at dark: the drivers had lain down to rest; the fires were blazing brightly, while the moon, half obscured in the smoke of ... battles, shone out red and lurid upon the field.... Here was this vast addition to our numbers—the dead to be taken out and buried, the living to be fed, and washed, and surgically dressed. Detailing our guard, we visited every ambulance, moving those who had died. One by one they were placed upon stretchers, their bodies hardly cold, their limbs in every position, and they were carried out to an adjoining field, where they were laid side by side. In the meantime, our kitchen was taxed to its utmost capacity ... and before midnight every man had an ample supper, such as we could hastily prepare. Our work went on. There were throbbing wounds to be dressed, and fevered limbs to be cooled by fresh water applications. With basins, sponges, bandages, and lint, and with clear spring-water, we went from ambulance to ambulance, bathing, cleansing, soothing wounds which were yet fresh and open, and some so ghastly as to make us almost faint. Arms, legs, shoulders, jaws, and feet had been carried away; many had received only the most hurried treatment upon the field, while others had not been attended to at all....

Moving through the train, we kept at work until all was still. The embers of the fires were dying out; perfect stillness reigned through the camp, with the exception of the moanings of the men who were to pass a sleepless night in pain. The dead were not to be left uncared for nor uncovered. There they were in one long row, laid side by side, stark and stiff, the moon looking calmly down upon them.... With a flickering candle we went over each body, examining clothing, marking every article, from gun-stopper to

watch, or photograph, or Bible; collecting data of wounds or death, with the address of their friends, to whom the news was yet to come of their burial in an enemy's territory by friendly hands. Then with tent-cloth and blanket we covered them....

At daylight we were on the field again, with fresh water, crackers, milk punch, and coffee, to give all the refreshment we could before starting them over those terrible roads between Fredericksburg and Belle Plain....

Roden, J. B., Pvt., CSA, en route to Guinea Station, Va.:

I started early next day and made fourteen miles, when I fell exhausted by the roadside. I was put into a wagon and hauled to the station, the remaining four miles. There I was put on a hospital train, but remained all night at the station.

The train arrived in Richmond the next Friday evening, when I was taken to Winder Hospital.

Joseph Johnston, realizing that Sherman's army was split because of the Union's flanking movement, decided to attack the Federal army piecemeal. Johnston sent Hood to attack the Federals. But Hood, wrongly believing that Federals were on his flank and at his rear, fell back on the defensive. Johnston then withdrew into defensive positions south and east of Cassville, where, when evening came, he fell back towards Cartersville and the Etowah River, followed closely by Sherman.

Grinsted, W., Surg., USV, 3d Div., 20th Corps, Cassville, Ga.:

On May 17th, we left for Cassville, and on May 19th, late in the evening, the troops having been in line of battle and marching, with frequent halts, they fought the battle of Cassville, capturing the town. Ten men were wounded, and they were placed in a comfortable house and immediately attended to, and then sent to the rear in ambulances. The weather was fine with occasional showers; the roads were in good condition, and the troops were in good health and spirits.... Two days' rest after the affair at Cassville, with facilities for washing and bathing, of which the men availed themselves, contributed greatly to the endurance of the subsequent fatigues....

May 20 (Friday)

As a result of military actions in Virginia, the Richmond, Fredericksburg & Potomac Railroad was largely in Federal hands, and the Virginia Central Railroad was put out of commission by Union raids. That left only the Orange and Alexandria Railroad open to move the Confederate wounded from the battles that had been raging since Grant had crossed the Rappahannock earlier in the month. The number of wounded placed great stress on the hospitals in Gordonsville (the former Exchange Hotel) and the hospitals in Lynchburg as they filled with most of the more than 48,000 Confederate men wounded during the month. Lynchburg would admit more than 10,000 of these sick and wounded, among which 127 would die in May alone.

McKenzie, Thomas G., Med. Purveyor, Army of the Potomac, Washington, D.C.:

Having remained at Belle Plain until the morning of May 19th, I was ordered to turn over the remainder of my supplies ... and report to ... Washington City. I left Belle Plain,... and reported to the Acting Surgeon General, May 20th.

The same night, the steamer *Planter* was ordered to report to me, and I was instructed to load her with all the supplies then in the warehouse at Alexandria. Two barges were also sent to load such stores as could not be transported by the steamer. In addition ... another barge was ... loaded exclusively with portions of a requisition made by ... Brinton.... An extract ... accompanying this requisition, I here quote: "It is also desirable that he procure a barge and load it with three thousand iron bedsteads or wooden cots, three thousand mattresses, ten thousand sheets, seven thousand pillows, one hundred brooms, four hundred rubber cushions with open centre, ten thousand pillowcases, five thousand suits of hospital clothing, two thousand blankets, three thousand counterpanes, five hundred wooden buckets, twenty caldrons, twelve cooking stoves with furniture complete, ten barrels of sulphate of iron for disinfectant purposes, two hundred pounds cocoa or chocolate, two hundred pounds cornstarch, one hundred dozen bottles porter, six hundred pounds oakum and one thousand bed sacks...."

In Georgia, Confederate Joseph E. Johnston passed through Cartersville, crossed the Etowah River, and took up strong defensive positions at Allatoona Pass. Union troops under Schofield followed closely through Cartersville.

May 22 (Sunday)

It seemed to be that just a few minutes after Lee had reached Hanover Junction, a short distance north of Richmond, Grant's blue columns arrived from Guiney's Station. Another close race had been won by the Confederates.

McParlin, T. A., Surg., Med. Dir., Army of the Potomac, North Anna River, Va.:

During the movement to the North Anna, on the 21st and 22d, fifteen ambulances moved in the rear of each division.... The number of stragglers, especially on the 22d, was large.... Instructions have been given to return all empty wagons not at Fredericksburg and Belle Plain Landing loaded, after which, so soon as the wounded are removed from Fredericksburg, that place and Belle Plain Landing will be abandoned, and the depot established at Pt. Royal on the Rappahannock.

Roden, J. B., Pvt., CSA, in Winder Hospital, Richmond, Va.:

On Sunday morning the surgeon in charge, Dr. Tyler, dressed my wound, nothing having been done to it since Wednesday except the use of cold water to keep down inflammation.

For the first few days things went well, but I grew weaker and the rations became distasteful. I was given a little bread and rye coffee for breakfast, and for dinner a small piece of half-baked corn bread, a little fat bacon, with a few stewed beets and potato-vine leaves for salad. One morning I requested the nurse not to bring any dinner unless he could find something more palatable. He replied that he would continue to bring the same diet, which he proceeded to do. Upon my taking him to task, he became insolent, and as he turned to leave I threw my chunk of corn bread at him. The nurse reported me to the ward master, who threatened to put me in the guardhouse. A comrade wounded about the same time I was and who lay on a cot to my right handed me one of his crutches, and we planned, though neither of us could raise our heads, to attack the ward master if he attempted to execute his threat.

The doctor came just before supper and found me in a fever. On learning the cause, he sent for the ward master and reprimanded him.

Johnston's Army of Tennessee, in fairly strong defensive positions near Allatoona on the Chattanooga-Atlanta railroad, waited for Sherman to attack. As usual, Sherman ordered a move around Johnston's left flank, going towards Dallas, Ga.

May 23 (Monday)

As Sherman moved his entire army across the Etowah River and headed towards Dallas. Johnston, having little choice, his left flank turned again, prepared to move towards that same location.

At Hanover Junction, Va., near the North Anna River, Lee waited for Grant to arrive. Late in the afternoon, Warren's Federal Fifth Corps crossed the North Anna. About 6 P.M., A. P. Hill's Confederates hit Warren's corps, made some initial gains, and then were stopped. Wright's blue-clad corps was crossing the river and would arrive the next morning to help Warren. Hancock's Second Corps attacked the Confederates near Old Chesterfield, on the north side of the river. Lee's opportunity to attack the Union Army piecemeal was lost because of his indisposition and lack of coordination.

Reed, Wm. H., Union hospital, Fredericksburg, Va.:

Monday, the 23d of May, 1864, was a most lovely day. The breeze came fresh and cool from the north; the air was pure and clear; the sky perfectly cloudless.... The wounded from the Wilderness and Spotsylvania were daily swelling the numbers of our patients. One ambulance and wagon train, which reached the Heights, discharged their living freight of five hundred wounded men upon the ground, there being no nook or corner or shelter in any building in the town. We were almost overwhelmed by the accumulated work which every hour seemed to be bringing to us. Surely such a day of horrors the sun had rarely looked upon. These sufferers had not eaten food in days. They were exhausted with hunger; many were dying at that moment from want of nourishment; and the ghastly undressed wounds made us heartsick. Five hundred wounds to be examined, bathed, and dressed; five hundred men to be fed and washed, and with but our little company of aides to do it!

May 24 (Tuesday)

Near Hanover Junction, Va., Meade's Union Sixth Corps moved to the right of the Fifth Corps and took up positions. Hancock's corps, the Second, crossed at the Chesterfield Bridge farther east. Burnside's Ninth Corps also crossed the river. The Army of the Potomac was now divided into three parts by the bend in the North Anna River and by Lee's protruding line. The Union forces weren't in a good position for mutual support.

McParlin, T. A., Surg., Med. Dir., Army of the Potomac, North Anna River, Va.:

On the 24th, a train was organized for the purpose of conveying the wounded from the field hospital to Pt. Royal.... Two hundred and ninety-one sick, five hundred and twenty-one wounded, forty-two ambulances and one hundred and eight wagons.... The train rendezvoused at Milford, near which point, the main trains of the army were parked. A cavalry escort of four hundred men accompanied it, and it reached Pt. Royal,... by dusk of the 25th.

Perry, John G., Asst. Surg., USV, 20th Mass. Vols., near Hanover Junction, Va.:

I can scratch only a few lines, being up to my elbows in blood. Oh, the fatigue and endless work we surgeons have! About one night in three to sleep in, and then we are so nervous and played out that sleep is impossible.

The hospital is fast filling up with poor fellows who last night charged upon the enemy's works on the other side of the river. We are some fifteen miles nearer Richmond than when I last wrote, and the strongest works of the Confederacy are at this point and at the South Anna River.... We have had a deal of forced marching lately, and the heat has been almost intolerable. At times it has seemed as if the sun's rays would lay us out, yet we march all day, and through volumes upon volumes of dense dust....

It seems to me I am quite callous to death now, and that I could see my dearest friend die without much feeling. This condition tells a long story which, under other circumstances, could scarcely be imagined. During the last three weeks I have seen probably no less than two thousand deaths, and among them those of many dear friends. I have witnessed hundreds of men shot dead, have walked and slept among them, and surely I feel it possible to die myself as calmly as any—but enough of this. The fight is now fearful, and ambulances are coming in with great rapidity, each bearing its suffering load.

In Georgia, Confederate Gen. Joseph Wheeler and his cavalry were at Sherman's rear, attacking wagon trains and creating havoc. Johnston, realizing Sherman was around the Confederate left flank again, ordered the Southern army towards Dallas, via New Hope Church, closer to Atlanta.

May 25 (Wednesday)

In New Hope Church, Ga., in the middle of rolling thunder and driving rain, Hooker's corps drove against Hood's Confederates along Pumpkin Vine Creek. New Hope Church, about twenty-six miles northeast of Atlanta, was to be (until about June 4th) the scene of the struggle for Atlanta.

Foye, John W., Surg., USV, 20th Corps, New Hope Church, Ga.:

The command left Resaca on May 16th, in pursuit of the enemy, and after a series of skirmishes, again met him in force at Dallas and became engaged from May 25th to 29th inclusive. The troops were much exhausted by long and heavy forced marches. Our supplies of stimulants, surgical appliances and shelter were ample. The field hospitals were located one-and-a-half miles from the front; but our lines advanced two miles in the evening of May 25th, and the hospitals were moved on the following morning…. The slightly wounded were placed in army wagons and sent to Kingston, Ga., and the more serious cases were sent to the same point in ambulances…. Two days' rations were sent with the train and the wounded were fed thrice daily while in transit…. Twelve hundred and sixty-four wounded were treated in the three division hospitals.…

Grinsted, W., Surg., USV, 3d Div., 20th Corps, New Hope Church, Ga.:

On May 23d, we crossed the Etowah River, and on the 25th we suddenly met the enemy at New Hope Church, before Dallas. When I found that a battle was impending, I turned the regimental panniers, stewards, etc., to the right and rear, and established a hospital at the house of one Hawkins, a mile-and-a-

half from the front, on a good smooth road. I was ordered still farther to the rear, across Pumpkin Vine Creek; but the roads being full of advancing troops, I was unable to obey. The hospital train was cut off, but by strenuous exertions it arrived at six o'clock A.M., on the 26th.…

Near Hanover Junction, Va., the confrontation between Lee and Grant was a stalemate. Grant wouldn't assault the strong Confederate positions, and Lee was too ill to conduct an offensive operation, even against Grant's divided army.

McParlin, T. A., Surg., Med. Dir., Army of the Potomac, North Anna River, Va.:

The first train of wounded … reached Pt. Royal … on the evening of the 25th. The steamer *Hugh Jenkins*, loaded with hospital supplies,… had reached that point a few hours before, as had also a barge load of stores belonging to the Sanitary Commission. Col. Cuyler had also arrived, bringing with him a number of medical officers, who were immediately employed in dressing the wounded. No buildings had been prepared for [the wounded's] reception, and as it was raining heavily, it was thought best to leave them in the wagons or ambulances during the night, hot coffee, soup, etc., being served to them. On the 26th, they were removed from the wagons into the houses and made as comfortable as possible.…

On this date the Ninth Corps was added to the Army of the Potomac, and that corps' medical director reported to Surg. McParlin, Medical Director of the Army of the Potomac. An inspection of the Ninth Corps' medical capabilities by Asst. Surg. J. S. Billings, McParlin's medical inspector, found that the equipment on hand was wholly inadequate for operations. Equipment was missing; a three-month supply of medical stores issued at Annapolis, Md., had been left there; the organization of the ambulance corps as directed on April 12th had begun but wasn't complete; the few ambulances available were broken-down and ill-equipped; civilians had been hired as ambulance drivers initially, but those civilians fled the scene at Fredericksburg, necessitating using stretcher-bearers as drivers; hospital wagons intended to be used to haul medical supplies were being used to transport officers' baggage; stretcher-bearers didn't go to the field to recover the wounded, but remained with the ambulances during action. The corps' medical department was a mess.

May 26 (Thursday)

Grant decided that it was futile to attack Lee's position at North Anna, so the Union general began a movement towards Hanovertown, south and east around Lee's right flank, Sheridan's cavalry leading the advance. The total number reported to have been sent from Fredericksburg and Belle Plain was: Union sick and wounded, 26,191; Confederate sick and wounded, 319; Union malingerers turned over to the Provost Marshal in Washington, 600.

Reed, Wm. H., Nurse, Union hospital, Fredericksburg, Va.:

Our work at Fredericksburg was nearly ended. The flank movements of Gen. Grant from Spotsylvania to Hanover C.H. left the town exposed. The government ... was completing the railroad to Aquia Creek,... to transfer the wounded rapidly to Washington. Two or three trains had passed safely through, but the guerrillas ... had broken the communications, and it became necessary to use all the river transportation that could be made available....

It was announced that the evacuation of Fredericksburg must be hurried forward.... Those who could walk, either with or without crutches, were sent forward on foot to Belle Plain. Probably many fell and died by the roadside. We know that many lives would have been saved had it been possible for them to remain quietly where they were. From our own building several were sent off who died before they reached the landing; while to remain was to linger in the hands of an enemy.... The evacuation went on. Our own men were sent away; and when we reached the wharf, the steamers were refusing to receive another man. Hundreds were left through the night in a pouring rain. The Sanitary Commission steamer *Kent* came at last, loaded with stores for the new base; and after other transports were loaded, we took the remainder, forty stretcher cases, all being amputations, on our decks....

Roden, J. B., Pvt., CSA, in Winder Hospital, Richmond, Va.:

A few days later erysipelas developed in my wound, and four negroes carried me on my cot across the field to the erysipelas camp.... I was placed in a tent by myself, where I remained two weeks, then was taken back to the hospital and placed in a ward in charge of a Dr. Braxton, who was very kind to me.

At New Hope Church, Ga., McPherson moved his Union troops to the general area of the church. The entire Union Army moved forward slowly, skirmishing nearly all the time. The Rebels waited.

Grinsted, W., Surg., USV, 3d Div., 20th Corps, New Hope Church, Ga.:

On May 26th, the line of battle was advanced, and the hospital tents were pitched a mile-and-a-half in the rear. The location was good, well protected, wood and water in abundance, and on a good road. The army medical supply train here came up, and our supplies, though not yet exhausted, were replenished.

The sick and wounded were sent on May 29th to Kingston, the graver cases in ambulances and the slighter cases in army wagons—the only time, I am happy to say, that we had to use such transportation during this campaign....

May 27 (Friday)

When rations were issued to the Army of the Potomac on the 26th, the wagons were placed under the control of the Medical Director to be used to transport the wounded. Today, a train of 40 ambulances and 112 wagons carried 262 sick and 477 wounded to Pt. Royal, where the train arrived before dark.

May 28 (Saturday)

Lee, outflanked when Grant moved around the Confederate right flank, rushed southeast and finally got to Cold Harbor, south of Grant's army. Union forces were crossing at Hanovertown, with heavy cavalry fighting on the Pamunkey and Totopotomoy rivers.

McParlin, T. A., Surg., Med. Dir., Army of the Potomac, North Anna River, Va.:

Early on the morning of the 27th, seven hundred of the slightly-sick and wounded were placed on board the quartermaster's transport, *City of Alton*, and started for Washington. About noon the hospital transport *Connecticut* arrived, and all the more serious cases were placed on board of her at once. She took a thousand wounded to Washington. The second train of wounded arrived in the evening, and they were at once placed on board the *Connecticut* and *State of Maine*, which had arrived during the afternoon.... The total number of wounded sent from Pt. Royal ... twenty-one hundred....

The Confederates under Hardee took heavy casualties when Johnston ordered a reconnaissance in force against McPherson near Dallas, Ga.

May 29 (Sunday)

McParlin, T. A., Surg., Med. Dir., Army of the Potomac, en route to Cold Harbor, Va.:

... during the movement from the North Anna to the Pamunkey.... The Cavalry Corps had by this time returned from the Richmond expedition, and two divisions were in advance. A large number of the horses had been so much exhausted as to die on the road, along which they were scattered at tolerable regular intervals of from fifty to one hundred yards, and the infantry following had the full benefit of the results of their putrefaction. This march of thirty miles was made rapidly over very dusty roads, and on a hot and sultry day, and the number of men who fell out of the ranks was very large. All the ambulances were filled to overflowing, and a few men were unavoidably left behind....

In the afternoon, the cavalry engaged the enemy near Hawe's shop, and had about two hundred and fifty wounded. The advance hospital was at a small house near Hawe's shop, and the greater part of the operating and dressing required was performed at this point.... The medical officers ... displayed great gallantry, as the hospital was at times under heavy fire, several shells striking the building, and one falling under the operating table, fortunately, however, without exploding....

Reed, Wm. H., Nurse, Union Hospital, Pt. Royal, Va.:

Pt. Royal, an unimportant ... village in Caroline Country, Va., twenty-five miles below Fredericksburg, on the Rappahannock, was, for two or three days, a temporary base of the army. Its quiet harbor was filled with transport steamers and barges, waiting orders.... Here we rested, enjoying the beauty of the river....

At midnight the cry of fire started us to our feet,

and but a few rods away was a barge of hay burning. The heat of the flames was even then felt upon our decks. The paint would blister, and the wood begin to char, unless we could drop immediately down the stream. Bales of burning hay were dropping off the barge and floating towards us. Our fires were out. Here were forty helpless men depending upon us for succor. The fire soon enveloped the barge, and shot up red and lurid in hot forks of flame. The heat became intense, and it was soon an impossibility to face it. For a time our fate seemed inevitable; the officers of the boat were at their posts, the fires under the boilers were kindling, the steam was rising slowly, and, at the moment when our position seemed to be the most critical, the beam of the engines moved, and in half an hour we were anchored out of danger. The next day our wounded were transferred to the hospital transport *Connecticut*, and were taken to Washington, and our decks were cleared....

May 30 (Monday)

In Virginia, Grant arrived at Lee's defenses at Cold Harbor, north of the Chickahominy. Grant ordered probing attacks prior to a full-scale assault.

McParlin, T. A., Surg., Med. Dir., Army of the Potomac, Cold Harbor, Va.:

During the 29th, the army moved into position on Tolopotomoy Creek. Sites for the field hospitals were selected, and ambulance roads cut through the woods to the front.... On the 30th, the cavalry moved to Cool Arbor, where they had a sharp engagement. The infantry also had a series of skirmishing and partial engagements during the day, from which about five hundred wounded were received into the field hospitals....

At New Hope Church and around Dallas, Ga., the lines remained much the same, with skirmishing and an occasional outburst of artillery.

May 31 (Tuesday)

Grant, now at Cold Harbor, moved around Lee's right flank, so Lee also adjusted the Confederate lines. On May 1st, Grant had been north of the Rapidan and Lee had been quietly lying at Orange C.H. In less than thirty days, Grant was outside Richmond and had Lee heavily engaged. Lee couldn't go anywhere.

McParlin, T. A., Surg., Med. Dir., Army of the Potomac, Cold Harbor, Va.:

On the 31st, the skirmishing continued, and ... a brisk fight ensued about four o'clock P.M., from which seven hundred and thirty-two wounded were brought in. The depot hospital boats and barges, together with the transports conveying the Eighteenth Corps, had arrived at White House on the 30th, and, during the afternoon of the 31st, a train of ambulances and army wagons [was] organized ... for the purpose of conveying the wounded and seriously sick to that point.... [The] total [was] one hundred and ninety-four sick and eleven hundred and one wounded. The train crossed the river at Hanover Town during the day, and moved down the north bank of the river, as the direct road on the south bank wasn't considered safe. It reached a point opposite White House on the 2d of June.

Reed, Wm. H., Nurse, Union hospital, White House, Va.:

We reached White House at sunset on the 30th of May.... While we were waiting the arrival of the wounded, we went in search of the Fortieth Massachusetts Regiment. The[ir] headquarters were under a thick bower of magnolia leaves, and we received a cordial welcome.... As we sat in this cool, shady spot, a staff officer rode up with orders to have the regiment prepared to move at a moment's notice, and we left the column ready for its march.... The regiment joined its brigade, marched to Cold Harbor, and, before another sun had set, the colonel and one hundred of his brave men were dead....

The sights of a field of carnage must not be described. But in the rear of it we can see groups of men sitting under trees, or lying in agony, having crawled to some shady spot, to a brook side or ravine, where they may bathe their fevered wounds or quench their thirst, while waiting their turn to be removed in ambulances to the hospital. The Sanitary Commission's supply wagons, which have been pushed forward to the field, are stationed where they can afford the most relief....

In the ambulances are concentrated probably more acute suffering than may be seen in the same space in all this world beside. The worst cases only have the privilege of transportation; and what a privilege! A privilege of being violently tossed from side to side, of having one of the four who occupy the vehicle together thrown bodily, perhaps, upon a gaping wound; of being tortured, and racked, and jolted, when each jarring of the ambulance is enough to make the sympathetic brain burst with agony. How often have I stood on the step behind, and heard the cry, "O God, release me from this agony!" and then some poor stump wound be jolted from its place and be brought smartly up against the wooden framework of the wagon, while tears would gather in the eyes and roll down over furrowed cheeks. And then some poor fellow would take a suspender and tie it to the wagon top, and hold on to that, in order to break the effect of the jolting ambulance, as it careened from side to side, or went ploughing on through roads rendered almost impassable by the enormous transportation service to the army. And yet, as a class, these ambulance drivers were humane men. I have been with them at their camp fires, and have shared their rough evening meal....

McKenzie, Thomas G., Med. Purveyor, Army of the Potomac, White House, Va.:

Having completed the loading of the steamer ... I was ordered, on the morning of May 26th, to proceed to Pt. Royal, Rappahannock river, Virginia, where I arrived on the evening of the 28th, remained during the night, and left next morning at daylight for White House, Virginia, Pamunkey river.... Arriving at White House, May 31st, I selected an eligible position, apart from the other departments, at a point near the wagon road, made a bridge of my barges, and commenced operations.... From that period until June 14th, I remained at White House....

In Georgia, Sherman had moved quite a distance since early May. Now he was knocking on the very outside door of Atlanta.

June 1 (Wednesday)

The early-morning mists seemed ghostly at the old Seven Days' battlefields in the vicinity of Cold Harbor as the Union forces faced the dug-in Confederates. A sharp fight between Sheridan's cavalry and the infantry of R. H. Anderson's corps livened up the morning.... Anderson's troops attacked Sheridan's twice and were thrown back. Action occurred on both flanks of the lines until late afternoon without significant gains for either side, only adding to the number of dead and wounded.

McParlin, T. A., Surg., Med. Dir., Army of the Potomac, Cold Harbor, Va.:

The Eighteenth Corps, which had made a forced march from White House, joined ... on the morning of June 1st, and during the afternoon, a general engagement took place.... The Sixth Corps hospitals were situated in the edge of a grove of pines, on the south side of Cool Arbor and Old Church road, near Burnett's house. Tents were pitched, and supplies on hand.... The number of wounded ... total, two thousand one hundred and twenty-five....

Welch, S. G., Surg., 20th S.C. Vols., field hospital, Chickahominy River, Va.:

There was not much fighting yesterday. It was only skirmishing. A few men were wounded in our brigade, only one of them being in my regiment. About an hour ago I heard heavy musketry on the extreme right of our lines, but it was far to the right of the division....

Jack Teague wrote me that Jim Spearman had been conscripted and assigned to light duty. Jack is very anxious for me to return to South Carolina as soon as possible, but it is no use to hand in a resignation at such busy times as these. I may send it in, though, whenever we get quiet again, so that it will be attended to.... The weather is becoming quite warm. The dust is very bad and we are needing rain again....

The Army of the Potomac reported that the Ambulance Corps, as of May 31, had: 620 ambulances; 40 medicine wagons; 174 army wagons; 15 forges; 1882 horses and 870 mules; 767 stretchers; and 57 officers and 2092 enlisted men.

Federal cavalry under Stoneman captured the pass at Allatoona, Ga., providing Sherman with his rail link to Chattanooga, ensuring that his supply line would be open. Fighting occurred near New Hope Church.

June 3 (Friday)

Federal cavalry entered Ackworth, Ga., as Sherman again outflanked Gen. Joe Johnston near New Hope Church.

At Cold Harbor on the previous day, Grant had planned an attack for early morning, but delays in the distribution of ammunition and the fatigue of the Union troops caused a postponement of the attack till late afternoon. Then it rained, and the attack was called off entirely for the day. It was all probably just as well, since the troops on both sides were frazzled by this time.

The Union charge began at 4:30 A.M. all along the Rebel line. The Confederates, having had two days to prepare, were well fortified. The Union attack was a head-on crash against the Rebels. The Federals relied on the sheer weight of numbers to breach the Confederate lines. A few problems developed. The Federal lines were enfiladed and the slaughter was terrible; the number of Federal killed and wounded was very large. The South lost about 1500 from a strength of some 60,000. At about noon the attack was called off, and the Army of the Potomac prepared to move to the left again.

The 11th Connecticut Volunteer Regiment, which took part in the assault at Cold Harbor, lost within five minutes nearly one half of its strength in killed or wounded.

McParlin, T. A., Surg., Med. Dir., Army of the Potomac, Cold Harbor, Va.:

By order of Gen. Meade, a full issue of rations was made on the evening of the 2d, and the empty wagons turned over to the medical department for the ... wounded. A train of army wagons and ambulances was organized on the morning of the 3d in the usual manner.... The number of wounded sent ... total, two thousand one hundred and seventy-seven....

At half past five o'clock A.M., a general attack was made by the army on the enemy's works.... The number of wounded brought off was ... two thousand eight hundred and sixteen.... About eleven hundred wounded were left on the field from the day's engagement, it being impossible to remove them....

Reed, Wm. H., Nurse, Union hospital, White House, Va.:

The dead at Cold Harbor were left unburied, and the wounded were rapidly sent to White House, where eight thousand arrived before a hospital was established to receive them. The vast plateau was, however, soon covered with tents; kitchens and feeding stations were established, and the regular routine of hospital work went on....

The refugee problem, both black and white, in St. Louis had again increased over that of September last year, and it was decided that the Army would provide a portion of Benton Barracks outside the city for the housing of these indigent refugees. In addition, a ward of the military hospital would be set aside for the use of the refugee civilians as required, and a school was organized where 140 children received instruction while awaiting relocation.

A new building, meant to house 2000 people, was constructed south of the city, in which the refugees housed and subsisted by the government at Rolla, Springfield, Pilot Knob, etc., were to be collected. This provided a more efficient system for handling them and centralized the support services for them. Between this date and October 26th, the Benton Barracks facility provided shelter and support services for 104 men, 222 women, and 421 children.

Rations, in all cases, were provided only for those who had no other resources. The operation of the facilities was in the hands of army chaplains, who were required to certify that those served were indeed needy. The relief given was to be only temporary.

The railroads provided free passes, for most who needed them, to get to the Sanitary Sanitary Commission facilities. In other cases, either the Sanitary Commission paid the fares or they were paid by the government.

The Sanitary Commission provided not only shelter but clothing for the refugees. During the course of the war literally thousands of coats, undergarments, dresses, shoes, shawls, and other garments were donated to the Commission and distributed to the needy. In some cases, articles necessary for housekeeping such as stoves, pans, bed frames, and other furniture were distributed to the refugees.

In Washington, Joseph K. Barnes, Acting Surgeon General, notified Secy. of War Stanton that the Lincoln General Hospital in the city had been designated as the place of treatment for the Confederate wounded. Barnes explained:

Upon arrival of large numbers of wounded it has been impossible in all cases to distinguish the prisoners from our own men, but at the earliest possible moment after reaching hospitals a careful examination is made and they are then transferred to the Lincoln Hospital.

In a few cases the nature of wounds and condition of the prisoners render their transfer impracticable at the time, but the invariable rule in this and other places is to collect them in one hospital as soon as it can be done.

The diet table, medical supplies, and surgical treatment are the same in all U.S. general hospitals.

June 4 (Saturday)

Today all was fairly quiet at Cold Harbor. The day was spent collecting the dead and wounded from in front of the Confederate entrenchments. An additional 1701 Union wounded were recovered and sent to the depot hospital at White House. At the end of the day, a second train of 544 wagons and ambulances carried another 161 sick and 2794 wounded back to White House.

Perry, John G., Asst. Surg., USV, 20th Mass. Vols., Cold Harbor, Va.:

I have not had a moment to write for nearly a week. It has been fight, fight, fight. Every day there is a fight, and every day the hospital is again filled. For four days now we have been operating upon the men wounded in one battle, which lasted only about two hours; but the wounds were more serious than those from former engagements. I am heartsick over it all....

Near New Hope Church, Ga., Gen. Joe Johnston began to move his Confederate troops in a rainstorm from the area around New Hope Church to the vicinity of Pine Mountain.

Hand, D. W., Surg., USV, Med. Dir., New Bern, N.C.:

On June 4, 1864, two large torpedoes were accidentally exploded at Bachelor's Creek, an outpost of New Bern, instantly killing thirty-six soldiers and eight negroes, and seriously wounding twenty-nine men attached to the 132d New York Volunteers. Many of the latter casualties involved compound fractures and extensive lacerations of the soft parts. Almost without exception these cases did well, and from the most terrible injuries the men recovered with useful limbs....

June 5 (Sunday)

Confederate Joseph Johnston moved his troops to near Marietta, Ga. There was some minor skirmishing near Pine Mountain as Sherman shifted closer to the railroad.

At Cold Harbor, Va., the long siege of continuous fighting took its toll on the troops' mental and physical health. Grant petitioned Lee for a truce to remove the wounded and dead. Pending the agreement, both sides withheld their fire as comrades of the wounded recovered them from the field.

Surg. Thomas A. McParlin, Medical Director for the Army of the Potomac, wrote a letter to Maj. Gen. Meade on this date which pointed out that the army had been in continuous contact with the enemy for 32 days. During this time, no vegetables had been issued; the water was increasingly bad; the ground around the camps was strewn with the bodies of dead animals and the offal of the slaughtered animals; few of the regiments had dug sinks for the use of the men, and human waste was deposited on the hillsides and was washing down into the streams that were used for water for drinking and cooking. These unsanitary conditions caused disease, especially diarrhea.

Meade took action on McParlin's letter and brought in large quantities of fresh vegetables to White House, where they were sent to the troops at Cold Harbor, and especially to the hospitals.

Earnhart, T. M., Pvt., Battery D, 10th N.C. State Troops, Petersburg, Va.:

Sometime during the first of June 1864, our battery took position in front of Petersburg, Va.... As we were on a line considerably in the rear of our infantry, and the lines of opposing infantry were ... at that time half-a-mile apart, the Miniés from sharpshooters were pretty well spent when they reached our position, but were still swift enough to penetrate one-inch-thick palings around the yard and garden in which we were entrenched....

I was just returning to my pit and stopped a few feet away from it to get a drink from a bucket sitting under an apple tree when one of those spent Miniés struck me in the right arm near the shoulder. It felt as if someone had struck me a heavy blow with a club or heavy piece of board. I had no idea that the bullet had broken the skin until blood commenced streaming down my body into my shoes. One of my comrades called to me to come into the redoubt, where we would be out of danger, and he tore my shirt into strips and bound up the opening in my shoulder blade where the bullet had entered and partly stanched the blood.

One of our company was detailed to take me back to the rear, where there was an ambulance. There I found an assistant surgeon, who examined my wound and found that the bullet had lodged in my arm and made quite a lump under the skin. He got some kind of a knife (I do not know whether it was a surgical instrument or a pocketknife) and said he would remove the bullet. He made two or three strokes over where the bullet lodged, but did not scratch the skin; then he said he would leave it until I got to the hospital, where possibly there was a knife that would cut the skin. So they loaded me into an ambulance and drove out and through Petersburg to the field hospital, which consisted of tents for surgeons and flies for the wounded.

Shortly after I arrived at the hospital, Dr. Buist, assistant surgeon, examined my wound; and after extracting the bullet and probing the hole with his finger, he said the bone was badly shattered, and amputation or resection was the only way to treat it. I asked him what resection meant, and he said to take out the bone. I begged him then to save my arm if possible, and he promised me he would. He then said that Dr. Post, the ranking surgeon, was over in Petersburg, and he would prefer that he was present while making such an operation. So he waited for a while, but finally said if he waited longer it might be dark before he got through, and that with what assistance he had he could do it himself. I was placed on a board, propped up on some kind of scaffold, and the chloroform administered. I soon felt as if I would float away, and I knew no more until I found myself sitting on a stool by the table, with my arm bound up and in a sling.

Afterwards, Dr. Buist's assistant told me that when Dr. Buist had started to operate, Dr. Post arrived and asked what he was trying to do to me, and Dr. Buist said he was trying to save my arm. Dr. Post berated him and said he had better cut it off, as there would be less danger, and I could better care for myself and be less trouble. After talking it over, Dr. Buist said he thought he could save the arm, and he had promised to do so; that Dr. Post ranked him and could amputate if he wished, but he (Buist) declined to do it. "O, well," said Post, "if you feel that way, go ahead. If you lose the man, it will be your fault." If this was so, and I have no reason to doubt it, all honor to Dr. Buist [who] told me that he took out about five inches of the bone, including the head of the bone humerus.

I was then very weak from shock and loss of blood, as I was from strenuous work and reduced rations at the time I was wounded. I was then removed to a fly stretched in a lean-to position and made comfortable by having a single blanket spread on the ground, with my coat or army jacket for a pillow, as I was practically helpless. The position of the wound made bandaging to prevent bending of the wounded arm impossible. Lt. Myers, of our company, came to see me next day.... When he went back to the line he had a man detailed and sent to take care of me....

June 6 (Monday)

In Georgia, Mother Bickerdyke and Mrs. Porter were following Sherman's Fifteenth Corps, doing all they could for the sick and wounded. One major problem was the lack of medicines and drugs, since the army made little provision for the treatment of the patients. This was the period when Bickerdyke's knowledge of botanical medicine came into play. For her, the woods abounded with plants (weeds, to some) that could be used effectively. Blackberries were plentiful, and blackberry cordial could be used to treat diarrhea. Painkillers could be made from the jimsonweed, and heart stimulants from wild cherry and bloodroot. Chigger bites, always a big problem when living in the woods, she treated by rubbing the bite with a bit of wet soap, saying that the scratching was the problem, not the bite.

Bickerdyke wasn't the only one in the South to use "homegrown" remedies. With the blockade of the Southern ports cutting off most of the supply of drugs and other medicines, the "old" recipes for specifics were dug out from grandmothers' cookbooks and used liberally. The slaves' medicinal lore was also tapped for treatments. Many of such medicines were very effective.

Earnhart, T. M., Pvt., Battery D, 10th N.C. State Troops, in hospital, Petersburg, Va.:

The next day I inquired about the care of my wound

and was told that it would not need to be dressed for the first forty-eight hours. My bloody clothes had been left on me, and blood had clotted and dried and made a frightful mess; but no attention was paid to me for two nights by the doctors and very little by the nurse. The first night I was feverish and restless; the second night I was, I think, partly delirious, and something seemed to be buzzing around my head all night.

June 7 (Tuesday)

Grant and Lee still faced off at Cold Harbor, and Grant sent Sheridan, with two divisions of cavalry, to Charlottesville, Va., to assist "Black" Dave Hunter in what would later become known as the Trevillian Raid. Grant also shifted the Union Fifth Corps from the right of the Federal line to its center. The next morning, the Fifth Corps took possession of Long Bridge and the Chickahominy there.

Perry, John G., Asst. Surg., USV, 20th Mass. Vols., Cold Harbor, Va.:

For the first time, I believe, since this campaign commenced, I am lying upon my blankets at twelve o'clock, noon. This morning early we sent almost every man in the hospital to the "White House," to make room for others....

Pease, R. W., Surg., USV, Sheridan's Cavalry, raid at Trevillian, Va.:

Orders were given ... that but four ambulances to each division and two for headquarters should accompany the expedition. Instructions were immediately issued to have one ambulance loaded for each division, and an army wagon was well filled with supplies of all kinds, and taken with the headquarters train. The command marched on the morning of June 7th, crossing the Pamunkey river at New Castle Ferry, and moved towards the Virginia Central railroad, intending to strike it near Trevillian Station....

Earnhart, T. M., Pvt., Battery D, 10th N.C. State Troops, in hospital, Petersburg, Va.:

On the second morning when daylight came I found that I was literally covered with maggots. I don't think I ever before or since felt so disgusted and discouraged, as I did not know what the result would be if worms got into the wound. I called the nurse and begged him to call the doctor, but he demurred, saying the doctor was not yet up and would be displeased if awakened. I considered my life at stake, and what I said to him was more forcible than polite, but he would not budge. I finally prevailed on him to help me up and lead me to Dr. Buist's tent, which was not more than two hundred feet from where I was lying. When I got to the doctor's tent, with my good arm I raised the flap and turned my back toward the couch where the doctor was sleeping and called: "Doctor, look at me." He threw back the cover, raised to a sitting posture, and looked me over. He then said: "Don't be alarmed. Go back and lie down, and as soon as I can dress I will be down and attend to you." It was not long before he came, but it seemed to be hours. He immediately stripped me, dressed my wound, cutting one stitch and filling the wound with calomel to destroy the maggots that had gotten in, and had me bathed in cold water and clothed in clean white underwear. After that for ten days or more he dressed my wound himself and had me bathed and my clothes changed every morning.

June 9 (Thursday)

Fighting flared up near Big Shanty in Georgia. After slogging through knee-deep mud to get to Big Shanty, Sherman was about to move against Johnston at Pine Mountain.

At Cold Harbor, Grant ordered the building of fortifications to cover the Union movement to the left towards Petersburg.

Roden, J. B., Pvt., CSA, in Winder Hospital, Richmond, Va.:

Someone had stolen my knapsack; and as I had failed to get my clothing from the quartermaster's, I had no change of raiment. Fortunately for me, though not for the other fellow, an old black mammy came along with a basket of clothes, saying to me: "I'se bin looking for de man what gim me dese close to wash and can't find him." Said I: "You have found him now." "Law, chile, is you de one?" As necessity knows no law and she could not find the other fellow, I laid claim to those clothes....

June 10 (Friday)

Col. William Hoffman, Federal Commissary-General of Prisoners, wrote Brig. Gen. Joseph T.

Copeland, commander of the prison at Alton, Ill.:

… in relation to the employment of Sisters of Charity at the prison hospital.… As you will perceive by my letters to Col. Sweet the employment of these sisters has not been authorized by me, and as their services can be obtained only on unusual conditions, viz, the renting and furnishing a house for them and the hire of a servant, their continued employment at the hospital is not approved.…

If there is an absolute necessity that female nurses should be employed, please report the number required, the services they are to perform, and the compensation they should receive.

I am under the impression that the Sisters of Charity take advantage of their position to carry information from and to prisoners, which is contraband, and if this is so they cannot under any circumstances be employed at the hospital.…

June 11 (Saturday)

John Hunt Morgan's raid through Kentucky brought on an engagement at Cynthiana, where several of his cavalrymen were captured during the confused fighting in the town. Among those captured was Frank O. Anderson, lately joined from the 14th Tennessee Regiment, and recuperating from wounds received at Chancellorsville. Anderson was captured and sent to Camp Douglas, Ill., but managed to escape from the train prior to arriving at that prison. After his escape, he was assigned to an organization that was to raid the prison at Camp Douglas and free the prisoners. This operation was abandoned when it was found to be impractical. Anderson returned to Richmond, and was paroled in June 1865, when he returned to Clarksville, Tenn. He later became a lawyer in Clarksville, married, raised a family, and died there on April 28, 1928, at age 87, still carrying the minié ball with which he'd been struck at Chancellorsville, Va., on May 2, 1863.

June 12 (Sunday)

The Army of the Potomac pulled out of Cold Harbor and raced to the previously situated pontoon bridges to begin moving across the James. This was one of the most brilliant moves of the war. The Union Army moved rapidly to positions near Petersburg. Warren's Corps was left behind to cover Grant's movements and to hold off Lee's forces as long as possible. Sheridan was still engaged near Trevillian Station.

Pease, R. W., Surg., USV, Sheridan's Cavalry, raid on Trevillian, Va.:

Our march was uninterrupted until the morning of the 11th, when, about four miles east of Trevillian Station, we came upon the enemy in force. The engagement continued with great fury until about four o'clock P.M., the Rebels being driven about five miles beyond the railroad. Our loss was about one hundred and sixty wounded. These, with about seventy wounded Rebels, were brought to our field hospital.... At eleven o'clock P.M., all but thirty-six severely wounded were placed in army wagons and moved to the station. Those remaining were placed in [the] charge of Asst. Surg. R. Rae, 1st New York Dragoons ... with ... five hospital attendants ... rations for five days, [and] medical supplies....

The greater part of the 12th was occupied in destroying the railroad. At five o'clock P.M., the enemy was found about three miles west of the station in a strong position, entrenched and fully prepared for an attack. A spirited engagement ensued, which continued until after dark. Our loss, in this attack, amounted to about three hundred and sixty-six wounded. Our hospital was established at the station in a large and commodious building. Orders were received at eleven o'clock P.M., to be ready to move our wounded by midnight. Thirty army and twelve ammunition wagons were assigned for the purpose. All who could not be transported in these wagons and in our ten ambulances were placed in carriages and other vehicles, which we had impressed on our route. In addition to our own wounded, we had about forty severely wounded Rebels. All were brought along on our return except the Rebels, the thirty-six wounded left after the first day's fight, and ninety-four severely wounded on the 12th. The latter were left at Trevillian Station....

Roden, J. B., Pvt., CSA, in Winder Hospital, Richmond, Va.:

The following Sunday a member of my command, Dr. Shaw, of the Ordnance Dept., came to see me, and kindly asked if he could serve me in any way. I gave him my $22 and asked him to buy me some eggs or nourishing food. I then craved something to eat....

June 13 (Monday)

While in Georgia, Sherman waited for the weather to clear. In Virginia, Lee finally discerned the movement of the Army of the Potomac from Cold Harbor and began to shift his troops rapidly to cover Richmond and Petersburg. Grant moved rapidly across the James. Hancock's Corps reached the James in the late afternoon and waited to cross. Lee, not really understanding the purpose of Grant's move, detached Early's Corps towards the Valley to stop Hunter.

McParlin, T. A., Surg., Med. Dir., Army of the Potomac, Cold Harbor, Va.:

The hospitals of the Second Corps moved to the Tyler house on the 7th, an open elevated location, with excellent water. The wounded and seriously sick were sent back to White House almost daily. The total number sent from June 5th to June 13th was ... one thousand four hundred and sixty-two sick and two thousand three hundred and sixteen wounded.

The number of sick in the army increased largely during the first half of June, and the severity of the cases became greater. The constant labor and watchfulness of the previous month began to manifest its effects. The country was low and marshy in character ... and the condition of the men in the trenches was very bad in a sanitary point of view. For over a month they had had no vegetables, and the beef used was from cattle which were exhausted by the long march through a country scantily provided with forage. The men had to lie close behind their breastworks, as it was almost certain death to expose one's person at certain parts of the line, and their cooking was imperfect and of the rudest kind. Dead horses and offal of various kinds were scattered over the country everywhere, and between the lines were many dead bodies of both parties, unburied and decomposing in the burning sun....

Roden, J. B., Pvt., CSA, in Winder Hospital, Richmond, Va.:

The next day I received two dozen eggs with receipted bill. My two months' pay had gone for two dozen eggs, but it was one of the best investments I ever made.

Dr. Braxton called to see me, when I told him I was "living high" on my investment. He then asked for the remainder of the eggs, which the ward master had in charge, sent them to the commissary department, had my money refunded, and prescribed two eggs each morning and evening. I soon regained strength, and left Winder Hospital, after a stay of eight weeks, with glad heart, feeling thankful I had been spared … though I am still unable to reach my mouth with the hand of that shattered arm.

June 14 (Tuesday)

Before Lee could understand what was afoot, the Army of the Potomac had crossed the James on pontoon bridges and by boat, rushing to gain the railroad center of Petersburg.

McParlin, T. A., Surg., Med. Dir., Army of the Potomac, on the road to Petersburg, Va.:

On the 11th, preparations for a move began. As fast as the tents could be emptied they were taken down, and by the 14th, the hospital was packed and ready to move. Each corps or organization was kept separate, and had a separate barge allotted for its transportation. The depot hospital boats and barges, together with those of the medical purveyor, moved on the 15th, passing first to the vicinity of Jamestown island, and finally reaching City Point on the evening of the 17th. The depot at White House was not entirely broken up, however, the trains of the Cavalry Corps being retained … until the Cavalry Corps should return from the Gordonsville expedition.…

At Pine Mountain, Ga., Lt. Gen. Leonidas Polk, along with Gens. Johnston and Hardee, were watching the Federal movements in front of Pine Mountain when Polk was hit by shot from a Federal cannon. The shot struck him in the chest, killing him instantly. His body was sent to Atlanta.

Jackman, John S., Pvt., "The Orphan Brigade," Pine Mountain, Ga.:

Cloudy early this morning but cleared up at 7 o'clock. The Adjt. and I having made a bed on a brushpile, "spliced blankets"; I slept well last night. Enemy shelling to our right.

Was wounded a few minutes after making the notes, June 14th, and I did not write any more in my journal for nearly three months. I shall try and give an account of my hospital experience during the time named in a brief manner:

About 9 or 10 o'clock A.M., 14th, Capt. G. and I were sitting by the Col.'s fire a little to the rear of the regiment. For two days not a shell had been thrown at our position and when a shell came shrieking over the mountain to our left I remarked to the Captain that some General and his staff, no doubt, had ridden up to the crest of the hill and the Federal batteries were throwing shells at them. "Yes," said the Captain, "and I hope some of them will get shot. A general can't ride around the lines without a regiment of staff at his heels." About this time we heard the second shell strike—I thought it struck into the side of the hill; but it had struck Lt. Gen. Polk. Where he was killed was not a hundred yards from us but the trees were so thick we could not see from where we were what was going on; and we did not learn what had happened for some minutes.

Soon after an order came for a report to be sent to brigade HdQtr and I sat down to write it out. Several of the enemy batteries had opened fire but as we were a little under the hill I thought we were in no great danger from the shells which were flying over— in fact we had gotten so used to bombshells that we scarcely noticed them. I was only a few minutes writing the report and turned my head to ask the Colonel if I should sign his name to the paper and had bent over and was about finished signing the paper when suddenly everything got dark and I became unconscious. If I had been sitting erect when the fragment of shell struck me, I never would have known what hurt me. When I came to my senses, Dr. H., our Asst. Surg., and Capt. G. were lifting me up off the ground. I stood on my feet and not feeling any pain I could not imagine what was the matter. The first thought that entered my mind was that my head was gone. I put my hand up to ascertain whether my head was still on my shoulders. I did not hear the piece of shell coming and it was such a quick, sharp lick I did not feel it strike. The fragment probably weighed little more than a pound. It came like a minié ball. After glancing off my head it struck against a rock and bounced and struck Col. C. on the leg but did not hurt him severely. There were several sitting around close together and they said there was a sudden scattering of the staff.

After Dr. H. bound up my wound there was so little pain I thought it no use to go to the hospital— my head only felt a little dizzy—but the Dr. said I had better go to the field hospital and stay a day or two as I was not very well anyway. He wished to send his horse back and I rode him back to the field hospital. Dr. B. again dressed my wound putting a ligature on a vein that was cut. He would not let me eat anything at dinner and in the evening had me sent to Marietta. He told me that the wound would turn out to be more serious than I thought, for after arriving at the Distributing hospital in Marietta my head got quite sore and painful.

At 9 o'clock P.M. took train for Atlanta. Gen'l Polk's remains were taken down on the same train. I slept on a bench at the distributing hospital in Atlanta the remainder of the night.

June 15 (Wednesday)

In Georgia, with moderate fighting, Gen. George "Slow Trot" Thomas moved his Union corps beyond Pine Mountain towards Kennesaw Mountain. Sherman pressed Johnston's Confederate lines.

Grinsted, W., Surg., USV, 3rd Div., 20th Corps, Golgotha, Ga.:

I regret to state that on June 2, 1864, Surg. H. S. Potter, 105th Illinois Volunteers, was killed by an unexploded shell, which struck him in the forehead.... Until June 9th or 10th, this division was held in reserve. For two weeks it had rained heavily, and the roads were much cut up.... On June 15th we had a sharp fight at Golgotha.... One hundred and eleven wounded were received into the hospital that night. By working until nearly daylight, all were well attended.... The wounded were sent to Ackworth....

Jackman, John S., Pvt., "The Orphan Brigade," in hospital, Newnan, Ga.:

The breakfast was tough beef, old bakers bread and coffee that had flies in it and I longed for the hardtack and cornbread which I had left at the front. Maj. C. having given me a letter of introduction to his aunt in Covington, 40 miles towards Augusta, I wished to go there but my name was put on the Newnan list. At 10 A.M. the train left for Newnan, Ga. and arrived there at noon. I was taken to Ward No. 1, Bragg Hospital, Dr. Goss of Bloomfield, Ky. in charge. The room in which I was placed—the Masonic Hall—had about 30 beds but few of them occupied and mostly by men from our brig. The room was clean as could be and the beds really comfortable. I had been dreading the hospital all the time (never having been in but one general hospital before which I did not like much) but I was agreeably disappointed at finding everything so nice.... I immediately went to bed for a sleep and scarcely waked until the next morning. For several days after being in the hospital, I imagined I could hear the whizzing of minié bullets and the thunder of artillery, I had become so accustomed to such sounds....

June 16 (Thursday)

Pulling all but a few troops from the Bermuda Hundred lines, Beauregard reinforced the Petersburg line against the onrushing Federals. There were severe setbacks on both sides as the fighting continued.

McParlin, T. A., Surg., Med. Dir., Army of the Potomac, Petersburg, Va.:

The movement from the James to the position taken up in front of Petersburg was rapidly made in hot and sultry weather; the troops were fatigued, and fell out of the ranks in large numbers, especially in the Ninth Corps. Many cases of heat-apoplexy occurred, and all of the ambulances were filled to overflowing. The assault made by the Second Corps on the afternoon of the 16th resulted in heavy loss, and but a part of the wounded could be brought in.... Five hundred and forty-five wounded were collected at Dr. Bailey's house, which afforded a shelter for the worst cases; soup and hard bread were distributed, and operating and dressing went on all night. The train came up about ten o'clock P.M., tents were immediately pitched, and the ambulance corps set to bringing in the rest of the wounded....

Mrs. Bickerdyke may have had her problems with finding medicines, but food wasn't a problem. Everywhere she set up hospital her soldier assistants would raid the countryside for chickens, pork, cornmeal, milk, eggs, and any other food they could find to feed the patients. There was always beef or chicken broth and *panado* when the patients needed them.

Foye, John W., Surg., USV, 20th Corps, Battle of Pine Hill, Ga.:

For sixteen days following the battle of Dallas, the men were exposed to a very annoying fire from the enemy who was entrenched in front of Pine Knob, and on June 16th, an advance was made with a view to dislodge him. This action is known as the battle of Pine Hill. The troops were worn-out and exhausted by continued marching and building of breastworks, and the roads were heavy from an almost incessant rain for ten days. The action commenced at two o'clock P.M., and continued until dark.... The field hospital was established about two miles from the line of attack. Water and food were abundant. There was more suffering from the constant rain and previous exhaustion than from other causes. The wounded were removed from the field depots on litters and thence to ambulances to the hospitals.... Six hundred and forty-three wounded were admitted to hospital, and thence sent to Ackworth in ambulances, and thence in boxcars to Chattanooga....

Jackman, John S., Pvt., "The Orphan Brigade," in hospital, Newnan, Ga.:

The next day after being in the hospital had to take medicine for something like intermittent fever—I had been unwell for a week or so. Several days before I got up. My head did not give me a great deal of pain at first but after being in the hospital perhaps a little more than a week my wound became inflamed and gangrene ensued which threw me in a high state of fever. Old Dr. Estell of Tenn., our ward surgeon, and who was seventy-five years of age and had been practicing surgery for more than fifty years, soon got the gangrene out by applying nitric acid, iodine, etc. The fever still kept with me and the doctors thought I would "go up." Dr. E., about this time, took sick and Dr. Goss prescribed for the ward. He immediately commenced giving me medicine to reduce my system. In about a week the fever left but I was so weak I could not get up and had to keep to my bed for some time.... While in this condition a force of Federal cavalry came to Moore's bridge on the Chattahoochee [River] about 10 miles from town and threatened a raid on the place. The evacuation commenced about dark.... The citizens all left too. A moving mass of carriages, carts, wagons, "lowing herds," horses, sheep, goats, and people moved through the streets. Soon the town was left in a manner desolate. The night wore away and no raid came.... Late in the evening all of the refugees came back and matters went on as usual....

Earnhart, T. M., Pvt., Battery D, 10th N.C. State Troops, Winder Hospital, Richmond, Va.:

After eleven days I was moved to Winder Hospital and assigned to a cot in a ward of probably one hundred cots. Here was every kind of misery conceivable, and some of the worst cases got well, while many with only scratches died. The ward was full of gangrene and erysipelas, which were said to be highly communicable. My wound being so near the body made it nearly certain death to me if it became infected. Each patient had his own wash pan and sponge, which were intended to be used on no one else; but as nurses were largely exempted from active service and often hardened and indifferent to suffering and death, it was up to me to keep a lookout that my pan and sponge were used on no one else and that no one else's were used on me. But I got through all right and in six weeks was entirely well, and my wound has never given me any trouble since. Of course I did not have the use of my arm as I had before, but it was far better than no arm at all.

While in the field hospital the doctor gave me a quarter of a grain of morphine every night after the second night to make me sleep; but after I went to Winder Hospital the doctors refused to let me have it, and I had a few bad nights. However, nature soon asserted herself, and I slept all right.

The worst thing that happened to me at the Winder Hospital was on account of the food. Badly hurt as I was and as weak as a cat, I was listed as convalescent and of course had convalescent's food, which consisted largely of corn bread and tomato soup, neither of which I could relish. When I went to the hospital I could walk if helped to my feet; after a week or two I would get dizzy and blind if raised up in bed. I realized that I was daily growing weaker and that to be strong enough to bear the journey home when the railroads were again in repair I must have something different to eat. I understood there was a matron in charge of our ward who had the ordering of suitable food so far as it was obtainable, but I had never seen her. I appealed to the nurse to let her know that I would like to see her, but nothing came of it. I then wrote a note and hired a boy to deliver it, and the next day she came to see me. She was a kindly, motherly-appearing lady. I explained to her that I would like to maintain my strength against the time I could go home, but instead I was daily growing weaker and could no longer stand on my feet. She ordered me two wheat biscuits per meal and some other food that I could eat; so in a few days I began to regain my strength, and by the time I was ordered home I could walk alone again. Even after that I often had to fight for what was sent down for me, as the nurses liked hot biscuits and other good things, and often they had favorites to divide [them] among. Of course I would have liked to share with other poor devils worse off possibly than I was, but self-preservation was then, as now, the first law of nature.

June 17 (Friday)

Heavy skirmishing continued around Petersburg. Lee, finally convinced that Grant intended to invest Petersburg, sent the remainder of the Army of Northern Virginia to the city's defenses. The casualties were heavy, 2722 wounded being taken to field hospitals on the Union side.

McKenzie, Thomas G., Med. Purveyor, Army of the Potomac, City Point (Hopewell), Va.:

On June 14th, I left White House under orders to proceed to Jamestown island ... and there await further instructions. I arrived there on the evening of the 15th of June, remained during the night, and, on the afternoon of the 16th, proceeded as far as North Bend, at which point a pontoon bridge was laid, over which troops were passing. About midnight, I left this point for City Point, where we arrived at early dawn, and, after considerable trouble, I succeeded in obtaining a position aside from the other departments, where I again constructed a bridge of my barges and commenced issuing [medical supplies]. There being no further necessity for the wagon train with supplies,... the wagons were unloaded, and their contents stored on the boats. Asst. Surg. Brinton then took charge. A pontoon bridge having been constructed on the Appomattox river, in close proximity to the corps hospitals, for the especial purpose of affording greater facilities for issuing, as, also, of being near the hospitals, we accordingly moved up to that point.

June 19 (Sunday)

In Virginia, Sheridan's Trevillian Raid continued. While accomplishing little of tactical value, the raid further consumed the already depleted resources of the South.

Pease, R. W., Surg., USV, Sheridan's Cavalry, raid on Trevillian, Va.:

On the 19th, we reached King and Queen Courthouse, and from thence sent the wounded to Washington, via West Point. Seven of the wounded died before reaching Washington. On the morning of the 20th, we resumed our march for White House, Virginia, being hastened by a message that the place had been attacked. We made the march of twenty miles in four hours, but found the enemy had been repulsed....

Sherman, in Georgia, found that Confederate Gen. Joe Johnston had pulled back, so the Federals advanced through the rain and mud *again*. Sherman *always* seemed to be fighting in the rain.

In Virginia, Grant let his troops take a breather, and Lee put his men to work digging entrenchments. The depot hospital having been moved to City Point, on the James, a train of wounded, consisting of 502 wagons and ambulances, carried 3715 wounded to City Point from the lines around Petersburg. The trip from Petersburg to City Point would get to be a very familiar trip, the siege being long.

June 20 (Monday)

Chief Surg. Isaiah H. White, at Andersonville, Ga., reports:

The report of sick and wounded for the month of April exhibits a ratio per 1000 of mean strength, 306.1 cases treated, and 57.6 deaths. May, 640.33 cases treated, and 47.3 deaths.

The daily ratio per 1000 of mean strength for the twenty days of present month has been 1⁵/₇ deaths.

June, which taken as an average for the thirty days would make 51.4 deaths per 1000 of mean strength for month of June.

The morning report of C.S. prison shows: Remaining in hospital, 1022; in quarters, 2665; deaths, 40; strength of command, 23,911.

The number of medical officers on duty at the prison is inadequate to perform the duties required of them. There are in all twelve, seven of whom attend sick call and five on duty at hospital; of this number five are employed by contract. I would suggest that the medical force be increased by ten additional officers....

June 21 (Tuesday)

In Virginia, the only action seemed to be in the Petersburg area. Both Grant and Lee were digging in, and Lee would be pinned for the next several months, indeed, until the end of the war. The period through the 21st of July would be fairly quiet, and the medical departments took the time to set up hospitals and prepare for the coming casualties.

When the boats and barges arrived at City Point on the 18th, they found chaos and confusion. Wharves were being built for the use of the Commissary and Quartermaster departments, and there was no room for additional landing craft. The buildings previously occupied by Gen. Butler's Negro troops weren't suitable for hospital use, so a hospital site was selected on the south bank of the Appomattox, about three-quarters of a mile from the main headquarters. The site was about 35 feet above the water and on level, open ground. The first wounded arrived on the 18th, and more arrived on the 19th in a large train of ambulances and wagons. The worst cases of the 19th were placed on the transports *George Leary* and *Connecticut*, and sent to Washington; the remainder were placed in the new hospital. On the 20th, a pontoon wharf was made on the river side, near the hospital, and it was used exclusively by the medical department.

Perry, John G., Asst. Surg., USV, 20th Mass. Vols., hospital near Petersburg, Va.:

Gen. Grant has made a strategical movement, and here we find ourselves, after a very circuitous but rapid march, south of the James River and pegging away at the side door of Petersburg.... The day we started, all surgeons were ordered to join their respective commands, but I, being attached to the hospital, was obliged to remain with it. In other words, I had to follow the hospital wagons, look after the stores, and attend the sick and wounded in the ambulances. These wagons took the same route as the troops, but kept far in their rear. The heat each day was intense, and the dust beyond any expression of which I am capable; but suffice it to say that most of the time I could not even see the head of my horse. The whole train was fifty miles long, the roads sandy, and we moved with the heavy draw of great bodies. We marched about sixty miles in four days and nights, halting every six or eight hours to bait horse and man. Little opportunity was given us for sleep, and ... I felt at times tired and restless, as the officers near me were disagreeable fellows, who often amused themselves by entering the houses along the route and stealing everything they could lay their hands on....

Pease, R. W., Surg., USV, Sheridan's Cavalry, raid on Trevillian, Va.:

On the 21st, the corps moved to Jones's bridge, skirmishing nearly all day. Thirty-seven were wounded. Five or six of the 1st Pennsylvania Cavalry fell into the hands of the enemy; two were wounded by bushwhackers; making a total loss of forty-five men. Orders were received to send our sick and wounded to Washington the next day. Forty wounded and eleven sick were sent....

June 22 (Wednesday)

Having been sent to the Confederate left flank, Hood attacked at Zion Church, but the attack was broken up by the alerted Federals. The dead and wounded on both sides made a useless sacrifice.

At White House, Va., Sheridan, chased by Hampton's cavalry, took charge of a supply train of 900 wagons that Sheridan was to escort to Grant's lines near Petersburg.

June 23 (Thursday)

McParlin, T. A., Surg., Med. Dir., Army of the Potomac, Petersburg, Va.:

On the 21st and 23d, the steamers *Continental, Western Metropolis,* and *De Molay,* which were regularly fitted up as hospital transports, and provided with medical officers and attendants, reported ... and were employed during the rest of the summer, in conveying wounded to Philadelphia, New York and other points.... The hospital transports *Connecticut* and *State of Maine* were employed on the inland waters running to Washington, Annapolis and Baltimore. The barge *New World,* containing eight hundred beds, intended to be used as a receiving ship for serious cases, and, when full, to be towed to some point in the north, arrived on the 30th, and was brought up to the wharf near the hospital. Upon examination, it was found that she was entirely unfit for the purpose for which she had been designed, as not over two hundred men could be safely placed upon her. She had three decks, one above the other, ventilation was exceedingly imperfect, and erysipelas and phagedaena made their appearance in forty-eight hours after wounded were placed on board She was used for a few days as a receiving ship for slight cases, and was then turned over to the quartermaster's department, the bedsteads, bedding and hospital stores on board being transferred to the hospital. The boats of the medical purveyor were brought to the hospital wharf, and, as no further necessity existed for the train of thirty-five wagons, the stores were placed on the purveyor's boats, and the wagons turned over to the quartermaster's department....

June 24 (Friday)

Perry, John G., Asst. Surg., USV, 20th Mass. Vols., hospital near Petersburg, Va.:

I am up to my neck in work. It is slaughter, slaughter. Our brigade has met with a sad loss by having three regiments gobbled up as prisoners. The Twentieth fortunately escaped....

Welch, S. G., Surg., 20th S.C. Vols., in a letter to his wife, from a field infirmary near Petersburg, Va.:

When I wrote to you two days ago I said appearances indicated that we were about to have a fight. Sure enough, about half an hour after I had finished writing the battle began. Our division was engaged. McGowan's Brigade did not suffer much. It supported Wright's Georgia Brigade of Anderson's Division, and, as the men were not engaged, they had the privilege of lying down. Consequently most of the missiles passed over them. The brigade lost only thirty or forty, and the Thirteenth Regiment had but one killed and two wounded.

We were very successful. It is estimated that we killed and wounded about two thousand. We captured about the same number and four cannon. Our loss was about four hundred. We are still in our old position.... Just as I began to write this letter I had two wounded men to come in. They were hurt by a shell early this morning.

I had my third mess of beans yesterday, and a big one it was too. I shall have rather a poor dinner today—only bread, meat and coffee. We have been getting enough coffee and sugar to have it twice a day ever since I got back from home in April....

Sheridan, en route with his long train of wagons, skirmished on the 23rd near Jones's bridge across the

Chickahominy, taking a few casualties but saving the train. On the 24th, Hampton's cavalry again attacked Sheridan's 2nd Division and pursued the Union forces for a period of time. The wagon train, however, remained intact and would be delivered to Grant on the 26th.

Pease, R. W., Surg., USV, Sheridan's Cavalry, raid on Trevillian, Va.:

On the 23d, during a skirmish near Jones's bridge, on the Chickahominy, we had four killed and nine wounded. We received into our hospital ten of the 28th U.S. Colored Troops, wounded at the same time.

On the 24th, the 2d division was attacked by the Rebel cavalry while on the St. Mary's church road, parallel to the Charles City Courthouse road, on which a train of eight hundred wagons, left at White House for this command to guard to the James River, was moving. The division was driven back to Charles City Courthouse, and lost about two hundred men. The severely wounded fell into the hands of the enemy.

On the 26th, I received an order from Gen. Sheridan to go with the wounded and sick to Washington....

Grinsted, W., Surg., USV, 3rd Div., 20th Corps, advance on Atlanta, Ga.:

On June 19th, we crossed Moses's Creek with the hospital, and received some twenty-five wounded, when, from the position of the enemy immediately in our front, we were obliged to leave that location in haste....

On June 22d, we received some two hundred wounded, as our division was sharply engaged. Four deaths occurred here.

On June 24th the wounded were removed to Ackworth, and one section of the hospital moved with the forces to Culp's farm, on the Marietta and Sandtown road. Here we remained several days.... The brigade organization of hospitals was now abandoned and the whole consolidated into a division hospital....

June 27 (Monday)

Sherman's armies of the Cumberland and the Tennessee attacked the Rebel works at Big and Little Kennesaw Mountains in Georgia, with the Army of the Ohio attacking the Confederate left flank. The slaughter of Union troops was one of the worst yet in the west, with nearly 2000 killed or wounded. The attack failed to break the Rebel lines and many of the troops held on by their fingertips to the ground they had gained. This was a defensive victory for the Confederates, but it was a victory. It was also the last time that Sherman would use direct assault on the Confederate lines.

Perry, John G., Asst. Surg., USV, 20th Mass. Vols., hospital near Petersburg, Va.:

When our division was withdrawn from the extreme front,… we surgeons looked for a little less arduous work; but now the artillery brigade has been placed under our care, and we have as much to do as ever.

It has not rained for a month, and the poor wounded fellows lie all about me, suffering intensely from heat and flies. The atmosphere is almost intolerable from the immense quantities of decomposing animal and vegetable matter upon the ground. Many of the surgeons are ill, and I indulge in large does of quinine. Horses and mules die by the hundreds from continued hard labor and scant feed. The roads are strewn with them, and the decay of these, with that of human bodies in trenches, causes malaria of the worst kind.

War! war! war! I often think that in the future, when human character shall have deepened, there will be a better way of settling affairs than this of plunging into a perfect maelstrom of horror.

June 29 (Wednesday)

Perry, John G., Asst. Surg., USV, 20th Mass. Vols., hospital near Petersburg, Va.:

Rumor says that the Twentieth is to be mustered out of service on the 18th of July.… Our division has again been put in the front line of rifle-pits, and again the poor wounded fellows will be coming in. All this accumulation of experience quickly changes careless boys into sober and thoughtful men, men who trust, and who feel that whatever happens, in the end it will somehow be for the best; men who value what has not cost them a thought before.…

June 30 (Thursday)

McParlin, T. A., Surg., Med. Dir., Army of the Potomac, in front of Petersburg, Va.:

The hospitals at City Point were fairly organized and in good working order by the end of June. For a time they were somewhat overcrowded, the capacity … amounting to forty-five hundred beds, while six thousand men were present.… Supplies and stores of all kinds were abundant.… The cooking arrangements were ample and worked well. The extra diet kitchens were under the supervision of ladies, whose services were thus made available, and who were of much more use than when employed as nurses in the wards.… Upon application by the medical director, an order was issued … directing that the negro women who should be brought within the lines of the army should be sent to the depot hospital to act as laundresses.…

July 1 (Friday)

Sherman was moving his troops, trying to find a way to gain an advantage over Gen. Joe Johnston. Light skirmishing took place at Howell's Ferry, Allatoona Gap, and Lost Mountain.

Foye, John W., Surg., USV, 20th Corps, advance on Atlanta, Ga.:

From June 17th to July 1st, a series of skirmishes occurred along the edge of Nancy's or Moses's Creek, on which our command was in position. These skirmishes were a part of the general operations for the possession of Kennesaw Mountain. The field hospital was moved seven times to accommodate itself to the ranging positions of the command. Twice it was driven from position by the shells of the enemy. Five hundred and four patients with gunshot wounds … were admitted into hospital. The wounded were transported in ambulance to Ackworth.…

The Army of the Potomac, in Virginia, reported that the Ambulance Corps of that army had on hand at the end of June: 615 ambulances; 45 medicine wagons; 197 army wagons; 14 forges; 1935 horses and 1019 mules; 851 stretchers; and 55 officers and 2114 enlisted men.

July 2 (Saturday)

In Georgia, Gen. Joseph E. Johnston pulled the entire Confederate line back from the Kennesaw Mountains to a line near Marietta, to escape being outflanked by Sherman.

July 3 (Sunday)

In the sixty-day period after Grant began his drive on Richmond, the U.S. Sanitary Commission provided to the hospitals for the soldiers of the Army of the Potomac the following: 30,197 quilts; 13,500 blankets; 42,945 sheets; 35,877 pillows; 49,906 pillowcases; 2269 pillow-ticks; 11,716 bed ticks; 87,904 shirts; 48,303 pairs of drawers; 80,232 pairs of socks; 14,984 pairs of slippers; 43,606 handkerchiefs; 65,164 towels; 10,235 wrappers; 3684 flannel bands.

July 4 (Monday)

Washington was getting jittery as Confederate Gen. Early's troops skirmished with Federals at Patterson's Creek Bridge, South Branch Bridge, and at other points, as the Rebels prepared to cross the Potomac.

Perry, John G., Asst. Surg., USV, 20th Mass. Vols., hospital near Petersburg, Va.:

Water is very scarce here; wells have to be dug to the depth of forty feet, and then the water not only runs in slowly, but is very muddy. Ice found in a house on one of the plantations has been a godsend to the hospital during this heat, but it has all gone now.

The question of my going home with the regiment still absorbs me. At one hour I am told there will be no difficulty in being mustered out with the others, and then some order comes from the War Dept., or from the surgeon-general, and I am left high and dry in doubt. For two weeks this has continued, and it wearies me. The medical director of the corps says he cannot spare me, and yet I am sorely needed at home.

After fighting at Big Shanty and Sweetwater Bridge yesterday, Sherman moved past the Kennesaw Mountain towards Johnston's new line at Nickajack Creek. Today, Gen. McPherson's Federals, on Sherman's right flank, were now closer to Atlanta than was Confederate Joe Johnston. Johnston again retreated to prepared positions on the Chattahoochee.

July 5 (Tuesday)

Gen. Jubal Early, near Harpers Ferry, decided that the place was too difficult to take for the time being, so he crossed the Potomac at Shepherdstown into Maryland, causing skirmishing at Point of Rocks,

Noland's Ferry, and other points on the river. This caused Lincoln to call for 24,000 militia from New York and Pennsylvania to help defend Washington. Lee thought that if enough pressure was put on Washington, the Federals at Petersburg would go to the relief of the capital and he could escape Grant's hold on the Confederate Army.

Sherman, now with his right flank on the Chattahoochee near Atlanta, pressed Joe Johnston closely, skirmishing at Turner's Ferry, Howell's Ferry, and other points on the river. Sherman was looking for a weak spot in Johnston's lines.

Foye, John W., Surg., USV, 20th Corps, advance on Atlanta, Ga.:

On July 5th, the command left Kennesaw Mountain and followed the enemy to Chattahoochee, skirmishing the entire distance; but with few casualties, seventy-one being the number admitted to hospital for a period of nineteen days....

At LaGrange, Tenn., another Federal cavalry force went in search of the elusive Nathan Bedford Forrest. This time the Federals were commanded by Maj. Gen. Andrew Jackson Smith, a man very different from Sturgis, who'd tangled with Forrest last time.

July 6 (Wednesday)

Confederate Gen. Jubal Early's forces captured Hagerstown, Md., and were skirmishing at Big Cacapon Bridge in W.Va. and Antietam, Md. The Confederate John McCausland demanded $20,000 from the citizens of Hagerstown in retribution payment for "Black Dave" Hunter's burning and looting in the Shenandoah Valley.

Near Atlanta, Sherman and Johnston's forces skirmished at Nickajack Creek with some action around Allatoona. Sherman's men were suffering from the usual camp diseases, diarrhea in particular. There were thousands of cases, resulting in what one of the patients in a tent hospital described as "... hundreds of thin disgusting sick patriots that creep around these grounds [to] form a sight that I loathe with every power in me." Enteritis, an inflammation of the mucus membranes of the small intestine, took a dreadful toll of the soldiers, both North and South.

It was here that Mrs. Bickerdyke managed to stay in one spot for several days. The railroads had been rebuilt to Chattanooga and the supplies were coming through, including the Sanitary Commission supplies consigned directly to Mrs. Bickerdyke. Field dressings, clothing, dried and canned food, cooking utensils, laundry equipment, writing paper, pencils, and myriad other items came to her to use or to distribute to the patients. Here it was that Sherman sent to Nashville for a large number of revival tents to be used by the patients. The tents were quite large, holding about 100 men, and the hospital encampment was soon called Mother Bickerdyke's "circus." Bickerdyke, going along with the idea, made lemonade from extract and colored it with raspberry juice to be served to the patients, an idea so popular that it became standard fare in the hospital.

Welch, S. G., Surg., 20th S.C. Vols., near Chaffin's Bluff, Va.:

In recent raids by the Yankees they cut both the Weldon and Danville railroads. I do not know that the way is open yet, but I will write anyway.

We remained at Petersburg just two weeks and then came back here last Saturday night to relieve two brigades of Heth's Division which were here on picket duty. We had a very pleasant time in Petersburg. I succeeded in getting plenty of vegetables to eat. The Yankees are shelling the city, but the shells do very little harm and have killed but few. The people are not at all frightened by them. I would often see young ladies sitting on their porches reading quietly while shells were occasionally bursting nearby....

July 7 (Thursday)

McParlin, T. A., Surg., Med. Dir., Army of the Potomac, in front of Petersburg, Va.:

During the first week in July, three thousand iron bedsteads were obtained and placed in the hospitals. Two fire engines, two steam pumps and a reservoir were also received and used.... One hundred and sixty adult contrabands were kept employed in the hospitals as cooks, laundresses, etc. The washing of the hospital was no small item, amounting to six thousand pieces per week.

July 8 (Friday)

After skirmishing for the past two days, Maj. Gen. Schofield, on Sherman's left flank, crossed the Chattahoochee at Soap Creek with little opposition. Johnston, finding his right flank turned, evacuated his lines and withdrew to prepared positions near Peachtree Creek, closer to Atlanta.

The Third Division, Sixth Corps, Army of the Potomac, in Baltimore, formed up and prepared to advance against Jubal Early's Confederate force now coming towards Washington. Maj. Gen. Lew Wallace would use these Union troops and others gathered near Frederick, Md., to oppose Early.

Perry, John G., Asst. Surg., USV, 20th Mass. Vols., hospital near Petersburg, Va.:

The Twentieth Massachusetts is to be consolidated into a battalion of seven companies, and an order just issued by the War Dept. says that officers not having served three years from the last muster will be retained, if needed. According to this order, not an individual officer, except the quartermaster, can be mustered out on the 18th, when the regiment is supposed to go home.

It is intolerably hot, and has been for some time. No rain has fallen since the last of May. Our hospital is now in the woods close to the highway, and we have the benefit of the dust, which so incessantly sweeps over us that we eat and breathe it until almost suffocated by it.

July 9 (Saturday)

Maj. Gen. Lew Wallace collected some 6000 Federal troops—many of whom were raw recruits, troops on leave, etc.—to face Jubal Early's nearly 18,000 at Monocacy River between Frederick, Md., and Washington. The Union troops put up a stiff fight but finally broke, losing nearly 2000 casualties, about 1200 of whom were captured. Early's force suffered about 700 casualties, the wounded being sent back to Harpers Ferry. Grant sent two divisions from the Sixth Corps at City Point, Va., by steamer to Washington. Lee's hoped-for reaction of getting Grant to pull most of his men out of the trenches to defend Washington didn't occur. Instead, Meade ordered further pressure on Lee's army and a probing action around Lee's right flank.

In Georgia, Joe Johnston, outflanked again, took his Army of Tennessee back to the very gates of Atlanta. Pres. Davis, alarmed, sent Gen. Braxton Bragg to Atlanta to discuss Johnston's plans.

Richmond, in this third summer of the war, seemed to be short of everything. The Confederate currency was of little value and the Confederate Congress refused to raise the allowance for the support of the hospitals to meet the depreciation of the currency. Consequently, the food and supplies furnished the hospitals was of poor quality and, as often as not, short of the quantity requested. Another factor was the lack of railroad transportation to move food and other materials necessary for the treatment of the wounded. Mrs. Phoebe Pember, matron of Chimborazo Hospital No. 2 in Richmond, wrote of severe shortages of flour, cornmeal, milk, eggs, and other types of food so necessary for the treatment of the sick and wounded. Another major problem was the starving rats that infested the hospitals. Not only were the rats skillful at dodging the traps set for them, they also seemed to have other, more useful, skills. Mrs. Pember wrote:

They even performed a surgical operation which would have entitled any of them to pass the board. A Virginian had been wounded in the very center of the instep of his left foot. The hole made was large, and the wound sloughed fearfully around a great lump of proud flesh which had formed in the center like an island. The surgeons feared to remove this mass, as it might be connected with the nerves of the foot, and lockjaw might ensue. Poor Patterson would sit on his bed all day gazing at his lame foot and bathing it with a rueful face, which had brightened amazingly one morning when I paid him a visit. He exhibited it with great glee, the little island gone, and a deep hollow left, but the wound washed clean and looking healthy. Some skillful rat surgeon had done him this good service while in the search for luxuries, and he only knew that on awaking in the morning he had found the operation performed....

July 10 (Sunday)

Jubal Early's Confederates were now close to Washington, at Rockville and Gunpowder Bridge, Md. Grant's two divisions from the Sixth Army Corps were en route to the city from City Point, Va.

In Virginia, Grant established a huge supply point at City Point at the confluence of the James and Appomattox rivers. Rail lines were being laid rapidly around the Union works at Petersburg.

McParlin, T. A., Surg., Med. Dir., Army of the Potomac, in front of Petersburg, Va.:

The water for the use of the hospitals [at City Point] was at first obtained from springs in the riverbank. Wells were afterwards dug, and yielded water of excellent quality. The weather was very hot and sultry, and the dust soon became a great nuisance in the hospitals. The main road from the front to City Point, by which all the supply trains moved, passed close to the hospitals, and clouds of dust were constantly settling over the tents. To obviate this, a number of water carts were procured and the ground freely sprinkled. Screens and arbors of evergreens were also erected as fast as possible.

In Georgia, Johnston had his back to Atlanta and Sherman laid his plans to invest the city. At Decatur, Ala., Maj. Gen. Lovell Harrison Rousseau began a very successful cavalry raid against the railroads operating between Montgomery, Ala., and Columbus, Ga.

Grinsted, W., Surg., USV, 3d Div., 20th Corps, advance on Atlanta, Ga.:

On Sunday, July 3, 1864, we moved forward toward Marietta, and had three men wounded by shell on the march, whom we transported in ambulances several days, but who did well notwithstanding. The command moving slowly, one section of the hospital was always up with it. There was skirmishing for some two weeks, but with few casualties. Scorbutic affections increased, and on July 10th, seventy-five men were sent to Marietta general hospital. The weather continued fine and warm....

July 13 (Wednesday)

Sherman directed his cavalry around Atlanta to tear up the railroads and create havoc, while he crossed the Chattahoochee to advance on the city.

In northern Mississippi, Gen. Andrew Jackson Smith's cavalry was moving nearer to Forrest as the Confederates entered the city of Tupelo. Fighting was hot for a period at Camargo Cross Roads as the Confederates moved in for the attack against more than 14,000 Federals. Smith took up a strong position on a low ridge and awaited results.

The Sanitary Commission headquarters at Pilot Knob attended to a large number of refugees during its operations. During this month, the number of individuals provided assistance was 1346. The Sanitary Commission reports described these people:

They are, with a few exceptions, poor people from southeast Missouri and Arkansas, ignorant, unable to read and write, accustomed to live in squalid wretchedness, the poor "white trash" of the South, a class from which the Rebels have largely recruited their armies by conscription, and left their families, widowed and orphaned, to find their way to our lines to save themselves from starvation. They uniformly claim to be Union people, are willing enough to take the oath of allegiance, but do not really understand what is essential to loyalty.... Nevertheless they are human beings; and although in the lowest stage of civilization, they are thrown upon our charity.... Another and better class of them, however, have been faithful to the Government under every form of persecution, and are not only refugees but soldiers' families, who deserve all the sympathy and aid that can be given....

July 14 (Thursday)

Nathan B. Forrest was handed one of his two defeats today when he failed to rout Maj. Gen. Andrew Jackson Smith's Federal force at Harrisburg, near Tupelo, Miss. Smith's troops repeatedly repulsed the Confederate assaults with heavy Rebel casualties. Of Smith's nearly 14,000 men, only 674 were lost by all causes, less than 5 percent, while the Confederate losses were about 1350 out of about 9500, nearly 16 percent.

At White's Ford, near Leesburg, Va., Jubal Early's Confederate force had recrossed the Potomac and was safe for the time being. It was close however, since Gen. Horatio Wright's Federals were at Poolesville, Md., just north of the crossing.

July 15 (Friday)

Near Leesburg, Va., Jubal Early's Confederate forces were sorting themselves out after their attack on Washington.

At Tupelo, Miss., Union Maj. Gen. A. J. Smith waited until midafternnon for another Confederate attack, when he pulled up stakes and headed back to Tennessee, closely followed, but not attacked, by Gen. Nathan Bedford Forrest's cavalry. This kept

Forrest where Smith could watch him for a while and away from the vital railroad link carrying Sherman's supplies from Chattanooga to Atlanta.

July 17 (Sunday)

Pres. Davis, after several days, had reached a decision that Gen. Joseph Johnston would have to go. The command of the Department and of the Army of Tennessee would go to John Bell Hood, one of the corps commanders. In this case, the command went from wily Johnston, who conserved his troops, to a brawler (Hood) who would destroy the Army of Tennessee.

During the Battle of Kennesaw Mountain on June 27, Capt. William G. Ewin, 20th Tennessee, was wounded in the leg, which was then amputated. He was removed to Forsyth, Ga., where his leg healed without any serious complications. He wrote his sisters, Susan and Mary Elizabeth:

I am, thank Providence, nearly well with the exception of one or two little places, all of which a fourpence would cover, my leg is entirely healed and I am sitting up in a chair as I write. Had I a pair of crutches I could walk a little. I expect to have a pair in a few days. I am in the ... hospital at this place but stay in Dr. Du Pu's tent and am very comfortably situated. The Dr. has been very kind to me. As soon as I reached Atlanta, Uncle Elbridge Pearl obtained permission and carried me to his house where I received every kindness and attention that I could wish. They couldn't have treated me better had I been a son. His wife is one of the nicest ladies I ever met. I shall ever think of them affectionately. Since being here the ladies have been very kind and have brought me many nice eatables. A Mrs. Asbery was particularly kind....

My recovery has been very rapid and remarkable, not one unfavorable symptom having made its appearance, and it suppurated from the first. The operation was well done and with but little loss of blood. Have fallen away but very little and feel almost as strong now as I did before being wounded. I have much to be thankful for. I have the piece of shell that shattered my leg and will save it. It is nearly three inches square....

Unable to perform active service, Ewin remained connected to the Confederate Army, serving where he could help. He was paroled in May 1865, and returned to Nashville. He died in Humphreys County, Tenn., on July 30, 1882, at age 40.

All of the collecting points for refugees drew both blacks and whites. This month, Pilot Knob saw 160 black refugees provided assistance. There was a marked difference between this class of refugee and the "poor white trash," which also collected at Pilot Knob:

> … there were about as many colored refugees at Pilot Knob as whites, but they have been far more self-supporting, and taken much better care of themselves. Last summer, colored refugee women, of their own accord, planted their dooryards with vegetables, and kept them looking clean, and their children healthy, while the white refugees utterly neglected any such efforts to help themselves, or improve their condition. Such has been the paralyzing effects upon the industry of the poor whites of the South by their contact with the system of slavery, rendering them a far less hopeful class of our population than the negroes whom they so much despise, and affect to consider so much inferior to themselves.

July 18 (Monday)

At Atlanta, Confederate Gen. Joseph Eggleston Johnston turned over the command of the Army of Tennessee to Lt. Gen. John Bell Hood and left the city for North Carolina.

Perry, John G., Asst. Surg., USV, 20th Mass. Vols., hospital near Petersburg, Va.:

> I am retained, and Gen. Hancock says I must remain. Dr. Hayward and I have our quarters back of the hospital in a little nook, with green boughs to cover us. I visit the Twentieth about once a week, but it is almost too sad to go there, as so many of the old familiar faces are gone. I still hope that I may be mustered out of service before very long, however.

July 19 (Tuesday)

Near Atlanta, Union Maj. Gen. George Thomas and his Army of the Cumberland were north of the city, somewhat separated from the other two armies that made up Sherman's forces. Hood decided he would attack Thomas, believing his Confederates could defeat Thomas before Federal

help could arrive. Hood massed his forces for an assault the next day.

The Federals of "Black Dave" Hunter and Maj. Gen. George Crook were looking for Jubal Early's Confederate force and found it near Berryville, Va., where a sharp fight took place at Berry's Ford. Early threw in a number of troops against the advancing Federals, and then he left the area and headed for Winchester.

July 20 (Wednesday)

Hood's attack on Thomas north of Atlanta began three hours late, but was furious for a time. When the attack failed, it revealed that the Confederates had taken dreadful losses. Thomas, with about 20,000, lost about 1800, somewhat less than 10 percent. Hood, with about the same number of men, suffered losses of nearly 4800, almost 25 percent of his force. Nothing had been accomplished except that Hood now had fewer men and no way to replace them. The wounded were either carried, or staggered, to the field hospitals.

Foye, John W., Surg., USV, 20th Corps, advance on Atlanta, Ga.:

> On July 20th, about three o'clock P.M., the battle of Peach Tree Creek was fought. It consisted of a series of assaults on the part of the enemy, each of which was repulsed with great loss to them, and they finally retired. Our field hospitals were situated about one mile from the battlefield, and with one exception, were in working order by the time the wounded began to arrive…. We received into the three division hospitals during and subsequent to the battle, one thousand and fifty-one Union wounded, and one hundred and six Confederate wounded. One hundred and sixty-nine amputations and forty-two excisions were performed during the night and day following the battle. The wounded were sent to Marietta, and thence transferred to the field hospital of the Department of the Cumberland.
>
> On the morning of July 21st, the command moved forward and took a position about two miles from the centre of … Atlanta. Fortifications were erected and the siege of the city lasted forty-two days, terminating on September 2d in [its] occupation … by our forces.

Grinsted, W., Surg., USV, 3d Div., 20th Corps, advance on Atlanta, Ga.:

On July 20th, we met the enemy, and after a sharp fight of three or four hours, we drove him with severe loss. In this action … three hundred and forty-five men were wounded. There were also one hundred and ten Confederate wounded brought into hospital…. The wounded were fed and attended to as promptly as possible…. The wounds received during this action were of a severe character, the enemy charging boldly. The Confederates received were very severely wounded, many having from three to five wounds; a single wound being exceptional. Six died on the same night they were received, and some thirty more prior to their transportation….

Day, D. L., Pvt., Co. B, 25th Mass. Vol. Inf., 18th Corps hospital, Point of Rocks, Va.:

Thus far I have been unable to discover any charms in hospital life. With fair health, the active camp is far preferable. This hospital is divided into three departments. The first is the officers' ward, the second is the hospital for the wounded and very sick, and the third is the convalescent camp. The first two are in large hospital tents and are furnished with cots, mattresses and other necessary conveniences. In the third are more than 600 men, quartered under shelter tents. I am in this department.

It is not supposed that there are any sick men here. They are all either deadbeats or afflicted with laziness, and a draft is made from among them twice a week for the front. I had been here only four days when I was drawn, but Garland of Company C, who is an attaché at Dr. Sadler's office, saw my name on the roll and scratched it off. Although there are none here supposed to be sick, there seems to be a singular fatality among them as we furnish about as large a quota every day for the little cemetery out here as they do from the sick hospital. But then in a population of 600 or more, three or four deaths a day is not surprising.

I have been here three weeks and have been drafted four times, but with my friend Garland's help, I have escaped. I should be pleased to be back with the boys if I was only half-well, but I reckon I shall not be troubled with any more drafts. Dr. Hoyt sent a man back the other day. The next morning he was sent up with a sharp note to Dr. Sadler saying that he didn't send men to the hospital that were fit for duty and didn't want them sent back until they were. That roused Dr. Sadler's ire and he says when Hoyt wants his men he can send for them.

Dr. Sadler has the whole charge of the convalescent camp and has several young fellows, assistant surgeons so-called, on his staff. Some of these fellows I should think had been nothing more than druggists' clerks at home, but by some hook or crook have been commissioned assistant surgeons and sent out here. Every morning all who are able in all the ten wards go up to be examined and prescribed for by these new-fledged doctors, and those not able to go seldom receive any medical attendance, but it is just as well and perhaps better that they do not go as the skill of these young doctors is exceedingly limited. Dr. Sadler is a fine man and a skilful surgeon. He comes around occasionally, visiting those who are not able to go out and prescribes for them, and for a day or two afterwards the assistants will attend to those cases. These assistants make the examinations and draft the men for the front, after which they are examined by Dr. Sadler and frequently a number of them will not be accepted, and the assistants oftentimes need not feel very much flattered by some remarks of the doctor.

The convalescent camp holds its own in spite of all the drafts made on it. Recruits arrive daily and the drafts are made twice a week, sending back 50 or 100 at each draft. When a draft is made, one of the assistants comes into a ward and orders it turned out, and every man not down sick abed turns out. The ward master forms them in single rank and the inspection begins. They commence on the right and go through the ward, making the same examinations and asking the same questions of every man in the ward They feel the pulse and look at the tongue, and [if] those are right, they are booked for the front. They remind me of horse jockeys at Brighton examining horses. Some of the boys who are well enough but are in no hurry to go back, chew wild cherry or oak bark to fur their tongues and are thus exempted until Dr. Sadler gets hold of them, when they have to go. We get some recruits from the other hospital, for as soon as a sick or wounded man there is declared convalescent he is sent here.

A good joke occurred one morning when one of them was drafted for the front. He had been slightly wounded in the leg and was getting around with a crutch. When his ward was ordered out for draft he fell in with the rest and the doctor, not noticing the crutch, but finding his pulse and tongue all right, marked him as able-bodied. When Sadler inspected them he said to the fellow: "What are you here for?" "Going to the front, I suppose; there is where I am ticketed for." Sadler laughed and said: "I'll excuse you." Then turning to his assistant, remarked: "We are not yet so hard up for men as to want three-legged ones." The assistant looked as though he wished he was at home under his mother's best bed.

This whole hospital is under the management of a Dr. Fowler, and as far as I am able to judge, is well and skillfully managed. The cuisine is excellent and far better than could be expected in a place like this. The hospital fund as fast as it accrues is expended for vegetables, fruits, milk, butter, cheese, preserves and many other things which the government is not supposed to furnish. The kitchen is in two departments, one where are cooked and served out the meats, soups, vegetables and other food for the convalescent. In the other are cooked the roasts, steaks, broths, beef tea and all kinds of light diet for the officers' ward and the sick and wounded department. The light diet is presided over by an angel of mercy in the person of a Miss Dame, who is the hospital matron.

July 21 (Thursday)

The period between June 16 and July 21, 1864, was one of little movement around Petersburg. The siege tightened, but it would be about 10 months before attrition had its effects. The troops had settled in, on both sides, and endured the hot weather in varying degrees of discomfort. On the Union side, water was obtained from wells dug 8 to 30 feet deep, and the water was of good quality. Sick call was held regularly and was always well attended. During this period, 11,191 sick were received into the army's hospitals and 11,526 wounded were treated, giving a total of 22,717—the equivalent of one corps. Of these, 15,427 were sent to the hospitals at City Point; 3566 were returned to duty; and 797 died of all causes. The loss of over 16,000 men from the Union Army was unfortunate, but they could be replaced fairly easily. The same number lost on the Confederate side would have been devastating. Overall, the Union hospitals were in fine shape.

McParlin, T. A., Surg., Med. Dir., Army of the Potomac, in front of Petersburg, Va.:

These hospitals were fitted up with wooden bunks for

the patients, kitchens for extra diet, etc., and accumulated a very considerable amount of hospital fund, which was expended for butter, eggs and other delicacies…. The inmates of the hospitals experienced great annoyance from dust, and from the swarms of flies which seemed to spring up everywhere. For the first evil, there could be but little remedy. A large number of mosquito-bars procured and distributed served to abate the latter nuisance to a great degree. Regiments whose term of service had expired were leaving almost daily, taking with them their medical officers, and in this way a number of the most experienced and valuable surgeons were being lost to the service.…

It was extremely hot in Atlanta. Gen. Hardee's troops were sagging as they took a long march of 15 miles south, and then east, in an attempt to outflank Union Gen. James B. McPherson's Army of the Tennessee, which was east of Atlanta at Decatur. McPherson, meanwhile, had moved farther west towards Atlanta, closing in on Hood. Maj. Gen. Francis P. Blair, Jr., one of McPherson's commanders, attacked Leggett's Hill successfully, despite valiant efforts by Gen. Patrick Cleburne's Confederate division to defend it.

July 22 (Friday)

The Battle of Atlanta took place amid high temperatures that took a terrible toll on the troops on both sides. Hardee's Confederate corps, after a hot, long, night march, attacked the left flank of McPherson's corps located between Decatur and Atlanta without knowing that two Federal divisions had been moved into that location during the night. Confederate Gen. Cheatham's men fought fiercely on McPherson's front, but to no avail. The overall attack failed, with about 3700 Federal losses from nearly 30,000 engaged—slightly more than ten percent. The Confederate losses were estimated to be from 7000 to 10,000, out of about 40,000 engaged. This was the second loss of 25 percent Hood's army had taken. Two tries, two failures. Neither time was Hood on the field in direct command of the Confederates.

Maj. Gen. James Birdseye McPherson, USA, was killed, as was Maj. Gen. W. H. T. Walker, CSA. Hardee, again, was selected by Hood as the scapegoat. Union Maj. Gen. John A. "Blackjack" Logan assumed command of McPherson's Army of the Tennessee.

In the Shenandoah Valley, Federal forces were building up near Winchester and Early had withdrawn towards Strasburg. Gen. Horatio Wright's Sixth Corps returned to the siege lines at Petersburg. Grant was trying to decide what to do about the Valley.

Billings, J. S., Asst. Surg., USA, Army of the Potomac, near Petersburg, Va.:

The anaesthetic commonly used has been a mixture of ether and chloroform, in the proportion of one part of the latter to two of the former. Pure chloroform has been much used however, and several deaths have occurred from its effects....

The character of the surgery performed in the field hospitals during the campaign has been unprecedentedly good. The majority of cases have been properly dressed, and operated on, before being sent to the rear, and, for this reason, the number of primary operations has been very great. The great majority of wounds have been caused by the conoidal ball, but a few wounds from grape or canister hav[e] been observed. The treatment of flesh wounds has been simple and uniform, consisting of a small piece of wet lint placed on the wound, or wounds, and retained in position by a turn of bandage, or slip of plaster. The common adhesive plaster has been less frequently used than in former campaigns, partly because means of heat are necessary to apply it properly, and partly because it is thought to be somewhat irritating to the skin, and liable to produce erythematous inflammation. Gelatine plaster has been more largely used, and, in many cases, where formerly a bandage would have been applied, its cleanliness, ease of application, and the facilities it affords for examining or redressing the part being the principal arguments in its favor.

July 23 (Saturday)

In the Valley, Confederate Gen. Jubal Early unexpectedly turned on Gen. "Black Dave" Hunter. Early was coming down the Valley from Strasburg, north towards Kernstown, just south of Winchester. Union Gen. Crook went out to meet Early at Kernstown.

In Georgia, the armies of Sherman and Hood were busy tending the wounded and burying the dead after the fierce fighting of the day before.

Gen. Andrew Jackson Smith and his troops returned to Memphis after their engagement with Forrest and S. D. Lee at Tupelo.

July 24 (Sunday)

On the Shenandoah Valley Pike south of Kernstown, Va., Jubal Early was heading north over the old battleground of 1862. Maj. Gen. John C. Breckinridge commanded Early's right, with Gen. Ramseur's troops going around to the west, aiming for the Union right flank. Forcing the center after Breckinridge attacked the Union left, Early broke the Federal line and the footrace was on to Harpers Ferry, yet again. Federal losses in matériel were high; the loss in men was about 1200, mostly captured. Early followed at a leisurely pace.

In Georgia, the cleanup of the battlefield after the Battle of Atlanta continued. On the Confederate side, the wrangling and placement of blame also continued. Hood was *never* at fault—at least not according to J. B. Hood.

Grinsted, W., Surg., USV, 3d Div., 20th Corps, advance on Atlanta, Ga.:

On July 24th, we moved on the Marietta and Sandtown road to within a mile of our lines north of Atlanta, and lay there one month, during which time I was relieved from my duties ... and ordered to report ... as surgeon-in-chief of the Artillery Corps.

July 25 (Monday)

In the Shenandoah Valley, the Federals got a chance to cool off during their hot retreat when a heavy rainstorm began that turned the roads to mire. Early followed Crook's retreat up the Valley Pike to Bunker Hill. Heavy skirmishing took place in the rain at Martinsburg, W.Va., and Williamsport, Md.

At City Point, Grant, hoping to draw off some of Lee's army, sent two cavalry divisions north of the James to tear up railroads and create havoc.

July 26 (Tuesday)

Sherman, having sent Maj. Gen. Lovell H. Rousseau to destroy the rail link between Montgomery, Ala., and Columbus, Ga., earlier in the month, now sent Gen. George Stoneman and his cavalry on a similar raid towards Macon, Ga., to destroy the railroads in that area.

In the Shenandoah Valley, Union Gen. Crook crossed into Maryland, pursued by Early's infantry. Early now set his men to tearing up the Baltimore and Ohio Railroad near Martinsburg, W.Va.

In the evening, Mr. Yeatman, president of the Western Sanitary Commission, based in St. Louis, was called to the levee on the Mississippi to assist a group of refugees. There he found:

A group of fifty families, old, decrepit men, sickly and feeble women, puny and diseased children, clothed in rags, lying in bundles of miserable bedding, landed on the levee, without food or money to procure either food or a place of shelter for a single night.... Teams could not be had that night to convey them to Benton Barracks. The President of the Commission went and provided them with bread and coffee for supper and breakfast, and they remained all night on the levee, sleeping there with no shelter.... The next day a dozen Quartermasters' teams conveyed them to the refugee quarters at Benton Barracks; rations were procured for them; the sick (being full half the number) were taken to a ward of the general hospital set aside for the purpose; and the Commission furnished shoes and clothing to the most naked and destitute, and articles of necessity for the hospital ward, with a matron and cook to assist in its management.

As these people recovered their health, they were assisted with transportation to reach homes in the country, and directed to places of employment; thus making room for others subsequently arriving in the same condition. Many deaths, however, occur of the more feeble and sickly; and sometimes whole families of orphans are left on our hands, by the death of their parents while they are here.

July 27 (Wednesday)

In Georgia, Sherman, organizing the siege of Atlanta, put his cavalry to work tearing up track. Stoneman had gone to Macon. McCook would raid the Atlanta and West Point railroad, southwest of the city. Garrard was sent towards South River. Maj. Gen. John "Blackjack" Logan was relieved of command of the Army of the Tennessee and the command was given to Maj. Gen. Otis O. Howard, a move very unpopular with some people, especially Logan's troops. Joseph Hooker, then a corps commander,

resigned because he outranked Howard. Hooker felt that *he* should have received the command.

In the Shenandoah, Early's Confederates had ripped up enough track to slow down the Union forces, and now the Rebels contemplated recrossing the Potomac back into Maryland.

At Petersburg, Hancock's Second Corps and two divisions of Sheridan's cavalry crossed the James and headed towards Richmond—a diversionary tactic used to bring pressure on Lee and wear down his troops.

July 28 (Thursday)

With his cavalry running all over Georgia, Sherman now sent infantry down the western border of Atlanta to extend his lines. Gen. O. O. Howard had moved from the eastern side of the city to the western and was sent to disrupt the railroads south of this line. Hood sent Gens. Stephen D. Lee and A. P. Stewart to counter Howard's move and they met in a sharp dustup at Ezra Church. Howard, in good defensive positions, easily held off the Confederate attacks, losing only about 600, as opposed to Rebel losses of about 5000.

In Virginia, north of the James, Hancock and Sheridan found that Lee had shifted some forces around and that the Confederate lines were stronger than they'd believed. The momentum slowed, and the Federals returned to their lines at Petersburg.

July 29 (Friday)

Confederate Jubal Early again sent John McCausland across the Potomac west of Williamsport, near Cave Spring, while another Confederate cavalry unit demonstrated against Harpers Ferry. Skirmishing was reported at Hagerstown, Md., and Mercersburg, Pa. At Petersburg, the mining operation for the Battle of the Crater was in progress.

In Georgia, Union cavalry met resistance as it attempted to destroy the railroads at Lovejoy's Station and Smith's Crossroads.

July 30 (Saturday)

For more than a month, former coal miners, men of the 48th Pennsylvania, had been digging a tunnel 510 feet long, under the siege lines at Petersburg. When it was completed, the galleries were packed with gunpowder and a long fuse laid to the entrance. Today, at about 4:45 A.M., the fuse was lit and the powder exploded. The result was a hole in the Confederate entrenchments that was 170 feet long, nearly 80 feet wide, and 30 feet deep. About 280 Confederate soldiers died, never knowing what happened to them. The Federal assault began immediately, and by about 8:30 A.M., there were nearly 15,000 Union troops in the cratered area, many of them Negroes. Confederate Gen. Mahone's troops contained the Federals, and around 2 P.M. the order was given to Union forces to pull back. It cost 4000 Union killed, wounded, and missing, and about 1500 Confederates.

Mrs. Pember, at Chimborazo Hospital No. 2 in Richmond, recorded that the explosion of the crater at Petersburg caused a basic shift in the way the Confederate patients looked at their Union counterparts. Prior to this event, Johnny Reb may have disparaged Billy Yank in many ways, but there was an underlying respect in the Southerners' talk. After the explosion, the patients' respect turned to a smoldering hatred for what they called "a dirty trick."

July 31 (Sunday)

The ratio of the number of officers wounded in the Army of the Potomac during the month of May was 22 percent of the number assigned, somewhat greater than the 20.9 percent for enlisted men. This was largely due to the heavy fighting which had begun in the Wilderness, and which continued for the month of May. The ratio dropped during the months of June and July to a point where the enlisted percentage was greater. The higher toll of officers was due to the philosophy that officers led their men from the front, where, naturally, they became targets for every rifle the enemy could bring to bear.

August 1 (Monday)

At City Point, Va., Grant appointed Maj. Gen. Philip Sheridan as the new commander of the Army of the Shenandoah. Grant sent Sheridan to Harpers Ferry by the first train. Sheridan's task was to rid the Valley of Jubal Early's Confederates once and for all.

Day, D. L., Pvt., Co. B, 25th Mass. Vol. Infantry, 18th Corps hospital, Point of Rocks, Va.:

The ward next me on the left is a colored one, and contains from 60 to 80 men, according to recruits

and drafts. Until recently they have been pretty much on their own hook, no one seeming to care for them. Some days ago Dr. Sadler asked me if I would take charge of them. I said I should like to do anything where I could be of use. He gave me my instructions and some blank reports and set me up in business. My duties are to attend roll calls, surgeon's calls, keep an account of arrivals, discharges, desertions, deaths, march them up to the kitchen three times a day for rations and make my report to him every morning. Entering on the discharge of my duties, the first thing I did was to set them to work cleaning and fixing up their quarters so they would be more comfortable.

A couple of hours' work showed a great improvement in the condition of things and while it was being done it gave me a chance to find out who among them were the worst off and needed the most care and favors....

The kitchen is about 30 rods from the camp, and when I march them up there, there are so many lame ones, they straggle the whole distance. Dr. Sadler called my attention to this, and said he should like to see them march in a little better order. I replied: "Surgeon, come out in the morning and see the parade; you will see them marching a 28 inch step and closed up to 18 inches from stem to stern." He promised he would. The next morning at breakfast call I formed every one ... that carried canes on the right, and the lamest I put at the head of the column, and gave them a send-off. It was a comical show, they marched at the rate of about one mile an hour, and those in the rear kept calling out to those in advance: "Why don ye goo long dar! Hurry up dar; shan get breakfas' fo' noon." They kept closed up better than they kept the step, as the rear crowded the advance to push them along. We were cheered along the route as almost everybody was out to see the fun. We marched in review before the doctor and by the way he laughed and shook himself I thought he was well satisfied with the parade; at any rate he complimented me on my success when I carried in my morning report....

August 2 (Tuesday)

In Springfield, Mo., Chaplain Fred H. Wines, Superintendent of Refugees, had a large influx of them from southwest Missouri, Arkansas, and Texas.

Many of these people were destitute but were willing to help themselves if means were available. Wines reported that if money were available for seed to plant corn or other grain, some of the people could subsist themselves. However, they couldn't afford clothing, food, *and* seed. While the government furnished each person with half a soldier's ration of flour, bacon, beans, and hominy (and a coffin in the event of their death), neither coffee nor sugar was provided, because if they had been, multitudes of others who could support themselves very well without help would seek to draw rations to obtain these luxuries. No clothing of any kind was provided by the government, but medicine and the rations were given free. After an appeal to St. Louis for more assistance, more clothing, food, and other goods were provided, although not nearly enough to completely alleviate the suffering of the people. Chaplain Wines wrote on this date:

I wish to express to you my sincere thanks and the thanks of the sufferers at and around this post, for the relief which you have sent them in the shape of goods.... There is much sickness here, and the doctors frequently apply to me for delicacies for their indigent patients.... The supplies sent to the hospital were received and duly appreciated.... They relieve a great deal of suffering.... The refugees coming to this post, are, almost without exception, soldiers' families, the destitute wives and children of the U.S. Volunteers from the State of Arkansas. They have been driven from their homes; they have been robbed of all which they once possessed; they have been set down in our midst, homeless, friendless, and penniless. Hundreds of them lie day and night by the roadside, exposed to the scorching sun and the pelting storm, without so much as a blanket to shield them from the sky.... I ask where upon earth can families be found whose necessities are so pressing as those of the naked and famishing wretches, who arrive here by hundreds with every Government train from the south? They are not to be found.

August 3 (Wednesday)

The diet of the Army of the Potomac, under the watchful eye of Surg. McParlin, got a boost when the chief commissary officer, Col. T. Wilson, brought in tons of fresh fruits and vegetables for issue to the troops on the line.

August 4 (Thursday)

After a series of raids by the Union on the Confederate railroads around Petersburg, and to the west of Richmond, the flow of patients to hospitals was reduced to a trickle. Wounded couldn't be moved to medical care, and this resulted in many avoidable deaths. In one such incident, Mrs. Phoebe Pember, matron of Chimborazo Hospital No. 2, recalled seeing a man sitting in an ambulance, apparently forgotten by the attendants:

... a dilapidated figure, both hands holding his head which was tied up with rags of all descriptions. He appeared to be incapable of talking, but nodded and winked and made motions with head and feet.... I took him under my especial charge. He was taken into a ward, seated on a bed, while I stood on a bench to be able to unwind rag after rag from around his head. There was no sensitiveness on his part, for his eye was merry and bright, but when the last came off, what a sight!

Two balls had passed through his cheek and jaw within half an inch of each other, knocking out the teeth on both sides and cutting the tongue in half. The inflammation caused the swelling to be immense, and the absence of all previous attendance, in consequence off the detention of the wounded until the [rail]road could be mended, had aggravated the symptoms. There was nothing fatal to be apprehended, but fatal wounds are not always the most trying.

The sight of this was the most sickening my long experience had ever seen. The swollen lips turned out, and the mouth filled with blood, matter, fragments of teeth from amidst all of which the maggots in countless numbers swarmed and writhed, while the smell generated by this putridity was unbearable. Castile soap and soft sponges soon cleansed the offensive cavity.... The following morning I found him reading the newspaper.... His first request ... was that he wanted a looking glass to see if his sweetheart would be willing to kiss him when she saw him....

August 5 (Friday)

Once in position, the engineers of the Army of the Potomac wasted no time in designing and building a railroad to serve the Union forces. Engines and freight cars were brought to City Point and placed on the rails as fast as the rails were ready. This was an outstanding feat of warfare for that time.

McParlin, T. A., Surg., Med. Dir., Army of the Potomac, in front of Petersburg, Va.:

Early in August.… The weather was generally dry. The soil contained enough clay to make the roads, after rain, almost impassable for loaded trains;… The ground occupied was subject to malarial influences. Personal movements and labor were restricted in those portions of the line exposed to fire. Wells had been dug and good water secured both in camps and entrenchments. The extension and use of the railroad made heavy trains, to a great degree, unnecessary after September 14th.

August 6 (Saturday)

At 5 o'clock this warm morning the Sisters of Charity who had been at Point Lookout, Md., tending the wounded for the past two years, were at their morning meditations in their small chapel when a loud noise was heard When they reached the door they found the air darkened with whirling sand, lumber, bedsteads, stovepipes, and even the roofs from some of the buildings. A raging tornado was tearing up the encampment from the river to Chesapeake Bay. The little chapel was shaken and the doors and windows blown out. The hospital wards were torn apart, with sick and wounded strewn about the grounds. One Sister seized hold of the tabernacle, fearing that it, too, would be swept into the Bay. One house was seen sailing through the air almost intact. Although the storm lasted only several minutes, the damage was major, and it took weeks to repair and return the facility to normal.

August 8 (Monday)

Perry, John G., Asst. Surg., USV, 20th Mass. Vols., hospital near Petersburg, Va.:

It is very quiet here in front of Petersburg, but, oh, so hot! And the combined efforts of flies, fleas, and blackflies make life almost hell. At four o'clock in the morning, which means dawn, I am awakened by the buzzing and humming of these busy insects at their pestering task, and this labor does not cease till we poor mortals are again lost to them in the darkness of the night.

Yesterday was Sunday, and all the employees and agents of the Sanitary Commission collected together and read their Bibles aloud, sang psalm tunes, and recited prayers, for I can call it nothing else. The effect was doleful in the extreme, and I never want to repeat such an experience while I am in the army. Let men pray by themselves as much as they please, and read their Bibles in solitude, but not fill every man's ears with their sins and offenses.… The flies bite so I cannot manage my thoughts and must therefore stop scribbling.

Welch, S. G., Surg., 20th S.C. Vols., near Chaffin's Bluff, Va.:

The weather for the last few days has been intensely hot. It is very dry, and I hope we shall soon have some rain. My health is excellent. We get plenty of blackberries, and all we need is plenty of sugar to go with them.

I expect we shall soon go back to Petersburg, but I am informed that Kershaw's Brigade and several thousand cavalry have left for the Valley. This indicates that the seat of war may soon be around Washington instead of Richmond. I hope we will not be sent to the Valley again, for I detest those tedious marches.…

Word was sent from the headquarters of Wilcox's Brigade to McGowan's that a negro was captured at Petersburg the day Grant's mine was sprung (July 30), who claims to belong to a medical officer of McGowan's Brigade. On the provost marshal's register is the name of "William Wilson of New York." He always claimed that to be his name. I believe it may be my servant, Wilson. If so, the remarkable part of it is that he was captured charging our breastworks. If I get him, I shall regard him as something of a curiosity in the future.…

August 10 (Wednesday)

Jackman, John S., Pvt., "The Orphan Brigade," in hospital, Macon, Ga.:

The hospitals being broken up at Newnan with other sick to be transferred to Macon, Ga., I took train for Atlanta at 10 o'clock A.M. During the afternoon we got to East Point, [some] miles from Atlanta, where the Macon and Western road branches off, and had to lie over until dark. The brigade hospital being at East Point, I saw Dr. B. and several of the boys from regiment.… The train was very much crowded with wounded and sick and having learned our baggage was stored at Griffin, I got off the train at that place to get mine. I slept until morning on a pile of crossties....

August 12 (Friday)

McParlin, T. A., Surg., Med. Dir., Army of the Potomac, in front of Petersburg, Va.:

1st to the 12th, comparative quiet existed, but, at this last date, movements were initiated having in view the seizure and destruction of the Weldon railroad.... The sick and wounded of that corps [the Fifth] were sent by ambulance to the depot field hospital at City Point. The corps marched in the afternoon, and camped at City Point at night, awaiting transport vessels....

August 13 (Saturday)

About this date a large influx of patients who'd been improperly vaccinated arrived at Chimborazo Hospital in Richmond. Evidently, the serum used for vaccination had either been unstable, or had been contaminated with a virus.

The letters of Asst. Surg. John G. Perry ended on this date. Shortly thereafter, Perry returned to Boston, where his wife was extremely ill. Following his return to Petersburg, several letters to the War Dept. requesting his release from active service because of his wife's health and his own ill health finally brought his mustering out.

Perry returned to Boston and after a short time resumed his medical practice there, where he'd remain for the rest of his life.

August 14 (Sunday)

McParlin, T. A., Surg., Med. Dir., Army of the Potomac, in front of Petersburg, Va.:

The [Fifth] corps embarked on the 13th, and reached Deep Bottom, north of the James. On the 14th, it disembarked, advanced to the west of the New Market road and took position. The day was excessively hot; the men had been exhausted, and many fell out of the ranks, some insensible or in convulsions; in many cases, death resulted. Twenty ambulances for each division were crossed over the pontoon bridge from Jones's Neck, and were at once occupied with these cases and those wounded in skirmishes. One medicine

wagon and one army wagon, loaded with tent flies and cooking utensils for each division, also crossed.... Hospitals were formed near the lower pontoon bridge, on the north bank of the river, where a landing place was constructed, by which to send the wounded on boats to hospital at City Point. These were sent by quartermaster transports on the 15th. Skirmishing continued on the 16th and 17th....

August 18 (Thursday)

McParlin, T. A., Surg., Med. Dir., Army of the Potomac, in front of Petersburg, Va.:

On the 18th, the enemy attacked,... along the line of the Tenth Corps.... The field hospitals ... were placed near the Deserted House.... Military considerations made it proper to take only ten ambulances to each division, the residue ... went into park in the vicinity of the Burchard house. There were received ... five hundred and forty-two wounded....

August 19 (Friday)

McParlin, T. A., Surg., Med. Dir., Army of the Potomac, in front of Petersburg, Va.:

On the 19th, one division of the Ninth Corps was sent to join the Fifth Corps, near the six-mile station, on the Weldon railroad.... The field hospitals of the Fifth and Ninth Corps were relieved of their inmates by the ambulances of the Sixth Corps, the patients being carried to City Point....

August 20 (Saturday)

Day, D. L., Pvt., Co. B, 25th Mass. Vol. Infantry, 18th Corps hospital, Point of Rocks, Va.:

I have read a great deal in the papers of the Christian and Sanitary commissions, of the noble and humane work they were doing and the immense amount of money contributed for their support by the people throughout the north and west. I have taken a great interest in these commissions and have supposed they were a kind of auxiliary to the medical and surgical department of the army, carrying and dispensing some simple medicines, pouring in the balm of Gilead and binding up gaping wounds, giving comfort and consolation to the sick, weary and distressed; but in all this, so far as my observation has gone, I find I have been laboring under a delusion.

Since I have been here is the first I have ever seen of the workings of these commissions, and I have watched them with some interest and taken some pains to find out about them. Here is a branch of each located midway [between] the convalescent camp and sick hospital and I find they are little else than sutler's shops, and poor ones at that. These places are said to furnish without money and without price to the inmates of this hospital and the boys in the trenches such little notions and necessities as we have been accustomed to buy of the sutlers, and in consequence of this no sutlers are allowed to locate anywhere in this vicinity. The boys are not supposed to be fooling away their money to these thieving sutlers when our folks at home are willing to supply our little needs, free gratis for nothing. So when we happen to want a lemon or a pencil, a sheet of paper or a piece of tobacco, or whatever other little notion we require, all we have to do is to apply to one or the other commission and make known our wants; after answering all the questions they are pleased to ask, we are given a slice of lemon, a half sheet of paper, or a chew of tobacco. These are not wholesale establishments.

Fortunately for me I have stood in very little need of anything [that the Commission had]. I seldom solicit any favors and those are granted so grudgingly I almost despise the gift.... This is the first place I ever got into where I could neither buy, steal nor beg. I notice the officers fare a little better; they get in fair quantity almost anything they call for.... Sometimes a person calling for an article will be told they are out of it, but expect some when the team comes up from the Point. In a little while after, perhaps some officer will call for the same thing and get it....

August 21 (Sunday)

By decree, the Chimborazo Hospital No. 2 in Richmond was cleared of all patients except those from Virginia and Maryland. This created several problems for the hospital staff. Mrs. Phoebe Pember, matron of the hospital, found that families and friends would visit the wounded or sick and stay for long periods of time, often having to be physically removed from the wards. Mrs. Pember often used other means to get rid of them, at least temporarily. On one occasion, an entire family, including two young ladies, came to visit their relative, who was recovering from typhoid fever. They brought food which was inappropriate for the patient, and then appropriated food from the ward kitchen meant for other patients. The entire family entered Mrs. Pember's quarters at ten o'clock one night demanding sleeping accommodations. She finally housed them in the laundry for the night—they stayed for six days, raiding the kitchen and creating problems. In one case, a woman stayed with her husband for some time, and when he was returned to duty she refused to leave the hospital. Her stated reason was that she'd heard a battle was imminent and she would wait for her husband to be brought back in, wounded. Sure enough, he was back within a week with a bullet in his neck. This same woman, a month later, gave birth on her husband's bed. After much confusion, mother and child were moved to another ward and put to bed. At the end of the month, mother and child were sent to the railroad depot to return to western Virginia. The driver of the ambulance returned with the baby, but not the mother. The father was then given a furlough, the baby a quart of milk, and both were sent after the mother. The mother wasn't entirely without gratitude; she named the baby Phoebe.

In the area of Harpers Ferry, Sheridan pulled back to Halltown and dug good defensive positions, which Early refused to assault.

South of Petersburg, Warren still held the Weldon Railroad despite the efforts of A. P. Hill's Confederates to dislodge him. In extreme heat and occasional rain, the Rebels made repeated assaults on the Union lines, but were repulsed. The rail link to Petersburg and Richmond was lost, and Lee knew it. In four days the Federals had suffered about 4500 casualties (mostly captured) out of about 20,000 engaged, roughly 22 percent. Lee's losses were about 1600 out of 14,000, roughly 11 percent. Grant could afford the loss, Lee couldn't, and things would only get worse for the Rebels.

McParlin, T. A., Surg., Med. Dir., Army of the Potomac, In front of Petersburg, Va.:

... the Second Corps, taking ten ambulances to a division, advanced from Deep Bottom to the position on the Weldon railroad occupied by the Fifth Corps, and, facing southward, continued to destroy the road as they advanced until the 25th, when, reaching Ream's Station, they encountered the enemy. On the

21st, the enemy attacked the Fifth Corps ... but was repulsed with heavy loss, leaving one hundred and sixty of their wounded in our hands.... The labors of the ambulance corps were severe. Two sergeants were killed, six men were wounded, and nineteen captured. Eight stretcher-bearers were killed. Shells passed through two ambulances....

August 22 (Monday)

At St. Louis, Mo., a refugee family arrived at the levee on the Mississippi from the White River country in Arkansas. The woman was sick, and she took all the children, except for the oldest boy, to Benton Barracks to obtain assistance. The boy was left on the levee with the few possessions that couldn't be carried, and the understanding that his mother would return for him. The young boy waited all night and all the next day before he was found by agents of the Sanitary Commission, who informed him that his mother had died shortly after arriving at Benton Barracks and the hospital. All the children were sent to the Mission Free School and later placed in foster homes.

The Union governor of Arkansas also had his problems with refugees. Thousands fled the state into Missouri and across the river into Tennessee and Mississippi to escape the guerrillas and outlaws who preyed on the helpless. The Union Army had withdrawn into enclaves within Arkansas, and most of the countryside was overrun with marauders. Gov. Isaac Murphy wrote the president of the Western Sanitary Commission on this date:

Dear Sir: Enclosed I send you the report of the Refugee Committee. It gives a very imperfect conception of the extent of the destitution and suffering pervading the entire state. Since Steele's retreat, the army has occupied a few posts, but all beyond the pickets has been held at will by the Rebels, and their conscription has swept the country up to the picket lines, accompanied by the murder and pillage of all the loyal element outside of the pickets. Families, stripped of everything, have fled to the military posts, and to other states, for protection. Nothing, scarcely, has been raised for food, in the state. Unless those portions of our country which God has blessed with peace and security come at once to our aid, Arkansas will be a wilderness....

August 25 (Thursday)

In the Valley, Sheridan sat in his fortifications at Halltown, while Early reentered Maryland at Williamsport and moved a force towards Shepherdstown.

In Georgia, Sherman began his advance, intending to isolate Atlanta completely. He sent his blue columns to cut off the area south and east along the south side of the city, towards Jonesboro.

Today, the Battle of Ream's Station took place south of Petersburg on the Weldon Railroad. Confederate A. P. Hill, with a reinforced corps, struck Federal troops under Hancock in a surprise attack that cost the Union 2372 losses, nearly 2000 of them being captured. The Confederate losses were around 720. The attack accomplished little. Hill returned to the Petersburg lines and Hancock continued the destruction of the railroad.

McParlin, T. A., Surg., Med. Dir., Army of the Potomac, in front of Petersburg, Va.:

The Second Corps occupied a position at Ream's Station on the 25th, quite exposed to ... attack from several directions, and were more distant from permanent base and field hospitals. Its wounded [were] temporarily received in Ream's church, where the hospital staff of each division made their rendezvous. The field companions and ambulances furnished the required dressings and appliances. The cavalry division ... had with it a medicine wagon, which was very useful. The medical director of the Second Corps sent back for one for his command, but it did not arrive; indeed, it only escaped capture by the sergeant in charge prudently returning with it again to the park, observing that the enemy occupied the road.

The church was far from being a place of security; indeed, no such place was attainable. The line of defense described *two thirds of the circumference of a circle with a radius so small that bullets fired on the left coursed over the enclosed area and struck down men in position on the right.* [Italics added.]

During the more vigorous assault at two o'clock P.M., the ambulances, the wounded, medical officers and attendants retired about a hundred yards to a shallow ravine affording partial shelter. The ambulances, once filled, were sent at some risk via the Geary church road to the Williams house, and empty vehicles were sent for. The fresh trains reached the corps safely, prior to the final assault made by the enemy at five o'clock P.M. The attack was so severe from all sides that the portion of the railroad which had been destroyed and the position at that point were relinquished. The ambulance officers succeeded in loading up with such of the wounded as could not retire; others were carried by stretcher men or aided by stragglers. None of the wounded behind the breastworks were left, but those on the advanced pickets could not be removed. Four medical officers, two hospital stewards and ten stretcher men were detailed to remain and care for them....

The train of wounded from Ream's Station proceeded to the Williams house, and, aided by ambulances of the Ninth Corps, the wounded were sent to City Point, after receiving necessary surgical attention.... The number of wounded brought to field hospital after this affair was ... one thousand four hundred and sixty-one; total deaths, eighty-seven....

August 26 (Friday)

Jubal Early's Confederates found the Union positions around Halltown, W.Va., too strong for their liking, and they moved back to west of the Opequon River towards Bunker Hill and Stephenson's Depot, Va. Some minor skirmishing occurred, but nothing serious.

Coxe, John, Pvt., Hampton's Legion, Charles Town, W.Va.:

In going toward Harpers Ferry we passed through the pretty little village of Charles Town at an early hour on the 26th of August, 1864. It was a lovely country ... We halted a short distance beyond town and formed line on the edge of a wood on the right of Harpers Ferry Pike.... Pickets were posted in the woods on the hill in front, and I was one of them, my post being on our extreme left in trees near the pike.... Between 5 and 6 P.M.,... I was relieved....

I was very tired and hungry when I got down to ranks, and while I was boiling some green corn and hardtack in a frying pan, it was suddenly announced that the enemy was advancing against us from over the hill.... Our pickets scampered down into ranks with the cracking rifles of the enemy just behind them. We were behind a weak improvisation of rails. The Federals were in heavy line of battle and thought to run over us, rushing up to within a few yards of our line and

delivering their fire.... Randolph Bacon, of my company, but then color-bearer of the regiment, was shot through the heart and fell dead, but still held on to the flag.... The next moment I was shot.

For a few seconds the shock completely paralyzed me. At first I thought a piece of shell had hit me in the throat; but it was a rifle ball that had entered my throat and, passing to the left of the windpipe, by which it was slightly deflected, went on clear through me and passed out between the back of my neck and left shoulder. And, as if not satisfied with all that, the ball kept on and ripped through the corner of my knapsack, leaving a jagged hole in the oilcloth. Blood rushed out from both holes, and my clothes were saturated with it. Then an officer shouted, "Get to the rear!" and I started. But I didn't get back more than fifty yards, just out of the woods into a field of pretty timothy and red clover, when I fell, being too weak to stand any longer. Meanwhile the blood continued to flow, but I felt good and supposed I would pass away shortly.

The fight in front continued only a few minutes after I fell, during which a few Federal bullets cut through the tall timothy near me.... It was getting late, and after the Federals were driven back I heard voices near me and tried to call, but found I couldn't speak above a whisper. Neither could I be seen except at very close range, so well was I screened by the tall hay. At one time I saw the head of Pvt. Jake Miller, of my company, and tried my best to attract his attention, but in vain. Then I heard the sound of horses' feet, and a moment later a party of mounted officers rode right up to me and stopped. It was Maj. Goggin, of the division staff, and others. The major looked down into my face with a sympathetic expression and said: "Are you badly hurt, young man?" I couldn't speak, but nodded my head in reply. He then turned and said something to an orderly, who galloped away. Then saying, "I'll have you looked after promptly," the party rode slowly away. The orderly returned soon with two men bearing a stretcher, and as they tenderly put me on it the expression of their faces indicated that they thought I was "done for."

It was dark when I was laid down on the green grass floor of the field hospital tent in the edge of town. Others badly wounded were there already. Our regimental surgeon was working hard, but I saw no other surgeon. Still more wounded were brought in until the tent was full. When the surgeon hastily examined me, I was so weak I could hardly move a muscle. He seemed surprised to see so much blood and me still alive. As he turned away to another I heard him say to an attendant: "No, the hemorrhage has ceased." I received no more attention that night, nor was it possible, with the help at hand, to give much attention to any one person.

Sometime during the night a great thunderstorm struck us. There was much thunder, wind, and rain, the latter coming down in torrents and flooding our tent. Then the tent blew down on us, and we came near being drowned or smothered till the storm passed and the tent was reerected.

August 27 (Saturday)

Coxe, John, Pvt., Hampton's Legion, Charles Town, W.Va.:

About 2 A.M. I heard the rumble of vehicles outside, and soon after I, with another young fellow of my regiment, but not of my company, [was] carried out and placed in an ambulance, and the driver was told to go to Winchester. The pike was level and smooth, and there was not much jolting. After daylight I found that my companion was wounded in the upper left arm. It seemed to be a flesh wound, but the ball was still in him. To my whispers he told me that he was suffering great pain and was not inclined to talk much. Then I whispered and said: "You'll be all right in a short time, but look at me." He laughed faintly, but said nothing more. Two days afterward the poor youth died from lockjaw.

Arriving at Winchester at 2 P.M., we were carried into a church building then being used as a hospital. My clothes were dry and so stiff that they had to be cut from me. Clean mattresses were on the floor, and kind ladies of the city assisted in looking after the many wounded, who, for the most part, were from the battlefields of Early's campaign to Washington. The next day my relatives had me removed to a private home. Dr. Shine, our brigade surgeon, looked after my medical needs, and in every other way I had the best attention, to all of which I believe I owe my life.

August 28 (Sunday)

Yesterday, Sherman completed his organization to cut the final link into Atlanta. Hood, so far, hadn't provided much resistance to Sherman's buildup.

Today, Sherman was on the move around Atlanta. Maj. Gen. George Thomas's Army of the Cumberland reached the Atlanta and West Point Railroad at Red Oak, where some fighting occurred. Otis O. Howard's Army of the Tennessee was on the same railroad near Fairburn, and Schofield's Army of the Ohio was at nearby Mt. Gilead Church. Slocum manned the Union lines immediately around Atlanta. The city was almost sealed off.

In the Valley, Sheridan came out of his fortifications at Halltown and advanced towards Charles Town, W.Va., with light skirmishing.

August 30 (Tuesday)

The Confederacy lost the West Point-Atlanta rail link today when Sherman's bluecoats occupied the line and continued their advance towards Jonesboro. Only the Atlanta-Macon rail link remained. Hood, trying to stop Sherman, sent Patrick Cleburne with Hood's old corps and the corps of S. D. Lee to head Sherman off before he got to Jonesboro. This attempt proved to be futile.

In the Valley, Sheridan assigned Maj. Gen. Crook as the major commander in W.Va., replacing "Black Dave" Hunter. Sheridan then shifted his own advance towards Berryville and the Valley Pike.

August 31 (Wednesday)

Schofield's Army of the Ohio cut the last rail link to Atlanta when that army crossed the Macon-Atlanta line between Jonesboro and Atlanta. Hood had sent Hardee to attack Otis O. Howard's Army of the Tennessee near Jonesboro. The Confederate attack wasn't pressed vigorously, and it failed, with heavy Southern losses. With most of the Confederates now south of Atlanta, Sherman told Slocum to try to enter the city, if possible.

September 1 (Thursday)

Atlanta was being evacuated, and the munitions dumps and railroad yards were blown up by Hood's retreating Confederates. Fires broke out in the area of the explosions, and little was done to extinguish them, as the Confederates rushed to escape. Hood had failed in his task of holding the largest rail terminal in the South.

Meanwhile, Confederate Gen. S. D. Lee's corps had started back towards Atlanta, and then been delayed by Hood at Rough and Ready. Hardee's corps was going against Howard's army and elements from both Thomas's army and Schofield's Army of the Ohio. The Battle of Jonesboro started at about noon, and within a reasonably short period of time the Federals had decimated two Rebel brigades, although other Confederates held their ground. At dark Hardee pulled back to Lovejoy's Station to join with Hood and the remainder of the Army of Tennessee. By the end of the second day of fighting around Jonesboro, the Confederate Army was ruined.

The refugee problem at Ft. Leavenworth, Kans., was severe. Many of the people reaching there were fleeing from the guerrilla raiders of Missouri and eastern Kansas. Mr. J. R. Brown, Superintendent of Refugees at Leavenworth, wrote the president of the Western Sanitary Commission in St. Louis:

We have our Freedman's Home under full operation, have a school in one part of one of the buildings, and we can already see the benefit of our enterprise in many ways. Our plan, in short, is to take in the worn down and helpless, just up from below, suffering with all sorts of diseases, induced by every exposure by the way. Our washhouse is the first apartment to enter, where all filthy and infecting clothing is removed, and a thorough cleansing takes place. The office is the next place, where names and particulars are recorded. Then the dining room is opened, and wholesome food is furnished, and then rest is allowed, and in one or two days, these tired, wretched beings look and act like men, women and children. We advertise to furnish help of every kind desired, and when we have calls for it, we know just who are in condition to go out, and such are called into the office, and at first sight present a wholesome appearance, and are almost sure to please. Then again, persons wishing to hire help, come there expecting to pay a reasonable price, and put themselves under obligations which they would not feel if they had picked up their help in the street, or it had been urged on them by some poor starved seeker of work. Then again, we can feed, doctor, teach, and shelter them, at less expense in this way than any other....

September 2 (Friday)

On the Petersburg line, the Federals were again operating on the Weldon Railroad, securing more of that line and tearing up track. There was skirmishing at Yellow Tavern and at other points. With all the combat, the construction of the railroad from City Point to service the entrenchments at Petersburg and bring in the wounded was continued apace.

McParlin, T. A., Surg., Med. Dir., Army of the Potomac, in front of Petersburg, Va.:

During September, the hospitals of the Second Corps were at the Burchard and Deserted Houses. The prevailing diseases were diarrhea, dysentery and fevers of the intermittent and typhoid type. The average number on the daily sick report was a little over five percent. The railroad was continued, by the 14th day of September, from Cedar Level, Seven-miles Station, on the City Point and Petersburg railroad, to Warren Station, the point on the Weldon railroad seized and held by the Fifth Corps.

From Atlanta, to Chattanooga, to Nashville, to Louisville, to Washington, D.C., the telegraph lines hummed with the message from Gen. Sherman to Pres. Lincoln: "Atlanta is ours, and fairly won!" Lincoln could have received no better news at this time. It relieved considerable political pressure on him and showed the Northern pessimists that the war could be won.

Southeast of Atlanta, Hood regrouped around Lovejoy's Station with the tattered remains of the Army of Tennessee, while Union Maj. Gen. Slocum's corps actually entered the city. Sherman's men took a breather while Sherman went to Atlanta to survey it city and plan his next move.

In the Valley, there was much skirmishing at Darkesville and Bunker Hill, while Sheridan readied his offensive. Lee felt the shortage of troops at Petersburg. Lee pressured Early to return to the Army of Northern Virginia the troops Early had "borrowed."

September 3 (Saturday)

Sherman was in Atlanta and planning for the next step. Hood, at Lovejoy's Station southeast of the city, regrouped, pulling his scattered remnants of units together and taking stock of what he had.

Sheridan was moving up the Valley Pike with his now-enlarged army. Early followed Lee's order and detached R. H. Anderson's corps, sending it back to Petersburg. However, en route, Anderson's corps accidentally ran into one of Sheridan's, much to the surprise of both generals. This brought on a sharp fight that caused Early to rethink his decision about returning Anderson to Lee.

Hand, D. W., Surg., USV, Med. Dir., New Bern, N.C.:

… early in September an epidemic of yellow fever appeared in New Bern, and seized on nearly every soldier who was exposed to it. The regiment doing provost guard duty, the 15th Connecticut Volunteers, was immediately moved outside the town, and all the patients in the hospital able to bear transportation were, as fast as possible, removed to Morehead City and Beaufort. About six hundred soldiers had the fever, of whom two hundred and eighty died.

September 4 (Sunday)

Sherman was in Atlanta, and already the civilian authorities were arguing with him about who was responsible for the debris littering the streets, how they could feed the population left in the city, and who had control of law and order. Hood, southeast towards Macon, was still collecting his battered units, and counting noses.

After the fight around Berryville between Anderson's corps and Sheridan's army, Early pulled his entire line back up the Valley.

September 6 (Tuesday)

Ft. Scott, Mo., also a major collecting point for refugees, was in dire straits because of a combination of weather and lack of medicine, clothing, and food. Chaplain Charles Reynolds sent an urgent appeal for assistance to J. R. Brown of the Sanitary Commission:

I have been able to get transportation for but a few of these people north as yet. I have now over 200 in camp, and they are in a most deplorable condition. A severe storm arose last evening, which continues this afternoon, with no prospect of abatement. Dr. Slocum and myself removed about twenty of the sick to a hospital tent in the Plaza, and I have a mother with her dying babe in my office. The rest are in camp, in a condition next to death. Most of them have no shelter but what the trees afford, and their rations, which I distributed yesterday morning, are ruined. The river has risen over thirty feet and is still rising. I have communicated with them twice today, by boat, and have sent over bread for the living, and

coffins for the dead. Your agent here has no funds, no tents, nor clothing. Do for heaven's sake send something along *at once*…. I would respectfully call upon the ladies of this post, to aid at once in relieving the sick women and children who are without shelter and naked. Two poor creatures died during last night's storm, and several others are very ill. Two sick children are entirely destitute of clothing.…

September 7 (Wednesday)

Today, Sherman ordered the evacuation of Atlanta. Everyone other than those in his army was to leave, some 1600 people, comprising about 446 families. The mayor of the city, Gen. Hood, and everyone else who could reach Sherman protested, to no avail. Sherman said he would have enough trouble feeding his own troops and wouldn't feed the civilians. Those who wanted to go south, could go in that direction; all others could go north.

September 10 (Saturday)

Phoebe Pember, matron of Chimborazo Hospital No. 2 in Richmond, found one of her most onerous duties was that of telling a wounded man he wouldn't survive when he was unaware there was any imminent danger of death. Pember also described other problems:

Irritability of stomach as well as indifference to food always accompanying gunshot wounds, it was necessary, while the fever continued, to give him as much nourishment in as small a compass as possible, as well as easily digestible food, that would assimilate with his enfeebled condition. Beef tea he (in common with all soldiers and I believe men) would not, or could not take, or anything I suggested as equivalent, so getting his consent to drink some "chemical mixture," I prepared the infusion.

Chipping up a pound of beef and pouring upon it a half pint of water, the mixture was stirred until all the blood was extracted, and only a teaspoonful of white fibre remained; a little salt was added, and favored by the darkness of the corner of the ward in which he lay, I induced him to swallow it. He drank without suspicion, and fortunately liked it, only complaining of its being too sweet, and by the end of ten days his pulse was fairly good and there had been no accession of fever.…

September 12 (Monday)

The "Virginia reel," "danced" in the Valley by Sheridan and Early, was taking a rest, much to the dismay of both Lincoln and Grant. Sheridan didn't seem to be able to get things moving.

Sherman began the second day of evacuation of the civilians from Atlanta amid curses, pleas, and threats coming from all sides. There was no relenting however; all must go.

September 13 (Tuesday)

In the Valley, skirmishing, however light, showed that the armies of Sheridan and Early weren't entirely asleep, as Lincoln had been thinking. In Georgia, Sherman and Hood were into the third day of a ten-day armistice and the evacuation of Atlanta's civilians.

September 14 (Wednesday)

In Atlanta the cleanup and clean-out continued. Sherman's troops were restoring the rail link to Chattanooga, and the civilians in the city were evacuating.

Grant and Lincoln pressured Sheridan to do something in the Valley about Early. Early was being pressured by Lee to return R. H. Anderson's (borrowed) corps to the Army of Northern Virginia. Lee badly needed these troops to bolster his thinning ranks. Today, Early released Anderson to move his men back to Petersburg.

Welch, S. G., Surg., 20th S.C. Vols., in a letter to his wife, from near Petersburg, Va.:

It seems that you have not received the bundles I sent to you. I sent some gunpowder home recently, and you should get some of it for your brother Jimmie, if he wants it.

You express some apprehension that I shall not be able to get home this fall. I will try very soon to get off, but if I am disappointed you can come on here. I believe our brigade will remain about Petersburg this winter, and if we do I shall make some arrangements for you to be with me.... The greatest difficulty in a man's keeping his wife here is finding enough for her to eat, but we intend to have supplies sent to us from home. You must begin to make arrangements to come and be ready between the 15th of November and Christmas, if I do not get home before that time myself.

September 16 (Friday)

In Augusta, Ga., Joseph Jones was nearly recovered from an illness, and was preparing for a visit to Andersonville Prison. His wife, Carrie, suffering from a nervous breakdown, wasn't seriously ill enough, in Jones's opinion, to postpone his trip yet again. Leaving Augusta in the company of Louis Manigault and his Negro servant, Titus, Jones travelled to Americus, Ga., and then to Andersonville, arriving about the 18th.

Jackman, John S., Pvt., "The Orphan Brigade," Americus, Ga.:

Took train on southwest road for Americus at 8 A.M. and arrived at A. at 12 P.M. Went to Bragg Hospital.

I again got in Ward No. 1, the same attendant being in charge save Baldridge and Smith. I also was placed in the Masonic Hall, a large room with nearly fifty beds in it, but there were few patients in the room. All the "rats" were glad to see me back again. My head was hurting me from loss of sleep, etc., and I went to bed.

September 17 (Saturday)

Jubal Early, with about 12,000 men, now weakened by the loss of R. H. Anderson's corps, moved down the Valley towards Martinsburg and the Baltimore and Ohio Railroad, which had been repaired after his last track-bending visit.

September 19 (Monday)

In the Valley, north of Winchester, Sheridan sent 40,000 troops against Early's 12,000. The main force of Sheridan's infantry drove up the Valley Pike around Berryville and hit the Confederates hard. Confederate Gen. Robert E. Rodes was mortally wounded during action that saw the Confederates drive into a gap in the Federal line, but the Federals held and, in turn, drove the Rebels back. The Union cavalry drove Gen. Breckinridge's division from north of the city to a new line east of Winchester. About 4:30 P.M., Sheridan ordered another advance and Early withdrew up the Valley. Federal casualties ran about 10 percent—4000 out of 40,000. Confederate losses were heavier in percentages—nearly 30 percent—3921 out of about 12,000. Early retreated with a much-weakened force.

Ghiselin, J. T., Surg., USA, Med. Dir., Sheridan's command, Shenandoah Valley, Va.:

At daylight on the morning of September 19th, one division of cavalry, which had the advance, engaged the enemy near Opequan Creek, five miles from Winchester, and drove him from his position, which it held until relieved by the infantry. The battle, during the morning, was fought with great obstinacy.... About half-past three o'clock P.M. a combined advance of infantry and cavalry was ordered ... and the enemy fled from the field, routed and demoralized. That night we occupied Winchester. The field hospitals were established during the day, on or near the Opequan Creek, and their locations were well protected from the shot of the enemy by wooded hills. They were all in the immediate vicinity of good roads. The wounded, as a general thing, received good care, and had nourishing food....

During the latter part of the day, however, it was impossible to collect all the wounded, as the army pushed on so rapidly, thereby increasing the distance for the ambulances. Quite a large number, therefore, remained on the field that night, many being concealed in the thick woods where they had fallen. At nine o'clock P.M., the same night, the general commanding ordered me to have all the wounded taken to Winchester, and the field hospitals broken up as rapidly as possible. For this purpose, a detail of medical officers to remain was made from each corps, a certain proportion of ambulances was ordered to be left, and the chief quartermaster placed at my disposal all the empty army wagons.... That night I informed you [the Surgeon General of the Army] by telegraph of the result of the battle ... and requested you to send forward to Winchester twenty medical officers, hospital supplies for five thousand wounded, and an experienced surgeon to take charge of the hospitals. Several weeks previously, the chief quartermaster, at my request, ordered the post quartermaster at Harpers Ferry to keep on hand three hundred hospital tents for such an emergency.

September 20 (Tuesday)

At Atlanta, the Confederate cavalry under Wheeler was creating supply problems for Sherman. Wheeler had been tearing up track and stopping the supplies for several days now. Forrest was loose and heading for middle Tennessee to do what he did best—create havoc.

In the Valley, Sheridan's troops chased Early's retreating columns through Middletown and finally stopped when the Confederates were south of Strasburg on Fisher's Hill. The Federals entrenched north of the town. Early was later to remark that Sheridan missed a chance to annihilate him at Winchester.

At Andersonville, Ga., Dr. Joseph Jones had arrived and set up his camp about three-quarters of a mile from the prison pen. He immediately began his investigative work and had no problems getting access to the hospital or to the "dead-house." Capt. Henry Wirz, the commandant of the stockade, absolutely refused Jones permission to visit the stockade until Brig. Gen. John H. Winder, senior officer present, intervened on Jones's behalf. The doctor's initial statistics showed that there were nearly 5000 sick Union prisoners in the prison hospital and within the stockade. Prisoner deaths averaged 110 per day at this time, there having been nearly 10,000 deaths in the prison since March, when it was opened. Jones immediately began his search for the cause of sickness and death at the camp. He didn't have to search far, for the main culprits were diarrhea, dysentery, scurvy, and gangrene, most of which could have been prevented had a proper diet been provided. His main investigative effort, however, was pointed towards gangrene, which was rampant and nearly always fatal.

September 21 (Wednesday)

In the Valley, at Strasburg, Sheridan advanced on Early's fortifications on Fisher's Hill. Fighting took place in the town of Strasburg, at Fisher's Hill and at Front Royal. After dark, Sheridan sent Gen. Crook with one of the Federal corps to the right and around the left flank of the Confederates to a position of attack.

Ghiselin, J. T., Surg., USA, Med. Dir., Sheridan's command, Shenandoah Valley, Va.:

Dr. Du Bois reported to me on the 21st that he had seized a portion of the army train, unloaded it, and with the ambulances left him, had transported all the wounded from the field to hospitals which he established at Winchester in the churches, public buildings and such private dwellings as were suitable.

These hospitals he organized by corps. Being almost destitute of food for the wounded, the commanding officer of Winchester took, at his request, eight thousand rations from an army train which was going to the front. This embarrassment arose from the fact that no subsistence train accompanied the army. Things were soon systematized, and over four thousand wounded were safely transferred to the hospitals of their respective corps, competent surgeons placed in charge, and the most experienced and expert operators designated to perform the operations.

At Andersonville, Ga., Joseph Jones's report indicated that the major problem with the prison was the overabundance of vermin and insects. Mosquitos and gnats filled the air and fleas teemed in the sandy soil. Jones was covered with so many bites that he looked as if he'd had measles. The prisoners in the compound were in worse shape, since they had fewer clothes to keep the critters off.

Jones attached no blame on the Confederate officials who chose the site of Andersonville, feeling that the site was in an "elevated and healthy locality, which was more salubrious than one half of the territory of South Carolina, Georgia, Alabama, Mississippi, and Louisiana." He remarked in particular on the quality of the water in the area being especially good—of course, that was before it made its trip through the prison compound. He commented on the purity of the water prior to its entrance into the compound and compared that with its exit, where it was "loaded with filth and human excrement" and created "an intolerable and sickening stench." He further commented that "standing as I did over these waters in the middle of a hot day in September, as they rolled sluggishly forth from the Stockade, after having received the filth and excrements of twenty thousand men, the stench was disgusting and overpowering; and if it was surpassed in unpleasantness by any thing, it was only in the disgusting appearance of the filthy, almost stagnant, waters moving slowly between the stumps and roots and fallen trunks of trees and thick branches of reeds, with innumerable long-tailed, large white maggots, swollen pease, and fermenting excrements, and fragments of bread and meat."

September 22 (Thursday)

Ghiselin, J. T., Surg., USA, Med. Dir., Sheridan's command, Shenandoah Valley, Va.:

Some skirmishing occurred on the 21st, and, during the afternoon of the 22d, an assault was made, which resulted in the complete rout of the enemy, and his broken army was pursued to Woodstock, a distance of twelve miles. The pursuit occupied the entire night, and the troops did not bivouac until four o'clock the following morning. Fortunately the casualties on the march were few....

On the evening of the 22d, Surg. J. H. Brinton, USV, arrived with five medical officers, and relieved Dr. Du Bois, who returned to headquarters on the following day. Four hundred hospital tents, ample supplies, and ten additional surgeons arrived on the 23d. About three hundred hospital tents were pitched on a well selected site near the town, and a camp hospital organized under the designation of Sheridan field hospital....

Dr. Joseph Jones also found that personal hygiene among the prisoners was almost nonexistent. One morning, he found the outline of a prisoner clearly depicted in the dirt and mud of the compound. When Jones asked about this, he was told that the dead, according to custom, were removed from the shelters and were left outside at night, ready for pickup the next morning. The rain would wash the accumulated dirt and carbon from the clothes and body of the prisoner, and this would provide an outline of the body in the dirt.

The treatment of the prisoners as regards food and shelter was not alleviated. The Confederacy had fewer resources now than it had had earlier in the war, and at this time the prison population was increasing. Little was done to get the collected trash and garbage out of the compound for a number of reasons—the primary reason being that wagons and mules weren't available to move it. A large mound of decaying food, bones, and other garbage several feet high and nearly thirty feet across was the breeding ground for millions of flies, which infested the camp and further spread disease.

September 23 (Friday)

At Fisher's Hill, Sheridan was poised to attack Early's diminished forces as soon as Crook got into position on Early's left flank. Late in the afternoon, Crook's Federals came roiling over the Rebel entrenchments, attacking them at their rear and flank. The Union troops in front attacked at the same time across the Tumbling Run ravine and up Fisher's Hill. During the melee, Confederate Lt. Col. Alexander Swift Pendelton, called "Sandie," was mortally wounded in the abdomen and died a short time later. The Union bluecoats chased the Confederates for four miles up the Valley before Early could get his lines together. Early lost 1235 more from his steadily diminishing force.

Ghiselin, J. T., Surg., USA, Med. Dir., Sheridan's command, Shenandoah Valley, Va.:

… orders were given to the chief medical officers to be prepared to send their wounded to the rear. By the afternoon of the 23d, all were comfortably loaded in an empty supply train and sent to Winchester. At Strasburg and Woodstock a few Confederate wounded were found, destitute of all supplies, and unable to bear transportation. These men were attended to by their own surgeons, who were furnished with all the necessary medical and subsistence stores.

Earlier in the year, on June 5th, the opposing forces in the Shenandoah Valley had fought at Piedmont, located about seven miles southwest of Pt. Republic, Va. The battle, which lasted from late morning until late afternoon, matched 5600 Confederates under Gen. W. E. "Grumble" Jones against about 8500 under Union Gen. "Black Dave" Hunter. The results were worse for the Confederates. "Grumble" Jones was killed and the Confederates routed. During the seesaw battle, the possession of the Union wounded at the field hospitals changed with the tide of battle. At the end, one such field hospital was in possession of the Confederates. This hospital was in the charge of Asst. Surg. William Grumbien, whose report of the aftermath of the battle was later recorded.

Grumbien, William, Asst. Surg., 20th Penn. Vols., Staunton, Va.:

I was detailed on June 7th, and left Staunton on [the ?] of September for Richmond, and was sent from thence through the lines on September 23d. The convalescent men that I sent off at first were taken to Charlottesville and Lynchburg, but the rest to Richmond. I think they were nearly all exchanged, except those that were again fit for field service. I had four hundred and twenty-seven wounded and sick

men under my charge. Forty-five died, and eight I left in the hospital, not being able to be moved. I left with them three nurses. Of every man that died, I preserved some relic, which I sent to his friends on coming to our lines, and wrote a letter informing his friends of his death. Some left a little money, which I placed in the packages; but on coming to Libby [the Confederates] searched them all, taking the money, promising to give it back when I left, which promise, however, they did not fulfill. I reported this to Capt. Hatch, Confederate commissioner of exchange, and he asserted that he would get it and send it to me by Maj. Mulford. If he does, I will send it to the friends of the deceased.

I had my own cooks, stove and cooking utensils, and feel a great satisfaction in certifying that my cooks, Charles Anderson and Daniel Pray of the 18th Connecticut, spared no pains in preparing palatable dishes for the men. My nurses were, as a general thing, efficient, especially L. T. Spencer of the 18th Connecticut, who did everything in his power to lighten my labors. The mortality, ten and a half *per centum,* may, at first sight, appear large, but it must be taken into consideration that about one hundred and twenty of the slightly wounded were sent to Martinsburg soon after the battle, so that none but the worst cases were left in my hands. Also, that the men brought from the valley, by the Confederates, on heavy lumber wagons, often being conveyed for four or five days without any care, were in such a condition that recovery in some was impossible, not from the severity of their wounds, but from neglect. That the number of sloughing wounds was extraordinary, I attributed to the impure air, and heat, and drought prevailing in June and July, and to the lack of vegetable food. The proper medicines were generally wanting. Nitric acid and chloride of zinc, which I regard as the best caustic agents in sloughing wounds, could not be had. Sulphate of copper was the only available escharotic, and I had no tincture of iron, the best of all tonics. The want of proper stimulants and tonics was severely felt. The apple brandy we used, I thought did more harm than good; it is unfit as a stimulant for a sick man. The regular rations of bread and meat were sufficient, and, generally, of good quality; but such articles are as most desired by the sick, I could not obtain in adequate quantities. The Confederate wards were furnished first, and what remained was turned over to us. In spite of their assurances that my men should fare the same as theirs, and all their assertions to that effect, I know that there was a desire to deceive me, perhaps not as much by those in authority as by their subordinates.

To Dr. Merrill, the surgeon in charge for the first few months of my stay, I cannot express my regard too much. He has been kind and aided me whenever he could, and has shown a great deal of sympathy for my men. The other surgeons, as a general thing, were clever....

The men that were sent to me from the valley were stripped of their clothing, and many were barefoot and hatless. I made a requisition for shoes, shirts, and socks, but it was never filled. This difficulty I overcame by making shoes out of overcoats and blankets, and was thus enabled to send my convalescent men off fully clothed. I also made a haversack for each man that was not already supplied; but these were taken from them on entering Libby prison. The clothing of the men that died I had washed and given to those who stood in need....

September 24 (Saturday)

In the Valley, Sheridan set his men to burning crops, barns, and anything else usable to the Confederacy, while he slowly advanced up the Valley towards Early. The smoke columns marked the progress of the blueclad columns as they advanced. Early needed everything, mostly men.

At Andersonville, Ga., Dr. Joseph Jones had been very busy, not only conducting autopsies and examining the sick, but also investigating the prison compound and developing statistics with the assistance of Louis Manigault. The amount of data collected was varied by type and amount. An accurate description of the prison pen was prepared with no detail overlooked or omitted. Statistics, at least the numbers available, were prepared on types of illness, numbers of patients with specific illnesses, the mortality rate by illness, percentages of those ill to the total prison population, and a great deal of other data that would eventually be written into Jones's report to the Confederate Surgeon General.

September 25 (Sunday)

Sheridan's army moved south towards Staunton and Waynesboro, Va., destroying all in its path. Ear-

ly was forced back to Brown's Pass in the Blue Ridge near Waynesboro. Tall columns of smoke were seen from horizon to horizon to mark the passage of the Union Army.

Ghiselin, J. T., Surg., USA, Med. Dir., Sheridan's command, Shenandoah Valley, Va.:

We arrived at Harrisonburg on the 25th, where there were several Confederate hospitals, containing three hundred and thirty-five sick and wounded, attended by five Confederate medical officers. The surgeon in charge reported that he was in need of subsistence and a few essential medicines, all of which he was at once furnished with. One hundred and thirty-five sick and wounded were selected, who could bear transportation without injury, and sent to Winchester by a returning subsistence train. The medical officers here seemed to have some regard for hygienic principles in and about the hospitals, and their patients were probably as comfortable as they could make them with their restricted means; but at every other place, from Woodstock on, where Confederate wounded were collected by their own surgeons, the most extreme filth and positive indications of neglect were seen.... The army made no important movement up to October 6th, when a retrograde march was commenced. The enemy's cavalry followed us....

September 28 (Wednesday)

Things were quiet on the Petersburg line, just the usual sniping and occasional shot on the picket line, casualties low but steady. In Atlanta, most of the civilians had now been evacuated, and the city was full of soldiers, with very little action going on. Forrest was roaming central Tennessee.

Having been at Andersonville nearly two weeks, Dr. Joseph Jones began packing to leave, which he would do within the next two days. He'd go from here to the headquarters of the Army of Tennessee, and later to Augusta, Ga., where, beginning in April 1865, he'd write his report.

September 29 (Thursday)

In the Valley, Sheridan's troops and Early's Rebels engaged at Waynesboro, Va., with light contact.

Two separate, yet related, actions occurred in the Petersburg area. Grant wanted to extend his left flank beyond the Weldon Railroad to encompass the

South Side Railroad and the Appomattox River crossings. Near Peebles' Farm, Gen. George Meade and 16,000 Union troops began an operation that would last for four days without the Federals making major contact with the Confederates.

Grant had also sent the Tenth and Eighteenth Corps north of the James to keep Lee's army busy, so that the Confederates wouldn't be able to send reinforcements to either the South Side Railroad or to Jubal Early in the Valley. The Eighteenth Corps advanced rapidly and Gen. George Stannard's division took Ft. Harrison, a major Confederate defense bastion, in the defense line, and some of the surrounding entrenchments. The Confederates prepared to counterattack, with Lee personally directing the assaults.

In Elmira, N.Y., Col. B. F. Tracy, Commanding Prison Depot, received explicit instructions from Col. Wm. Hoffman, Federal Commissary-General of Prisoners, concerning the movement of sick prisoners of war to be sent South for exchange.

... all the invalid prisoners of war in your charge who will not be fit for service within sixty days will be in a few days sent South for delivery to the Rebel authorities, and, as directed in my telegram of yesterday, you will immediately prepare duplicate parole-rolls to accompany them and an ordinary roll for this office. None will be sent who wish to remain and take the oath of allegiance, and none who are too feeble to endure the journey. Have a careful inspection of the prisoners made by medical officers to select those who shall be transferred. Detail to accompany them a medical officer or two, if necessary, with as many attendants and nurses, taken from the well prisoners, as may be required, and have them organized into companies of convenient size, so that all may receive proper attention.

You will send suitable guard under a field officer in charge of the prisoners, and give instructions in writing as to the service to be performed. The guard and prisoners will be furnished with cooked rations for two days. Require transportation of the quartermaster's department to Baltimore, and see that the cars are of a suitable character and well provided with lights and water. Direct the commanding officer not to give a certificate for the transportation unless the contract is fully complied with. The quartermaster at Baltimore will be directed to provide transportation

to Point Lookout. Furnish the commanding officer with a list of all moneys placed in his hands belonging to prisoners, which list, with the money, will be delivered to the Rebel officer who receives them.

One of the parole-rolls, with the officer's receipt, will be returned through you to this office as evidence of the delivery. On arriving at Point Lookout the officer in charge will report to the commanding officer, Brig. Gen. Barnes, and, if relieved from charge of the prisoners, he will turn over to the relieving officer the rolls, money, &c., taking a receipt therefore.

P.S. Report by telegram to the quartermaster at Baltimore, Lieut. Col. C. W. Thomas, and to this office the time at which the prisoners will leave at least twenty-four hours before their departure.

September 30 (Friday)

Ft. Harrison, north of the James and on the Richmond defense line, was now in Union hands and, despite repeated counterattacks by the Confederate troops under Lee, would remain Union. The Confederacy now constructed new works to face Ft. Harrison, and these new positions were occupied rapidly.

To the south of Petersburg, there was considerable fighting at Peebles' Farm, when Confederate Gen. A. P. Hill caused confusion by driving his corps between the two Federal corps of Warren and Parke. The Union line held, and the two Union corps finally joined again, causing the Confederates to spread their line a little thinner.

October 2 (Sunday)

Welch, S. G., Surg., 20th S.C. Vols., in a letter to his wife, from near Petersburg, Va.:

Last Thursday [September 29] afternoon we received orders to be in readiness to move to the north side of the James River, and at about nine o'clock that night we started. We traveled until about two hours before day, and were nearly to Drury's Bluff when we were ordered back because the Yankees were making a demonstration on our right. That afternoon [September 30] our brigade and Lane's North Carolina had a considerable fight on the right. We drove [the Federals] nearly two miles to their breastworks. It was a nice victory for us and our loss was small.

The Fifteenth Regiment lost eight killed on the field and had about twenty wounded. I have never before known so large a proportion to be killed. Spencer Caldwell was killed. Col. Booker of the Twelfth Regiment and three officers of the Thirteenth Regiment were killed—none that you know. Billie was in it, but was not hurt. His company had one killed and but one wounded. Lang Ruff's boys were both in it, but were not hurt. I saw them this morning and everybody was in fine spirits.

Our cavalry had a fight yesterday afternoon on the extreme right, and it is reported that Gen. Dunnovant was killed. We are expecting the Yankees to attack us again. Grant is evidently doing his best for Lincoln's election.... I hope to hear good news from Forrest. If Sherman is forced away from Atlanta and we can hold Richmond this winter, I believe we shall have peace.

We need ten or fifteen thousand more men here, and we could easily get them if the able-bodied exempts would come on here, but they seem to have become hardened to their disgrace. If the South is ever overcome, the contemptible shirkers will be responsible for it. They should have seen our poor fellows Thursday night coming in wounded and bleeding and shivering with cold; but these very men who suffer and have often suffered in this way are the last ones to say surrender....

October 3 (Monday)

Things were fairly quiet both at Petersburg and in the Valley. Lee's army kept dwindling as his men were wounded, killed, or taken prisoner. Desertions were on the rise also, as the men slipped through the pickets at night and went to the Union lines.

Things livened up yesterday at Big Shanty and at the Kennesaw Water Tank in Georgia, when Hood's Army of Tennessee reached Sherman's rail link with Chattanooga. The Confederates tore up the track of the Western & Atlantic Railroad and interrupted service on the line.

Jackman, John S., Pvt., "The Orphan Brigade," Americus, Ga.:

Great consternation among the "rats," [when] the "ironclad" Med. Ex. Board from the army examined the attendants of the hospital and the convalescents, sending all who were able to pull a trigger to the front. The Board made nearly a clean sweep of the hospital. I witnessed the examination and it reminded me more of traders examining stock than anything else....

October 4 (Tuesday)

Sherman had looked at the situation near Big Shanty and Ackworth, Ga.; he left one corps to hold Atlanta and took the rest back up the railroad line to "discuss" the situation with Hood.

October 5 (Wednesday)

Hood's Army of Tennessee attacked Union troops at Allatoona Pass, Ga., where Union Brig. Gen. John M. Corse refused the surrender demands of Maj. Gen. S. G. French, who'd moved into position during the night. From atop Kennesaw Mountain to the southeast, Sherman could see the smoke of battle around Allatoona, 18 miles away. The Confederates, assaulting the Union garrison, couldn't take the pass, and the Southerners suffered high casualties. Both sides lost about 35 percent of their forces. French, receiving a report (which later proved to be erroneous) that a Union force was coming to relieve Corse, pulled up stakes, leaving the Union in charge of the field. The Union resistance was a classic example of determination and guts.

October 9 (Sunday)

McParlin, T. A., Surg., Med. Dir., Army of the Potomac, in front of Petersburg, Va.:

About September 28th,... steps were taken for a movement towards the South Side railroad. The sick in the hospitals were sent to City Point.... September 30th, the troops advanced up the Squirrel Level road beyond Poplar Spring church, and position was taken by Gen. Warren at the Pegram house, three miles from Yellow tavern.... The Fifth Corps bore the brunt of the attack.... The wounded ... were soon attended to near Poplar Grove church, and ... Peeble's house. They were afterwards sent to City Point. Rain continued on October 1st and 2d, with cold weather, exercising an unfavorable influence upon the troops and the roads.... At this time, our works before Petersburg were occupied by divisions extended so as to fill the place left vacant by troops sent to the left. The movement was complete by the

6th of October, when quiet was established,… until October 26th, when affairs were put in readiness for the movement to Hatcher's Run.…

At Tom's Brook, Va., in the lower Valley near Fisher's Hill, the site of Early's last fight with Sheridan, the cavalry of Gen. A. T. A. Torbert was sent against the Confederates who had been harassing Sheridan's troops. Gens. Custer's and Wesley Merritt's divisions attacked and chased the Confederate cavalry of Gens. Thomas L. Rosser and L. L. Lomax for several miles back up the Valley, capturing 300 prisoners.

Ghiselin, J. T., Surg., USA, Med. Dir., Sheridan's command, Shenandoah Valley, Va.:

On the 9th, near Woodstock, our cavalry attacked and routed that of the enemy, driving him a distance of twelve miles. Our loss was very slight, and all the wounded were sent to Winchester the following day.

October 10 (Monday)

In the Valley, Sheridan moved to a position straddling the Valley Pike near Cedar Creek and held, awaiting developments. Early was coming down the Valley.

Ghiselin, J. T., Surg., USA, Med. Dir., Sheridan's command, Shenandoah Valley, Va.:

We moved to Cedar Creek on the 10th, and took up a strong line of battle, with the apparent object of remaining there to wait for the development of the enemy.

Immediately after the battle of Fisher's Hill, our base being changed to Martinsburg, Acting Asst. Surg. E. Ohlenschlager, USA, acting medical inspector, was ordered there to take charge of the transportation of the wounded, who were sent to that place as fast as they could bear transportation, and, for this purpose, advantage was taken of every returning train. The wounded were loaded in wagons, bedded with hay or straw, without crowding, and a large number of blankets were sent with them, as well as stretchers, for some of the most severe cases. The wounded in these trains were fed and dressed on their arrival at Martinsburg, and were then placed in cars which were sent to Frederick or Baltimore.…

With the fall of Vicksburg, Miss., and its occupation by the Union forces, the Western Sanitary Commission established facilities there to support the needy and provide services to the local Union hospitals. As a part of this support, a Refugee Home was established and a school for the children was opened. A Miss Grace D. Chapman of Exeter, Me., was hired as a teacher for the school, but she fell ill after several weeks and returned to Maine. She did, however, write a letter to the president of the Western Sanitary Commission when she regained at least part of her health:

Dear Sir: I have not *forgotten* that I am to give you some account of my short term of labor in the Free School for Refugees at Vicksburg, but have been waiting to get stronger, and to decide about trying to finish, or, rather, *continue* a work but fairly well begun. After seven weeks of anxious toil, I had succeeded in awakening an interest in the school, and had the satisfaction of seeing a marked improvement, both mentally and morally. If Southern temper is fast, the Southern *intellect* is very slow. I had no difficulty in managing those under my care, but they had not the slightest idea of order or discipline; and, like a boy we read of, must be told a thing twenty times, because nineteen would not make him remember. They thought me very *strict*, but did not attempt to disobey.…

I had my first room in the Refugee Home, used also for chapel and charnel house. Often two or … three dead bodies were there at a time, and school must be suspended. The first day there were but five scholars, all in the ABC's; the next I went round *conscripting*, and impressed a few more, but it was like taking them to prison; they had never been to school; their parents were deplorably ignorant and indolent, and must have been for generations, to transmit such sluggish, inferior brains, as I found to deal with.…

… We are to have the vestry of a church for schoolroom soon, and I shall be glad. It is rather bordering on the *awful* here.

A few days after we moved up to the vestry, and scholars about town began to come in. There was some feeling in regard to the "Free School," and young Secesh came to annoy my poor little refugee flock, and abuse their teacher by throwing brickbats and calling names. When the storm of missiles had abated, and it was sage to venture out, I quietly asked my scholars to keep their seats a few moments, while I stepped over to the Soldier's Home. Mr. Mann promptly sent a few of the boys to my assistance, when, true to their Southern instinct, the army from the "Pay School" "skedaddled." While I was at dinner they came back, threw mud and sticks at my children, drove them out of the house, and tossed their books on the floor. Again the bluecoats went after them, and threatened them so hard that they troubled us no more....

October 12 (Wednesday)

Welch, S. G., Surg., 20th S.C. Vols., in a letter to his wife, from near Petersburg, Va.:

Grant has come to a dead halt before Petersburg and Richmond. It is believed that the next fight will take place across on the north side of the James River....

About twelve thousand men from Richmond have been sent into the trenches at the front. Many of them were in the Government service and many others were gentlemen of leisure. The authorities sent everybody. The police would capture men in all parts of the city and send them under guard to some point to be organized and put under the command of officers who happened to be in Richmond from the Army. A man told me these officers were seized in the same way on the streets, and that the authorities would even send out and capture a colonel and put him in command of a whole battalion. A medical officer would sometimes be seized. He would plead that he was due at his command and that he was a noncombatant, but they would tell him he was the very man they needed to attend to the wounded. It delights soldiers to hear of these things. It does them good all over. The soldiers are accustomed to these sudden dashes at the front, but the miserable skulkers almost die of fright.

We are building chimneys and fixing up things in our camp as if we are to remain here. If I were sure of it, I would have you come out and stay with me a while. It is useless for me to try to get off now while we are so tightly pressed.

I saw Billie this morning. I carried a haversack full of biscuits and ham to him. I will have ham, light bread and coffee for breakfast in the morning. I have been living well this year.

We have a new chaplain in our brigade named Dixon. I heard him preach yesterday, and he does very well. If Congress would pass a conscription law bringing the preachers into the army we could have

chaplains. They have acted worse in this war than any other class of men....

October 13 (Thursday)

In the Valley, skirmishing occurred around Cedar Creek as the Confederates probed from their old lines at Fisher's Hill against Sheridan's troops astraddle the Valley Pike.

Today the medical director at Baltimore, Md., Surg. J. Simpson, wrote Col. Hoffman, Federal Commissary-General of Prisoners, about prisoners arriving in that city. These were the prisoners about whose shipment from Elmira, N.Y., Hoffman had sent instructions on September 29th:

... a train of over 1200 Rebel prisoners arrived in this city today from Elmira, en route for City Point. The officer in charge report[ed] to me that many of the prisoners were exceedingly ill and that five had died on the road. I made a personal inspection of the men and found a number unable to bear the journey. I directed that they should be admitted to the West Hospital, and gave Surg. Chapel instructions to examine those on board the boat. As soon as a report from Surg. Campbell, who continued the inspection, is received, I will forward it, with a full report of the case to you. The physical condition of many of these men was distressing in the extreme, and they should never have been permitted to leave Elmira.

The instructions given to Surg. A. Chapel by the medical director at Baltimore were explicit as to the extent of his duty:

You will receive such sick and wounded Rebels into the hospital under your charge as may be sent you by Surg. C. F. H. Campbell, U.S. Volunteers, from those now *in transitu* through this city from Elmira, N.Y., and receipt for them on the customary rolls to Maj. E. A. Roberts, in charge of the squad. As it is possible that some cases might have been overlooked you will visit the steamer on which the prisoners are embarking for exchange, and admit to the hospital under your charge such as humanity requires should be taken care of. You will report to this office in the morning the number thus received.

October 14 (Friday)

Today, Surg. A. Chapel, Baltimore, Md., reported to Surg. J. Simpson, Med. Dir., Baltimore, on his inspection of the Rebel prisoners en route to City Point from Elmira, N.Y.:

I went on board the steamer loaded with prisoners of war last evening,… and examined the worst cases. I found at least forty cases that should not have been sent on such a journey, most of whom were in a very feeble and emaciated condition, but as my hospital had been more than filled by those sent by Surg. Campbell, and they were all very anxious to continue the journey with their comrades, I thought it better not to remove them. I found no medical officer, hospital steward, or nurse aboard the boat with the worst cases. Someone, in my opinion, is greatly censurable for sending such cases away from camp even for exchange.

Surg. C. F. H. Campbell, Asst. Medical Inspector, at Baltimore, had inspected the prisoners on the train which had come from Elmira, N.Y., on the afternoon of October 13th and today submitted his report to Surg. Simpson, Med. Dir., in Baltimore:

I yesterday proceeded to inspect the physical condition of the Rebel prisoners then in transit through this city from Elmira, N.Y., to City Point, Va., for exchange. The train was composed of over 1200 men, from which number I selected sixty men as totally unfit to travel and sent to general hospital. These men were debilitated from long sickness to such a degree that it was necessary to carry them in the arms of attendants from the cars to the ambulances, and one man died in the act of being thus transferred. Such men should not have been sent from Elmira. If they were inspected before leaving that place in accordance with orders it was most carelessly done, reflecting severely on the medical officers engaged in that duty and is alike disgraceful to all concerned. The effect produced upon the public by such marked displays of inefficiency or neglect of duty cannot fail to be most injurious to our cause both at home and abroad. Five men had died on the train on the road to this city from utter prostration and debility, their appearance after death bearing evidence of this fact. Thus it will be seen six men have died from the number sent, and if the above selection of men had not been made and sent to general hospital many more deaths would have been added to this number ere they reached City Point.

Surg. Simpson, medical director at Baltimore, forwarded the reports from the other surgeons to Col. William Hoffman, Federal Commissary-General of Prisoners, in Washington. With the reports he stated: "The condition of these men was pitiable in the extreme and evinces criminal neglect and inhumanity on the part of the medical officers making the selection of men to be transferred."

October 16 (Sunday)

Capt. Munger, USA, inspecting the prison camp at Elmira, N.Y., reported:

I have made the weekly inspection of camp,… and find the police of grounds, quarters, &c., good. Drainage as perfect as the situation of camp will allow. During the past week over 1200 invalid prisoners, 300 of whom were from hospital, were paroled and sent South for exchange. There are now in hospital 588 patients, and receiving medical treatment, 1021 prisoners. During the four days since the removal of the sick there have been forty-four deaths. The cause of this amount of sickness and death is a matter of deep interest. That the existence of a large body of filthy, stagnant water within the camp has much to do with it can admit of no doubt. Low diet, indifferent clothing, and change of clothing doubtless have some effect. Most of the causes may be removed, and that it be done seems the plainest duty of humanity.

October 17 (Monday)

In Georgia, Hood's Confederate Army of Tennessee moved from harassing Sherman's rail lines and deployed towards Gadsden, Ala., relieving some of the pressure on Sherman. The torn track Hood left behind would be replaced shortly, and the trains would be running again.

October 19 (Wednesday)

Early this morning, Sheridan was in Winchester, looking at the town's defenses, when Jubal Early's Confederates crept through the fog and surprised the Union Eighth and Nineteenth Corps in an attack that sent the Federals flying north down the Valley. Wright's Sixth Corps was the next victim of assault, but Wright held his ground fairly well for a period, falling back in an orderly fashion to north and west of

Middletown, W.Va. Many of the Confederates stopped in the evacuated Union camps to loot the departed Yankees' tents and to eat the breakfasts still on the cooking fires. At this point, Early had captured most of the artillery, ammunition, and much of the equipment of Sheridan's force.

Sheridan arrived from Winchester at about 10:30 A.M., organized his force again, and attacked Early at about 4 in the afternoon. The attack wasn't expected, and the Union troops were out to redeem themselves for having run that morning. Early, with a force of 18,000 men, was chased by Sheridan back to Fisher's Hill, with Confederate losses that reached about 2900, including Maj. Gen. Stephen D. Ramseur. Sheridan had lost nearly 5700 from a force of about 30,000. While Early was badly beaten, he'd proven that his Confederate Army was still a dangerous adversary.

Ghiselin, J. T., Surg., USA, Med. Dir., Sheridan's command, Shenandoah Valley, Va.:

At dawn,… the enemy attacked and turned the left flank of our army. Their attack was so sudden and unexpected that our troops were thrown into confusion, and it was not until we had fallen back four miles, that another line of battle was established and confidence restored. In the early part of the action, the Nineteenth Corps lost all its medicine and army wagons, loaded with medical supplies and hospital tents, and thirty ambulances, but the latter were recaptured by the cavalry in the afternoon. The other ambulances and wagons had been ordered to the rear and were out of reach. Before the second line of battle was formed, but few of the wounded got off the field; those who did so were such as were able to walk, and a few who were carried in the ambulances of the cavalry, or in blankets slung on muskets. Division field hospitals were now established in and near Newtown, six miles from the original line of battle, and two from the second.

The wagons and medical supplies arriving from the rear, the medical officers of the Sixth Corps promptly pitched their tents; before this, however, each division formed a temporary hospital in rear of the line of battle, and, up to this time, had performed a few capital and a large number of minor operations. The medical officers of the Nineteenth Corps took possession of the churches and several houses in

Newtown, and prepared them for the reception of the wounded, as all their tents had been captured. The cavalry had only a comparatively small number of casualties, and, for this reason, were enabled to care for their wounded in ambulances until a favorable opportunity offered to send them to the rear.

October 20 (Thursday)

In the Valley, fighting still went on as Early's stragglers fell back towards Fisher's Hill. Sheridan reorganized for an advance.

Ghiselin, J. T., Surg., USA, Med. Dir., Sheridan's command, Shenandoah Valley, Va.:

On the morning of the 20th, there being no immediate prospect of hostilities, but a military necessity for removing the wounded farther to the rear, all the ambulances of the army, and a large train of army wagons, properly bedded with straw, were loaded with wounded. The ambulances were used for the most severe cases.… Knowing that the hospitals at Winchester were unable to accommodate the large number of wounded to be disposed of, the chief medical officer of that place was instructed to retain only those who would be injured by further transportation, and to feed, dress and furnish the remainder with all things needed, and send them on to Martinsburg.

October 21 (Friday)

Ghiselin, J. T., Surg., USA, Med. Dir., Sheridan's command, Shenandoah Valley, Va.:

By the afternoon of the 21st, the whole number of wounded, with the exception of fifteen mortal cases, had been removed from Newtown. All the corps were amply supplied for this emergency, with the exception of the Nineteenth, but its urgent wants were relieved by the others, until several wagons, loaded with medical stores, which had been kept at army headquarters to meet accidents of this kind, could be brought from Winchester, whither they had gone in the morning to prevent capture.

The general commanding not wishing that even a temporary hospital should be established at Martinsburg, the wounded had to be placed in the cars immediately on their arrival. Owing to a deficiency of transportation, as well as to the difficulties of loading a number of cars in a confined depot at that place, a portion of the wounded of each train were placed in the churches, which were fitted up as field hospitals. Dr. Du Bois, who had been sent with orders to take such means as might be necessary to prevent any accumulation of wounded, reported that the trains generally arrived in excellent condition, few cases of neglect being observed, and most of these owing to the excessive fatigue of the medical officers. With each train was sent a surgeon in charge, a proper proportion of medical officers, stewards and attendants; also, cooked rations, anodynes, stimulants, dressings, etc., more than sufficient to last the usual number of days in making a trip. On arriving at Winchester these trains were divided among the different hospitals, and every man was dressed and fed during the night by a large detail of surgeons and attendants, and the same was repeated at Martinsburg before transfer to the cars. A responsible medical officer provided with supplies, together with a proper number of attendants, accompanied each train. As the army was liable to move suddenly, I did not consider it advisable to let sick and wounded accumulate, but sent them to Winchester, which had been made a receiving depot, using ambulances when the distance was not great and it was expedient to do so. Notwithstanding the distance, [the] wounded were transported in army wagons, in some instances as far as a hundred miles. Very few died on the road, which, fortunately, was a fine turnpike.

October 25 (Tuesday)

Welch, S. G., Surg., 20th S.C. Vols., in a letter to his wife, from near Petersburg, Va.:

I have a bright fire this morning. There is a nice chimney to my tent, which makes it almost as comfortable as a house…. Everything is very quiet on the lines…. The health of all the men appears to be about as good as if they were at home under shelter and with suitable diet…. They get nothing to eat now but bread and meat. We have eaten nearly all the beef Hampton captured recently in rear of Grant's army, but we have received some from North Carolina which is very nice and tender.

Your brother Edwin is to be appointed a lieutenant in the Fourteenth Regiment. I took dinner with him yesterday. Lt. Petty, with whom he messes, had just received a box from home, and I fared sumptuously. My box has not yet arrived. Boxes now

take about two weeks to reach here…. I have a nice little Yankee axe, which is so light that it can be carried in a knapsack, but it just suits a soldier for use in putting up his little shelter tent or for making a fire. All the Yankees have these little axes, and many of our men have supplied themselves with them, as they have with almost everything else the Yankees possess.

Are you making preparations to come out here this winter? Col. Hunt will have his wife to come out again, and a great many other officers are arranging for their wives to come on soon. Some are here already…. When we were on the Rappahannock River last fall some of the officers carried their wives along by having them wrap up well and putting them in the ambulance; and if you were here and we had to move I could easily take you along that way….

October 26 (Wednesday)

McParlin, T. A., Surg., Med. Dir., Army of the Potomac, in front of Petersburg, Va.:

On the night of October 24th, the 2d and 3d divisions of the Second Corps were withdrawn from their positions in front and massed for movement, and, on the 26th, the Ninth Corps was prepared also. The sick of all the corps were sent to City Point on that day…. On the 26th, the 2d division of the Second Corps also moved, with the medical transportation allowed, to Ft. Duchesne, whence all but fifteen ambulances to each division were sent back to the Gurely house to await orders from the front….

October 27 (Thursday)

In one of the last major actions before settling into winter quarters, the Federals around Petersburg took another stab at capturing the South Side Railroad. Two Union corps, Warren's and Hancock's, numbering nearly 17,000, were met by Confederates at Hatcher's Run, under Heth and Mahone, with Hampton's cavalry thrown in for good measure. As a part of a diversion to the attack at Hatcher's Run, the Army of the James skirmished with the Confederates north of Petersburg towards Richmond, at Fair Oaks and on the Darbytown Road. The Union troops attacked, the Rebels repulsed the attack, and everyone went home to settle in the thirty-five miles of trenches, redoubts, mudholes, and louse-ridden hovels for the winter.

McParlin, T. A., Surg., Med. Dir., Army of the Potomac, in front of Petersburg, Va.:

The movement was commenced on the 27th, the Ninth Corps passing along Squirrel Level road beyond Ft. Cummings, formed in line of battle two miles and a half in advance, its left being near the Clements house. The hospital in this corps established at Peeble's [was] sufficiently accessible,... and did not require to be moved. The Fifth Corps advanced on the left of the Ninth, and soon engaged the enemy's pickets. The transportation allowed was half the ambulances, one medicine wagon and one army wagon to each brigade.... The ambulances of the Ninth Corps advanced to the vicinity of an abandoned Rebel fort and promptly carried back to the field hospital all the wounded, some seventy-five in number.

The 2d division [Second Corps], which had advanced on the Halifax road before dawn ... met the enemy at the crossing of Hatcher's Run, and drove them from their earthworks. Application was made to send the wounded, eighty in number, to the Gurley house rendezvous, with or without an escort, in the ambulances which were then to return, but this was overruled by the corps commander, the road having become infested by the enemy's cavalry. They were, therefore, carried with the troops along the Boydtown road, where Hill's corps and Hampton's cavalry attacked the 2nd division and Gregg's cavalry. Several attacks were made by the enemy after four o'clock P.M., the casualties resulting being over four hundred in the infantry and one hundred in the cavalry. The primary rendezvous for the wounded was first made at Rainey's house, on the Boydtown road, but as [the house] soon came within musket range of the advancing enemy, and seemed likely to be captured, the wounded were removed.... The ambulances were loaded and moved to a grove of pines ... where the exposure was materially less. The assault ceased at dark, and, after some hours, it was ascertained that the struggle would not be renewed. Preparations were then made to withdraw. The ambulances were loaded ... and, escorted by a regiment of infantry, proceeded to the field hospital park near Gurley's....

... for want of ambulances, the wounded collected at the Rainey house had to be left, and fell into the hands of the enemy.... The number of wounded left at the house and on the field was estimated at two hundred and fifty.... It rained very hard during the night. The wounded reached Gurley's early in the morning, and by night, on the 29th, were in hospital at City Point.

October 29 (Saturday)

Welch, S. G., Surg., 20th S.C. Vols., in a letter to his wife, from near Petersburg, Va.:

I suppose you have heard how we whipped the Yankees on both this side and the north side of the James River. The killed and wounded fell into our hands here at Petersburg, and we have been attending to their wounded all day today. Our loss was very small.... We now have strong hopes of being able to hold Petersburg and Richmond.

This war can never end until the fanatics, both North and South, are gotten rid of. They are influenced solely by their blind, senseless passions, and reason never enters their heads. It is always such discontented, worthless wretches who bring about revolutions. The North is still infested with such characters, and the South is not far behind. If we could get those hotheaded fools in South Carolina who composed that meeting at Columbia recently and put them in the army and get them all killed off, it would be much better for us. What a pity we cannot have them killed, but they cannot be made to fight....

My box is not here yet. I will continue to keep on the lookout for it until it arrives. My dinner will soon be ready and I think it will be fine, for I shall have white cabbage, bacon, potatoes and biscuit.

As soon as I can I will send you one hundred and fifty dollars to pay your expenses in coming out. The Government owes me about five hundred dollars, which I hope to be able soon to collect....

November 1 (Tuesday)

McParlin, T. A., Surg., Med. Dir., Army of the Potomac, in front of Petersburg, Va.:

Investigation into the cause of sickness in certain regiments of the Ninth Corps, the 179th and 186th New York and the 31st Maine, in which typhomalarial fever was reported, developed from the fact that the men "burrowed" to some extent. Their camps were on low ground, near a swamp, and the issues of vegetables had been neglected. In order to secure vegetables in that corps, two pounds of coffee in each one hundred rations were dropped, and, in lieu, sixty pounds of potatoes and seventeen pounds of onions were furnished....

In Elmira, N.Y., Surg. E. F. Sanger reported to the Surgeon General of the U.S. Army in Washington concerning the health conditions of the camp. The report portrays bureaucracy at its worst:

... forward the monthly report of sick and wounded of prisoner's hospital, Elmira, N.Y., for the month of October. The ratio of disease and deaths has been fearfully and unprecedentedly large and requires an explanation from me to free the medical department from censure.

Since August, the date of my assignment to this station, there have been 2011 patients admitted to the hospital, 775 deaths out of a mean strength of 8347 prisoners of war, or 24 percent, admitted and 9 percent died. Have averaged daily 451 in hospital and 601 in quarters, an aggregate of 1052 per day, sick. At this rate the entire command will be admitted to hospital in less than a year and 36 percent die.

The prison pen is one-quarter of a mile square, containing forty acres, located in the valley of the Chemung River. The soil is gravel deposit sloping at two-thirds of its distance from the front towards the river to a stagnant pond of water 12 by 580 yards, between which and the river is a low sandy bottom subject to overflow when the river is high. This pond received the contents of the sinks and garbage of the camp until it became so offensive that vaults were dug on the banks of the pond for sinks and the whole left a festering mass of corruption, impregnating the entire atmosphere of the camp with its pestilential odors, night and day.

On my arrival the subject of drainage, sinks, enlargement of the hospitals, providing a kitchen, mess hall, laundry, dead-house, offices, and storerooms were all considered and their importance impressed upon the commanding officer.

On the 13th of August commenced making written reports of the following dates: August 13, August 23, August 26, September 3, 5, 16, October 5, 9 and ... 17, calling attention to the pond, vaults, and their deadly poison, the existence of scurvy to an alarming extent (reporting 2000 scorbutic cases at one time); recommended fresh vegetables daily to scurvy patients and an increase in the capacity of the hospital; pointed out the necessity of a kitchen, laundry, mess-room, and dead-house, and presented plans for the same; called attention to improvements in cooking and method of serving the rations; great delay in filling my requisitions for the hospital; the sickness and suffering occasioned thereby; a more general observation of the sanitary laws governing human beings herded in crowded camps and the inevitable consequences following neglect. How does the matter stand today? The pond remains green with putrescence, filling the air with its messengers of disease and death, the vaults give out their sickly odors, and the hospitals are crowded with victims for the grave.

A single ration of vegetables was given for a while and discontinued. Three rations in five of onions and potatoes were allowed from the 1st of October for a fortnight and discontinued. The men are hurried in to their rations of bread, beans, meat, and soup, to half gulp it down on the spot or to carry it hastily away to their quarters in old rusty canteens and improvised dirty dippers and measures.

Hospital wards, with the addition of three barracks, buildings poorly adapted for hospital purposes, are insufficient to accommodate the sick. Kitchen half large enough. Washing and drying done in the open air at a time when we have not been able to dry our clothes for a month. Nurses, full-diet patients, &c., eat in the wards, kitchen, or wherever they can. Postmortems performed in a little tent exposed to the gaze of the camp and an office 12 by 20 feet, in which are crowded together drugs and druggists, stewards and clerks, doctors and dressings, commissary clerks and hospital supplies, in a state of confusion worst confounded.

While Lt. Col. Eastman, of the Regular Army, was in command I reported directly to him, and was able by direct communication to expedite business, personally explain the wants of the hospital department, and to a limited extent act as medical adviser of the medical interests of the prisoners. Since Col. Tracy, of the U.S. Colored Troops, has been in command, all direct communication has been cut off, and I am ordered by him to report to a junior military officer in camp, who has merely a forwarding power. So far as garrison duties are concerned, I do not object to reporting to a junior military officer, but in the administrative duties of a large hospital department, the surgeon in charge must have direct communication with the commander, who is the only authorized executive officer. My provision returns, my bill of purchases, my requisitions for hospital fixtures and medical supplies, must all be forwarded to him, subject to his approval or disapproval, without any medical representations to advise or guide in the exercise of opinions and actions based upon common sense alone. Common sense is a very good thing, but does not work in physic. To illustrate: The requisition for medicine sent October 7 through the intermediate channel for approval was never heard from; the second was delayed two or three days; my provision returns are often forty-eight hours getting back to me, and applications for straw and fixtures for hospital are frequently made some three or four weeks before I receive the articles. My application for straw, put in October 21, for beds, is not filled yet, and the patients are compelled to lie on the floor. My application for caldron, stovepipe, and cover for washing purposes, put in on the 5th and 16th of September, was finally filled October 28. I was ordered to feed patients in quarters, and yet my requisition for cooking utensils came back disapproved. When the sick were sent from here for exchange I received no official information, nor was advised in reference to the matter. I was informed by a captain of the examining board, in the original examination, not to send those who were unable to travel. I was totally ignorant whether the journey would exceed two or three days, only as I judged from the number of days' rations required, viz, two; although the day for forwarding prisoners' returns was the day before the prisoners started, October 11, and mine went in promptly. I did not receive my supplies, and the patients were sent off without coffee or sugar. The train started without reporting to the medical officer, and before the nurses were assigned, blankets distributed, and many had been fed after a fast of more than twelve hours. I was ordered to appoint a given number of nurses and doctors, and my application for an increased number received no attention. A camp inspector is appointed who takes the liberty of entering my wards at all times, instructs my ward masters and nurses, finds fault to them of my management, and quizzes them in regard to the medical officers. Medical officers have complained that he changes beds of the patients, corrects and changes their diet, directs the washing of my wards without regard to my rules, orders pneumonia patients with blisters on their sides bathed, &c. I have entered a written protest without avail. I cannot be held responsible for a large medical department of over 1000 patients without power, authority, or influence. Our post is without a medical representative, and as senior medical officer of this post the whole administrative duties should be intrusted to my care, when it would be hoped that the interest of the sick would be consulted.

The report above, received at the Surgeon General's office in Washington, caused immediate reaction. On the 10th, C. H. Crane, Surgeon General of the U.S. Army, directed that an inspection be made of the Elmira facility and action taken to correct the deficiencies noted in Sanger's letter.

November 3 (Thursday)

Welch, S. G., Surg., 20th S.C. Vols., in a letter to his wife, from near Petersburg, Va.:

We are still quiet. Nothing is going on except the continual fighting of the skirmishers, which amount[s] to little more than a waste of powder and lead, although a man gets killed or wounded occasionally....

We are having rain. It fell all night and continues today. Billie's big coat came just in time for this cold spell of weather. He is as fat as a bear. The health of our troops is excellent....

We shall know in a few days who is elected President of the United States. In my opinion Old Abraham will come in again, and I believe it would be best for us. McClellan might have the Union restored, if elected. I should prefer to remain at war for the rest of my life rather than to have any connection with the Yankees again....

A man by the name of Simeon Werts is going home today on sick furlough for thirty days, and I shall send this letter to you by him. I shall also send my father some smoking tobacco, which we have been drawing monthly as part of our rations, and I shall send Dr. Clark some rolls of blistering ointment which we captured from the Yankees at Chancellorsville. I have more of it than I could use in two years....

Our box of provisions from home still holds out, and if you will hurry up and come on, we may have some of it left when you arrive. I have just finished my breakfast, which consisted of hash, potatoes, biscuit, molasses and coffee. I do not mind the war as long as I can have plenty to eat and comfortable quarters....

November 5 (Saturday)

Forrest left the area of Johnsonville, Tenn., to join Hood, going by way of Corinth, Miss., after causing an estimated $6,700,000 worth of damage at the Johnsonville depot.

November 7 (Monday)

In Richmond, the Second, and last, Session of the Second Congress of the Confederate States of America gathered for its meeting. The message read from Pres. Davis was unduly optimistic in tone, playing down such things as the loss of Atlanta. Davis also sent a message to Gen. John Bell Hood urging him to beat Sherman so that he'd have no obstruction on his (Hood's) optimistic plans to march to the Ohio.

November 8 (Tuesday)

Abraham Lincoln was reelected President and Andrew Johnson elected as Vice-President by a 55 percent plurality of the popular vote of the people of the United States. Lincoln-Johnson received 212 electoral votes to McClellan's 21. Interestingly, the soldiers' vote was almost entirely for Lincoln. The war would continue.

November 9 (Wednesday)

At Kingston, Ga. a decision had been made concerning Sherman's armies. Sherman would imitate Grant's Vicksburg campaign, when Grant crossed the Mississippi, plunged into the interior of Mississippi towards Jackson, without long supply trains, planning to live off the land.

First, however, the army had to be reorganized. The four corps were divided into two "wings," the left and right. The left wing would be commanded by Maj. Gen. Slocum and would consist of the Fourteenth and Twentieth Corps. The right wing would contain the Fifteenth and Seventeenth Corps, under Maj. Gen. Otis O. Howard.

Second, there would be no long "trains" in this army. The regiments would make do with one wagon each, the companies with none. Wagons would be reserved for ammunition and other "essentials," and all comforts were to be left behind. A liberal policy of acquiring draft animals, etc., en route was

established as was the policy for "drawing rations" from the local populace.

Another problem was the sick and wounded then in Atlanta. These were to be evacuated north by rail to the general hospitals. Both Mrs. Bickerdyke and Mrs. Porter rode several trains north and returned to take more on the journey. Sherman was adamant that Mrs. Bickerdyke not go with the army on the coming march. She was to return North and prepare to meet him on the coast when he emerged from his travels. Try as she might, Bickerdyke couldn't convince him otherwise. Sherman suggested to her that she might spend some time with her own "young'uns" while up North. This brought a flash of anger from her:

> Don't you worry about my young'uns, Uncle Billy. You never worried about Jim and Hi when you needed me. You think you don't need me now. You think because you picked out a bunch of healthy fellows they're going to stay that way. If that ain't just like a man—never thinks he's going to be sick till he is, and then he's worse than a baby. Well, all right. If you want to be pigheaded about it, you'll just have to find out for yourself. Reckon I can find plenty to keep me busy in the hospitals up North. But mind you, let me know when you want me, and I'll come a-running.

Mary Ann Bickerdyke took the last train to leave from Atlanta before the Union troops burned the depot, adding to the flames and the pall of smoke that hung over the city.

November 10 (Thursday)

In the Valley, Jubal Early's force was now very weak. Early did, however, make a demonstration north from the New Market area towards Sheridan.

In Tennessee, Forrest was moving, slowly, towards Hood. The confluence of the two forces would provide a formidable force to face Thomas at Nashville.

Sherman continued his organization of his armies, preparing to move back to Atlanta. One item on the agenda was to direct Surg. John Moore, Sherman's medical director, to notify the Surgeon General that Sherman wanted three months' medical supplies for 60,000 men, and a 5000-bed hospital ready for delivery to his army when he emerged on the coast.

November 11 (Friday)

In Georgia, Sherman ordered the railroads destroyed. At Rome, Ga., the Union troops tore up the tracks, destroyed mills, foundries, etc., while the garrisons around Kingston were sent to pull up the rails and send them back to Chattanooga for later use.

November 12 (Saturday)

In the Valley, Sheridan and Early sparred at Middletown and Cedar Creek, with light contact.

In Georgia, Sherman had sent his last message to Grant. Sherman's army was tearing down Atlanta, except for the houses and churches, and Sherman's force of 60,000 men and 5500 artillery was ready to march.

Gill, H. Z., Surg., USV, 1st Div., 20th Corps, preparing for the March to the Sea:

> The division was composed of fifteen regiments,... the men were generally in good condition,... well clothed before leaving Atlanta.... The transportation of the division consisted of one hundred and seventy-seven six-mule wagons, thirty-eight of which carried ammunition.
>
> The transportation of the division hospital consisted of three army wagons and one medicine wagon, carrying sixteen tent-flies and the usual monthly allowance of the most useful medical supplies. The transportation of the sick and wounded consisted of thirty two-mule ambulances, under the supervision of a captain and one lieutenant for each brigade, to which were added, near the close of the march, three army wagons for conveying knapsacks and equipments of such men in the regiments as were not fit for hospital and who would return to their regiments at night.
>
> The ambulances carried two hundred pounds of hard bread for the hospital, which was much needed after the commissary's supply was exhausted ... also a quantity of beef essence. The sick and wounded of the command had been mainly sent to the rear before we left Atlanta....

November 13 (Sunday)

Yesterday, a Union brigade comprised of the 8th, 9th, and 13th Tennessee Cavalry regiments fought an engagement at Bull's Gap on the Tennessee and Virginia Railroad line. Today, the brigade moved from the gap and got into a world of trouble.

Carrick, A. L., Surg., USV, Tennessee Cavalry, Bull's Gap, Tenn.:

> On the 13th, when orders were given to retreat from Bull's Gap, there were eight of our wounded who could not be removed, four being patients whose limbs had been amputated the day before. These, I left in charge of Dr. Drake, a surgeon of experience and reputation, who resides at the Gap. He volunteered to take charge and I left him a sufficient supply of medicine, dressings, etc. The remainder of our sick and wounded, I took with me in our ambulance train.
>
> All went well until we reached Russellville, when our train was fired upon by the enemy concealed in the woods. This created the greatest confusion and alarm.... The train retreated precipitately to Morristown, the enemy being close behind. When we neared Morristown, we found the railroad train from Knoxville in waiting, with some reinforcements. I then considered all danger passed as our forces were formed in line to resist the enemy, and I went over to make arrangements to get all my sick and wounded on board ... but before I could get anything done the enemy, from various points, attacked in overwhelming force, and the train started back to Knoxville.
>
> Our artillery opened on the enemy with grape and canister. Our forces rallied and made a vain effort to stem the torrent; the ambulance and wagon trains were hurried forward, but I regret to state a panic seized our men. They broke in confusion and disorder, and in less than twenty minutes ambulances and wagons were upset on the road. Fifteen of the sick and wounded got out and escaped, some on the cars, others on horseback. The remainder, together with all the ambulances, hospital stores, and medical supplies, fell into the hands of the enemy. This catastrophe occurred at midnight, rendering the scene doubly frightful....
>
> The enemy continued to pour volley after volley into our retreating column, rendering it impossible for any of the medical officers to go to the assistance of the wounded. Next day, when I arrived at Strawberry Plains, I found many of the sick and wounded, whom I thought captured, had arrived there before me. These I sent to general hospital at Knoxville.

On her way north, Mrs. Bickerdyke stopped in Cairo, Ill., staying overnight at the Soldier's Home. This Home, newly constructed in January, was operated by Mrs. A. F. Grant, the same woman who Bickerdyke had recommended to run the Pest House hospital in Memphis in 1863. The Home was described:

> The Home was, in its construction, a model of convenience. "It could not possibly be improved," is Mrs. Grant's testimony. She made it a model of order. Washing scrubbing, cleaning, cooking, and all household processes, went on under her remarkable administration as regularly as in a private house. The dining tables were scoured after every meal, and were kept so white that tablecloths were a superfluity. There were regular days for the scrubbing of floors, porches and water barrels.... The kitchen was the pride of the establishment. Its huge apparatus for cooking was kept in shining order.... Three tubs were permanently arranged for dishwashing. In the first, the dishes were washed; in the second they were rinsed, and by a rule of Mrs. Grant's, the water in this tub was so hot as to necessitate taking them out with a skimmer. In the third, they drained for a moment on a rack. Then they were wiped while hot, and passed through a window into the dining room where the tables were instantly reset, to be ready for fresh guests.

Somehow, that kitchen doesn't recommend itself as a place for the summer, and the idea of resetting the tables when the flies were about doesn't sound too sanitary, either.

In the Valley, Jubal Early's weak force was further weakened when some of his troops were sent to Richmond to bolster Lee's shrinking army. Although not as famous as Jackson's Valley Campaign, Early's defense of the Valley was better conducted and he faced a Federal force that was larger and more experienced than had been the case previously. Jackson's campaign of 1862, while brilliantly executed, couldn't compare to the efforts made by Early, who'd fought 72 engagements and had marched nearly 1700 miles in about a five-month period. The end, however, was approaching.

November 14 (Monday)

Federal cavalry under Gen. Judson Kilpatrick left Atlanta and headed towards Jonesboro and Savan-

nah. Sherman's left wing, Maj. Gen. Slocum, went out to Decatur and Stone Mountain, where they demolished the railroad, bridges, and anything else of military value.

In Nashville, George H. Thomas was assembling his troops, and Schofield's two corps at Pulaski were positioned as a blocking force. Hood, near Florence, Ala., waited for Forrest to come up from Corinth, Miss., before they'd enter Tennessee.

November 16 (Wednesday)

Sherman left Atlanta in ruins, creating an emotional scar that never healed, the economy wrecked and the people without means of livelihood. He rode out with the Fourteenth Corps towards Lovejoy's Station. Skirmishing was light, mostly with local militia.

In lower Tennessee, the Federals, at Pulaski, waited for Hood to enter the state. Forrest had finally arrived, increasing Hood's force with a good cavalry arm.

November 17 (Thursday)

McParlin, T. A., Surg., Med. Dir., Army of the Potomac, in front of Petersburg, Va.:

> Fine bathhouses existed in all the hospitals and in many of the regiments. Among those especially mentioned by the medical inspector for excellence were the ones established by the 35th Massachusetts, the 3d Maryland, the 9th New Hampshire and the 1st, 2d and 8th Michigan. The troops in reserve adopted, as winter approached, a nearly uniform system of huts. In the forts, shelter tents and bomb-proofs were used, and covered ways connected the forts at points exposed to sharpshooters. The bomb-proofs consisted of long trenches roofed over and covered in, on the aspect facing the enemy, by means of heavy logs, protected by a thickness of two or three feet of earth and sandbags. Generally no attempt was made to make them impenetrable to rain. Two or three fireplaces were built in each bomb-proof along the open rearward side, and sleeping bunks were constructed. The huts were generally six feet by ten and not less than five feet and a half to the eaves, roofed by shelter tents, and intended for four men....
>
> Five hundred barrels of apples, received from the patriotic merchants of New York,... were distributed to the hospitals.... The colored division of

the Ninth Corps having left this army ... the hospital for such troops was broken up....

November 19 (Saturday)

Gov. Joseph Brown of Georgia had long been at loggerheads with the Confederate government about the use of Georgia troops, often refusing to send conscripts from his state to the Confederate Army. On more than one occasion, he'd refused to turn over to the central government muskets which had been produced in the state, reserving them for militia use.

Gov. Brown now called for all the able-bodied men in the state to come forward to defend their homes from the depredations of Sherman's marching columns. Brown got very little response from anyone; most were content to let Sherman's 60,000 men go where they pleased, since any small Confederate force would be completely annihilated.

November 21 (Monday)

Hood moved with about 30,000 infantry and over 8000 cavalry, including Forrest's, from Florence, Ala., into Tennessee. His first objective was to get between Schofield at Pulaski and Thomas at Nashville, and to try to defeat the Federals piecemeal. Sherman soundly defeated the Georgia state militia at Griswoldville, Ga.

November 24 (Thursday)

In Tennessee, Schofield's two corps, and Gen. Jacob D. Cox, arrived in Columbia, just ahead of the Confederates. Forrest's cavalry, leading Hood's army, was repulsed by the strong Union infantry. Schofield also secured a bridge crossing on the Duck River on the road to Nashville.

November 26 (Saturday)

At Columbia, Tenn., Hood arrived in front of Schofield's entrenched Duck River line and began to plan an attack.

November 28 (Monday)

Forrest's cavalry crossed the Duck River in Tennessee during the evening, soon to be followed by more of Hood's men. The crossing was above the city of Columbia, Tenn., where Schofield's Federals were skirmishing with other elements of Hood's army.

Welch, S. G., Surg., 20th S.C. Vols., in a letter to his wife, from near Petersburg, Va.:

The mails seem to be greatly deranged again, for I have not heard one word from you in two weeks. These clerks in the post offices are the contemptible imps of cowardice who seek all the soft and safe places. They should be placed in the ranks and made to fight, and their places given to the young ladies who are refugees from within the enemy's lines and who would be glad to secure such employment.

Everything is quiet here now—only an occasional gun. Kershaw's Division has come back from the Valley [and] is now on the north side of the James River. The Yankees have not shelled Petersburg for several weeks, and it is beginning to have a quiet air of business....

A man is going home today on sick furlough, and I shall send this letter by him to be mailed to you from Columbia. I am glad you have decided positively to come on to Virginia. I will have everything ready for you when you arrive....

November 29 (Tuesday)

Near Spring Hill, Tenn., Forrest's cavalry had crossed the Duck River last evening and was skirmishing around Spring Hill by noon. Schofield was still on the Duck River line, disengaging his troops and sending them north along the turnpike between Columbia and Spring Hill. This road was being held open by Gen. David S. Stanley's Union troops. By some quirk, all of Schofield's men went up the turnpike without being attacked by Hood's Confederates. The entire Federal force, wagon trains and all, escaped to take positions near Franklin.

Heard, J. T., Surg., USV, Spring Hill, Tenn.:

On the morning of 29th of November, the Fourth Corps consisting of three divisions, and the Twenty-third Corps of two divisions, were in position on the north bank of Duck River opposite Columbia, Tenn. The enemy, or the larger portion of the Rebel army, was upon the south bank.... At nine o'clock A.M., the 2d division of the Fourth Corps marched for Spring Hill, accompanied by and guarding all the trains of the army, with the exception of twenty ambulances left with the 1st and 3d divisions of the Fourth Corps, which divisions were ordered to remain with the Twenty-third Corps until dark and then to withdraw with the rest of the army.

About two in the afternoon, the head of the column being within one mile of Spring Hill, the commanding general was informed that the cavalry of the enemy was pushing back our cavalry and rapidly approaching the town. The troops were at once pushed forward at double quick, and having passed through the town, charged the enemy, checked him, and finally caused him to retire....

About four o'clock, the right brigade ... was furiously attacked by two brigades of Rebel infantry. The attack continued until nearly dark, when our right gave way towards the pike and was followed by the enemy. Fortunately all trains had then passed, and had been parked north of the town where, also, division hospitals had been temporarily organized, and the wounded provided with primary dressings and comforts. A few wounded men were unavoidably lost when the right gave way. One hundred and fifteen wounded were brought to hospital. Shortly after dark, orders were given to break up hospitals, load ambulances, and be ready to move.... The rest of the army reached Spring Hill about ten P.M., and continued their march through town towards Franklin. The hospital and ambulance trains moved at the same time, reaching Franklin at ten in the morning of November 30th, without loss....

November 30 (Wednesday)

Hood caught up with Schofield at Franklin, Tenn., where the Union general was dug in south of town. Schofield was faced with the problem of dealing with Hood while repairing bridges to get his wagon trains up to Nashville. Hood came driving north up the turnpike from Columbia, swung his troops to the left and right, into line of battle, and attacked the well-fortified Yankees about 4 P.M. The Confederate line came in well, drove the Federals back to their second prepared line, and then pulled back.

The casualties for the Rebels were very heavy— nearly 6300 out of a force of 27,000, more than 23 percent. Among them were six Confederate generals: States Rights Gist, H. B. Granbury, John Adams, O. F. Strahl, and the incomparable Patrick Cleburne. John C. Carter was mortally wounded. The dead generals were laid on the porch of a local house. Hood also lost 54 regimental commanders

killed, wounded, or captured. He now had fewer than 18,000 effective infantrymen. Federal losses were about 2300 from nearly 27,000 engaged. At night, Schofield pulled his men out of Franklin and headed up the road to Nashville.

Heard, J. T., Surg., USV, Battle of Franklin, Tenn.:

The wounded and sick were sent by rail to Nashville early in the afternoon. The two divisions of the Twenty-third Corps with the 1st and 2d divisions of the Fourth Corps remained south of the Harpeth River and entrenched themselves. The 3d division of the Fourth Corps crossed to the north side of the river and was not engaged in the battle.

About one o'clock in the afternoon of November 30th, the enemy appeared in force opposite our lines. At half past three o'clock in the afternoon, as it was determined to withdraw at dark toward Nashville, orders were given to send all trains, except half the ambulances of each division, to Nashville. Soon after the trains were fairly on the road, the enemy commenced a furious attack upon the entire line. Six distinct assaults were made, and by hard fighting were repulsed with great loss to the enemy. As soon as the firing commenced, orders were sent for the hospital wagons to be parked in the nearest field, and the tents to be temporarily pitched; all ambulances to return and cross the river. Efforts were there made to obtain a train of cars for the wounded; the commanding general, however, did not deem it best....

Owing to the intense darkness and imperfect provision for crossing and recrossing the river, the movement of ambulances was necessarily retarded. The wounded were collected at hospital as rapidly as possible; the town was thoroughly searched for wounded; orders were issued for the withdrawal of troops at twelve o'clock; the ambulances worked constantly until eleven o'clock P.M., and were then loaded ... with wounded at hospitals. Such slight cases of disease as remained were loaded upon army wagons; the hospitals and ambulance trains were the last to draw out, and were closely followed by the troops. Five hundred and fifty wounded were brought off. From all that can be ascertained, it is probable that from seventy-five to one hundred wounded of this corps were left in the hands of the enemy. Many Rebel wounded fell into our hands, but were left for want of transportation. The ambulance train reached Nashville at nine o'clock A.M., December 1st, and the wounded were placed in general hospitals....

In Virginia, the Army of the Potomac had little or no activity during November. For the month, the aggregate number of wounded admitted to the field hospitals was 293.

December 1 (Thursday)

At Nashville, Schofield entered the Union lines after eluding Hood's forces at Spring Hill, Columbia, and Franklin, Tenn. Maj. Gen. George H. Thomas had formed his defenses for Nashville in a semicircle, with both flanks resting on the Cumberland River. Hood brought his much-reduced and weary army to the front of Thomas's defenses and surveyed his options. Hood could now either attack Thomas, or bypass Nashville, in his drive to the Ohio, leaving Thomas to the rear of the Confederates. This could be an unhealthy situation for Hood.

December 3 (Saturday)

McParlin, T. A., Surg., Med. Dir., Army of the Potomac, in front of Petersburg, Va.:

To collect the sick and wounded from the front line immediately before Petersburg, picket stations for ambulances had been designated.... Each ambulance, when used, returned to its park from the division hospital and was relieved by another. After a short stay in division hospital, serious cases were sent by railroad to depot hospital at City Point, and thence, if no improvement was noticed in them, they were transferred to the general hospitals north. For this service, the transports of the Surgeon General were exclusively used, except when great emergencies made it proper to send more rapidly than the regular medical steamers permitted.... The steamers conveying the sick and wounded from City Point were the following: Steamer *State of Maine*, Surg. Janes in charge; capacity, five hundred beds. Steamer *Connecticut*, Surg. Hood in charge; capacity, four hundred beds. Steamer *Western Metropolis*, Acting Asst. Surg. W. M. Hudson, USA, in charge; capacity, four hundred and fifty beds. Steamer *De Molay*, Surg. Seaverns in charge; capacity, three hundred beds. Steamer *Baltic*, Asst. Surg. Thomas McMillen, USA, in charge; capacity, five hundred beds. Steamer

Atlantic, Surg. D. P. Smith, USV, in charge; capacity five hundred beds. The last two ocean steamers came only to Fortress Monroe, where patients were sent for transfer to them. Steamers of more convenient draught and entirely seaworthy, such as the *Ben De Ford* and *S. N. Spaulding*, were sent to City Point, after their superiority became evident. Patients were sent direct from City Point to Washington, Point Lookout, Annapolis, Baltimore, Philadelphia and New York.

December 5 (Monday)

McParlin, T. A., Surg., Med. Dir., Army of the Potomac, in front of Petersburg, Va.:

In the depot hospital at City Point, preparations were made for the winter by the construction of stockade buildings with open fireplaces. Many fine wards were thus added. The tents which were kept in use were supplied with frames.... At the same time, the division hospitals at the front were made ready for winter. The ambulance corps put up very comfortable stockades and stables for the men and animals at points convenient to their division hospitals.... Since August last, the duties of nurses, attendants, cooks and orderlies at the depot hospitals have been, to a great extent, performed by detailed musicians, the services of able-bodied men being required with their regiments. An efficient officer of the line was detailed by each corps commander for the general charge of the musicians of his corps....

December 7 (Wednesday)

South of Petersburg, Va., the Weldon Railroad, connecting Richmond with North Carolina, was a major means of transport for supplies to the beleaguered Confederacy at both Petersburg and Richmond. To further tighten the stranglehold on the Confederate capital, Grant ordered a raid on the railroad in early December. Asst. Surg. Charles K. Winne, USA, reported on the medical aspects of the operation.

Winne, Charles K., Asst. Surg., USA, Weldon Railroad expedition, south of Petersburg, Va.:

An expedition, composed of the Fifth Corps, the 3d division of the Second Corps, four batteries, Gen. Gregg's cavalry and a bridge train of canvas boats, having been ordered to move on daylight on December 7th, the flying hospital, composed of one medicine wagon and one hospital wagon for each brigade, with one half of the ambulances, accompanied the command. All the field companions and hospital knapsacks were directed to be filled. One hospital tent fly to be carried in each ambulance, and the boxes to be supplied with hard bread, sugar and coffee, while the hospital wagons carried stimulants, anodynes, dressings, blankets, hospital clothing, rations and hospital tents. The field hospitals of the troops about to move were left intact in charge of assistant surgeons, and all who were unable to march were sent thither....

... the troops moved, the ambulances following their respective divisions, the flying hospital with the [supply] train in rear. The command moved south of Yellow tavern, Gurley and Temple houses to Jerusalem plank road, and down this road to Hawkinsville, nineteen miles from Petersburg, where it halted until the pontoon bridge was thrown across the Nottoway river, at Freeman's Ford A wagon having been overturned on the bridge, the crossing was so much retarded that it was dark before all were over, and the troops bivouacked on the south side of the river.

A battalion of cavalry was detailed to collect all stragglers on the road north of the river and take them to army headquarters. Eight hundred and fifty were found.... It rained steadily the whole morning, but the soil being sandy, the march was but little retarded.

December 8 (Thursday)

Winne, Charles K., Asst. Surg., USA, Weldon Railroad expedition, south of Petersburg, Va.:

December 8th, we broke camp at three o'clock A.M., marched through Sussex Courthouse and Corman's well, to the North Cross house, on Halifax road, thirty miles from Petersburg, where the pontoon and other trains were parked. The weather, clear at starting, changed and became colder, with high wind at night, and heavy frost. The ambulances had been comparatively free during the day, many men requiring only a short rest to enable them to resume the march, and the remainder being returned to their respective commands on going into camp. During the night the troops were engaged in tearing up the railroad and destroying the road as far as practicable.

December 9 (Friday)

Winne, Charles K., Asst. Surg., USA, Weldon Railroad expedition, south of Petersburg, Va.:

The troops were engaged all day destroying the railroad, the cavalry going as far as Bellefield, opposite Hicksford, on Meherrin river, found the bridge at that point protected by seven or eight guns, supported by infantry in fieldworks, and it was not deemed advisable to attempt to force a passage. Here a short engagement occurred with some loss in the cavalry. It was very cold all day, with rain and sleet at night. Many of the men became intoxicated on apple whiskey, found in nearly all the houses on the road.

December 10 (Saturday)

Sherman, now in front of Savannah, had his cavalry probing the city's defenses. Gen. Hardee, with somewhat less than 18,000 men defending the city, had flooded the rice fields of the area, leaving only a few roads available for an approach. Sherman, after a reconnaissance, ordered investigation of Ft. McAllister, south of the city. The fort guarded the Ogeechee River, the obvious approach to the sea. While rations weren't short, forage for the horses and other draft animals was quickly used up. Some supplies were required.

Winne, Charles K., Asst. Surg., USA, Weldon Railroad expedition, south of Petersburg, Va.:

December 10th, the return march commenced, with the wagon train in advance, guarded by the 1st division, and the ambulances in advance of their respective divisions, two only following in the rear of each. The cavalry, with the exception of one brigade, returned to Sussex C.H. by the road we marched out, the infantry marched by another road. It was thawing, and the roads were very heavy during the day. We bivouacked a mile south of Sussex C.H. The 3d division, bringing up the rear, was attacked twice by Rebel cavalry,... two men received flesh wounds.

December 11 (Sunday)

Sherman quickly laid siege to Savannah, waiting to obtain his link to the sea, where the Union Navy waited. The Confederates had destroyed the bridge across the Ogeechee River to Ft. McAllister; the bridge had to be rebuilt. Sherman's troops fell to with a will and, using axes to fell trees and parts of dismantled houses, started rebuilding the 1000-foot span. Surg. Gill recorded what happened during the march.

Gill, H. Z., Surg., USV, 1st Div., 20th Corps, Savannah, Ga.:

On the march, men were admitted to ambulance or hospital on passes signed by the regimental medical officers. One medical officer of the hospital corps and one steward accompanied the ambulance train each day to regulate admissions and attend to the wants of the sick. During the campaign seven hundred and seventeen sick and seventy-four wounded men were admitted to hospital. At the close of the siege at Savannah, the number in hospital was only one percent of the entire strength of the command.... The weather was unusually fine during the campaign, there being but three rainy days, though there were also a few light showers....

Winne, Charles K., Asst. Surg., USA, Weldon Railroad expedition, south of Petersburg, Va.:

I visited the cavalry hospital at Sussex Courthouse on the 11th and learned that forty men had been wounded since the expedition started. We reached Nottoway river about noon, the troops all crossed before dark and camped on the Jerusalem plank road from Hawkinsville to the Belcher house.

December 12 (Monday)

Winne, Charles K., Asst. Surg., USA, Weldon Railroad expedition, south of Petersburg, Va.:

... the march was resumed and troops went into camp between Halifax and Jerusalem plank road by five o'clock P.M. During the expedition, the troops were exposed to great vicissitudes of weather and endured great fatigue and hardship. Two fractures were treated at the flying hospital, one received in tearing up the road, the other in felling timber.

December 13 (Tuesday)

The attack on Ft. McAllister was made across the 1000-foot bridge by the Fifteenth Corps at about 5 P.M. Sherman and several officers had climbed atop a rice mill to watch the show. On his elevated plat-

form, Sherman could see the sea. The long-sought goal was there!

As Sherman watched the Fifteenth Corps go into the attack, a man yelled, "A steamboat!" Sure enough, black smokestacks and the Union flag were seen coming upstream on the river. A signal flag on the steamer asked: "Who are you?" Sherman's signalman replied: "Gen. Sherman." The boat then asked: "Is Ft. McAllister taken yet?" Sherman replied: "No, but it will be in a minute."

At Nashville, the weather was still icy and everyone waited. Grant had ordered Gen. John Logan to Nashville to relieve Thomas if the latter didn't attack when the weather cleared.

December 15 (Thursday)

The first day of the Battle of Nashville began when George H. Thomas's blue lines of about 35,000 men slowly edged their way through heavy fog and struck Hood's left flank. The Federal onslaught was almost irresistible, driving the grey-clad veterans more than a mile to the rear, where they held on the Franklin Pike, but barely. The weather was cold, wet, and sloppy with melting ice. The lines were adjusted somewhat during the night.

Heard, J. T., Surg., USV, Battle of Nashville, Tenn.:

On the morning of December 14th, orders were received to be ready at six o'clock A.M. December 15th, to move upon the enemy's position. The hospitals of this corps which, since the 2d of the month, had been located near the city on the Franklin pike, were ordered to be broken up, and the hospital train to be parked on the Hillsboro' pike, there to remain until further developments. The sick were transferred to general hospital.

At seven o'clock A.M. December 15th, the troops of this corps moved out by the Hillsboro' pike, in front of the line of works.... The hospitals of the corps were at once established directly on the Hillsboro' pike, and about a quarter of a mile [to the] rear of the line of works. The site selected was the lawn in front of a large brick house; water was abundant and good. Detachments from each division's ambulance train were close [to the] rear of the troops, the remaining ambulances were parked [to the] rear of the works and ready to move out when required. The stretcher-men were with their respective regiments.

During the fighting ... the line of this corps was advanced nearly two miles. The loss in wounded was not severe, being only two hundred and three men. The wounded were promptly removed from the field and cared for at division hospitals.... After dark, the fighting having ceased, and all operations and dressings having been attended to, the wounded were transferred to general hospital. As the position of the corps had now changed from the Hillsboro' to the Franklin pike, the hospital train was ordered to be loaded and ready to move at daylight on December 16th....

December 16 (Friday)

The second day of the Battle of Nashville was fought today. At 6 o'clock in a morning filled with rain and snow, Thomas's troops moved into the assault. The Confederate right was pressed back and then held at the line of their main entrenchments. The Union cavalry got in behind Hood's left flank and the Confederates' rear was threatened. Late in the afternoon the Federals made their main assault and the firing became almost continuous for a period of time. The Confederate left caved in first, moving back, then the center folded, leaving the right to play rear guard. Thomas described the Confederates as being "hopelessly broken." The Confederate rear guard held off the pursuing Federals until late in the afternoon, when the entire line gave way and the Rebels fled the field. Hood lost most of his artillery and many of his wagons.

Thomas had engaged about 55,000 men and had suffered 3600 casualties, mostly wounded (2562). Hood's force had little more than 20,000 men, and he lost 4500 captured and another 1500 killed and wounded—over 25 percent lost. The Army of Tennessee was now an army in name only.

Heard, J. T., Surg., USV, Battle of Nashville, Tenn.:

The hospitals were located on the right and left of the Franklin pike at the Springs,... the ambulances were near the troops. The fighting today was much more severe than that of yesterday, although the casualties were wonderfully slight. Four hundred and ninety-five men of this corps were wounded and tak-

en to hospital.... At night the wounded, after being attended to, were to be transferred to general hospital, and the hospital trains to be loaded and ready to move at early daylight, either for the establishment of the hospitals near the troops in the event of another battle, or to be ready to follow the corps in case ... the enemy should retreat....

Sherman was busy unloading supplies of ammunition and other necessities from the ships of the Union fleet. His troops bent willing backs to unload the cargo as fast as the ships could be docked on the Ogeechee River. Another, more precious, commodity, *mail*, was also aboard the steamers in anticipation of a Federal land-sea linkup.

December 17 (Saturday)

Mrs. Bickerdyke had been kept busy during her visit North. First, she settled her sons with a farm family in Wisconsin, and they were happy with their lot. Second, Mrs. Livermore had plans for Bickerdyke to go on a fund-raising tour and to appear at the new Sanitary Fair that was being planned. Livermore was about to go east to New York and Philadelphia, entering the territory of the U.S. Sanitary Commission to raise money.

It was in Philadelphia that Sherman's call reached Mrs. Bickerdyke. She was to come to Savannah as soon as possible, with all the supplies she could muster. Sherman even provided a steamship for her use.

Although she was in the territory of the rival Christian Commission, she didn't hesitate to call on them for help in gathering the needed supplies. Their response was tremendous. Mr. George H. Stuart, the Commission president, took over filling her ship for her. Stuart went to the Philadelphia merchants and obtained dried and canned fruits, clothing, crackers, butter, cheese, tea, sugar, condensed milk, tapioca, extract of beef, cornstarch, lemons, oranges, tin cups, a span of mules and an ambulance, and many other useful things. In record time the ship was loaded and ready to go.

Federal cavalry under James H. Wilson plus some infantry chased Hood's retreating Confederates down the Pike south from Nashville towards Columbia, Tenn., where skirmishing broke out with Hood's rear guard at Franklin, Hollow Tree Gap, and West Harpeth River. The rear guard held Wilson at bay until the rest of the Rebels made their escape.

December 18 (Sunday)

Wilson's cavalry pursued Hood to Rutherford Creek, near Columbia, Tenn., where the Federal chase was called off when the Federals found the stream flooded and impassable. As the news of the defeat at Nashville was telegraphed North and South, all believed that a serious blow had been dealt the Confederacy, one which would contribute greatly to its defeat.

Sherman waited quietly, resupplying his troops with new uniforms, etc., while Hardee, who the day before had refused Sherman's demand for surrender, pondered his next move. Sherman wrote Grant that he wanted to drive for Raleigh, N.C., burning and tearing up track all the way, forcing the Confederates to evacuate Richmond.

December 21 (Wednesday)

Sherman's medical director had ordered a 5000-man hospital to be sent to the coast of Georgia for use at whatever point the army emerged from the interior. The hospital, with all its equipment, was aboard a ship off Savannah and ready for use, but it wasn't required. The men were extremely healthy, aside from the usual broken bones, cuts, scrapes, etc. The expected disease rate didn't materialize because of the rapid movement of the force and the availability of fresh meat and vegetables on the march route. The season of the year also played an important part in the health of the men—the weather being much cooler.

December 23 (Friday)

On the way south along the coast, Mrs. Bickerdyke's ship stopped at Wilmington, N.C., to take on water. While there, Bickerdyke went into town, and there she found some of the prisoners from Andersonville who'd been returned to Savannah and then sent on to Wilmington, where they were being received by Union officials. With the first look, Bickerdyke decided that these men needed her more

than Sherman, and that the supplies she had were certainly needed here more. She ordered the ship unloaded, sent a hastily scribbled note to Sherman with the ship, and went to work.

The prisoners were a dreadful sight. Those who could walk were walking skeletons, repulsive with the ugly running sores of "prison pox," a skin disease attributed to exposure, starvation diet, and rat bites. The stretcher cases suffered from worse ills, such as septic wounds.

The army had taken over many of the public buildings in Wilmington to serve as hospitals, and this is where the former prisoners from Andersonville were sent. There, too, went Mrs. Bickerdyke. These men needed bathing, clean clothes, decent food, and the loving attention that she had in abundance.

For the next several months, Bickerdyke would labor in Wilmington, helping with the Andersonville prisoners, as well as with those from other prisons in the South. When her hospitals were emptied, she'd return to Washington and rejoin the Fifteenth Corps and her "boys," for the parade in May 1865.

December 26 (Monday)

John Bell Hood's bone-weary Confederates crossed the Tennessee at Bainbridge, Ala., and the Army of Tennessee, for all practical purposes, passed into history. The dream to reach the Ohio and draw Sherman out of Georgia became a hazy memory, to be remembered as a montage of long, cold marches, colder nights, and periods of hellish gunfire.

December 31 (Saturday)

McParlin, T. A., Surg., Med. Dir., Army of the Potomac, in front of Petersburg, Va.:

I estimate the total number of wounded attended to by this department during the year ending December 31, 1864, at *sixty thousand three hundred....* There is every reason, also, to believe that the number of sick reported, viz., *one hundred and seventy-three thousand and sixty-three,* fall short of the actual number. [Italics added.]

1865

January 1 (Sunday)

The first day of the year found Surg. E. J. Marsh, assigned as the Chief Medical Officer of the 2nd Division, Cavalry Corps, Army of the Potomac, on the siege lines around Petersburg. The division was encamped on the Jerusalem Plank Road, beyond the rear line of earthworks, and near the crossing of the Blackwater. The weather was very cold as the troops waited out the long winter for the spring campaigns to begin.

Marsh, E. J., Surg., USA, Chief Med. Off., near Petersburg, Va.:

> The total number of medical officers present for duty on the 1st of January was twenty-six.... There was a full complement of men, wagons and ambulances, the number of ambulances being twenty-six, with three medicine wagons and fifteen army wagons. The ambulances were mostly old, but in good repair and serviceable.

January 2 (Monday)

The siege lines at and around Petersburg, Va., developed nearly an urban air during the winter of 1864-65, when action along these lines was intermittent. The Fifth Corps Artillery Brigade, Army of the Potomac, was camped near the Weldon Railroad, the men housed in log/canvas shelters which were heated with fireplaces and, in some cases, Sibley stoves. A

hospital had been constructed for the brigade and was under the management of the brigade surgeon, who related how the hospital was laid out.

Haynes, C. F., Surg., USV, Artillery Brigade, Fifth Corps, Petersburg, Va.:

> This hospital was located at Parke's Station, near to the Aikin house, at a point quite central to batteries. It consisted of three hospital tents and tent flies, pitched upon ground favorable for drainage and ventilation, where pure water was obtained by sinking a deep well. It was heated by a brick fireplace on the north side of the middle tent, the three tents being arranged end to end, forming a continuous ward. This ward contained twenty beds, raised upon bunks two feet wide and one foot apart. A passage two feet in width ran through the centre. The ground being hard, it was not thought necessary to construct a floor. Ventilation was effected by separating the flaps at each end by a cross stick. The dispensary was built of logs and covered by a tent fly. Ample supplies were drawn monthly from the medical purveyor at City Point. The kitchen was built like the dispensary, and divided into two apartments, one used as a cook room and the other as a dining room. The attendants, eight in number, occupied four log huts. The hospital grounds were neatly enclosed by a fence and evergreens, and were at all times thoroughly policed. The burial ground adjoining the hospital was neatly enclosed. At the head of each grave a board was

placed, upon which was legibly engraved the full name, rank, regiment, and battery of the deceased....

January 3 (Tuesday)

After the disastrous attempt by Maj. Gen. Benjamin Butler to capture Ft. Fisher, in Wilmington, N.C., Grant assigned Maj. Gen. Alfred H. Terry, a westerner, to command the army during the next assault. In Grant's instructions to Terry, he said: "I have served with Admiral Porter and know that you can rely on his judgment and his nerve to undertake what he proposes. I would, therefore, defer to him as much as is consistent with your own responsibilities." Grant also notified Porter that Terry was coming as the commander of the army troops.

January 4 (Wednesday)

Pulling out all the stops, Admiral D. D. Porter ordered that all available sailors and Marines from the fleet were to be formed into landing parties to disembark on the beach on the seaward side of Ft. Fisher, while the army, under Gen. Terry, was to assault the landward side. The sailors, armed with cutlasses and pistols, were to be backed up by the Marines, who would provide rifle fire, the sailors "boarding" the fort in the accustomed naval manner.

January 8 (Sunday)

The transports containing Maj. Gen. Terry's Union expeditionary force from Hampton Roads, Va., arrived today off the coast of Beaufort, S.C.

January 12 (Thursday)

Today, the largest American fleet ever assembled under one command sailed from Beaufort, S.C., up the coast towards Wilmington, N.C., and Ft. Fisher. The army forces under Maj. Gen. Terry met with Admiral Porter's fleet and the assault on Ft. Fisher began. The armada arrived off the beach at Wilmington, and the navy prepared for the bombardment which was to precede the landing of 10,000 Union soldiers, sailors, and Marines.

January 13 (Friday)

Early this morning, off Wilmington, N.C., the U.S.S. *New Ironsides*, Commodore William Radford, led the monitors *Saugus*, *Canonicus*, *Monadnock*, and *Mahopac* to within 1000 yards of Ft.

Fisher and opened with their naval guns. The defenders, 1500 men under Col. Lamb, replied with spirit, at least initially. The U.S.S. *Brooklyn*, Capt. Alden, led the heavy wooden-hulled ships into line behind the ironclads and the bombardment lasted all day and into the night. Maj. Gen. Terry, in command of army forces, landed his 8000 men on a defensible beachhead, out of range of the fort's guns. Terry prepared for the assault on the fort.

The first weeks of the new year were very busy as the Army of the Potomac entered its last year of war. Late in the previous year, a new medical director was appointed who remained with that army until the end of the war, and who saw the troops mustered out and the army disbanded. Surg. Thomas A. McParlin was of the Regular Army and had had several years' service before the war started. His report at the end of August, 1865, sheds much light on the conditions existing in the closing months of the war.

> McParlin, T. A., Surg., USA, Med. Dir., Army of the Potomac, near Petersburg, Va.:
>
> During December, 1864, the supply of fresh vegetables ceased. This deprivation continued so long that,... it was brought to the attention of the commanding general.... It should be remarked that the deficiency of fresh vegetables was attributed by the subsistence department to want of transportation.
>
> ... it was recommended that cooking by companies be enforced and attention reinvited to existing orders requiring it (General Orders No. 52, Headquarters Army of the Potomac, May 15, 1863).

January 14 (Saturday)

Meanwhile, Gen. Terry had prepared defensive works facing the approaches from Wilmington to protect the Union rear from a possible assault by the 6000 Rebel troops under Gen. Braxton Bragg, at Wilmington. During the day, the C.S.S. *Chickamauga*, based at Wilmington, came down and fired on Terry's Union troops from her position on the Cape Fear River.

Terry visited Porter aboard the flagship *Malvern* to coordinate the attack for the following day. The plan called for 4000 of Terry's troops to hold a defensive line and the other 4000 to attack the land face of the fort in midafternoon. At the moment of Terry's attack, 2000 sailors and

Marines would assault the sea face of the fort on the northeast bastion.

January 15 (Sunday)

In the relative silence that followed the constant crashing and exploding of shells within the confines of Ft. Fisher, the Confederate gunners manned the guns that were left and began firing on the assaulting Federals. The naval landing force was the first target available, the army troops having farther to come, and as the landing party crossed the beach the defenders' fire was point-blank, "ploughing lanes in the ranks." The naval landing force, under the command of Lt. Commander K. Randolph Breese, pressed the attack, with one group headed by Lt. Commander Thomas O. Selfridge reaching the top of the parapet and temporarily breaching the defenses, but they were driven back. Ensign Robley D. Evans, later to become a rear admiral with the sobriquet "Fighting Bob," described the command problem of the assault: "All the officers, in their anxiety to be the first into the fort, had advanced to the heads of the columns, leaving no one to steady the men behind; and it was in this way we were defeated, by the men breaking from the rear."

The Confederates were cheering the repulse of the naval force when they realized that Terry's men had occupied the western end of the fort in strength. A counterattack was immediately launched and hand-to-hand fighting soon ensued. Reinforcements rushing to the western end from other points of the fort were hit now by naval gunfire. Its pinpoint accuracy destroyed the Confederate columns as they moved. Other ships fired on the riverbank behind the fort to prevent any reinforcements from that direction. Gen. Whiting, commander of the fort, was mortally wounded during the assault, and command was passed to Maj. James Reilly, after Col. Lamb was hit in the hip by a bullet. Reilly fought doggedly and well, but was overwhelmed by the onrushing Union troops and the naval gunfire. The Confederates were driven from the fort, and Reilly surrendered his men later that night.

Union casualties were heavy, nearly 1000 killed or wounded, compared to about half that for the Confederates. The magnificent cooperation between Terry and Porter signalled the end of the last haven for blockade runners supplying the Confederacy. Admiral Porter wired Secretary Welles, "Ft. Fisher is ours."

January 16 (Monday)

At Ft. Fisher, celebrating Union soldiers, sailors, and Marines were firing their weapons, when one shot accidentally set off a powder magazine whose explosion killed about 25 and wounded nearly 70. Thirteen men were never found.

Hand, D. W., Surg., Med. Dir., New Bern, N.C.:

... in January, Maj. Gen. Terry, with a portion of the army of the James, stormed and captured Ft. Fisher, N.C. Two hundred and ten of the wounded from this battle were brought to Mansfield general hospital, at Morehead City, where the necessary operations were performed by Asst. Surg. J. M. Palmer, 85th New York Volunteers. The wounds of these men healed with remarkable rapidity, and the men nearly all recovered much sooner than was expected. I have thought that the stimulating effects of the victory they had won had much to do with it.

January 17 (Tuesday)

The aftermath of the Battle of Franklin, Tenn., followed by the Battle of Nashville, in December 1864, left many Confederates wounded on the fields. One such individual must have led a charmed life for the entire period of the war.

Synnamon, James, Capt., Co. I, 6th Missouri Inf., CSA, Ft. Delaware, Del.:

At Wilson Creek I was wounded in the head and shoulder and lost the sight of my right eye.

At Corinth, Miss., the 6th Missouri went into battle with three hundred and forty-seven men, and at roll call after the battle only thirty-five answered for duty, the rest having been killed or wounded (none captured). In this battle I was wounded in the foot, the side, and through the shoulder.

At Pt. Gibson I was knocked senseless by a shell and left for dead, and have been deaf in one ear ever since.

At Black River, when the 61st Tennessee gave way on the railroad that crossed our works, Col. Riley, of the 1st Missouri Regiment, left the works on our right, crossed our rear at a double-quick, formed, as we thought, on our left, and opened fire on the Federals in our works. He then left us and retreated across the bridge. As we were the only troops now left, Col. Cooper ordered us to fall back to the riverbank and cross the bridge. Not being much of a runner, I did not get to the bridge until it was a mass of flames; but being a good swimmer, I swung my boots about my neck, plunged in, and made the other side.

At the siege of Vicksburg I was constantly in the trenches, and received there several slight wounds. On one occasion I was buried under the dirt torn up by an exploding shell, and had to be dug out along with Capt. Lile, who had involuntarily shared the same misfortune.

When the men were paroled after the surrender [of Vicksburg], I was put on provost marshal duty on the Mobile and Ohio Railroad until exchanged, when I reported to Gen. Hood in Atlanta.

I was with Gen. Stuart in the battle of Franklin and was in the last charge, about sundown, when Stuart and Cheatham attempted to take the works from which our troops had been repulsed. It seemed to me that the air was all red and blue flames, with shells and bullets screeching and howling everywhere, over and through us, as we rushed across the cotton fields strewn with fallen men. Wounded and dying men lay all about in ghastly piles, and when we reached the works at the old cotton gin gatepost only two or three of my companions were with me. They went into the ditch, but I was tumbled over by a Yankee bullet and was dragged over and laid prisoner by the old gin-house. That night I was put into an ambulance and taken to Nashville and placed in a hospital....

January 22 (Sunday)

On the 15th, Sherman's army began its march north from Savannah, Ga., and Beaufort, S.C. The army moved in stages, not as one force. The objective was to reach Goldsboro, N.C., on March 15th, fewer than 60 days away. The movement of Slocum's left wing was slow because of heavy rains, which had turned the dirt roads into bottomless pits.

Sherman's headquarters left Savannah for Beaufort by steamer, with a stop at Hilton Head, S.C. The march along the coast included one column along the railroad running to Branchville, S.C. Sherman notified Gen. Blair *not* to destroy the railroad,

since it would possibly be needed later. Sherman gave all indications of heading towards Charleston.

Moore, John, Surg., USA, Med. Dir., Sherman's Army, en route to South Carolina:

The several corps left Savannah at various dates from the 15th to 22d of January. Before marching they were disencumbered of all men not supposed to be able to endure active duty in the field, these sick or disabled men being placed in their respective corps hospitals.... Before entering Savannah, about two hundred men, eighty of whom had been carried in ambulances from the vicinity of Macon, had been sent on a hospital steamer to the hospitals at Hilton Head....

January 24 (Tuesday)

Maj. Gen. Wm. Tecumseh Sherman's headquarters headed north along the coast of South Carolina, having crossed the Savannah River. The Union Navy was providing support along the river at any point to which gunboats could ascend, providing firepower, supplies, and evacuating personnel when necessary. Admiral Dahlgren was determined that no stone would be left unturned in the support of the drive northward.

Marsh, E. J., Surg., USA, Chief Med. Off., near Petersburg, Va.:

... by permission of the acting medical director of the army, I issued a circular directing the surgeons-in-chief of brigades to turn over the medical property in the ambulances to the surgeon in charge of the division hospital, and placing upon him the responsibility of keeping the boxes filled. I did this because the ambulance property is used exclusively in the field hospital, over which the surgeons-in-chief of brigades have no control, and confusion of accounts often arise[s] from the fact of several officers being responsible for property in the same hospital.

January 25 (Wednesday)

Sherman was notified by Grant that Lee *wouldn't* send any troops from Petersburg to bolster the Confederate forces in the Carolinas. Sherman's armies moved through a flooded countryside, the past four days having been nothing but rain.

January 27 (Friday)

Sherman's army was now widely scattered and wet. The incessant rains had been a problem in both forward movement and supplies. The stationary positions used up the supplies quickly, and no foraging could be done. For the movement, Sherman again "stripped" his army of excess baggage.

January 30 (Monday)

Sherman turned northwest and headed his avalanche of blue towards Columbia, S.C. This irresistible tide would smash South Carolina, while it had only "touched" Georgia.

January 31 (Tuesday)

Sherman continued his march towards Columbia, the smoke rising from burning buildings like signal fires, his troops building corduroy roads through the swamps, movement never stopping. What little resistance they met was outflanked and brushed aside.

February 1 (Wednesday)

Gen. Slocum, commanding Sherman's left wing, was having a hard time with flooded rivers and streams and getting his troops across the Savannah River at Sister's Ferry, despite the assistance of the Federal Navy. Gen. Howard, on the right, encountered burned bridges and felled trees that presented few problems to Sherman's trained engineers and Pioneer battalions. They had plenty of experience with those obstacles before. Progress was slow but steady.

Moore, John, Surg., USA, Med. Dir., Sherman's Army, in South Carolina:

The right wing, under command of Gen. Howard, began the march from Pocolatigo, S.C., on February 1, 1865. These troops had been encamped for two weeks in low marshes, and it was again found necessary to disencumber the two corps,... of about two hundred sick, who were sent to hospitals in Beaufort, S.C. At about the same date, the two corps,... forming the left wing under Gen. Slocum, began the march from two points, about thirty miles apart, on the north side of the Savannah River. To facilitate the progress of the army, the four corps marched by as many different roads. By far the most serious

obstacle encountered ... was the bad condition of the roads. The face of the country was intersected with innumerable streams, spreading over a wide extent of bottom, through which the water flowed in numerous channels, with intervening marshes, impracticable for roads except by continuous corduroy and bridging. To do this work,... great numbers of men were wading through water and mud from morning till night....

Marsh, E. J., Surg., USA, Chief Med. Off., near Petersburg, Va.:

I received orders from the medical director to send off all the sick and wounded who would be unable to accompany the command in case of a move. At three o'clock P.M., I sent one hundred and eighty-one patients to City Point. A few, however, arrived from one of the regiments too late to be sent, and were placed in hospital.

February 2 (Thursday)

Sherman's right wing, commanded by Maj. Gen. Otis O. Howard, was into the swamps, and Confederate troops were delaying the advance as much as the terrain. Heavy skirmishing took place along the crossings of the Salkehatchie River. Sherman's Seventeenth Corps cleared Confederate forces from Rivers' Bridge by crossing three miles of swamp, sometimes up to their shoulders, outflanking the Confederates. From this point on the Salkehatchie River, the blue columns moved rapidly towards Columbia.

Moore, John, Surg., USA, Med. Dir., Sherman's Army, en route through the Carolinas:

The enemy disputed the crossing of the Salkahatchie River at Rivers' Bridge. After a short skirmish, a crossing was effected with the loss of sixteen killed and eighty-five wounded. The wounded from this affair were sent back to Beaufort. After this there was no other considerable skirmish until the arrival of the right wing at Congaree Creek, near Columbia....

February 3 (Friday)

Today, Clara Barton wrote Pres. Lincoln requesting both authority and endorsement for a plan in which she would:

...act temporarily as general correspondent at Annapolis, Md., having in view the reception to and answering of letters from the friends of our prisoners now being exchanged. It will be my object also to obtain and furnish all possible information in regard to those who have died during their confinement.

February 4 (Saturday)

Sherman's whole front was now in motion, headed for Columbia. Slocum's problems getting across the flooded Savannah River had been solved and he was making good time in the higher, less swampy, terrain. There was skirmishing at several points across the front. The smoke was still rising from burning houses, barns, etc.

Marsh, E. J., Surg., USA, Chief Med. Off., near Petersburg, Va.:

February 4th, we received orders to move at three o'clock A.M., next morning. I was directed to take fourteen ambulances, but no wagons were allowed on account of the condition of the roads. Surg. Lovejoy was to take charge of the field hospital, with half the attendants of the division hospital....

February 5 (Sunday)

McParlin, T. A., Surg., USA, Med. Dir., Army of the Potomac, near Petersburg, Va.:

Preparations for a military operation were made early in February, and it became necessary to clear the field hospitals and commands of all who were unable to participate in it. Over two thousand were sent down to the depot hospital in thirty-six hours, chiefly at night, the railroad conducting its ordinary business in the meantime. On the 5th of February, the movement to Dabney's Mill and Hatcher's Run began.... The roads were corduroyed and the railroad extended correspondingly to the left. The wounded were not very far from their established division hospitals, and after receiving surgical attention were sent from Patrick Station, very promptly, by rail to City Point.... On my application hospital cars were placed on the military railroad, greatly improving the mode of transporting sick and wounded to City Point....

Marsh, E. J., Surg., USA, Chief Med. Off., near Petersburg, Va.:

February 5th, at three o'clock A.M., the division moved by the Jerusalem Plank Road and Geary's Church to Ream's Station; and after a short halt, proceeded by the Halifax and Malone roads to Malone's bridge, over the Rowanty. Here we found a small force of the enemy on the opposite bank of the creek, and after a short skirmish drove them from their line of breastworks, and captured several prisoners.... We then proceeded by some country byroads to Dinwiddie Courthouse. We met no force of the enemy at that place.... We then returned by the same road by which we had advanced to Malone's bridge.... During the day the weather was mild and pleasant but the roads were very muddy, especially the wood and field road by which we advanced. In returning they were almost impassable. We reached the Rowanty about dark. One brigade ... crossed, and the others camped on the south side.

February 6 (Monday)

Sherman's columns were fighting for every ford and bridge on the numerous rivers bisecting their route. The delays were usually neither long nor costly, but there were delays. There was fighting on the Little Salkehatchie River, at Fishburn's Plantation, and near Barnwell, S.C. Most of the Confederates were outflanked rather than taken head-on.

Marsh, E. J., Surg., USA, Chief Med. Off., Hatcher's Run, Va.:

At half-past twelve A.M., we again started on the road to join Gen. Warren at the crossing of the Vaughan and Quaker roads. The weather had grown cold after dark, and when we started, the roads were completely frozen and we suffered greatly from the cold. On joining Gen. Warren, we found his command marching to Hatcher's Run, and followed in his rear. We were ordered to mass in some open fields before crossing the run, and put out skirmishers expecting the enemy.... After some time the enemy appeared in our rear and some skirmishing occurred. There was not much fighting, however, until afternoon, when they attacked in some force. They were, however, easily repulsed, but we had several officers and men killed and wounded. The wounded were temporarily dressed on the field, and sent back in the ambulances to the hospital at the Cummings house.

February 7 (Tuesday)

Marsh, E. J., Surg., USA, Chief Med. Off., Hatcher's Run, Va.:

On the morning of the 7th, it rained hard and continued raining nearly all day.... About two o'clock, the Fifth Corps was ordered to advance and proceeded by the Dabney's Mill road. At the same time the 2d brigade of the cavalry division was ordered to drive the enemy down the Vaughan road and across Gravelly Run if possible.... This brought on a general engagement along our line.... The firing was quite heavy and we had a number killed and wounded.... The wounded were, as far as possible, dressed temporarily and removed rapidly to the hospital. The ambulance corps did remarkably well.... The ambulances were brought as far to the front as possible, and two ambulance horses were wounded by bullets.... As soon as the fighting was over and all the wounded removed from the field, I went back to the hospital. Here I found fifty-five wounded. Surg. Lovejoy had taken some outhouses for hospital use and had also put up tent-flies; had procured straw for bedding, and had fed all the patients. The wounds were mostly dressed and some of the necessary operations had been performed. Others continued to occupy the surgeons until midnight. In the evening I received orders ... to send as many as were dressed and could be carried in the ambulances to Patrick's Station, where cars would be ready to receive them. About thirty were sent off and the rest made comfortable for the night....

February 8 (Wednesday)

Sherman's advance continued, the blue columns outflanking the Confederate positions, the Confederates withdrawing. In addition to the burning of the houses and barns, the railroads were demolished as the army progressed. Fighting for the fords of the Edisto and South Edisto rivers continued. An escaped prisoner from Florence, S.C., reported that the Union prisoners there were in desperate straits, very low on rations.

Marsh, E. J., Surg., USA, Chief Med. Off., Hatcher's Run, Va.:

The next morning some more operations were performed, and all the remainder of the wounded, but four or five, were then sent to the railroad. On the 8th it was clear, and the 1st and 3d brigades were

ordered back to their old camps at the Jerusalem Plank Road.... I broke up the hospital at the Cummings house and took the few remaining wounded to the division hospital.

February 10 (Friday)

McParlin, T. A., Surg., USA, Med. Dir., Army of the Potomac, near Petersburg, Va.:

Although all able-bodied soldiers, detailed as attendants at the depot hospital, had been replaced by musicians, their commanders still made frequent applications for the relief of their detailed bandsmen, drummers, buglers, etc. It became therefore desirable to have the services of hired nurses or of numbers of the veteran reserve corps for duty in the hospital. After consultation with the assistant adjutant general, the subject was brought to the attention of the Surgeon General, but reliable contract nurses were difficult to obtain and the great demand upon the veteran reserve corps for nurses, cooks, etc., for general hospitals, precluded any detail for the depot hospitals at City Point. *Had a hospital corps been properly organized during the war, I am persuaded that good material would have* [been] *attracted to it, and the public service would have been greatly benefitted thereby.* [Italics added.]

February 11 (Saturday)

Sherman's troops were now in position between the Confederates on the coast at Charleston and those in Augusta, Ga. In neither place did the South have sufficient men assembled to oppose the Union forces successfully. There was fighting in the vicinity of Orangeburg, Aiken, and around Johnson's Station.

February 13 (Monday)

Sherman's army now approached the Congaree River, S.C., which the troops would cross on the 14th (Tuesday). The weather remained clear. Progress of the columns was marked again by rising columns of black smoke as the troops burned the countryside.

Marsh, E. J., Surg., USA, Chief Med. Off., Hatcher's Run, Va.:

During the remainder of the month, the division remained in camp; the picket duty was increased by the recent lengthening of the lines towards the left.

The health of the command was, however, good, and there were but a few admissions into hospital. Unfortunately, but very few vegetables could be issued, and, in the latter part of the month, the patients admitted showed spongy gums, and a few cases of scurvy appeared....

February 14 (Tuesday)

Sherman's troops were across the Congaree River, using some fords that were discovered somewhat by accident and some bridges that were hastily secured against destruction by the Rebels.

Moore, John, Surg., USA, Med. Dir., Sherman's Army, en route through the Carolinas:

The crossing was opposed by cavalry under Wade Hampton; but the crossing was soon effected, with a loss of five killed and fourteen wounded. Two days afterward the army entered Columbia....

February 17 (Friday)

With the capture of Ft. Fisher and the arrival of Maj. Gen. Schofield, Surg. Hand switched responsibilities from Medical Director of North Carolina to Medical Director for Schofield's Union forces. These forces were then being concentrated for the drive on Wilmington and the linkup with Sherman, who was advancing north through the Carolinas.

Hand, D. W., Surg., Med. Dir., New Bern, N.C.:

During the latter part of February, all the available troops in the former district of North Carolina were concentrated at New Bern under command of Maj. Gen. Palmer. The 1st Division of the Twenty-third Corps, under command of Maj. Gen. Ruger, arrived there from the west. A provisional division, made up of recruits and stragglers (who'd been left behind when Sherman left Atlanta) from Sherman's army, arrived as well. The whole of this force, about thirteen thousand strong, was commanded by Maj. Gen. Cox, and was moved out from New Bern on March 3d....

February 20 (Monday)

Sherman's columns left Columbia, passing through a fertile country for about five miles, and then they passed into an area of hills with stunted pines, sandy soil, almost barren. A large train of refugees consisting of several hundred white people followed the army as it left. There were many reasons for the exodus; some left to escape starvation; some to escape conscription; some to escape persecution. All were a bother to the army and made many demands for protection, provisions, etc., which couldn't be met. Sherman ordered them expelled from the columns.

Moore, John, Surg., USA, Med. Dir., Sherman's Army, en route through the Carolinas:

After a rest ... in Columbia, the army resumed its march, taking roads leading to the north, and in two days reached Winslow.... The country passed over from Columbia to the Wateree, a distance of nearly fifty miles, was high and rolling, with occasional outcroppings of the granite formation, more so than any passed over in South Carolina....

March 2 (Thursday)

The Army of the Potomac's Second Corps was encamped near Patrick's Station in the Petersburg siege lines today, and had been there for some period of time. The troops were waiting for the spring offensive to begin. The medical department of the corps was getting prepared for field operations with an eye towards the loading of the medical ambulances and supply wagons. Asst. Surg. C. Smart reported the activities.

Smart, C., Asst. Surg., USA, Med. Inspector, 2nd Corps, Patrick's Station, Va.:

With the view of avoiding the recurrence of what happened at Ream's Station and on the Boydton road, where, while the engagement was in progress, all the medicine wagons were, by order, lying in park many miles in rear, the surgeons-in-chief of the 2d and 3d divisions had recourse to a plan which they hoped would enable them to provide for the wounded even during the temporary absence of their Autenrieth and Perot wagons. They caused the boxes of several of the ambulances to be filled with battlefield supplies; chloroform, morphine, lint, plaster, rollers, and whiskey, instead of the beef stock and hard bread directed by the supply table. The ambulances so loaded were marked, and the ambulance officer directed to take them along in all movements in which a portion of the hospital train, only, was permitted to accompany the troops. About this time, also, the medical transportation of the corps was ordered to be reduced from forty-four wagons to thirty-seven. But thirty of these were available for carrying medical supplies, seven being used as forage wagons for the ambulance train....

As a further preparation for active operations, an application was made,... to have the drummers and musicians of the command report to the surgeon in charge of the field hospital at the commencement of the campaign. This application was approved....

March 3 (Friday)

Hand, D. W., Surg., Med. Dir., New Bern, N.C.:

... following the line of railroad to Kinston and Goldsboro', N.C. The transportation of the Twenty-third Corps not having arrived, all the ambulances that could be spared from the post of New Bern were sent with this force under charge of an officer who was temporarily attached to the staff of Gen. Cox. Not more than one ambulance to each thousand men was thus provided; but as the troops were ordered to proceed only on the line of railroad, and little faster than the track could be relaid behind them, this amount of transportation for the wounded was found sufficient.... These [medical] officers were directed to send their sick to New Bern by railroad, and, in case of battle, to keep their temporary hospitals as near the line of railroad as possible....

In New Bern, preparations were made for a large increase of patients, and by extending the hospital accommodations mainly near the railroad, we were enabled, notwithstanding our deficient ambulance force, to transfer the sick and wounded rapidly from the front to our wards.

Dr. Spencer G. Welch married Cordelia Strother on February 13, 1861, at her family's plantation, "Fruit Hill," in Edgefield (now Saluda) County, S.C. Their first child, George Strother Welch, died at the age of two on December 7, 1863.

Welch's wife, Cordelia, came to Petersburg, Va., to stay with her husband, arriving on December 7, 1864. After her arrival, she wrote several letters to her sister, Georgia Strother, who was still at "Fruit Hill." Cordelia was a keen observer of her surroundings.

Welch, Cordelia S., Petersburg, Va., to Georgia Strother, "Fruit Hill," S.C.:

Your letter received yesterday shows that you have missed all the letters I have written you from here, so I'll begin at the very beginning.

Mrs. Hunt and I reached here on the night of Dec. 7, our trip via Columbia, Chester, and Danville being comparatively comfortable and uneventful except for having to sit up all night at Danville. Gen. Scales and his wife were with us there and we were indeed glad of this. Altho' we had telegraphed to our husbands several times on the way, the telegrams failed to reach them, so nobody met us. Gen Scales took us to the hotel for the night. Next morning Dr. W. and Col. Hunt came for us in an ambulance and took us across the Appomattox River to a Mr. Hamilton's where they had engaged rooms for us. Here we have been very comfortable. I have a very good servant. Army rations are issued to us; then we can buy chickens, eggs and vegetables.

The weather has been continuously cold—very—all the winter, tho' we have had only one heavy snow. Over here we have good wood in abundance, and keep roaring fires all the time. I wish our soldiers on the lines were as fortunate. Wood is scarce there and then only green pine, for which they have to go some distance into the country.

You ask how we spend our time. Well, it is surprising how rapidly it has passed. I cannot realize that I have been here nearly three months. Very pleasant people are here in the house. Dr. Huot and wife of Charleston; Maj. Brailesford and wife of Sumter; and Capt. Arnold and his wife, from Warrenton, Ga.

Dr. Huot is a Frenchman, having been brought over from France when a boy by Dr. Fair, and lived with the Dr. in Columbia.

One day we spent pleasantly with the Hunts, who are at the boardinghouse right near the lines. We crossed the river on a pontoon bridge and went the rest of the way in an ambulance.

Another day, the Huots, Hunts, and we went to the lines to visit Col. Newton Brown of Anderson. We had a fine dinner in his tent. From the door of the tent could be distinctly seen the Yankees constructing a tower along their lines to enable them to see over into ours. Apparently it was only about a mile away.

Last Sunday we attended service at an Episcopal Church in Petersburg, where we saw Gen. Lee and his staff march in. Col. Marshall was the only one we knew. Gens. Longstreet, A. P. Hill, and Wilcox sat not far from us. Gen. Lee's face bespeaks the character of the man. He seemed to all appearances oblivious of everything except the sermon and the service.

Yesterday we spent the day with Edwin, who as you doubtless know, is Sergeant in Capt. Petty's Pioneer Corps. We ate dinner in his tent and a pretty good one it was too—not a great variety but plentiful and nicely prepared—tender beef in abundance, delicious tomatoes and bread made from home-ground meal. The crowning piece, however, was an apple roll that Edwin unrolled steaming hot from a towel—the best substitute he had! Nevertheless, the roll was good.

Very often friends from S.C. and others too, come over to the Hamiltons' to spend the evening with us. Dr. Bailey, Chaplain Wallace Duncan, Gen. McGowan and Capt. Petty are among our frequent visitors. Edwin, Billie Welch, and Robert Land come too, right often. As the weather is beginning to be more pleasant, Edwin is urging me to make my plans for leaving. He seems uneasy for fear, that if I continue here much longer, fighting may begin in earnest and then [I] can't get away.

You know I brought a quantity of woolen yarns from home. I wish I had kept an account of the numbers of pairs of sox I have knit for the soldiers. Then, too, I have done lots of patching and mending for them. It takes a good deal of work and planning to keep our own clothes presentable.

Mrs. Huot's father, who is a blockade runner, sent her recently two of the most exquisite silk dress patterns I ever saw. She offered to sell the prettier one to any of us for $300, but nobody was able to buy it. She took it over to Petersburg and exchanged it for a much-needed suit of clothes for her husband.

You ask if I had heard a battle. Only once since I came has there been one, and 'tho Gen. Lee said of it: "Our loss was small; that of the enemy not great," nevertheless several were killed on our side, one of them being Pegram of Virginia. His young bride who was in Petersburg, knowing that he was in the neighborhood of the firing, went out when it ceased, to meet him, as she supposed, flushed with success. Instead she met his dead body being borne back.

I shall see Mrs. Hunt in a few days and will then write you when to expect me.

March 8 (Wednesday)

At New Bern, N.C., Gen. Jacob D. Cox, commanding the Union buildup, was attacked by elements of Braxton Bragg's Confederates from Wilmington, near Kinston, N.C. During the attack, some of the Federal troops broke, but the remainder held and fought off Bragg's force. The Confederates weren't really strong enough to sustain the attack.

March 9 (Thursday)

Again today, Bragg's Confederates attacked the Union forces near Kinston, N.C., with no more success than they'd had the day before.

March 10 (Friday)

Bragg, at Kinston, finding that he couldn't dislodge Cox, broke off the engagement and left for Goldsboro to join Confederate Gen. Joseph E. Johnston's force, which was getting ready to deal with Sherman.

Hand, D. W., Surg., USV, Med. Dir., New Bern, N.C.:

On the 8th, 9th and 10th of March, the enemy, under Gen. Hoke, attacked our forces near Kinston, N.C., but was driven back each day. They captured, however, seven hundred of our men, and killed and wounded about three hundred. The wounded were promptly removed from the field, and all of them conveyed to New Bern within from twelve to thirty-six hours after the action. The more serious cases were, as fast as they became able to travel, transferred by hospital steamer to the north.... Gen. Schofield, who arrived at the front on March 8th, assumed command of the whole force.

Sherman's army approached Fayetteville, N.C., in rain and on muddy roads. Movement was very slow. The soil was very sandy and made necessary the corduroying of the roads to get the wagons over them. Quite often the logs used for the corduroying would sink after one or two wagons passed. If wagons strayed off the roads, they would sink to their beds with little hope of getting out.

March 11 (Saturday)

Sherman's armies nearly surrounded the town of Fayetteville, N.C., waiting to go in. Scouts sent in were met with firing from Confederate cavalry, which was soon dispersed, the cavalry leaving town by the bridges over the Cape Fear River. The old U.S. Arsenal at Fayetteville, destination of the rifle-making machinery removed from Harpers Ferry in 1861 by Thomas J. Jackson, was occupied and would be destroyed. Sherman's messengers to Schofield had reached Wilmington, and Union boats were on their way upriver to Fayetteville.

Pres. Lincoln appointed Miss Clara Barton to the position she'd requested on February 3rd, that of establishing correspondence with the friends and families of the prisoners who'd died during captivity. This work would consume her (small) personal fortune, because she initially undertook to pay for the operations herself. Congress then arranged for her to have her list of prisoners printed at the Government Printing Office, and to have the list mailed using one of the Congressmen's franking privileges.

March 12 (Sunday)

Sherman's men fell to with a will to destroy the arsenal and other military facilities in the city of Fayetteville, N.C., a town of about 3000 inhabitants. A Confederate steamer had been captured below the city on the Cape Fear River, and this would be loaded with Negroes and refugees, and then sent to Wilmington.

March 13 (Monday)

At Fayetteville, the destruction went on, Sherman's men tearing the place apart while waiting for supplies to come up from Wilmington. A steamer and two gunboats arrived at the city from Wilmington carrying an officer of Gen. Terry's staff who was critical of Sherman's method of operations—but not of Sherman.

March 14 (Tuesday)

Sherman's armies at Fayetteville were cleansing the army of sick animals, replacing them with captured stock. The sick and wounded men were being sent to Wilmington by steamer to be sent North to the hospitals. The remainder of the Negroes and refugees were being sent to Wilmington, under escort, to further lighten the load. Some supplies had come up, mostly sugar, coffee, and several thousand pairs of shoes—still not enough to fill the armies' needs. There was a desperate shortage of uniforms; some men were in rags.

Moore, John, Surg., USA, Med. Dir., Sherman's Army, en route through the Carolinas:

A halt ... was made at Fayetteville, during which about three hundred sick and a few wounded were sent on river transports to Wilmington....

March 17 (Friday)

At Mobile, Ala., Maj. Gen. E. R. S. Canby began moving his 32,000 Union troops against Mobile's defenses. One force moved up from Pensacola, the other moved from Mobile Point and up the east side of the bay. Brig. Gen. R. L. Gibson had only 2800 Confederates to defend the city, although these troops were in some strong forts.

Smart, C., Asst. Surg., USA, Med. Inspector, 2nd Corps, Patrick's Station, Va.:

... a telegram from the medical director of the army ordered the immediate removal of all those unable to accompany the command on a march, to the depot hospital at City Point, and it was further ordered that in future the hospitals should be kept in as mobile a condition as possible. In accordance with these orders, on the 15th, 16th, and 17th of March, there were sent to the rear seven hundred and seventy-nine sick and seventy-one wounded. A large proportion of the sick were trivial cases, and many of them were returned to their regiments for duty in the course of a few days....

March 18 (Saturday)

At Mobile, Ala., a column of 1700 Federals left Dauphin Island and started up the west side of Mobile Bay as a diversion to draw off some of the Confederates in Mobile. The main thrust was to be on the east side of the bay.

March 20 (Monday)

Gen. E. R. S. Canby's Federal column from Pensacola departed for Mobile to add weight to the assault on Spanish Fort and the Confederate defenses.

Willis, P. A., Surg., Chief Med. Off., Union forces from Pensacola, Fla.:

The command, consisting of Brig. Gen. C. C. Andrew's division of the Thirteenth Corps, Brig. Gen. J. P. Hawkins's division of U.S. Colored

Troops, and Brig. Gen. Lucas's brigade of cavalry, numbering in all about twelve thousand men, moved from Pensacola, Fla., on the 20th of March, 1865. The command was in excellent sanitary condition, having left all the sick and disabled in hospital at Barrancas.... The command was supplied with the full amount of medical stores, hospital tents and ambulances allowed by the existing orders.

On the first day's march from Pensacola it began to rain and continued, almost without intermission, for forty-eight hours, rendering the roads almost impassable. The condition of the men during this long rainstorm was miserable in the extreme, as they were unable to dry their clothing during the time, and, owing to the flat condition of the ground, could not find a dry place to sleep or rest. But little sickness resulted from this exposure....

On the 20th, the whole command was put on one-fourth rations and large details were employed each day in laying corduroy bridges, while others assisted in extracting artillery and wagons from the mud. In many places the trains had to be moved entirely by the men, since it was utterly impossible for the animals to get through....

March 23 (Thursday)

Hand, D. W., Surg., USV, Med. Dir., New Bern, N.C.:

After resting the troops at Kinston six days, waiting for the rebuilding of the railroad bridge over the Neuse River, they were, on March 20th, put in motion for Goldsboro', which place was reached without opposition the next day. Maj. Gen. Terry, with a portion of the Tenth Corps from Wilmington, now joined Gen. Schofield and, on March 23d, Gen. Sherman arrived with his whole army.... Temporary hospitals were prepared by Surg. Shippen at Goldsboro', but all serious cases were transferred to New Bern; so, also, were the sixteen hundred wounded brought by Gen. Sherman from the battles of Averysboro' and Bentonville, N.C., and all the sick of his army.... Anticipating the demand for increased hospital accommodations as soon as Gen. Sherman should reach Goldsboro', I immediately reopened this hospital at Beaufort, and increased its capacity to six hundred beds. By this hospital and the Foster at New Bern, with a capacity of three thousand beds, we were now enabled to receive all the

sick and wounded from Goldsboro' until they could be shipped north by the three hospital steamers at that time ordered to Beaufort Harbor....

March 24 (Friday)

Canby, at Mobile, was advancing his positions for the assaults on the various forts defending the city, while Wilson's cavalry continued towards Selma, Ala., north of Mobile.

March 25 (Saturday)

At three o'clock this morning, a group of Confederates appeared at Ft. Stedman, a major Union bastion in the Petersburg siege lines, and announced themselves as deserters. An hour later, 4 A.M., Gen. Gordon threw his troops against the Union strongpoint and completely overwhelmed it, surprising the garrison along the line of entrenchments.... The Confederates swarmed over the defenses and some selected units headed for City Point. There was, however, not enough weight behind the attack, and it faltered, giving the Federals time to regroup and drive the Confederates back to their own lines, with the exception of Ft. Stedman, which the Confederates still held.

At about 7:30 A.M., a Union division was sent against Ft. Stedman, and the Confederates were routed back to their own lines. The Union line was whole again. Grant had lost about 1500 in casualties; Lee, about 4000, many more than he could spare. The line quieted again.

The expected assault at Mobile Bay got under way, with Gen. Canby coming up to Spanish Fort on the east side of the bay. Brig. Gen. R. L. Gibson's 2800 Confederates had little hope of holding against Canby's 32,000 Federals without some immediate help—and none was in sight.

Willis, P. A., Surg., Chief Med. Off., Union forces from Pensacola, Fla.:

On the 25th we reached the vicinity of Bluff Springs, where we found Brig. Gen. Clanton with a small force prepared to oppose our further progress. Brig. Gen. Lucas, commanding the cavalry forces, ordered the 2d Louisiana Cavalry to charge, which it did in fine style, killing several and capturing Gen. Clanton with one hundred and forty men. Gen. Clanton was wounded through the body and left with the other wounded of his command in a small house near the battlefield....

Smart, C., Asst. Surg., USA, Med. Inspector, 2nd Corps, Patrick's Station, Va.:

Very early on the morning of the 25th, the enemy assaulted Ft. Stedman on the right of the Petersburg front. They captured it, but were subsequently driven out of the work.... At nine o'clock A.M., the Second Corps moved out of the fortifications and advanced westward, in line of battle, for about a mile, when the works of the enemy were discovered, and a brigade of the 3d division was sent forward to charge the first line of rifle-pits. These ... [pits were captured], losing but very few men in the assault. The wounded were speedily conveyed to Patrick's Station, where a couple of tents were pitched to accommodate them.... After four o'clock,... the enemy, having massed in front of Miles's division, assaulted [the Union] line with great vigor. The fighting was sharp.... As usual during an engagement, all the medical officers but those attached to the division field hospital reported at the points where the stretcher-bearers of each brigade transferred the wounded to the ambulances, and rendered such aid to the wounded as was necessary before sending them to the rear.... Shortly after the termination of the engagement,... all the wounded [were] lodged at Patrick's Station, where the hospitals had been established. The surgeons in charge were instructed that their patients must be ready to be moved to City Point by ten o'clock the next morning....

March 26 (Sunday)

Sheridan's cavalry crossed the James and headed towards Grant's position at Petersburg. This provided Grant with about 15,000 aggressive cavalry, and with an even more aggressive commander. Lincoln was on hand to watch the long lines of blue cavalry cross the river and move on west. Sheridan remained at City Point to confer with Grant on further movements, and Lincoln reviewed the troops. Lee was getting ready to evacuate Petersburg and move west, hopefully, to join with Johnston in North Carolina.

At Mobile Bay, the Federals began their approach to Spanish Fort, provoking heavy skirmishing.

Smart, C., Asst. Surg., USA, Med. Inspector, 2nd Corps, Patrick's Station, Va.:

Cars reported at Patrick's Station at noon ... and by one o'clock P.M., all the wounded were on their way to City Point. All had been attended to, every operation deemed necessary performed, and every wound dressed before the departure of the train.... The troops retired from the line of captured rifle-pits to within the fortifications....

Lidell, J. A., Surg., USV, City Point, Va.:

On the 26th of March, the depot field hospital at City Point, which already had a capacity of five thousand nine hundred and thirty-five beds, was ordered to be enlarged one thousand beds....

March 27 (Monday)

The second major military unit involved in the siege of Richmond was the Army of the James, located at this time to the rear and slightly north of the Army of the Potomac. The Medical Director for the 24th Corps, which was part of the Army of the James, was Vol. Surg. J. B. Morrison. He related that corps' actions in the closing days of the war.

Morrison, J. B., Surg., USV, Med. Dir., 24th Corps, James River, Va.:

On the evening of the 27th of March, the 1st division,... crossed the James and Appomattox rivers during the night. The march was continued until the evening of the 28th, when we bivouacked in the rear of the Second Corps, south of Petersburg.... We started with twenty-five ambulances in each division....

March 28 (Tuesday)

McParlin, T. A., Surg., USA, Med. Dir., Army of the Potomac, near Petersburg, Va.:

The chief medical officer at City Point had been instructed, March 28th, to be prepared to expand his hospitals to the utmost capacity at short notice, to send off in hospital transports as many of the cases as were proper for general hospital, and, upon the contingency of a great battle, to telegraph to the Surgeon General for additional facilities for transportation.

Smart, C., Asst. Surg., USA, Med. Inspector, 2nd Corps, Patrick's Station, Va.:

... the command was again placed under marching orders. The sick and wounded, one hundred and forty-two in number, were sent to City Point, and the hospitals at Patrick's Station were in readiness to move after the troops. Special requisitions ... had replaced the supplies expended during the fight on the 25th.

Marsh, E. J., Surg., USA, Chief Med. Off., Hatcher's Run, Va.:

March 14th, orders were received to send all sick to City Point, which was done, and nearly all the hospital tents were taken down and packed, preparatory to a move. Two wards were left standing, to admit cases until the command actually moved.

March 28th, the remainder of the sick were sent off, and everything completely packed ready to move. On this day, the division was detached from the Army of the Potomac, and ordered to report to Maj. Gen. Sheridan.

Lidell, J. A., Surg., USV, City Point, Va.:

On the 28th, a medical purveyor's train of thirty-six wagons, loaded with extra battlefield supplies,... was brought up from City Point to the headquarters of the army.... Due attention had also been paid to the subject of transportation,... ambulances on hand, five hundred and twenty-five; army wagons, one hundred and fifty-four; medicine wagons, fifty-five; forges, sixteen; horses, one thousand six hundred and sixty-six; mules, nine hundred and ninety-four; stretchers, nine hundred and seventy-nine. The ambulance corps, at this time, consisted of forty-four officers and eighteen hundred and sixty-eight men.

At Petersburg, Va., the Appomattox campaign began with the movement of Grant's army to the southwest and Sheridan's large cavalry force towards Dinwiddie C.H. Lee, trying to defend more than 30 miles of entrenchments, was running out of men. The whole purpose of the Union movement was to force Lee out of his entrenchments and into the open, where he could be defeated by the larger Union force.

March 29 (Wednesday)

Smart, C., Asst. Surg., USA, Med. Inspector, 2nd Corps, Cumming's House, Va.:

At six o'clock on the morning of the 29th, the 2d division moved across Hatcher's Run on the Vaugh-an road, and was followed by the 3d and 1st.... In the order of march,... it was directed that one medicine wagon and one army wagon to each brigade, and one-half of the ambulances should accompany the troops, and that each train would follow in rear of its division, but as the road was narrow and a rapid movement into line of battle expected, this order was modified, the trains being directed to remain on the left back of Hatcher's Run until all the troops and artillery had crossed.

After the troops were formed into line of battle, half a dozen ambulances were sent forward to the immediate rear of each division, while the hospital organization remained at the Cummings' house, where it was intended the hospital should be established if a fight took place....

Late in the evening of the 29th, twenty of our ambulances were sent to the field hospital of the Fifth Corps to aid in conveying the wounded of that command to Humphrey's Station.

March 30 (Thursday)

Amid pouring rain, Sheridan got his troops, cavalry and infantry, organized for a push on the Confederate right flank. The rain, which turned the dirt roads to slop, delayed the advance. There was some skirmishing at Hatcher's Run and near Five Forks. Gen. Humphreys pushed his Second Corps up to the Rebel works at Hatcher's Run, while Warren's Fifth Corps moved on Gravelly Run. Lee's lines were getting weaker as he concentrated his forces southwest of Petersburg to protect the South Side Railroad.

Smart, C., Asst. Surg., USA, Med. Inspector, 2nd Corps, Cummings' House, Va.:

On the morning of the 30th, however, the advance of the troops rendered ... advance on the part of the trains necessary. They were moved over to the west side of the run [Hatcher's] and parked to await events.... About a hundred wounded cavalrymen, belonging to Gen. Sheridan's command, were admitted to the 2d division hospital, dressed, and then conveyed across the run for railroad transportation to City Point....

Morrison, J. B., Surg., USV, Med. Dir., 24th Corps, Patrick's Station, Va.:

On the morning of the 29th, we relieved the Second Corps, and established our headquarters at the point occupied by its headquarters. On the mornings of the 30th and 31st, the sick of the command were sent by railroad from Humphrey's Station to City Point, there to take the boat for the Point of Rocks hospital.... We had some fighting near Hatcher's Run. I established the field hospital of the corps on the Vaughan road, about a mile in rear of the troops. The wounded were received and cared for with promptness. They numbered one hundred and nine. Next morning they were sent on the cars to City Point....

In Alabama, the march against Mobile was "on hold" for a day while some of the Federal troops replenished their supply of cornmeal.

Willis, P. A., Surg., Chief Med. Off., Union forces from Pensacola, Fla.:

On the 30th we reached Stockton, where we found large quantities of corn and a gristmill and the command halted twenty-four hours in order that a supply of meal might be obtained....

March 31 (Friday)

As the rain ended southwest of Petersburg, Sheridan sent his large force of Union cavalry and infantry towards Dinwiddie C.H. on the Confederates' right flank. Lee had about 10,000 men against more than 50,000 Union men on the western lines. The Confederates initially drove Sheridan back, but not for long. At night, Pickett realized that Warren's Fifth Corps and Sheridan's mix of cavalry and infantry was too strong for him, so he withdrew to Five Forks. Humphreys' Second Corps repulsed an attack at Hatcher's Run and held without difficulty.

McParlin, T. A., Surg., USA, Med. Dir., Army of the Potomac, near Petersburg, Va.:

The wounded of the Second and Fifth Corps during the extension of our lines to the left, March 29th, 30th and 31st, numbered fifteen hundred and fifty-five; they were received on the field at Spain's house, Quaker church, the "Chimneys" and the division hospitals near the Cummings' house.

In the actions around Dinwiddie and Five Forks, the wounded of the cavalry and Fifth Corps, three hundred and eighty-two in number, were sent to the Methodist church field hospital April 1st, and

thence by ambulances and wagons in great part to Humphrey's Station, on the railroad; the remainder accompanied the Fifth Corps and were sent to Sutherland Station, on the South-side railroad, ten miles from Petersburg.

Smart, C., Asst. Surg., USA, Med. Inspector, 2nd Corps, Cummings' House, Va.:

Very early on the morning of the 31st,... the enemy was discovered in heavy force in front of the Fifth Corps.... The hospital of the 1st division was directed to move forward from the Vaughan road to a clearing about half a mile distant from the Dabney Mill road on the north, and the Quaker road on the west. At noon, immediately after the hospital train had reached this point, the 1st division became heavily engaged, and at two o'clock P.M., the 3d division participated to some extent. The wounded were brought off the field with great promptness. The hospital train of the 3d division was ordered, at midday, to move to some spot near the position occupied by the 1st, but it was midnight before it succeeded in reaching this point.

The Vaughan road and the wood roads were in a miserable condition on account of the heavy rains of the previous day, and, moreover, they were blocked up by ammunition and other heavy wagons, which had found them impassable, until roughly corduroyed. The wounded of the 3d division, however, did not suffer from the absence of these wagons. They were treated at the 1st division hospital by the medical officers of their own division until the arrival of the train.... The 2d division hospital remained at the Chimneys, as this position was still near enough to the part of the line held by the troops of that division.... In the afternoon ... the medical officers were instructed to have all operations performed and every case attended to and ready to be sent to the rear by the following daybreak. The reserve train of ambulances were sent for to carry the wounded to Warren's Station, where a train of cars was expected to be ready at nine o'clock on the morning of the 1st....

Lidell, J. A., Surg., USV, Hatcher's Run, Va.:

Late in the afternoon, Gen. Sheridan was heavily engaged with the enemy near Dinwiddie Courthouse. In the evening, it was reported that he had several hundred wounded for whom he had no transportation. Gen. Meade, therefore, ordered the Sixth

Corps ambulance train to proceed to Dinwiddie Courthouse and bring them in to Humphrey's Station. At the time, these ambulances were much needed to remove the wounded of the Fifth Corps from the Spain house to Humphrey's Station, since nearly all the ambulances of that corps had been ordered to proceed at once to the assistance of Gen. Sheridan's cavalry. In consequence, a considerable number of the wounded of the Fifth Corps had to be transported in army wagons, about six miles, over very rough roads, to Humphrey's Station.

April 1 (Saturday)

Today, Lee's right flank caved in under overwhelming numbers. Grant ordered an assault on the lines for the following morning and all night the artillery thundered in preparation. Ft. Sedgewick's heavy guns belched forth to sustain its knickname of "Ft. Hell." Lee withdrew from Petersburg during the night.

Smart, C., Asst. Surg., USA, Med. Inspector, 2nd Corps, Cummings' House, Va.:

It was not, however, until about ten o'clock on the morning of the 1st, that the ambulances succeeded in reaching the field hospitals. They had experienced much delay on account of the condition of the roads. By the time they arrived the wounded had all been properly cared for. [The ambulances] were immediately loaded up and sent to the railroad station.... The Fifth Corps moved off to the left toward Five Forks, while the Second extended toward the left to hold the portion of the line this left unguarded. No fighting took place during the day, but toward evening and during the succeeding night, heavy cannonading and occasional musketry fire was heard before Petersburg and near Five Forks....

Lidell, J. A., Surg., USV, Hatcher's Run, Va.:

Throughout the day nothing transpired along the line but a small amount of picket firing. At the field hospitals of the Second and Fifth Corps, the medical officers were busily occupied ... getting off the wounded ... to the depot hospital at City Point. In the morning the roads were still so muddy that the transportation of the wounded over them was slow and difficult, but during the day they dried rapidly. During the morning thirty cars loaded chiefly with wounded, but carrying also a few sick, left Humphrey's Station for City Point. At four o'clock P.M., a train of fifteen cars loaded in

the same manner was sent to the same destination. About six o'clock P.M., the ambulance train of the Sixth Corps, which had been sent to Dinwiddie Courthouse to bring in the wounded of the cavalry, arrived.... Before night all the wounded had been conveyed in ambulances or army wagons from our division hospitals to the station.

In Alabama, Canby's assault on Mobile and Blakely continued.

Willis, P. A., Surg., Chief Med. Off., near Mobile, Ala., with the Union forces from Pensacola, Fla.:

On the 1st of April we arrived in the vicinity of Blakely, having marched one hundred and twenty miles over the worst of roads; many estimating that thirty miles of corduroy bridge had been built.... Field hospitals were established in the rear of each division; the corps of operators reported promptly and everything was made ready to care for the wounded. The hospitals had to be moved several times on account of the shells from the Rebel gunboats reaching so far to the rear.... The ambulances were stationed in localities which were easy of access from the several regiments, and the wounded were promptly removed from the field to the ambulance stations on hand-litters. Gen. Hawkins's division suffered severely on the 1st, 2d, and 3d from shells thrown from the Rebel gunboats, but after these were driven off the daily list of casualties was small until the evening of April 9th....

April 2 (Sunday)

At 4:40 A.M., the Federals advanced through heavy fog against the Petersburg lines. Little resistance was met. In some cases, the Confederate battle line simply vanished. Along the Boydton Plank Road near Hatcher's Run, Lt. Gen. Ambrose Powell Hill, one of Lee's best generals, was killed. Lee notified Pres. Davis: "I think it is absolutely necessary that we should abandon our position tonight...." Lee ordered the evacuation of Petersburg and designated Amelia C.H., 40 miles west, as the concentration point for all units.

McParlin, T. A., Surg., USA, Med. Dir., Army of the Potomac, near Petersburg, Va.:

The number of wounded during the general assault upon the forts and works before Petersburg, April

2d, was nineteen hundred and seventy-two; they were received in the regular division hospitals of the Sixth and Ninth Corps. The wounded of Gen. Miles's division of the Second Corps, on the same day, numbered two hundred and seventy-two. They were received at Moody's house, near Five Forks.

Smart, C., Asst. Surg., USA, Med. Inspector, 2nd Corps, Five Forks, Va.:

At eight o'clock A.M., April 2d, an advance of part of the 3d division was ordered, with the effect of driving the enemy from his advanced works in the neighborhood of Burgess's Mills. This was followed,... by the evacuation of his main line of works. No sooner was this discovered than the Second Corps was started in pursuit.... The hospital of this division [3d] followed in the rear of the troops, and was established at a suitable point on the road [to the] rear of the line.... The ambulances and hospital train of the 1st division had followed the troops, carrying the wounded along as they picked them up, until the train being loaded, they were compelled to halt at Moody's house, where a field hospital was formed. During the afternoon and evening, all the wounded of the 1st division, two hundred and sixteen in number, were carried to this place. Fifty-nine were received into the hospital of the 3d division, and eight into that of the 2d division....

Morrison, J. B., Surg., USV, Med. Dir., 24th Corps, Ft. Gregg, Petersburg, Va.:

On the morning of 2d of April, we attacked the enemy's lines and carried them, continuing our march until we reached Ft. Gregg, near Petersburg, which we captured with a loss of five hundred and ninety killed and wounded. Early the same morning, I had ordered the hospital on the Vaughan road to follow the troops, and the ambulances left on the north side of the James river, when we commenced our march, had arrived, making, in all, seventy-six ambulances with our two divisions. I established the hospital about half a mile from Ft. Gregg. All the wounded were well cared for, and sent to Warren's Station in ambulances, to take the cars for City Point, and from thence by boat to Point of Rocks. About one hundred and fifty were sent on the night of the 2d, and all the others on the following day. The wounded were well cared for and the dead properly interred.

Hand, D. W., Surg., USV, Med. Dir., Goldsboro, N.C.:

I ... hastened immediately after the occupation of Goldsboro'.... I arrived there on April 2d, and found Surg. George C. Jarvis, 7th Connecticut Volunteers, acting as chief medical officer. Surg. Jarvis was working hard, and, with the medical officers under him, doing all he could for the sick; but there was a sad want of system, and owing to the death of several prominent medical officers, and the sickness of most of the others, the records of the hospitals were in a very confused and unsatisfactory condition.

At that time there were in Wilmington fourteen district hospitals, with an aggregate of twenty-three hundred patients. Some of these patients were exchanged prisoners, but most of them were recruits and other soldiers taken sick on their way to join Gen. Sherman's army, and colored soldiers sent to the rear by Gen. Terry while on his march to Goldsboro'. The sick were in dwelling-houses, railroad depots, and other unsuitable places, and the mortality among them had been very great, although at this time greatly reduced. Of eighty-six hundred exchanged prisoners received at northeast North Carolina on February 25th and 26th, thirty-six hundred were so ill as to require immediate hospital treatment, and to be unable to travel on common transports. These men were first placed in the temporary hospitals to which I referred, where an epidemic fever broke out, carrying away many of them, and extending not only to the troops stationed there, but to the citizens in all parts of the town.... At the time of my visit, April 2d, that fever still prevailed in Wilmington, and the city being very filthy, it was thought best to remove all the men in hospital from this place as soon as possible.

The two regiments doing duty there had already been encamped outside the town. With that view, arrangements were at once made to open a general hospital of a thousand beds at Smithville, on the Cape Fear River, twenty-three miles below Wilmington. The hospital steamer *Gen. Barnes* arrived at that time, and we took on board the remainder of the exchanged prisoners. Most of the small hospitals were closed, and two large churches were seized and prepared for use as hospitals until such time as the balance of the white sick could be moved. The colored soldiers were all removed to a hospital just outside the town.... Not many patients were after this sent to Wilmington, and by May 1st the hospitals were nearly empty, and the city quite healthy....

April 3 (Monday)

McParlin, T. A., Surg., USA, Med. Dir., Army of the Potomac, near Petersburg, Va.:

The Rebel wounded found in Petersburg April 3d, were allowed to remain in the Confederate general hospital under charge of their own surgeons, and generally throughout the campaign they were moved as little as possible until they were able to be paroled and sent home.

Smart, C., Asst. Surg., USA, Med. Inspector, 2nd Corps, Five Forks, Va.:

Early on the morning of the 3d, part of the reserve ambulances having returned from Warren's Station, a train was formed to carry the wounded to Petersburg for railroad transportation to City Point. About the same time, the 3d division joined the main body of the Corps at Well's Church, and the whole command, followed by the hospital wagons and the few ambulances which could be spared, moved westward along the Namozine road. The corps camped for the night near Namozine church.

Morrison, J. B., Surg., USV, Med. Dir., 24th Corps, Sutherland Station, Va.:

On the morning of the 3d, the troops moved for Sutherland Station, where they arrived in the evening, and bivouacked for the night. Here I found eight wounded Rebels in a car. I had them cared for and sent to Petersburg in ambulances next morning.

April 4 (Tuesday)

Lee retreated towards Amelia C.H. with Sheridan in hot pursuit. Sheridan's cavalry occupied Jetersville on the Danville Railroad, south and west of Amelia C.H., thereby blocking the use of the railroad by the Confederates.

Smart, C., Asst. Surg., USA, Med. Inspector, 2nd Corps, Deep Run, Va.:

... the march was resumed, but before proceeding far, the cavalry divisions with their trains, blocked up the road in front and impeded our progress. The corps encamped at Deep Run.

Lidell, J. A., Surg., USV, Hatcher's Run, Va.:

... the weather continued pleasant. The Second and Sixth Corps moved at dawn, marching up the river road in a westerly direction. The Ninth Corps was left behind at Petersburg, and the Fifth was still with Gen. Sheridan. The medical director of the Sixth Corps reported that the ambulance horses of that corps were much jaded from overwork.... The day's march was long, and over almost impassable roads.

Morrison, J. B., Surg., USV, Med. Dir., 24th Corps, Wilson's Station, Va.:

We moved at half past eight o'clock A.M., on the 4th, and advanced on the Cox road toward Wilson's Station, where we halted for the night. On the march I found nearly forty wounded Rebels and four of our own wounded who had been left by the Rebels in buildings on the roadside. There were two Rebel medical officers with them. I left them several days' supplies of food, medicines, dressings, etc.

April 5 (Wednesday)

Lee and the Army of Northern Virginia arrived at Amelia C.H. to find that the expected supplies weren't there. Sheridan's cavalry was to Lee's front at Jetersville. The Danville Railroad to Farmville wasn't usable to bring supplies to Lee from Lynchburg. Sheridan, restrained by Meade, waited.

Smart, C., Asst. Surg., USA, Med. Inspector, 2nd Corps, Jetersville, Va.:

At midnight, we were again on the move, and again the cavalry and trains interfered with the advance. By eight o'clock A.M., the road was clear and the corps pushed on to Jetersville, which was reached in early afternoon....

Morrison, J. B., Surg., USV, Med. Dir., 24th Corps, Burkesville Junction, Va.:

At Wilson's Station on the morning of the 5th, we left some sick under the care of Surg. Ainsworth, USV. Two ambulances and supplies were left with them. At Burkesville Junction we found a Rebel hospital containing some thirty or forty sick and wounded Rebels, under the care of two Rebel medical officers. Here we established our corps field hospital.

April 6 (Thursday)

Lt. Gen. Richard S. Ewell's entire Confederate corps was captured today at the Battle of Sayler's Creek—the last battle between the fabled Army of Northern Virginia and the Army of the Potomac. The last to surrender was the naval brigade from Drewry's Bluff, commanded by Commodore John R. Tucker, CSN, who gave his sword in surrender to Brevet Brig. Gen. J. Warren Keifer, USV. Years later, Keifer returned the sword to Tucker.

Smart, C., Asst. Surg., USA, Med. Inspector, 2nd Corps, Sayler's Creek, Va.:

On the morning of the 6th, these works were abandoned, and an advance toward Amelia Courthouse was commenced, in progress of which, near the Sulphur Springs, the rear of the enemy's column was found. This changed the direction and manner of the march. A line of battle was formed, and the enemy was pursued through Deatonsville, towards High Bridge on the Appomattox. Skirmishing with their rear was kept up till eight o'clock P.M., when the corps bivouacked on Sayler's Creek, where a large portion of the Rebel wagon and ambulance train had been captured. The hospital of the 1st division was established early in the day at Amelia Springs, those of the 2d and 3d divisions at the Vaughan house, about a mile from this. Sixty wounded were collected at the hospital of the 1st division, and one hundred and seventy at that of the 3d division.... Of these, a dozen belonged to the cavalry, and twenty-five were Rebels.... In the evening, all the ambulances that could be spared from the advance reported at the hospitals, to carry as many of the wounded as possible to Burke's Station, where a depot hospital had been formed....

Morrison, J. B., Surg., USV, Med. Dir., 24th Corps, Rice's Station, Va.:

On the 6th, the corps moved toward Farmville to meet the retreating Rebel army and check its progress, which was successfully done in the afternoon, about seven miles from Burkesville Junction near Rice's Station. Part of the hospital was left at Burkesville, with several medical officers and a good quantity of supplies, while the other portion accompanied the troops, and was established at a farmhouse near the battleground ... receiving and caring for fifty wounded, who were properly attended to and sent back to Burkesville in ambulances during the night.

April 7 (Friday)

At Farmville, Va., against Federal resistance, the Confederates crossed the Appomattox River and continued their retreat west on the river's north bank. Having obtained rations at Farmville, Lee's troops were in better shape, although they'd been delayed. Lincoln told Grant, "Gen. Sheridan says, 'If the thing is pressed I think Lee will surrender.' Let the *thing* be pressed."

McParlin, T. A., Surg., USA, Med. Dir., Army of the Potomac, near Petersburg, Va.:

Several days elapsed before the railroad from City Point was available beyond Petersburg, and it was necessary to repair and change the gauge of the railroad from Petersburg toward Danville, April 7th. When it was completed as far as Wilson's Station, the sub-depot hospital was moved to that point and received several hundred wounded, chiefly from the cavalry of Gen. Sheridan. The wounded from the operations around Jetersville, Amelia Springs, Sayler's Creek, High Bridge, Farmville and beyond were sent from those places and from the Brooks and Vaughan houses and Appomattox C.H. to Burke's Station, after April 6th.... The medical purveyor's train was at Burke's Station and ready to supply whatever was required at the depot or at the front. For this last purpose it passed on to Farmville on the 9th of April.

Smart, C., Asst. Surg., USA, Med. Inspector, 2nd Corps, Farmville, Va.:

On the following morning, the rear of the enemy was again struck at High Bridge, and skirmishing recommenced, continuing, with more or less activity, until about nine o'clock P.M., when the corps bivouacked near Farmville, on the right of the army.... During the early part of this day's running fight, no hospitals were established, but the wounded were carried along after the advance until near Farmville, where the enemy made a determined stand. On this field hospitals were established [at the Brock's house], about a mile-and-a-half ... [to the] rear of the line of battle. The cases received numbered as follows: 1st division, one hundred and fifty; 2d division, twenty-four; 3d division, thirty-five.... These were operated on during the night....

Morrison, J. B., Surg., USV, Med. Dir., 24th Corps, Farmville, Va.:

On the 7th, we moved for Farmville. At the Watson farmhouse, about three miles east of Farmville, we found about thirty of our own wounded and twenty-five Rebels, who had been wounded the day before in the fight near High Bridge. I left medical officers and supplies with them. They were soon afterward sent to Burkesville. We arrived at Farmville on the afternoon of the 7th. Here we found a large Rebel hospital containing about one thousand patients, with plenty of medical officers and a fair supply of provisions and medicines.

Lidell, J. A., Surg., USV, Burke's Station, Va.:

On the morning of April 7th,... I proceeded to Burke's Station for the purpose of assisting in the arrangements for the reception and care of the sick and wounded at that place until the railroad to Petersburg could be put in running order.... Having reached Burke's Station about noon, I found ... that the hospitals of the 2d and 3d divisions of the Ninth Corps were on their way, and would arrive in the afternoon, together with the ambulance trains of those divisions. I also learned that the railroad was only open as far as Wilson's Station, twenty-seven miles distant, and that several days must elapse before the cars could get up to Burke's Station.... It was also known that several hundred wounded were already on their way.... The hotel buildings at Burke's Station had been in use for a considerable time as a Rebel hospital, and were already filled to overflowing with Rebels who were unable to be moved when their forces retreated.... All the vacant warehouse rooms at the railroad depot were also taken possession of, and made ready.... In the evening, about seven hundred and fifty wounded from the Second and Sixth Corps arrived, and were promptly cared for.

April 8 (Saturday)

In Virginia, the road to Lynchburg, passing through Appomattox C.H., was filled with Lee's legions. Close behind was Meade's Army of the Potomac and the relentless Grant. Sheridan was to the south and in front of Lee, between Lee and Lynchburg. Lee refused a general engagement with Meade regardless of the unremitting skirmishing between the two armies. Sheridan had seized the supplies and the trains at Appomattox intended for Lee. Grant, at Farmville, had received a letter from Lee on the previous day. Grant replied, "Peace being my great desire, there is but one condition I would insist upon, namely that the men and officers surrendered shall be disqualified from taking up arms again against the Government of the United States until properly exchanged." Lee answered later in the afternoon: "I did not intend to propose the surrender of the Army of Northern Virginia, but to ask the terms of your proposition." Lee was still indicating a willingness to talk to Grant.

Smart, C., Asst. Surg., USA, Med. Inspector, 2nd Corps, New Store, Va.:

... in the morning, [the wounded were] dispatched to the depot at Burkesville, in a train consisting of ambulances belonging to the Ninth Corps, some of which had been captured from the Rebels, and a few of those belonging to this command.

In the meantime, the enemy having evacuated his Farmville defenses, the troops were advancing in pursuit through Buckingham County, but they did not overtake the enemy so as to engage him. At midnight they bivouacked about a mile west of New Store....

Lidell, J. A., Surg., USV, Burke's Station, Va.:

... the warehouses at the depot, and the hospitals of the Ninth Corps,... were capable of sheltering sixteen hundred wounded, and this was entirely independent of the Rebel hospital ... and the dwelling houses in the neighborhood used by the cavalry for their wounded. Capt. J. H. Alley, hospital commissary of the Ninth Corps, sent out a foraging train today, under suitable escort, to obtain subsistence for the sick and wounded. It brought in three wagon loads of provisions, consisting of flour, meal, potatoes, hams and bacon. Capt. Alley also sent to City Point for enough sugar, coffee and candles to last four thousand men eight days.... He also began to repair the large oven of the hotel,... and, placing a safeguard upon a neighboring gristmill, he set it to grinding flour and meal.... Foraging wagons were also sent out for straw.... During the day and evening, about five hundred and fifty wounded and sick arrived.

April 9 (Sunday)

Gens. Lee and Grant met at Appomattox C.H. for the purpose of the surrender of the Army of Northern Virginia. After the surrender in the McLean house, Lee returned to his disheartened troops and Grant notified Washington of his actions. Lincoln, returning to Washington from City Point, learned of the surrender that evening when he landed at Washington.

Smart, C., Asst. Surg., USA, Med. Inspector, 2nd Corps, New Store, Va.:

After settling in camp for the night, commissary stores were issued, and in the morning, the empty wagons were started for the Vaughan house to carry the wounded left there on the afternoon of the 6th by the 3d division, to Burke's Station. But, as was afterward ascertained, these wagons were not required, some ambulances belonging to the Ninth Corps having already transported the wounded from that point to the depot.

On the 9th, no fighting took place on account of the negotiations then in progress between the commanders of the two armies, which terminated on the afternoon of that day in the surrender of the enemy. According to the regimental reports, the casualties during the month were ... seven hundred and ninety-eight....

Morrison, J. B., Surg., USV, Med. Dir., 24th Corps, Appomattox, Va.:

On the 8th, we marched thirty-three miles. On the morning of the 9th, we encountered the retreating enemy on the Lynchburg road, about one mile west of the Appomattox Courthouse. On the same day the Rebel army surrendered. The field hospitals of the corps were then established at Appomattox Station. When the cavalry of Gen. Sheridan were ordered away, their wounded, eighty or ninety in number, were left in my charge. I furnished medical care, food, etc., and had them sent in ambulances to the railroad station, and placed on the cars with our own wounded and a number of wounded Rebels. At Farmville, wagons met them and conveyed them to Burkesville. Those who could not

endure wagon transportation were left at the Rebel hospital at Farmville.

In Beaufort, N.C., Mother Mary Ann Bickerdyke was busily attending the wounded when the church bells began to ring in a wild cacophony. Word had been received that Lee had surrendered and that the war, for all practical purposes, was ended. Bickerdyke was too busy to take the time to celebrate.

Willis, P. A., Surg., Chief Med. Off., near Mobile, Ala., with Union forces from Pensacola, Fla.:

... the evening of April 9th,... the works were carried by assault, and hundreds of wounded were carried to the hospital. Finding the hospital accommodations in Gen. Andrew's division inadequate, I had the wounded removed to the house of Mr. O. Sibley where there was plenty of shelter and excellent water in abundance. By ten o'clock P.M., all the wounded had been removed from the field and before morning every man had received attention.... The supplies of food, water, stimulants, and medical stores were abundant.... The wounded were removed to the steamship *St. Mary* at the landing below Spanish Fort and shipped ... to the general hospitals in New Orleans. Most of the wounded ... were shipped on the 12th, and the remainder ... on the 13th of April.

April 10 (Monday)

At Appomattox C.H. the Union forces, working with their Confederate counterparts, began preparing the lists of troops for parole.

Lidell, J. A., Surg., USV, Burke's Station, Va.:

Sunday, April 9th, Capt. Alley again foraged successfully for provisions and straw. About two hundred and sixty wounded and sick were brought in.

Monday, April 10th, the bakery began to turn out soft bread of first-rate quality, working at the rate of two thousand rations per diem. Provisions and straw were again obtained by foraging.... In the evening, the Ninth Corps ambulances returned from the front, bringing about two hundred sick and wounded. One hundred and fifty hospital tent-flies had arrived in wagons from Wilson's Station, so that we now felt easy on the subject of shelter....

Reed, Wm. H., Union Nurse, Burke's Station, Va.:

The surgeons with whom I started from City Point established their hospital at Wilson's Station,... instead of at the front, where they were ordered to go. They had ample hospital equipage, medical stores and commissary supplies in abundance, with but half a dozen patients ... while a few miles beyond were thousands who were suffering for the very stores and attention they were sent to supply....

Leaving my companions, I pushed on alone to Burkesville with a few private stores, and found wagon and ambulance trains arriving at the Junction filled with these maimed and bleeding men. They came creeping slowly over the hills, as if to soften the agonies of such transportation. Every shed and building was filled at once. The men were laid upon the ground under the shelter of brush, in freight depots, in the open air, under extemporized roofs of rubber blankets, the mud up to one's knees, and the moving from point to point almost an impossibility. There were but few surgeons, and these were overworked at the operating tables, while three thousand men were lying in this squalid suffering.

In two or three open sheds and in one railroad building were six hundred men without even straw for bedding, and no blankets to protect them from the rain which soaked through these long wards of misery.... Several were dying; and upon the spot my brandy flask was soon in use, restoring two or three sufficiently to get from them their names, and to write some last message to their friends.... Men were sitting up bathing their own wounds, when they could get the water, or were helping each other, while there were moanings and cries for help, to all of which it was impossible to respond....

In one shed were two hundred Rebel wounded. A surgeon of their own sat there and smoked his pipe, never showing sympathy enough to dress a single wound, so far as I could see, while our own soldiers acted as nurses, treating them as tenderly as they could....

Hand, D. W., Surg., USV, Med. Dir., New Bern, N.C.:

On April 10th, Gen. Sherman's whole army marched against Gen. Johnston,... sending to New Bern all the accumulated sick of the two weeks of rest....

April 11 (Tuesday)

Lidell, J. A., Surg., USV, Burke's Station, Va.:

There were about two thousand two hundred sick and wounded at Burke's Station, of whom about one thousand six hundred belong to the Army of the Potomac, about two hundred and twenty to the Army of the James, about one hundred and eighty to the Cavalry Corps, and about two hundred were prisoners of war....

The railroad cars came up ... for the first time, and preparations were immediately made to load them with wounded on their return to City Point. In this way about one thousand four hundred and fifty sick and wounded were sent to City Point. The last train started at five o'clock P.M. The cars for the wounded were well bedded with straw. Two days' rations were provided for the patients, with two attendants to each car, and medical officers to accompany them to City Point....

Between the army surgeon and a volunteer nurse who was present at the time, there seemed to be some differences in the description of how the trains were handled.

Reed, Wm. H., Union Nurse, Burkesville, Va.:

... the railroad was opened, and it was taxed to its utmost in transferring the wounded to City Point. There were long trains of twenty freight cars, as closely packed inside as the men could lie, and covering every foot of space upon the top, with no blankets or straw for a wounded limb or an amputated stump.

In this train was work for fifty pairs of hands. Their wounds were throbbing with fever, and needed the cooling of only [a] sponge full of water. There were one thousand men; they had been placed in the cars in the early afternoon, and were to have been started before dark. Many would not live to reach City Point, and their last hours in this jolting train would necessarily be hours of keenest suffering. With cold springwater I went through each car, bathing their heated stumps. It was dark, and there were no signs of starting. For hours they had been lying in this state neglected,... It was heartrending to pass from car to car and see their condition, to hear their cries for even a cup of water to moisten their lips, or a drop to wet their fevered wounds, and to see their silent appeal by the holding up of undressed limbs. The surgeon in charge of the train for whom these thousand were waiting and suffering, was found at midnight in a comfortable room half a mile off, enjoying a cigar and a game of euchre. He was reported to the Medical Director. Even this faithless surgeon would have been melted had he seen their gratitude as the sponge was squeezed, and the cold water flowed smoothly over the stiffened, clotted bandages, softening them, and reaching the wound, which was soothed and refreshed by the application....

The men were hungry, and had had nothing since their early dinner twelve hours before. I went up to our tent, built fires, had large "containers" of beef tea prepared, and gave a little to each, also filling canteens, and supplying other needs of the moment....

April 12 (Wednesday)

Lidell, J. A., Surg., USV, Burke's Station, Va.:

... sent to City Point at noon, by railroad, about six hundred sick and wounded, the trains being provided in the same manner as those sent on the 11th. This evacuated Burke's Station of all the sick and wounded, except about one hundred and fifty Rebels, who would also have been taken if there had been enough transportation. During the latter part of the day the ambulances of Cavalry Corps arrived.... They brought ... about two hundred and fifty sick and wounded, most of whom were Rebels....

Reed, Wm. H., Union Nurse, Burke's Station, Va.:

At two o'clock in the morning the train started with its living freight of shattered, suffering men. This was hardly over before a long train of army wagons of wounded, just from the field, reached the camp. Basins, sponges, bandages, lint, and plaster were again in requisition, and making a heavy draught upon the medical wagons. Candles gave out, we were left in the dark. We had to do the best we could, the men lying on the ground covered only by tent flies, which hardly shed the rain; and so we worked until morning, dressing and feeding men who for five days had been without care or nourishment....

April 13 (Thursday)

Morrison, J. B., Surg., USV, Med. Dir., 24th Corps, Appomattox, Va.:

I sent a large train of ambulances to Burkesville, conveying the Rebel wounded and some sixty of our own wounded. Many of the ambulances in this train had been turned over to us by the Rebels.

Lidell, J. A., Surg., USV, Burke's Station, Va.:

... four hundred and fifty sick and wounded were sent to City Point. A majority of them were Rebels. This relieved us of all sick and wounded then on hand who could safely be transported.... Up to this time about twenty-five hundred sick and wounded had been sent to City Point by railroad. Of this number it was estimated that about two thousand were wounded....

April 14 (Friday)

In Beaufort, N.C., the bells rang again. This time it was a mournful tolling for the assassination of Pres. Lincoln, who'd been shot at Ford's Theater in Washington. Mrs. Bickerdyke took time to attend a memorial service at the hospital chapel and then returned to the wards and the wounded.

Bickerdyke had her hands doubly full with the wounded and convalescent soldiers in the hospital. With the end of the war, the men almost well enough to return to the line were now looking to go home rather than back to war. Their insistent clamor for release only added to the confusion. Bickerdyke, in cooperation with the hospital authorities, began the process of clearing the hospital.

Smart, C., Asst. Surg., USA, Med. Inspector, 2nd Corps, Burkesville, Va.:

On the 11th, as the troops were under orders to move to Burkesville, the few severe cases of sickness in the command were placed in ambulances and sent on ahead, that they might avoid the fatigues and delays incident to transportation in the rear of their commands.

On the morning of the 12th, the march was commenced, and on the afternoon of the 14th, the corps went into camp in the angle formed by the Lynchburg road and that leading to Danville.... The march to this place was very fatiguing. The delays experienced on account of the bad character of the roads, the labor required to improve them, and the exposure to the rain which fell almost unremittingly during the march, had considerable influence in inducing the increased sickness in the command, which showed itself immediately after settling in camp.

The men encamped under shelter tents which they raised from the ground on uprights about a foot and a half high. The bunk or bed place in each was likewise raised. Those regiments which encamped in the open ground where there was no shade, built arbors over their quarters for protection from the heat.... The division field hospitals were established on good sites in the vicinity of their commands....

April 15 (Saturday)

Having returned to City Point from Burke's Station aboard one of the trains, Nurse Wm. Reed took a day to visit the city of Petersburg. Here he found a city largely deserted, but not destroyed. It was a welcome interlude after his trip to the horrors of Burke's Station.

Reed, Wm. H., Union Nurse, hospital, City Point, Va.:

At this point, Mr. J. W. Paige, Jr., of Boston, was in charge of the Sanitary Commission. In his tent under the magnificent pines,... which gave shade to the Fair Grounds Hospital, I found him engrossed in the most laborious duties of administration.... The relations between the Medical Dept. and the Sanitary Commission were harmonized by a quick perception and no little diplomatic skill, which resulted in making both more effective than either would have been alone.... To avoid the dangers of a dreadful infection, the gangrene ward was established in an icehouse, apart from the main hospital. Here, where the most loathsome and hopeless cases were awaiting death, where was every type of this horrible disease, was the scene of many of his most touching ministries. Here were limbs which could only be cleansed, not dressed; amputations where the flaps had been eaten away, and the flesh was ragged and fallen from the bone; wounds into which the gangrene was making its fearful ravages day by day—a charnel house, indeed, where was opportunity for such service as is rendered at the bed of death, where the sufferer is past all healing.

April 16 (Sunday)

At about this time, Dr. Joseph Jones had completed his reports for the Confederate Surgeon General,

but had no place to send them. The Union had decided to prosecute Capt. Henry Wirz for his role at Andersonville, and Jones was fearful that his report would be used against Wirz. His worst fears were realized when the Union demanded the reports and Jones appealed. To no avail, the reports were finally given over to Union prosecutors on October 3rd.

April 18 (Tuesday)

Morrison, J. B., Surg., USV, Med. Dir., 24th Corps, Farmville, Va.:

We left Appomattox Courthouse on the 17th, and marched eighteen miles toward Burkesville, encamping for the night at Prospect Station. Next morning we started for Farmville, where we arrived early in the afternoon. We bivouacked for the night about three miles east of Farmville. At Farmville I found in the Rebel hospital about one hundred and forty wounded belonging to the different corps of our army.... I had all who could bear transportation in ambulances started on the morning of the 19th for Burkesville, where they arrived that afternoon. I was obliged, however, to leave about forty of them, whose condition was such that could not have endured transportation.

Mrs. Cordelia Strother Welch, wife of Surg. Spencer G. Welch, CSA, left Petersburg, Va., on April 1, 1865, for South Carolina. She departed just one day ahead of the Federal offensive.

Welch, Cordelia S., Newberry, S.C., to her Mother at "Fruit Hill," S.C.:

This is just a note to tell you that I am *at last* in Newberry, and will leave here day after tomorrow to see all of you.

At Chester, trains stopped and I sent Alex (our negro who came with us from Petersburg) on foot to Newberry for a wagon. He made the trip over and back in four days. Gov. Bonham had arranged for us to come on the wagon train to Newberry, after Alex started from Chester. Luckily we met him not far out from Chester coming in a wagon, to which we transferred. They made him wait long enough anyway at Mr. Welch's to pack up a box with enough good things in it to last us a week. We did enjoy it for the two days on the way!

A report is current here that Lee has surrendered, but it is not confirmed....

April 20 (Thursday)

Smart, C., Asst. Surg., USA, Med. Inspector, 2nd Corps, Burkesville, Va.:

On the 20th, a train of twelve ambulances was dispatched to Amelia Courthouse with supplies for some wounded Rebels quartered there, with orders to transport such of them, as were in proper condition to endure it, to the Farmville hospital....

During the remainder of the month there was an increase of sickness in the corps, not so much in the number taken sick, as in the gravity of the cases. The cases of diarrhea, which was the prevailing disease, became obstinate, and were accompanied with very great and rapidly increasing prostration, resembling the disease as seen during the Peninsular Campaign of 1862. The fatigue of recent active service, and the bad water in the second division had, no doubt, their influence in producing this condition, but I attribute it chiefly to the lack of a proper supply of vegetables. Since the camps near Hatcher's Run were broken up there had been issued but one or two rations of potatoes and a small quantity of beans to a portion of the command. Nevertheless, no well marked cases of scurvy are recorded by the medical officers, except in one or two instances of men recently returned from southern prisons....

April 26 (Wednesday)

Morrison, J. B., Surg., USV, Med. Dir., 24th Corps, Richmond, Va.:

We arrived at Burkesville on the 19th, and remained until the morning of the 22d, when we started for Richmond. Meantime, I had all the sick and wounded sent by cars to Petersburg, under the care of efficient medical officers. The troops arrived at Manchester on the 24th, crossed the James River, and passed through Richmond on the 25th. We are now encamped about three miles from the city.

In regard to the medical and hospital property turned over by the Rebels, I have to say that there is but little. It was sent over in parcels, and at different times, and before it could be collected, some of it was lost or destroyed by our own men, there being no guard on the wagon park. However, Surg. Guild, Gen. Lee's medical director, informed me that there was but little to transfer. In the midst of the general bustle and confusion, I did the best I could to collect it.

April 29 (Saturday)

Smart, C., Asst. Surg., USA, Med. Inspector, 2nd Corps, Burkesville, Va.:

On the 29th, the Confederate hospital at Farmville, now under charge of Surg. O. Evans, 40th New York, having been placed under the control of the medical director of the Second Corps, a train of ambulances was sent to carry to their homes, in the vicinity of Petersburg, a hundred of the inmates, who were so far recovered from their wounds as to be able to travel. They were brought to Burkesville and placed in the cars for Petersburg. On the same night, three thousand rations were sent out to supply the necessities of those still remaining in this hospital, six hundred and fifty in number, among whom were twenty-seven of our own men, who were unable to be removed on account of the character of their wounds.

Hand, D. W., Surg., USV, Med. Dir., New Bern, N.C.:

... the right and left wings of Gen. Sherman's army marched from Raleigh for Washington and home, leaving in the department of North Carolina the Twenty-third and Tenth Corps, and a division of cavalry under Maj. Gen. Kilpatrick. The sick were, at this time, gradually brought down to the hospitals at New Bern and Beaufort, and transferred to the hospital steamers whenever they came in. This process continued through the months of May and June, and until a large proportion of troops in the department were mustered out of service....

April 30 (Sunday)

McParlin, T. A., Surg., USA, Med. Dir., Army of the Potomac, near Petersburg, Va.:

About two thousand wounded and five hundred sick were received at Burke's Station from the different corps. The sub-depot hospital established by Surgeon V received from April 9th to 30th, six hundred and sixty sick, and one hundred and ninety-two wounded. Of these, five died, and eight hundred and thirty-eight were sent by railroad to the hospital at City Point. The ambulance train of the Ninth Corps and the captured ambulances and empty wagons were used in addition to the other ambulance trains in the collection and transfer of wounded from the battlefields, of which Burke's Station was the depot. After the surrender of the Army of Northern Virginia, several hundred Confederate wounded, and those of our own whom it was improper to move, at Farmville, were cared for in a most comfortable hospital there..... The last of our wounded were sent down from Burke's Station April 13th, to City Point, but scattering cases continued to be received in depot hospitals at City Point, until April 20th.

April 30th, I ordered the assistant medical purveyor to discontinue the sub-depot at Burke's Station, and proceed with train and supplies to City Point....

May 1 (Monday)

At Beaufort, N.C., Bickerdyke had nearly cleared the hospital of its patients. The patient strength had fallen from about 2000 to only about 200 by this date.

May 2 (Tuesday)

Today at Beaufort, Bickerdyke received a telegram from Maj. Gen. John Logan, then en route to Washington. The telegram informed Bickerdyke that Logan was on the way but was short on rations and could get very few. Logan's instructions were terse. He wired: "Go up [North]." Bickerdyke responded in her usual fashion.

Learning that a steamer would leave in a short time for the North, she had all the Sanitary supplies packed for shipping, gave the bedding and clothing to the colored folks, told all [patients] who were able to look out for themselves, took the nine worst cases into her special care, and in two hours time from the receipt of the dispatch was ready to sail.

Welch, S. G., Surg., 20th S.C. Vols., in a letter to his wife at Fruit Hill, from Newberry, S.C.:

It was well you left Petersburg when you did, for the very next day (April 2) our extreme right was attacked, and, as our line was very thin, it was easily broken. Billie was digging a rifle pit when some Yankees charged it and captured all who were at work on it, and he is now a prisoner.

During the day a few prisoners were brought back, and among them was a smoke-begrimed captain with gray hair. I invited him into my tent and gave him something to eat. He had been in some of the hardest fighting of the war, and he said to me: "You see these gray hairs. When I came into the army they were all coal black."

As night came on many wounded were brought back to some huts lately occupied by soldiers, but now used by us as a hospital. Among them was Mose Cappocks, and I amputated his thumb. Gen. Hill was killed.

The next day we began to leave, and there was continuous fighting. Our march soon developed into a disastrous retreat, and we were pushed to the extreme every hour of it for eight days. At Sailors Creek we were compelled to abandon our wagons, and they were burned. In one of them I had a new case of the finest surgical instruments. They had recently run the blockade and I hated to see them destroyed. Gen. Kershaw and his young son were captured here. I saw some Yankee spies in gray uniforms marched along with us under guard They had been captured in our lines, but the surrender occurring so soon afterward saved them from being hung.

Our retreat was most trying, and when we reached Appomattox on the morning of the 9th, Gen. Gordon had a fight and captured a battery. Appomattox is in a basin with high hills on all sides. The Yankees seemed to have surrounded us, and their blue lines, with white flags here and there, came moving in slowly and silently. There was a report in the early morning that we had surrendered, and this made us think it might be true.

I heard some of our men yelling, and saw Gen. Lee and his staff riding towards us, and as he stopped to dismount the men crowded around him to shake his hand and every man was shedding tears. Sad as was the sight, everyone felt relieved that it was all over.

The Yankees camped on the hills, and men from both armies went back and forth on apparently friendly terms. Their wagons, mules, harness and entire equipment was the very best and everything was in perfect condition throughout. All of their wagon covers were white and new. Ours made a sorry spectacle in comparison. I unhitched a little mule from an ambulance, and that afternoon Col. Hunt, Lt. Col. Lester, Capt. Copeland and I started together for South Carolina.

We had a little fly tent under which we slept at night. Bill Byers, who was mounted on a tall, gaunt horse, joined us before we reached the Catawba River. Copeland's horse gave out and he continued with us on foot. The river was swift and deep at Island Ford, and in crossing only the face and ears of my little mule remained above the surface. We found a farmhouse nearby, where we stood before a blazing fire to dry. The people were very kind to us and gave us the best they had to eat, but our clothes were too dirty and vermin-infested for us to sleep in their houses, so we slept in the barns.

At one house where we stopped and asked for something to eat the man's wife was in a pitiful condition with cancer, but was without medicine to alleviate her suffering. I happened to have a bottle of morphine in my haversack, which I gave her and which was enough to last her for the short time she could live.

We were three weeks on the way, and when I reached my father's home nobody was expecting me. I was completely exhausted, but after getting on some clean, whole clothes and sleeping in a bed once more I felt greatly refreshed. Father has given me a good horse in exchange for my little mule, and I hope to be rested enough to leave here after tomorrow and go through the county in a buggy for you.

Dr. Spencer Glasgow Welch remained in South Carolina for the rest of his life, dying at Newberry on January 5, 1916, at age 81. His descendants still live in Newberry. Cordelia Strother Welch, his wife of 54 years, died at Newberry on July 5, 1915, at age 76.

May 6 (Saturday)

McParlin, T. A., Surg., USA, Med. Dir., Army of the Potomac, near Petersburg, Va.:

The Sixth Corps was then at Danville, where it remained for some time. Other corps of the army marched for Alexandria early in May. The depot hospital, Army of the Potomac, at City Point, was ordered to be reduced [by] twenty-five hundred beds April 30th, and to be moved to Alexandria, May 4th, and to be finally discontinued May 25th. After the cases had been disposed of by transfer to general hospital in Washington and Alexandria for discharge from service, the establishment ceased to exist....

May 7 (Sunday)

In Washington a whirlwind arrived in the form of Mother Mary Ann Bickerdyke. She was looking for rations for Gen. John "Black Jack" Logan's troops now en route to that city. Her first call was at the office of the quartermaster for the capital area, Gen. Easton, who declared that he'd no rations to spare.

Her next stop was at the Sanitary Commission, where she received the same answer.

Not to be deterred, she sent a wire to Dr. Bellows at his church in New York. Bellows, in the middle of a sermon when the wire was handed him, immediately stopped the sermon and began an appeal for food donations for Logan's army. The food wholesalers, meat packers, etc., in the congregation did not disappoint him. By midafternoon a five-car freight train was bound for Bickerdyke in Washington and for Logan's troops, now headed to Alexandria, Va.

Bickerdyke was at Alexandria when the first weary troops began filing into the bivouac site. Their first question was usually, "When do we eat?"

The train from New York arrived at 10 P.M. and records were set unloading the rations. The Washington quartermaster wanted to store the rations until the next day, an idea that drew immediate fire from Bickerdyke—those troops had to be fed tonight!

Bickerdyke, and the rations, arrived at Alexandria about midnight, and the remainder of the night she spent cooking steaks, bacon, potatoes, etc., until all were fed.

May 9 (Tuesday)

The Washington area was a giant beehive of blue uniforms which seemed to swarm about the miles-deep lines of white canvas tents surrounding the city. Tens of thousands of troops from the western armies were arriving daily to add to the throng. Most of the western troops hadn't been paid for eight months, and the town went on a spree as the soldiers tried valiantly to drink it dry, even though the capital was still in mourning for Lincoln.

May 16 (Tuesday)

The cleanup work of clearing the hospitals went on. At Point Lookout, Md., Brig. Gen. James Barnes called Gen. Hoffman's attention to the number of prisoners remaining at the prison hospital and urgently requested disposition:

General: I beg leave to invite your attention to the patients in the prison camp hospital. There are in this hospital 1859 men, including the attendants, belonging to the following states, viz: Maryland, 6; Virginia, 391; North Carolina, 521; South Carolina, 184; Georgia, 233; Florida, 25; Alabama, 154; Louisiana, 20, Mississippi, 216; Arkansas, 19, Tennessee, 60;

Kentucky, 4; Missouri, 7; Texas, 22; numbering in all as above, 1859. Some 1600 of them could be sent home with proper means of conveyance, say, by steamer, to the most advisable ports. The oath of allegiance could be administered to them all, for they all are ready to take it and would be glad to be sent home. Many are disabled by loss of limbs and otherwise by wounds and the expense of taking care of them here is considerable. You will be able to judge of the places which they might be sent by the statement above of the states to which they belong. These steamers would take them, say to Wilmington, Savannah, and Mobile. There would remain between 200 and 300 not in condition to be furloughed for the present....

Hoffman, Commissary-General of Prisons, recommended to the Secretary of War that this action be approved on May 18. At last, many of the Confederates who'd struggled so hard and lost so much would be permitted to return home.

May 22 (Monday)

Today the black crepe and bunting was removed from the houses along Pennsylvania Avenue in Washington, to be replaced by the red, white, and blue. Mourning was over and the workmen were busily constructing reviewing stands along the Avenue for the Grand Review which was to begin the next day.

May 23 (Tuesday)

Today was the day for the Army of the Potomac. They paraded down Pennsylvania Avenue in their newly brushed uniforms, and their short, seemingly choppy, 15-inch step. Regimental flags proudly bore such names as Gettysburg, Antietam, Chancellorsville, Cold Harbor, and scores of other names where these men, and those of their number who lay in graves, had fought with valor and dedication. The crowds roared their approval and appreciation.

Throughout this day and well into the night, the men of Sherman's armies worked getting ready for the next day. There would be four corps with nearly 65,000 men. Leading the Fifteenth Corps was to be Maj. Gen. John "Black Jack" Logan on his horse Slasher. Riding next to him, in an old familiar place, was to be Mary Ann Bickerdyke, astride Old Whitey.

Bickerdyke had been given a brand-new velvet basque and plum-colored riding skirt in New York, and she planned to wear this in the parade. Old Whitey had been furnished with a blanket of blue flowers.

May 24 (Wednesday)

The day of the parade, and Bickerdyke arrived at the assembly point early. Here she found that "her boys" had a lady's sidesaddle for her that had been "borrowed" from some Southern plantation months ago. Eager to try the saddle, since she didn't think it did much for a lady's dignity to ride astride a horse, she hopped up onto this soft, red-leather creation to try it out. While riding up and down the street atop her newfound throne, the bugle called for the troops to line up and Mary Ann went off to the parade in her everyday calico dress, bonnet hanging down her back by the drawstrings, leaving the new finery still on her bed.

The parade was one to be remembered forever. Unlike the easterners, these western soldiers had a long, swinging stride that had eaten the miles from Donelson to Savannah. They had an air of cocky, devil-be-dammed, efficiency that seemed to flow with them down the Avenue.

At the head of the Fifteenth Corps came Maj. Gen. "Black Jack" Logan and Mary Ann Bickerdyke, both to the wild acclaim of the crowds. Sherman described his feelings for the parade:

> When I reached the Treasury building and looked back, the sight was simply magnificent. The column was compact, and the glittering muskets, looked like a solid mass of steel, moving with the regularity of a pendulum.... The steadiness and firmness of the tread, the careful dress of the guiders, the uniform intervals between companies, all eyes directed to the front, and the tattered and bullet-riddled flags, all attracted universal notice. Many good people, up to that time, had looked upon our Western army as a sort of a mob. But the world then saw and recognized the fact that it was an army in the proper sense.... It was, in my judgment, the most magnificent army in existence.

Bickerdyke declined an offer, almost an order, to join the reviewing party in their box, preferring to go to two tents she'd ordered to be set up in a vacant lot at Pennsylvania Avenue and I Street. One tent contained iced lemonade for the thirsty marchers and balm for their blistered feet. The other covered a newly dug latrine vault. Customers weren't long in coming.

May 29 (Monday)

With so many troops in the Washington area, rations were very short. To counter this, Bickerdyke opened the Sanitary Commission stores to help feed the soldiers. Bickerdyke, along with Mrs. Porter, then turned her attention to helping send the soldiers home as rapidly as possible. In a frantic pace, the hospitals were emptied, the patients being sent home with relatives when this could be done.

June 3 (Saturday)

At about this time, Clara Barton found a former Andersonville prisoner named Dorrence Atwater who'd worked as a clerk in the administration office at the prison. The great find was that Atwater had secretly kept a roster of those who'd died at Andersonville, and had managed to retain it after being liberated.

Barton arranged for Atwater, forty coffin makers, and a crew of grave diggers to go with her to Andersonville, where they began the work of exhuming the dead for identification and reburial. This certainly wasn't the most pleasant of tasks—there were more than 12,000 dead at the prison.

June 9 (Friday)

Mary Ann Bickerdyke spent her remaining time in Washington having tea at the White House, dining with Dorothea Dix, and watching the number of soldiers dwindle. She helped whenever and wherever she could, aiding soldiers in getting paid, getting tickets, and packing that all-important sandwich for the train ride home.

Bickerdyke's beloved Army of the Tennessee left for Louisville about this time, but Bickerdyke and Mrs. Porter remained to help where possible.

At last, Mrs. Bickerdyke returned with an Illinois regiment to Camp Butler, near Springfield, Ill. The slow process of mustering out the troops delayed her departure until March 21, 1866, when she submitted her resignation to the Sanitary Commission. She was then nearly forty-nine years old. Her job for "her boys" was done. On November 8, 1901, she died of a stroke in Kansas, and was buried in Galesburg, Ill., beside her husband.

June 25 (Sunday)

Hand, D. W., Surg., USV, Med. Dir., Goldsboro, N.C.:

Most of the patients in general hospitals were mustered out of service, and ... the expenses of the medical department were rapidly reduced in May and June. Nearly all the contract surgeons and nurses were discharged. The Mansfield general hospital at Beaufort, and the Wilmington general hospital, were closed on June 25th....

June 30 (Friday)

On the 30th of June, 1865, the Army of the Potomac ceased to exist.

July 1 (Saturday)

McParlin, T. A., Surg., USA, Med. Dir., Army of the Potomac, Washington, D.C.:

Of the fund in my hand accruing from tax on the sales of newspapers in the Army of the Potomac, I have applied to the purchase of luxuries for the hospitals and necessary articles for the transaction of the business of the medical department since last report, five thousand and seventy dollars and thirty-five cents. The amount received since January 1, 1865, has been six thousand three hundred and eighty-four dollars. On hand December 31, 1864, per last report, nine thousand and twenty-five dollars and thirty-nine cents. The balance remaining in my hands upon the breaking up of the Army of the Potomac, June 29, 1865, was, therefore, ten thousand three hundred and thirty-nine dollars and four cents. This balance, pursuant to proceedings and recommendations of the board appointed by Special Order No. 163, headquarters Army of the Potomac, and approved by the commanding general, was turned over by me, July 1, 1865, to the Surgeon General in trust, to be made a donation from the Army of the Potomac to the Nation Asylum, created by the act of Congress approved March 3, 1865.

July 3 (Monday)

McParlin, T. A., Surg., USA, Med. Dir., Army of the Potomac, Washington, D.C.:

The following statement, showing the number of sick and wounded during the half year ending June

30, 1865.... Remaining, December 31, 1864, in field hospitals, two thousand five hundred and sixty, in depot hospital, two thousand eight hundred and ninety-five, in Northern general hospitals (approximate number), seventeen thousand eight hundred and sixteen; taken sick and wounded from January 1 to June 30, 1865, seventy-five thousand four hundred and eighteen; returned to the army from furlough and desertion, two hundred and fifteen; aggregate to be accounted for, ninety-eight thousand nine hundred and four. Of this number there were returned to duty from field hospitals, fifty-seven thousand and thirty-seven, from depot hospital, twelve thousand one hundred and ninety-two, from Northern hospitals, four thousand nine hundred and forty-nine; transferred to the veteran reserve corps, eight hundred and sixty; discharged from service, from field hospitals, six hundred and eighty-three, from depot hospital, ninety-three, from Northern hospitals, five thousand one hundred and twenty-two; deserted, five hundred and twelve; died in the field, six hundred and fifty-five, in depot hospital, five hundred and seventy-two, in Northern hospitals, one thousand five hundred and eighteen; furloughed from the depot and field hospitals, six hundred and one; remaining, June 30th, in regimental hospitals, one thousand six hundred and fifty-two, in Northern hospitals (approximate number), twenty-two thousand four hundred and fifty-eight.

July 11 (Tuesday)

Through the sweltering heat of the Georgia summer Clara Barton and her crew of coffin makers and grave diggers kept at their appointed task, guided by Dorrence Atwater's list of the dead at Andersonville. In all, 12,800 Union bodies were exhumed and reburied in graves four feet deep. Four hundred Confederate dead were also identified, where possible, and reburied. The work wouldn't be completed until early October.

August 15 (Tuesday)

McClure, Joseph, Co. A, 18th Texas Cavalry, Ft. Worth, Tex.:

I was captured at Arkansas Post January 13, 1863, and imprisoned at Camp Douglas, near Chicago, and was exchanged at City Point, Va., in April, 1863. We were for some time recruiting and in service around Lynchburg, Petersburg, and Richmond. Remnants of the 15th, 17th, and 18th Arkansas, and 10th Texas were consolidated into one regiment. We were transferred to Gen. Bragg at Tullahoma, Tenn. We were placed in Gen. Granbery's Texas Brigade, under Pat Cleburne and Hardee. We were in nearly every fight from Tullahoma, Tenn., to Atlanta, Ga., where at daylight on July 21, 1864, the enemy had a cross fire on us, and I was wounded twice by balls from two directions. I was carried to Griffin Hospital, where I lay for thirty-two days. Then using crutches, I was granted a sick furlough for sixty days, and a grand, good lady, Mrs. John M. Garrick, called at the hospital for a Texan that she could take out and care for. This noble woman cared for me and washed and bandaged my wounds and supplied me with good clothes from August 24, 1864, to July 14, 1865. Then she gave me money to use on my way home.

I started home on July 15, using crutches much of the way. The railroads were destroyed in so many places that I had to walk about halfway to Vicksburg. I arrived there on Sunday. Soon a nice gentleman, seeing my condition, asked me where I was from and where I was going. He kindly gave me a five-dollar United States bill and said I would need it on my way. This cash came in good time, for that which Mrs. Garrick gave me was Georgia and Alabama State money, and was not good for my needs across the river.

I walked on my crutches from Vicksburg, Miss., to Mt. Prairie, Tex., where I rested three days with a friend who furnished me a young but wild mule to ride home; but to control the mule I had to leave one crutch. That ride almost wore me out; it was very hard on me. The mule trotted very hard, and I kept him in a gallop most all the way to Alvarado, where I landed at home on August 15, 1865, just one month on the trip....

October 7 (Saturday)

In Washington, near the end of the Henry Wirz trial, Dr. Joseph Jones was called to testify concerning his work at Andersonville in September 1864. During the testimony, Jones was never allowed to explain the overall problems at Andersonville as he saw them, and extracts of his report were introduced into evidence without the substance of the report being presented. The Union trial was rigged; Wirz became the sacrificial lamb.

Jones returned to Georgia after the trial. He eventually joined the faculty of what was to become Tulane University in New Orleans, where he remained until his death in 1896.

October 17 (Tuesday)

After months of toil supervising the exhumation of the prison's dead at Andersonville, Ga., identifying them where possible, and reinterring them in over 12,000 marked graves, Miss Clara Barton today raised the national flag at a ceremony dedicating the new National Cemetery at Andersonville. Miss Barton later commented:

> Then, I saw the little graves marked, blessed them for the heartbroken mother in [their] old Northern home, raised over them the flag they loved and died for, and left them to their rest.

October 30 (Monday)

The Union troops were finally leaving North Carolina after so many months. Their departure obviated the need for large hospital facilities, and, at last Surg. Hand was running out of work. Near Wilmington, the last of the large hospitals closed on this date. Surg. Hand would remain to "tie up the loose ends" until November 18, 1865, when he was relieved from duty as Medical Director of the Dept. of North Carolina.

Hand, D. W., Surg., USV, Med. Dir., Goldsboro, N.C.:

> The Foster General Hospital was removed from New Bern to the hospital buildings at Morehead City, and its capacity reduced to four hundred beds. The Smithville general hospital was also reduced to two hundred beds, and all surplus property turned in to the quartermaster and medical purveyor. During the summer months, the number of troops in the department was constantly reduced by muster out, the medical staff being reduced in the same proportion. On September 17th, the Smithville hospital was finally closed, and on October 30th, the Foster general hospital at Morehead City was broken up....

EPILOGUE

Although the war ended with Lee's surrender at Appomattox C.H., for those who'd been maimed during the war by shell or shot, the war would continue for years, causing endless pain and suffering. Too, those countless numbers of men, North and South, who'd suffered the ravages of diseases such as malaria, dysentery, and diarrhea would agonize their effects for the remainder of their lives. Congress finally granted pensions to the victims of camp and battle, but often this came too late for the intended recipient, who was already dead.

The often-crude surgery performed on the injured during the war led to amputations that would have been found to be most unacceptable by today's standards. Gangrene, the silent killer of amputees, was hardly understood by the doctors treating the wounds. Gangrene caused more deaths by ignorance than could be thought possible. The makers of substitute limbs, especially legs, were in great demand at the end of the war.

Although much had been learned by doctors dur-ing the Civil War, such knowledge mostly concerned surgical techniques for amputation. Hospital organization developed during the war was carried back to the civilian communities by the discharged doctors and put to good use. It's unfortunate that the U.S. Army didn't continue to use the medical organization it had so laboriously developed. Almost immediately after the war, the medical department reverted to prewar organization and wouldn't advance much until the late 1890s.

The true monuments to the war, attesting to the magnitude of death and suffering, are the tens of thousands of graves scattered over the country containing sons, husbands, brothers, or fathers. The tens of thousands who survived would for years recall their experiences and relive the *days of glory*, often forgetting the spectre of death which accompanied those days.

The endurance of the soldier, North or South, to fight on for his beliefs became a standard of fidelity and courage.

Let us never forget.

BIBLIOGRAPHY

Adams, George Worthington. *Doctors in Blue: The Medical History of the Union Army in the Civil War.* New York: Henry Schuman, 1952.

Baker, Nina Brown. *Cyclone in Calico: The Story of Mary Ann Bickerdyke.* Boston: Little, Brown & Co., 1952.

Barber, James G. "Alexandria in the Civil War." Blacksburg, Va.: Virginia Polytechnic Institute & State University [Master's thesis], 1977.

Barnes, Joseph K., et al., eds. *The Medical and Surgical History of the War of the Rebellion, 1861-1865.* 12 vols. Washington, D.C.: U.S. G.P.O., 1870-88.

Barton, George. *Angels of the Battlefield.* Philadelphia: Catholic Art Publishing Co., 1898.

Boulware, James, M.D. *Diary.* Columbia, S.C.: University of South Carolina, South Caroliniana Library.

Breeden, James O. *Joseph Jones, M.D.: Scientist of the Old South.* Lexington, Ky.: The University Press of Kentucky, 1975.

Buckingham, Clyde E. *Clara Barton: A Broad Humanity.* Alexandria, Va.: Mt. Vernon Publishing Co., 1977.

Cashman, Diane Cobb. *Headstrong: the Biography of Amy Morris Bradley, 1823-1904.* Wilmington, N.C.: Broadfoot Pub. Co., 1990.

Chicago Medical Journal. 1862.

Chisolm, J. Julian, M.D. *A Manual of Military Surgery for the Use of Surgeons in the Confederate States Army.* Columbia, S.C.: Evans and Cogswell, 1864.

Confederate Veteran. Anderson, Charles W., Maj., CSA, Vol. IV, 289-90

    Bloomer, Sam, 1st Minnesota Reg., Vol. XVII, 169

    Bradwell, I. G., Pvt., CSA, Vol. XXIX, 224-25

    Coxe, John, Pvt., Hampton's Legion, Vol. XXIV, 407

    Curtis, Finley P., Pvt., Co. B, 1st N.C. Infantry, Vol. XXIV, 401

    Dalton, R. H., Surg., 11th Mississippi Vols., Vol. I, 181

    Donoho, A. G., Surg., Calhoun, Ga., Vol. XXV, 27

    Earnhart, T. M., Pvt., Battery D, 10th N.C. State Troops, Vol. XXVI, 528-29

    Ellis, F. P., Co. I, 13th Mississippi Regt., Vol. XVII, 456

    Leadbetter, M. T., Pvt., Co. C, 5th Alabama Battalion, Vol. I, 243-45.

    Lokey, J. W., Pvt., 20th Georgia Regt., Vol. XXII, 400

Roden, J. B., Pvt., CSA, Vol. XXI, 549

Semple, Mrs. Letitia T., Williamsburg Hospital, Vol. II, 141

Stevens, James A., Pvt., CSA, Vol. XXVII, 318

Synnamon, James, Co. I, 6th Missouri Infantry, CSA, Vol. XXI, 582

Thomas, D. C., Texas Cavalry, CSA, Vol. IV, 126

Ward, W. C., Pvt., Co. G, 4th Alabama Regt., Vol. VIII, 345-49

Duncan, Louis C., Capt., Medical Corps, U.S.A. *The Medical Department of the United States Army in the Civil War.* U.S. Army Publication, [ca. 1905].

Edmonds, S. Emma E. *Nurse and Spy in the Union Army.* Hartford, Conn.: W. S. Williams & Co., 1865.

Formento, Felix, Jr. *Notes and Observations on Army Surgery.* 1863.

Gettysburg Compiler. Gettysburg, Pa.: National Military Park files

Gillett, Mary C. *The Army Medical Department, 1818-1865.* Washington, D.C.: U.S. G.P.O., 1986.

Hart, Albert G., Maj. *The Surgeon and the Hospital in the Civil War.* Washington, D.C.: U.S. G.P.O., 1906.

Hoke, Jacob. *The Great Invasion of 1863; or, General Lee in Pennsylvania.* Dayton, Ohio: C. S. Shuey, 1887.

Houck, Peter W. *Confederate Surgeon: The Personal Recollections of E. A. Craighill.* Lynchburg, Va.: H. E. Howard, Inc., 1989.

Johnston, Joseph E. *Narrative of Military Operations.* New York: D. Appleton & Co., 1874.

Lester, C. E. *The Light and the Dark of the Rebellion.* Philadelphia: George W. Childs, 1863.

Locke, E. W. *Three Years in Camp and Hospital.* Boston: Geo. D. Russell & Co., 1872.

Maxwell, William Quentin. *Lincoln's Fifth Wheel: The Political History of the United States Sanitary Commission.* New York: Longmans, Green & Co., 1956.

Medical and Surgical History of the War of the Rebellion (1861-1865). 3 vols., Washington, D.C.: U.S. G.P.O., 1875-88. Allen, J.M., Surg., USV; Bache, Dallas, Asst. Surg., USA; Barrell, H.C., Asst. Surg., USV; Billings, J.S., Asst. Surg., USA; Blair, W.W., Surg., USV; Breed, B.B., Surg., USA; Brickett, George E., Surg., USV; Brinton, John H., Surg., USA; Brown, H.E., Surg., USA; Brown, J.B., Surg., USA; Brumley, J.D., Surg., USV; Campbell, A.B., Surg., USV; Carrick, A.L., Surg., USV; Church, C.W., Surg., USV; Cooper, George E., Surg., USA; Craven, J.J., Surg., USV; Crosby, A.B., Surg., USV; Dalton, R.H., Surg., CSA; Davis, Philip C., Asst. Surg., USA; DeGraw, C.S., Asst. Surg., USA; Derby, N.R., Surg., USV; Donoho, A.G., Surg., CSA; Foye, John W., Surg., USV; Ghiselin, J.T., Surg., USA; Gill, H.Z., Surg., USV; Goodbrake, C., Surg., USV; Gray, C.C., Asst. Surg., USA; Grinsted, W., Surg., USV; Grumbien, William, Asst. Surg., USV; Gugin, D.S., Surg., USV; Hammond, J.F., Surg., USA; Hammond, William A., Asst. Surg., USA; Hand, D.W., Surg., USV; Hart, Samuel, Asst. Surg., USV; Hatchitt, J.G., Surg., USV; Haynes, C.F., Surg., USV; Heard, J.T., Surg., USV; Howard, B., Asst. Surg., USA; Hubbard, George H., Surg., USV; Ingram, Alexander, Asst. Surg., USA; Irwin, B.J.D., Asst Surg., USA; Kellogg, G.M., Surg., USV; King, W.S., Surg., USA; Letterman, Jonathan, Med. Dir., USA; McDougall, Charles, Med. Dir., USA; McGill, George M., Asst. Surg., USA; McKenzie, Thomas G., Med. Purveyor, USA; McParlin, Thomas A., Surg., USA; Magruder, D.S., Asst. Surg., USA; Majer, Adolph, Surg., USV; Marsh, E.J., Surg., USA; Melcher, S.H., Asst. Surg., USA; Menzies, S.G., Surg., USV; Mills, Madison, Surg., USA; Moore, John, Surg., USA; Murray, Robert, Surg., USA; O'Leary, Charles, Surg., USV; Peale, J.B., Surg., USV; Pease, R.W., Surg., USV; Perin, G., Surg., USA; Perry, John G., Asst. Surg., USV; Peters, D.C., Asst. Surg., USA; Phelps, A.J., Surg., USV; Read, Ezra., Surg., USV; Richardson, T.G., Surg., CSA; Sanger, Eugene F., Surg., USV; Schell, H.S., Asst. Surg., USV; Shummard, G.G., Surg., USV; Smart, C., Asst. Surg., USA; Smith, A.H., Asst. Surg., USA; Smith, David P., Surg., USA; Sprague, H.M., Asst. Surg., USA; Stearns, H.P., Surg, USV; Sternberg, G.M., Asst. Surg., USA; Swift, E., Surg., USA; Swinburne, John, Acting Surg., USA; Vollum, E.P., Med. Insp., USA; White, W.H., Surg., USV; Willis, P.A., Surg., USA; Winne, Charles K., Asst. Surg., USA; Wright, J.J.B., Surg., USA.

Mitchell, Mary Bedinger. *A Woman's Recollections of Antietam*. Battles and Leaders of the Civil War: Vol. II, The Struggle Intensifies, New York: Century Magazine, 1887.

Nevins, Allan. *A Diary of Battle: The Personal Journals of Colonel Charles S. Wainwright—1861-1865*. New York: Harcourt, Brace and World, Inc., 1962.

Olmsted, Frederick Law. *Hospital Transports: A Memoir of the Embarkation of the Sick and Wounded from the Peninsula of Virginia in the Summer of 1862*. Boston: Ticknor & Fields, 1863.

_____. *A Journey in the Seaboard Slave States, with Remarks on Their Economy*. New York: Dix and Edwards, 1856.

Perry, Martha D. *Letters from a Surgeon of the Civil War*. Boston: Little, Brown & Co., 1906.

Pressley, J. G. Extracts from the diary of Lt. Col. John G. Pressley, 25th South Carolina Volunteers in *Southern Historical Society Papers*, 1886.

Quaife, Milo M. *From the Cannon's Mouth: The Civil War Letters of General Alpheus S. Williams*. Detroit: Wayne University Press and The Detroit Historical Society, 1959.

Reed, William H. *Hospital Life in the Army of the Potomac*. Boston: William V. Spencer, 1866.

Ropes, Hannah. *The Diary and Letters of Hannah Ropes*. Riverside, Calif.: University of California, Riverside. Rivera Library, Special Collections Dept.

Steiner, Paul E. *Disease in the Civil War*. Springfield, Ill.: Charles C. Thomas, 1968.

Stillé, Charles J. *History of the United States Sanitary Commission, Being the General Report of Its Work during the War of the Rebellion*. Philadelphia: J. B. Lippincott & Co., 1866.

Tripler, Charles S. *Manual of the Medical Officer of the Army of the United States: Part I, Recruiting and the Inspection of Recruits*. 1858.

United States Congress. *The Reports of Committees of the House of Representatives made during the Third Session of the Fortieth Congress, 1869*. Washington, D.C.: U.S. G.P.O., 1869.

United States Sanitary Commission. *Report No. 22, Appointment of the Sanitary Commission*. Washington, D.C.: 1861.

_____. *Report No. 23, Report on the Conditions of the General Hospitals in and around Washington*. Washington, D.C.: 1861.

_____. *Report No. 40. Report on the Sanitary Condition of the Volunteer Army, December 1861*. Washington, D.C.: 1861.

_____. *Report No. 48, Report on the Operations after the Battle of Sharpsburg, Md., September 1862*. New York: 1862.

_____. *Report No. 55, Report on the Operations at Perryville, Ky.*. Louisville, Ky.: 1862.

_____. *Report No. 57, Report on the Operations at the Battle of Fredericksburg, Va., December 13, 1862*. Washington, D.C.: 1862.

_____. *The Sanitary Commission of the United States Army: A Succinct Narrative of Its Works and Purposes*. New York, 1864.

Virginia Medical Monthly. 1894.

War of the Rebellion: A Compilation of the Official Records of the Union and Confederate Armies (OR). 69 vols., Washington, D.C.: U.S. G.P.O., 1875-88.

Welch, Spencer Glasgow. *A Confederate Surgeon's Letters to His Wife*. New York: Neal Publishing Co., 1911

Western Sanitary Commission. *Report on Operations ending June 1, 1863*. St. Louis, Mo.: 1863.

_____. *Report on the White Union Refugees of the South*. St. Louis, Mo.: R. P. Studley & Co., 1864.

Wormeley, Katherine Prescott. *The Other Side of War with the Army of the Potomac. Letters from the Headquarters of the United States Sanitary Commission during the Peninsula Campaign in Virginia in 1862*. Boston: Ticknor & Company, 1889.

INDEX